THE JOURNALS AND
LETTERS OF
FANNY BURNEY

Fanny Burney

By Daniel Gardner

With the permission of the owner and of the Mellon Collection

THE JOURNALS AND
LETTERS OF
FANNY BURNEY
(MADAME D'ARBLAY)

VOLUME XI

MAYFAIR 1818–1824

LETTERS 1180–1354

Edited by

JOYCE HEMLOW

with

ALTHEA DOUGLAS *and* PATRICIA HAWKINS

CLARENDON PRESS · OXFORD

1984

Oxford University Press, Walton Street, Oxford OX2 6DP
London New York Toronto
Delhi Bombay Calcutta Madras Karachi
Kuala Lumpur Singapore Hong Kong Tokyo
Nairobi Dar es Salaam Cape Town
Melbourne Auckland
and associated companies in
Beirut Berlin Ibadan Mexico City Nicosia

Oxford is a trade mark of Oxford University Press

Published in the United States
by Oxford University Press, New York

British Library Cataloguing in Publication Data

Burney, Fanny
    The journals and letters of Fanny Burney.
    Vols 11 and 12: Mayfair 1818–1824 and
    Mayfair 1825–1840: letters 1180–1354 and
    1355–1529.
    1. Burney, Fanny–Biography
    2. Authors, English——18th century——
    Biography
    I. Title   II. Hemlow, Joyce
    III. Douglas, Althea
    IV. Hawkins, Patricia
    823'.6   PR3316.A475
    ISBN 0-19-812563-1

Library of Congress Cataloging in Publication Data
(Revised for Volume 11)

Arblay, Frances (Burney) d', 1752–1840.
    The journals and letters of Fanny Burney (Madame D'
Arblay).
    Vol. 2 edited by Joyce Hemlow and Althea Douglas.
    CONTENTS: v. 1. 1791–1792, letters.——39.——v. 2.
Courtship and marriage 1793, letters 40–121.——[etc.]——
v. 11. Mayfair 1818–1824, letters 1180–1354.
    1. Arblay, Frances (Burney), d', 1752–1840——Corre-
spondence. 2. Arblay, Frances (Burney), d', 1752–1840
——Diaries. 3. Novelists, English——18th century——Biography. 4. England——Social life and customs——18th
century. 5. England——Social life and customs——19th
century.
PR3316.A4Z552   823'.6[B]   72-189680
ISBN 0-19-812563-1

Typeset by Joshua Associates, Oxford
Printed in Great Britain
at the University Press, Oxford

ACKNOWLEDGEMENTS

Persons mentioned in the Acknowledgements of 1972 (volume i of this series), especially the distinguished scholars concerned with the organization of Burney Project I, are here gratefully remembered, though some of them the years have carried away. For unfailing help and permissions to print priceless manuscripts, I wish to thank, among their successors, Dr. Lola L. Szladits, Curator of the Henry W. and Albert A. Berg Collection of the New York Public Library; and Dr. Stephen R. Parks, Curator of the James and Marie-Louise Osborn Collection at Yale University, who kept us informed of new Burney accessions, as did Mr. Herbert T. F. Cahoon of the Pierpont Morgan Library, New York. I am grateful to Mr. John Sparrow, *lately* Warden of All Soul's, for the opportunity to read his Collection of Burney letters; to Mr. John R. G. Comyn for hospitality and access to the riches of his family collections; and to Mr. Michael Burney-Cumming for permission to print family letters that have come to him.

As the exciting discoveries of Burney letters, some of them still in their eighteenth-century folds, and the happy years of cataloguing new caches of manuscripts, large and small, progressed to the exacting work of listing, compiling, transcribing, proof-reading, editing, and as the annotation of the text involved long searches, group- or team-work became necessary and consequentially, steady financial support. The persons and the institutions *but for whom* the work could never have been undertaken or completed include first of all McGill University, the successive Principals and Deans of Graduate Studies and Research, who provided liberty, freedom, luxurious space, and of late years, a part-time salary. The Committee on Research at McGill has never once in thirty years refused an appeal for help, though doubtless relieved, considering the claims of others, when the appeals were well spaced.

The Social Sciences and Humanities Research Council of Canada, formerly called the Canada Council, provided a continuous series of grants, large or small, as the exigencies of the work required; and the Humanities Research Council in earlier years, summer grants. To the Canadian Federation for the Humanities, using funds provided by the Social Sciences and Humanities Research Council of Canada, the publisher as well as the editors must be grateful for a subsidy applicable to the costs of publishing these last two volumes of the series.

Fellowships awarded by the John Simon Guggenheim Memorial Foundation, and especially the first Fellowship of 1951, led to the discovery of the Barrett Collection of Burney Papers, now in the British Library. The Foundation also allowed, initially, publication grants both for the edition and the *Catalogue*.

Gratitude is proportionate not only to the size or continuance of grants but also to the relief afforded when even a few thousand dollars may prevent a halt or a delay in the work. Such in former times Mr. D. Lorne Gales, Director of Developments at McGill, used to procure from McGill Alumnae. The work was aided in early stages by the Nuffield Foundation with its summer travel grants; and in critical stages by the British Academy, for research in England; the American Philosophical Society; and the American Learned Societies. To one and all deep gratitude is here expressed.

Among persons who helped with the annotation of the text I have pleasure in thanking Mr. Warren Derry, editor of volumes ix and x (the Bath Volumes), who kindly bent his mind to Bath problems in volumes xi and xii; those sharing specialized information, Patricia D. Crown on Edward Francesco Burney, the artist; Linda René-Martin, on Marianne Francis; Olwen Hedley, author of *Queen Charlotte*, who prevented my blundering into the wrong royal cottages in Old Windsor or Kew; Slava Klima, for his detection of errors of all kinds; Lars E. Troide, for research in the Yale Library; John Kerslake, Keeper, the National Portrait Gallery, for access to the richly grangerized Diaries of Fanny Burney and for his identifications of artists painting Burney subjects; Professor Patrick Bridgwater of the University of Durham, for help with the Cumberland Burneys; Messrs. Hoare, Madame d'Arblay's bankers, of 37 Fleet Street, whose Ledgers, beautifully preserved, explained investments and provided full names for the servants, tradesmen, and pensioners, thus illuminating the amalgam of domestic life in Mayfair in the

Acknowledgements

1820s and 30s; the Librarian and Archivist at the Church Commissioners, 1 Millbank Street, for documents explaining d'Arblay's career in the Church; the Church of Jesus Christ of Latter-Day Saints, for their Computer File Index, supplying dates of births and marriages; the skilled archivists of County Record Offices, who produced Land Tax Assessments, parish records, and other documents, and supplied information; the incumbents of remote parish churches, the custodians of parish registers and of parish chests, who replied to letters; Andrea Smith and Dr. Martin Bowman who searched parish registers in Edinburgh.

An omnivorous reader with a phenomenal memory, Fanny Burney had a wide range of works to call on for illustrative material. For the identification of literary allusions in her letters credit must go first to Professor Curtis D. Cecil of McGill University who read the full text (some 1,500 letters), isolating, indexing, and identifying most of the sources; and then, among others, to knowledgeable readers of the *TLS* who kindly replied to the editor's queries; and to Mr. Anthony W. Shipps of the Indiana University Libraries, who concluded the long search for the 'unhappy divinity stuck in a niche' (i. 35 and viii. 500) in Anstey's 'An Election Ball'.

In London the BL, the PRO, the GLRO, the Guildhall Library, the Genealogical Society, Somerset House, St. Catherine's House, and the Wellcome Library seemed always to harbour identifications of the hundreds of persons emerging in the Burney manuscripts. Like Dr. Burney, who prided himself on the wide range of his acquaintance, his daughter Fanny Burney (Madame d'Arblay) also knew or met the most humble cottagers, the most humble Londoners, tradesmen, men and women of letters, courtiers, *émigré* Frenchmen, Louis XVIII himself and Talleyrand, the highest nobility, the Princesses of England and the Queen of the realm. The editors will remember most gratefully the many persons who helped to explain her pages, a veritable kaleidoscope of names and events.

CONTENTS

LIST OF PLATES

xi

ABBREVIATIONS

MEMBERS OF THE BURNEY FAMILY
AND SOME OF THEIR FRIENDS

AA	The Revd. Alexander Charles Louis Piochard d'Arblay, 1794–1837
CAB	Charlotte Ann Burney, 1761–1838
CBF	after 1786 Mrs. Francis
CBFB	after 1798 Mrs. Broome
CB	Charles Burney (Mus. Doc.), 1726–1814
CB Jr.	Charles Burney (D.D.), 1757–1817
CF	Clement Robert Francis, 1792–29
CFBt	Charlotte (Francis) Barrett, 1786–1870
CPB	Charles Parr Burney (D.D.), 1785–1864
EBB	Esther (Burney) Burney, 1749–1832
FB	Frances Burney, 1752–1840
FBA	after 1793 Madame d'Arblay
GMAPW	Georgiana Mary Ann (Port) Waddington, 1771–1850
HLT	Hester Lynch (Salusbury) Thrale, 1741–1821
HLTP	after 1784 Mrs. Piozzi
JB	James Burney (Rear-Admiral), 1750–1821
JCBT	Julia Charlotte (Barrett) Thomas, 1808–64
JCBTM	after 1842 Mrs. Maitland
M. d'A	Alexandre-Jean-Baptiste Piochard d'Arblay, 1754–1818
MF	Marianne Francis, 1790–1832
SEB	Susanna Elizabeth Burney, 1755–1800
SBP	after 1782 Mrs. Phillips
SHB	Sarah Harriet Burney, 1772–1844
TT	The Revd. Thomas Twining, 1734–1804

SHORT TITLES

Standard encylopaedias, biographical dictionaries (both national and professional), peerages, armorials, baronetages, knightages, school and university lists, medical registers, lists of clergy, town and city directories, road guides, almanacs, and ephemerides of all kinds have been used but will not be cited unless for a particular reason. Also consulted were annual Navy, Army, and Law Lists, *Royal Kalendar*, and the many editions of Edmund Lodge's *The Peerage of the British Empire as at Present Existing* and of Sir John Bernard Burke's *A Genealogical and Heraldic History of the Peerage and Baronetage* and *A Genealogical and Heraldic History of the Landed Gentry of Great Britain and Ireland*. In all such dated series, though the wording of titles varies somewhat, citation will be to the commonly used short title with the date of the volume or edition.

Altick	Richard D. Altick, *Richard Owen Cambridge: Belated Augustan*, Philadelphia, 1948.
AR	*The Annual Register, or a View of the History, Politics, and Literature* . . . , 1758- .
Barrett	The Barrett Collection of Burney Papers, British Library, 43 vols., Egerton 3690–3708.
Berg	The Henry W. and Albert A. Berg Collection, New York Public Library.
BL	The British Library.
Bunsen, *Life*	*The Life and Letters of Frances Baroness Bunsen*, ed. Augustus J. C. Hare, 2 vols. in 1, New York, 1879.
Bunsen, *Memoirs*	*Memoirs of Baron Bunsen*, ed. Frances Baroness Bunsen, 2 vols., 1869.
Burford Papers	*Burford Papers, Being Letters of Samuel Crisp to his Sister at Burford; and other Studies of a Century* (1745–1845), ed. William Holden Hutton, 1905.
Burney, Fanny Anne	*A Great-Niece's Journals* . . . , ed. Margaret S. Rolt, 1926.
Catalogue	*A Catalogue of the Burney Family Correspondence 1749–1878*, compiled by Joyce Hemlow, with Jeanne M. M. Burgess and Althea Douglas, New York, 1971.
Clifford	James L. Clifford, *Hester Lynch Piozzi (Mrs. Thrale)*, Oxford, 1941, 1952, 1969.
Cobbett	R. S. Cobbett, *Memorials of Twickenham*, 1872.
Computer File Index	Compiled by the Church of Jesus Christ of Latter-Day Saints.
Comyn	The John Comyn Collection of Burney Papers, The Cross House, Vowchurch, Turnastone, Herefordshire, England.
Crown, Patricia	'Edward F. Burney: an Historical Study in English Romantic Art', unpublished dissertation, Univ. of California, Los Angeles, 1977.
Delany [Mrs.]	*The Autobiography and Correspondence of Mary Granville, Mrs. Delany: with Interesting Reminiscences of King George the Third and Queen Charlotte*, ed. Lady Llanover, 1st series, 3 vols., 1861, and 2nd series, 3 vols., 1862.
Derry	Warren Derry, *Dr. Parr / A Portrait of the Whig Dr. Johnson*, 1966.
Diary	Mme d'Arblay's 'Mayfair Diaries', kept in small pocket books and extant (Berg) for the years

1819-21, 1823, 1826, and 1828, with widely spaced entries or memoranda for the years 1827, 1837-9 (Berg), and selected entries for the year 1818 copied in the hand of Charlotte Barrett. The typescripts (some 600 pages) it has proved impractical to print in this series but the Diaries may be read in the original in the Berg Collection, the NYPL, or in typescript in the Hemlow–Burney Archives, McGill University.

DL (1842-6)	*Diary and Letters of Madame d'Arblay*, ed. Charlotte Barrett, 7 vols., 1842-6.
DL	*Diary and Letters of Madame d'Arblay (1778-1840)*, ed. Austin Dobson, 6 vols., 1904-5.
ED	*The Early Diary of Frances Burney, 1768-1778*, ed. Annie Raine Ellis, 2 vols., 1907.
Farington	Joseph Farington, *The Farington Diary*, ed. James Greig, 8 vols., 1922-8.
FB & the Burneys	*Fanny Burney and the Burneys*, ed. R. Brimley Johnson, 1926.
Furneaux	Robin Furneaux, *William Wilberforce*, 1974.
Gazley	John G. Gazley, *The Life of / Arthur Young / 1741-1820*, Philadelphia, 1973.
Glenbervie	*The Diaries of Sylvester Douglas (Lord Glenbervie)*, ed. Francis Bickley, 2 vols., 1928.
GM	*The Gentleman's Magazine*, 1731-1880.
Greatheed	Bertie Greatheed, *An Englishman in Paris*, ed. J. T. Bury and J. C. Barry, 1953.
Harcourt Papers	*The Harcourt Papers*, ed. Edward W. Harcourt, 14 vols., Oxford, 1880-1905.
Hayward	Abraham Hayward, *Autobiography, Letters, and Literary Remains of Mrs. Piozzi (Thrale)*, 2 vols., 1861.
Hedley	Olwen Hedley, *Queen Charlotte*, 1975.
HFB	Joyce Hemlow, *The History of Fanny Burney*, Oxford, 1958.
Highfill	Philip H. Highfill, K. A. Burnim, *et al.*, *A Biographical Dictionary / of / Actors, Actresses, Musicians, Dancers, Managers . . . / 1660-1800*, 6 vols., 1973- .
Hillairet	Jacques Hillairet, *Dictonnaire historique des rues de Paris*, 2 vols., 1973.
Hoares' Ledgers	Customers' Personal Account Ledgers (1673-) and Bank Income & Expenditure Ledgers (1718-), preserved by Messrs. C. Hoare, Bankers, 37 Fleet Street, London.
Holland, Lady [*Letters*]	Elizabeth, Lady Holland, [*Letters*] *to her son, 1821-1845*, ed. the Earl of Ilchester, 1946.

Holland, Lady *Journal*	*Journal, 1791–1811*, ed. the Earl of Ilchester, 2 vols., 1908.
Hyde	Mary Hyde, *The Thrales of Streatham Park*, Cambridge, Mass., 1977.
Jerningham Letters	*The / Jerningham Letters / (1780–1843) / Being Excerpts from the Correspondence and Diaries of the Honourable Lady Jerningham and of her Daughter Lady Bedingfeld*, ed. Egerton Castle, 2 vols., 1896.
JRL	The John Rylands Library, Manchester, England.
Lamb, *Letters*	*The Letters of Charles Lamb . . . [and] Mary Lamb*, ed. E. V. Lucas, 3 vols., 1935.
Locks of Norbury	The Duchess of Sermoneta [Vittoria (Calonne) Caetani], *The Locks of Norbury*, 1940.
Lonsdale	Roger Lonsdale, *Dr. Charles Burney*, Oxford, 1965.
Manwaring	G. E. Manwaring, *My Friend the Admiral: the Life, Letters, and Journals of Rear-Admiral James Burney, F.R.S.*, 1931.
Memoirs	*Memoirs of Doctor Burney, Arranged from His Own Manuscripts, from Family Papers, and from Personal Recollections*, by his daughter, Madame d'Arblay, 3 vols., 1832.
'Memoirs'	Autograph Manuscripts of Dr. Burney's Memoirs, fragments of which survive in Berg, Osborn, and BL.
Moore, Thomas	*Memoirs, Journals, and Correspondence*, ed. Lord John Russell, 8 vols., 1853–6.
Morley (SHB)	Edith J. Morley, 'Sarah Harriet Burney, 1770–1844', *Modern Philology*, xxxix (Nov. 1941), 123–58.
NPG	The National Portrait Gallery, Trafalgar Square, London.
NYPL	The New York Public Library, Fifth Avenue and 42nd Street, New York.
Osborn	The James Marshall and Marie-Louise Osborn Collection, Yale University Library, New Haven, Conn.
Phil. Trans.	*Philosophical Transactions of the Royal Society*, 1665– .
PML	The Pierpont Morgan Library, 33 East 36th Street, New York.
PRO	Public Record Office, London.
Queeney Letters	*The Queeney Letters, being Letters Addressed to Hester Maria Thrale by Doctor Johnson, Fanny Burney, and Mrs. Thrale-Piozzi*, ed. the Marquis of Lansdowne, 1934.

R.H.I., Windsor	Royal Household Index, the Queen's Archives, Windsor Castle.
Richardson, Joanne	*The Disastrous Marriage. A Study of George IV and Caroline of Brunswick*, 1960.
Robinson, *Diary*	Henry Crabb Robinson, *Diary, Reminiscences, and Correspondence of* . . . , ed. Thomas Sadler, 3 vols., 1869.
Scholes	Percy A. Scholes, *The Great Dr. Burney*, 2 vols., 1948.
Shelley (Cameron)	*Shelley and his Circle*, ed. Kenneth Neill Cameron, Cambridge, Mass., 6 vols., 1961- .
Six	Georges Six, *Dictionnaire biographique des généraux et amiraux français de la révolution et de l'empire (1792-1814)*, 2 vols., 1934.
Stuart, *Dtrs. Geo. III*	Dorothy Margaret Stuart, *The Daughters of George III*, 1939.
Teignmouth	Charles John Shore, 2nd Baron Teignmouth, *Reminiscences of many Years*, 2 vols., Edinburgh, 1878.
Thraliana	*Thraliana, The Diary of Mrs. Hester Lynch Thrale (Later Mrs. Piozzi), 1776-1809*, ed. Katharine C. Balderston, 2 vols., Oxford, 1942.
Walpole	*The Yale Edition of Horace Walpole's Correspondence*, ed. W. S. Lewis, 49 vols., New Haven, 1937–83.
Welvert	Eugène Welvert, *Princesse d'Hénin, histoire d'une grande dame du temps passé*, Versailles, 1924.
Windham Papers	*The Windham Papers / The Life and Correspondence of the / Rt. Hon. William Windham 1750–1810* . . . , ed. the Earl of Rosebery, 2 vols., 1913.
'Worcester Journal'	A typescript of a family chronicle entitled 'Memoranda of the Burney Family, 1603–1845', once in the possession of Dr. Percy A. Scholes (as described in Scholes i. 1 n., and ii. 391). Dr. Scholes allowed the Editor to take the copy now in her possession.

INTRODUCTION

The scene of Madame d'Arblay's widowhood was Mayfair. For ten years (1818–28) she lived at 11 Bolton Street, nine years (1828–37) at 1 Half Moon Street, for a year at 112 Mount Street, and finally at 29 Lower Grosvenor Street, at the corner of Davies Street, where she died on 6 January 1840. As a residence, London was her choice for the social, literary, and professional advantages it offered to her son the Revd. Alexander Charles Louis d'Arblay (1794–1837), who having graduated in 1818 tenth Wrangler from Christ's College, Cambridge, and having been made a Fellow of Christ's in the same year, was seeking a living in the Church, if possible, a lectureship in London. For herself she favoured Mayfair for its proximity to green spaces, the Green Park and Berkeley Square, where residents of the time must have seen her on long daily walks ('one of my chief Delights') with the dog Diane and the devoted servant Elizabeth Ramsay of Ilfracombe. The address was respectable, one where the fashionable carriages of the high-ranking friends of her old age would not look amiss. Among these were the Princesses Augusta, Sophia, and Mary, Duchess of Gloucester,[1] whom as young girls Fanny Burney had known in court in the 1780s when she served as Keeper of the Robes to Queen Charlotte. Now they sent warm carriages conveying her to and from Buckingham House, Kensington Palace, or Gloucester House, and on one occasion Frogmore. On one of these visits she saw the infant Victoria, and she lived to see her ascend the throne. In 1819 a magnificent French equipage entered Bolton Street almost daily[2] carrying the wife and the sister of General d'Arblay's distinguished French friend General Victor de Latour-Maubourg, who served for part of this year as French ambassador to the Court of St. James. His sister Marie de Maisonneuve was Madame d'Arblay's most intimate friend during her Paris exile and a correspondent through life. From

---

[1] Some 300 letters, notes, and invitations from the Princesses of England to FBA survive in the Berg Collection of the New York Public Library.

[2] See Diary for the year 1819.

France also came members of the Beauvau family, Marc-Étienne-Gabriel de Beauvau, 3rd prince de Beauvau-Craon, his wife, who was related to the Harcourts, their sons and daughters.

Cherished among English friends were still Mrs. Locke of Norbury Park, now residing at Eliot Vale, Blackheath, and her daughters Augusta, now Lady Martin, nearby in Hertford Street, and Amelia, wife of John Angerstein of Woodlands, whose town house was in St. James's Street. A faithful friend of earlier days was Queeney Thrale, now Viscountess Keith, wife of Admiral Sir George Keith, of Tullyallan, Scotland, a fashionable caller in the London season when the Houses were in session. In a gem of a house facing the Green Park lived the wit, poet, banker, and socialite Samuel Rogers, who, with his sister, often made his way to Madame d'Arblay, bringing on one occasion the poet Crabbe and on another, written large in her Diaries, Sir Walter Scott.

In the Burney family the best and most affectionate feelings lay near at home. A positive influence, pulling Madame d'Arblay out of the depths of her sorrow of 1818, was her brother James, who lived with his wife and daughter Sally *later* Payne at 26 James Street, Buckingham Gate, within walking distance across the Green Park. In 1821 he was at long last gazetted Rear Admiral, more in recognition perhaps of his geographical works and Voyages of Discovery than for actual service on the seas. His death in 1821 was grief anew.

The greatest comfort and support of the next seventeen years was the youngest of the original Burney family, Charlotte Ann Burney, Mrs. Broome, who, herself in her sixties, mother and grandmother, took lodgings for months, even years, when her family affairs permitted, in Bolton Street or Half Moon Street to be near her sister d'Arblay. She seemed to need, her daughters said, no other company. There was perfect confidence between them, deep affection, shared memories. On long evenings and long Sundays such society was a boon and a comfort, and when separated they wrote, usually on Sundays.

Old ladies commonly died of starvation, they thought, and the letters of their advanced old age were filled with anxious remedies and prescriptions: 'a seed Cake—an Egg beat up with warm water & sugar . . . a sponge biscuit dipt in a 1/2 of a glass of good sherry—the yolk of an Egg beat up with a little sugar & 3 Table spoonfuls of . . . milk & one desert spoonful of brandy'. Mrs. Broome understood the note of panic or desperation: 'Having lost so many darlings, only renders us still more distracted at the thoughts of fresh Bereavements.'[1]

On Sunday evenings Edward Burney, the artist, would arrive with his niece Fanny Burney, on one occasion bringing a portfolio of his decorative works—a new set of adventures for John Gilpin and a study of 'Drawing in all its Branches', drawing the long bow, drawing teeth, drawing straws. 'All his figures, notwithstanding the fun & absurdity of the ideas, are so extremely beautiful, that one is never tired of looking at them.'[2]

Humble connections on the Sleepe side of the family also made their way to Bolton Street. James Sansom, who on the death of Charles Burney, master of Greenwich School, migrated to the protective kindness of James, came with his wife and his son in the evening, the recipient of charities, as were also the Sleepe cousins Esther and Frances of Little Britain. Charity, a virtue that Fanny Burney had studied seriously in *Cecilia*, she practised regularly all her life. Named in her Diaries were the needy persons at the door, the mendicants in fixed stations in the lanes of nineteenth-century London—a matchwoman, a musselman, peddlers of thread or sheets of music. Distressed singers and actresses, the destitute and the unfortunate, even a Burney imposter, knew they could elicit help from her. In her Mayfair Diaries, even in her Last Will and Testament, is the reflection of a wide range of society from the *mendiante* in the alley to the Queen on the Throne.

Among other calls of duty was the fulfilment of promises made in happier times. General d'Arblay, foreseeing that after his death, set tasks in writing might help to fill the empty hours, had asked her to record adventures of the past for their son. In the years 1818 to 1825, therefore, she wrote partly from memory, partly from Pocket Book Memoranda or from correspondence, the Dunkirk Journal, her Presentations

---

[1] See xii, L. 1492, dated 6 [March 1837] and n. 1.
[2] See xii, L. 1387, dated [24]-25 October 1826, n. 10.

to Louis XVIII and to the Duchess d'Angoulême, the Water-
loo, Brussels, and Trèves Journals, and the Ilfracombe Journal,
accounts which, printed in the chronological order of their
occurrence in volumes vi–x of this series, would run to a
volume in themselves, some 200 pages.

To fulfil the expectations of her father Charles Burney
(1726–1814), Mus. Doc. (he *'designed & wished & bespoke
me for his Editor'*),[1] she undertook to edit his correspondence, the proceeds of which, when published, were to be
shared with her sister Esther Burney as joint residuary legatee. This was a task to daunt a professional editor of much
younger years or even a team of cataloguers and editors.
Learning in 1828 of restrictions in the copyright law that
prevented her from publishing letters written *to* her father
without the consent of the writers and realizing that, as the
distribution then was, most of Dr. Burney's letters were still
in the hands of their recipients, she undertook, until the
letters could be recalled, a full-scale biography of her father
The Memoirs of Doctor Burney (3 volumes), which was published in 1832. An act of piety and more a hagiography than
an objective biography, it was received, nevertheless, with
gratitude, if one may judge from long newspaper reviews and
extensive quotations. Readers were happy to be introduced
to the 'pleasant and buoyant genius of Burney himself'[2] and
to personages by that time legendary—Dr. Johnson, Garrick,
Burke, Gibbon, Sir Joshua Reynolds, Mrs. Thrale, and Bruce
of the Nile, of whom there were no descriptions at that date,
it was said, 'of greater vivacity and strength than those contained in these volumes'. Far from the natural style of the
journals and letters, the artificial style, probably fabricated to
accord with the pious matter, was disastrous and to readers
of *Evelina* a matter of astonishment. The work brought from
the dreaded reviewer John Wilson Croker, accusations of
'literary vanity' and the intention to deceive.[2] Resentful letters arrived from descendants of persons mentioned in the
Memoirs and from connections of the Burney family dis-
agreeing with her readings of old monetary transactions. One
armigerous member of the family argued that the names of

---

[1] See xi, L. 1238, dated [25]–28 November 1820; also Ll. 1304, 1307.

[2] For reviews, see xii, L. 1424 n. 1; L. 1529 n. 5.

the maternal forebears of the Burneys, Sleepe and Dubois, once residents of the Poultry and Threadneedle Street, could well be left in oblivion. The biographer's correspondence of 1833 (she was then 81 years of age) reflects octogenarian efforts to cope with the aftermath of the *Memoirs*, pleasant and unpleasant.

Highly visible on the actual manuscripts to this day are the editorial marks of some twenty years' toil over the accretions that, by the deaths of her sister Susan (1800), her father (1814), her husband (1818), and eventually her son (1837), had successively fallen into her care. To preserve for her son's 'Fire-side Rectory' and for posterity what might be of interest and value but to remove from the public eye all letters or passages in letters reflecting the painful or less creditable events within the family history—this was her aim. Her methods, described at some length in the Introduction to this series (i, pp. xxxvi–xliv)[1] and shown as well in a facsimile (*facing* p. xl; and *HFB*, p. 432), were drastic. The final decision to be made concerning the annihilation or preservation of the correspondence,[2] she discussed at length in a letter of [25]-28 November 1820 (xi, L. 1238) to her sister Esther, a document that may be taken as her editorial *apologia*. The work had its physical cost. At night bending over the trunks of papers and once in the very act of obliterating '*passages* of letters that I wished not wholly to destroy' she was seized with dizziness.[3] Periodically she fell into feverish illnesses brought on, her doctor said, by '*a Head over-worked, & a Heart over-loaded*'. In 1839 she could work no more. Sacks full of papers she consigned to the flames, and still there was a residue of thousands more. What shall I do 'with this killing mass?' 'Shall I Burn them?'[4] To Mrs. Broome must be given much of the credit for their survival. Applying her wise head and 'feeling heart' to the question she came up with an

---

[1] See also Joyce Hemlow, '. . . Establishing the Text', *Editing Eighteenth-Century Texts*, ed. D. I. B. Smith (Toronto, 1968), pp. 25-43.

[2] Much deplored and condemned is the mutilation and partial destruction of the 'Memoirs' or Recollections of his own life that Dr. Burney prepared in the years 1782-1806. See Roger Lonsdale, *Dr. Charles Burney* (1965), chap. xi. The surviving fragments of the work have been assembled and edited by Professor S. Klima *et al.* of McGill University.   [3] See xi, Ll. 1304, 1307.

[4] See xii, L. 1518, dated [20 April 1838] and n. 3; also i, p. xlii.

evaluation of the manuscripts almost prophetic with respect to the Burney d'Arblay papers and her own.[1] Following her advice, Madame d'Arblay willed one division of the papers to Mrs. Broome's daughter Charlotte Barrett, to whom also had come by that time all her mother's papers.[2] To Charles Parr Burney she returned the papers of his father and his grand-father, which came down to his descendants, who still retain many of them.[3]

The past and its memorials by no means obliterated the present, and Madame d'Arblay's greatest concern in the years 1818-37 was her son, his health and his prospects in the world. No one could argue that she was a wise mother and many perhaps can point to where she went wrong. Less clear, except to psychologists perhaps, is what, as it were, ailed him. She expected him to be a Burney, like her father or her brother Charles, the Grecian, who could combine solid achievement with an active social life; but, with intellectual capacities (particularly in mathematics) that made young d'Arblay the friend of many eminent men of his age—Charles Babbage, Herschell (the younger), William Whewell, Richard Jones and other Cantabs of his years—he attained little dis-tinction. 'He *might* have been, everything', his tutor affirmed, but he had wasted his college years, not in vice, but in idle-ness, chess, and poetry, Lamartine and Byron vying in favour. 'Son goût pour la Poésie absorbe tous les autres', observed Mme de Maisonneuve. With an 'apathy and nonchalance' im-penetrable, he could not, in spite of years of nagging on the

---

[1] See p. xxiii, n. 4.

[2] For the initial division of the archive, see Madame d'Arblay's will (PRO/PROB/11/1922/88, pr. 17 February 1840), printed xii, pp. 976-81. The Burney-d'Arblay papers willed to Charlotte Barrett, together with those of her mother Mrs. Broome *née* Charlotte Ann Burney, came down in the Barrett-Wauchope family. With sales of the twentieth century this collection was again divided, most of it reaching the Berg Collection of the NYPL with a large supplementary adjunct eventually to the BL. For curators' reports of these acquisitions, see i, pp. xxv-xxvi; also Joyce Hemlow, *et al.*, *A Catalogue of the Burney Family Correspon-dence, 1740-1873* (1971), a list of about 10,000 items to which some 300 can now be added.

[3] The papers willed to Charles Parr Burney (1785-1864) were handed down to his descendants until in 1954 a large division was placed on the market and, acquired by the late James M. Osborn, is now in the Osborn Collection at Yale University. Still in the possession of the Burney family are the Comyn Collection (see i, p. xxvii) and a number of letters owned by Mr. Michael Burney-Cumming. Doubtless some are still retained by other members of the family.

subject, be brought to advance his own interests. He lacked the Burney drive or ambition, being, like his father, the comte d'Arblay, too gentlemanly perhaps for that. As Talleyrand said, the comte knew not how to petition. In forty years of life Alexander never gained what his mother termed 'a knowledge of the world and its ways',[1] and he remained at the age of 40 pretty well the young man she observed at his reading party in Ilfracombe in the summer of 1817, aged 23. His imagination held 'impetuous sway over his Actions'. Absorbed in the composition of 'some Ode, some Elegy, or some Scene in a Tragedy',[2] he could not be brought to attend to practical matters at hand, least of all studies leading to his degree. In feverish absorption in writing he resembled his mother more than she ever realized, but without her success, he remained, as the body of his work would suggest, more Poetaster than Poet.

Ordained in St. James's Church, Piccadilly, in 1818, he was seeking with no great eagerness or *empressement* a living in the Church. His clerical mentor and supporter was his mother's friend the Revd. George Owen Cambridge, Archdeacon of Middlesex, with whose help he obtained a living of sorts as Perpetual Curate to one of the new Commissioners' churches in Camden Town, with a stipend of £200 per annum. For the onerous pastoral duties of this large working-class parish he had neither the physical strength, however, nor the temperament. After preaching two sermons on Sundays 'il se tomba mal à s'évanouir de fatigue le soir', he confessed to his mother's friend Madame de Maisonneuve. Genuinely religious, however, and conscientious as far as his strength permitted, he wrote structured or literary sermons, which he delivered in the declamatory or highly theatrical style of his favourite actors Talma or Kean, he versified the psalms, established an infant school, and looked in vain for a lectureship in London.

In London he was to be found in bookshops or with his friends the wealthy Angersteins at balls, plays, or operas. 'He dresses like a gentleman', reported Sarah Harriet Burney, the novelist, 'and goes into good society and is remarked for his

---

[1] For Mrs. Broome's studies of d'Arblay's artlessness and simplicity, see xii, L. 1492 n. 4; L. 1494 n. 2.
[2] x, L. 1094, dated 21–9 June [1817].

clever countenance; and in favour with those he gets into conversation with.'[1] With his mother's phenomenal memory, which she had trained from his infant days in recitation, he could entertain with whole scenes from Molière or recite, to Thomas Moore's gratification, the whole of *Lalla Rookh* (some 6,000 lines). 'Il est impossible', adjudged Madame de Maisonneuve, 'de mieux parler d'avoir une organe plus agréable et un meilleur choix d'expression   il est si instruit qu'il peut avoir les conversations les plus savantes et avec les personnes ordinaires il parle de tou[tes] choses avec un gayeté et un esprit rempli d'agrémens et originalité.'[2] He seemed in London a Frenchman, in Paris, an Englishman. The double nationality assigned to him by birth and the dichotomy as well between his life style and his actual circumstances ran him into visionary hopes and disappointments, more than once, in love and marriage. Despair afforded a subject for verse but failed to spur him to the exertion necessary to improve his clerical lot. Advancement in the church depended on the favour of a bishop, and the pursuit of bishops, not unmarked in the Burney family, became the subject of one of Sally Payne's jokes, when Aunt d'Arblay sent Alex fifty miles, she said, in fruitless pursuit of one bishop only to miss one near at hand.

In 1835, to the relief of his immediate patron, the Vicar of St. Pancras, he resigned his curacy at Camden Chapel. Once again Archdeacon Cambridge came to the rescue obtaining for him the ministry of Ely Chapel in Holborn. The beautiful thirteenth-century building had been closed for years. Damps clung about it, and d'Arblay preaching there in December 1836 contracted an influenza that brought him, on 17 January 1837, the death he had long seemed to desire.

To this devastating blow Madame d'Arblay bore up well, it was said, but the Letters, Diaries, and Notebooks of her final years testify to racking grief and desolation. She lived on till 6 January 1840, meeting death with the courage that had sustained her through a long and eventful life.

Shy, gentle, retiring, affectionate, home-loving, and outwardly conforming but adventurous in spirit, mind, and action, she lived her life in full. Often in a front seat as major

---

[1] In a letter (Berg) of 25 April 1828 (cited, xii, L. 1401 n. 4).
[2] See xii, L. 1412 n. 7.

events of her time unfolded as upon a stage, she was more than most writers *present* in history and industriously she recorded it for family, friends, and for posterity. At the end her mind wandered, it was said, over wide bournes in shifting memory and conceivably in imagination to that perfect land where firmly she expected to meet those who had gone before. 'I know I am dying but I am willing to die; I commit my soul to God, in reliance on the mercy and merits of my Redeemer.'

[26 James Street, Westminster],[1]
2–7 October 1818

To Esther (Burney) Burney

A.L.S. (rejected Diary MSS. [7144–7], p. 3 numbered 7146, Berg),
2–7 Oct. 1818
Double sheet 4to   black edged   4 pp.   *pmk* 〈   〉 wafer
Addressed: Mrs. Burney / Lark Hall Place / near / Bath
Endorsed by EBB, p. 4, *address panel*: Answered by Post / Oct. 12th
Docketed in old brown ink: 1818

2[d] Octr. 1818

I know how anxious my kind Hetty will be to hear from me—& I would have written yesterday but my hand & head were too unsteady—I am quieter to-day—though all my nights have been feverish & restless—Here, nevertheless, I have *necessarily* so much more of assumed calm that it is possible it may hasten the period of its becoming natural. I have been received by All here[2]—James at the head—with the

---

1180. [1] JB's house (the 'Freehold Messuage or Tenement with the outbuildings and appurtenances' at 26 James Street, Buckingham Gate, Westminster) had been bequeathed to him in 1792 by his father's friend John Hayes (i, L. 10 n. 10). It was to be immortalized for its whist parties through the writings of Charles Lamb, H. Crabb Robinson, Hazlitt, John Rickman, and the Ayrtons, father and son. See Lamb, *Letters, passim*.

Though invited by her brother to remain with his family all winter, FBA moved on 8 Oct. 1818 to 11 Bolton Street, Piccadilly, and there established a London home for her son Alexander, now aged 23. As is shown in Rate Books (Westminster Library) the proprietor was Frances Wheatley or Whitley (*fl.* 1807–54), daughter of the artist Francis Wheatley (1747–1801) by his marriage to the model and artist Clara Maria Leigh (d. 1838), *later*, Pope (see *DNB*). For the years 1818–28 she would rent the greater part of the house to Mme d'Arblay at £180 per year (see FBA's Account Books, Berg). Marked by a plaque placed by the National Trust, No. 11 is now occupied, along with the house next door, by a firm of solicitors.

[2] Those present would have been James himself, now 68 years of age, the 'Captain Burney' described by H. Crabb Robinson (*Diary*, i. 300), who had met him at Lamb's house in 1810, as 'a character, a fine noble creature—gentle, with a rough exterior, as became the associate of Captain Cook in his voyages round the world, and the literary historian of all these acts of circumnavigation'. James's wife Sarah *née* Payne (1758–1832) emerges attractively in Lamb's essay 'Mrs. Battle's Opinions in Whist' and in her correspondence (Manwaring, pp. 275 ff.). Their son Martin (1788–1852), a 'certified attorney', was an 'odd joker', 'whitesouled' according to Lamb, and according to Sharon Turner (1768–1847), under whom he had articled, 'a man of great honour and integrity'. 'He never told me

most touching affection & commiseration—more than I had ever flattered myself with expecting—& so much as to reconcile me to having missed arriving while the house was empty — — They had all returned from Lynn on the Tuesday. Alex, after a night's Journey, had preceded me only on the same day,[3] Wednesday. I will leave him to tell his own history, as he means to write it to Maria & Sophy—I will only tell I you that he *has not been plucked*—il s'en faut de beaucoup—& that he was the only Candidate for orders who was at the Palace,[3] where my very amiable & constant Friend the Bishop of Salisbury made him live quite *en famille* with Mrs. & the Miss Fishers, & his Nephew, Archdeacon Fisher.[4] The good Bishop made him, also, one of his own family in taking him to a great dinner given by Mr. Hume,[5] one of the Canons of Salisbury—. Archdeacon Fisher himself shewed him—& another fellow of Christ College, Mr. Graham,[6] all

a lie in his life!' (Manwaring, p. 292). The daughter of the house, Sarah, now about 22 years of age, was in a few years to give Lamb his subject for 'The Wedding'.

[3] Madame d'Arblay had left Bath on Wednesday 30 Sept. 1818. Previous to this, on 13 Sept. (see x, L. 1178 n. 2) she had received a letter from her old friend John Fisher (i, L. 3 n. 36), formerly canon of Windsor, Bishop of Salisbury (1807), inviting her son Alexander for a visit with his family at the Palace from the 23rd to Sunday 27 Sept., the day on which he was ordained deacon in the Church of England. For his ordination papers, see x, L. 1178 n. 1. After this, Alexander, now a Fellow of Christ's College, Cambridge, had gone to London, arriving on Wednesday 30 Sept., but he had departed for Cambridge on Tuesday 6 Oct. For his friendship with his cousins Maria Bourdois and Sophia Elizabeth Burney (i, p. lxix), who lived at 5 Ainslie's Belvedere, Bath, see ix, x *passim*.

[4] FBA's friendship with the then Canon Fisher and his wife Dorothea *née* Scrivener (i, L. 3 n. 36) dated from 1786, the first year of FB's appointment as Keeper of the Robes to Queen Charlotte (*DL* iii *passim*).

The elder daughter Dorothea (*c.* 1797–1889), as heiress of her grandfather the late John Preston Scrivener (*c.* 1730–97) of Sibton Abbey, Suffolk, was to marry on 9 Apr. 1839 John Frederick Pike (d. 1 Oct. 1866), who with the Scrivener fortune took the name Pike-Scrivener. The younger daughter Elizabeth (d. Dec. 1880) was to marry on 16 Oct. 1823 John Campbell Mirehouse (1789–1850).

Dr. Fisher's nephew would have been John Fisher (*c.* 1767–1832), vicar of Osmington, Dorset (1813), Archdeacon of Berkshire (1817), and canon residentiary of Salisbury (1819).

[5] The son of John Hume (*c.* 1706–82), Bishop of Salisbury (1766), the Revd. Thomas Henry Hume (1765–1834) was prebendary of Salisbury (1795), canon residentiary (1803), and treasurer (1806).

[6] Born in 1794 (the year also of AA's birth) and like him, a Wrangler, a Fellow of Christ's, and ordained deacon in 1818, John Graham (d. 1865) was to attain, in marked contrast to d'Arblay, high places in University, Church, and State. Proficient in mathematics as well as classics (see *DNB*), he was to be appointed

the Lions of the City—& Mr. Graham took him to the superb domain of Lord Radnor,[7] in its neighbourhood: & Mr. Douglas,[8] a prebend, of Salisbury, & son of a very famously learned former Bishop of Salisbury, who was also one of my Windsor Friends, invited him to see his noble library, & then, kept him on an additional day, to give him a great ¦ dinner, with Mr. Hodgson,[9] secretary to the Archbp of Canterbury, who came down to aid the ordination.

See how involuntarily I am running into his history!—I have seen nothing yet that has suited us for a residence—& James is most averse to my fixing one—but alas I am in great want of the power of utter seclusion without calling for indulgence in so doing. Yet it is impossible utterly impossible for consideration to be greater or more delicate than I meet with here from All—but it is myself who am in requisition *with* myself; for I do not think it right to accept their hospitality & not endeavour to meet its kindness with apparent revival. But my loaded heart is but the more ponderously heavy for all forced exertion. Yet, could I have seen you All at Lark Hall place as I *now* see All here, I should lament that I had not made the so long intended visit—but for *once* it

Master (1830–48) and Vice-Chancellor (1831, 1840), Bishop of Chester (1848), and at Court, Clerk of the Closet to the Queen (1849).

[7] This would have been Longford Castle, Wiltshire, near Salisbury, the occupant at this time being Jacob Pleydell-Bouverie (1749/50–1828), 2nd Earl of Radnor (1776).

[8] The Revd. William Douglas (*c.* 1769–1818), F.R.S. (1800), held prebends in Salisbury Cathedral (1792–9), Fordington (1799), and Westminster (1807). He was canon residentiary at Salisbury, Precentor (1804), Archdeacon of Wiltshire (1799–1804), Chancellor of the Diocese (1799), and Warden of St. Nicholas Hospital, Salisbury (1792). A mural tablet in Salisbury Cathedral states that he was interred in St. George's Chapel, Windsor, 'near the remains of his venerable and learned father, John Douglas, D.D., late Bishop of this Diocese'. The latter, FB and CB had known as early as 1786 when he was Canon of Windsor (*DL* iii. 148; and iv *passim*). See also i, L. 23 n. 47.

[9] A friend of CB Jr., Christopher Hodgson (1784–1874) was an 'ecclesiastical lawyer', whose aid was often sought in the collection of church revenues. In 1806 or 1807 he was appointed 'chapter clerk, registrar, and bailiff of the manors and bailwicks to the dean and chapter of St. Paul's'. In 1809 he became Secretary to the Archbishop of Canterbury, and within ten years, Secretary as well to the Bishop of London and the Archbishop of York. For almost fifty years (1822–71) he acted as Secretary or Secretary-Treasurer to the Queen's Bounty, Dean's Yard, Westminster. For his publications and his services to the Church, its prelates and incumbents, see G. F. A. Best, *Temporal Pillars* . . . (1964), pp. 226–30 and *passim*.

would ill have answered—for distressful indeed to me—& I believe all round—was my first Evening here.—

Should you meet with any opportunity, through the Brannans[10] or Mrs. Payne,[11] I beg you to send my thanks, mixt with my scoldings, to the too kind Miss Wilson[12] for a Basket of Grapes & Biscuits which were put into my hands just as the Horses were driven off from Bath. |

I have a Letter from poor Charlotte,[13] who seems in a state of debility alarming to herself!—She is at Brighton—so is *Sarah Harriet*. I have a Letter also from Charlotte Barret, from Geneva; but she is really coming home[13]—though with a view to return to the Continent for another Tour next year! They are to spend a 12 month at Bradfield. I forgot to put up the little old mourning Ring mementos—but will send them by the first opportunity. Alex is not quite well—hurry—high

[10] John Brenan or Brannan (*c.* 1763-1826) and his wife Anna Maria *née* Hayter (*c.* 1775-1850) of 23 Great Stanhope Street, Bath, with whom the d'Arblays lodged in the years 1816-18 (ix, L. 1011 n. 14).

[11] Mary Ann Payne (*c.* 1787-1824), practical nurse, employed by the d'Arblays in Bath (x, L. 1170 n. 83).

[12] Harriet Wilson (*fl.* 1797-1840) was apparently the illegitimate daughter of the wife of Joshua Wilson (d. 1797) of Crofton Hall, Yorkshire, and the half-sister, therefore, of Henry Wright Wilson (*c.* 1757-1832), formerly a captain in the 1st Regiment of Life Guards, heir by his father's will (PRO/PROB/11/1295/580, pr. 2 Aug. 1797) to Crofton Hall and the manor of Pontefract, Yorkshire, and resident in Grosvenor Square.

Having been employed as a governess, Harriet was encouraged to give up her post in lieu of an annual allowance offered to her by her half-brother, who, according to her story, soon discontinued the pension, leaving her without support. She is soon to appear in London, where she visits FBA, in whom apparently she had confided her story, a story that would emerge publicly in *The Times* (22 Feb. and 27 Nov. 1823). An action that she had initiated in the Court of the King's Bench to recover arrears in her allowance was non-suited on 21 Feb. 1823, and a second appeal on 26 Nov. was similarly dismissed. Her half-brother seems to have ignored the suggestion of the Court that he 'be generous and give what he did not chuse to yield', and Harriet lived in ever-increasing poverty, first in Red Lion Square and later in Camden Town, appearing in FBA's charity lists (Berg) and eventually in her will, dated 6 Mar. 1839, with a bequest of £40. A number of Harriet's letters are extant in the Berg Collection (see *Catalogue*).

[13] FBA's sister Charlotte Broome (i, p. lxxii) and her half-sister Sarah Harriet, the novelist (i, p. lxxiv). Mrs. Broome's daughter Charlotte Barrett (with her husband and elder daughter) had embarked in July on a three-month continental tour, the stages of which are shown in the datelines of the series of letters (see *Catalogue*) that she sent to Arthur Young of Bradfield: Boulogne (13-15 July), Paris (28 July), Tours (3 Aug.), Lyons (17 Aug.), Sesto (28 Aug.), Milan (30 Aug.), then by way of Turin and Mount Cenis to Lausanne (7-15 Sept.), Geneva (16 Sept.), Chamonix on the Jura (25 Sept.), and back to Paris (6 Oct.), with plans to embark from Dieppe to Brighton. See also Gazley, pp. 690 ff.

living, travelling by night, & kept down, but potent secret anxiety have evidently shaken him. I wish to have him tranquilly under my care—but he must soon go to Cambridge & it is uncertain for how long. This is not gay!—Oh my dear Esther—but adieu—keep well; all here send Loves—My revered poor Queen lingers on![14]—

Remember me kindly & particularly to my dear Blue,[15] who I hope has better news from Worcester? & give my love to Mr. B. Amelia[16] & the Belvedere[17]—

Henry's letter is charming, dear little fellow.[18] Mrs. Payne has done so well & had so much trouble, I shall send her one pound when I can, w[ith th]anks—

I forgot to give this for the Post!—I have now to thank Maria & Sophy[3] for their Letters—Mrs. Payne's parcel is arrived safe & well.

I began this the 2^d—but have only gone on by bits to this morning, the 7th—I *cannot* do any thing *de suite*. ⎟

[14] The health of the Queen, a matter of concern since June 1818, when her indisposition had caused the postponement of the marriage of the Duke of Cambridge, had steadily worsened. On 5 Sept. FBA had been saddened by a letter written by the 'Dowager Lady Harcourt on the visibly approaching dissolution of my dear—honoured—precious, & truly exalted Royal Mistress', a letter written at the request of Princess Mary, now Duchess of Gloucester, 'to save me the shock of surprise' (see x, L. 1176 n. 1). Bulletins issued regularly since mid-September described nights devoid of rest and days unchanged for the better, though the Queen was to linger on until 17 Nov. 1818, dying at Kew Palace in the seventy-fifth year of her age (Olwen Hedley, pp. 297-8).

[15] The sister of Charles Rousseau Burney (L. 1189 n. 10), 'Blue' or Elizabeth Warren Burney (i, p. lxxv) of Worcester, who lived for long periods of time with EBB's son, the Revd. Richard Allen Burney (i, p. lxix) in his rectories at Rimpton and Brightwell. FBA hoped for encouraging news of the health of Blue's sister Ann, the widow of the Revd. John Hawkins (d. 19 June 1804). Mrs. Hawkins, who had in effect adopted EBB's daughter Cecilia (see iii, L. 132 n. 5), had on 2 Apr. 1813 taken a house on Barborne Terrace, near 'the old family dwelling, Barborne Lodge' (see 'Worcester Journal').

[16] Amelia Maria (i, p. lxix), EBB's fifth surviving daughter, now aged 26, was shortly to take the name, unofficially at least, of 'Emily'.

[17] See n. 3.

[18] Henry (b. 6 June 1814) was the son of the Revd. Richard Allen Burney (1773-1836). Presented in 1801 by the Bishop of Winchester to the living at Rimpton, Somersetshire (v, L. 462 n. 8), Richard owed to the same family, namely to the Revd. William Garnier (c. 1772-1835), prebendary of Winchester (1800), and husband of Bishop North's daughter Henrietta (1771-1847), a curacy at Brightwell, Berkshire ('Worcester Journal'), and in the years 1815-31, the use of the rectory there; and to his father-in-law he owed the living of Buckland Dinham, Somerset (ix, L. 1078 n. 11).

PS. If you or Maria or Sophy, see Mr. Hay,[19] I beg you to mention how sorry *we* were to quit Bath without receiving his Account—& to give my Direction at my Brothers, & entreat that it may follow me— |

May I entreat you to trust me with 5^s to Mrs. Payne for a Mrs. Abrams,[20] added to my mournful—mournful cards? —I can pay it by some opportunity ere long.—

Y^r truly affect^e sister F. d'Arblay.

1181   [26 James Street, Westminster],
6 October 1818

To Alexander d'Arblay

A.L. (Berg), 6 Oct. 1818
Single sheet 8vo   black-edged   2 pp.
Addressed: To the / Reverend Alexander d'Arblay / Christ College, / Cambridge.

Tuesday Noon
6th Oct^r
1818.

My dear Deacon,

I will not let you wait the slow arrival of the waggon for your Linnen, which I therefore send off as soon as it appears. Your kind Uncle has taken charge of your Trunk & Hat Box. —I accompanied him—& had not moved a step ere I met Charles Parr![1]—I knew him not at first—& was painfully

[19] George Edmund Hay (1778-1844), the apothecary who attended General d'Arblay in his last illness (see x, L. 1170 *passim*). For his reluctance to present his account, see L. 1189 n. 18.
[20] Possibly Jacob Abraham (*fl.* 1799-1842), optician and mathematical instrument maker, of 7 Bartlett Street, Bath (x, L. 1179 n. 9).

1181. [1] In looking over the papers of CB Jr. (d. 28 Dec. 1817), Charles Parr Burney had come upon references to the theft of books that had resulted in his father's explusion from Cambridge in 1777 (see *HFB*, pp. 72-6; x, L. 1150 nn. 2, 3; also Ralph S. Walker, 'Charles Burney's Theft of Books at Cambridge', *Transactions of the Cambridge Bibliographical Society*, III. 4 (1962), 313-24. After a correspondence with his aunt d'Arblay on the subject (x, Ll. 1150 and 1158), CPB had come to consult her at Bath (x, L. 1158 and n. 1; J. 1170. 867).

struck when I recollected him—I think he was nearly the last person who saw our departed Angel.—for Angel must he be—who, so like an Angel already, sunk to Earthly rest! —Heaven—Heaven grant us but to re-join him! — — —

I go certainly on Thursday, Oct. 8th to No 11. Bolton Street, Piccadilly.

Why do I give you that Address?—Can you conjecture, my dear Deacon? ǀ

I would have *Yours* my first Letter there.

Do not forget my message to *Dr. Kaye.*[2] Nor to consult *Mr. Ebden*[3] about your Furniture—nor to write to *Dr. Gibbs.*[4] And mention to me when you have done it. But above all tell me truth of your Cough.

NB. Try, Mr. Deacon, to separate the Thin fine cambric frills from the thick common calico.

And tell me they all arrive safe & are welcome.

1182   26 James Street, Westminster,
                                     6 October 1818

To Mrs. Broome

A.L.S. (rejected Diary MSS. 7148-[51], Berg), 6 Oct. 1818
Originally a double sheet 4to (8.9 × 7.2″)   4 pp.   black edge
The second leaf was cut and pasted as described in Textual Notes
pmk ⟨O⟩C wafer
Addressed: Mrs. Broome / Broad Street, / No 9. or / Post office / Brighton
Endorsed: Sister d'arblay / Octr 6th 1818 / ansd
Edited by CFBt.

[2] John Kaye (1783-1853), D.D. (1815), Bishop of Bristol (1820), of Lincoln (1827), at this time Master of Christ's College. A former pupil of CB Jr., he had helped in AA's difficulties at Cambridge (ix, x *passim*).
[3] AA's friend the Revd. James Collett Ebden (viii, L. 840 n. 28), a Wrangler (1816), Fellow of Christ's College (1816-17), of Trinity (1817-28). See ix, x *passim.*
[4] George Smith Gibbes (1771-1851), F.R.S. (1796), M.D. (1799), physician at Bath, kt. (1820). See ix, L. 1037 n. 4.

Westminster
James Street—
6th Octr 1818

Long indeed I have found it to be without any communication with my dearest Charlotte & oh how more than long —how direful has been the period of silence!— to prepare to quit the last spot in which all that was most dear to me has perished!—the spot so fatal in which I lost him—yet that I quitted with deepest emotion for it was the spot on [which] I last was blest by him—Oh my dear Charlotte—how bitter has been my toil in all this mournful preparation! the harrass of my body too has been terrible—I thought I should never have done, so innumerable were the objects to remove, dispose of—or abandon. And All connected with some latent subject of regret—all conveying in themselves some little history to make their sight—their touch—tragic! tragic! —— But it is over—& I am now writing from our worthy James's most hospitable roof.[1] I have found in that excellent Brother a feeling for me, a sense of my loss that has softened my grief by its tenderness. It will be a real & true comfort to me to be near him for the rest of my days. And if our long meditated plan can be brought to ǀ bear that will join me with my ever dear & tender Charlotte that—with Alexander —may revive me—perhaps—not to happiness. never— never more!—but to a supportable existence—& a sense of gratitude to the Almighty that such blessings are yet in store, maternal & fraternal—

I have just taken the greatest part of a house in Bolton Street, all, indeed but the Parlour & a Garret & one Kitchen.[1] —It is dear, but Alex, whom I make my leader in all, prefers any œconomy to that of sparing a handsome dwelling, & ample room for his Books & our Pictures. Our income is yet uncertain, but we must live according to its utmost smallness in all points but House rent, till we have paid certain sacred Bills, & seen what may be obtained from just—but difficult claims from abroad.[2]

1182. [1] See L. 1180 n. 1.
  [2] For the payment of arrears owing to General d'Arblay, see L. 1191 n. 9 and L. 1280 n. 5.

You recommended to me a Girl of 14 as a young servant —pray give me her direction. A maid of my own,[3] for needlework for us both, & to attend me when I am ill, &c, is to come to me, from Ilfracomb: an excellent & very pleasing young woman, who never yet has served, & who will be a great solace to me. But she is not maid for *all* work, or for hard work, & must have some one under her. I think your Richmond young Girl will just suffice. And if so, I shall try house keeping for ourselves instead of Cooking by the Hostess or her servants. Pray tell me what ought to be the wages. |

I rejoice—what a word!—that our beloved Charlotte is returning. I have had a very kind Letter from her dated Geneva.[4] Shall we not be much together this winter, my dearest Charlotte? Alex goes to Cambridge to-morrow[5]— Dismal will be my home without him! I go to it on Thursday. Our kind James would fain detain me here—but I am really only fit for general seclusion, broken in upon by occasional attempts at sociality. A residence away from my own Cell is beyond my force. While Alex is away, if my dear Charlotte could come & take his room!—That would indeed be soothing to me.—

Let me know my chances—& when you leave Brighton. Stay there however as long as [the] sea air is salubrious. Your health is far dearer to me even than your sight. I beseech you to regain it by every possible effort.

I am very much obliged to Mrs. Cooke.[6] I was sure of

[3] Elizabeth Ramsay (1798–1873) was the second daughter of Robert Ramsay (*c.* 1753–1843) of Ilfracombe, a shoemaker, with whose family FBA and AA had lodged in the summer of 1817 (see x, L. 1095). Devoted to FBA and a great comfort to her (see L. 1189) but hopelessly inefficient as a servant, FBA reluctantly encouraged her return to Ilfracombe in 1822 (see Ll. 1304, 1307, 1314).

[4] This letter is missing but CFBt had joined her mother in Brighton *c.* 12 Oct. 1818 (see L. 1180 n. 13). [5] Thursday 8 Oct. 1818.

[6] A cousin of Jane Austen's mother, Cassandra *née* Leigh (1744–1826) and her husband the Revd. Samuel Cooke (1741–1820), vicar of Great Bookham (1769), were neighbours and friends of the d'Arblays in the years 1793–7 (see iii and iv *passim*). 'In all y^r extensive range of Admirers', Mrs. Cooke had remarked in a letter of condolence (Berg) of 18 Oct. 1818, 'None could more sincerely estimate your great deprivation than those of this Vicarage! for few could know as We have had the happiness of witnessing the high, the superior Qualities in every Character, of y^r long & patient Sufferer—'.

For reasons of health (v, L. 469 n. 3), the vicar, his wife, and his daughter seem to have spent parts of the last twenty years in Bath or Brighton, where they

her real concern for a loss she had learnt to appreciate by knowing the excellencies of which it was composed—Oh my Charlotte What excellencies!—what sweetness what nobleness combined!— ׀

[*The bottom of page 3 is missing; the top of page 4 continues:*]

apparently best. She[7] has more of the activity of health than any of her Children.—I am very—very anxious for better accounts of your own health, my dearest Charlotte —give them as soon as possible to your truly affectionate F. d'A.—

Mrs. Burney is indefatigably kind—zealous—& affectionate. Sarah greatly improved in all points—& Martin steadily good friendly & worthy.—The family[8] are unusually all well together & their Chearfulness insensibly does me service—

1183   [11 Bolton Street,
                                   13 October 1818]
To Mrs. Piozzi

A.L. (Diary MSS. viii. 7152-[4], Berg), n.d.
Double sheet 4to (8.9 × 7.2″)   black-edged   1 p.   mutilated *pmk*   14 OC. 818   black seal
Addressed: For / Mrs. Piozzi, / Gay Street, / Bath.
Edited by FBA, p. 1 (7152) *annotated and dated*: ⌐N° (5)¬   15. Oct[r] 1818   *also numbered* 40 and X 7174
p. 4 [7154] *docketed by* FBA: 9th Oct[r]
Edited also by CFBt, who copied on p. 3 of the 4to the close (date line and signature) of FBA's original. Also edited by the Press. *See* Textual Notes.

Dear Madam,

From my general seclusion during this late mournful period, I only, & by accident, heard of your return to Bath

met CBFB. For Mrs. Cooke's correspondence with members of the Burney family, see *Catalogue*.
[7] Probably EBB.   [8] For JB's family, see L. 1180 n. 2.

just as I was quitting it[1]—I should else, I think, have trusted to the kindness of old remembrances—that with me can never die,—for soliciting to have seen you for a moment before my departure. As it is, however, I will venture, upon the same grounds, to hope that when circumstances call you to town—whither my son has now drawn me for our chief present residence—you will not forget that there now dwells in Bolton Street an old Friend who with ever invariable attachment sincerely signs herself

Dear Madam,

1184   11 Bolton Street,
                                 17 October 1818

To Alexander d'Arblay

A.L. (rejected Diary MSS. 7158-[61], Berg), 17 Oct. 1818
Double sheet 4to   black edged   4 pp.
Addressed: Rev[d] Alexander d'Arblay, / Fellow of Christ College, / Cambridge,
Edited by CFBt. *See* Textual Notes.

1183. [1] After the General's death FBA had apparently called more than once on Mrs. Piozzi looking (conjecturally, and if so, in vain) for sympathy. 'Madame D'Arblay writes and comes, and cries', wrote Mrs. Piozzi on 15 Oct. 1818, 'and goes to live at London with her son. She is very charming: she always was; but I will never trust her more' (x, L. 1174 n. 2). Not from her could FBA expect expressions of condolence or sympathy much less regret at her departure from Bath. ' "Nothing so dull as a consolatory letter" ', opined HLTP on a similar occasion (16 July 1820; Hayward, ii. 311), quoting from 'some pert wit of the last age'. Her reply (Berg) of [*pre* 17 Oct. 1818] to FBA's letter (*supra*) obtruded no 'insipid consolation' therefore. Not 'dull for that reason' it was rather her usual breezy missive, commenting on mutual friends and recent books, including the 'hideous Tale called Frankenstein' ('How changed is the Taste of Verse Prose & Painting! since *le bon vieux Temp!*'). Her letter, with a request for verses on October written by CB, is printed but incorrectly dated (*DL* vi. 388-9).

FBA was grateful for the speed of the reply and that her former friend 'had had enough of old kindness to write so readily'. The letter itself she found 'strange & fantastic [and] ill adapted to my state of mind,—which, probably, she does not devine nor understand' (Diary, 17 Oct.). HLTP's request she was to deal with only on 15 Dec. 1820 (L. 1239), when a correspondence reminiscing on old times was renewed.

Bolton Street, Piccadilly. N⁰ 11
17. Octr 1818.

Your Letter,[1] my dear Deacon, required too much consideration for an immediate answer, & it will be better we should agree that you should never expect a return of Post, as it is so seldom such a one can be satisfactory. And, in truth, you gave me a whole morning's work in hunting for Mange,[2] as the Books are none of them unpacked, for I am still in our Hostesses own Apartments,[3] our own not being yet vacated. But I sent a line that my search was successful, as I take an additional Day not only for looking out, from my innumerable packages, cravats & *Bas*, but, yet more, to allow myself cool time for deliberately weighing the 4 propositions that all are deeply interesting & important, to which you desire my *sisterly* reply.

Sisterly they shall be, my Alex; I will not ask to guide your determination: I will only lay before you my opinions, & reflections, & ideas, that you may weigh them with your own before you decide.

The 4 Great points are, Your *Pupils;*[4] Y^r *Apartm^{ts} A*— & y^r *Work. 1st* To begin with what is least near our hearts, because merely affecting our purse, *The Apartments.*

I regard it as singularly fortunate that all these contrarieties & incertitudes have kept you from having any in your College.——

How so? You cry.

Because you cannot furnish them Now without augmenting the *embarrassment* we are under with regard to our Bills from Bath, &, should they run very high, turning it into *distress.*

1184. [1] AA's letter is missing.

[2] Gaspard Monge (1746–1818), comte de Péluse, French mathematician, whose *Géométrie descriptive* (1799) may have been the work in demand.

[3] The 'Parlours & a Garret & one Kitchen', mentioned in L. 1182, were evidently retained, at least temporarily, by Frances Wheatley, the owner or 'occupier' of the house 11 Bolton Street (L. 1180 n. 1).

[4] Cf. AA's letter (Berg) of 10 Mar. 1818 to his parents: 'I have only just time, on account of the duties of my new situation, to write that I was elected Fellow of Christ's College on Friday last! and that the first year I am not to touch a farthing of the emoluments, according to the practice of this College—The expenses of this term are a little lessened by my having had a pupil—and I am to have two for the next—which begins on April 1 . . . I have *no rooms* in College, till next year—the fellowship at first is a *new expense* instead of a help—but it repays afterward.'

Rest satisfied, therefore, with your Rooms *en Prince*[5] while you can have them; & when their right owner returns, resign them with good humour, & good sense, for such as will be more *en Deacon*; but still only *hire* rooms till our affairs are more in our own hands; & frankly—gayly, *avow* the delay to be convenient.

Every one, then, will respect it.

Added to This, the principal motive to *wish, Here*!!! for procrastination, another strong one is, That I may have Time to collect you excellent Furniture in *Town*, better fashioned & more commodious, from the frequent Sales of Gentry going to the continent—almost as good as New, at a 1/4 the Price, & which the waggon will convey to you in perfect safety. |

2ᵈ I shall next come to 2. for I will not, even initially, aggrandize him to A.[6] You were quite right to receive him civilly, yet not return his call speedily. I would never accept an Invitation from him; & never make him one: *but* always Bow when I met him, silently, unless He spoke first, & then Answer civilly, but add no new speech of your own, & separate as if hurried by some affair. Yet, should he *ask* you to help him, do it readily, though only in your own Cell. This would elevate you much more than *refusal*. But *offer* nothing. That would now be duplicity, for you can never be Friends again. Each side has been too offensive as well as offended. Yet by This conduct, if persevered in steadily, you will keep off Hostility, which is always best avoided, &, *peu à peu*, as it becomes gradually known, you will shew your change to be the result of characteristic disapprobation, not of petulant resentment, or transient pique.

NB. Read over the above after every meeting with 2 *this Term.*

3ᵈ *The Pupils*!!! Here I sigh! & my Alex knows why!— *sisterly* indeed, as sagaciously he desires, I must be here, for maternally I could but remind him of the opinion of Him of whom he ought now to be the honourable Representative.

As *myself*, I can have no objection: the Maternal side of

---

[5] AA was apparently occupying the quarters retained by one of his friends.

[6] Edward John Ash (*c.* 1799–1851), Tancred Student in Divinity of Christ's. AA had complained of his friend (ix, L. 1064 n. 6) but the friendship was apparently repaired, see L. 1320 n. 4.

your Family have All risen to the respectable place they hold in the community by the exertion, & remuneration, of Talents.

But, I shall never forget—or rather never cease to reflect on these Words, pronounced by your incomparable Father, while yet in the Drawing Room, & while pensively looking at his own dignified Portrait.[7] '*Tout le monde dira à Alex qui est sa mere; mais—qu'il n'oublie pas qui a été son pere!—C'est pour cela que je lui ai consacré et fait faire ce Portrait.*' —— ——

I need make no comment; I *can* make none! I leave you here to your own Guidance, only enjoining you to take no measure precipitately, or pre-maturely, that can never be *re-called*. To whatever that last word belongs, rigorous care & scrupulous foresight must be given, so that what is done may be never *repented*. ⎪

4ᵗʰ The Work projected.[8] I come now to your *4ᵗʰ* Article, reserving it, as you have led the way, to the *bonne bouche*, because I meet in it all your wishes. I *like* the plan, & *desire* to see it adopted. It is most natural that the rage of Author-ship, so prevalent now in the World, & so peculiarly general in my family, should have bitten you: I am therefore greatly pleased that you have started a subject which Mr. Peacock[9] thinks fitted to your abilities.

To This, therefore, Give your best Thoughts, Time & studies, for it seems to open fairest to all your Favourite views in Life.

I only, & earnestly, recommend to you to begin in such a way as You may go on: c. à d: with Foresight as well as Eagerness; with Good Sense, as well as with Enthusiasm.

For this purpose Commence by resolutely refusing your-self to Work in an *Evening*. Give *all* your Evening to *Society*,

---

[7] For M.d'A's portrait, painted by the Vernets in Paris, see *HFB, facing* p. 234; and the *frontispiece*, x.

[8] AA was encouraged by his friends Charles Babbage and J. F. W. Herschel to publish, as they had, papers on mathematics that might gain the attention of the Royal Society (L. 1185 n. 6). On 19 Feb. 1818, for instance, Herschel had read a paper 'On circulating functions, and on the integration of a class of equations . . .', *Phil. Trans.*, cviii (1818), 144–69.

It seems, however, to have been a translation of some French work on mathe-matics that AA had in mind at this time, to which effort he was encouraged by his friends Herschel and the Revd. George Peacock (n. 9), lecturer in mathematics at Trinity (*DNB*).

[9] The Revd. George Peacock (1791–1858), mathematician, fellow of Trinity College, Cambridge, junior moderator for the tripos (1818), F.R.S. (1818). For the active part he had played in AA's career so far, see ix, x *passim*.

14

when you can get it, either at home or abroad; or to some *amusement*, when any is attainable; otherwise, to agreeable *Reading*, which is *always* to be had: I mean Books of polite Literature, or of Fancy.

And pray, pray retire to *Rest Early*, & from chearful, not studious ideas & occupations. So, only, can you *rise* with your powers all awake.

If you would have Health & Vigour for your Undertaking, —which I am earnest should succeed—Divide Your Mornings between *work* & *walk*: *study* & *Exercise*. And don't— (a hint!) call Noon that Morning!—

Force yourself to *rise Early*, my dearest Alex,—all of your prosperity, & *preservation*, hangs on that!

Your Health & Your Composition will certainly, in the long run, thrive or fade together.

Therefore *Rise Early*! work ardently, & Repose socially. |

I shall talk to you in my next of our Financial affairs— but this long deliberative Letter—the First I have written this half year!—has cost me much pain.—I *think* I could only have done it for my dear Alex! Writing is become a great toil to me—it is ungenial—*recollective*—laborious—recol- lective!—for oh what precious—what encouraging Value did He who is ever present to me in his absence bestow on all that dropt from my Pen!—

Nevertheless, I have more, & consequential, I wish to say to you before you take any measure—but I am now ex- hausted—& uncertain whether you may not already be decided.—If not, Answer this quickly, & you shall have the rest to consider over before your *audit*. But—if your Deci- sion is made, spare me further writing.

[⌐]Mean while⌐

Turn in your contemplations every way, & weigh in detail This Question: *why* should you not pass All this next *Winter*, perhaps the *only* one you may command, wholly unfettered, to see London?

NB. If you wish for more *Bas*, or *Cravats*, or your Great Coat, write me but a word, & I will make a further rummage & unpacking with pleasure. God bless my dear Deacon, & direct him. Indeed you ought to write to Dr. Gibbes.[10]

[10] Physician at Bath (L. 1181 n. 4).

P.S.2d Your Cousin Richard[11] is a very noble young man —the wealth is *his*, not his Family's; & he has turned aside from all selfish indulgence, or wild extravagance, to improve his own Mind & Education, & to *Give* an Education to 4 of his Brethren, whom he has brought over to England, & placed in seminaries, at his own complete expense: 2 Girls & 2 Boys.[11] one of the former is said to be lovely & Elegant:—

'Tis impossible for you to conceive how melancholy is my loneliness—Yet how I prefer it to ⟨H Ely⟩[12]

P.S. I have got your Sacramental Certificate,[13] but as you do not name it; I keep it for a Frank, in the fear of any accident to a stage parcel.

NB. I have received your Arms from France[14]—of which in my next.

---

[11] Son of FBA's half-brother Richard Thomas Burney (1768–1808), headmaster at Kidderpore, India (i, p. lxxiii), Richard Burney (1790–1845) was a Lieutenant, and in 1824, Captain, in the Bengal Army. Arriving in England at the age of 28, he was admitted on 22 May 1818 as Fellow-Commoner to Christ's College, Cambridge, graduating B.A. in 1822, in later life donating the 'Burney Prize' to the University. In England at this time or soon to arrive were his sisters Caroline Jane (1802–71) and Sarah Ross Burney (1808–91). The brothers were probably James Christian (1797–*post* 1828) and John (1799–1837), who returning to India in the following year, enlisted as cadets in the H.E.I.C.

[12] Conjecturally an invitation extended by the Cambridges, the Revd. George Owen (*HFB*, pp. 187–93), prebendary of Ely Cathedral, and his wife Cornelia (L. 1205 n. 6).

[13] Presumably from the rector of Walcot Church, Bath (x, L. 1170 n. 120). Among the conditions of holding a Fellowship at Christ's College, to which AA had been elected on 6 Mar. 1818, was, as he explains in a letter (Berg) of 27 March to his parents, that he take the sacrament within three months, as he mistakenly thought, of his election. For his confusion and his father's anxiety on the matter, see x, L. 1161 n. 10; L. 1167 n. 4.

[14] The arms of Alexander Charles Louis Piochard d'Arblay (1794–1837), comte d'Arblay, were similar to those of the Piochard family, which are blazoned in *Nobiliare Universel de France* (20 vols., 1872), i. 183: 'Un écu d'azur, à trois étoiles d'argent posées deux et une; écartelé de gueules à une aigle d'argent, les ailes étendues; et sur le tout d'or à une bande de gueules.' The d'Arblay arms are drawn and described by the Revd. David Wauchope in the Scrapbook (Berg) 'Fanny Burney and Family 1653–1890', p. 35, and are reproduced in the genealogical table, vi, *facing* p. 476.

11 Bolton Street,
22 October 1818

To Alexander d'Arblay

A.L. (rejected Diary MSS. 7162-[5], Berg), 22 Oct. 1818.
Double Sheet 4to   black edged   4 pp. *pmk*   22 OC .818   wafer
Addressed: Rev^d / Alexander d'Arblay / Christ College, / Cambridge.
Edited by CFBt. *See* Textual Notes.

Bouton Street
London.
22^d Oct. 1818

O fie, Mr. Deacon, fie!
Wasting Time still?—still *about nothing*! Why, then, did you make me send you *Monge*?[1] Merely to employ me in the Hunt?
Fie, Mr. Deacon, fie!
When are you to Work?—And *where*?
The Walking I highly approve, if Working preceded & followed; & regularly, not furiously.
As to The Pupils—
Read over what I have said in my last, attentively, for I have Nothing to add! The subject with me is awful, for it is not my own. I have explained already. Pray Read more carefully. And weigh well *ere you decide*. And *afterwards, never turn to the pros & cons again*.
What I had *more* to say, if your determination was still open, regarded the *Mathematical Lectures*, or any other appointment that may be offered to you at the approaching Audit.
Upon This I will now speak fully & plainly.
My confirmed opinion is That you ought to spend one complete Year free of all forced occupation, save your essential preparation for taking Priest's orders speedily.[2] My Reasons are: That you should Give one Winter & Spring to seeing the

1185. [1] See L. 1184 n. 2.
    [2] AA would be ordained priest on Easter Sunday 11 Apr. 1819 at St. James's, Piccadilly (see further, L. 1203 n. 2) by the Revd. George Henry Law (1761-1845), D.D. (1804), Bishop of Chester (1812-24).

humours of the Capital while you can do it without quitting any Duty, or Call. |

And *This* may be your last & only winter at full Liberty.

You may gain by it, if active & observant, a degree of Knowledge of the World, & of Things in general, of which you are eminently deficient; with an acquaintance with celebrated Characters, that will raise your consequence, & therefore your happiness at Cambridge, by & bye, in giving you more self-confidence, & better *forms*; a fuller supply of general subjects of discourse, & a greater flow of easy language, without stuttering & hesitation.

But if you begin a settled Collegiate Life immediately, I plainly foresee you will soon fall into all your old habits—of Indolence—of Chess—of Ennui—of late rising—&c. &c!! so destructive to your health, so dangerous to your Character & Reputation, & so abortive to all your rational prospects of celebrity.

And For What?

Were we *distressed*, it would be Prudence & Duty: but we are only *embarrassed*, & a small sacrifice, with great œconomy, will speedily set us clear. I have had a Letter from M. Laffite,[3] to assure me I shall receive our French Dividend in the course of November. I have had assurances, on another hand, of £25: *This* quarter: secure, therefore, your Fellowship, & we shall be rich enough, till you Marry, for our moderate desires & peculiar tastes. Strict œconomy-privation, rather, for myself, during this period, will cause me no pain! If I practice it for my Alex, it will procure me pleasure. |

[3] Jacques Laffitte (1767–1844), banker, régent de la Banque de France (1809), provisoire gouverneur (1814).

As may be seen in the ledgers preserved by FBA's bankers, Messrs Hoare, of 37 Fleet Street, a sum of £71. 11s. 4d. was duly received on 7 Nov. 1818 from the Paris banker. For the next twenty years dividends on investments in France were to be sent half-yearly (usually in April and October) to FBA by Laffitte (and later by Baignères) and credited to her account with Messrs Hoare, whose ledgers show for the remainder of her life (1818–39) an income from this source amounting to £140 or slightly less annually.

The £25 mentioned for the quarter would have been her pension (£100) from the Queen, which was to continue for her life.

Alex's stipend as Fellow of Christ's varied with the income of the College and took no account of commons. In 1819 he was to receive in payments made in April and October about £120. See Mr. Warren Derry's note (x, L. 1157 n. 3) for AA's first year.

Enjoy, then, your fair opening prospects unfettered, & go to the Audit[4] next Wednesday prepared with a grateful & respectful declining, if any appointment should be offered. Place it, if you will, upon my broken health & loneliness: That will surprise no one, & leave you open, hereafter, when you have had this necessary holy day, to Acceptance.

At all events —— stay at Cambridge This Term, & spend it in diligently dividing your time between preparing for Priest's orders at Christmas, & collecting materials from the various Libraries, & from your scientific Friends, for your projected Work.

That done, you can go on with it as well Here as There, for a while, with the noble Public Library of the Museum, which contains all that is most rare & old, & the fine Private Library at Sr Joseph Banks,[5] which contains all that is scarce & expensive & modern. You will also here have fresh excitement & assistance from Babbage,[6] Jacob,[7] Herschel,[8] & continual Foreigners at Sir Joseph's.

---

[4] So that the Fellows of a College 'shall have knowledge of its estate', it was fixed by Statute that 'twice in each year, once within a month of Easter and a second time within another month of the Feast of Saint Michael the Archangel [29 Sept.], all the Fellows . . . being present, or at any rate the majority of the same, the Master or Keeper shall render a true and faithful account of all things relating to his office and administration, what he has spent, what he has received, and what remains to be received, what the College owes and what in turn is owing to the same. He shall compel the bailiffs and tenants at the same time to make their accounts in the presence of the Fellows, in order that the entire estate of the College may be . . . clearly apparent to all.' See H. Rackham, *Early Statutes of Christ's College, Cambridge* . . . (1927), p. 53.

According to FBA's letter (*supra*) the audit was held on 28 Oct. of this year, and mentioned in her Diaries and Letters of October or April (1819-36) are at least seven such obligatory journeys on AA's part to Cambridge.

[5] Besides CB's acquaintance with Sir Joseph Banks (1743-1820) and his library at Soho Square, FBA may have had in mind JB's access to it 'with permission to take away . . . whatever appeared connected with my pursuit'. See his dedication to Sir Joseph in his history of . . . *Discoveries in the South Sea or Pacific Ocean* (v, L. 538 n. 7). Sir Joseph's library of some 16,000 volumes was eventually given to the British Museum (*DNB*).

[6] Charles Babbage (1792-1871), famed for his invention of an analytical engine, see Anthony Hyman, *Charles Babbage: Pioneer of the Modern Computer* (1981). Always a social being, he frequented among other sets at Cambridge a group of first-class chess players, where he would have found d'Arblay, who was a member as well of the Cambridge Analytical Society (ix, L. 940, n. 9), of which Babbage and Herschel produced a volume of *Transactions* (1817). The son of a banker, Babbage had married in June 1814 Georgiana Whitmore (1792-1827) and lived with his family in his father's house at 5 Devonshire Street, Portland

[*See p. 20 for n. 6 cont. and nn. 7 and 8*]

And—

Cambridge will still be always open for visits long or short, as occasion, & inclination, & information, may invite.

But, if you accept an appointment, you can only sojourn at London when it is empty: i.e. during the long Vacation.

And Now, that I have detailed my opinion, & its motives, Act as you will; only let it be deliberately, not capriciously, And *Ponder* Now: not when you *have* acted, & to change is too late. Beware of that!—

Remember, too

If I had refused your request, & remained at Bath — — how would you have sighed for such a London Home as I now invite you to in Bouton Street, Piccadilly!—

Adieu—adieu— ׀

Place, carrying on his experiments in 'a workshop on the upper floor of the coach house'.

In a charming letter (Berg) on the occasion of his father's birthday 13 May 1817 ('Quand passerons nous donc ce jour-ci ensemble; cher Papa? Pourquoi faut-il que depuis six ans j'aie toujours été séparé de vous le jour de votre fête?') Alexander went on to speak of Babbage, 'qui vient d'inventer un nouveau Calcul, et qui vient d'envoyer ses Memoires à Mr de Laplace, s'est rendu à Cambridge il y a quinze jours pour prendre son dégré de M.A.—et a occupé pendant huit jours des appartemens dans la même maison que moi. Pendant ce temps, nous avons été beaucoup ensemble à causer de Mathématiques; Il prétend me faire recevoir l'année prochaine membre de la Société royale de Londres, pourvû que je fasse, quand j'aurai pris mon dégré, quelque bon mémoire sur l'analyse.'

[7] Edward Jacob (x *passim*), Senior Wrangler, Fellow of Caius College (1816), and tutor to the group of students, including AA, who read for the summer of 1817 at Ilfracombe. At this time reading law at Lincoln's Inn, he was to be called to the bar on 28 June 1819.

[8] Son of Sir William Herschel (*DNB*), the astronomer, whom CB used to visit at Slough (iv *passim*), John Frederick William, later Sir John (ix *passim*), was, with Babbage, the founder of the Analytical Society of Cambridge (ix, L. 940 nn. 8, 9). AA had known him since 1814, and in his letter of 13 May 1817, op. cit., he speaks of Herschel who 'en ce moment-ci s'occupe à écrire une Algebre élémentaire, dans laquelle il s'attachera surtout à exposer la partie philosophique de la science, trop négligée dans nos ouvrages, et à rassembler en un seul corps et systême uni les doctrines et théories éparses dans plusieurs recueils.

Mais il ne se contente pas d'exposer ce qu'ont fait les autres; il vient de publier dans les Transactions philosophiques des mémoires superbes, où il a résolu des problêmes de Calcul Intégral que l'on avait jusqu'ici crû irrésolubles, et sommé des séries qui résistaient à toutes les méthodes connues jusqu'à ce jour. En même temps il s'occupe à apprendre de son père l'art de faire des télescopes; et travaille fortement à la chimie.—'

In 1821 AA was to accompany the mathematicians Babbage and Herschel on a tour of Switzerland.

I shall long for your decision—

Keep me no longer in suspense than you may be in, by your own incertitude, yourself — —

I have much to say—but will not mix matters—& I am much fatigued by thinking & writing this

May it help you to a fortunate decision! without retrogation—

1186   11 Bolton Street,
                                      24 October 1818

To William Tudor

A.L.S. 3rd person, copied by FBA (Berg), 24 Oct. 1818, written on pp. 3 & 4 of the reply, A.L.S. 3rd person, from William Tudor to FBA, 26 Oct. 1818   1p.   addressed: To / Madame D'Arblay / 11 Bolton Street / Piccadilly / London.
Double sheet 4to   paged 1, 2, 3, 4   2 pp.   red seal
See FBA's explanatory opening (below).

24th Octr 1818.

To William Tuder, Esqr.
NB. This, *à peu pres* is the Letter[1] to which the other side was

1186. [1] Concerned in a series of misapprehensions were FBA's friends of long standing Sarah Martha Holroyd (ix *passim*) of Bath, now nearly 80 years of age, and the surgeon William Tudor (x *passim*), who had attended General d'Arblay in his last illness.

The misunderstanding originated apparently with FBA's asking her friend to remind the surgeon Tudor and Hay, the apothecary, to send their accounts. The kind-hearted Miss Holroyd, who before this had herself offered her friend 'a little pecuniary assistance' ('I have fifty or sixty pounds at your command ready to give directly'), had undertaken not only to assure Mr. Tudor of FBA's sense of his having done 'all *that could be* done' but also to acquaint him with what she conceived to be FBA's circumstances. Though it was reported, she said, that Madame d'Arblay had had 'a *large* acquisition' from her brother CB Jr. (deceased), she felt that her style of life proved the contrary. 'To save for a beloved Son & to give every indulgence to the dear General himself accounted to me for the considerable economy with which you lived.' See letters of [May], 18 and 28 Oct. 1818 (Berg).

The surgeon, troubled by these representations (see his letter of 17 Oct. 1818, Berg, to Miss Holroyd), sent in an account so modest that Madame d'Arblay thought fit to double the amount with the comments above.

the Answer. The *motive* was hearing that Mrs. Holroyd, in a mistaken zeal to serve F. d A. had essayed to induce Mr. Tudor to diminish his Bill.

Mad^e d'Arblay presents her best Comp^ts to Mr. Tudor, & assures him she is sincerely concerned to find, by his Note (to Mrs. Holroyd)[1] that he has been tormented by what he calls 'This unpleasant business;' Unpleasant, indeed,—painful, rather, must be all that belongs to so fatal a Catastrophe! but if her excellent Friend has supposed Mad^e d'Arblay to have harboured so ungrateful, or so wrong an idea, as that of making any representation to Mr. Tudor that might induce him to diminish his just & well-earned Rights, she has been completely mistaken. Mad^e d'Arblay had merely expressed her anxiety to know what those Rights were. from the fear of erring through ignorance; which would both have shocked & grieved herself & her Son; &, consequently, the Sum of 30 G^s mentioned by Mr Tudor, as remuneration for his attendance, &c, makes them now decide to double it; with their united & sincere acknowledgments for the kindness & zeal—never to be forgotten—of his Attendance to the last moment on All they held most dear upon Earth!

Mad^e d'Arblay entreats that Mr. Tudor, should he mention this act of Justice to that most excellent Friend—alluded to, will forbear | shewing her this Note, as Mme d'Arblay is truly grateful for her amiable intentions, & would not hurt her for the World

The £63 will be forwarded for Mr. Tudor to Sir Benjamin Hobhouse, on Monday 26. Octr by Messrs Hoare.[2]

11. Bolton Street, Piccadilly.

---

[2] The bankers concerned were Messrs Hoare of 37 Fleet Street, London; and in Bath, Hobhouse, Clutterbuck & Co., Milsom Street (ix, L. 1060 n. 3).

1187 [11 Bolton Street,
14 November 1818]

To Alexander d'Arblay

A.L. (Berg), n.d.
Double sheet 8vo   black edged   1 p.   *pmk*   14 NO .818   black
seal
Addressed: Revd Alexander d'Arblay / Christ College / Cambridge—

Unreflecting Alex!
Does then no 'Still small voice' within, ever whisper,
    'Have I a Mother?
    'What is her health?
    'What are her spirits?
    'What are her Occupations?
    'How does she support her altered life?—
    'How, my Silence? my Absence? my Neglect?
'Does she grieve at them?—
     'or Cease, at length, to care for them or for Me—
'What are her plans?
'What does she know of mine?
Of all these things, what do I know? What have I Enquired?
             of None!
I have never thought about the matter. Neither from any sense
of filial Duty, Nor from any tender pity for her lonely sad-
ness, & lost peace & happiness.—
            Unreflecting—
for still I forbear to *say*, to *think*, unfeeling
                      Alex!—

1188 11 Bolton Street,
15–16 November 1818

To Mrs. Broome

A.L.S. (Berg), 15–16 Nov. 1818
Double sheet 4to   black edged, half of the address page being separated from the remainder of the letter   4pp.   *pmk*   17 NO 1818
black seal

Addressed: Mrs. Broome / German Place / Brighton / Sussex
Endorsed by CBFB: Sister d'Arblay / Nov[r]—1818 / ans[d]
Edited by ?CFBt. *See* Textual Notes.

⟨15⟩. Nov[r] 1818
11. Bolton Street—Piccadilly

Your tender & cordial invitation, my Charlotte, would draw me from my Cell could any thing produce that effect at this period—but I have no courage for any sort of enterprise—& Brighton might not to me be the private retreat I require. Many are the accidents by which I might there be known—& I should be afraid, as at Bath, to move abroad lest I should subject myself to some visit. For the present, therefore, we must be content—if we can!—with each our separate home.—I ought not perhaps—to talk to you of my disappointment in the news that seemed awaiting my arrival in search of you, that you were established 50 miles off!—Yet my silence could no more make you doubt it than my Naming it can be interpreted into blame. No—I see its *right*, & therefore necessity—but I had not anticipated it, & therefore felt—& feel cruelly annoyed by the circumstance. 'Tis well it was not surmized at Bath! where all that reconciled Hetty to my departure was the idea we should nearly, at least, live together. From Bath—fatal Bath!—it is true it was Alex, his desire & his plans that brought me away; but when once his project & wishes were known, you rose before me to ˡ stand highest & most conspicuous—Near as was our worthy James—for forming some comfort to myself in my compliance:—I would not name this for useless chagrin—but *could* you doubt it? or *wish* to doubt how near you are to my heart? No, no,—let me therefore with all that heart *thank* you, most sincerely, in the midst of my disappointment, for making your health a serious study.[1] That alone

1188. [1] Mrs. Broome was often to describe the health and strength she derived from the sea breezes at Brighton as they were drawn inland with the rising tide. Her daughter Marianne Francis (1790–1832), who disliked the place, explained in a letter (JRL) of 8 Dec. 1818 to Mrs. Piozzi: 'My poor dear Mother has a complaint for which it is hard to find a name, but the effect is that of taking away all her strength, so that the grasshopper is a burthen. For this she is, for the present, prescribed sea air; so here we are, at Brighton; & here I like not to say or think, how long we may probably remain.' They were to remain for ten months (*c.* 12

can be true kindness for those who love you completely—
for Life without it can only selfishly be covetted for us by
our Friends—while only painfully be endured by ourselves.
And let me, for our Mutual satisfaction add, that I have much
hope the Sea Breezes so closely followed up may restore you
to such a state of recruit as may enable you, with Safety, to
still come hither—& winter our days together—Bolton
Street is the healthiest spot, nearly, in London. The Green
Park is its conclusion—Hyde & St. James Parks Blow fresh
to it—Berkeley Square is at its end, & the spacious Gardens
of Devonshire House & Lansdown, with those of the Duke of
Portland, give air to my dwelling from every direction. The
street too is clean & quiet. It is only half a thorough fare for
carriages, & I can walk up & down the pavement, when it is
too bad weather to go further, as unobtruded upon & as un-
observed as in a country village. ¹

—15 Novr 1818.

I live very—very secluded—I see no one but by appointment; for my spirits cannot bear any surprise—or any meeting unexpected—The absence, so long, of Alex is truly
afflicting to me. Life seems to linger as if Time travelled with
leaden feet.——'Tis from self constrait, from the force of my
sense of duty alone that I can employ one moment! If I permitted myself to be natural, I should but sit & ruminate all
day long—upon what is past & gone! Mingled with prayers
—fervent prayers—for what is to come But the present—
save by struggle—is null!

I am told Clement is greatly improved by his Travels.²

Oct. 1818-14 Aug. 1819), as MF would report (27 Oct.) to Mrs. Piozzi, this time
from Ormond Place, Richmond: 'Mama's health being much reestablished, she
was anxious to find herself once more in the neighbourhood of dear Charlotte
[Barrett] & her 5 beautiful children, from whom our abode is but the distance of
5 minutes walk.' See letters of MF to Arthur Young and to Mrs. Piozzi (*Catalogue*).
² Clement Robert Francis (1792-1829), B.A. (8th Wrangler, Caius College,
1817), had been elected Travelling Bachelor (see x, L. 1125 n. 12). Having set out
in the spring of 1818 for a tour of Italy and Greece, he had proceeded to Constantinople, and his Asiatic travels are recorded by his sister Marianne in her
letters (JRL) of 26 June, 23 Sept., and 8 Dec. to Mrs. Piozzi.
  Marianne's sister Charlotte Barrett, with her husband and eldest daughter
Julia, had taken the continental tour described in L. 1180 n. 13. Marianne herself
had visited the old family friend Arthur Young (1741-1820) at Bradfield for the
summer, taking with her the younger Barrett daughter Henrietta, aged about 7. In

I think, at Xmas, when Alex is here I may be glad to see him
—the exertion now would be too painful to give *him* pleasure
any more than myself. Not so with our Charlotte—I trust to
her peculiar affection—& her consciousness of mine, for believing she will prefer the melancholy interview to lengthened
separation. She will come to me on Wednesday. Mrs. Lock &
Mrs. Angerstein came last Friday[3]—it was a terrible meeting!
they stayed the whole morning to wear away its terror for
the next—which will take place on Thursday. Oh my dearest
Charlotte—get stout & well, that when we are together we
may do one another nothing but good! I earnestly desire it.
The kind Mrs. Cooke has written me a most affectionate Let-
ter[4]—I have begun an answer.—Their true & fond | respect
& regard for all I must eternally lament—makes their condoleance, & will make their society welcome to me. They
talk of London for the winter—& I shall receive them with
far more readiness than the most sprightly, or celebrated.

Mutually we must indeed hope—& plan—hereafter—
when our Alex & clement quit us, to meet *solidly* at each
others' Homes. Those will be the periods we shall most want
each other, & the periods, at the same time, when we can
best accommodate each other. I look forward to This as a
plan of permanent intercourse for our future lives—when
your health & my spirits will bear change of abode. I do not

her letter of 8 Dec. (*supra*) she tells how in mid-October all three travellers con-
verged on their mother Mrs. Broome at Brighton '& that without any kind of
prior concurrence'. 'It was like a scene in dramatic life.' Clement was soon to be
called away by his 'College duties, fellowships, & Lectures' (he intended to take
orders) and Charlotte, beginning 'to yearn for the sight of her little boys, left at
a school in Richmond', returned to Richmond, while Marianne remained with her
mother at Brighton. Charlotte's visit to her aunt at 11 Bolton Street, FBA duly
records in Diary, 18 Nov. 1818.

[3] After William Locke II sold Norbury Park in 1819, his mother 'found a little
house at Eliot Vale, Blackheath' near her 3rd son the Revd. George Locke (1771–
1864), since 1803 rector of St. Margaret's at Lee, which living he was said to owe
to the Princess of Wales. While Mrs. Locke was furnishing Eliot Vale, says the
Duchess of Sermoneta, *Locks of Norbury*, pp. 279–80, she stayed with her daughter Amelia Angerstein (1776–1848), either at Woodlands, Blackheath (iv, L. 333
n. 2), or in the Angerstein town house in Cumberland Place. In the years 1797–
1801 at Camilla Cottage (West Humble) or at Norbury Park, the d'Arblays and
Lockes met almost daily. In an acquaintance of over thirty years both families
had known sorrow, and it was the innumerable associative memories that made
the first meeting after d'Arblay's death so 'terrible'. For subsequent meetings, see
Diary, 18, 19 Nov.

[4] For Cassandra Cooke's letter of condolence, see L. 1182 n. 6.

understand what you say of Alex, save that it is very partial & very kind—but he writes me nothing! no accounts whatsoever—nor more than a few lines of hasty *bulletin* when I press him. He is terrible for that. But I must look at his *other* side, & see my good fortune. How does Marian like Brighton? My kind Love to her, I beg, And to Sarah Harriet if still with you,[5] whose amendment in health gives me warm satisfaction—pray tell her so—& how few things can do it! adieu, my own dearest Charlotte, God bless & preserve you! prays earnestly & tenderly

your aff^{te}
F d'A.

Pray do not *Sit* too much by the sea side! Let the air come to your house—& your walks: but beware of the Rheumatism—& pain in the Face! *Pray* mind this in time—I have been frightened by the history of your stool so late in the year.——Be careful, I entreat— | Tell me a little how you pass your time, Have you any agreeable Neighbours?

1189   [11 Bolton Street,
                    c. 26 November]–4 December 1818

To Esther (Burney) Burney

A.L. (rejected Diary MSS. 7166–9, Berg), *internal dating* 3 or 4 days before 30 Nov. 1818 *concluded* 4 Dec.
Double sheet 4to   black edged   4 pp.   wafer
Addressed: Mrs. Burney / Lark Hall place / near / Bath.

sent along with

A.L. (Berg), 4 Dec. 1818
Single sheet 4to   2 pp.   wafer
Addressed: Mrs. Burney / Lark Hall place, / Bath.

[5] That Sarah Harriet Burney (1772–1844) had visited Mrs. Broome in Brighton is indicated by the joint letter (Berg) that they addressed to MF and Henrietta Barrett at Bradfield, 24 Aug. 1818. It was probably after Mrs. Broome's children had dispersed in different directions for the summer that Sarah found an opportunity to visit her favourite half-sister.

Endorsed by EBB: Decr 4. 1818 / Answered / Jan. 11th 1818
Arithmetical scribbling in pencil p. 4.

Your Letter[1] touches me to take my pen the instant I have
read it, my own dear Hetty—I have been self-accused for not
writing before I received it,—but I wanted to be able to
write more chearfully—& chearfully!—Oh 'tis a word so far
so far from all within! — — Nevertheless, I have many more
motives to comfort than I had when I wrote last, & I will
carefully collect them for the kind heart that I am sure will
give them such kind welcome—

And First—I have seen Mrs. Lock & Mrs. Angerstein—&
the first meeting over—which was terrible![2] almost baleful
—every other has been balsamic—& they come to town at
least once a Week expressly to pass a whole morning with me.
—& always write first, that I may expect them

2^{d}ly my maid is arrived from Ilfracomb,[3]—& she deserves
a long paragraph, for it will be a pleasant one to your feelings.
When I left you, it was arranged, you may remember, that she
was to wait at her Father's, & learn clear starching & fine Work,
&c till I sent for her, after I was settled, & had a little maid for
all work to act under her. When I took the dwelling I now
occupy, I wanted no one,—or rather, I could *have* no one, for
I entered it while my intended apartments were still in the
possession of those I was to succeed. The truth is, I was so
low, so full of anguish, that I languished for an entire retirement; & notwithstanding the real & warm rivalry of kindness
between our affectionate James & his worthy wife to detain
me, I felt myself a gloom upon their fire-side, ⎸ even while
existing myself inwardly in the most painful & laborious manner to seem more chearful. I engaged the proprietor of the

1189. [1] In a letter filled with loving kindness and concern (Barrett, Eg. 3690,
ff. 122-3b), 11 Oct. 1818, Esther had tried to rally her sister's spirits: 'Grieve you
must in a degree as long as life lasts.—*all* who *knew* the distinguished & Exalted
Character, and truly amiable Qualities of your lamented partner, *do* & *will* Sympathise with you—and long deplore his loss.—for *you* my poor Fanny! a little
forced Exertion perhaps may not be deemed improper,—the tender sorrow that
overwhelms your broken heart,—would I greatly fear, (if receiving no Check—)
entirely ruin y^r health.—take Care my Dear love! and try to dwell on promises
solemnly asked and as solemnly acceded to! — —'
[2] See L. 1188 n. 3; and FBA's Diary, 18, 19 Nov. 1818.
[3] Elizabeth, daughter of Robert Ramsay (L. 1182 n. 3).

House[4] therefore to take lodgings for herself, while I inhabited the Parlour. But there was no chamber empty for my maidens. This lasted 3 weeks:—the most forlorn that can be conceived even by the darkest Imagination! a seclusion complete from all but sorrow—save, my dear Hetty, Prayer & Future Hope. —Without those, I think I had surely sunk. And with them, this solitary affliction was so nearly heart-breaking, that I seemed to myself living in a Hearse! — — Yet I did all I could—& walked out daily with Diane—& made short visits to James street very frequently—but the long—dreary afternoons & Evenings were always alone.—When my apartments —the same as at Bath—became vacant, a new embarrassment arrived: I heard that not one of the documents for the Sale in Paris, upon which so much depended, had arrived at Mr. Le Noir's![5] They were carried over by Chas Parr in June![6] &

[4] Frances Wheatley (L. 1180 n. 1), proprietor of 11 Bolton Street.

[5] An employee in the ministère de l'Intérieur, as d'Arblay was formerly, and one of his most faithful friends in Paris (see x *passim*), Marie-Alexandre Lenoir (1762–1839) had been appointed in 1800 administrator of the *Musée des monuments français*. Some aspects of his work are described by Bertie Greatheed (p. 23).

It was to M. Lenoir that FBA and AA had applied in June for assistance in their Paris affairs, and, taking advantage of Charles Parr Burney's plans for summer travels on the Continent (L. 1191 n. 8) and his offers of service (see n. 6), AA wrote to him from Bath on 28 June 1818 (Comyn), explaining:

> My mother sends you her kindest love and many thanks for your offers of service, and begs that you will be so kind as to deliver two letters of important business for us according to their directions at Paris. She will send them (having no means to get a frank) in a parcel by the Mail that sets off this af[ternoon] from Bath, and she entreats that somebody, if you are too busy, should write word of it's safe arrival, or non arrival.
>
> We have six trunks of books and drawings in a magazine at Calais; which have been there ever since the year 1815, under the care of M[r] Quillac, Master of the Great Hotel. the great expense of their carriage &c has always hindered my dear father from claiming them. if it were possible you could make some inquiry about them and what is due for their remaining at the Magazine or any other 'renseignement', we should be greatly obliged to you. Indeed the best way w[d] be in telling M[r] Quillac the calamity which has happened, to beg he would himself send an account addressed to me. . . .

For continued negotiations on these matters, see L. 1194 n. 2; L. 1229 n. 1.

[6] In an affectionate letter (Berg) of condolence to AA, 17 May 1818, CPB had offered, as he knew his father would have done, his 'very best services' to his Aunt d'Arblay: 'He, who could, & would, have supported her,—is not now with us,— but entreat her never to forget, that that beloved Brother left a son, who would be proud, & happy, & honoured in performing any one act of duty, or of kindness, which that favourite Brother would have rushed forward to discharge. To you I say the same, & mean all, which I do say, in its fullest, & kindest extent.' See further, L. 1191 n. 8.

have never been received! To this was added that the Papers we had sent, for an immediate large sum, to the War office, had also never been heard of, & were supposed to be at Aix la Chapelle, whither M. le C^t de Caraman was gone.[7] What we have else to expect—or demand!—cannot even be claimed till this previous affair is arranged. I was now so embarrassed, two of my 3 sacred Bills of Bath still unpaid!—that I was obliged, for the present, to relinquish Miss Ramsay, & to content myself with a little maid recommended to me by our Charlotte, who was living at Richmond. I sent a £1. Note to Mr. Ramsay,[8] with my regret, &c —— —— but I received an immediate answer, that if I would accept the services of his Daughter, she would prefer herself to come for every thing, rather than wait any future chances. Much pleased at this further proof of her desire to live with me, I accepted the offer; & she is now my sum total. She is no servant!—None, in any way! which I am very sorry for, & somewhat distressed at: but she is good, sincere, modest, very desirous to improve, & ready for any thing; & so much above, though not equal to a servant, that I am pleased to talk with her, ‖ & have her walk with me, & work in the room with me. I believe & hope she will become a serious comfort to me. The poor creature was so much affected by the change—the dire Change she saw in me since we had parted at Ilfracomb, that for the first day she would never look at me without tears. I am sure my dear Esther will be happy to hear I am now no longer thus apallingly lonely: & that I have a person innocently & really & warmly attached to me always at hand.

3dly. I have had a letter from M. Laffite of Paris,[9] to assure me our stock was safe, & that the half year's next dividend should be ⟨paid⟩ in this Month.

Without this, I must have quitted Bolton Street.

These 3 things will I am sure give you pleasure—and

[7] Georges-Joseph-Victor de Riquet (1790-1860), comte de Caraman, attaché at the Hague (1808-10), the United States (1812-14), chargé d'affaires in London (1816-20). Third son of Victor-Louis-Charles, duc de Caraman (1762-1839), he was a nephew of the marquise de Somméry (L. 1206 n. 1), whom the d'Arblays knew in Bath (ix, x *passim*).

[8] See L. 1182 n. 3. FBA had spent most of the summer of 1817 in Ilfracombe (*c.* 30 June to *c.* 4 Oct.).

[9] The banker (L. 1185 n. 3).

pleasure You have given to me, in hoping my dear Mr. Burney is in a way to do better.[10] May you be able to realize that hope speedily! Alex is always at Cambridge, alas! —— —— I am very sorry for poor Maria[10]—yet always *wished* your hand to prove Gouty. I am glad Sophy is better.[10] I wish her to try *Gum Guiacum*[11] for her Gums. I believe it would cure them. Mrs. Locke tells me to recommend to her a blister on the *back*. She says that that cured *her* of pains in the Gums & jaws & Teeth that had nearly distracted her during 6 years, & had resisted all other discipline, even *blisters* placed behind the Ears, or elsewhere. 'Tis surely worth the experiment. Mrs. Locke has never had but occasional & short fits, from colds, since. It operated like Magic for the cure, with only the pay of a few Hours suffering from the Blister.——

How sorry I am for poor Mrs. Hawkins![12] & for dear feeling Cecilia![12] May she be *better* when you write next! I kept our valued Edward[12] here to tea the other Night—a great effort for me! but I am glad I made it. He will send you money at Xmas, when I shall join the £3:6:6—& pray tell me what more. |

I forbear to begin upon the Queen![13] so much I should

[10] Charles Rousseau Burney (1747–1819), one of the Worcester Burneys, EBB's cousin and husband. He had played in the orchestra of Drury Lane for seven years and had given music lessons in London for about forty years, moving to 5 Lark Hall Place, Bath, in May 1817 (see ix, L. 1074 n. 7). For his daughters Hannah Maria Bourdois (iv *passim*), now aged 46, and Sophia Elizabeth, aged 41, see L. 1180 n. 3.

[11] See n. 24.

[12] Ann *née* Burney (i, p. lxxiv), a sister of Charles Rousseau (*supra*), who had in effect adopted his daughter Cecilia, now 30 years of age. For the illness of Mrs. Hawkins, see L. 1180 n. 15, and L. 1191 n. 1.

A brother of Charles Rousseau (*supra*), Edward Francesco Burney (1760–1848), artist, book illustrator, etc., lived at 25 Clipstone Street. 'E.B. is an artist of no common powers; in the fancy parts of designing, perhaps inferior to none', stated Lamb in his essay *Valentine's Day*, 'his name is known at the bottom of many a well-executed vignette in the way of his profession, but no further, for E.B. is modest, and the world meets nobody half-way.' 'He is our Agent in Town', EBB had explained in her letter (op. cit.), 'and any little Money-Matters between us— may be settled thro' him—.'

[13] On Tuesday 17 Nov. FBA had solemnly recorded in her Diary:

This Day—at 1 o'clock—breathed her last, the inestimable *Queen of England*. Heaven rest & bless her Soul!

She was full of Virtues & made up of good Intentions. She was timid by

have to say upon that venerable & Venerated admirable & virtuous Sovereign—whom I honoured from the bottom of my
heart—& from the bottom of it, lament! None of the princesses know—or believe me in town[14]—I see no one—& keep
doubly retired from a consciousness I ought else to present
myself when I feel no power—no strength for appearing.—
The distress of those sweet Princesses added to my own at
their sight—what good could it do to either party? When you
see Mrs. Payne,[15] tell her the saddle is at her service. I had
forgotten all about it. I wish her a good place heartily. Oh
yes, my dear Esther, it was a grievous blow to me Charlotte's
Brighton! Yet I encourage her to stay there. I have no force
to join her, though she solicits me most affectionately. I am
very glad of your Beaufort additional society.[16] M^rs. Locke has
somewhere heard they are *bien aimable.* You will be glad to
hear I have now—after many difficulties, paid Mr. Tudor,[17]

Nature, and shrunk from coming forward through the fear of not acquitting
herself according to her notions of right.

In a separate Memorandum Book, now lost, FBA penned a recollective sketch
entitled 'Queen Charlotte's Character', which Charlotte Barrett transcribed (Berg)
and printed with editorial deletions in *DL* (1842–6), vii. 338–40 (reprinted in
Austin Dobson's edition, *DL* vi. 378–80). Deleted were accounts of the Queen's
⌐partiality and unspeakable⌐ condescension, her 'openness and ease' in conversation, the moments of intimacy: ⌐'And so successful was her graciousness, that
from the moment the page shut us up together, I felt enlivened into a spirit of
discourse beyond what I felt with almost any one. All that occurred to me I said
with vivacity.'⌐ The Queen knew, FBA explained, ⌐'she might divest me of awe
without risking familiarity'.⌐

[14] On Wednesday 9 Dec. 1818 (see Diary) FBA was to write a letter of condolence to the Duchess of Gloucester, who replied 'the very moment she received it'
(11 Dec., Berg): 'I can not let so kind so aff^te and so soothing a letter remain unanswered a moment.' She would have been 10 years old when FB came to Court
as Keeper of the Robes and writing as if to 'an *old Friend*', she told of the watch
kept by herself, the Princess Augusta, and her two elder brothers at Kew and of
their consolation to see their mother expire after so much suffering 'without
a pang, & a sweet smile on her face'. [15] See L. 1180 n. 11.

[16] Henri-Claude-Raimond de Beaufort (*fl.* 1814–18) and his wife Rosalie Eliza-
beth Wilhelmina lived at No. 8 Lark Hall Place, a few doors from EBB (No. 5).
The baptisms of their daughters Elizabeth (26 June 1814) and Juliana Cecilia
(10 Aug. 1817) are recorded in the registers of the parish of St. John, Bath.
Roman Catholics and friends of the marquise de Sommèry, they are described by
EBB in her letter (Barrett, Eg. 3690, ff. 124–5b), 22 May [1819], as 'Agreable
neighbours' and 'A Charming Couple,—sensible, *witty* and Polite.—Mad^e de
Beaufort—is very young & pretty, and her Children are charming.'

[17] Cf. L. 1186. In letters (of 26 and 27 Oct. 1818, Berg), William Tudor acknowledged FBA's 'polite note, & the handsome & flattering manner in which she ...
remunerated his past & painful services' (double the account presented).

& received from him a Letter of warm acknowledgement. I am much relieved to have satisfied him. Mr. Hay still sends no account, though Mrs. Holroyd has written to him to ask for it, as Alex did a week before we left Bath.[18] Probably he chuses to send all his Bills in at Xmas. I shall not now *apply* again till I can do it do it better, though I will *pay coûte qui coûte* when he gives in his memoir. Have you heard of the Organ affair?[19] Alex is a very naughty correspondent indeed! You make me love more & more your excellent & attached & generous-spirited Beckford[20] & Hayes[21]—What a blessing

[18] In a letter (Berg) of 18 Oct. Martha Holroyd assured FBA that she had written to the apothecary desiring him 'to send me his bill for you'.

A draft of AA's letter of ⟨16⟩ Sept. 1818 to Hay written on the *verso* of an A.L.S. from CB Jr. to FBA, 18 Nov. 1816, FBA preserved, as she did the belated reply (Berg):

Bladud Building, Bath
April 27—1819

Dear Sir—

I have, as you say, received numberless Orders to send in the account of your dear Father which I have neglected under the hope and expectation that it might pass over and be forgotten! I did not dare to say that I would not send in an Account and yet I wished for the privilege and satisfaction of feeling that what has passed between us might be on the score of friendship for indeed My dear Sir, I never met with any One I more sincerely loved, esteemed, and respected, nor whose loss I more deeply regretted!—In conformity however with your desire I state below what appears upon our books in his name not against him, for I had written 'Settled' at the bottom of the page long since.

I beg my respectfull remembrance to your good Mother

I Remain Dear Sir
Your obliged humble serv^t
Geo Edm Hay

The ⟨Acc^t⟩ of the late Genl D'Arblay
By Bill for Medicine &c a⟨s of⟩ Book   To Hay & Phinn.—
from Febr^y 1817. To May 1818. £19. 3. —

For FBA's reply, see L. 1210.

[19] Lost with EBB's letters, but possibly an allusion to some post as organist in one of the churches. In 1823 a 'fine-toned organ', built by Flight and Robson, was installed in the Concert Room, the Assembly Rooms, Bath (see *Keene's Bath Journal*, 15 Dec. 1823). This organ, Mr. Warren Derry has noted, is now at Corsham Court.

[20] Charlotte *née* Hay (d. 24 May 1833) of 5 Upper East Hayes, Bath, who had married in 1773 William Beckford (*pre* 1756-99), the historian of Jamaica (*DNB*), one of CB's friends (see *ED* i. 221). The son of Richard Beckford (1712-56), he was a cousin of the author of *Vathek* and a nephew of William Beckford (1709-70), Lord Mayor of London and twice M.P. for the City.

[21] Anna Maria (*c.* 1774-1847) and Elizabeth Frances (*c.* 1781-1838) were the daughters of Horace Hayes (d. 1807), Governor (1782-8) to the Princes (see x, L. 1179 n. 16), Commissioner of Taxes. His widow Elizabeth *née* Thirkell (*c.* 1745-1837) lived at 3 Marlborough Buildings, Bath, until her death on 14 Nov. 1837, at the age of 92.

such Friends in *neighbours*! I rejoice indeed in your *Doctor* Friends,[22] too. I have promised James you will come to us next spring. Such views lighten absence—nay, life. He would else, he says, go to have a peep at *you*. All his old & native affections, are as warm & cordial as ever. Edward has offered me a conveyance for This—Adieu, my dear my Very dear Hetty — — I am certainly *better*.—Mrs. Locke loves you very sincerely—she blessed the sight of your hand writing, yesterday, on my Table. I began this 3 or 4 days ago. 'Tis now 30. Nov[r]. 1818.

Turn back to last P.S. [*on margins*]
Make kind messages for me, my paper being full—& address these as I should myself—

Last P.S.
4th Dec[r] I open This to say I missed Edward's opportunity —& the melancholy that pervaded me on the approach & execution of my dear & honoured Royal Mistresses Funeral[23] made me omit sending it.—I am now more tranquil—

---

[22] An allusion lost with EBB's letter, but if to medical men, probably Sandford (i, p. lxxv), Phinn (ix, L. 1059 n. 19) and others. See her letters of 22 May and 19 July 1819 (Barrett, Eg. 3690, ff. 124–7b).

[23] The State Funeral of Queen Charlotte on 2 December, the funeral cortège, and the interment in St. George's Chapel, Windsor, are described at length in *AR* lx (1818), 'Chronicle', 170–80. MF remarked that the length of the Queen's illness had all but 'worn out the stock of public concern', and yet, according to Charlotte Barrett, her husband Henry had gone to Kew and climbed a wall 'to see the Queen's funeral pass, he says the crowd was great,—fine ladies pushed into the mud and splashed up [to] their eyes — — . . . . After all there was nothing to see . . . the grandeur . . . will not commence till the procession arrives at Frogmore—.' See A.L. (JRL), MF to HLTP, 8 Dec. 1818, and CFBt to Arthur Young, 1–2 Dec. 1818 (Barrett, Eg. 3703A, ff. 74–5b).

Among genuine tributes to the Queen were those of Charlotte Barrett (ibid.): 'I, whose only virtues are negative ones, begin to think that the Queens negative good qualities are not sufficiently appreciated. She certainly deserves some gratitude from the Nation for not having given into Faro playing when surrounded by all her gambling Duchesses—and for not falling in love with any of the fine young Dukes about the Court—and for not spending and dressing extravagantly when she had power and example to tempt her. she has set a good example in domestic life & been as St Paul commanded her, a stayer at home for fifty years —and now I hope she has found a home in Heaven through the mercy and merits of our blessed Saviour who went to prepare one for all who should trust in him.' For FBA's tributes and sense of loss, see n. 13 and x, L. 1176.

4ᵗʰ Decʳ 1818—

I now enclose this to send by our valued & truly valuable
Edward, to whom I have just paid £3:11:0.—which he tells
me is the sum you have mentioned. If any thing is omitted,
he says he has frequent opportunities of parcel sending—
I have been so additionally gloomy these last days that I had
forgotten my Letter was not gone—I have yet no news of
Alex relative to his arrival—adieu again, my dearest Esther—

I really wish *you*—but yet more *Maria* to try *Gum Guiacum*²⁴—first asking Mr. Sandford if he sees any objection.
I have known it do wonders for rheumatic constitutions. The
mode is to pour half a Teaspoonfull into a Tumbler of warm
water, & drink it in going into Bed: & the next day not to
walk out in the morning, as it opens the pores—which is its
chief operation—though it has, gently, two others. But to
warm the blood without heating it, it is really incomparable,
where it agrees. I If *Sophy* tries it, for her Gums, it must be
only by holding every morning 10 or 12 drops, in a mouthful
of warm water, in her mouth. This has cured me of pains in
the Jaw that kept me constantly restless. I never tried it till
since my present residence—but have heard of it all my life,
from old Mr. FitzGerald, whom you must remember.

Fortunately I met Edward in returning rather prematurely,
from my melancholy morning stroll; & *fortunately*, in this
case, I had forgotten again my Letter—which I here enclose.

Kind love to Mʳ B. *in chief*—& thence around

---

²⁴ A pharmaceutical substance prepared from the resin of guaiacum, a genus
of hard-wooded tropical American tree (lignum-vitae). A non-irritating stimulant,
it was used as a remedy for arthritis, gout, and cutaneous erruptions, being particularly effective 'when given early in cases of sore throat, especially of rheumatic origin' (*Encl. Brit.*, 11th edition).
Introduced into Europe by the Spaniards in the early sixteenth century and
appearing in the *London Pharmacopœia* (1677), it was used (FBA recalls) by the
old neighbour, friend, and landlord of the Burneys in Poland Street, the experi-
mental scientist Keane FitzGerald (d. 29 June 1782). See iii, L. 222 and n. 3.

To Alexander d'Arblay

A.L. (Berg), n.d.
Single sheet 4to   black edged   2 pp.   *pmks*   PICCADILLY / 3
P.P.P.   RICHMOND / 29 DE 1818   29 DE 1818   black seal
      Addressed: Revd Alexander d'Arblay, / Henry Barrett's Esq,[1] / Richmond / Surry.
      Readdressed: 11 Bolton S^t / Piccadilly

If you wish me to come either *to* you, or *for* you, let me know it without scruple, my Alex—if the former, entreat kind Mr Barrett to get us apartments, as his house is full[1]—& it cannot hurt you to go to them in a Chair—& *besides* want of room, the jocund juvenile group—that erst would have so delighted me, would now be over powering—2 quiet, well aired, & comfortable Bed Rooms would be all we should want for this occasion—for as soon as you can dine, &c, *out* of a Bed Room, Bolton Street will be most convenient.

What can I say to our Charlotte! the truly worthy Child of the tenderest of Mothers! Her Letters are so comforting,[2] &

1190. [1] AA had arrived at 11 Bolton Street on 17 Dec. (Diary) to celebrate his 24th birthday (18 Dec.) with his mother but had departed before the 25th to spend the Christmas season with his cousins, the Barretts, at Richmond.

[2] CFBT's letters of this time to FBA are missing, but in a Letter (Barrett, Eg. 3703B, ff. 78-9b) of 23 Dec. [1818] to Arthur Young, she comments on both her aunt and cousin: 'My poor aunt d'Arblay is still nervous & low & cannot bear general conversation. her son Alexander is with her, [&] is pursuing theological studies with great avidity. I hope he may become a pious & useful clergyman—'.

It seems to have been at this time that, at the invitation of Archdeacon Cambridge, AA read prayers for the first time in the 'small neat' Twickenham or Montpelier Chapel, built in 1727, 'a unique and most unecclesiastical structure, deriving all the interest it possesses from its age and the eminent men who have ministered in it'. See R. S. Cobbett, *Memorials of Twickenham . . .* (1872), pp. 143-4. The 9th minister, admitted for life in 1805, was the Revd. George Owen Cambridge (1756-1841), from whose proprietorship the chapel was known in the Barrett family as 'the archdeacon's chapel'.

Rector of St. Michael's, Mile End, Colchester (1791), and collated in 1793 to the rectory of Elme, Cambridgeshire—a living valued at £1,640 (Altick)—prebendary of Ely (1795), archdeacon of Middlesex (1806), Cambridge was a churchman of some prominence and influence in local ecclesiastical affairs. To FB the cause of much anguish of heart in the past (see *HFB*, pp. 189-93), he was to be her son's chief patron and adviser.

well judged, they keep off all vain alarms——& indeed, I have
no doubt but this attack has been *brooding* ever since your
change of *Beverage*. Dr. Bourdois, M. Moreau, & Dr. Larey,
& Dr. Esparron,[3] all said, upon trial, & proof, & examination,
that Wine, even in *France*, was inimical to your Constitution.
You remember the mischief of your mushrooms? —— &
now Ham, too!—My poor Alex! to what privations & self
denials you must submit if Health be dearer to you than
luxury! God bless you my own Alex!—though you have not
frightened me, you have taught me—by my anxious concern
& restlessness, how valuable & dear an interest I yet have in
life! |

My kindest Compliments & Thanks to Mr. Barrett—& tell
him I rely much on his medical skill. I can find no message
half good enough for our Charlotte—I must wait till I can
embrace her. I think the Stage *better* for you than a hackney
post Chaise, which would be too cold. You can stop at the
bottom of the street & come up in a Coach with y^r parcel.
I will say nothing of how I long for you! —— ——

Nevertheless—but for the terrible intrusion on your Cousins, I would not, for my *own* sake, hurry you—but I trust
you may come in safety to-morrow. Let Mr. ⟨Julius⟩,[4] however, guide your *Hosts* to Guide *you*!

Pray do not forget to pay all your *little pecuniary* debts!

Our Charlotte will write while your stay is prolonged—
I am sure—Her Letters are all that Letters can be.—Your
good Uncle James was here yesterday—

I know you will be very sorry for Lady Crewe[5]—for me,
I am quite grieved.

---

[3] FBA's mind had reverted to the physicians she knew in Paris: the fashion-
able Edmé-Joachim Bourdois de la Motte, baron Dominique-Jean Larrey, and
Jacques-Louis Moreau de la Sarthe (vi, L. 595 nn. 4, 9, 16). M. d'A had consulted
Pierre-Jean-Baptiste Esparron (x, L. 1089 n. 15 and *passim*).

[4] Unidentified.

[5] Daughter of CB's early patron Fulke Greville (*c.* 1716-1806) of Wilbury
House, Wiltshire, Frances Anne (1748-1818), later Lady Crewe (1806), the Whig
beauty and wit, one of Dr. Burney's strongest friends and supporters and a constant friend of his family as well, including FBA (see iv *passim*), had died at Liverpool on 23 Dec. See *GM* lxxxviii (1818), 646; also *Memoirs*, i. 24-61, 109-17;
iii. 134-40, 208-11, 229-38, 242-7, 342-3. 'Apropos, poor Lady Crewe is dead',
remarked HLTP in a letter of 12 Jan. 1819 (Hayward, ii. 262), 'an object of defor-
mity! The greatest beauty of her time: at least, the most admired woman . . . but
palsy shook her frame, and cancer gnawed it.'

1191   11 Bolton Street,
                                          1 February 1819

To Esther (Burney) Burney

A.L. (rejected Diary MSS. 7170-[3], Berg), 1 Feb. 1819
Double sheet 4to   black edged   4 pp.   with marginal writing con-
nected sequentially by numbers 1-5   *pmk*   2 FE 1819   black seal
Addressed: Mrs. Burney / Lark Hall Place / near / Bath
Endorsed by EBB: answered by / favor of Miss ⟨Herb^t⟩ / 1819
Docketed in old brown ink, p. 4 [7173]: 1819
Edited by CFBt. *See* Textual Notes.

                                   11. Bolton St. 1st February
                                   Berkeley Square.——1819

Could I have devized any thing to say of a solacing sort—
especially to poor Mr. Burney,[1] whose own sufferings, &
whose nearer parentage make me, in this last melancholy
event, think of Him the most, I had assuredly forced myself
to write as soon as I had read Sophy's sad tidings: but oh my
dear Hetty!—a fresh Death Bell that tolls is, to me, but a
New peal to that which has cut off the Joy of my existence!
& my own spirits were in no state to enable me to struggle for
raising yours. *My* struggles are almost all directed not to curb
the juvenile propensities, so natural, & so *desireable*, of my
young companion, & to bear with his flights & exentricities.
And to this purpose I assume an appearance of chearfulness
that beguiles him into thinking me revived, & that suffices
to leave him Master of his own animation. And by these endeavours, with others of a still higher sort, joined to the all
subduing influence of Time, I am certainly less an alien to
society & to Myself than when I left Bath. There, indeed,

1191. [1] Charles Rousseau Burney's sister, the widowed Ann Hawkins (L. 1180
n. 15; L. 1189 n. 10) had died in Worcester on 16 Jan. 1819 (see 'Worcester Journal' and for her will, L. 1248 n. 7). After the funeral another sister Rebecca (i,
p. lxxv) and her husband William Sandford (1759-1823), a surgeon with the
Infirmary at Worcester since 1793, had taken Charles Rousseau's daughter Cecilia,
their niece, to their home in Bridge Street, Worcester, later conducting her to her
parents in Bath. Cecilia was not to recover from the effects of the long attendance
on her aunt Hawkins, probably a consumptive patient, and was herself to die of
that complaint in her early thirties (see further, L. 1244 n. 3, L. 1245 n. 1,
L. 1246 n. 1).

38

Revival was impossible! every object presented a regret—&
my loss—my irreparable loss was pointed out to me, freshly,
& continually by All & Every thing that surrounded me—In
London I never had the happiness to live with *Him*; my deprivation, therefore, Here—though *Internally* forever the same
—is not so acutely goaded on by All that is *ex*ternal also.

I did not mean to write all this—but my pen is unruly—
I meant merely to talk of good & lamented Mrs. Hawkens, of
my dear Mr. Burney, & of sweet Cecilia, whose tender heart
I doubt not has been severely assaulted by sorrow.[1] But I
thank Sophy[2] for mentioning that Mr. Sandford has comforted you with an assurance that the dear Girl has borne the
stroke rather better than he had ⎮ expected. Her inconsolable
feelings, & hopelessness, previously, had spared her, at least,
the horrours of disappointed Hope!—Her task was the harder
& more cruel while she nursed her beloved adopted Parent;
but her Recovery will certainly be more speedy & natural.
I wish much to know her destination, & the state of her
affairs, & prospects, & intentions, & proceedings. When you
are able, my dear Hetty, I *beg you* to be copious on a subject
so near to you, & to me truly interesting. I conclude the
house at Barborne[3] must immediately be relinquished. I have
seen nothing of Edward or Fanny[4] since this event; the latter
called this morning while I was taking my Exercise—a thing
I never omit without a return of those restless—tumultuously
restless nights, that threatened me with many a frightful
symptom at Bath.

I am admirably situated here with regard to Exercise, for
I am within a minute's reach of the Gravel Walk round the
Bason in the Green Park: & either there, or in Berkeley Square,

[2] Charles Rousseau's 3rd daughter Sophia Elizabeth (L. 1180 n. 3).

[3] The house that early in 1814 Mrs. Hawkins had taken in Barborne Terrace,
Worcester (L. 1180 n. 15).

[4] Frances Burney (1776-1828), EBB's 2nd daughter, who, unlike her sisters,
had perforce to earn her living as a governess. Beginning in 1794, she was employed by Lord Beverley (iii, L. 142 n. 3), then in the family of Sir Thomas
Plumer (1753-1824), Attorney General (1812), the father of five sons and two
daughters (see *DNB*); and thereafter by Sir Henry Russell (1751-1836), an Indian
Judge, with at least two daughters (see further, L. 1293 n. 4). For her literary
work, see L. 1200 n. 5.

or in the quiet part of Hyde Park, Diane & I, & commonly, Ramsay, take the air daily. Alex goes further afield. I would by no means confine him either to my pace or my limits.

He has now, alas, left me again. He returned yesterday to Cambridge, & I have but small hope of seeing him till Easter. I am sorry he has not written again to Maria & Sophy—& so is he; but he grows worse & worse in Epistolary communication, & hates it, he says, past cure! He often regrets that his Cousins are not within a *walk*, that he might carry his verbal excuses, & enjoy their society vis à vis:—for they always are, & always will remain, amongst his highest Favourites & those whom he most willingly seeks, & enjoys. He was here quite upon a relaxing plan this time, & hardly pursued any study; but he is gone to work hard, now, for taking Priest's orders.[5]

Our good Brother James called upon me yesterday, looking so well, & so blyth, & so *well accoutered*, it would have given you pleasure to see him. He is preparing for the Press, & means to ¦ bring out his new memoir on the Northern Passage in April.[6]

I have seen Sarah only once,—& consequently only with sadness—but she looks well, & has been much benefitted by Brighton.[7] I have no hope of Charlotte in Town!—& *ought* to have none, she is so much better at Brighton—yet it is a cruel disappointment.—Sarah assures me she is looking well, & joining in society with new awakened chearfulness.

[5] See L. 1185 n. 2 and L. 1232 n. 10.

[6] For the whole of the year 1818, according to Manwaring, pp. 260-1, JB had been engaged in writing *A Chronological History of North-Eastern Voyages of Discovery; and of the Early Eastern Navigations of the Russians*. This, his last major work, was to appear in June 1819.

The last chapter deals with the controversy raised by a paper he had read to the Royal Society in December 1817, *A Memoir on the Geography of the North-Eastern part of Asia, and on the Question whether Asia and America are contiguous, or are separated by the Sea* (1818). See also *Phil. Trans.*, 108 (1818), 9-23, reprinted in the *Quarterly Review*, xviii (1817-18), 431-58, where JB's conclusions were queried.

[7] On a visit of August 1818 to her half-sister Mrs. Broome at Brighton (see L. 1188 n. 5), Sarah Harriet Burney had evidently introduced to her Maria *née* Harvey (d. 11 Sept. 1822), widow of George Wilbraham (1741-1813) of Delamere Lodge, Cheshire, M.P. (1789-90). SHB was formerly a governess in this family, her chief charge being the youngest daughter Anna (c. 1790-1864), who was to become in 1831 the 2nd wife of Field-Marshal Thomas Grosvenor (1764-1851). Governess and pupil were to remain life-long friends. See correspondence, *Catalogue*.

She has made acquaintance with Mrs. Wilbraham,[7] & they like each other mightily.

Your kind concern relative to our (Alex's & mine) affairs abroad I can easily conceive:—the loss of the original documents by which we could claim our rights, & which we trusted to Charles Parr,[8] is really frightful. Books, Furniture, Cloathes, Paintings, Drawings, Mineral[s] & innumerable curiosities, collected with excellent choice, & great expence, & ordered for sale, we can obtain no account of! Alex has written 3 Letters, & we have no answer! — — The arrears of the Pension, however, we have recovered.[9] The War Minister accorded it as soon as I sent over, in form, my claim & Title.—Alas! how melancholy that I never should have written my name by my dear Husband's Honours but for a claim on his Departure!— our limitted income, & the decided English destiny of Alex, determined our dropping the Title bestowed by the French King at Ghent,[10]—but as it is entered at the *War Office*, & at the *Bank*, I can, Now, make known no Right but by taking it up. In other circumstances, how proud should I have been of a distinction that so marked his Sovereign's sense of His services! but I always thought it would be an awkward

[8] CPB, with his cousin Henry Foss (*c.* 1790-1868), had set out, apparently, in mid-July for a tour of Switzerland. Having delayed in Paris, he saw Talma in Racine's *Britannicus*: 'I wanted more grace,—more finish,—more dignity. . . . His eye is animated & expressive,—but—. He is a good, impassioned Actor for parts of strong emotion,—but fails, I should think, in all the softer, & more delicate delineations of character.' CPB had reached Stein, Switzerland, on 28 July, and in a letter (Osborn) of that date to his mother, tells of his plans to return via Brussels and Antwerp, then 'by Lille, or Cambray, to Calais'. 'It is my intention to be home this day fortnight.'

The documents entrusted to him were eventually to reach M. Lenoir (L. 1194 n. 1) at Saint Denis (see L. 1200).

[9] Receipt (8 Jan. 1819) of a sum of £84. 14s. 11d. is shown in the Ledgers preserved by Messrs Hoare, bankers, Fleet Street, and also in FBA's Account Books (Berg), where it is described as 'From the residu of the War Debt to my late revered Husband—transmitted by M. Benier to Messrs Laffitte, & by them, for me, to Messrs Hoare.'

Mr. Warren Derry, who has studied the d'Arblay finances (x, Appendix), thinks that FBA recovered at this time 'what was due on M. d'A's retraite from 1 July 1817 to 3 May 1818 (his death)—i.e. for 10 months approximately 10/12 of 4,000 fr. = 3,333 fr. *minus* (as being received abroad or 'hors de France') 1/3 = 2,222 fr. = approx. in English money after the exchange, etc, £84. 14. 11.' For receipt of a further £40, arrears in M. d'A's *retraite*, see L. 1280 n. 5.

[10] 'La Comtesse Veuve Piochard d'Arblay' was the title, FBA explains in 1827 (xii, L. 1390), under which she had received arrears due to her husband.

embarrassment, rather than an elevation, to Alexander, as an English Clergyman; & if we had retained the Title here, he must necessarily have inherited it, or not have seemed our son: & the tenderest & noblest of Father's gave up that *civil* Rank for the idea of his Alexander's following a straiter path, & avoiding any false ambition, without it; contenting himself with avowing, Here, only his own *military* Rank, which, as Lieutenant General, I stood next in height to the Marechals: —& I, from the same motives, more eagerly studied to decline & avoid a Title than any one else can have done to acquire one:—What a strange fatality does it seem, that Now, when we can no longer *Share* it, I am destined to write myself la Comtesse d'Arblay in every application!—I have, at least, however, the great consolation to see the uncommon judgement & propriety with which my dear Alexander not only resigns unmurmuring this part of his really rightful inheritance, but honestly & thoroughly approves & abets its renunciation. We are now joining in a reclamation for those Debts owing to his honoured Father from the Mission of Louis 18 to Luxembourg & Treves.[11] I only wait to know our success for a public manifestation of *whom* & *what* we have lost in the Church & Church Yard of Walcot! — — but whether success or Failure ensue, I am equally anxious to settle with Mr. Hay,[12] & can form no idea why he will not send his account; nor why he has never answered Alex's Letter the week before we left Bath; nor my message to him by Mrs. Payne;[13] nor a Note to demand it from Mrs. Holroyd.[14] When Maria & Sophy see him, I wish they would give him mine & Alexander's Compliments & tell him we are quite in consternation at his silence. —Remember me most kindly to my dear Mr. Burney. I am sure you will hasten to me good news when you can, certain no one will receive it more thankfully. I have been very ill —seriously ill, for a little while, but am now tolerably well. How I long for better news of your poor fingers!—Mrs. Lock is beautifully well.—poor Mrs. Angerstein far from it!—L^y

---

[11] This gives the impression that back-pay was owing to the General, but see Mr. Warren Derry, x, Appendix.

[12] L. 1180 n. 19.

[13] L. 1180 n. 11.

[14] L. 1186 n. 1.

Martin[15] blyth & happy—was here t'other day. I have remembered the good Sansoms[16] & Sleepes[17]—I am quite shocked about Mary who I thought would have proved a treasure: Ramsay is perfectly good, & attached, &c—but will *never* make a good servant. How well they might *amalgamate!* Adieu, my ever dear Hetty! & God bless you!— ˡ

I have had a very alarming, though *sisterly* attack in my Hand; but I conquer it with pouring Hot Water on it for a quarter of an Hour night & morning: as hot as I can bear it, & then bathe it in a Basin. This succeeds, but demands constancy—I join my Guia⟨c⟩um—only 20 drops—Tell Maria but let her consult Mr. Sandford

[15] Mrs. Locke's elder daughter Mary Augusta (1775-1842), who had married as his 2nd wife Sir George Martin (ix, L. 938 n. 16). The couple lived at 8 Hertford Street, Mayfair.

[16] Related to the Sleepes and the Burneys was a James Sansom (1751-1822), who with his wife Elizabeth Margaret *née* Wood and their son James (bapt. 21 Oct. 1803) would pay evening calls from time to time on Mme d'Arblay in Bolton Street. The elder Sansom had been employed by CB Jr. (see v, L. 482, headnote) and while at Greenwich he had published a book, lavishly illustrated, *Greenwich, A Poem, Descriptive and Historical* (privately printed, London, 1808). The dedication to E.M.S., his wife of an 'unsullied round of twenty years' and as well the mention of Eliza, 'a perfect wife', establishes her as the Elizabeth Margaret Wood who on 24 July 1790 married James Sansom at the church of St. Mary the Virgin, Aldermanbury (Computer File Index). The subscription list comprises a roll-call of Burneys, their in-laws and friends (especially those of CB Jr.), Lady Crewe, Martin Davy, John Kaye, Sheridan, the Ogles (ten in number), and John Young (see *Sale Catalogue*) had a copy of the book and another was located by Cynthia Comyn, to the delight of the editors, in the Library of the Guildhall, London.

At this stage of their lives the Sansoms seemed to be under the protection of JB (see L. 1287 and x, L. 1177, headnote), being mentioned in his will (PRO/PROB/11/1653/56, pr. 6 Feb. 1822): 'to my Cousin James Sampson ten guineas and 10 sets of my Chronological history of South Sea Discoveries. To my cousins Hetty and Fanny Sleepe five guineas each and five sets of the said voyages.'

[17] Frances (*fl.* 1780-1838) and Esther (*fl.* 1780-1828) were daughters of James Sleepe (*c.* 1714-94), the illiterate relative and Jack of all trades, whose amiable nature and amusing malapropisms made him a great favourite with the Burneys (iv, v *passim*; *HFB*, p. 216). He may have been a brother or half-brother of CB's first wife Esther *née* Sleepe (1723-62). The Sleepes appear regularly as do the Sansoms as small pensioners in such of FBA's Account Books (Berg) as survive, e.g., in her 'Yearly Resumé of Expenditure' for 1819: 'Messʳˢ Sansom & Sleepes — — — £5.0.0.' For 1820 and 1821 the sum is £8. 0s. 0d.

I hope your valuable Friends Mrs. Beckford[18] & the Miss Hayes & ⟨Capt⟩[19] are able now to see you oftener. You have taught me to love them for your sakes— I

Pray make my very sincere condolence of kind remembrance to dear Blue[20] & dear Mrs. Sandford[20] when you write—& to excellent Mr. Sandford also—but above all, to Cecilia—

I *think* I have told you I have settled with Mr. Tudor, &, he assures me, quite to his satisfaction.[21]

I am truly glad to hear of the great improvement in *demonstrative* affection in Amelia[22]—my love to her— I

I conjure you, my dear Esther, not to let your Nursing break into your Walks, in *All* weather, but Rain & Snow.

I wish you could learn the name of the Book, due to Mr. Hayes.[23]

The illness I have alluded to was spasmodic, & very violent & painful, but short.

1192   [11 Bolton Street], 10 February 1819

To Alexander d'Arblay

A.L.S. (rejected Diary MSS. 7176-[9], Berg), 10 Feb. 1819
Double sheet   4to   black edged   4 pp.   *pmk*   10 FE .819 black seal

[18] See L. 1189 n. 20.

[19] Anna Maria Hayes (L. 1189 n. 21) and her brother Thomas (b. 15 May 1771), who, educated at Rugby, had 'applied to become a writer in the Bengal Establishment in 1790, remaining in the Bengal Civil Service until 1815' (I.O.R.: J/1/134. 110-14). At this time he was living in Derby House, Sunbury, Middlesex, where he died *post* 1838. It was probably in the local militia that he held the rank of Captain.

[20] Elizabeth Warren Burney (L. 1180 n. 15) and her sister Rebecca Sandford (n. 1).

[21] For the surgeon's letter of acknowledgement, see L. 1189 n. 18.

[22] Amelia Maria (L. 1180 n. 16), now aged 27.   [23] See n. 19.

Addressed: Revd A. d'Arblay / Christ College / Cambridge.
Edited by CFBt. *See* Textual Notes.

I was never more surprised!—How?—a Letter from Alexander by return of Post? — — — Astonishment upon astonishment! 'Tis an *Answer*! it shews my last Letter has been read—understood—& thought over—not cast aside, for a few words written just as the post is going, without any Response, or the smallest regard to its contents! — —

Oh naughty Alexander!—if you could guess the *approach* to something like a feel^g of pleasure which this unexpected promptitude of attention has occasioned, where Pleasure of every sort has so long stood sternly aloof,—it would surely disarm your Apathy of some of its marbleness.—

Be that as it may, I was *pleased* for the moment,—& I am glad to be *pleased* if only for a moment.—

You, that are a mathematician, may thence make Calculations upon the ballance of giving Pleasure, or keeping Apathy, — — that are far beyond *my* reach. — —

At all events, you have Earned my promised long Letter.

And 1st—like you, my dear Alex, I begin by a reply: after which, I have much to say.

With regard to the Cabinet,[1] I think all you say upon the subject perfectly just & well weighed, for the 'dowdy' effect, joined to the insufficiency, would only make it ornament the room to its cost,—without unloading our Chairs & Tables. But I had not represented it as a *completion* for our Library —Could you expect such a thing for £1:15^s 0?[1]—It certainly I would not hold a 3^d of what is contained in that which you have now stuffed up like a Book Stall, or, rather, a Broker's Shop. I had merely meant it as a decorated repository for about 50 of the best bound Volumes, half within the silken Curtains, the other half, exposed as external ornaments: But: the whole of it, now, upon your view of the matter, which I really think a fair one, is out of the question. I have seen a Book Case that would just have done, since; not *wider*

1192. [1] The sum duly appears in FBA's 'Yearly Resumé of Expenditure' for 1819 (Account Book, Berg): 'Mock Rose Wood Cabinet—1. 15. 0' with such related expenses as 'Carpenter for Shelves—2. 1. 6'. Entered similarly in 1820 was: 'Book Case my Alexander—8. 8. 0'.

than that we have at present, but as high as the Ceiling, & with 2 Compatments of Drawers down to the floor, for Pamphlets & unbound Books, or papers: the whole Glazed to the top, & sufficiently deep for folios, or 2 ranges: all in view solid mahogany; the shelves & back & sides of deal painted. But its price is 8 Guineas; & nothing of such dimensions, & in Mahogany, will be less costly. For which reason, had I been richer, I should myself have bought it, & gallantly have presented to my dear Alex, as I have done in that I have already purchased, the joint use of it. But I need not say this is, *Now, impracticable*, because it would be wrong.

⌣

Feby 10th I was interrupted by a visit to which I had consented for the sake of her mother, from Miss Frodsham;[2] & she was so gentle & soothing in her manners, & appeared—though silently & delicately, so feeling upon my unhappiness, that I was insensibly led to converse on with her till the post was gone by. She was surprised, & pleased, though ashamed, when she saw the hour. I have, nevertheless, you will be glad to hear, invited a repetition of the visit, some time hence, to shew her that she did me *good*, not *harm*. she enquired after you,—& we had some clerical discourse. She adores Mrs. Marsh,[3] as much as her mother does: & she is now with a friend in this neighbourhood, Mrs. Dickson,[4] who she asserts to be another of those uncommon characters that captivate all hearts. She made many efforts to effect an acquaintance

[2] Emma (*c.* 1784–1834) was the younger daughter of Captain John Frodsham (*c.* 1737–91), R.N., and his wife Anne *née* Leigh (*c.* 1751–1830), originally of Lymm, Cheshire, a relative of Samuel Crisp (1707–83), early friend of CB and of the younger Burneys (*HFB*, pp. 16–18; and Plate 1). It was this relationship that recommended Anne Leigh to FB in earlier days (i, L. 3 n. 89) and the memory of earlier days that now prepared a welcome for her daughter.

[3] Daughter of a Leipzig merchant, Marianne Émilie Charlotte *née* Lecarrière (*c.* 1775–1844), wife of the Rt. Revd. Herbert Marsh (1757–1839), Bishop of Peterborough (1819), had a London address near FBA at 11 Half-Moon Street. For her acquaintance with Mrs. Frodsham (*supra*), see x, L. 1170 n. 55.

[4] Possibly Susanne Jane Dickson (d. 15 Apr. 1821) of Cavendish Square, the widow of Alexander Dickson (d. *pre*-1820), 'formerly Lieutenant Colonel in . . . [the] sixteenth Regiment of Foot'. See *AR* lxiii. 235; and her will (PRO/PROB/11/1642/205, pr. 28 Apr. 1821). The sister of Sir John Henry Moore (1756–80), poet, and niece of Edward Long (1734–1813), author (see *DNB*), she had literary connections and presumably interests that, as FBA's friends seemed to think, could make her a congenial acquaintance.

there—but I can bear nothing save old friends, except what will be solely for *You*; & for You, my dear Alex, I will make my promised efforts as occasion, ¹ or Your request, shall invite.

⌐——⌐

I have this morning seen sundry more Book Cases: all that are of mahoghany are very dear: recollect, our's of £10 was only of deal, coloured, & bordered with Green baize. For such a one as you describe, you cannot give *less*, & only at an Auction, so little; if you will have drawers, also, as is now usual. I have seen one, just your dimensions, with Drawers & a secretaire 2ᵈ hand, at 30.Gˢ—If you give me a Commission, be precise how high you will go, & I will try to be within it, if I can: but not purchase *at all* beyond it: Pray be explicit on this point.

⌐——⌐

I have just been interrupted again, by your good Aunt Captain—with Sarah, looking so remarkably well, that I think her capable of new conquests without difficulty. Mr. Payne has sent me word he will call & look at the Books when I please.⁵ I must now to work with all my might to be ready with my Catalogue & assortment.

Oh my Alex! what an emotion shook my poor frame when I read in the Papers that Count La Tour Maubourg was appointed our Ambassadour!⁶—my dear Mad. de Maisonneuve

⁵ JB, his daughter, and his wife Sarah *née* Payne (L. 1180 n. 2), the sister of the bookseller Thomas Payne (1752-1831), who, inheriting his father's well-known bookshop in Castle Street, near the Mewsgate, had in 1806 moved the business to Pall Mall (south side). JB's daughter Sarah, now about 23, would marry in 1821 her cousin John Thomas Payne (*c.* 1796-1880), the natural son of Thomas above and so owned in his will (PRO/PROB/11/1831/234, dated 25 July 1821, pr. 20 Apr. 1831).

⁶ The most intimate and lasting friends that Madame d'Arblay made in France in the years 1802-12 were members of the Latour-Maubourg family, of whom, residing as neighbours in Passy in the years 1802-5 were d'Arblay's early associate among the Constitutionalists, the friend of Lafayette, Marie-Charles-César (v, pp. xlvi, L. 446 n. 12) and his family, including his son Just-Pons-*Florimond* (1781-1837), here mentioned, and his (César's) sister, Madame de Maisonneuve (1770-1850), whose letters to FBA survive to the number of 126 in the Berg Collection. See further, v, L. 515 n. 10; L. 518 n. 10; and for Florimond's career, L. 1196A.

It was neither César nor his son, the diplomat, however, who had been appointed on 29 January as 'ambassadeur à Londres à la place du marquis d'Osmond'

I imagined would accompany him——& the fullness of my Joy
& Sorrow was so great, & so equally preponderate, that my
heart swelled with a pain indescribable!—What would not
have been the exultation of happiness to our best & dearest
Friend had such an event been permitted during his mortal
abode! it would have given him more gratification, more
delight, than any thing upon Earth could do that was not
you, or *me* —— & surely to see again my Mad^e de Maisonneuve, even now, in my desolated state, would be the softest
solace I could receive —— Mrs. Burney, however, brings me
word it is neither the eldest Count, the *Chief* M. de Maubourg,
nor yet the noble warriour, Victor, but the Son & Nephew,
Florimond. This is a severe disappointment, chequered with
deep regret as was my satisfaction. That we hear nothing
from France, en attendant, is truly marvellous.

Maria is better,[7] but still confined to the house. She is
quite impatient for a Letter from you. Pray set about one at
once.

I am glad you were man of Business enough to answer M^r
Foss[8] off hand.

I am going to *parcourir* some Books I have looked out concerning ancient Philosophers, to see what I can recommend
to you. 'Tis droll you should only want classics, Now,—which
the museum could so fully have provided *here*:—& *when*
here, only sighed for analytics!—Don't retard dangerously
the Epistles, &c!—I understand that Sarum is the 1st week in
lent—& Lauds at Easter. Which will you try for?—

It is *thought* the new Evelina[9] will be here in the course of

but César's brother, the brave soldier Marie-*Victor*-Nicolas de Fay de Latour-
Maubourg (1768-1850), général de division (1807), who, serving in most of Napoleon's campaigns and grievously wounded more than once, had been created
baron de l'Empire (1808), comte de (1814), marquis de (1817), and a member of
the Légion d'honneur (1814). His name is inscribed on the Arc de Triomphe de
l'Étoile.

'He will display among you a character foreign to intrigues—a character
honourable and conciliating, like that which we witness in your Minister Pleni-
potentiary', the Paris Correspondent assured readers of *The Times* (3 Apr.).

[7] AA's cousin Maria Bourdois (L. 1180 n. 3).

[8] Probably Henry Foss (L. 1191 n. 8), apprentice to and connection of Thomas
Payne, the younger (n. 5), and since 1813 a partner in the firm Payne and Foss,
booksellers, Pall Mall (see *DNB*).

[9] Georgina *Cecilia* Locke (1798-1867), the 2nd daughter of Charles Locke
(1769-1804) of Norbury Park, and Cecilia Margaret *née* Ogilvie (1775-1824),

the spring—but not *decided*. The *negociation* is not *signed* yet! I shall soon know more—but poor Mrs. Lock is an Invalid with a feverish Cold, & cannot come to me till next week.

You ought to let Dr. Kaye know the extraordinary mystery of our Letters & papers, that he may comprehend the non-appearance of the Chinese Dictionary.[10]

I say nothing of *The* Pupil for 1/2 a term!—alas!—for how small a matter is this painful step taken!—

You don't speak of rising?—

Early rising is the First thing, either for your P[riest's] orders to be distinguished, or your Prize attempt successful, or your meeting with the New Evelina propitious!—What motives to discard sluggishness! Besides giving much comfort to la meilleure de vos amies—

F d'A

10. Feby 1819

1193   [11 Bolton Street], 11 February 1819

To Alexander d'Arblay

A.L. (rejected Diary MSS. 7180-[3], Berg), 11 Feb. 1819
Double sheet 4to (8.9 × 5.1″) black edged 4 pp. *pmk* [*blurred*] black seal [*with a large tear*]
Addressed: Revd A. d'Arblay / Christ College / Cambridge
Edited by CFBt. *See* Textual Notes.

whom the d'Arblays had known in Surrey in the years 1795-1801 (iv and v *passim*). After five years abroad Mrs. Charles planned to bring her two younger daughters to England and leave them with their grandmother Locke at Eliot Vale, Blackheath, while she returned to Genoa to be with her eldest daughter Emily Frederica (1796-1822), whose unhappy marriage to the conte da Viry (1792-1844) she had unfortunately assented to or arranged. See x, L. 1109 n. 12, and *Locks of Norbury*, pp. 281-306.

[10] *Dictionnaire Chinois. Français et Latin*, published in Paris in 1813 by Chrétien-Louis-Joseph de Guignes (1759-1845), a copy of which General d'Arblay intended as a gift for John Kaye (L. 1181 n. 2). See x, L. 1170 n. 107 and further, L. 1194 n. 5.

49

Sat^y 11. Feby 1819.

My own Alex—This last letter is very dear to me—'tis *conversation*—'tis an opening of heart to heart—& mine receives all that comes from your's *tout droit.*

I am sadly vexed by your confinement,—the *process* to that was not quite so well judged as the *process projected* to give pleasure to your best Friend.—But the lesson comes with the fault, therefore comment would be superfluous: simply let me entreat you to see some medical person, & have *leave* for walking forth before you quit your apartment. All hurts of the feet are dangerous if *ill-treated*, as well as if *neglected.* I hope you have not administered *ointment* without advice?

I will try to get more intelligence about the *New:*—[1] L^y M[artin] will tell any thing—every thing. She was here yesterday, but I was at my lonely Dinner, & could not receive her. *Mrs. Lock* writes me word she is better, & will come to me as soon as she may take the air. *Amine* is shut up with her Children, excellent Mother that she is; but her favourite Governess is recovering, & now at Eliot Vale; therefore I hope she will soon be at liberty to give me again her dear sight.

They will no where suffer shelves to be put up, as they leave marks along the Walls. I am glad *you* will be patient, for then *I* am in no haste. Here after, we may get *Mahogany* which costs much, but lasts for-ever, & always looks *comme il faut.*

I marvel I did not enquire about the Tour? I think of it often. *Less* than Mr. Ebden[2] has calculated would be impracticable. |

As to the *New*—it is not going to *Italy* would do the business, but having some situation *here* that seemed in a fair way to future high preferment. The Lady Mammy is already in

1193. [1] The 'new Evelina' or 'the beautiful Cecilia' Locke (L. 1192 n. 9), now about 20 years of age, whom AA had met in Bath. Much smitten, he had evidently asked his mother when she was expected to return to England, but as yet FBA had had no opportunity of applying to the persons most likely to have that information, namely, Cecilia's aunts Lady Martin (L. 1191 n. 15) or Amelia Angerstein (L. 1188 n. 3), or her grandmother Mrs. Locke (ibid.).

[2] The Revd. James Collett Ebden (L. 1181 n. 3), Fellow and Tutor at Trinity College, Cambridge, with whom AA was making plans for a tour of the Continent (see Diary, 12 July 1819).

disgrace for an imprudent connexion formed for the *Eldest*;[3] who is again upon her own hands, with a husband & Child into the bargain! & I hear she is very penitent & ashamed: —therefore she will now be any thing rather than *romantick*,

Clement is returned from Brighton, with his *two* sisters,[4] & they were all at Richmond the other day. I have not yet seen our dear *Charlotte*: but had good news of her by *Fanny* Raper,[5] who spent all yesterday morning with me. She talked with her usual great kindness of you. I mean to make my arrangement without loss of time for joining my dear sister *Broome* during your absence. This Letter closed, my next will be to her, for that purpose. She is, I thank God, much better.

I am very glad you have written to *Maria*.[6] I have no fresh news from Bath, & am very uneasy for good *M*ʳ *Burney*.

Edward has not called; *Fanny B*[urney] only once,[6] when I was out taking my usual & essential exercise with our *Diane*.

As to *Diane* —— —— her disconsolate search for you, & moaning Countenance at its failure, has been quite affecting. If your room door is open, she darts into it still, with a

[3] The unfortunate marriage in 1817 of Emily Frederica Locke (L. 1192 n. 9) to the conte da Viry (x, L. 1109 n. 12), an Admiral (at the age of 36) in the Sardinian navy and later Governor of Nice. Their first child Nina had recently been born, but the young wife, terrified and subdued by her husband's cruel and gloomy humours, soon sank into the hopeless unhappiness depicted by the Duchess of Sermoneta (*Locks of Norbury*, pp. 285-6, 297-303, and *passim*). For Emily's early death in a street accident at Boulogne, see L. 1294 n. 4.

[4] Mrs. Broome's family by her first marriage, namely, Marianne and Clement Francis and her married daughter Charlotte Barrett (i, pp. lxxii–lxxiii), on visits to their mother, who was to remain at 6 German Place, Brighton, until August 1819.

[5] A faithful caller and a friend to FBA to the end of her life was her niece Fanny *née* Phillips (1782-1860), SBP's daughter and the wife since 1807 of Charles Chamier Raper (*c.* 1777-1842) of the War Office. The couple lived at Field Cottage, King's Parade, Chelsea, and had one child Catherine Minette, now 11 years of age. Fanny Raper, like Marianne Francis, very 'religious' and a follower of 'enthusiastic' preachers like Irving, was the author of a pamphlet entitled *Pastoral Duties*, published by Hatchard (1818). 'It is intended for young clergymen', CFBt explained to Arthur Young in a letter (Eg. 3703A, ff. 46-7b) of 18 May [1818], 'who go into the Church just now by hundreds, merely because they cannot go into the army—& she thought they might attend to a short & simple & cheap new exhortation when they would not read the good old books on the same subject.'

[6] Maria Bourdois (L. 1180 n. 3); Edward Francesco Burney (L. 1189 n. 12), the artist; and EBB's daughter Frances Burney (L. 1191 n. 4).

precipitation that shews revived hope; but stands motionless & forlorn, when she is disappointed, for half an hour, if not called away. 'Tis the most constant & respectable *Friend* in the World.

I hope *Richard Burney*[7] is returned & that you see him often in your confinement.

⸺

I have not seen Lady Keith:[8] do tell me positively I whether you mean I should *write* to her your intention to keep free from engagement at present; or whether you desire that matter should be let to take its course?

The late Rising makes me sigh!—but you are kind to give me hopes the next Letter will announce improvement.

You are trying for many things, & Capable of many things; but a Sluggard, my dear Alex, *effects* nothing.

You have written exactly my feelings & reflexions as to Florimond. Had Victor—& Mad[e] de M[aisonneuve][9] not, momentarily, been thought of, I must have rejoiced in his appointment, for he is amiable, exemplary, &, I am sure, much attached to us both: ⸺ ⸺ but oh! Victor & Mad[e] de M.!—that would have been *all but* Fe[licity! but] *Felicity* nothing can be to me!—but *They*, & *You*, can still draw me within its outward circle—the *core*, indeed, is buried!

I have sent to *Mr. Hay* once more by my sister Burney; but received no answer.[10] The silence, however, of Mr. *Le Noir*[11] leaves all other wonders in the lurch. I fear he is removed from the ministry, & has missed all our papers!—

[7] Richard Burney (L. 1184 n. 11).

[8] A constant friend to FBA since the Streatham days of the 1780s, Hester Maria *née* Thrale (1764-1857) had married in 1808, as his 2nd wife, George Keith Elphinstone (1746-1823), Admiral of the Red (1801), Viscount Keith (1814). See also vi, L. 594 n. 8; xi *passim*.   [9] See L. 1192 n. 6.

[10] For the wishes of the apothecary that out of regard for the deceased his account might be forgotten, see L. 1189 n. 18. That FBA insisted none the less on paying is shown by an entry in her 'Yearly Resumé of Expenditure' for the year 1819 (Account Book, Berg): 'Mr. Hay! Bill & attendance. 50. 0. 0', a payment recorded also by her bankers Messrs Hoare, Ledger, 30 Apr. 1819: 'To [Jones & C°] for G E Hay with [Hobhouse & C°] 50'.

[11] M. Lenoir (L. 1189 n. 5), to whom FBA had sent £50 (see her Account Books, Berg), being the legacy bequeathed him by M. d'A. See further, L. 1194 n. 1. Remembering his kindness to M. d'A in 1817, she also would name him in her will (xii, Appendix) for £50.

Be sure Collect all the Creditor's accounts as fast as possible. Do not wait till you have *de quoi payer le tout*—it is right you should know how your means stand actually before you incur any new expence beyond necessity.

Do not neglect this, my dear Alex: we can make no estimates either as to Book Cases, or Travelling, or my Drawing Room, till you know your own situation. Richard,[12] I dare say, would go round & claim them for you. He is so friendly, & so much versed in business, that I wish you would trust him.

I shall do the very best I can, with *propriety*, about the Books. I ^l am quite of your opinion about the *Elder*,[13] & shall make a point that it be *him*—certainly I am not *bound*; & if what he advises, or says, seems unfair, or unpleasant, I shall be *free*.

I am very glad of your Cicero reading: that must, in every way, & upon every project, be good for your taste as well as instruction. I would I were erudite enough to enjoy it with you, as I did Bacon on Learning! What we *both* like, I would rather read with You, *Now*!!! than with any one, independently of *private motives*, as I think we excite pleasure in each other. Your Confinement has made me give this morning to writing to you, as I know well such a situation gives double zest to a Letter.

While I highly approve your *silent efforts* as to the ensuing prize, because its result must always be added information,[14] —yet forget not the *main-point*! the Priest's orders—for you cannot quit England & run the risks of the many accidents (boiling water not excepted!) that might interfere with your return in time for *preparing*: as you certainly would not *travel* to be studying for that!—& you have now little more than a month before you, I understand, for our own kind BP.[15]—though I was mistaken as to the first week in Lent. Get ready with *indispensables* as fast as possible. Add decorations

[12] Richard Burney (L. 1184 n. 11), who having secured an ample competence in the employ of the Bengal Army, had impressed FBA as a capable man of affairs.

[13] Conjecturally Thomas Payne, bookseller in Pall Mall, as compared in matters of business with his natural son John (L. 1192 n. 5).

[14] Cf. CFBt's report on AA's preparations for his ordination (L. 1190 n. 2).

[15] Probably Dr. Fisher (L. 1180 n. 3), Bishop of Salisbury. For AA's ordination, as priest, see L. 1203 n. 2.

& brilliancy *as* you can, & *if* you can. See but what constant application has done for Florimond! Who, I am sure, will see you with his old friendship & kindness—Give the News of your poor foot as soon as you can. Uncle James called upon me just now, blyth & well, bringing me his first Proof sheet.[16] Adieu—& Be well. I should not write so very quick but for y^r foot.

1194   11 Bolton Street,
                                          18 February 1819

To Alexander d'Arblay

A.L. (rejected Diary MSS. 7184-[7], Berg), 18 Feb. 1819
Double sheet 4to   black edged   4 pp.   *pmk*   18 FE 1819   seal
Addressed: Revd A. d'Arblay, / Christ College, / Cambridge.
Edited by CFBt. *See* Textual Notes.

                                   Bolton St. 18th Feby 1819.

What a blessing is This, my dear Alex! a Letter at last from M. Le Noir,[1] and
    Your beloved Father's invaluable posthumous Letter has been, at last, safely received by him!
    This has filled me with gratitude & satisfaction.

---

[16] For JB's works, see L. 1191 n. 6.

1194. [1] This letter is missing, though extant in the Berg Collection are M. Lenoir's letter of condolence of 19 May 1818, addressed to AA (who has lost 'le meilleur de Pères, le plus noble, le plus aimant, le plus généreux, le plus délicat, le plus droit des hommes, l'ami le plus dévoué, le plus tendre, le plus aimable—!') and a letter of 24 Sept. 1822 (Berg) to FBA, in which, with renewed lamentations for his friend, he acknowledges receipt of a legacy of £50, given to him 'par cet ami rare, ce coeur parfait, cette âme noble et sain modèle, que nous regrettons et pleurerons toujours'. He thanks Madame d'Arblay, who, though no will was made, took pleasure in fulfilling her husband's wishes.
    For the activities of the archaeologist in 1790-1816 in assembling the *Musée des monuments français* (chiefly from convents and churches), its closure by royal ordinance 18 Dec. 1816, and the restoration of the monuments to their original locations, see Larousse XIX. Formerly director of this enterprise, Lenoir feels himself, as administrator of the monuments in Saint Denis, 'oubliè et sans avancement, dans sa petite sphère, dans son modeste emploi; bien heureux encore que cet emploi nous procure des moyens suffisans d'existence!'

Au reste, you will find this poor M. Le Noir has been literally *disorganized* by his afflictions! *Coup sur Coup* have so assailed & shaken him, that the aggregate seems to have as nearly demolished him as the one so peculiar & dreadfully irreparable Coup has your poor Mother. You must write the kindest Letter to him that is possible, in both our Names, & yet leave me some space to add my own sympathies, and to give my procuration for his proceedings.

Au reste, you will write to me first, with a sketch of your notions & wishes.

The *Catalogue*[2] seems out of the question: there are so *many* Books nearly Valueless, that it would take more time —for a trusty Copiest, than the *Vente* would purchase.

The difficulties & expence of custom Houses & package & postage & Carriage, are so great, that you cannot demand too little. Nothing that can be dispenced with. |

M. Le Noir proposes excepting so many Books & Drawings or pictures, that I see he is utterly unacquainted with these enormous charges.

He knows not what this very circumstance still detains at Calais—nor the Sacrifice made—even by your dear Father *himself*!

With all his passionate love of Books of all sorts, to escape the terrible balance.

Nor does good M. Le Noir yet know that mille franc— 1500, Je crois, are destined to himself. £50.—

To raise This how many Books must be sold!—Meubles— Drawings, all!—

I shall except only His Portrait[3]—dear to my Soul! drawn by William Locke just at the period of our Marriage! & the *Pendant*, M. de Narbonne—with the Designs for Evelina & Cecilia given to me by our excellent uncle—[4]

And the *Pendule*—a Birth Day Gift!—

And the Chinese Dictionary for Dr. Kaye.[5]

[2] Some of the books to be catalogued were in the six trunks left in storage in Calais (see L. 1189 n. 5 and further, L. 1229 n. 1 and L. 1237 n. 3).

[3] William Locke's drawing of General d'Arblay is shown in volume ii, Plate I, *facing* p. x.

[4] A list of such possessions, shown as unsettled in 1822 and yet to be reclaimed from France, appears in FBA's Account Book, Berg.

[5] For the *Dictionnaire Chinois*, see L. 1192 n. 10. FBA's 'Yearly Resumé of

To recover That is a real joy to my poor spirits. For that must be the Book to which M. Le. N. alludes.

You will pardon I trust my opening the Letter? I knew M. Le Noir's Hand, & was sure the Writing must be for both. Oh how sweet is what he says of our best Friend! ⏐ 'avec qui mon coeur étoit si lieé avec qui je me sentais si *rafraichi!*—' There is the Word!—there the feeling of what I deplore!—

The poor poor M. Norry![6] quel coup inattendu!—oh what a world of woe!—

Alex! My dear Alex!—work well, & deserve well while yet you escape calamity! To enjoy your present days of peace, make them days of virtue!—Rise—& Work!—

Then Rest—& play!—

How fortunate that all the sacred renseignmens arrived safely! A Letter to me, from Paris, tells me we must expect very little from the *Vente*, so ill every thing sells, however dear it may have been bought. M. Le Noir does not mention Mme de Grandmaison—nor Mme de Cadignac, nor M. des Essards, nor M^e ⟨Lubin⟩[7]—

Certainly we shall submit the *manner* of the *Vente totally* to the judgment of M. Le Noir, as your dear Father prescribed. We must only join to beg he will merely *superintend*, & *direct*, not act, nor Count, nor waste his declining health & few moments of leisure in *execution*.

There are between 13 & 14 hundred *title pages!*—He little suspects the admirable Books & Engravings & MSS. we lost at Dover, not to pay *les frais!*[8] [il ne] faut absolument pas demander à reçevoir que le moins [precieux que] ⏐ nous serons encore forcés to *resign in mass* at Dover, as your dearest

Expenditure of 1820' (Account Book, Berg) includes the item 'Chinese Dictionary Binding, BP Kay 2. 2. 0'.

[6] Charles Norry (1756-1832), architect, author (x, L. 1089 n. 48 and *passim*), chef du bureau au ministère de l'Interieur, and a friend both of M. d'A and M. Lenoir. He had suffered the loss in September 1818 of his eldest son Charles Désiré, a student in architecture, aged about 22.

[7] FBA had hoped to hear news of friends she had known in Paris: Marie-Pierre *née* Sonnerat (1759-1848), who had married (1788) as her 2nd husband Alexandre-Paul-Millin de Grandmaison (1739-1811); Catherine *née* Hunter (*c.* 1773-1860), widow of the émigré Anne-Charles-Guy-Gérard Dupleix (1767-1804), comte de Cadignan; Louis-Hyppolyte Ragon des Essards (*fl.* 1783-1819), formerly mayor of Béon (vi, L. 561 n. 2); and Charlotte-Claude de Berthelot de la Villeheurnois *née* Drouyn de Vaudreuil (b. 1 Oct. 1760). For these friends see v, vi *passim*.

[8] For 6 trunks of books left at Calais, see L. 1189 n. 5.

Father did, per force, this time twelve month! What *argent* can be procured by the mass in France will be truly accept-able, for the £50 — — & the logement—& a *Fleurist* who has sent him a bill of about £3—If more, how properly it will help our sacred demands at Bath![9]

Think over all you have to propose, & to say, speedily; a Letter such as This ought to be answered as soon as pos-sible. With a *mind diseased*, like our poor excellent & too feeling friend's, he will else give over again the business with returned despondency. Alas—I know it all [*tear*]! How good of him to plan *seperate* distributions! [*tear*] could *ask* a Vente en masse, but his plan is 1000 times [*tear*]—worthy—*melt-ing* M. Le Noir! would I could see him!—

adieu, my Alex—This has been a great relief to me, on millions of accounts, melancholy as is the relief.

Nothing yet from Mr. Hay[10]—though Maria has spoken to his shopman. She & Sophy are highly pleased with an Epistle from You. I am very glad you have written—& *successfully*.

1195   [11 Bolton Street,
                              c. 27 February 1819]

To H.R.H. Princess Elizabeth
later Landgravine of Hesse-Homburg[1]

A.L. a preliminary draft (Berg), n.d.
Twenty-three pages (6 × 3.7″) written in a Memorandum Book kept

[9] These 'demands' would include payments for the memorial plaque within Walcot Church at Bath (see x, J. 1170 n. 121) and for a black marble gravestone (specified by the General himself, x, J. 1170.897) not now to be seen. In FBA's Account Book for the year 1820 (Berg), in the Ledgers of Messrs Hoare, bankers, and in the relevant correspondence (Berg) are the records of payments made (17 Apr. and 9 June 1820) to the statuary mason Thomas King (*fl.* 1804–33) of Bath, both for the gravestone and the mural plaque within the church:

Mr. King! Black Marble Tablet, in Walcot Church Yard! Bath!	13. 7. 0.
Mr. King, Tablet on Walcot Church	33. 0. 0.

His receipt for £46. 7*s.* 0*d.* in all is extant (Berg). See further, 'The d'Arblay Gravestones in Bath', xii, Appendix.   [10] See L. 1189 n. 18.

1195. [1] Of the princesses whom FBA had known when in the years 1786–91 she served as Keeper of the Robes to Queen Charlotte, she had had the opportunity

by CB (Berg),[2] marble covered, *entitled* 1796, but reversed by FBA and *entitled*: Les Princesses

CB's memoranda begin (1 Jan. 1796): stick of pomatum . . . [*but record his appointments, visits, and teaching engagements.*] For this draft FBA used the spaces ruled for the dates 31 Dec.–16 Oct. 1796, on which spaces CB had made diary entries for the dates 12–13, 20–2, 26–7, 31 Oct.; 7, 9, 11, 22–3, 29 Nov.; 3, 6–8, 10, 13–17, 20–2, 28, 31 Dec. 1796. He had entered, on the right, accounts for the weeks of 17, 24, 31 Oct.; 14, 21 Nov.; and 12, 19 Dec.

The *verso* of the second leaf written on by FBA (the space for Thursday 20 Oct.) has an entry in CB's hand: This fatal evening my poor Wife, Elizabeth, breathed her last, between 8 & 9 o'Clock! . . .

FBA's text (23 pp.) shows the deletions and the rewritings characteristic of a draft.

Princess of Hesse Homburg

⟵————,

Little able as I still feel to do *de suite* what I wish, my whole heart rises to pour forth immediately the fullness of its thanks for the sweet goodness that dictated so early an acceptance of so tardy a Letter.[3] Ah Madam, if condescendsion of so humane a tenour as that of y^r R.H. won not all hearts, of

to see in late years only the Princess Elizabeth (1770–1840), who had accompanied the Queen to Bath in the autumn of 1817 (see x. 846–52). On 7 Apr. 1818 the Princess had married Frederick Joseph (1769–1829), Hereditary Prince of Hesse-Homburg (x, L. 1165 n. 1), and had left England on 29 June, arriving at the Castle of Homburg on 14 July.

Now that the Princess was herself blest 'with the best of Husbands' (one whose 'character & principles . . . integrity & worth are proverbial here') she could feel 'doubly' for FBA's loss. 'Perfect happiness is not to be found on earth', she goes on to say in her letter (Berg) of *post* 29 July 1818, 'for I should have been at the summit of bliss had it not been for this sad & suffering illness of my poor & respectable Mother'. Little had she thought when at 'dear Bath' the Queen 'was so very well' that she 'should be so ill now'. It is fortunate that we cannot see into the future, 'for had I known how my happy marriage was to be clouded, what should I have felt, & how gone through it,—but I bless God hourly for my lot, & indeed I should have been much too happy for this world had I not had this very heavy affliction—'.

[2] The use of CB's Memorandum Books for scratch paper indicates that FBA was at this time examining her father's papers. See also the entry in her Diary for 7 May 1819: '—Finished 2^d examination of Cahier 1st of MS. Memoirs de Mon Pere'.

[3] It must have been late in the year 1818 (after the death of Lady Crewe on 23 Dec.) that FBA had written, as she says, a 'tardy' letter of condolence to the Princess on the death (17 Nov.) of her mother Queen Charlotte. The Princess's undated reply (Berg) ran to the usual discursive length of 4 pages 4to or more.

what stuff must they be composed? I am the more ready, at this moment, to resume some alacrity in writing, because I have to relate a circumstance in which my private feelings, which yr. R.H. so graciously commiserates are blended— most unexpectedly & even wonderfully, with a public event[4] I shall venture, therefore, to give ⏐ at some length a little Narrative which I have every reason to flatter myself will engage yr R. H^ss—kind interest. ⏐

When my honoured Partner in All carried me to his own Country, he had previously arranged my reception in a Circle of the first class of amiability amongst his widely spread connexions & acquaintance: & when he had given me, in detail, the characters of Those to whom he meant to introduce me, he finished with saying that the person upon whom he chiefly built, for best supplying the place of all I most grieved to ⏐ quit, was a lady of such exemplary conduct & sweetness of manners, & who had a mind so highly furnished with female excellence, that he should be greatly surprized if I did not think of her, & love her, as a Countrywoman as well as a Friend.

He divined justly—for he knew me well!—I found in Madame de Maisonneuve every thing united that Affection & Esteem could demand for forming a warm & permanent Friendship—Gentleness with dignity; Modesty, with arch vivacity; & Reserve with glowing Feelings. M. d'A — — who had known her from her ⏐ earliest youth, had instigated her to think of me with determined partiality; our first meeting, therefore, was already like that of two old friends, & we soon

---

[4] Anxious to secure a warm welcome in England for her French friend Madame de Maisonneuve (v, L. 515 n. 10 and *passim*), FBA wrote long accounts of her to the Duchess of Gloucester (L. 1196A) as well as to the Princess Elizabeth (*supra*).

The 'circumstance' was the receipt on 11 February (see Diary) of a letter (Berg) from Madame de Maisonneuve herself, announcing the appointment of her brother General Victor de Latour-Maubourg (L. 1192 n. 6) as 'ambassadeur en Angleterre'. Victor, a brave soldier, wounded in many battles and suffering from the amputation of a leg at the hip joint (and an ill-fitting artificial limb), was unwilling, his sister said, to accept the diplomatic post even temporarily. He was to arrive, however, on 7 Apr. accompanied by his sister, Madame de Maisonneuve, and by his wife Petronella-Jacoba (1772-1844), the daughter of the Dutch General Albert van Rijssel (1726-1805).

This was one of the more exciting and pleasurable events of FBA's later years, though the pleasure was marred by her grief that the General could not have been alive to welcome such old friends to England.

became so intimate, that we thought it a severe privation if a day passed in which we saw not each other.

To yr. R.H.——whose Heart, I am convinced, will ever be in the *tight little tidy*[5]——I may say, what to say *There* was rather impertinent, that her air, manner, look & discourse, as well as her most delicate conduct, were so *English* ⏐ that I could scarcely persuade myself she was not born on this side the Water. Another strong point of union between us was her little son,[6] an only Child, just of an age, though a year & more younger, to become a playmate with my Boy. The Children grew up together, went to the same Ecole secondaire, & were nearly inseparable.

Made de Maisonneuve lived in the ⏐ most extreme retirement. Her Family both of Birth & of Marriage were ruined by the Revolution, & her Pittance, for herself & Child, was so niggardly, that she had only 2 small rooms, narrow & ill furnished, up 2 or 3 pr of crooked, ladder like stairs, in which she lived with an œconomy hardly credible, for she had not above 80 a year, yet was always well, though simply dressed; kept one young Maid for every thing, the Child included; educated that Child in the best manner, ⏐ made his external appearance accord with his real, not fortuitous rank in life; while her own pleasing deportment & high character were so universally admired, that she was never seen but with distinction & pleasure whenever she could be induced to quit her Cell. Her disposition however, was of so quiet a cast, that she mixt with no society but of her family & its circle. To Me—— what a bond of union, was such a propensity to retirement—— rare even here, but in France almost ⏐ *unique*. What obligations did I not owe to her! She came to me daily, indulging my rooted sauvagerie in not demanding any return of visits: if I was sick, she Nursed me; if I was embarrassed or perplexed,

---

[5] From the popular patriotic song by T. J. Dibdin, *The British Raft* (1797). In letters of the years 1802–17 FBA often used the phrase in references to England (e.g. v, L. 543, and viii *passim*).

[6] 'Maxime' or Fréderic-Gérard-Bénoni-César Bidault de Maisonneuve (1797–1869), lieutenant-colonel des Grénadiers à Cheval de la Garde Royale, the son of Gérard-Joseph Bidault de Maisonneuve (v, L. 515 n. 10). Descriptions of Alexander and Maxime in their schooldays (1803–5) in Passy, and of the daily visits between the d'Arblays, Madame de Maisonneuve, and other members of the de Latour-Maubourg family are to be read in FBA's Diaries of 1802–12 (vi. 735 ff.) and her French Exercise Books (Berg).

in a strange land, with regard to customs, habits, & expectations, she relieved & enlightened me; she informed me of all it was necessary to know; she aided me in all it was necessary to do; if I wished to see any place, any Curiosity, any Spectacle, ¦ she procured me Tickets or Admission if I required retired exercise, she engaged the owners of great Chateaux to send me Keys of their Gardens, without exacting visits or acquaintance; if I wanted to make purchases, she accompanied me to the best *boutiques*—If I had any difficulty about my Alexander, she considered it as an affair of her own Maxime, & found means to remedy it accordingly. ¦

Here let me stop, not to fatigue yr. R.H. with too much minuteness, & come to the point: When I quitted this dear & excellent Friend in the year 1815, she was the last person I saw in Paris[7] — — She came to take leave of us at 6 O'clock in the morning, & descended into the Court yard to see the last of us. I wept even bitterly, though I was then by the side of All most dear to me upon Earth, from a well grounded apprehension of the precariousness of our ever meeting again: an apprehension ¦ that dejected me even while I was happy, & was a constant source of regret: ¦ Nevertheless, my dear General purposed frequent excursions to France, & This very ensuing Summer had been promised for a visit thither from us all 3 to the favourite Brother of my Mad^e de Maisonneuve, who was the favourite, the chosen Friend, of Genl d'Arblay —But—with the 3^d of last May This project, of course, was annihilated, with nearly All that made the peculiar & most rare happiness of my Earthly existence—& I believed myself as completely, though not as awfully, parted from my Mad^e de Maisonneuve as from Him who with such tender discernment had elected her for my Friend:—Your R.H. then may judge what were my sensations when, after such desolation ¦ of all prospect of re-union! ¦

I received—last week a Letter from the Marquis de Lally Tolendall,[8] a school fellow at the College d Harcourt with

[7] The farewell scene in the courtyard FBA described in her Trèves Journal, viii. 537.

[8] By the French diplomatic postbag FBA had received the letter (Berg) of 4 Feb. 1819 from Lally-Tolendal (v, vi *passim*), felicitating her on the arrival of her friend: 'je ne veux pas laisser partir Mr de Caraman, l'aimable précurseur de notre ambassadeur, sans vous dire avec quel attendrissement je songe à votre

M. D'Arblay, to tell me that *mon amie cherie Mad^e de Maisonneuve*, was coming over to England! her ⎮ favourite Brother having been appointed Ambassadour by the King of France to the British Court!

Imagination could not paint an event more truly unlooked for; and the utmost fancy of Fiction could not have devized any other means by which our meeting again could have been brought to bear; since for Me, a Voyage to France would now be heart-breaking; & for her, with an income so narrow, a Voyage to England seemed as utterly improbable as a Voyage to Japan. ⎮

I am more thankful & more soothed by this extraordinary circumstance than words can express. It is just what my best & tenderest Friend would most have wished for me, but that such a Nomination seemed out of the question, first from the exceeding mediocrity of the Marquis' fortune—& next, because he has never yet moved in the diplomatic line. The King, however, does honour to his own discernment—& indeed to our Country by the choice, for a Man of a ⎮ nobler mind does not exist. Alas! to me what of regret & sorrow will mingle with the soft satisfaction of so unexpected a meeting!⁹ I look forward to it with almost as much dread as gratitude!—it would have been a happiness to Genl d'Arblay surpassing all other!

Can yr. R.H. pardon this long history? I think so!—& should it prove that I do not too much flatter myself, my next shall contain as much of the brother as this does of the sister. ⎮

I entirely—however sadly—subscribe to the justice—the religious justice of all yr. R.H. says upon the 'duty of submission to Providence unmurmuringly,¹⁰ even upon our most

prochaine réunion avec Mad^e de Maisonneuve, et ses dignes parens. quelle consolation ils vous apporteront et de quel secours vous leur serez! que ne puis-je les accompagner et recevoir dans mon coeur toutes les effusions du Vôtre, et serrer votre Alexandre dans mes bras! . . .

'Adieu, chere Madame. un mot de vos nouvelles, de celles de Votre jeune savant, destiné, à ce qu'on m'a dit aujourd'hui, a être le doyen de Votre Saint Paul ou le Saint-Paul de votre Eglise. je suis à vos pieds. . . .'

⁹ This meeting, 'the most affecting I can have in this nether World', was to take place on 20 Apr. 1819 (Diary).

¹⁰ In reply to FBA's letter (n. 3) of condolence ('a painful one', remarked the Princess, 'as each had so much to mourn for'), she went on more forthrightly than one might have expected, to offer advice on the subject of mourning: 'Your *own loss* is a most afflicting one & a widow is what ought most to be pitied when wrapt up in her partner which I well know you were, but the sufferings of Mon-

heart-piercing deprivations—but without murmuring, there may be affliction! & where the heaviest of all possible subjects of affliction is given, it surely must be pardonable that it should be felt!

My intentions, however, to force myself, for my son's sake, out of my *melancholy* solitude, will ∣ certainly be strengthened by the encouraging approbation of yr. R.H.[11] But I have not yet been imperiously called upon for exertion; since my Son is almost wholly at Cambridge.[12] when his fellowship no longer makes him deem it right he should make the University his principal residence, I will surely do my best to put my purposes & my promises into execution.

My dear Mrs. Locke resides in a small house on Blackheath, named Eliot Vale. It is within ∣ a quarter of a Mile of the Living, at Lee, of her son George, whose Church is in sight from her habitation.[13] I am told it is an elegant little Dwelling, & I *mean* to go to it ere long. It is within a Walk of her sweet Daughter Amelia Angerstein, & consequently of 5 grandchildren,[14] the eldest of whom is now finishing his education at Brunswic. The other, & very amiable Daughter, L^y Martin, resides in my neighbourhood, in Hertford Street May Fair;[15] & visits her mother continually, with her husband Sir George.

sieur d'Arblay were so dreadful that You ought to bless the Almighty for removing what you have so dearly loved from all pain to a state of bliss, it is thus I am trying to submit to the loss of my ever to be regretted Mother & by being satisfied that She really is happy & meeting the just reward of a well spent life I bend with humility to the Will of God, which I am sure is what is best for us; & as he gives & grants us our blessings we ought with chearfulness to resign, when he thinks right to deprive us of them—it requires much trust in Him for one often loves too well & that we are told is wrong but how difficult to measure our affection!'

[11] Like the Lockes and Angersteins, the Princess inveighed against the deep seclusion into which FBA had withdrawn after the death of her husband. 'I am sure that it was not intended that we should shun society & become recluses, it injures not only ones health but ones temper & understanding.'

[12] Residence, apparently, was one of the conditions of the first year of AA's Fellowship at Christ's College, Cambridge. For other conditions, see x, L. 1161 n. 10.

[13] See L. 1188 n. 3. The information about Mrs. Locke and her family is FBA's response to the Princess's inquiries. 'Has she a House in Town? or where is she now that she has quitted Norbury Park? is it sold or lett, or what is become of it?'

[14] The six Angersteins, children of John Angerstein (*c.* 1773–1858), were John Julius William (b. 1800), Caroline (1802–79), Henry (1805–21), Elizabeth Julia (1806–70), Frederick (b. 1809), and William (1812–97).

[15] See L. 1191 n. 15.

She comes, also, very often to me. Mr. William Locke, with his Family, is now a resident of Paris.[16] There is still there such an Assemblage of Paintings, that he is content, for the present, not to travel further. I know not ˡ with exactness the fate of Norbury Park—dear Norbury Park! the seat—when I first knew it, of the most perfect Human Felicity I ever witnessed.

My very good Friend Ly Keith has just had the Honour & happiness of passing 10 Days at Brighton.[17] That the sweet Du^ss of Gloucester should have condescended to make even anxious enquiries about me, gratefully delighted, but could not surprize me—any more than if it had been the dear Princess of Hesse Hombourg— ˡ but I was indeed *surprized* as well as deeply gratified, to hear that the P^r R^t had deigned to join in the enquiry, & even, L^y Keith says, with *much kindness*, adding sundry questions relative to my son, with an air of interest in his proving to me a comfort. How does a little trait like this shew the sincerity of His R.H. devotion to his admirable Mother!—

Lord Keith has not yet forgiven! nor admitted to his presence, Mme de Flahaut,[18] L^y K. however, who acts with the highest honour in this business, thinks he will finally relent, though ever remain cruelly wounded by the alliance. Whatever there was against the connexion, little *astonishment* can belong to those who knew M. de F. for he is very remarkably what the French call *aimable*—& I really believe,

---

[16] After his sale of Norbury Park in 1819, William Locke II (1767-1847) lived abroad (*Locks of Norbury*, p. 280 and *passim*). He had married in 1800 Elizabeth Catherine Jennings (iv, L. 385 n. 2) and had two children William (*c.* 1802-32) and Elizabeth (*c.* 1805-77), who was to marry on 23 Sept. 1822 the 3rd Lord Wallscourt (1797-1849).

[17] It was on 22 Feb. (Diary) that FBA's staunch friend Lady Keith (L. 1193 n. 8), returning from Brighton, had called at 11 Bolton Street with first-hand news of the Royal family and their polite inquiries.

Characteristic of the Prince Regent was his kindness to his sisters and the instant tact with which, given the situation, he would have supported their concern for former friends or retainers. For the Duchess of Gloucester, see L. 1198.

[18] Margaret Mercer Elphinstone (1788-1867), Lord Keith's daughter by his first wife, had in 1817 married, in defiance of her father's wishes (see L. 1091 n. 24), Charles-Auguste-Joseph, comte de Flahaut de la Billarderie (1785-1870), son of the novelist Madame de Souza, and, some say, of Talleyrand. His gallant career in war and in love, particularly as the lover of Queen Hortense, by whom he had a child, is described by Constance Wright, *Daughter to Napoleon* (1961). For Lord Keith's objections and Lady Keith's appeal to FBA for information in the critical year of 1817, see ix, x *passim*.

in defiance of frailties & irregularities he has a good & feeling heart.

I shall be very attentive about the Plants when I see them. I know those roots require great circumspection in their cultivation.

I am very glad that a sense of the beauty of Purity, even *external*, begins to spread around certain Gardens.[19] I think there will surely be effected a great & memorable change, ere long, ǀ in those departments—& indeed in All that can have a superintendent as patient & judicious as she is elegant & full of taste.

I was much struck with the solemnity of yr. R.H. kind funereal visits[20]—How must the Prince value such a testimony of regard! I am grieved so excellent an old lady was not spared to yr R.H. longer.—I am truly, truly grateful for the promise of yet more interesting details—the rooms—& their ⟨habiliments⟩[21]—

[19] Probably seeds or roots sent to the Duchess of Gloucester or some of the Royal Family, though the reference is lost in the missing parts of the Princess Elizabeth's letter. Extant, however, are her allusions to the garden at the Castle of Hesse Homburg, 'which was so filthy when I came, I was astounded'. Though at present she could only undertake 'to keep the Garden *clean*', in five years time this daughter of 'Farmer George' was to write happily of her fruit trees in 'greatest beauty', 'folliage improving every hour—our grass magnificent & bidding fair for a fine hay season', borders of 'Strawberries all in blossom looking quite pretty', and in the nursery gardens, experiments with fruit trees that she hopes will be of 'use to the country'. 'I think every hour my passion for flowers grows greater', she was to add in her May Day letter (Berg), 27 Apr.–1 May 1824. A rose garden, the geraniums, 'lovely, quite fresh', and the 'little wood' in high beauty appear in her printed *Letters*, ed. Philip C. Yorke (1898), and the Plate *facing* p. 256.

[20] 'The Prince's Great Aunt is dead', the Princess had informed FBA in her undated letter of [1819], 'a most charming old Lady, of seventy six'. This was Princess Magdalena Sophie *née* Von Solms-Braunfels (1742-1819), widow of Prince Victor Amadeus of Anhalt-Bernburg (1723-90). She was the sister of the hereditary prince's paternal grandmother, the Landgravine Ulrike Louisa (1731-92), wife of the Landgrave Frederick IV (1724-51), and she had died on 21 January, aged 76, as the princess says.

The 'funereal visit' is explained as the Princess continued her narrative: 'I have done all I can, for since she breathed her last I have visited her every day: it is a painful visit, but I feel it is a duty, & knowing the Prince's attachment for her, I feel it pleases him; I shall see her again to day, & then it is over, for to morrow she is to be buried.—'

The Landgravine was grateful to the deceased. 'She was kind & good to me from the moment of my arrival, & I used regularly to go every other evening to her. I felt when I was mixing her cards for *Patience* that I was still near my mother.'

[21] The Landgravine's offer, if not in the missing pages of the undated letter

My Son will remain at Cambridge till Easter! How I miss him! In this hope, I have the high honour to remain, Mad^e yr. R.H. ever & ever most

1196A   [11 Bolton Street,
                                        pre 4 March 1819]

To H.R.H. Princess Mary Duchess of Gloucester

A.L. draft incomplete (Berg), n.d.

Nine pages (6 X 3.7"), written on the blank introductory pages of CB's Memorandum Book of 1796, as described in the headnote of L. 1195.

From the bottom of the first leaf a segment (*c.* 2 X 3.5") previously written on by CB had been torn away before FBA had begun her draft. The *verso* of this leaf has an entry in CB's hand: King's band ab^t—40, 0, 0 [*and a total*] £517. 0. 0. The *recto* of the third leaf written on has a list of CB's 'Scholars this Year. / L^y Banks / . . . / L^y Aug. Lowther [*eleven names in all*]

Duchess of Gloucester

Madam,

The most distant hope of having any thing to say that may awaken any interest in yr. R.H. gives me courage to resume my pen, & it seems to me that the new Embassade from France cannot be wholly without a chance of exciting yr. R.H^{ss} attention. In the flattering hope, therefore, ┃ that the subject will not be entirely without attraction, I will venture to write some account of the La Tour Maubourg Family,[1] with which I was very particularly acquainted during the whole time of my residence in Paris.

(*supra*) appears also in that of [*post* 29 July 1818]: 'You shall have a full description of all my rooms.'

1196A. [1] Well known to the d'Arblays were the three brothers Latour-Maubourg, César (L. 1192 n. 6), General Victor (ibid.), and Charles (v, L. 485 n. 7), their wives, their sister Mme de Maisonneuve (ibid.), and their aunt Catherine de Fay (vi, L. 554 n. 5).

The eldest brother César and his wife Marie-Charlotte-Hippolyte *née* Pinault de

[pre *4 March 1819*]

The Chief of the House, M. le Comte de la Tour-Maubourg, has been represented, & *mis* represented, a thousand ⎸ ways, at various times, with regard to his public & political conduct:[2] but with regard to his private life, & moral character, Calumny itself has never dared to cast a stain upon him, & There he remains spotless. If I could enter into his history, I think I could clearly shew him to be really upright & noble: for his motives would always be the apology for his actions. where he has appeared to be politically wavering, he has only been urged, or distressed, how to save his wife & 7 Children from the horrours of the Guillotine, or the miseries of Emigration. ⎸ His confinement in the Tower at Olmutz, with M. de La Fayette & Mr Bureau de Pusy, is well known.[3]

When I arrived in France, in 1802, he resided at passy, a village about 2 miles from Paris, where an alarming Cough which our son had at Paris, induced us, also, to fix: & here I soon became intimately acquainted with him, & his excellent & dignified wife, upon whose jointure he lived, his own fortune being all confiscated; his eldest Daughter, Mad[e] Pinkney, was just married, but his other 6 Children lived with him, & nothing could be more conjugal, more maternal, nor more respectable than the manner in which he spent his days.

Obliged, afterwards, either to serve under Buonaparte, or to emigrate to America, Europe, at that time, having no Asylum open to him, he accepted the command of Cherbourg, & other appointments—in the course of which he owed, unhappily, personal obligations to Buonaparte, that involved him imperceptibly into a species of adherence that has removed him from the counsels & the Peerage of Louis 18.

Thenelles (v, L. 446 n. 12) lived near the d'Arblays in Passy in the years 1802–5, and FBA came to know their seven surviving children, four sons and three daughters: Florimond, the diplomat (L. 1192 n. 6); Alfred, killed in battle in 1809; Rodolphe (1787–1871), an army officer; and Septième, now 18 years of age. Their eldest daughter Éléonore-Marie-Florimonde (1779–1831) had married c. 1802 Charles Lucas Pinckney-Horry (1769–1828), expatriate American (v, L. 515 n. 22); Adèle (1782–1811), the marquis de Courcival (v, L. 448 n. 9); and Marie-Stéphanie-Florimonde (1790–1868), the comte d'Andréossy (x, L. 1101 n. 25).

[2] See L. 1192 n. 6, and for his acceptance from Napoleon of the governorship at Cherboury, vi, L. 605 n. 2.

[3] For the careers at this stage of César (*supra*), Lafayette, and Jean-Xavier de Pusy (1750–1805), see ii, pp. xvii–xviii, viii *passim*, and André Maurois, *Adrienne . . .* (1961), 'The Prisoners of Olmutz', pp. 275–315

His Eldest son, Florimond, was a decided Bourbonite, & would not enter the army of Buonaparte. He was a young man of extraordinary beauty, & of the most amiable qualities, with perfect rectitude of conduct; But he was of too conspicuous a Family for Buonaparte to leave him in obscurity; he applied himself, therefore, to the | study of diplomacy, in Germany, & was soon sent as a secretary to Constantinople, under Sebastiani.[4] This, he thought, as it was an office of Peace, not War, was serving his Country, & not the usurper, as far, at least, as the distinction could be made with safety. He acquitted himself with so much sence & prudence & sagacity, that when Sebastiani was called away, to head his Regiment, Florimond was left Minister; — — but when the King was restored, he immediately, according to the custom for young men of Family in France, went | into the Army. The King took him instantly into favour, & meant to send him Minister to Hanover. He had the honour to be presented to the Duke of Cambridge,[5] during His R.H[ss] visit at Paris, with that view: what occured to change it, I have not yet heard: but I believe he is at some other German Court.

I come now to the Ambassadour, the Marquis victor de La Tour Maubourg. He is the much younger Brother of the Chief, & the nephew[6] of Florimond. He is a man of | whom may be said, I believe, what is said of the Duke of Cambridge, That he has his first fault to make. Certainly he is one of the most exemplary Characters I have ever known. He began life by being placed in the King, Louis 16. Garde du Corps,[7] &, on the famous 5th of October, it was He who saved the Queen, Marie Antoinette.

---

[4] Horace-François-Bastien Sébastiani de la Porta (1772–1851) maréchal and diplomat, was sent as Ambassador to Constantinople on 2 May 1806 and recalled to direct troops in Spain on 22 Aug. 1808 (Six). A running commentary on the diplomatic career of Florimond de Latour-Maubourg is to be found in the letters of his aunt Mme de Maisonneuve (Berg). See also ix, L. 1019 n. 7.

[5] By the treaty of Vienna (Oct. 1814) the electorate of Hanover was made a kingdom, and in November 1816 Adolphus Frederick (1774–1850), Duke of Cambridge, was appointed to the viceroyalty (*DNB*).

[6] For nephew read uncle.

[7] Sous-lieutenant in the gardes du corps, Victor, according to Six, 'protégea la reine et la conduisit auprès du roi le 6 octobre' [1789]. This was at the time the mob marched on Versailles.

1196B   [11 Bolton Street],
4 March 1819

To H.R.H. Princess Mary
Duchess of Gloucester

A.L.S. a second draft (Berg), 4 Mar. 1819
Nineteen pages (6 × 3.7″), written upside down on blank spaces of
CB's Memorandum Book for 1796, as described in the headnote of
L. 1195. The draft occupies the spaces ruled for the dates 3 Oct.–5 Aug.
1796 and shows the deletions, obliterations, and overscorings character-
istic of a draft.

Of the pages thus used, CB had made diary entries for the dates 6,
11–13, 20, 22, 24, 26 August; 3, 7–10 September; 4, 8 October and he
had entered accounts for the weeks of 8, 15, 22, 29 August and 26 September.

Duchess of Gloucester[1]

4. March
1819.

The new marks of y^r R.H. sweetness to me, which my kind
Friend L^y Keith has been eagerly recounting,[2] make me hope
I may offer some degree of pleasure to yr R.H. benevolent
mind by relating that, from a wonderful Vicissitude of circumstances, an approaching public event promises to bring my
afflicted heart a great & most unexpected private consolation.

1196B. [1] For the marriage of Princess Mary (1776–1857) to her cousin Prince
William Frederick (1776–1834), Duke of Gloucester, and their residences at Bagshot Park and Gloucester House, Park Lane, see ix, L. 1004 n. 2, L. 1012 n. 3 and
passim; also Stuart, *Dtrs. Geo. III*, pp. 205–58.

On 9 Dec. (Diary) FBA had written a letter of 'attempted condolence', to
which the Duchess had promptly replied on the 11th (see L. 1189 n. 14) with
touching accounts of Frogmore, Windsor, and the meetings with the Queen's old
servants and with her sister Sophia. She had retired to Bagshot Park but hoped to
see FBA at Gloucester House in January, when she expected the Duke to return
from the Continent. The Duke arrived in March (see *The Times*, 6 Mar.) and on
the 2nd the Duchess wrote to say that on 'Friday, or Saturday at latest, I shall be
at Gloucester House, & as soon as I can after having arrived, I will appoint a day
to see You'. FBA's correspondence with the Duchess was to flourish (see *Catalogue*), and the audience that was to take place finally on 27 Mar. (Diary) was the
first of a long series of visits.

[2] For Lady Keith's report of her conversations with members of the Royal
Family at Brighton, see L. 1195 n. 17.

69

But before I enter upon this little narration, may I not be permitted to express my deep & sincere Gratitude that His R.H. the Pr Regent I also had deigned to join in the gracious enquiries? Every condescending attention towards the old servants of Her Majesty seems to me an added tribute of filial devotion to her venerated Memory &, as such, makes my satisfaction in it almost sacred. I

Thus, therefore, encouraged, I shall venture to my subject without further preface:

When, in 1802, I joined, with my little Son, my honoured & most honourable Husband in Paris, he presented me to a Circle of his chosen Friends whom he had prepared to receive me with kindness. Amongst them, I was most struck & charmed with Mad^e de Poix, whose Husband, the Prince, I had known in England, where, with his elegant son, now Duke de Mouchy,³ he had emigrated; the sweet Ma^{de} de Beauvau,³ also, & the charming Victorine,⁴ afterwards Duc^{ess} de Crussols, to whom I had messages from the P^{ss} Eliza, & Letters I from Mrs. Ly. Harcourt, were of this sett;⁴—all which, in its various branches, gratified General d'Arblay by receiving me immediately as one of their Party: but many as there were amongst them to love & admire, it was one who appeared in the circle the seldomest that won my best affections—won them from a similarity of taste for retirement, & a sameness of position in having each an only Child,⁵ a narrow income, a necessity for

---

³ Anne-Louise-Marie de Beauvau (1750-1834), who had married in 1767 Philippe-Louis-Marc-Antoine de Noailles (1752-1819), prince de Poix, and their son *Charles*-Arthur-Tristan-Jean-Languedoc de Noailles (1771-1834), *styled* duc de Mouchy, were among the persons the d'Arblays knew in Paris (see v, L. 513 n. 16; L. 526 n. 2).

⁴ In April 1802 FBA had been entrusted with messages from Princess Elizabeth and a letter from Lady Harcourt (*c.* 1750-1833) to members of the French Harcourt family, namely, Nathalie-Henriette-Victurnienne de Rochechouart de Mortemart (1774-1854), who in 1792 had married Marc-Étienne-Gabriel de Beauvau (1773-1849), prince de Beauvau-Craon (1793); and her sister Catherine-Victurnienne-*Victorine* (1776-1809), who had married in 1807 Adrien-François-Emmanuel de Crussol d'Uzès (1778-1837), duc de Crussol (1830). For these meetings, see v, L. 513 n. 1 and *passim*.

⁵ Marie-Françoise-Elizabeth *née* de Fay de Latour-Maubourg (1770-1850), who had married in 1791 and divorced in 1800 Gérard-Joseph-Bidault de Maisonneuve (*fl.* 1770-1800), soldier and diplomat, the 'unworthy husband', about whom FBA was long curious (see her French Exercise Books, Berg). 'Maxime' de Maisonneuve (L. 1195 n. 6) was three years younger than Alexander d'Arblay, but they were playmates in Passy for about two years.

œconomy, & an inclination for social life that made all our meetings as chearfully happy, ⏐ as they were confidentially affectionate, &, far from a murmur, I never remember even a regret at the smallness of our fortunes, nor a wish for their increase, save for the future prosperity of our Sons.——But on Her side alone was all the virtue of this philosophy; I needed none! for while she was tied, by a French early marriage, to a man she could neither love nor esteem, I had the rare felicity to be united to a person whom every Day's setting sun shone upon the brightness by some new motive for love & for Honour —— ⏐

Not that then, even then I knew perfect contentment! the condition of humanity allows not of that! my forced absence from my dear Country, & all to which I was natively & tenderly attached was a constant worm that eat, even then, into my peace of mind. This lady, Made de Maisonneuve, however, whom M. d'A had been acquainted with from her earliest Youth, & whose Brothers[6] were his particular friends, he presented me to as the person the most highly fitted for supplying to me all I valued & all I missed— ⏐ He knew— & judged me well! I found in her a perpetual consolation for all I had quitted. Her excellencies are not of a brilliant or glaring species, but they are those of sentiments the most refined, of a zealous ardour to do good, of unaffected piety, & of the purest conduct. To all this, she then joined great & Raphaël like Beauty: but I speak of 17 years ago.——Her understanding is very good, & her manners, when she wishes to please, infinitely engaging; but with English virtue, & English modesty, she joins English Reserve, & English coldness; so that she captivates only when she herself feels partial propensities.

From the hour of our first meeting, each prepossessed in favour of the other by M. d'Arblay, we conceived a desire of ⏐ intimacy that grew so fast upon our feelings, that soon not a day passed without some intercourse, or much regret. A stranger in the land, & naturally shy even to mauvaise honte,

---

[6] Marie-Charles-*César*-Florimond de Fay de Latour-Maubourg (v, vi *passim*) and his brothers Jules-*Charles*-César de Fay (1775–1846), who had married in 1798 Lafayette's daughter Anastasie (1777–1863), and General Victor (L. 1195 n. 4), the brave and active soldier, much respected during the Empire and Restoration alike.

I owed to her obligations incessant, & innumerable, for counsel, assistance, hints, & kind offices. Her son, Maxime, was the constant Play fellow, as well as school fellow, of my Alexander; & her favourite Brother, whom she loves with a twin-like love, was next to M. de Narbonne,[7] the Friend in all France whom M. d'Arblay prized the most ardently; these ꟾ circumstances made our connexion a general pleasure to all parties,—&, during my whole long residence in France, she was a continual resource, comfort, & delight to me.

During this time, ruined by the Revolution, she lived in two small closets, rather than rooms, up a winding, narrow, dangerous stair Case, 2 or 3 stories high, ꟾ at Passy, where we also for some years dwelt. Her Pittance, for herself & her son, was so small, it would not be believed in this Country, if told; but her character was so much esteemed, & her conversation was so pleasing, that, whenever she suffered herself to be drawn forth, she was always signalized by universal admiration & respect. ꟾ

Even since the Restoration, though her affairs, in common with those of her Family, have been somewhat ameliorated, & though she is removed to Paris, her life has been nearly as retired, though not quite so obscure or parsimonious; but her habitation was still up 2 pr. of stairs, in 2 small rooms, though not closets, where she never received any evening society, or scarcely even a Friend in the morning, passing the whole of her days at one of her Brothers.

Thus, in my last visit to Paris, in Nov. 1815—I left her with flowing Eyes & ꟾ a sorrowing heart;[8] though General d A always purposed an excursion to France every year & he made one in 1816. & another in 1817—but my son's necessary studies at home, with his delicate health, kept me stationary in England:—in 1718. a long & awful Voyage was made to stop all others—but of a similar sort!—

In the midst of my grief—I regretted my now final separation ꟾ from this beloved friend, whose sympathy would have been more soothing than any other, as she better knew what I had lost—& participated, even for herself, in my affliction

---

[7] For d'Arblay's friendship with Louis, comte de Narbonne, see ii, iii, v, vi, vii *passim*.

[8] See L. 1195 n. 7.

—but I now wept over even her remembrance, though she was living, from losing all hope, all prospect of ever seeing her more—she joined in bewailing the same privation—but inscrutable Providence teems with wonders such as the mind of Man, in its most fanciful, nay ǀ romantic Imagination never could invent. Fiction would scarcely dare to frame the one only event which could re-unite us — — Yet is it preparing to take place!—This tender Friend—whom I left 6 years ago a modest & willing Recluse—is now coming over to England in all the splendour of a French ambassade!—Her favourite Brother—the favourite Friend of General d'Arblay —is nominated Ambassadour to the Court of Great Britain, & she will accompany hither her belle soeur!—

For 2 or 3 days after this news reached me I thought it a dream—a dream, however, from which I now hope I shall be spared awaking — — Yet is all my satisfaction sullied by acutest regrets—that it comes too late to be shared by Him to whom it would have given bliss unutterable!

What rendered this event the ǀ more unexpected, is that the Marquis is a younger Brother &, though his Birth, like that of all the La Tours, is noble, & his Great Uncle[9] was a Marechal de France he has no fortune but from his appointments, & he has never been in the diplomatic line. He has, however, a clear & good understanding, a manly mind; a firm love of his ǀ Country, manners, when his reserve wears away, singularly pleasing, & the highest, the most exalted sense of Honour. Nothing can more strongly prove the sincerity of the King of France's desire of a good intelligence with this Kingdom, than such a choice, for the Marquis is utterly incapable of duplicity or intrigue of any description. He has commonly been called *un vrai chevalier français*; — — alas, his departed Friend, where best known, had the same appellation—!

What an enormous Letter! But the gracious words & feeling Message delivered by L^y Keith give me a real belief that yr R.H. will hear with generous pleasure that a solace so unexpected should by means ǀ so unlooked for, be brought to bear & under the influence of this belief I will not lengthen

[9] Probably Jean-Hector de Fay de Latour-Maubourg (*c.* 1674–1764).

my Letter by apologies, but simply entreat permission to sign myself

Madam

yr R.H.

&c &c

F d Arblay,

1197   11 Bolton Street,
5 March 1819

To Alexander d'Arblay

A.L. (rejected Diary MSS. 7192-[5], Berg), 5 Mar. 1819.
Originally double sheet 4to (8.9 × 7.2")   black edged, mutilated and pasted as described in Textual Notes   *pmk*   5 MR .819   black seal
     Addressed: Revd Alexander d'Arblay, / Christ College, / Cambridge.
Edited by CFBt. *See* Textual Notes.

March 5. 1819.

Bolton Street

London

Oh my dear Alex what an Event!—what an inconceivable—yet blessed Event!—It is *Victor* who is our new Ambassadour! & Madame de Maisonneuve—my dear tender—sympathizing darling Madame de Maisonneuve will accompany him! — — — Never never can I be grateful enough to pitying Providence as for this unlooked for Unhoped for Consolation!—For several days it almost *disorganized* me, bodily & mentally, — — more nervous I grew, more spasmodic than ever—torn with unspeakable anguish that it had not happenned sooner! yet melted with gratitude that it happenned at all! but so marvellous it seemed—in every way,—that a sensation of *Incredulity* made me fear I could not be awake—& my poor head felt as nearly deranged as my heart—my poor heart felt afflicted.—But I now see it as no illusion—I have had Letters the most satisfactory,—& the violence of my sensations begins to subside—& to give place to the ┃most devout thankfulness that the exact solace is thus wonderfully accorded me for which my soul was hopelessly pining! 'tis the precise blessing your blessed Father would have wished for me! would have directed!—Oh Guardian Spirit! if such you are, how will this alleviating balm gratify your exquisite tenderness!—

Even yet—I know not how to be calm—the tumult of my mind is indescribable!—how I shall support the Meeting[1] I know not, greatly as I covet it!—I tremble—I shrink—every moment I think of its taking place!—

In this agitated state, that unfits me for all things but my own preparatory efforts to repress the excess of my grief—my anguish to meet his best friends when he cannot share their society—Mrs. Marsh,[2] the amiable Mrs. Marsh makes new & stronger advances for beginning an acquaintance for which I am now so utterly unfit.—She has sent a proposal—most pressingly—to come to me at once, with our mutual Friend Mrs. Frodsham. I am fearful to repress a kind predilection that may be useful to my Alex—but I know not how to conquer my averseness to a new ¦ acquaintance — — —

But why do you thus delay to answer M. Le Noir?[3] or even to tell me your thoughts & wishes on his subject? Reflect that it is our business, not his; yet that it is his trouble, & not our's. And then think of our obligation to his present intentions, & of the necessity of explaining that we know his avocations too well to *desire*—or even *consent* that he should do more than *superintend*. His time is fully occupied, & his gentle & feeling soul is dejected, almost disabled, by his misfortunes.

This is my 3ᵈ Letter unanswered!

I am always apprehensive at such silence!

I have millions of things I should commune with you about had your '*process*' continued.

However, I would not keep from you this amazing news—Help me—I call upon you! to be thankful! for I know not how to pour forth with sufficient devotion my own thanks to Providence for this wonderful Event! The only one in the

1197. [1] See Diary, 20 Apr. for the first of a series of meetings.

[2] For Anne Frodsham and the wife of the Bishop of Peterborough, see L. 1192 nn. 2, 3.

[3] See L. 1189 n. 5, and for a list of effects the d'Arblays left in Paris, FBA's Account Books, Berg.

Chapter of *possibilities* by which I could ever, in this World, have obtained again the sight of my beloved Mad^e de Maisoneuve—

What is the *Manie* of the present moment? Early Rising?— Chess?—Analytics?—the philosophies?—Priest's orders?— Politics? or Poetry?—*Hey*?—

France has kept me, [*part of line cut away*]

I I98   [I I Bolton Street],
                                           6 March 1819

To H.R.H. Princess Mary
Duchess of Gloucester

A.L.S. draft (Berg), 6 Mar. 1819
Six pages (6 × 3.7″), written in CB's Memorandum Book (see described in the letter to the same, *c.* 27 Feb. 1819, L. 1195). The draft is written in the spaces ruled for 4–31 July, in which spaces CB had made entries for the dates 11–14, 16, 18–20, 23, 26, 28–9 with accounts for the week of 11 July.

Duchess of Gloucester

Madam,

One line I cannot resist of most grateful thanks for a Letter[1] breathing such condescending solace in the prospect of future intercourse—joined to such humane anticipation & allowance for the agitating Conflict between pleasure & anguish that will inevitably disturb the first meeting after events so irremediably calamitous—Well & most gratefully I remember the commiserating concern with which yr. R.H. saw me after my loss of my darling Sister Phillips[2]—Well

1198. [1] The letter doubtless of 2 Mar. (see L. 1196B n. 1), in which the Princess, writing from Bagshot Park, gave notice of her imminent arrival at Gloucester House and her willingness to 'appoint a day to see You'.

[2] For FBA's audiences with the Princesses on Wednesday 5 Feb. 1800 after the tragic death on 6 Jan. of Mrs. Phillips at Parkgate, see iv. 393–4: 'each of the

I remember ˡ too, the tender pity with which H.R.H. the Pˢˢ
Augusta deigned to embrace me—& the Pˢˢ Eliza—& Sophia
—& the Pˢˢ Amelia — — Ah!—What indeed have I to
remember that is not sweetness & condescendsion & generous
confidence in each excellent daughter of that best of Mothers
& of Fathers?

I have just read a Letter from Mᵐᵉ de Maisonneuve to tell
me she has had the honour of being presented to H.R.H. the
Duke of Gloucester, who has most agreeably brightened the
spirits of all the *ambassade* by making a visit *la plus aimable*
et meme cordialle to la Marquise Victor de La Tour ˡ Maubourg to console her disappointment in having been unable
to be presented to H.R.H. elsewhere, from a long continued
indisposition.[3] His R.H. has quite charmed by all this courtesy—And they are people of such uncommon worth &
unaffected goodness that they peculiarly merited such a distinction. Madᵉ de La Tour Maubourg is a most estimable
woman. She is by Birth *une Hollandaise,*[4] & perfectly gentle
& feminine, though her height is at least that of his R.H. the
Duke of Kent.[5] I hope ˡ yr R.H. will be prepared to see in the
Marquis *Victor* (for he is a younger Brother) de la Tour Maubourg, a maimed as well as a most valiant warriour. He had
a Leg—& almost a thigh, amputated in one field of Battle,
& his Jawbone broken in another—besides sundry wounds
no longer observable. But I ought, I think, to mention that
though he fought under the banners of Buonaparte, it was
not for Him, but—according to his own notions ˡ of patriotism, & to peculiar circumstances, it was for his Country,
which he loves passionately—though by no means indiscrimi-
nately that he fought: The King of France, & even Mᵐᵉ

Princesses saw me with a sort of concern & interest I can never forget. . . . my
own Princess Augusta . . . spoke to me in a tone—a voice so commiserating—
I could not stand it—I was forced to stop short in my approach, & hide my face
with my Muff—she came up to me immediately—put her arm upon my shoulder, & kissed me—I shall never forget it — — '

[3] This is Mme de Maisonneuve's letter (Berg) of 22 Feb. 1819 ('son A.R. a
bien voulu l'en dédommager en lui [Mme Victor] faisant la plus aimable et cor-
diale visite').

[4] See L. 1195 n. 4.

[5] The proportions of the Duke of Kent emerge somewhat ghoulishly in the
mention, *AR* lxii² (1820), 690, of the weight and unusual length (7′ 5½″) of his
coffin.

d'Angoulême,[6] are well acquainted with his history, & with the nobleness as well as bravery of his character, & at this very time his private audiences of leave from the whole of the Royal Family have been of the most flattering Nature. I am persuaded this excellent family will both please & be pleased in this dear ⏐ Country, from the native & most uncommon simplicity of their manners, joined to much unaffected elegance.

May I venture to entreat yr. R.H. permission to offer my most respectful—yet very warmest acknowledgements to their R.H. the P^{sses} Augusta & Sophia

I have the Honour to sign myself,

Madam. yr. R.H.
ever—&c &c
F d A^y

Sent 6 Mars. 1819

1199   11 Bolton Street,
[–19 February]–8 March 1819

To Mrs. Broome

A.L.S. (Berg), 8 Mar. 1819
Double sheet 4to   black edged   4 pp.   pmk   10 MR .819   black seal
Addressed: Mrs. Broome / German Street / Brighton / Sussex
Endorsed by CBFB: Sister d'arblay / March 8th 1819 / ans^d—april 11th—

My Charlotte—my dearest kindest Charlotte is the last to misconstrue, or take ill, my silence—yet her's—however naturally its consequence, appears to me — — I will not say a reproach,—She can do nothing that can wear that aspect to one she loves so partially,—but still, I cannot accustom

---

[6] Louis XVIII and his sister Marie-Thérèse-Charlotte de France (1778–1851), who had married on 10 June 1799 Louis-Antoine d'Artois, duc d'Angoulême (1775–1844). For their residence in England and return to France, see vii, viii passim.

myself to not seeing her dear hand, even when I seem least
to deserve it—Alas—to take up my pen is a weight upon my
spirits that necessity alone can make me support—but —
— —

I was interrupted in this—begun I know not now when—
but a Letter is come in the interval[1] that shews me my Charlotte's indulgent kindness is ever the same. I will not let the
pen go out of my hand again till the paper is ready to go also.
And indeed when once I have begun writing where my affections are ever so alive, it is rather a relief, a solace to me to go
on, than to stop—but I always dread & defer the beginning,
from the fear of infecting with my depression Her whom I
would do every thing in my power to chear. Our separation
at this period is indeed unfortunate, for I am sure I should
more revive with *you* than with any one—excepting always
my Alex—because we should mutually draw forth our
mutual sorrows, which sink but the deeper for suppression, &
the *natural* state which that would occasion, would soon lead
each of us to do the best we could to revive, for the sake of
the other. As Alex spends this whole term at Cambridge,
I should surely have been allured by you to Brighton were
I not peculiarly circumstanced; I could not there remain in-
visible, without shutting myself up from all air & exercise; for
though I should not be *thought of* at ˡ the Pavillon itself, so
many acquaintances & even Friends, visit it continually, that
I could not without incurring displeasure be at *Brighton*, that
is away from *Home*, & hide myself from all kind Enquirers.
But certainly I will conquer this antipathy to all intercourse
as soon as Alex is living with Me *here*; I have sacredly promised
that!—& then, once subdued at home, I shall be fitter for
being abroad. And then we will meet. And *Here* as soon as
your Health is better established, I shall build on your long
engagement to take Alex's room when he deserts it again for
any length of time. But I would not tempt you through kindness to quit the air that is so salubrious to you for the World.

1199. [1] This letter, now missing, had arrived on 19 Feb. (Diary). Scarcely yet
recovered from the long nursing of her consumptive son 'Dolph', who had died in
Bath on 27 Apr. 1817, Mrs. Broome was to remain in Brighton until August. It
was the attempt, mistakenly religious, to *suppress* grief, she afterwards said, that
delayed her recovery; and what she found invigorating at Brighton was to sit at
the waterside as the tide was rising and, as it was called, 'take the breeze'.

Our dear Charlotte gave me 3 views of her sweet countenance while she was in James Street.[2] I am thankful to tell you I was not struck with the altered looks you bemoan. I hope the fear is the exaggeration of your affection. I think her mind is too much *occupied* by her irresolution as to publishing her Journal.[3] I wish a *decision* to take place as speedily as possible. I can give no advice, for I have not my attention, or my faculties, sufficiently disengaged to dare read her composition with any view of counsel, except in *details*; & that I have sincerely offered: but for fixing her determination I am by no means, now! qualified. I can read nothing regularly; my own thoughts cleave to me so closely, that I know not, beyond a paragraph or two, what subject is presented to me. It must be difficult to find any thing new to say, at present, of an excursion on the continent. Charlotte has powers so pleasing, so natural, so intelligent, that she may have found combinations that may *youthify* old materials: but *new* matter I think scarcely attainable. Had she stayed longer, & mingled with the Inhabitants, & learnt customs & habits & foreign ways of life, she might have had a very good chance of making a Book more agreeable than nearly *any* that has preceded her: but the time was so short it could scarcely allow of authenticating even cursory or obvious remarks. All this, however, is only ¦ between ourselves. She told me her work was with you, & that she should be chiefly guided by your judgment. Sweet & dear Creature that she is, I wish her every success from the bottom of my heart if she makes the

---

[2] On a visit to her uncle JB, CFBt had called on FBA on 13, 14, 15, and 16 Feb. (Diary). On the 15th she had been accompanied by her daughter Julia, a budding beauty, aged 10.

[3] In the course of her continental tour of 13 July–12 Oct. 1818 (see L. 1180 n. 13), CFBt had written a series of travel letters to Arthur Young (see *Catalogue*) and has also, at his suggestion, taken notes on farm prices and the like, memoranda to be embodied in a Journal, which, transcribed early in 1819, had been sent to him and returned by 5 Feb., with approval and the offer to recommend it to Longman. At the moment, a part of the Journal was with Mrs. Broome at Brighton, the other part, with a cousin Fanny Raper. On 2 April it was in the hands of Martin Burney, who 'is very judicious in the verbal corrections', improving 'the style of what he looks over . . . —but he has business of more consequence which makes him slow' so that he could not be got 'to return it'. By 22 April, however, Martin stood ready, should the manuscript be rejected at Longman's, to send it to Murray's. Apparently it was rejected, and probably on the grounds that FBA suggested might obtain.

attempt. And indeed, my dearest Charlotte, I am rejoiced to tell you that *nobody* partakes your apprehensions as to her valuable——her *in*valuable health.

I am truly glad you have got your favourite Julia[2] with you. She is universally beloved, & seems to merit that high distinction by her modesty & good qualities, united with so much beauty. How happy she will be with you! She was delighted at going. You will know I am in a far more *natural* state than I have been——for these last dreadful months—— when you hear that I desired to see the sweet Girl——though the terrour I had of affecting such innocent little creatures had——till then, made me strictly decline meeting any children. 'Tis the same with musick: I have shunned it because the sound——the *concord of sweet sounds,*[4] overpowers me ——the organ at Church dissolves me!——Oh my dear Charlotte! What havock in all my existence has that dread dread blow occasioned!

But what is it you mean by the word surgeon? & knife?—— it is figuratively, I hope, *metaphorically* that you speak? Tell me, however. Clement, I am told, & that by our James, is much improved, in *manner* & *discourse*, by his excursion.[5] I am sorry I missed seeing him: but I risk no state of surprise I can avoid; & he did not let me know when he should call. When he can do that, I will receive him with great readiness. I have had a visit from Marianne,[5]——which, being arranged, went off serenely enough. I thought *her*, too, in manner & deportment, much improved; formed & fashioned with an air of being used to good company that becomes her much.

Alex says that, at the Archdeacon's Ball,[6] nobody was half as elegant as Charlotte. He is partial to Charlotte in the highest degree;——if to love & admire *her*, can be *partial*. I wish I could I see more of *Her*,——there is a soothing expression in her looks & voice that robs me of my distaste to society.

———

[4] *Merchant of Venice*, V. i.

[5] Clement Francis (L. 1188 n. 2) had included Italy, Greece, and Constantinople in his tour of 1818. He had called at 11 Bolton Street on 7 Jan.; his sister Marianne, on 27 Feb. (Diary).

[6] On 12 Jan. (Diary) AA had gone to a dance given at Twickenham Meadows by Archdeacon Cambridge (L. 1190 n. 2), returning on the 13th.

I know nothing yet of the Mathias business,[7] save that the *last quarter*, of January, has been sent me, unapplied for, by the poor Queen's Executor, Lord Arden & Genl Taylor.[7] Whether it be a leave taking, or a continuation, is not specified. I hope not the *former*; for it will be most unjust to stop the pensions accorded for *past* services by the judgement & award of the Queen & King: & I think the Parliament cannot have such an idea. Yet Lady Keith fears the opposition will succeed in cutting all such short!—!—I still hope not. But I live penuriously till I know what I have to trust to—& *This* year! this fatal year!—there *are*—& will be—such mournful expences that my utmost œconomy will difficultly save me from selling out, even though I should not *lose* a hundred a year.—But I have received one payment from France that has greatly helped me,[8] & I am in expectation of another— & another.—£ 14 of yours, my dear love, are still at Messrs Hoare; for Hetty & I agreed you ought not to have any thing to do with our dear Father's Monument.[9]

I saw Miss Cooke[10] this morning: poor Mr. & Mrs. Cooke are not yet well enough to come to me—& I — — go *nowhere*, except to Brother James. I walk out in the Green Park, or Berkeley Square, almost Daily, & take all the care in my power to keep off chronic disease or obstructions—I have much to tell you in my next of my hope to see a dearly loved Friend of my Beloved's from France. Adieu, my own Charlotte.

Yours with tenderest affection.

F. d A.

[7] In former times it was to one of CBFB's early friends Thomas James Mathias (*c.* 1754-1835), Queen's Treasurer (iii *passim*) that application had to be made for FBA's pension of £100 per annum. Mrs. Broome had doubtless inquired if the pension was to be continued after the Queen's death.

Charles George Perceval (1756-1840), a Lord of the Admiralty (1783-1800), Baron Arden (1802), was the Queen's Executor; Sir Herbert Taylor (1775-1839), diplomat, warrior, biographer of the Duke of York (see *DNB*), her private secretary (1811-18).

[8] On Friday 15 Jan. 1819 FBA recorded receipt (Diary) of a draft for £84 on Messrs Coutts 'from La Guerre!' And showing duly in Hoares' Ledgers was a 'Bill on Coutts & Co. £84.14.11'.

[9] The cost of Dr. Burney's Monument in Westminster Abbey was assumed by his residuary legatees (FBA and EBB) with the assistance of CB Jr. (see ix *passim* and ix, L. 1057 n. 3).

[10] Mary (b. 14 Mar. 1781), the daughter of the Revd. Samuel Cooke (L. 1182 n. 6), Vicar of Great Bookham, and his wife Cassandra *née* Leigh, had called on 9 Mar. (Diary).

Finished 8: March, 1819.
Bolton Street. N⁰ 11.
Berkeley Square

ˡ poor Mr. Burney is very suffering![11]—I fear! I fear!—
Our Esther is pretty well—& all else ditto. James is quite
blyth. Full of his new work, & of Hope renown & success.[12]
—amen!

1200 [11 Bolton Street],
12 March 1819

To Esther (Burney) Burney

A.L.S. (rejected Diary MSS. [7098–101], p. 3 being numbered 7100,
Berg), 12 Mar. 1819
Double sheet 4to   black edged   4 pp.   *pmk*   1⟨3⟩M⟨   ⟩1819
black seal
Addressed: Mrs. Burney. / Lark Hall Place, / near / Bath.
Endorsed by EBB: April 22ᵈ answered
Docketed by FBA, p. 4 [7101]: Character & conduct / of / Marie /
de / Maisonneuve— / to be kept as a Memorial / of her Excellence—&
Friendship
Docketed p. 1 (7098): ⌐1813⌐   1819
Docketed in old brown ink, p. 4 [7101]: 1819
Edited by CFBt. *See* Textual Notes.

12. March—1819.

My dearest Esther,
Now then—at last—& most wonderfully—I am enabled
to write something that, for *my* sake, will give pleasure to your
long afflicted kindness for me. An event has happened that
by means the most unlooked for—unhoped for—*unthought*

[11] For the illness of Charles Rousseau Burney, see L. 1209 n. 5 and L. 1217
nn. 2, 3.
[12] JB's *History of North-Eastern Voyages of Discovery* (L. 1191 n. 6) was to
appear in June 1819.

of, will bring me to the sight—I had believed lost forever—of the person to whom He whom I never cease to deplore presented me, in his own Country, as the one whom he thought, & wished, I should like above all others,—as one whom he augured I should love like another Mrs. Lock,—Madame de Maisonneuve.[1]—Such a recommendation from Him—who loved & liked so many of his native Friends, & who wished me to love & like them all, operated upon me at the time so as to open all my heart to partial feelings: & She, whom he had known from her earliest youth, & whom he had endeavoured to prejudice equally in *my* favour, met me at once as a chosen favourite: an intercourse, therefore, of the most frank & friendly sort took place, & was soon followed by the tenderest & most unreserved affection on both sides. The obligations I owe to her are countless—Countless!—She was always in motion to serve, oblige, amuse, or console me, according as any embarrassment, distress, *ennui*, or misfortune assailed me. A more devoted friendship can hardly be imagined; & it was the more striking, & the more touching, from the general coldness & reserve of her character. The happy prepossession given her by the tenderest of Husbands had thawed these icy qualities in my favour before our first encounter—& they never froze again.—We suited each other, in this point, most singularly. She never would enter our dwelling unless she heard I was alone,—& she paid me, without any comment, 20 visits for one. When the health of Alex obliged us to quit Paris, *She* was our motive to fixing upon Passy, for there she resided. For very many years, the Day hardly ever passed in which, early or late, we did not meet: neither Rain, nor Darkness—Cold, nor Wind, nor Frost, nor dirt, nor sultry heat, could prove to her any obstacle:—& at the time of my terrible operation[2]—her sufferings & her services, exceed description—when the dreadful moment came, she had had private information of its arrival, unknown to me, but at her own desire, & secretly entered the house—not to my room—which I could not have supported; not to the next, where were medical assistants in waiting,

---

1200. [1] See L. 1192 n. 6; and L. 1196B.
  [2] A mastectomy (30 Sept. 1811). For Baron Larrey (1766–1842), the famous army-surgeon, and the other physicians and surgeons concerned, see vi, L. 595.

whom she was too agitated to encounter,—not to the Library, where she feared she might intrude upon Him whose feeling tenderness made him—perhaps—a greater object of pity than myself, but — — *in the Kitchen*! & there, dissolved in tears, she spent the whole time of my agony, & afterwards nearly the rest of the day, in case female assistance, beyond that of my Nurse & femme de chambre, should be wanted, or even *permitted*; for no one was allowed to enter my room for the first 10 Days but with the direct leave of Dr. Larrey.[2] And for many, many long & affrighted months preceding this catastrophe, & many languishing & suffering ones after it, she ¹ was my constant & soothing companion, whenever my first —best—Oh best of all! was compelled by his affairs to quit my side. This lady—this precious Friend, this *Gift* of my Beloved Departed,—who has done nothing but repine at our separation from the time of my deadly unhappiness, is Now coming over to England!—It seems like a miracle, so utterly was it unlikely! but her favourite Brother is just named to be our Ambassadour,[3] & she will accompany him hither. Oh my dear Hetty! with all the gratitude I feel to Heaven for this extraordinary event, its opening almost demolished me! *Regret* that it happenned not when it might have been shared by my Partner in All, joined to my astonishment, & to so new a sensation as that of joy,—*Joy*, that seemed a Guest almost *ungenial* rather than welcome, so disordered me in a thousand ways, that I could not believe I was completely awake, or consciou[s.] I had a frightful incredulity of every thing about [it] & I spent some days as ill bodily as mentally —for Oh how blest would such an arrival have made Him! he has wished them here a thousand times!—Alas!—

But let me to Your Letter, lest this subject monopolize all mine. And to begin with what is continually on my mind, the long & cruel malady of my dear Mr. Burney[4]—I am truly grieved, but cannot be surprised, you have so little expectation of a cure till finer weather; but what you tell me of the constancy of his resisting inactive despondence, & keeping

³ Victor de Latour-Maubourg (L. 1192 n. 6; L. 1195 n. 4).
⁴ Charles Rousseau Burney (i, p. lxix), amiable and talented musician, was to live on with increased suffering until 23 Sept. 1819. See further, L. 1217 nn. 2, 3; L. 1219 n. 1.

alive all resources, of Music, Drawing, & Reading, in every interval of pain, gives me every hope of his *weathering the storm*, & meeting the fair season with fair recovery. God Grant it! No one surely, by patience & fortitude, more merited such a triumph. But I am not without some apprehension for *you*, my beloved Esther, who required all your time for indefatigable exertions on your *own* account & who must now have a *division* of attention for which your health & strengh must difficultly suffice. I *conjure* you, however, to take at least your exercise whenever it is fine, as without that, you will soon ׀ want the tender care yourself you are bestowing upon your dear Invalid. I thank you heartily for your details of my sweet God Daughter.[5] Give her my kindest condolence when you write to her. I am not in the least amazed at Maria's half yearly proposition, as I know her & Cecilia's mutual fondness for each other, & that Sophy warmly partakes of it:[6] but a report has reached me here that Mr. & Mrs. Sandford have enlisted her,[7] as an Inmate, with themselves. Is it true? I only pity those who have her *not*, & chiefly *you*, who love her so justly & tenderly. Yet I think it wiser, with a heart so wounded, that she should be kept from all sick rooms at present.

As to my affairs, they continue unsettled & unknown to *me*, both at home & abroad. The Papers, however, lost by Chas Parr have at length been found,[8] & we are called upon for new—melancholy—certificates, previously to any steps being taken as to our rights. With regard to my title, as *We* had agreed *together* not to take it up in England, for the reasons I have detailed, certainly I shall never take it up *singly*! In simply adhering to *Madame* I forbear to *disclaim* it, or

[5] His second daughter Frances Burney (1776-1828), the governess (L. 1191 n. 4), had lately published *Tragic Dramas chiefly intended for Representation in Private Families, to which is added 'Aristodemus', a Tragedy from the Italian of Vincenzo Monti* (1818), a copy of which she had presented to FBA on 29 Apr. (Diary). For her learning and accomplishments, see *FB & the Burneys*, pp. 366–71.

[6] The widowed Maria Bourdois (L. 1180 n. 3), who had taken her sister Sophia Elizabeth Burney (i, p. lxix) to live with her in Bath.

[7] EBB's fourth surviving daughter Cecilia Charlotte Esther (1788–1821), who after the death in Worcester of her aunt Ann Hawkins (L. 1189 n. 11), would live with her aunt Rebecca, wife of the surgeon William Sandford (L. 1191 n. 1), first at Bridge Street and later at Rainbow Hill, Worcester. The fifth daughter Amelia Maria (1792-1868) remained with her parents.

[8] For the documents entrusted to Charles Parr Burney, see L. 1189 n. 5.

assert it; for Madame only announces the *Wife* of a French Gentleman, but leaves uncertain whether she has any rank or not, being equally given to a Duchess & to a Washwoman. As *Mrs.* I should be an *alias*, for in the Bank of France my name was entered by his generous self, in devolving to me the sum there, as la comts^se d'A.—& the same at his Banker's, M. Laffitte.[9] In my applications, therefore, at those 2 places, as well as at La Ministère de La Guerre, for *residu* pension, I sign by that name—which, in fact, must *be my real signature*; or le Comte which is put to all His, would seem to have me his mistress, or house-keeper. Since my dear Alex, however, is now fixed an English Reverend, I speak of the Honour conferred on my noble Partner unreservedly, which I now hold to be a duty to his memory, & a Justice to the King of France; but I announced at the same time that I *drop* the title from motives of œconomy & love of simplicity. *This* much I think may be as useful & honourable to my Alex as *more* might be hurtful: for it makes known how high his honoured *Father* stood in his own country.—I would not have him appear only a *Mother's* son! I have said all this in answer to your enquiry that you may be [quite *au*] *fait*; & for another ˡ most melancholy reason of which in some future Letter.—I am quite sorry for that poor charming Miss Wood:[10] I drank Tea with James, &c, last Week: all well. I have had my Alex for one Day only! rember me most kindly to my dear Mr. B. Our Charlotte goes on better, thank God—My love to Maria Sophy & Amelia.

adieu, my dearest Esther

Ever yrs ⟨most truly⟩ F d'A.

I walk out daily with my Diane—& nothing so quietizes my shattered nerves. ˡ

---

[9] The banker Jacques Laffitte (L. 1185 n. 3).

[10] Probably the Miss Wood, teacher of pianoforte and singing, whose address in 1819 was 4 Terrace Walks, Bath. On 9 Apr. 1817 she sang at Mrs. Ashe's annual benefit; and on 18 Apr. 1822, at her own benefit, for which tickets were to be procured at her residence 49 New King Street. Her farewell concert was announced by the *Bath Chronicle* (10 Mar. 1825) for the 15th. She may be identified, with some uncertainty, therefore, as the Frances Wood (*c.* 1775-1835) of 3 Catherine Place, whose burial at the age of 60 is recorded in the registers of the parish of Walcot. For this information the editors are indebted to Mr. Warren Derry of Bath.

I have no room left for much I wish to say to my kind Bath Friends—speak for me therefore, I beg, to those you meet—especially the Thomas's[11] & Mrs Beckford[12] & Miss Hayes[13] &c

1201   [11 Bolton Street],
22 March 1819

To Alexander d'Arblay

A.L. (Berg), 22 Mar. 1819
Double Sheet 4to   2 pp.   *pmk* 23 MR .819   black seal
Addressed: Revd Alex. d'Arblay, / Christ College, / Cambridge.
Docketed in unknown hand: *C.* 19

22^d March, 1819.

[*Sent blank, as a reproof, except for a sentence written on the right fold:*]

I regret not having sent this Answer to your promised Letter sooner.

1202   [11 Bolton Street],
24 March 1819

To H.R.H. Princess Mary, Duchess of Gloucester

A.L.S. draft (Berg), 24 Mar. 1819
One page (6 × 3.7″) written in CB's Memorandum Book for 1796. The draft is written on the page ruled for the dates 4–10 July 1796, on

[11] CB Jr.'s friend the Venerable Archdeacon Thomas (1760-1820), his wife Susanna Isabella *née* Harington (1762-1835), and their family (ix, L. 947 n. 10 and *passim*).
[12] See L. 1189 n. 20   [13] See L. 1189 n. 21.

which spaces CB had made entries for the dates 4–9 July, and shows few emendations.

24. Mars.   To the Du^ss of Gloucester. 1819

Madam,

At the earliest Hour since y^r R.H. deigns to give me—so feelingly—the Choice—at 12 o'clock on Saturday Morning I will summon my utmost fortitude for the high honour of waiting upon yr. R.H.[1] I look forward to it with a mixture of sensations utterly indescribable—but Gratitude is at their head—& that, I hope, will keep every thing else in order, so as to make even this first admission recompence the benevolent intentions of yr. R.H. in proving an immediate comfort to y^r R.H^ss most devotedly—

Respectfully eternally attached
ob^d h^ble ser^vt
F. d'A

1203   11 Bolton Street,
                          [26 March 1819]

To Alexander d'Arblay

A.L. (rejected Diary MSS. 7174–[5], Berg), [*misdated*] 27 Mar. 1819
Single sheet 4to   2 pp.   *pmk* .819   black seal
Addressed: Rev. Alex. d'Arblay, / Christ College, / Cambridge.
Edited by CFBt. *See* Textual Notes.

I do certainly think that of all persons existing He who has got the easiest Conscience is a young fellow of a College!

So you really think such a miserable scrawl as you bestowed *3 minutes* upon in return to my

1202. [1] In letters of 11 December 1818 and 2 March 1819 (Berg), dated Bagshot Park, the Duchess of Gloucester had expressed the wish that on her arrival at Gloucester House, Park Lane, FBA might pay her a visit. Finally in a note (Berg) of 24 March she set the date for Saturday the 27th at 12 o'clock. See also Diary 24 and 27 March and for an account of the visit, L. 1210.

Speaking Answer
to a promised Letter that was to tell me, with Brotherly confidence—
The state of your Debts—
your expectations for their discharge,
Mr. Eb[den]'s plans for excursion[1]—
How you recovered your Morning Hours,
How you work for
(what is impossible)
The prize—
How you do *not* work for (what is essential)
the Priest's orders[2]—
AND
What answer you wish to give
(having Carte blanche)
to Mr. Le Noir's intentions & agency[3]
relative to the melancholy *Vente* at Paris—
My *Speaking Answer* to All this promised communication
—*told* You—I had not one item
to answer! — —

1203. [1] See L. 1181 n. 3; and L. 1193 n. 2.
   [2] Alexander d'Arblay was to be ordained priest (along with 52 other candidates) on Easter Sunday 11 April at St. James's Church, Piccadilly, by the Bishop
of Chester (L. 1185 n. 2). Assisting him was FBA's former friend the Revd.
Gerrard Andrewes (v. 16, 201), Rector of Mickleham (1800–13), of St. James's
(1802–25), and Vicar of Great Bookham, Surrey (1820).
   FBA witnessed the ceremony from the Gallery and marked the event with a
prayer (Diary): 'I fervently pray to God that my Son may meet this his decided
Calling with a disposition & Conduct to Sanction its choice!—' That she described
the ceremony in a letter, now unavailable, to Amelia Angerstein, is shown by the
reply of the latter (Barrett, Eg. 3698, ff. 82–3b), dated Saturday 24 [April 1818]:
   'I myself carried my M^rs d'Arblay's dear letter to Elliott Vale, . . . & shared
with my precious, bright, serene, mother in her own little fragrant abode the
almost overcoming pleasure of thinking of the dear tender mother in St James's
Church last Sunday attending a Ceremony so interesting & so replete with every
bright & consoling hope & every feeling most gratifying to maternal pride as that
which makes her Alex a member of our Church—We lifted up our prayers
together for him as we saw in idea the excellent Dean laying his hands in blessing
upon his young head. . . .'
   [3] For a list of effects the d'Arblays had left in Paris, 'Pictures, Engravings,
Drawings', 'les Mineraux', furniture, and objets d'art, of which, apparently,
M. Lenoir (L. 1189 n. 5) was to arrange a sale, see FBA's Account Book for 1822
(Berg).

Nor yet one enquiry relative to myself—! to the Ambassadour!—Whether or not at last he comes—! Mad^e de Maisonneuve—! *Maxime*—! &c &c &c ǀ

Nevertheless

Oh Shabbiest of the shabby!—

  as I can perhaps give you necessary information, I
will not hold back my — — so little invited pen—

I copy therefore this Paragraph from a small Book, to dis-
perse the darkness before your Eyes of *when is Palm Sunday*:
'Palm Sunday is the next before Easter, so called in memory
of our Saviour's triumphal entry into Jerusalem, when the
multitude strewed Palm Branches in his way.'

Recollect

If you do not hear from Mr. Hodgson[4]—
you must write to him for a remembrancer—

as it is Your own business, not his, that will occasion the
Correspondence—and as it is *you*—as has been shrewdly remarked to you by the B^p[5]—who is to be ordained—not *him*!

These hints I would not withhold—To-morrow week
it seemeth to me—
being Palm Sunday,
i.e. the day week you receive This remembrancer.

Your uncle James says he is very glad you are to be ordained by Dr. Sparkes[6]—as he has heard—from some of his
worthies who know him, that he is a sharp examiner '& therefore', adds the partial uncle—'Alex may gain credit.' ǀ

I sent your Keys by the Coach—Ramsay[7] ran after you
quite to the office—& Mr. Green[8] then took them to the
Book Keeper—I hear your kind thanks—

Saturday, 27. March 1819
NB. I have mistaken the date, this is Friday.

---

[4] Christopher Hodgson (L. 1180 n. 9), secretary at this time to the Bishop of London.

[5] Possibly FBA's friend Dr. Fisher (L. 1180 nn. 3, 4), Bishop of Salisbury (1807), and an experienced tutor of young persons, including formerly the Duke of Kent and the Princess Charlotte of Wales (see *DNB*).

[6] Bowyer Edward Sparke (1759-1836), D.D. (1803), was translated from the Bishopric of Chester (1809) to that of Ely (1812) and was not therefore the Bishop of Chester who ordained AA (see n. 2).

[7] Elizabeth Ramsay (L. 1182 n. 3).   [8] Unidentified.

1204 [11 Bolton Street,
2 April 1819]

To Alexander d'Arblay

A.L. (Berg), n.d.
Double sheet 8vo   2 pp.   *pmk* 2 AP 1819   black wafer
Addressed: Revd Alexander d'Arblay, / Christ College, / Cambridge.

In the hope this will meet you before your grand council,
& help you to a share of becoming Courage of deportment, I
write these few lines to tell you That a Friend has acquainted
me that the good—good Dr. Kaye[1] has expressed himself
about you—
To an Enquirer — —
with great kindness. — —
& said That you only wanted to value your time for Yourself as your friends valued its worth for you:—which he had
no doubt a little experience would urge you to do.

My authorities, for my last *admonition*, & for this *encouragement* shall be given you on Monday—
When, Alex, *shall* I return your Apathy! ǀ
If you again defer arriving,
a Word —
that I may not await you —

1205 [11 Bolton Street],
19 April 1819

To Mrs. Barrett

A.L. (Berg), 19 Apr. 1819
Double sheet 8vo   black edged   3 pp.   *pmks* 20 AP 1819 20 AP
.819   black seal
Addressed: Mrs. Barrett, / Richmond, Surry—
Docketed by CBFB *in pencil*, p. 1: From / Fanny

1204. [1] See L. 1181 n. 2.

19 April 1819.

To-morrow, I hope & trust, my two dearest Charlottes will have the mutual blessing of being in each other's arms.[1]

When my dear sister can come to me, I entreat to have a previous line—I wish to be as composed as I can—but for that I must have the power of preparation—we shall *both* need all we can muster of fortitude for a satisfaction mixt with such poignant pain — —

I have had—besides—& have still in reserve extreme agitation from meetings that almost tear me to pieces from deep profound regret that mingles with tender pleasure in seeing again the dearest Native Friends of All I most prized,—& most deplore[2] — —

Perhaps it may be better my dear sister may wait till the beginning of next week, & I then come to me for 5 Days following [*tear*] The certainty of keeping her, may take off much from the tumultuous sensations of our meeting—& Alex—who is with me till next Monday, will then go to Cambridge for 5 or 6 days[3]—She could therefore have his Room & Bed, & we could be together—entirely & tranquilly.

I think this will be best for us both.

Arrange this if possible, my Charlottes—&, not to lose any time so precious, endeavour to arrange it for *Monday* the 26th

1205. [1] On 13 and 15 April respectively FBA had received letters (now missing) from CBFB and CBFt (see Diary) with the news presumably of Mrs. Broome's intended visits to her daughter at Richmond and to FBA at 11 Bolton Street. Mrs. Broome was not to leave Brighton, permanently, however, until late August, when she settled at Ormond Place, Richmond. See headnote L. 1216 and text.

[2] The arrival of the French ambassadorial party was announced in *The Times* (9 April): 'Dover, April 7.—His Excellency the Marquis De Latour Maubourg, French Ambassador, landed this afternoon from *L'Antigone* French packet, . . . under a salute from the Citadel and a guard of honour; The Marchioness and two other Ladies accompanied the Marquis.' They had rested that night at Paris Hotel in Dover, arriving in London on the evening of the 8th.

On Friday 9 April Madame de Maisonneuve, in a reply (Berg) to a letter from FBA delivered to her by the secretary of the French Embassy on her arrival, wrote with kind messages from such French acquaintances as the Beauvau families, and on Saturday 10 April she arrived for a two-hour visit to FBA ('How marvellous —How soothing!—How Heartbreaking!—'). On the 12th and the 19th she called again; the marquise de Latour-Maubourg came on the 19th and the Ambassador himself on the 20th (Diary).

[3] Alexander, in London since Easter Sunday 11 April, when he had been ordained priest, was to leave for Cambridge on the 25th (Diary), probably for the audit (see L. 1185 n. 4).

God bless you both—
My Love to Marianne,[4] & remember me kindly to Mr. Barrett[5] ⏐

Pray thank the kind Mrs. Cambridge[6]—
    I shall always receive my ⟨dear⟩ Miss Baker[7] with open
arms.

1206   [11 Bolton Street],
                                            26 April 1819

To Madame de Somméry[1]

A.L. draft (Barrett, Eg. 3698, f. 248), 26 Apr. 1819
Written on p. 3 of an A.L.S., double sheet 4to, from C[écile] de
Somméry to FBA, 24 [Apr. 1819]   3 pp.   *pmks* 24 ⟨ ⟩ 181⟨9⟩
25 AP 1819   black seal   *addressed*: Madame d Arblay / Nº 11 Bolton
Street / Piccadilly / London   1 p.
    Edited by FBA, p. 1, *dated and annotated*: April—1819. on the
anniversary Mass to be performed on the fatal 3ᵈ May!—with the reply
—
    Docketed, p. 4: H

Answer

Dear Madam,
    It is a solemn gratification to me that through your hands,
& pious offices, this sacred duty may be fulfilled I am very
sure that could He for whom it is to be performed have indicated the measure, it is Madame la Marquise de Somerey[1]

    [4] CFBt's sister Marianne Francis (i, p. lxxiii).
    [5] CFBt's husband Henry Barrett (1756-1843).
    [6] Cornelia *née* Kuyck van Mierop (*c.* 1769-1858), wife of the Revd. George
Owen Cambridge (L. 1190 n. 2) of Twickenham Meadows.
    [7] Sarah Baker (*c.* 1744-1835) of Richmond, one of FBA's devoted friends
(iii, iv, v *passim*), would pay her a visit on 5 May (Diary) and eventually remember
her in her will (PRO/PROB/11/1842/67, pr. 19 February 1833).

1206. [1] For advice and help with respect to a memorial service for General
d'Arblay, FBA had evidently written to his Roman Catholic friend at Bath
Cécile-Agathe-Adélaïde *née* de Riquet de Caraman (1768-1847), marquise de
Somméry (ix, L. 967 n. 11 and x *passim*), aunt of Georges, comte de Caraman
(L. 1189 n. 7), at this time Secretary to the French Embassy in London.
    In a reply (Eg. 3698, ff. 247-8b) of 24 April 1819, the marquise, after a few

that He would have named for my Directress. I entreat that not less than £5. may be dedicated to this service; & since you are so kind as to undertake the superintendence, I shall venture to forward that sum to your Name, through Sir Benjamen Hobhouse,[2] in Bath, immediately—whence I hope you will have the goodness to send for it, & to appropriate it in such manner as to your own benevolence & piety seems most fitting — — certain of the perfect concurrence & true thankfulness of her who has the Honour to sign herself, Dear Madam,

Your much obliged
& &c

Monday 26. April
1819.

1207 [11 Bolton Street],
29 April 1819

To Esther (Burney) Burney

A.L. (Berg), 29 Apr. 1819
Double sheet 4to   black edged   2 pp.   *pmk* Old Bond / ⟨ ⟩
29 A⟨P⟩ 1819   black seal
Addressed: Mrs. Burney— / Lark Hall place— / near / Bath.
Refolded, secured with a red wafer, and readdressed (p. 3), *probably by* EBB: *Mrs. Bourdois*
Docketed in old brownish ink: 1819

reflections on the comforts and 'Conseils de notre sainte religion' and the hope of 'bonheur Eternel dans le céleste sejour', explained 'l'usage . . . parmi nous . . . au jour anniversaire de la mort de nos parents ou amis [qui] est de les faire recommander par le pretre de notre chapelle aux prieres de la Congrégation lors qu'elle est assemblée et d'annoncer ⟨que tel⟩ jour le S^t sacrifice de la masse sera offert pour le repos de leur âme'. Usual in such a case was a contribution of '10^{sh} ou 1£ comme vous le jugeras à propos'.

Knowing the consolation it would bring, she had sent FBA's letter to the priest the Revd. François Elloi (x, L. 1170 n. 85). 'Il est toujours bien infirme mai il n'a rien perdu du coté du zele et de la bonté du Coeur.'

For further remarks on the Memorial Mass, see Ll. 1209–10; and Diary, 26, 27 April and 3 May (the day of the Mass).

[2] The banker (L. 1186 n. 2).

My dearest Esther——
                 If you are well enough——
willing I am sure you will be —— —— I beg you to attend a
little Congregation that will be collected, by my desire, by
Madame de Somerey,[1] to pay a last public tribute to a
memory I so deplore—on *Monday*—the fatal anniversary of
my lost Earthly happiness —— —— but of His eternal bliss I
humbly hope & believe!——
    Maria   Sophy & Amelia will surely join.—That you are not
Roman Catholics need not interfere,—your prayers may be
fashioned by your own tenets & feelings,—but go, my dear
Hetty!—let me know that all of my family that could attend,
did—in this last outward testimony to their respect & affection. *All* Religions must unite in wishing to do Honour to
worth, Virtue, Goodness, exalted—sweet & Exemplary like
his!——
    I thank you for your kind Letter—which I cannot at this
moment answer—I have been considerably recovered—in
all ways—but this returning period brings with it—Hour by
Hour—such ˡ piercing recollections that I even *rejoice*, at
this moment, my Alexander is again at Cambridge.
    Madame de Somerey has accepted my melancholy commis-
sion with the most ⟨amiable⟩ eagerness, rather than assent. I
owe her much obligation. Pray let Maria or Sophy tell her so.
I have had—this very instant—an answer from Mr. Hay[2]—
& one that has extremely touched me. I believe indeed he
sincerely loved nay revered his blessed Patient.—Blessed!—
What tears that word when it's meaning suddenly impresses
me—dries up! —— ——
    I hope my ever valued Mr. Burney revives with the reviving
year? I feel anxious for sweet Cecilia[3]——
    God bless you, my dearest Hetty, ever!——

29ᵗʰ April—1819—

1207. [1] See L. 1206 n. 1.
    [2] For this letter (Berg), dated 27 April 1819, see L. 1189 n. 18.
    [3] Cf. L. 1200 nn. 4, 7.

1208 [11 Bolton Street,
c. 29 April 1819]

To George Edmund Hay

A.L.S. draft (Barrett, Eg. 3701A, f. 38b), n.d.
Written on *verso* of the first leaf of a double sheet 4to of an A.L.S., George Edmund Hay to AA, 27 Apr. 1819   *addressed*: A. D'Arblay Esqre / N° 11—Bolton Street / Berkely Square   wafer   p. 1, *annotated by* FBA: Last Bill of the Last Attendance! of Mr. Hay!—with the Answer.

Answer,

Dear Sir,

Your Letter[1] has extremely touched me, but the tears it has cost me were soothing, not bitter. I never doubted your attachment, & General d'Arblay was always warmly convinced of it:—it is therefore I will now beg of you to spare an hour next Monday morning—the anniversary of the fatal 3^d of May!—to join the little Congregation that will be collected at the Catholic Chapel to shew a last public mark of respect to his honoured—sacred Memory.—You are not a Roman Catholic; nor am I, who make the request: but no Religion can be offended by a personal testimony of reverence to a Character so eminently good, honourable, exemplary.

If Mr. Tudor,[2] also, could be so kind as to attend, it would be a great gratification to me.

My Son is at Cambridge; but we had agreed, as I know your hand, that I should open your answer, & reply in both our Names.

You must not contest our doing something more than doubling the most moderate account I ever saw. By tomorrow's Post, Messrs Hoare will forward £50, in your Name, to Sir B. Hobhouse.[3] From many extra circumstances, & your long & assiduous services, it is absolutely your due; for we attempt nothing that ought to make you uneasy; & should

---

1208. [1] To the account the apothecary had been persuaded to present (£19. 3s. 0d. for medicine, see L. 1189 n. 18), FBA and AA added '31. de plus pour extra—attendance' (Diary 29 April), L. 1193 n. 10, and L. 1210.

[2] The surgeon William Tudor (L. 1186 n. 1).

[3] For the bankers, see L. 1186 n. 2.

you, to our great vexation, return it, we should instantly re-inclose it to Miss Hay.[4]

I hope your health is perfectly re-established, & beg you to accept my best wishes, & to believe me—D[r] S[r]

Y[r] most—

F d'A.

1209   [11 Bolton Street],
18 May 1819

To Esther (Burney) Burney

A.L.S. (rejected Diary MSS. 7198-[201], Berg), 18 May 1819
Two single sheets 4to   4 pp.   *pmk* 19 MY .819   black seal
Addressed: Mrs. Burney / Lark Hall place / near / Bath.
Endorsed by EBB: answered— / May 22[d]
Edited by CFBt, *and possibly in a first stage, by* FBA. *See* Textual
Notes.

18. May 1819—

You *did* attend, my dearest Esther, since such was your effort as well as your wish & intention—& I am pleased accordingly. I should have been gratified that All my Friends at Bath should have shewn that little mark—the only one left—of Respect & Regard to the name & Character the little Congregation met to commemorate; but I could only *ask* it of Mess[rs] Tudor & Hay; & whether they complied or not, I have not heard. Their *Time* is so fully employed that it might not be in their power; or their *opinions* might be adverse, in which case I am the last to blame, or be hurt by their absence. For myself, if praying for the Dead make a Roman Catholic, I have been one all my life.—Yet am I nothing less; for their tenets, in almost all other respects, where there is any difference from those of the Protestants, I utterly disclaim. Long ere I thought of any distinction between the two Religions, my soul involuntarily lifted itself up in Prayer for the Dead,

---

[4] The apothecary's maiden sister Elizabeth (1766-1826), who ran a preparatory school at 7 Grosvenor Place for boys aged 4 to 10.

& surely, then, as innocently as it was spontaneously, for it was for our dear Mother—Well, well I remember, never getting into Bed without praying for my dear Mamma, & that I might be good enough to join her.[1] What, in short, is prayer, but the expression, equally humble & fervant, of the wishes which we direct, in the effusion of our hearts, to Heaven?—I am not without hope we think the same. |

I have had, since, a Letter from Mlle de Somerey,[2] which says that Mme de S. depuis quelques jours ne se portant pas bien, l'a chargée—to tell me qu'elle a rempli toutes mes intentions de son mieux—mais — — that she has vainly sent to Sr B. Hobhouse for the sum I had ordered—which, small as it is, is 4 times what Mme de Somerey had named to me. And I had done the same at the fatal first period. This *entre-nous*:—but imagine my inquietude, at this intelligence, joined to yours, which shewed that Mr. *Hay*, also, whose demand I have more than doubled, *nearly* trebled, is equally without payment.

Alexander was just returned, & I begged him to call upon Messrs Hoare, with these astonishing tidings. They said they had no direct dealings with Sr B. Hobhouse, but had transmitted my orders to Messrs Jones & Lloyd,[3] & would make instant enquiry. They have since wrote to me, that, by some mistake, in which *they* were blameless, the *regular advice* had not been given to Sr B. Hobhouse relative to the £5. but that for the £50, it had been sent.[3]—However I have had no news relative to either: I must conclude, therefore, as well as hope, that both sums are now with their right owners: nevertheless,

---

1209. [1] CB's first wife Esther *née* Sleepe had died in 1762 when her daughter Esther would have been about 13 and Fanny, 10 years old. 'Be assured my Dear Fanny', Esther had replied in a letter (Barrett, Eg. 3690, ff. 124-5b) of 22 May, 'that there is now no division of sentiment between us on the subject of Prayer tho' it must not be denied, that I was *far behind you*, (young as you were) in that article,—when we were both children, *my* heart I fear remained untouched long after yours experienced warm feelings,—towards the great disposer of all Events.—'

[2] Stéphanie-Cécile-Gabrielle du Mesniel (b. 1787), eldest daughter of Mme de Somméry (L. 1206 n. 1).

[3] A branch of Jones, Loyd, & Co., of London, a banking firm that had originated in Manchester in 1784. See F. G. Hilton Price, *A Handbook of London Bankers* . . . (1876). The transactions are recorded with exactitude in Hoares' Ledgers: 29 April 'To Jones & Co for Mad^e de Somerey / with Hobhouse & Co £5'; and on 30 April: 'To D^o for G E Hay with D^o £50.'

the first visit that Amelia pays at that part of the town, I shall be much ⏐ obliged to her to repeat the enquiry at Sir Benjamin's, &, should again a Negative be given, to transmit it to me without delay, after telling Sir B[enjamin], or his Partners, or Clerks, That Messrs Hoare have written me word that they Paid the Two Sums in my Name to Messrs Jones for Sir Benjamin to deliver to Mad^e de Somerey & to Mr. Hay.[3] But do not you, my poor harrassed Sister, quit your poor Invalide, or risk mischief to your so [prec]ious hands, by prematurely going forth. I know [you will] feel for me the impleasantness of such a suspense, & represent it to Amelia,[4] who will good-naturedly end it as soon as weather & Engagements will permit. I long, also, for better news of sweet Cecy, as well as of my ever dear Mr. Burney.[5] You were very considerate to assure me you were well next day. I thank God I have now my Alex to settle with me for some time. Hitherto, he has only come to go. My solemn promises I am preparing to put in practice — — for that, I shall have, I know, my dear Hetty's warm approbation—but oh my dear Hetty—for this Month—this piercing Month[6]—that completes a mourning year I had never believed I could have outlived—for This month I am forced to beg exception — — it has offered anniversary after anniversary so afflicting to Memory—so pointed for regret—that it retrogrades, not advances the recovery of any pleasure in this life — ⏐

It must be quite entre Nous, but I am much disappointed there was no music—& nothing extraordinary. I attribute this to the non arrival, *so unaccountable*, of the destined sum —At present, I must content myself that it will be assigned to the Priest or his Charities. It is truly wonderful, & very unpleasant, what can be the cause of the omission of the receipts

---

[4] For the members of EBB's family, see i, p. lxix and L. 1200 nn. 4–7.

[5] In a reply of 22 May, op. cit., EBB went into a clinical account of her husband's complicated complaints and sufferings. 'He is tormented almost beyond all endurance—*still* he is patient,—Oh, that such good men—should *so suffer!* —you *may* indeed my dear F.—feel for *me*—for it is most dreadful to witness such misery.—. . . by dint of opium [he] gets a couple of Hours sleep—& wakes in pain—sleeps again & during the forenoon, you might *sometimes* believe he was almost well,—on his best days, he plays the most beautiful & spirited things alternately, Exercises his fancy and his Memory. . . .'

[6] The last days of General d'Arblay, who had died on 3 May 1818. See also FBA's Diary for May.

of the money. To Mr. Tudor[7] what I ordered arrived at once, & he acknowledged it, very handsomely, by return of Post.

Your account of Mr. B[urney] is truly affecting—yet truly edifying. His persevering courage of occupation charms me— How do I wish him the reward of relief & ease!—And *you*, my dearest Esther—I feel for you with my whole heart: but I conjure you always to take what exercise you can, when you can, especially in the walks above you, where the sweet air must refresh & revigorate you. I am eager to know whether good Mr Sandford could devize any anodyne—at all events, I rejoice at his visit.

Alex has hurt his foot, & is just now a Prisoner:[8] not a very tranquil one! for he holds it on a chair half the day, while the other half he skips upon it as light as a Bird. James is well & flourishing, & his true attachment to his Sisters seems more warm than ever. My dear Mrs. Lock & Angerstein are both confined by Mr. Angerstein, Sen^rs continued illness;[9] but I see my beloved & tender friend Mme de Maisonneuve when- ever she can borrow the Ambassadrice's Carriage to come to me.[10] She is as sweet, as feeling, as pleasing, & as eminently good as ever. Oh yes!—you devined truly—the first inter- view was a conflict the most severe of Grief & affection.— I will write of the good Sansoms[11] in my next—
Adieu my dearest Hetty:
Sick or Well, gay or sad—y^rs forever
F d A

[7] See L. 1189 n. 17.

[8] 'My love to the Dear clumsy clergyman, Alexander', his aunt EBB was to reply in her letter of 22 May, op. cit., 'how & *why* did he hurt his foot—and why does he skip upon it?—has he performed Duty yet—in church or chapel—I shall long to hear him.—'

[9] Amelia Angerstein's father-in-law John Julius Angerstein (1735-1823), now 84, had emigrated from Russia at the age of 15, and, an underwriter at Lloyds, had created 'one of the most extensive mercantile connexions extant'. He was to leave 'half a million pounds' and a collection of pictures later bought by the nation for £57,000. See *AR* lxvi (1824), ⌐89⌐, 272; and Joanna Richardson, *George IV: A Portrait* (1966), p. 125.

[10] In May (see Diary), Mme de Maisonneuve had paid at least nine visits to Bolton Street.

[11] See L. 1191 n. 16. These obscure relatives of the Burneys and Sleepes appear regularly in FBA's charity lists and in her accounts of letters and visits received. e.g., her Notebook for 12 June 1819: 'D[onation]—Coat Sansom'.

I shall be glad to chuse my Ring by the first safe opportunity— I

Pray distribute my Love & Alexander's

1210 [11 Bolton Street],
20 June 1819

To Esther (Burney) Burney

A.L. (rejected Diary MSS. [7202-5], p. 3 being numbered 7204, Berg), 2⟨0⟩ June 1819
Double sheet 4to   4 pp.   with marginal writing connected sequentially by numbers 2-6   *pmk* 21 JU 1819   black seal
Addressed: Mrs. Burney, / Lark Hall Place / near / BATH.
Endorsed: answered / July 19— / 1819
Edited by CFBt. *See* Textual Notes.

2⟨0⟩ June. 1819.

Your little Note, my kind Esther, was my first, & only intelligence of the £5. but I have had, at length, a very satisfactory Letter, through the medium of Alexander, relative to the £50, from Mr. Hay, who appears *more* than content: & I hope he is so, as it is amongst the *necessities* to my peace that I satisfy All who had aided in the last attendance upon all my Soul held most dear — ! — The Bill of Mr. Hay was the most moderate possible; medicines—operations—attendance included, it was within £20.[1] Let all this of Money transaction rest between ourselves, or nearly, as it is not of a nature that ought to be spread abroad: but I thought you would like to know how the affair stood, as well as how it terminated.

A lowness—utterly unconquerable, of spirits, has kept me

1210. [1] In obedience to FBA's request of 18 May (L. 1209), EBB's daughter Amelia had inquired at the banking house, Hobhouse, Clutterbuck, & Co., on Milsom Street, for the funds sent by FBA through her bankers Messrs Hoare (L. 1186 n. 2), only to find, as EBB explained in her letter of 22 May, op. cit., that the £5 directed to Madame de Somméry for the General's Memorial Service had arrived, but not as yet the sum of £50 for the surgeon G. E. Hay (see L. 1189 n. 18 and L. 1193 n. 10).

from writing sooner —— — All April I passed in retrospection
of the April of last year, That Last Month we lived together!
—& all May in irrepressible sorrow that that was the month
of our final worldly separation.—Yet I did not forget the
Good with the misery of May! I owed to it the Birth, as well
as loss, of Him who for so many precious Years was the Joy,
the Occupation, the Pride, the Pleasure, & the Comfort of my
Existence! in *that* view I meet the Month with thankfulness
— — & next year, should I be here, I will seriously endeavour to Hail it in that sense.—Nor did I forget that to May
I owe my dear & excellent sister,[2] my valuable & truly loved
Esther — — & when, on the 24th I heard the Birth of our
New future Queen,[3] — — for such is the Daughter of the
Duke of Kent—I uttered an earnest wish she might be endowed with the spirit of Generosity, & the zeal of Charity ׀
that regularly through life have distinguished my dear Hetty
—though always narrowed by her limitted means: *Then*,
what a blessing to the Nation will the 24th of May become!
—May, too, gave existence to my dear & venerable Royal
Mistress,[4] for so many Years the brightest as well as highest
example of solid & efficient Virtue to all her subjects; & May,
also, gave breath to the charming Princess Elizabeth;[4] as
fragrant in the powers of pleasing, & as sportive in their exercise, as the Flowers, or the Birds, that bud, or that chirp in
that glowing opening of summer.—Shall I not seek, then, to
meet — — next Time!—That May, that eventful May, with
lessened bitterness, & deepened Gratitude?—Let us hope so,
at least.—Alexander is at length with me,[5] & my struggles
for amelioration of spirits become—in some sort—duties—
What a Call upon me does that word make!—

⌒⟶

[2] CB's eldest daughter Esther was born on 24 May 1749 (see *HFB*, p. 6).

[3] The birth at Kensington Palace on 24 May of Alexandrina Victoria, daughter
of Edward, Duke of Kent (1767–1820), who on 29 May 1818 had married
Victoria-Maria-Louisa (1786–1861), daughter of Francis Frederick Anthony,
Duke of Saxe-Coburg-Saalfeld (1750–1806). FBA would see the Duchess and 'the
New born presumptive Queen' on 18 July (Diary).

[4] Queen Charlotte, daughter of the then reigning Duke of Mecklenburg-
Strelitz, was born on 19 May 1744; her third daughter Elizabeth, on 22 May 1770.

[5] In London since 30 May, according to FBA's Diary, AA had been engaged in
a round of social life, opera, theatre, and was often with the Latour-Maubourgs.
His invitation to a dinner at the French Embassy on 26 août is extant (Berg).

How affecting are all your accounts of dear suffering exemplary Mr. Burney![6] I read them as lessons—if not Models, to all of our Family that I see, as well as to myself. To amuse himself so ingeniously, so patiently, so *wisely* — — while others consume their remnant strength in murmurs & apprehensions,—must make every interval afford double recruit to the mind, as well as the body;—indeed I honour his courage, as much as I grieve at its cause.

I have been just interrupted by our good James,[7] who entered amicably arm in arm with his Wife, to read to me certain

---

[6] See L. 1209 n. 5 for EBB's account of her husband in his hours of surcease from pain, playing and extemporizing as usual on pianoforte or harpsichord.

[7] In a Memorial or protest (PRO. ADM. 1. 5233) addressed to the Lords Commissioners of the Admiralty on 24 February 1818 (see ix, L. 1138 n. 1) James referred to the Order in Council of 19 December 1804, by which qualified Captains like himself, on shore for many years, could rise in the order of seniority 'to the rank and pension of superannuated Rear Admirals, as equivalent to active service at Sea'. See also Michael Lewis, 'The Naval Hierarchy: Rank, Promotion, and Appointments', *A Social History of the Navy, 1793-1815* (1960), pp. 181-227. The trouble was that not having been employed, notwithstanding many offers on his part of service, since 1785 and being high, therefore, 'on the list of Post Captains', he had been placed in 1804 on the 'list of Retired Post Captains' and thus, allegedly punished for his seniority, was 'set aside', 'passed over', and 'excluded from the common benefit'. This document bears the response: 'Feb 25 (Commission Branch) His request cannot be complied with.'
Pursuant to the above complaint and appeal for redress James sent to the Lords of the Admiralty on 18 August 1819 under the covering letter (ADM. 1. 1566) two letters from Earl Spencer and a letter from Earl St. Vincent, which letters approved his service at sea and exonerated him from blame for the years (1785-1804) of unemployment. It could only be 'by mistake', James suggested, that he 'had been precluded from the benefit of His Majesty's Order in Council of December the 19th 1804'. This document bears the same laconic response in the same hand: '18th Aug . . . His request cannot be complied with—'
On 24 February 1820 (ADM. 1. 1768) James was to write again asking the Lords to inspect the papers he had sent (*supra*) and consider his request for 'superannuation as Rear Admiral from the date of His Majesty's Order in Council of December the 19th 1804'. The response seemed already forged and ready: 'Feb. 26. His request cannot be complied with—'. The 'old Post Captain' was next to address an appeal to the King in Council, see L. 1241 n. 1. 'Brother James has sent us his Book', reported EBB in her letter of 22 May, op. cit., 'Mr. B. has read it through we are neither of us *extremely conversant* with the subject of it—but think the style not only manly & perspicuous,—but glowing in some places with the *warm* humanity of his own disposition: I think the independance that reigns thro' it,—& the better, because it cannot, at present clash with his interest,—when I have navigated the work—and collected my criticisms, I shall write to him—'

documents he has prepared for an appeal to the Admiralty—
& so well done is the address & Representation, that I am not
quite destitute of hope of its ǀ success—though I dare not
give way to expectation. He has made his claim, however, in
so Gentlemanly as well as spirited a manner, that it cannot
but redound to his honour, whether prosperous or not. Dear
James! how should I rejoice were he to gain his point! I read
to him Your Paragraph upon his Book, & its *style*, &c; & he
was much pleased, & extremely diverted by your waiting to
collect your Criticisms[7] before you wrote.

Alexander is so *à la Mode,*[8] that he is invited away from
me continually. I must not repine that he pleases, nor that he
is pleased; far from it: but yet, you can scarcely conceive
how little time he spends at home.—I have heard nothing
from our dear Charlotte—alas, I have not merited to hear!
since last March! but I am assured she is considerably better,
& my next Letter after this shall be to Her.[9] sweet Charlotte
Barrett I hear is quite well again. We hope to pass July &
August together: I mean the *elder* Charlotte. I am to go first
to dear Mrs. Lock—but I defer & defer & defer!—involuntarily—yet irresistibly!—Not once have I entered any house

[8] The preacher *à la mode* or the fashionable preacher, as ridiculed by Robert
Southey in *Letters from England* (1807), Letter XIX, was not the man perhaps
to be signalled out by the bishops for serious advancement. 'Thread-bare garments', said Southey, 'would have few charms for that part of the congregation
for whom the popular preacher of London curls his forelock, studies gestures at
his looking-glass, takes lessons from some stage-player in his chamber, and displays his white hand and white handkerchief in the pulpit. The discourse is in
character with the orator . . . sparkling with metaphors and similes, and rounded
off with a text of scripture, a scrap of poetry, or, . . . a quotation from Ossian. . . .'
    Of the red coat of the soldier and the black of the priest, black then carried
the day with the ladies. 'The customs of England do not exclude the clergyman
from any species of amusement; the popular preacher is to be seen at the theatre,
and at the horse-race, bearing his part at the concert and the ball, . . . he generally
succeeds in finding some widow, or waning spinster, with weightier charms than
youth and beauty.' Such a preacher, Southey said, hoped to 'make a fortune by
marriage' or to obtain 'a lectureship in some wealthy parish' or 'a chapel of his
own, in which he rents out pews and single seats by the year'.
    Though d'Arblay came naturally enough by some of these attributes and was
never self-seeking, there are parallels enough between his lifestyle and that depicted
by Southey to account for his curtailed career in the Church.
[9] See FBA's letter of 8 March (L. 1199). The visit planned by Mrs. Broome for
April (see L. 1205 n. 1) seems not to have materialized.

but that of James!—except to a Gracious Royal Command[10]
—which was unavoidable—& indeed I am glad it was so, for
I passed some *Hours* with the amiable Duchess of Gloucester
in a manner to do me good every way. She is made up of right
conduct, & kind feelings.—She received me, by her own
appointment, *early*, & *alone*—& she was all tender consideration & sweetness.—

I am truly glad Cecilia is recovering.[11] I am sure her abode
at the Belvedere will give great pleasure to her two sisters.
I desire my love to them all, with my thanks to Amelia for
her walks & information. I have never yet found out where or
how the delay occurred. Messrs Hoare only clear *themselves*: &
I inclosed their own Letter to Mr. Hay to shew *my* exactness.
Will you endeavour—through the Belvedere, or Mad^e de Beaufort,[12] to express to Mad^e la Marq^se de Somerey my regret &
astonishment at l the unaccountable slackness with which my
commission was fulfilled, & my very grateful acknowledgments for the pious service which I owe to her, with my best
thanks to Mlle de Somerey for her polite & obliging Letter.[13]
To all this, pray add les *hommages respecteux* of Alexander,
with a million of apologies that he has not himself written his
sense of the goodness of Mme la Marquise in complying with
his request of authenticating Mr. Brenan's hand writing.[14] The

[10] At Gloucester House on Saturday morning 27 March (L. 1202 n. 1).

[11] Cecilia Burney (L. 1200 n. 7), now visiting her sister Maria Bourdois (L.
1200 n. 6) at 5 Ainslie's Belvedere, Bath.

[12] See L. 1189 n. 16.

[13] For Madame de Sommèry and one of her letters at this time, see L. 1206
n. 1. The letter from her daughter Stéphanie (L. 1209 n. 2) is missing.

[14] Among the documents needed to settle business affairs in England and in
France was apparently a certificate of the General's death. In a letter, now missing, AA had apparently asked John Brenan (L. 1180 n. 10), occupier of 23 Great
Stanhope Street, Bath, where his father had died, to procure the death certificate,
for in a reply of 1 June (Barrett, Eg. 3701, f. 34) Brenan wrote of the pleasure it
gave him 'to perform such a duty for a . . . family I am so much indebted [to] for
so many past favours'. 'The expense incurred was only 3^s which Doctor Hay paid.'
FBA's Diary of 3 June records the receipt of the above letter 'with the melancholy certificate or affadavit for La Ministère de La Guerre à Paris to recover
Sums due to [her husband]'.

A Roman Catholic of the parish of St. John, Bath, Brenan would naturally
have called on Mme de Sommèry of the same parish and, as well, a friend of the
d'Arblays, to attest to his handwriting.

French Consul General, M. de Sequier,[15] accepted the signature of the Marquise in lieu of that of a Magistrate. We were ashamed to trouble her, but yet we know she takes pleasure in trouble that is to do good. Alex often sees her Nephew, le C^t de Caraman,[16] whom he much admires. The Ambassadour & his Family are all kindness to Alex. My most sweet & constant Mme de Maisonneuve gives me all the time she can spare,[17] & rather partakes than pardons my deplorable dejection.—She so loved—so esteemed—so admired its object, that she cannot wonder at its permanency!—Nevertheless, I am beginning, again, to gain some little ground in revival— &, *before company*, I am tolerably composed. Did I tell you how I gratified Charles Parr by your paragraph upon his Fanny?[18]—*Your* Fanny I saw for a few minutes, in her way to James Street, last Sunday—& had hardly time to give her the thanks you must long ere this know to have been her due from me. She has had a bad cold, & looked thin & fatigued. At first after she got rid of her work,[19] she looked so flourishing, I had hopes she was growing fat. Edward was with her, silent & elegant, yet observant & penetrating as usual. I have sent a Message at last to good Mr. Sansom,[20] to be so kind as to *call*, & talk over the Chinese &c. I could not sooner muster courage even for that! Indeed, left to myself, I still sink into utter solitude.—Should chance put Mr. Brenan into the way of any of the family, I beg he may receive Alexander's thanks for his obliging Letter, & our joint acknowledgment for his prompt execution of Alex's commission.[14] The melancholy documents we are thus called upon ∣ to repeat will, ultimately, I believe, answer in the recovery of our just claims—owing

[15] Armand-Louis-Maurice, baron de Séguier (1770–1831), consul, London (1816).

[16] Georges-Joseph-Victor de Riquet, comte de Caraman (L. 1189 n. 7), chargé d'affaires in London, had called on FBA on 29 March (Diary).

[17] Madame de Maisonneuve had written to FBA frequently and had called upon her at least four times thus far in June.

[18] CPB's daughter Fanny Anne (1812–60) had accompanied her father to Bath (register of arrivals for 7 January 1819). See *A Great-Niece's Journals / Being Extracts from the Journals of Fanny Anne Burney / (Mrs Wood) / from 1830 to 1842 /*, ed. Margaret S. Rolt (1926). CPB had visited his aunt on 1 May.

[19] Fanny Burney (L. 1191 n. 4) and her uncle Edward (L. 1189 n. 12), the artist, had called on FBA as recently as 14 June. Her *Tragic Dramas*, AA was reading aloud to his mother on 18 May.

[20] James Sansom (L. 1191 n. 16), from whom EBB had received a letter.

chiefly—perhaps totally, to the singular chance of my Mad^e de Maisonneuve's present influence.[21] Mrs. Lock—nor a Hetty could not work for us more vigourously. adieu, dearest Esther—yours ever & for-ever more—

F. d'A.

How are the poor dear Hands? Your writing is so good it prevents my thinking of them— |

If any of the Family happen to see Mr. Hay, also, pray thank him for his quick execution of Alexander's commission, with our joint best compliments.

I am much pleased with your account of les de Beauforts[22] —Pray remember me to the Thomas's—& M^rs ⟨Beckford⟩ Miss Hayes & all I know that remember *me*.[22] I have not written this Age to my excellent Friends, Mrs. Bowdler[23] & Mrs Holroyd:[24] but I received Mrs. H. Bowdler & Miss Frodsham[24] to *Tea*[25]—a great exertion but it did me certainly good

I had a visit last week from Sarah Harriet,[26] who was looking remarkably well. |

I am very sorry at your hint about the good Sandfords[27]— Will they continue at Worcester?

[21] For the satisfaction of this claim, see L. 1280 n. 5.

[22] See respectively L. 1200 n. 11; L. 1189 n. 20; and L. 1189 n. 21.

[23] Frances Bowdler (*c.* 1747-1835) of 2 Lansdowne Place East, Bath; and her sister Henrietta Maria (1754-1830) of 2 Park Street. See ix, x *passim* and Noel Perrin, *Dr. Bowdler's Legacy; a History of Expurgated Books in England and America* (1969).

[24] See L. 1186 n. 1; and L. 1192 n. 2.

[25] On 10 June (Diary).

[26] On 15 June (Diary).

[27] Possibly a hint on the retirement of the surgeon William Sandford (i, p. lxxv), now about 60 years of age. On 4 April 1820 the Sandfords were to move to 'a small house pleasantly situated on Rainbow Hill 3 qrs. of a mile from the centre of the town' ('Worcester Journal').

1211   [11 Bolton Street,
                                      10 July 1819]

To Mrs. Waddington[1]

A.N. (Berg), n.d.
Single sheet 4to   cut down to (4.4 × 7.2″)   1 p.

I am quite distressed but so engaged for my Alex who
leaves me to night for 3 weekes[2] that I dare not see my dearest Mary — — I have no room at this moment to receive her
                          I am quite
                                  quite grieved—

1212   [11 Bolton Street],
                                      5 August [1819]

To Mrs. Broome

A.L.S. (Berg), 5 Aug.
Double sheet 8vo   black-edged   4 pp.   *pmk* T.P. / Piccadilly
6 AU 1819   black seal
Addressed: Mrs. Broome, / at Henry Barrett's, Esq, / Richmond /
Surry.
Endorsed by CBFB: Sister d'arblay / 1819

                                      Friday 5th. Augst.

Every day—& all day long, for at least a week past I have
been expecting a line from—or of—my dearest Charlotte,
with news of her arrival at Richmond, & with documents
upon which to establish our so long—long delayed meeting:
but no intelligence reaches me—& at James Street ignorance
upon this subject is equally profound.

1121. [1] Georgiana Mary Ann *née* Port (1771-1850), whom FBA had known
since 1784 (i. 61; vii, ix, x *passim*).
    [2] On this very day 10 July (Diary) AA had left with his friend James Collett
Ebden (L. 1181 n. 3) for a tour of Switzerland; and in his absence FBA had intended to make a visit to Mrs. Locke at Eliot Vale (L. 1188 n. 3) and to the
Barrett family at Richmond.

I am at this moment in the greatest perplexity relative to this cruel—& it should seem endless procrastination—for Alex has given up his Swiss expedition, & is now in *Paris*[1]— or perhaps at Calais — — — where he has 2 days business —How do I wish my beloved Charlotte could come to me directly![2]—while ⎸I have yet [room] & Bed—all prepared —If you are now actually at Richmond, I earnestly entreat you to try to give me *one night* immediately—as to pass an Evening & a Morning together, entirely, will be really balsamic, after so fearful—so miserable a separation. You can arrive within a stone's throw of *N° 11*, & go back as easily—

Pray try, my dear love—you will want *no baggage*—night things will all be ready—& the tenderest reception from your affecte true & faithful

F d'A—

Most kindly to *our* Charlotte let me be remembered, & to all else [*tear*]. ⎸

N.B. I did not answer your dear Letter as it led me to hope for another so shortly. — —

P.S. Nevertheless—if it will hurry you too much, defer again! all is better than risk to your precious health—

otherwise—the *tête à tête* I propose will be invaluable to both— ⎸

one word I earnestly d[em]and, *Yes*—or *No*, By return of Post—to secure my being alone if happily you can come ⟨Do⟩ Charlotte endeavour!—

1212. [1] FBA had received on 12 July a letter sent on the 11th by AA from Dover and on the 15th, a letter from Calais. On 3 August she was surprised by a visit from Ebden with the curious information that he 'had left Alex at Paris— after Vainly endeavouring to conquer his *inertia* for proceeding on their Journey to Switzerland' (Diary).

[2] The sisters seem not to have met since the deaths in Bath of CBFB's son 'Dolph' in 1817 (see ix. 379–84) and General d'Arblay in 1818. Mrs. Broome was to arrive at Bolton Street on 7 August ('pangful was the 1st sight of this dear Sister after the Tragedy of our absence!') and to remain until the 18th ('after a week's soft intercourse of gentle soothing & perfect Confidence'). This sister was to be FBA's best comfort in her declining years.

11 Bolton Street,
12 August 1819

To H.R.H. Princess Augusta Sophia

A.L. draft (Berg), 12 Aug. 1819
Two double sheets 4to 7 pp. paged 1-7 showing the blots, lines
obliterated, and the rephrasings characteristic of a draft. The revised
version is printed here.

To the P^ss Augusta, in answer to a *volunteer* Letter of sweetest words of attachment & constant Regard.

⟨━━━⟩

12. August, 1819
Bolton Street.

Madam,

A sweeter surprize,[1] a more soothing pleasure, my life,
though fertile in events which, without being momentous, are
little common, has never yet, I think, [acco]rded me, than
the sudden & unexpected sight of the gracious hand of my
long loved as well as reverenced Princess Augusta. The feeling
kindness I have experienced from All your R.H^nesses since my
irreparable & ever deplored loss of a Partner in All the most
sympathising & most honourable, has been nearly formost
amongst my revivers to returning comfort in existence; & has
been received the more cheeringly, because that lamented

1213. [1] The surprise was Princess Augusta's letter (Berg) of 8 August 1819 ('*You
must forgive me* as *Dutchess Mary* says—for pouncing upon you quite unawares
like a Hawk upon an innocent Bird'), which FBA received on the 10th and answered on the 13th.

   She had been received by Princess Augusta on at least three occasions before
this: on 22 June, apparently at Buckingham House; on 15 July, when the Princess
'played to me, & Sang to me airs of her own composition . . . very pretty, &
prettily executed—with touching words of innocent ardour of sentiment'; and on
23 July, when she again sang 'to me sundry of her own Compositions, little airs, &
such, selecting, as had been favourites with the dear King'.

   Thomas Moore was to be delighted with the 'new airs' that the Princess had
composed for his songs 'The wreath you wove' and 'The Legacy' (18 May 1824,
Memoirs, iv. 193). 'She played also a march, which she told me she had "composed for Frederick" (Duke of York), and a waltz or two, with some German airs.
I then sung to her my rebel song, "Oh, where's the slave!" and it was no small
triumph to be *chorused* in it by the favourite sister of his Majesty George IV.'

Partner, when generously, in his last days, seeking to reconcile me to lengthened life without him, for the sake of our Alexander, mentioned himself—the condescending attachment, gracious, trusting, & unvarying, of the Queen & of the Princesses,[2] & announced his wish that I ǀ should approach *them*, as well as Mrs. Lock & Amelia Angerstein; adding that Both Now, besides being too narrow a sojourn for a rising young man, could no longer offer to me any happiness.— Exquisite was his foresight in those solemn hours![3]—& fully justified have been his expectations; for, as I have since heard, the *Queen*, my invaluable Royal Mistress, took so commiserating an interest in my situation, that Mrs. Beckedorff[4] wrote me word she had not dared *risk a spasm* by making known, at the time it happenned my affliction; & the *Princesses* equally fulfilling his ideas—have evinced a partiality of Regard in their pity just such as his kind spirit—already nearly immortal, had depicted—

Shall I apologise for all this egotism, & for recurrence to circumstances so personal? No,—for I am conscious of the humanity of your R. H^nesses purpose in designing to accord me this *melodious voluntary*:[5] I see it is *composed* with benign intent to confirm my confidence in ǀ your R.H^sses unchangeable goodness to me. And indeed I have the happiness to feel the firmest reliance on it—How could I do otherwise after reading the admirable maxim[6] that separates so rationally,

---

[2] FBA's Diary for June and July 1819 records letters from the Duchess of Gloucester and visits to Gloucester House, where on 26 July she was presented to the Duke. In his estimation *Evelina* 'was the first Book . . . *dans son genre*, in the Universe', and he led her to relate the 'history of its composition & publication'.

[3] See x. 879 for FBA's transcriptions of the General's last words and advice.

[4] Charlotte Beckedorf (*fl.* 1802-19), appointed Keeper of the Robes to Queen Charlotte on 3 February 1802, was in attendance ('nuit et jours') in the last six months of the Queen's life. The death of General d'Arblay had been kept hidden 'aussi longtems que possible a la connoissance de Sa Majesté', she had informed FBA in a letter (Barrett, Eg. 3698, ff. 23-4b) of 20 August 1818, 'depeur que cela ne causa le retour d'un spasme. à quoi toute Emotion donne toujours lieu; mais depuis que cette Auguste Invalide en est informée, Elle y'a pris la part la plus sensible, m'ordonnant de Vous témoigner combien Elle sent Vôtre perte, et participe à Vôtre juste Douleur, souhaitant que Votre Sante n'en souffre pas.'

[5] A play on voluntary as a musical term in reference to the Princess's voluntary opening of a correspondence.

[6] The Princess's 'admirable maxim' bore on the nature of friendship: 'It is has been an old saying of mine (*because it is the genuine Sentiment of my Heart*) that I love *too* sincerely the *few I do love* to have room for a *Crowd* in *my Heart*. I

the duties of general Christian Charity from the *platitude* of making an *Hospital* of *the Heart*, for the reception of all the diseases, as well as virtues, of our acquaintance? The Heart, in truth, can never be 'large enough for a Crowd'—where a multitude can find room, Heart is out of the question: the welcome, then, is made by Vanity, or Caprice, or Interest, or eagerness for something New, or Dissipation that has no discrimination, or *Ennui*, that has no resources. From all these, the Heart—where Heart there is, draws back, delicate, difficult, concentrated in its selections. Oh Madam! in Such a repository—so pure, so sacred, am I permitted to hope for a place? ˡ

I truly rejoice in your R.Hˢ deserved possession of beautiful Frogmore.[7] No wonder there should start so many concomitant circumstances to endear that fair maternal bequest; Frogmore was so long the favourite refuge from Ceremony, & relief from care of its august Founder that, some time hence, perhaps, in some deeply shaded spot, a small, elegant, funereal urn may be consecrated to Her revered memory.[8]

How just is that quotation from Pope relative to the famous — — I cannot say illustrious—Traveller![9] *Sense* certainly is wanting in the same proportion as Decency in such a Project. But perhaps the Report alone is spread to feel the pulse of the public. If not, two possible motives only strike me; Either, it may be believed that the arrival may avert condemnation,

cannot make an *Hospital of my Heart*. I wish everybody *well* like a Christian—but I can only love a *few as friends*:—and I am attached to You my Dearest Madame d Arblay. . . .'

[7] The Princess had expressed gratitude to her mother for having so 'considered my Comfort and Happiness' in giving her 'beloved Frogmore'.

[8] According to Olwen Hedley, the biographer of Queen Charlotte (1975), FBA's suggestion of a memorial urn at Frogmore was not carried out.

[9] 'What do you think of the *threatened* Visit from our *Illustrious* Traveller', Princess Augusta had asked. 'Its quite keeping up her dashing Character—' ' "Want of decency is want of Sense" ', she went on, attributing the lines not to Roscommon, *Essay on Translated Verse* (1684), i. 120, but to 'Pope'. 'Its really charity to think her Mad—and I am of opinion that if She has one friend left in the World *that friend* ought to advise her *not* to make the attempt.'

The 'Traveller' was, of course, Caroline, Princess of Wales (1768-1821), the highlights of whose spectacular appearances in half a dozen countries had now reached England. For accounts of her continental progress (1814-20), see Joanna Richardson, op. cit., pp. 170-6; *The Disastrous Marriage. A Study of George IV and Caroline of Brunswick* (1960); or Roger Fulford, *The Trial of Queen Caroline* (1967); or *AR* lxii¹ (1820), chap. ix.

in order to spare the horrours of Execution; or, there may have been as much delicacy practiced for Safety as there has been want of it for Morality, &, then, the coming forth is from fearlessness & defiance of conviction. ⏐ Should this latter be the case, every friend to the injured party must wish the *attempt at justice* not to be made, for Guilt that cannot be proved, even where it cannot be doubted, will always, by the culpable, & by the Mob, be called Innocence: & then —— — what hideous yells would rend the air with cries against Calumny & Defamation! If, on the contrary, the precautions of Cunning should be defective, & Truth & Law should blazon the turpitude of Crime: then, all artful calculations upon the dangers of public punishment may prove abortive, for a noble, & at the same time a politic Clemency might change the sentence from Death[10] to perpetual Captivity; avoiding by that means all popular clamour, & shewing that the point sought was not Vengeance, but merely a dignified desire to rescue the highest & most honoured name in this Country from being assumed by a Person who—in general Report, at least—bears a character the most disgraced. Unhappy Woman! how wilful & how inveterate must be her ⏐ blindness to Right!

Most softly flattering to me your R.H^sses gracious enquiries about my Son. He has relinquished, for this year, his Swiss excursion, the party he was to accompany having changed their plan:[11] he will content himself, therefore, with passing

[10] Adultery in a Queen of England could, as treason, be punishable by death; or so the biographers above as well as many persons of the time thought. In law, however, see *The Public and Private Life of Lord Chancellor Eldon* . . . , ed. Horace Twiss (3 vols., 1844), ii. 371, Caroline was in no danger of execution: 'The offence of a Queen Consort, or Princess Consort of Wales, committing adultery with a person owing allegiance to the British Crown, would be that of a principal in high treason, because, by statute, it was high treason in him, and as accessories in high treason are principals, she would then be guilty of high treason as principal. But as the act of a person owing no allegiance to the British Crown could not be high treason in him, so neither could a Princess be guilty of that crime by being an accessory to that person's act.' Or, as explained in the *AR*, op. cit., p. ⌐125⌐, because Queen Caroline's alleged adultery, even if it could be proved, was committed abroad and with a foreigner, it could not endanger the succession and would not therefore incur the death penalty.

[11] The responsibility for the change in plan FBA here deflects from AA himself to 'the party', namely Ebden. Cf. Diary, 10 July, 3 and 17 August. The visit to Richmond would take place from 9 to 28 September, that to Mrs. Locke was deferred to 13 December (see L. 1226 n. 2).

a few Weeks at Paris, whence I am almost daily expecting his return: after which we shall go for some time to Elliot Vale, to Mrs. Lock's new Cottage; & he will then visit Archdeacon Cambridge at Twickenham, & make some other social country rounds, during the residu of this summer.

My excellent French Friends, who are quite enchanted with their reception in this Country, think themselves, nevertheless, extremely unlucky that the 25th the only day that allows them the high honour of seeing your R.H. &c *Duchess Mary*, should have so many impediments in the way of their wishes. That sweet | *Duchess Mary*! How I enjoy for your R.H.nesses this sisterly fortnight! chiefly, however, for Pss Sophia,[12] who to such a circumstance alone can owe even a sight of her dear *Duchess Mary*.

I could not bring myself to write a shorter Letter—I was so much gratified by [y]r R.H.sses Voluntary.[5] I have always naturally loved Musick but no *ouverture* has ever pleased me quite so much. I will now, however, conclude, only allowing myself to ask one Question: if Such are the Hawks that hover over us for prey — — Who would not wish for a pouncing? For me, I hope to be pounced upon again with all my Heart.

I have the Honour to subscribe myself

Madam—

1214   [11 Bolton Street,
post 16 August 1819]

To Mrs. Barrett

A.L.S. 1st leaf (Berg); 2nd leaf (McGill), n.d.
Originally a double sheet 8vo (7.15 × 4.45″), the conjugate leaves of which have been separated   4 pp.   black seal
Addressed: Mrs. Barrett.
Endorsed by CFBt: Madame d'Arblay
Annotated in pencil and dated incorrectly p. 1: unfinished / n. d. / 1823–38
Docketed in ink, p. 4: Madame d'Arblay

[12] The Princess Sophia (1777–1848) evidently remained at Windsor while her father George III still lived but was later established at Kensington Palace.

Not alone my Consent but my greatest pleasure, my dearest Charlotte[1]—is to have Alexander with a friend whom his heart loves so completely as a favourite sister: I will not grieve you by going into any detail of the causes of disturbance given by the late non-appearance of my non-mi-ricordo; —but say that I certainly shall not now expect to see him till Tuesday:[2]—nor *then*, if he will but *write*, should he desire to prolong his stay. How can he be better, where so well, as with the playfully wise associate who knows how to blend her flattering encouragement to exertion with the ᛁ arch little episode of Mr. Puff Up?—admirable, my dear *good* Charlotte!

I send this by post because — — it — — might else— *entre nous*—be brought me back unread.—

My Etourdie came home last Monday with a rising Cold, from having forgotten to put up his Night Wig in his little packet. & he has been so much engaged by Evening parties since his return, that he has had no opportunity to nurse off the assault: he has, therefore, left me in a most sniffling state.

Now—

I earnestly entreat, should this cold be worse to-morrow, that you will pack him off by the earliest stage after his church duty—that I may pursue my long accustomed ᛁ methods of cure, to prevent an illness.

With respect to my Richmond so long delayed visit, I assure you it is my real desire to be amongst you—now that I am better able to enjoy, in some degree—What so lately I could scarcely bear—society — — but I shall beg my dear Sister to communicate to you my impediments. They are by no means painful—nor will be lasting: I am glad my Dick[3] is so manly. I have a great love for him. But don't let my Julia[3] be

---

1214. [1] Charlotte Barrett's letter, presumably an invitation to Richmond, is missing. She had called with her husband and family at Bolton Street on 12 August (Diary).

[2] Alexander arrived from Calais on Monday 16 August (Diary). Here another instance of FBA's recording on a given date what had in reality happened the day before. When at Richmond, he was usually invited by Archdeacon Cambridge to read the service or preach at Twickenham chapel (L. 1190 n. 2).

[3] Richard Arthur Francis Barrett (1813–81), FBA's godson, a schoolboy at Richmond, and his sister Julia Charlotte (1808–64).

jealous. *All* yours I must love and I do.——only the Stem before the Branches——Best compts to Mr. Barret——

yours with true affection
true & tender——F. d'A

It is long since I have seen our dear Fanny.[4]

1215A
11 Bolton Street,
[23 August 1819]

To James Burney

A.L. (PML, Autog. Cor. bound), Monday
Double sheet   12 mo   black edged   3 pp.   *pmks* T. P / Piccadilly 23 AU 1819   seal
Addressed: Captn Burney, / 26 James Street / Westminster.

Though I have never, myself, been uneasy about my Pension,[1] which, having been considered by the kind Queen & Gracious King *due* to me 30 years, nearly, ago, there seemed to me no reason to suppose would be now with drawn——: yet many of my Friends have been anxious upon the subject, & none with deeper interest, I am very sure, than my dear James——It will give, therefore, I know, great satisfaction to his truly Brotherly heart to hear that it has formally been assured to me, by a visit from Mr Vernon of the Treasury.[2] My ¦ Love to All——& God bless you——

You are the First to whom I have made this communication.

---

[4] SBP's daughter Fanny Raper (L. 1193 n. 5) was a faithful caller in these years at Bolton Street (Diary).

1215A. [1] A pension of £100 per annum (i. 2), granted in 1786 when FB retired as Keeper of the Robes to Queen Charlotte.

[2] Joseph Vernon (*c.* 1771-1851), Receiver of Fees at the Treasury (1794-1834). His visit to FBA must have taken place on 22 or 23 August, else she would have imparted the news on the 21st, when she drank tea at James Street (Diary).

Bolton St.
Monday Noon.

May this be de bon augur from the Treasury to the Admiralty!³—

Mr. Vernon said to me The Committee, Madam, voted the Continuance of your pension: the Parliament granted it; & the Prince Regent has signed your Warrant,—which you shall have in a few days.— |

Do not speak of this *publicly*, as it may excite envy & jealousy—but *privately* tell it to my always faithful friend your other half—

I am too courteous to say *better*, which always comes *best* from one of the Twain.

Alex is engaged, for the Day, or would have been the Bearer.

1215B   [11 Bolton Street,
                                    post 23 August 1819]

To James Burney

A.L.S. (BL, Add. MSS 43,688, ff. 158-9), n.d.
Double sheet 12mo   2 pp.   black edged   seal

I thank you heartily my dear Brother for your tidings of the Admiralty—

May it have its deserved success!—Alex forgot to give me your kind message last night—& when he thought of it this morning, late, he was going to Mᵐᵉ de Maisonneuve with a Book from M. de Lally. He promised to carry you my desire you would accept us any day *after* to-morrow, to Tea—that you please. To day he will be back late, & to-morrow I think he is engaged. But *Saturday*—or *Monday*—or *any* other day. I am not just yet up to a *Dinner*: you must take me as I am, my dear James!—& that is *Yours* with the truest affection.

F d Ay

³ See L. 1210 n. 7.

You will tell all this to your kind Half, who will allow for it with her constant partiality.——

I send this, lest Alex should be kept too late to call—or — — lest it should slip his Memory!—a thing not quite impossible—

1216   [11 Bolton Street],
                                    1 September 1819

To Mrs. Broome

A.L. (Berg), 1 Sept. 1819
Double sheet 8vo   4 pp.   black edged   *pmks* T. P. / Piccadilly
1 SP 1819   black seal
    Addressed: Mrs. Ralph Broome / Ormond place / Richmond.
    Endorsed by CBFB: Sister d'arblay / 1819

Sept[r] 1st
1819.

A little line only to my dearest Charlotte to thank her for her most welcome Letter,[1] & say how much I want to hear news of the ceasing of the 'littel complaint—' & moreover, to tell her I will no longer resist her touching desire to make me try—once more—a roof not my own.——

Will *Monday* next suit her to receive in her quiet dwelling & affectionate arms a guest wofully unfitted for almost every house but her own?[2]——

1216. [1] The invitation is missing, but FBA and AA were to set off (not on Monday the 5th) but on Thursday the 9th (Diary) for a visit of three weeks to Mrs. Broome, who on her return from Brighton had taken the house 6 Ormond Place, Richmond. FBA would return to Bolton Street on 28 September (Diary).
    [2] A view of Madame d'Arblay at this time as she appeared to the younger generation is supplied by her niece Marianne Francis (L. 1188 n. 1) in a letter of 29 September 1819 (Barrett, Eg. 3703B, ff. 154–5b) to Arthur Young: 'We have . . . had my Aunt d'Arblay & her son Alexander on a visit with us in the house for some weeks. . . . She is a most gentle & pleasant visitor, is quiet, & kind, & easily pleased—So is her Son, who is a person of fine abilities, & very amiable, poor dear fellow. He has an astonishing memory, so has his Mother; but it is impaired by trouble, for she is very low, & has by no means recovered the loss of her husband.' In her turn FBA found there 'all tender cordiality & kindness—& Marianne Francis all attention and obligingness'. Cf. the description of Madame d'Arblay in

Alex is not yet quite sure whether he shall make an excursion to Bath, which he has promised to Maria, *before* or *after* Richmond—so we will take no measures for his habitation till ⎮ he has an answer from Maria, to whom he writes by this day's post. Mrs. Lock's invitation we remit till after her Tunbridge water drinking. I think I shall better bear *beginning* to leave my own nearly sacred Cell with my dearest Charlotte— my partial, indulgent, ever tender Charlotte, than with any one else, however kind & sweet & attached; for we have notions upon sympathy that open our bosoms to each other with an unreserve that cannot but be genial & soothing to both.

As I can defer without the smallest inconvenience to some later period my arrival, I entreat you earnestly to answer me sincerely: only remembering, your *littel complaint* will rather hasten me *to* you, than *from* you, as it will en[able us] ⎮ to abscond from Company together:[3]—& I shall see the least I can of all but our Charlotte & her children till I am firmer in composure, & less fearful of giving pain to those who seek to give me pleasure — — pleasure! — — Oh my dear Charlotte—how wide is it from all within!—yet I am *infinitely* stronger in mind than I was, with respect to some renewed interest in society. Be quite sincere, my dearest Charlotte, I only name *Monday* as my first day possible—with no other preference. Heaven bless you.— ⎮

pray distribute my Love

1813 supplied by Thomas Campbell (vii, L. 660 n. 5) and by Mrs. Whalley (x, L. 1094 n. 25).

[3] The Diary of the month, however, shows almost daily visits from members of the Barrett family, Sarah Harriet Burney, the Cambridges, the Ellerker sisters (iv. 327), the marquise de Latour-Maubourg, and Madame de Maisonneuve, whose polite letter of 14 September (Berg) reflects her impressions of Mrs. Broome and the 'soulagement que m'a fait le petit moment que j'ai passé samedi avec vous chez Mad^e votre soeur dont la bonté nous a tous bien vivement touchés; et les agréments de sa charmante fille'. She will fix a date for a second visit to Ormond Place, 'ou je voudrais que nous fussions tous les jours, nous avons tous bien envie de faire une plus ample Connoissance avec la charmante famille de Mad^e votre soeur'.

[11 Bolton Street],
30 August–4 September 1819

To Esther (Burney) Burney

A.L.S. (rejected Diary MSS. 7210-13, Berg), 30 Aug.-4 Sept., 1819
Double sheet 4to   4 pp   black edged   *pmk* 4 SE 1819   black seal
Addressed: Mrs. Burney, / Lark Hall place, / near / Bath.
Readdressed: Mrs. Bourdois /As Belvedere
Endorsed by EBB: Augt 1819
Edited by CFBt. *See* Textual Notes.

30 Augst 1819

NB—Lisez ⟨premt⟩ à vous-même

As Alex is now planning a visit to Bath,[1] I will try to prepare for him a long Letter to my dearest Esther, for I have
many things to say to her,—though none so pressing as what,
alas, to say is needless, my true sympathy in my own dear
Mr. Burney's sufferings, & in her own from witnessing them
—alas!—alas!—

My swelling heart made me quit my Pen, my dear Hetty,
&, once out of my hand, I have sometimes a cruel difficulty
to take it up again—yet, when once *en train*, to You very
especially, I almost as unwillingly relinquish it. But Alex
thinks he shall set out to-morrow for the Belvedere,—for it
is now *Septr 3d*—& I cannot let him go without such signs of
Life as now remain in me to give. —— Your last Letter was
very very touching to me—my poor—poor—Esther!—Yet
'tis a very singular comfort that your favourite Mr. Sandford
could come a second time:[2] otherwise, the most corrosive of
all additions to distress of mind would have grown upon your
peace, with an idea that something might have been done
that was omitted. I believe you are rescued from that evil,
at least, by the perpetual recourse you have had to new &

1217. [1] On a change in the plans of his cousin Maria Bourdois, d'Arblay, post-
poning his visit to Bath, accompanied his mother to Richmond (L. 1216 n. 1).
  [2] In her letter of 22 May, op. cit., EBB had told of an operation performed on
her husband by his brother-in-law the surgeon William Sandford (L. 1191 n. 1),
'something resembling an issue—near the seat of the disease . . . little if any benefit has *yet* occurred'.

new resources, as fast as they could be suggested,—joined to your tender care & assiduous watchfulness.[3] How can you think a moment of apologising for not writing more frequently? In a situation such as yours no Letters at all can be expected by those who love you most, though news *from* you, & *of* you, is more than ever covetted. But Amelia would I am sure be your *Amanuensis* for a Bulletin of Health, when you are too much occupied, & too much oppressed, to take a pen yourself. I gather news of you as I can, & very anxiously, during the chasms ǀ in our—now—so melancholy Correspondence,—from James—from Clipstone Street,[4] (through James Street) & once from Maria to Alex previous to his Tour to the Continent,—& lastly, from Mr. Sansom,[5]— which was less exhilarating than any that had preceded it.— *Stationary*, he said, all seemed, when I sighed to hear it was not *ameliorating*! — — I know you will be glad I have seen that good creature, who is truly & fervently devoted to you, & that I was able to invite him to Tea, & an Evening's chat. It cost me much less pain & trouble than I had apprehended; for the *thought* of such an exertion had been very weighty upon my spirits. However, he has so much to say, & says so much, that there is not much effort required to give him entertainment. I do not write this epigrammatically; by no means; for his conversation is really sensible & good, though sententious & formal; but the latter is the simple effect of self-education, which, however, makes me but honour him the more. In truth, he is greatly improved, & I was very much pleased with him. He promised to tell you himself the history

[3] 'My poor Mr B. continues alas in such suffering state', EBB had stated in a subsequent letter of 19 July (Barrett, Eg. 3690, ff. 126-7b), 'that my attendance is required almost unceasingly, and you will believe this easily, when I tell you—that I have been but twice in Bath during the last month, or 5 weeks,— *You*, my poor Dear Fanny know better than I can describe the almost innumerable wants of an invalid . . . our Girls . . . cannot even be suffered to remain in the room with their poor Dear Father for more than half an hour at a time—oftentimes not so long.—'

[4] Charles Rousseau's brother Edward Francesco Burney (L. 1189 n. 12).

[5] James Sansom (L. 1191 n. 16), whom FBA had entertained on the evening of 24 August (Diary), was apparently prepared to dispose of the oriental musical instruments and a painting of the procession of the Great Mogul, for the provenance of which, see ix, L. 1052 n. 21. His wife Elizabeth Margaret (ibid.) had been employed by Marianne Francis (i, p. lxxiii) as a companion in her evening walks or outings.

of our Hindoo & Instruments, so I will not repeat it: but I have given him Carte blanche to adopt whatever measure you approve after his communication, that the matter may be brought to an issue. I am convinced not only that he may be fully trusted, but that he is in the way, better than any one else I know, to settle the business to our advantage. You will certainly have heard how his worthy *Wife* has been honoured?[5] his pleasure in that transaction it would be difficult to describe. She was not employed ǀ as the Work Woman, or Attendant,—but as the *Chaperon* of Miss Francis!—I should make you smile could I relate Mrs. J[ames] Burney's account of the good Sansom's exquisite exultation upon the opening of that proposition—But I cannot!—

It was a great comfort to me, indeed, to receive my dear Charlotte in the absence of Alex. She looks astonishingly better; & though her poor heart has been wounded to its inmost core by the loss of her darling Ralph,[6] she is recovering her spirits, her active life, & her health, & what is not *irre*-coverable of her happiness. I am going to her at Richmond as soon as I have parted from Alex for Bath. 'Tis my first attempt to bear any roof but my own, since that I made on my arrival in Town at our dear & excellent Brother's. That Brother is kinder & more amiable than ever. And his whole family have adopted the same plan of encreasing agreeability.

You must have been much surprised at the so quick return of Alex:[7] it has given a new fillip to my poor jaded existence that proves really serviceable to it. We shall go to-gether again to Richmond after his return—& perhaps, if I am strong enough, to Twickenham—but *certainly* to Elliot Vale, to Mrs. Lock, whose enquiries about you, & about dear Mr. Burney, are unfailing upon every Meeting, & every Letter.

---

[6] For CBFB's visit of 7–9 August (see Diary). Her son 'Dolph' (b. 1801) had died at Bath on 27 April 1817 (ix, Ll. 1064–71).

[7] AA had left for Paris on 10 May and returned *via* Calais on 16 August (Diary).

My pension has been announced to me as secure, which *you* will hear without surprize: but I see that *James*, more conversant with the politics of the opposition, which sought to annul all the benevolence, & even all the justice of the late revered Queen, had been so much alarmed for me, that he receives these tidings with as much pleasure as if they assured me of an *encrease* of income of £100 p^r annum—instead of the simple *continuance* of what I have regularly possessed for now nearly 30 years: & his affectionate heart was delighted in proportion to what had been its apprehensions. The confirmation, however, has been honourable & flattering. It was given by a visit from Mr. Vernon ׀ of the Treasury,[8] without any sort of application on my part. He told me that the secret committee on the Queen's affairs had Voted the continuance of my *annuity*; that the Parliament had granted it; & that the Prince Regent had signed its Warrant.[9]

I was not able to read with dry Eyes what you say of your *thankfulness* for all of *good* that has befallen your earthly abode, my dearest Esther, considering the affliction of the period in which you wrote it:[10] & especially I felt moved

[8] See L. 1215 n. 2.

[9] On 4 February 1819 the Prince Regent had sent a message to both Houses placing at the disposal of Parliament the sum of £58,000 per annum which, in the distribution of the civil list revenue, was to be appropriated to the maintenance of the establishment of the late Queen Charlotte. He pointed out that there existed certain claims on that sum from those who had served the Queen and asked that Parliament should grant such allowances to those individuals as it had been usual in the past for the Crown to bestow. See *J.H.C.* 74 (1819), 94–5; *J.H.L.* 52 (1819), 43. The Commons referred the matter to a Select (not a 'Secret') Committee and their report of 17 February was printed in an Appendix to *J.H.C.* 54 (1819), 1071, 1075, 'the general principle . . . being to suggest a provision for the female part of the Queen's Household, and for the domestic officers and menials, of whom the greatest portion have been for many years, and during the course of a long reign, attached to her service'.

The Act subsequently passed 'For the further regulation of His Majesty's Household' included the provision of £18,245 per annum to the late Queen's servants. The Act received Royal Assent on 6 April 1819 (59 Geo. III, cap. 22).

For this the editors are indebted to Mr. Maurice Bond, O.B.E., F.S.A., Records Office, House of Lords, Westminster.

[10] Such had been the hard life and the disappointments suffered by EBB and her husband as musicians and teachers of music in London that she could not feel sanguine about the success of JB and his appeal for favour nor indeed 'Expectations of any sort'. And she went on to review a career now drawing rapidly to a

by your recurrence to the origin of that Prize in the Matrimonial Lottery which was drawn so happily by your *first Born*.[11] The kindest of Partners in my every view—every wish—every feeling, gave to *me* then the *casting voice*, though himself always most partial to Maria, never accompanied me to the Belvedere without hailing with fresh satisfaction its remembrance—& in seeing, to use your own expressive words, that *it shed a happy influence over all the family*. I always, too, reflect with satisfaction that while to Maria it proved so every way propitious, it was perfectly congenial to her excellent Mate; who was certainly one of the most indulgent of Husbands, & always seemed happy in his lot. How sincerely have I ever regretted that the union was of such short duration!

I have much to tell you of my sweet Friend, Mme de Maisonneuve whom I see frequently, & with infinite consolation. But I must begin a

---

close. As to disappointments in the way of business, 'my worthy & in[d]ustrious partner has had *many* heavy ones,—of which you may be certain I bore a share — —. On many Occasions where in—had merit received it's deserts, his Applications *must* have been successful,—which however was far from being the Case —in 19 times out of 20.—& this circumstance kept us long in straightened Circumstances.—*Many* nevertheless, and *great* have been the blessings bestowed upon us, through the generous & affectionate aids of our dear & much loved relatives,—who in some degree made our Children their own.—in referring to this latter circumstance believe me—I do not forget your great kindness, thro' which our Dear first born,—gained a Prize, in the Matrimonial line—wch has shed a happy influence over all her family. of Dear blessed Susan, I will not speak—because I could *never* say Enough!!! — — The Dear good Barborne family have behaved like guardian Angels to us.—and our Dearly beloved Father was kind in life & his kindness did not terminate with his life!—upon the whole—I must be ever grateful for the large portion of happiness with which my abode in this World has been favored.—*far exceeding* it's miseries.—Yet—my Dear Fanny.—*if my* own Existence is *prolonged* Misery & affliction must *Encrease*—I say encrease,— because a larger portion than I now feel—is surely in store for me "Poor M^r B" —*tho' not now in immediate danger* is in a most precarious state.—& grows weaker.—Nothing does more than for a short time to *mitigate* suffering—You will see by what I have said, that I write *to you*, more than I should think proper for him to see.—' (Letter of 19 July, op. cit.)

[11] For the arranged marriage of 30 October 1800 between EBB's daughter Marianne and General d'Arblay's friend Antoine Bourdois, see iv, Ll. 379, 381, 394. The couple moved to Paris in 1802, but Bourdois died on 6 August 1806 (vi, L. 574 and *passim*).

Septr 4th

Alex has just received a Letter from Maria that leads him to postpone his visit—my dearest Esther! How I shall *now* desire to hear how *you* are as well as your dear—valuable Sufferer!—This being so ready, meant for *Alex*, I think I had best send it p^r post, to prevent uncertainty to Maria—for Alex is out, & though he intended to return, the post is in the street—& he could not write—

adieu & God bless & sustain you, my dear dear Etty

prays your true F d AY. |

Alex will now accompany me to Richmond—but all Letters will be forwarded to me from France—How shall I yearn for some—

1218   Ormond Place, Richmond,
                                        [*c.* 23] September 1819

To Mrs. Locke

L., copy in hand of CFBt (Diary MSS. viii. 7216-17, Berg), Sept. 1819
Single sheet 4to   2 pp.

To Mrs Locke

Ormond Place
Richmond. Septr 1819

How very your own kindest self was this so speedy & satisfactory intelligence of our Amine's safe arrival on the Continent![1] Heaven grant relief to that invaluable & most beloved

---

1218. [1] In these years Mrs. Angerstein, along with many of her compeers in the highest society, regularly went to Spa, in Belgium, for rest and change of air. 'Fashion and fancy, quite as strong in regard to remedies as to other objects in life, carry the periodical swarm of real or imaginary invalids to . . . the . . . springs of Spa', observed the fashionable physician Sir Henry Holland (1788–1873), *Recollections of Past Life* (1872), pp. 152–8, unabashedly recording that it was to the four consecutive summers he spent in Spa he owed 'those connections upon which professional success in London greatly depends'. The 'plea of health often put in at the end of the London season, to obtain sanction for a watering place

of Many! Anxiously I shall wait & watch the progress to be hoped for from the waters. At all events, the change of air will be beneficial & the change of scene must needs be recreative.—Mʳˢ Carter herself found amusement at Spa, from a variety of characters which she might not have met with, or have bestowed time to observe & devellope elsewhere:[2] for, in fact, almost every well inhabited spot contains as much diversity of the 'Human *Race* divine'[3] as it does of Cattle, Vegetation & Minerals—'tis only that which we see without trouble we see without interest, & where we are not forced to some expence of *money* we spare ourselves any of *thought*.

At Spa, & at other water drinking places, people open their Eyes & Ears because they must needs open their Purses, & therefore, as they pay ǀ well, they make some effort to be well paid.

⟶

I have been here above a fortnight with Alexander in the quiet dwelling of my good & tender Sister Charlotte.[4] She

abroad instead of a country house at home, is one which taxes both the conscience and judgment of the physician'.

According to Mrs. Locke, her 'poor harrassed Amelia' had need enough of rest by reasons of thinness, cough, and the trials incident to the illness of her aged father-in-law John Julius Angerstein (L. 1209 n. 9). 'She had all his letters of 3 weeks to answer & for the last 4 days never wrote less than from 10 to 13 out pʳ day' and she had had the pain of dismissing 'a person whom Mʳ A— had determined without any reason shoud not remain in the House'. The family had been upset also by the approaching nuptials of the octogenarian with a 'Lady of Quality' [Lady Rothes], half his age, plans that fell through, Farington said, when the Lady demanded 'a Carriage for herself & a separate bed' (ii. 229, 241).

Sir George and Lady Martin (L. 1191 n. 15) had set out on 14 August and John Angerstein, his wife, and three children, on 9 September. See Mrs. Locke's letters (Eg. 3697, ff. 196-205b) of [March] to 8 September 1819.

[2] In 1763, Lord Bath, to whom Spa had been recommended for his health, had made up a party including his friends Mr. and Mrs. Montagu (i, L. 3 n. 82) and her friend Elizabeth Carter (1717-1806), whose colourful account of the visit (16 June-17 August) FBA could have read in *Memoirs of the Life of Mrs. Elizabeth Carter . . .* , ed. the Revd. Montagu Pennington (1807), pp. 183-219. It seemed the 'high season', she said, 'for Princes and Princesses . . . *Serenissimos* and *Altesses*' and as well for 'Grave Bishops . . . English Lords and Ladies, High Dutch Barons, Low Dutch Burgomasters, and Flemish fat gentlewomen'. The Countess Spencer was there and Lady Mary Coke, and, on the walks, 'Priests and Hussars, Nuns and fine Ladies, stars and crosses, cowls and ribbons, all blended together in the most lively and picturesque manner imaginable'. See also Elizabeth Montagu's letter of 9 August, *Mrs. Montagu 'Queen of the Blues', her Letters and Friendships, 1762-1800*, ed. Reginald Blunt (2 vols., 1923), i. 53-4.

[3] *Paradise Lost*, iii. 44.   [4] Since 9 September (Diary).

permits me to live as like a *Recluse* as I can desire, without opposition even in her wishes, for her gentle Nature seeks only to accommodate & indulge those of others. My Alex, however, & my own promise—both urged with penetrating exhortation by my admirable Made de Maisonneuve, unite to keep me in order, notwithstanding the dangerous temptation of finding the reins of my self-government in my own hands. I am much better, therefore, prepared for Elliot Vale than while I resisted your kind summons, from terror of only carrying unhappiness unmitigated in return for your and my Amine's sweet sympathies.—& yet.—oh how changed I feel! how blighted—if not blasted! — —

1219   6 Ormond Place, Richmond,
                             26–27 September 1819

To Esther (Burney) Burney

A.L.S. (rejected Diary MSS. 7218-12, Berg), 26-7 Sept. 1819
Double sheet 4to   black-edged   4 pp.   *pmks* R.L. 27 SP 1819
⟨   ⟩.819   wafer
Addressed: Mrs. Burney / Lark Hall place / near / Bath.
Endorsed by EBB: answered.—
Edited by CFBt. *See* Textual Notes.

                          Sunday—Septr ⟨26⟩ 1819
                          6. Ormond Place, Richmond.

What can I say to my poor Esther—but Blessed be her excellent Partner![1] Blessed in the World to which he is translated as he was virtuous in This which he has left! Your preparation has been more—far more than sufficient, for

1219. [1] Charles Rousseau Burney had died on 23 September 1819, at the age of 71, and was buried at Batheaston. His obituary, copied into the 'Worcester Journal' from the *New Monthly Magazine*, xii (1 December 1819), 608, extolled his 'friendly and domestic virtues' and his 'genius for music'. '[He] excelled on a variety of instruments, but the piano-forte was his favourite. . . . His execution was rapid and brilliant, his precision and feeling were exquisite; his taste matured by the finest judgment. . . .' As a composer, his 'fancy and invention' were manifested in 'extempore performances . . . [and] for hours and days he poured forth unpremeditated strains of harmony, at once original, energetic, & impressive. . . .'

from the time you were Yourself convinced the Cure was *hopeless, I*, even *I* conceive the wish to retain him, on terms of such ineffectual sufferings, must have passed away — — must have changed into wishes for his release — ? — heart-breaking wishes, even while leading to resignation for his loss. — — Poor Cecilia's terrible account to Sarah,[2] which the latter sent to Charlotte Barrett last night, & which reached Charlotte & myself about 10 o'clock, when we were left alone, all else being retired, was truly mournful to us,—yet shewed a dreadfulness of malady to ward off all murmurring at the final event, with all its awful sadness:—but of our poor dear sister, our truly loved Esther, & her affliction, we sate talking with deepest interest & pity half the Night—we knew not how to separate, such tender hold of us had the subject. Anxiously, most anxiously shall I wait for some news of you. What you must yourself have gone through, however short of what your beloved Patient indured, must yet have been direfully trying for your Constitution as well as your poor Heart.—Charlotte & I have been thankful we were together, for our mutual interest soothed our grief, & we could have found no third that in an equal degree ǀ would have felt with us—I mean for tender *discourse*—& retrospec-tions of dear old scenes: not for active *service*; *there* our excellent James will be left behind by no one. I shall not even wonder should he set out to you to Bath. If he believes you to wish & want him, I am sure he will not hesitate, for I think his heart grows kinder & warmer towards his sisters every day. Edward I hope is arrived at your melancholy Dwelling[3]—for Cecilia mentions that Maria had written to invite him.—Him, indeed, I shall pity to have missed the sight of his excellent—& last Brother!—yet to have arrived sooner, where the disease was so desperate, could only have aggravated your distress from the distress it would have ex-cited in Edward's feeling mind. Surprize, however, no part of the family can have experienced, so long & grievous have been the preparatory strokes.—

If—at this calamitous period, there should be any Ex-pence which £.40 could help, I could spare that Sum—from

---

[2] Cecilia Burney's letter to SHB or to Sally (JB's daughter) is missing.
[3] Edward Francesco Burney (L. 1189 n. 12), the artist, brother of the deceased.

particular circumstances for which it is here after destined, *many months*, nearly a year,—without the smallest inconvenience; & I could transmit it, from Messrs Hoare to Sr B. Hobhouse, by a single line, at a day's *notice*.[4] Believe me, my dearest Esther, it would be a true & warm satisfaction to me that you should permit me to do this, which without your leave I dare not.

I beg my true condolences to Maria—Sophy—& Cecilia —But oh how I rejoice they are with you! They will give themselves up, I am sure, to endeavours to offer ⎸ & ⟨prevenir⟩ you comfort. Fanny & Amelia will hereafter, I hope, take their turn, with Richard—

But Friday, I was writing to Mrs. F Bowdler upon the advantage, in events of this afflicting nature, to have many Children, instead of one child—such various & varying interests in life help to make it supportable under Heaven's severest dispensations: And, with all the dispersions of a large family, 2 or 3 always remain.[5] — — But *one* is continually absent. —We have been here, however, Alexander & I, above a fortnight—& the change of air, & necessary exertions, have certainly done good to my health—& forced my spirits also from their heaviness & profound dejection.—I have promised in October to go to Mrs. Lock,[6] whom hitherto I have not been able to muster courage for visiting, though I have received her with consoling thankfulness. *She*, I am sure, will feel for you with great tenderness—though she has long been expecting the blow—But what expectation can impede it's severity?—

I do not speak for our good Charlotte, who is determined to write herself. God bless & sustain you, my very dear Esther! & spare your Health—to preserve your dear & valuable life Prays your truly affec^te sister

F d'A^y

I beg my direction to be always 11. Bolton Street—Berkeley Square — — whence my Letters safely follow. ⎸

[4] For the bankers, see L. 1186 n. 2. The sum of £40 was duly sent. See Diary for 9, 10, 11 November. Also Hoares' Ledgers, 10 November: 'To Bank Post Bills sent to M^rs E Burney £40.'

[5] FBA's letter of 24 September to Frances Bowdler (Diary) is missing.

[6] FBA's visit to Eliot Vale was to take place in December (see L. 1226 n. 2).

Monday—Charlotte has just told me she will defer writing to the end of the week, to keep our commerce more up without fatiguing you too much, as I have written—she is sure—the sentiments of both—

I think I shall return to-morrow or next day to Town from business that calls me there—once more God Almighty bless & keep you dearest Esther—

How I shall be glad should the £.40 be of any use! I can extend to a *year*—or even more, upon further calculations—

1220   [11 Bolton Street],
30 September [1819]

To Mrs. Broome

A.L.S. (Berg), 30 Sept.
Double sheet 8vo   4 pp.   black-edged

Thursday 30. Sept^r.

Unwillingly—& ungayly we left you, my ever dear Charlotte—you & your *Charmante famille*, in the words of my dear Mme de Maisonneuve,[1] & I have wished to write almost as soon as I could no longer speak: but the desire to give you some tidings of our poor Esther kept me quiet yesterday, when I could not obtain any—but shall not keep me silent to day, though I am still completely without intelligence. To my great surprize I found no Letters here, except *Foreign*; not a line from Bath, nor any news whatsoever, save that poor Edward called here on the *Thursday,*[2] to enquire for me, & whether I had any commissions or | Letters for Bath, whither he was going *next day*, Friday, having received intelligence that his Brother was very dangerously ill indeed. Ramsay says he looked in great distress. How sorry am I for him if he entertained any hope of again seeing poor good Mr. Burney!

1220. [1] See her letter (Berg) of 14 September (L. 1216 n. 3).
   [2] Thursday 23 September. See L. 1219 and n. 3.

—At the time he was talking with Ramsay[3] already his poor Brother had breathed his last!—Alexander went yesterday to James Street; but the whole Family was out—& the maid said were gone to Fanny Raper's.[4] Probably some old or customary engagement for Michaelmas Day. The weather to day has detained me at home—but if Alex, who goes again, returns before the post parts hence, I will add what I can gather from him.

All here of our house find me looking better than when I left it. To that I am now indifferent; but not to the *inference*, that my dearest Charlotte's sympathizing & ⏐ soothing society has been every way beneficial to me. I always felt it would be so—May as much for the Future be in store for me as in the Past has been denied me!

I delight in thinking my loved Charlo*ttina*[5] amending in health & strength: yet she was fatigued & seemed heated the last afternoon—I hope that is passed, & that she is now all her own sweet self.

My kind love, & many thanks to Marianne[5] for her numerous attentions & daily augmenting hospitality of manner. Her kindness to Alex was so exactly of the right sort that I regret he has not such a Cousin continually at his Elbow. So does he, I promise you! Julia is budding forth with resemblances to her dear Mother: Dick is a noble Boy—& I doubt not when I have spirits—if ever!—for the *renconntre*, I shall delight in all five. Meanwhile, distribute my kind love around you, with best ⏐ Compliments to Mr. Barratt—& to my valued old Friend the Archdeacon, & his amiable Partner.[6] How kind did we find every body! yet *entire repose* will, for a short season, be good for me—so great a change of life, for *me*, was that of Ormond place. I have even put off Mme de Maisonneuve for a few days. I have, also, very much *Home*, though not *social* occupation in preparing to live in the front Drawing room. Alex will bear no further delay; & I have people there Now all day long, hammering, cleaning, Nailing, brushing, & what not? But to make this exertion at once is

---

[3] FBA's maid (L. 1182 n. 3).

[4] See L. 1180 nn. 1, 2; and L. 1193 n. 5.

[5] For the members of Mrs. Broome's family, see i, pp. lxxii–lxxiii.

[6] See L. 1190 n. 2; L. 1205 n. 6; and *HFB*, pp. 187-93 and *passim*.

all that can make him forgive my not living & dying in Ormond Place.

Adieu, my dearly loved Charlotte—be, very very careful of yourself I earnestly entreat—& always prepare for a *month's* Brighton, that the winter may be safe, after it, for Ormond Place & Bolton Street—Heaven bless you, my love, as I think you deserve!—

F. d'Ay

1221   11 Bolton Street,
                                  4 October 1819

To Esther (Burney) Burney

A.L.S. (rejected Diary MSS. 7222-5, Berg), 4 Oct. 1819
Double sheet 4to   black-edged   4 pp.   *pmk* OC⟨   ⟩   black seal
Addressed: Mrs. Burney / Lark Hall place / Bath.
Endorsed by EBB: answered / Oct, 6. / 2ᵈ answer by / Parcel— / Oct, 27ᵗʰ
Edited by CFBT. *See* Textual Notes.

4ᵗʰ Octʳ 1819
Bolton Street, Berkeley Square.

I receive your Letter[1] with great thankfulness, my dearest Esther, & even—in the midst of its sadness,—& of my own —with a species of *Joy*, for I had terrified myself with many an apprehension lest your poor hand should have retrograded by your long sufferings. — — his I account yours!—& have reduced you again to an amanuensis, as at Turnham Green.[2] I am truly relieved by the sight of your own Writing, & I may say *edified* by the resigned composure of your sorrow under so deep an affliction. Yet I conceive that I — — even I— should have given a similar example, had as deadly a preparation preceded my bereavement!—but though for some weeks

1221. [1] This letter, received by FBA on 4 October (Diary), is missing, but for a partial paraphrase and a commentary, see L. 1222.
[2] EBB was afflicted with rheumatism or arthritis in her hand since 1814-17, when she lived at Turnham Green.

awakened—wretchedly awakened to a fear of *danger*, &, at times, agonized with a view of its encrease, I never was *hopeless*!—I *always*—*nearly* always—thought his constitution would give time for the cure, & surmount the disease! This, while it spared me your previous pains, has rendered my subsequent woe so profound—so permanent—so desolating! — — And yet, my dearest Esther, neither You nor I would have changed our lots with those of our 2 dear sisters who could never have known such grief:[3] 'twas our superiour happiness that has made our affliction—& I would not part with I the *recollection* of my rare felicity for the *enjoyment* of any other the World could offer!—I write so immediately because I cannot help it, my mind is so full of you; but I by no means expect an answer for a good while to come. so do not read me with any of that sort of worry upon your poor spirits. I will execute your commissions to James Street, Richmond, & Chelsea. I hope Edward, the excellent Edward, is with you still. Fanny I have heard is still at Sandgate. The two Charlottes charged me to beg you would not think of replying to them this month. I left them 2 or 3 days ago— not without some difficulty; but I resisted their kindness from a real necessity to be again in perfect repose. My long seclusion from any family or social general intercourse, made me seem to live in a whirlwind, quiet & retired, for all others, as was my sojourn with our tender & considerate Charlotte. However, the *break* is made—& I shall now, probably, glide into common life imperceptibly—not gaily! not cordially! —but indispensably, &,—I hope—chearfully! — — — Alex demands it unceasingly, & Alex is my first duty & comfort on Earth.

I see clearly, by your Letter, what I had soothed myself with anticipating, that many survivors of a beloved object necessarily lighten the burthen of the calamity they share. My *only* Alex has been so much away from me, &, when with me, is so occupied by his studies, that, dear as he is to me— indescribably dear! I have often—often regretted I had not also a *Daughter*: a female has a thousand ways both to I occupy & to console a Mother that a male cannot approach:

[3] If as widows, they had been called on to mourn for Molesworth Phillips (iv *passim*) and Ralph Broome (v *passim*), respectively.

a *male* rarely gives; he always *wants* aid: & that want, indeed, is what has constantly kept me from inertion, by calling forth continual employment for all my faculties. I am extremely gratified by all you say to me on this subject of your Daughters, to whom I beg to be kindly remembered. It is easy to me, indeed, to conceive how they must cling to you at such a moment.

James was with me on Saturday: he is about a New Work![4] How happy is this activity of mind in the midst of much disturbance as to the prospect of his affairs! He told me he had pressed you to James Street, for change of scene. It was truly like him, & I can be his *Garantee* that you would, & will give him the most lively pleasure should you accept his hospitable invitation.

Shall I tell you m[y] own idea for you? My *advice*, permit me to say, & my *wish*? It is that you would go, as early in November a[s] you can arrange your affairs, &c, to the seaside:[5] *Brighton* seems the favourite spot of our family; but the *sea-side* at any rate would brace & revive you above all things. It would be best for your *hands*, against Winter, & the change of air would strengthen & brighten you. It would certainly do *good*, also, to the delicate Cecilia, & could not do *hurt* to Amelia; I earnestly therefore desire you should break up house keeping at Bath for a few *Months*, & try that totally new life, for your real & solid recruit. I should think that even Maria & Sophy would be all the better for a similar plan. With respect to expence I must now add my sincerest Thanks for your *promise* to give me the preference; what you tell me of *Blue* I could have *guessed*;[6] so, she has ever been, kind, generous, useful, but you have given me great pleasure by the anecdote of Chas Parr, whom I shall love I the better for it all

---

[4] Possibly *A Commentary on the Systems which have been advanced for explaining the Planetary Motions* (privately printed, 1819), a work dedicated to Sir Joseph Banks. See Manwaring, chapter xi, for the publication of JB's last years and the papers he delivered at the Royal Society.

[5] EBB, with her daughters Cecilia and Amelia, was to spend the months (May–October 1820) at Minehead, Somersetshire.

[6] EBB's sister-in-law and cousin Elizabeth Warren Burney (L. 1180 n. 15).

my life.[7] I hope you will not be angry, my dear Etty, to receive from me an old Muff Box, by the Coach, containing the melancholy Bonnet & Cap first made for me at Bath Venns & Bristows,[8] which I have never worn but 3^{ce}——once, to church at Bath, & 2^{ce} to the D^{ss} of Gloucester's;[9] as Mrs. Payne[10] made me duplicates so admirably, that,——stirring out so little ——I never had occasion for them during my first deep outward mourning, & Now they are useless to me. You will be supplied, no doubt; but they may serve to save what is fresher. I send also the warm Gloves I wore while I thought no *Muff* sufficiently black. —— —— This is a sisterly liberty, & therefore so dear a sister will take it in good part. Alex is with me till about the middle of October, when he goes to Cambridge; I *hope* not for long. He begs his best remembrances & best thanks to Maria & Sophy for their very affectionate Letters to him. He *read himself into Church* at Twickenham, in Mr. Archdeacon's Chapel,[11] in an Evening Service, while

[7] Some account doubtless, of CPB's characteristic generosity, but lost with EBB's letter. Cf. L. 1189 n. 6.

[8] This was a dressmaking and millinery concern, established in 1814 by the three ladies Mary Ann Bath, Frances Venn, and Maria Briscoe, with a 14-year lease of the premises No. 8, Old King Street.

Daughter of Griffith Briscoe (1742-95), hatter and haberdasher of 35 Broad Street, Bath, and his wife Susanna *née* Webb (1748-1820), Maria Briscoe (1782-1862) would marry on 5 November 1819 as his 2nd wife the Revd. William Sturges (*c.* 1760-1829), vicar of Wakefield, Yorkshire, where she later resided. Frances Venn (1787-1870), youngest child and 7th daughter of Henry Venn (1738-1806) of Payhembury, Devonshire, would marry at Walcot Church on 27 December 1819 Maria's brother Thomas Webb Briscoe (1777-1853), who, inheriting his father's business (*supra*), was to add to it an undertaking concern and eventually to move it to 22 Market Place, Bath. Mary Ann Bath (b. 18 March 1792) was the eldest daughter of William Bath (*fl.* 1760-92) of High Littleton, Somerset, by his wife Dorothea *née* Venn (1767-1823), eldest sister of Frances (*supra*). See John Venn, *Annals of a Clerical Family, being some account of the Family and Descendants of William Venn, Vicar of Otterton, Devon, 1600-1621* (1904), p. ⌐276⌐.

According to Indentures (dated 31 August 1814), which were kindly supplied to the editors by Dr. P. A. Briscoe of Leeds University, Miss Briscoe was to superintend the dressmaking and millinery; Miss Venn, to keep the books; and Miss Bath, to take charge of the housekeeping and all domestic matters. The firm was to survive, under various managements, until 1833 or a little later.

[9] Since 27 March 1819, the date of FBA's initial summons to Gloucester House, she had made at least five visits, and on 26 July was presented to the Duke (Diary).   [10] See L. 1180 n. 11.

[11] The Twickenham or Montpelier Chapel (L. 1190 n. 2), where AA read prayers on 19 September and again on the 26th. For a further trial, see L. 1230 n. 4.

we were at Charlotte's — — & *Well*, Well, Well—I was There, & melted, overpowered with the sounds of his really fine voice—in so solemn a service & a place. Mr. Cambridge said to me, afterwards—'The General Thanksgiving I never heard read with more feeling, taste, or piety, by any body! — —' Imagine my grateful sensations!

adieu, dearest Esther.

I beseech you to walk out, when you can—you are well situated to do it quietly—& it is *essential* to you. I go into the Green park almost daily, with great advantage. You were very good to give me that hint about your affairs. *All*, I hope, is in, & to *pass through*, your hands—& that Long all may continue so, is the true prayer of y^r aff^e.

FdAy

1222 [11 Bolton Street,
pre 5 October 1819]

To Mrs. Locke

L., copy in hand of CFBt (Diary MSS. viii. 7214-15, Berg), 1819
Single sheet 4to   1 p.

To Mrs Lock

1819

— — — — —My invaluable Madame de Maisonneuve with her admirable Brother & truly *digne* Belle Soeur, are all spending a week or so with the Duke de san Carlos,[1] the Spanish

1222. [1] A descendant of several great families of the Spanish-American nobility, Don José Miguel de Carvajal Vargas y Maurique, 3rd duque de San Carlo (1771-1828), was born in Lima, Peru. A diplomat, immersed always in intrigues, he was appointed ambassador to Vienna (1815) and to London (1817-20).

A lover, by the way, of Mme de Talleyrand, he had married as his second wife Doña Maria Eulalia de Queralt y Silva (*fl.* 1808-19), daughter of Juan Bautista de Queralt y de Pinos, conde de Santa Colma, marqués de Besora (d. 1803). See Alberto Garcia Carraffa (1882-   ), *Enciclopedia héraldica y genealogica hispano-americana* (90 vols., 1919-). Mme de Maisonneuve's letter (Berg) of 8 November was written from their residence Nay Place, Crayford, near Blackheath.

Ambassador & his Lady.[1] Oh what a letter had I yesterday from that excellent Mme de M.! a Masterpiece of tender but forcible exhortation, calling upon me to quit my secluded mode of life in terms nearly—nay, in great measure, *quite* resistless![2]—I felt so piercingly the truth of most of what she urged, that I was almost annihilated by its effect half the day, —so fondly do I cling to all from which she would drag me!
— — But when I found, by that shake to my whole system, that she must be *right*, or I could not so have been affected by her representations, I determined, *coute qui coute*, to try, at least, to yield to her persuasive admonitions; for I *felt*— I *feel*—that He whom I so heart-brokenly mourn, would have joined in her injunctions had his noble & disinterested Spirit anticipated my misery.

I will shew you her beautiful Letter,[3] or send it I you, that you may participate in her desire to be known & loved by you—

1223   [11 Bolton Street,
                         5]–15 October [1819]

To Mrs. Broome

> A.L.S. (rejected Diary MSS. 7140-3, Berg), -15 Oct.
> Double sheet 4to   4 pp.   black edged
> *Addressed*: Mrs. Broome / Richmond / Surry
> *Dated in pencil*, p. 1: Oct 15 1819
> *Edited by* CFBt. *See* Textual Notes.

'Twas a kind surprise to see your hand so soon, my dearest Charlotte.—a surprise I shall give in return, by so quick a sight again of mine, but not—I am very sure, an unwelcome one — — I enclose, for she desires it, my Letter from our poor dear Esther.[1] You will find she took, as I meant, all I said

[2] Cf. L. 1222 n. 7.   [3] See further, L. 1223 n. 7.

1223. [1] Letters from CBFB and from EBB, received on 4 October (Diary) are missing.

of concern & interest & affection as from us both. I received this yesterday morning—& devoted the day to answering it. Her composure & resignation are very touching, & moved my heart—but I see with great satisfaction, what I have always observed elsewhere, how much less insupportable is such a deprivation where there are many to share its calamity. With *6 Children*, how various are the interests in life necessarily keeping off the gloom of seclusion! 4 of these are under her Eye, & 2 of them, probably entirely at her disposal, Cecilia & Amelia. I saw with concern that the latter, Fanny, & Richard are not numbered among her consolers:[2] but it may be they are omitted only from having been absent. I hope it! for the dear soul will be very susceptible indeed to any omission of regard & attention from them at such a dreadful epoch.—dreadful, in defiance of all ǀ preparation! & even of her *prayers for his release*! poor dear Esther! I am glad you have written, as well as my other Charlotte, notwithstanding her injunction to the contrary: I know all marks of sympathy are welcome, when they do not demand immediate acknowledgement: & I have told her, in my Letter of yesterday, that you had *both* desired me to add my assurances to your own that she would not think of burthening her poor shattered spirits by any reply.

You will be as glad as I am at the hint at the end relative to the Will. I fancy she is left sole Executrix & Residuary Legatee.[3] Her account of Maria is very comforting. I hope, therefore, she will settle gently & affectionately in the bosom of her children, yet come hither to visit her Brother & Sisters, & go to the sea side to brace her harrassed nerves. You will be glad to observe the consolation she justly desires from her own conscious acquittal of every tender duty the cruel malady called into exertion. Mr. Burney, the good & innocent Mr. Burney, deserved them all from her hands, for never was husband more fondly & more even exclusively devoted to his

---

[2] The Revd. Richard Allen Burney (L. 1180 n. 18), Rector of Rimpton, Curate of Brightwell (ix, L. 1017 n. 12), seemed never to be in good health. His sister Frances (L. 1194 n. 4) had gone to Sandgate.
[3] No will has been found.

wife. You will be glad, too, that Chas. Parr took so kind &
considerate a part in their mutual sufferings.[4] *Blue's* so doing
seems but of course, equally from her double relationship &
her known generosity of Character.[5]—But—how I feel for
her that there was no one to undertake the last dread offices!
—Alas!—oh my Charlotte, what a vision—a mere vision is
this mortal life! ¹ how quick it passes away, even in its longest
term! How well not only I, but *you* must remember this good
Mr. Burney a shy, modest, embarrassed, half-formed youth!
—though perhaps your memory only extends to him as a
Married Man, for you were quite a little Girl at the time of
the wedding.[6] The *End* brings to remembrance the *Beginning*,
as if no interval had separated them!—I think of him more,
therefore, from my first recollections than from all that
occur of later date: & I think of him with constant esteem
for his worth & innocence. He was really & truly *without
Guile*.

My excellent & pious Mad^e de Maisonneuve's Letter,[7] or
rather exhortation, I certainly meant to shew to my sweet
Charlottes both, & I hope it is the *right* one I had put apart,
& have left; is it in *two* small sheets? If so, read at your leisure: & preserve it carefully till we meet—or rather transmit
it to me by post in some future Letter: for it extorted from
me an engagement of exertion that ought to make me re-read
it occasionally, to keep in mind the tie, & excite my reluctance into activity — — Not very easy, with a soul so oppressed with heart-pierced sorrow!—but her words are Truth,
dressed in tenderness, & I will not struggle against them. Wishing & loving to shew the character Religious, & Noble, sincere

---

⁴ Cf. L. 1221 n. 7.   ⁵ See L. 1180 n. 15.

⁶ The marriage of the cousins had taken place on 20 September 1770. See *ED*
i. 96–7, 101–2: 'Hetty, my dear Hetty, has given herself away from us. She has
married at last her faithful Charles. God send her happy!'

⁷ The letter is missing but see FBA's paraphrase (L. 1222). Mrs. Locke,
apprized of its contents, seconded from her heart Madame de Maisonneuve's
recommendation that FBA cease to live as a recluse and resume her place in
society. 'In so doing we fullfill the sacred wishes of *Him* who depended on us for
withdrawing you gradually from that unrestrained grief which if indulged wou'd
deprive His & Your Alex of his remaining guide & shelter,—I ought to have said
only *his Alex*. For *self* even there, will always be a weak motive with my beloved
Friend—I am charged by our Am^e to add her entreaties to M^e de M^s & mine that
however painful you will tear yourself from seclusion. . . .' See her letter of 8 September, op. cit., and a letter (Barrett Eg. 3697, f. 206) of [June 1820].

& tender, of my dear chosen Friend—Chosen by my Friend of Friends, who gave us to each other on my first entrance into his Country, — —

What a break is there between the time I began this Letter, & this moment, *15. Oct^r* when I finish it!—overwhelming sensations stopt me in the last paragraph at the time, & before my pen could again be in movement, accidental ׀ occurrences intervened, & I then meant to send this by Alex—but his motions were so *abrupt*, after being so *retardy* that he went off in a whirl[8] — — of which you know the consequence!—what a *whirligig* he is! He sends his love & duty & 10000 thanks for your kindness, & your loan & he hopes to give the one & return the other in person as soon as he returns from Cambridge, whither he goes next week.

Mrs. Lock is at Elliot Vale, from Tunbridge,[9] & awaiting us, but I cannot yet fix our visit, as we have French business now in hand that necessitates our staying at present in town. The excellent Ambassadress has been very ill—which excited me to visit her — — the entrance into the house of the dearest Friend of my beloved & honoured Departed—affected me greatly:—It was right, however, & I am glad it is over. I have been there once since, to Tea.[10] The Ambassadress is better, & her amiable Husband & Sister are quite well. They

---

[8] On Saturday 9 October AA had gone on a visit to Archdeacon and Mrs. Cambridge at Twickenham Meadows, returning on Monday the 11th. On 26 October he was to return to Cambridge, presumably for the audit (L. 1185 n. 4). In the intervening time he read a good deal of French drama to his mother at home, and when abroad was often the guest of the French ambassador and his family (Diary).

[9] In the absence of her daughters at Spa, Mrs. Locke set off on 9 September for a two-week visit to her old friend Lady Templetown (1746–1823), who with her daughter Sophia Upton (1780–1853) seems to have been at this time at Tunbridge Wells. See Mrs. Locke's letters of [13 August] and 8 September, op. cit. It was on her return that she hoped FBA and AA would visit her at Eliot Vale, a 'high satisfaction' she had been trying all summer to arrange.

[10] FBA's visit, her 'First to the Dwelling of my dear Ambassador and Mme de Maisonneuve', was made on 6 October (Diary). 'I embraced my sweet Friend —& gave my hands to her amiable Brother, with still more of anguish, than of pleasure! for Oh! what a Void—What a Chasm . . . was the absence of Him who would . . . have felt transported with delight *so* to behold his noble Friend.' The visit was repeated on the 8th, however, and returned. Madame de Maisonneuve called at Bolton Street at least nine times in October.

were here to day. All enquire after you, & desire kind remembrances. Your *prescription* has done me, I think much good. This will please my dearest Charlotte: Tell it also to dear Marianne, on account of the interest she takes in poor Mr.   , whose Family, I hope, is recovering.[11] Do you know yet when to expect Clement?[12] When you are *aware* of his movements, pray tell me—& I shall not come to you *the less*, my kindest Charlotte, for coming a little *the later*. Our good James was here yesterday, perfectly well. Edward is returned from Bath, where all are tolerably well. I am not yet settled in my Front Room. Adieu, sweet sister!

ever & ever yours
F d'Ay—

pray keep the Brush till we return—

To Day I have had a visit from poor Beckey. Her Sister Mrs. Waters, Molly,[13] has again married: & the other sister, Maria, has taken George for her Spouse—He is 5 or 6 years at least her Junior. They have set up a China Shop at Chelsea. Beckey lives with her Father & Mother, much regretting, she confesses, that she did not take a husband also, when one, or

[11] Probably one of the 'poor families' of Richmond whom Marianne Francis visited, her sister said, 'in all weathers'. Strongly influenced by Arthur Young and by the Wilberforces, to whom in 1811 he had introduced her (see Gasley, pp. 602 ff.), she made friends among the active evangelists of her time. Having devoted her life to social betterment and to study (languages and music), during one of her extended visits to Kensington Gore she had taught young Samuel Wilberforce (later Bishop of Oxford and Winchester) Latin and in 'a school over the stables . . . 45 children'.

[12] In the summer of 1819 a group of Cambridge students, including Clement Francis (L. 1188 n. 2), had formed a reading party in the Lake District and he may have gone on to Scotland. '[He] is at the Lakes & Keswick', reported CFBt in a letter (Barrett, Eg. 3703A, ff. 112–13b) of 23 August 1819 to Arthur Young, 'sowing his last crop of wild oats before he begins reading for the church, preparatory to taking orders'. Charles John Shore (1796–1885), 2nd Baron Teignmouth, who had joined the party, remarked on Clement's health and 'the occasional overclouding of his mental faculties' (*Reminiscences*, i. 222–4).

[13] Rebecca More (*fl.* 1794–1819), formerly CB's cook, later housekeeper, and so denominated in his will (PRO/PROB/11/1554/202, dated 12 January 1807), by which date she has served him 13 years. A daughter of the 'Old Molly' mentioned in JB's will (PRO/PROB/11/1653/56, pr. 22 February 1822), she had a sister Mary (*fl.* 1793–1819) or 'young Molly', also one of CB's servants, who had married *pre* 1804 a Mr. Walker, a whitesmith (ii, L. 68 n. 30), for whose child CB stood godfather on 28 September 1804 ('Memoirs', Berg). Remarrying, she may be the 'Mary Standhal', also mentioned in JB's will (*supra*). A third sister, Maria, seems to have married CB's houseman or servant of the years 1813–14.

two, offered themselves, at the time she was younger. 'I might as well, she added, for fear I should not have another such opportunity, for I shall never think myself settled, if I don't get a husband at last |

Kiss sweet Julia for me, & be my Deputy to receive from my *God Boy* one of his best Bows[14]—& embrace your dear name sake tenderly in my Name—my Love & my thanks to Marianne & ⟨best⟩ comp^ts to Mr Barratt & at Twickenham

1224   11 Bolton Street,
                              12–17 November 1819

To Mrs. Waddington

A.L. (Berg), 12–17 Novr 1819
Double sheet 4to   4 pp.   *pmk* 17 NO .819   black seal
Addressed: Mrs. Waddington / Llanover House / near Abergavenny.

12th Novr 1819
Bolton Street Berkeley Square
No. 11.

Your very touching Letter my dear—*ever* dear Mary—I have had no courage to answer—yet every Day since I received it I have wished to write.[1] I will suffer, however, no longer procrastination that I may bear no longer silence total from Yourself. The heavy visitation You have had ought rather to approximate than to separate us.—if you were at hand—the true & tender interest with which I should enquire into every circumstance, & listen to every detail of that fair Flower, so untimely cropt, would soften your grief, by giving

---

[14] For the Barrett children, see i, pp. lxxii–lxxiii.

1224. [1] This may have been a reply (now missing) to the letter of condolence that FBA had written on 19 August (Diary) to Mrs. Waddington on news of the death on 12 April 1819 of her second daughter Emelia. A semi-invalid for most of her life, Emelia had married at Rome on 19 May 1817 George Manley (*pre* 1793–1858), originally of West Buckland, Somerset, Colonel and Adjutant-General of the papal troops at Rome (ix, L. 1063 n. 6). The marriage was by no means a happy one, and she had returned to Llanover, as she said, to die. See Bunsen, *Life*, i. 136–8.

it vent, & lighten the heavy swellings of the poor o'er burthened heart, by committing it to Nature. Then—perhaps
— — you, too, might draw me into a reciprocation of those
sympathies which alone have power to bestow any bosom-
soothing after calamities so irremediable. — — Write to me,
my dear Friend, of your Fanny,[2]—tell me *her* plans, & hopes,
& *your's* for your future re-union. To that alone I look forward for your restoration to any contentment that is not
factitious. I myself, to whom Happiness in this nether sphere
is cut off for-ever, I am now beginning—or rather trying to
begin—to drag myself out of my dread obscurity from the
earnest representations of my family & friends, and — —
far far more, from the agitating impatience of Alexander,
who thinks that my retirement is killing to myself while it is
cruel to him.—Such motives there is no obstinately with-
standing,—for though I have withstood them so long it has
been from incapacity to do otherwise almost as much as from
repugnance. Time, even in a woe like mine, wears away,
through the uniting operations of Religion, for Resignation,
& Despondency, for resistance, the acuteness of Grief;—but
the weight of sadness, the sick heaviness of a wholly changed
inside Time itself, with all its aids, & all its Concomitants,
never can wear away!—I have a constant feel as if half my
internal composition were converted to literal lead — —

For the sake of my Alexander, I might have prevailed
upon myself to make an earlier struggle for returning to my
Friends, & some of the interests of mortal life; but the truth
is I could not believe I could ever have survived This stroke:
what Killed my Happiness I thought would Kill my Existence.

Tell me of your Fanny—

Your description of *Her* blessed lot, with her sense of it,
has resemblances that move me greatly.

---

[2] FBA's god-daughter Frances *née* Waddington (see *DNB*) had married in
Rome on 1 July 1817 the Prussian linguist, savant, and diplomat Christian Charles
Josias Bunsen (1791-1860). For his distinguished career, an account of his courtship, the happiness of his marriage, the births and the loss of some of his children,
see Bunsen, *Memoirs*, i. 79-113. Of the twelve children born to the couple, the
eldest Henri George (1818-85), B.A. (Oxon., 1840), rector of Donnington, was
a Biblical scholar. Ernest (1819-1903) was the 2nd child. The daughter that FBA
wished for was to be born on 22 July 1820 but to die within the year.

I wish to convey to you the Letter of Mrs. Drewe that you
[|] sent me this time twelve month, with intention, kindly, to
let it prove a speaking lesson³—Alas! it will now come home
closely to your own situation—for an angel she calls & describes her own so early plucked plant.——Where is your sister
Harriet,⁴ who loves you so devotedly? I would have her by
your side. Augusta⁵ I am sure wants no feeling for you, but
her extreme youth should rather make her spared from effusions of too poignant, & too lasting affliction, than awakened
—or excited to all its suffering sensibility. You bid me not
judge Mr. M[anley]¹ too severely?—you probably imagine
you have given me some history that has never reached me,
for else, *why* should I judge him severely? I am wholly ignorant of his conduct & Character, except as I have gleaned
them from you, & seen them estimated, & *extolled* in paragraphs copied from his best Judge.——

How affecting is what falls from you of description! my
poor poor Friend!—yet I heard the event with a thousand
times more of sorrow than of Surprize—& I flattered myself *You* would have had less of surprize still, since I had
always been more sanguine for her life & recovery than either
You or Fanny.——*Fanny* had positively owned to me, with
a disconsolate voice, that she had not *any hope* her dear
Emily's health could be ever restored,——& that so long ago as
when she set me down, in your Carriage, at the Queen's
House, in the year 1812—or 13.——I forget which—she herself, also, seemed always prepared for her End; not only by
the virtues of her Character, but also by a steady belief her
Complaints were incurable.——What you say [|] of your thank-
fulness that she was permitted to return to you I comprehend
through every Nerve—it was my first & immediate consolation

---

³ One of the Allens of Cresselly (ix, L. 995 n. 3), Pembrokeshire, old friends
of the Waddingtons, Caroline (1768-1835) had married in 1793 the Revd.
Edward Drewe (1756-1810) of Broadhembury, Devonshire, rector of Welland,
Worcs. Their eldest daughter Caroline Elizabeth (b. 1796) had died in 1812, and
conjecturally it was a pious and improving letter on this event that GMAPW had
send FBA. The widowed Mrs. Drewe had accompanied the Waddingtons to Italy
in 1817, attending the Baroness Bunsen with 'tenderness and zeal' on the occasion of the birth of her eldest son Henri (Bunsen, *Life*, i. 131).

⁴ GMAPW's unmarried sister Harriet Port (1781-1824).

⁵ Augusta Waddington (1802-96), who was to marry on 4 December 1823
Benjamin Hall (1802-67), M.P. (1831-59), kt. (1838), 1st Baron Llanover (1859).

for *you*, because I am convinced it saved *her* pangs that would have been insupportable. Where the separation is made final during a separation meant to be happily terminated, then, indeed, the misery has no Alleviation—such was mine in my *First* Death Blow—when I lost—away from me!—& with every internal persuasion *I* should have revived her, my darling sister![6]—my 2[d] blow—though heavier yet! was spared at least a circumstance that must have maddened it!

— — —

Is Fanny's new child a Girl? I wish it, as she has already a Boy. How would my lot for my remnant existence be softened if my Alexander had a sister!—A *son* is continually away, & it seems a duty to encourage his absence, & seek objects & subjects to promote it:—&, at least till I can bear to give more chearfulness & Variety to his Home, I must adopt that course. My admirable Friends—my own best Friend's Friends, the La Tour Maubourgs,[7] exert themselves in his favour in every possible way, of amusement—improvement & advancement; I have the highest obligations to their active Friendship, & the tenderest to their consoling sympathy. I know this will give you pleasure. Adieu, dear—sweet Mary! Heaven bless you!—My love to Augusta. Finished 17th Nov[r] |

Alex is with me—thank God.—He gave up his Swiss Excursion, from staying too long in Paris to think it the moment for going further. Norbury Park, you will have heard, is sold![8] — — Mrs. Locke resides upon Blackheath, between her son George & her Daughter Amelia — —

---

[6] The death of FBA's sister Susanna Elizabeth Phillips on 6 January 1800 (iv. 382-3).

[7] For frequent letters, visits, and invitations, see FBA's Diary April–December 1817.

[8] A large and prominent notice advertising the sale of Norbury Park by auction on 16 June 1819 had appeared in *The Times* on 20 May 1819. On an eminence facing Box Hill across the river Mole, here described as 'one of the most romantic and interesting spots in England', it still stands in a large Park, preserved by the National Trust. For successive owners, see F. B. Benger, 'Norbury Park, Mickleham', *Proceedings of the Leatherhead & District Local History Society*, 1, No. 8 (1954), 14-19. For modern owners, see Ruth Hall, *Marie Stopes. A Biography* (1977), pp. 274, 282, 325.

1225 [11 Bolton Street],
3 December 1819

To Mrs. Locke

L., incomplete copy in the hand of CFBt (Diary MSS. viii. 7226-8, Berg), 3 Dec. 1819
Double sheet 4to   3 pp.

To M[rs] Locke

3[d] Dec[r] 1819

Never was good news more seasonable nor kindness more salutary than the arrival of my sweet Amine and the letter of her dearest Mother at the moment of their reception in Bolton Street. The unexpected *sunderment*[1] of which I had then so recently had the information, had given me a shake that penetrated to every nerve.—I had indulged myself in believing that these inestimable Friends would have been stationed here for very many years—The Ambassador knew & loved England; he had emigrated here in 1792,—had studied the language, & admired the Constitution, & liked the habits & customs, generally speaking, of the Inhabitants: so that, to an ardent patriotism for his own Country, he joined a Good will to this, that made him an Ambassador of Peace from his inmost heart.

He has highly pleased here wherever he has been known—

1225. [1] On 23 November (Diary) FBA learned that General Victor de Latour-Maubourg, lately appointed ministre de la Guerre in succession to Laurent, marquis de Gouvion Saint-Cyr (1764–1830), was to leave London immediately. On 24, 26, 27, 30 November and 2 December she made a series of farewell visits to her French friends, who on most of the intervening days paid return visits (Diary).

Mme de Maisonneuve's farewell note posted in London 2 December is extant (Osborn), and in a long letter (Berg) of 14–15 December she described her journey from London to Paris. Setting out on Thursday 2 December, the three ladies waited in Rochester while the Ambassador toured the naval base of Chatham, and Victor, who had surprised everyone by his agility in clambering up and down ladders and over the forts, came back with enthusiastic accounts of the defence works. They embarked the next day (Friday the 3rd) in lovely weather and on water so clear and transparent that they could see the fish swimming as in a garden pool. Becalmed all day, they saw a gorgeous sunset, followed by a magnificent moonlit night with the lighthouses of both Dover and Calais discernible in the bright air. At Calais they were greeted by martial music and by authorities both civil and military.

& as highly he has been pleased:—— | and his excellent Wife has won all hearts by her conciliating manners, her frankness, and her unaffected goodness & sense: While my Madame de Maisonneuve, though less prominent from the excess of her native timidity & reserve of character & disposition, had only to be known, to be esteemed, loved, & admired. The sudden break up of intercourse I had fondly considered as *Heaven-sent*—has done me no small mischief,—the stroke was so abrupt, & the disappointment so severe. Yesterday morning they set off: Mme de M. had engaged to come to me first, as the Ambassador was to go before *ces Dames*, with his Secretaries, Consuls, &c. to visit Chatham, & they were all to meet for dining together late at Rochester: but in the night a Courier express arrived that hastened all their motions; & instead of Mad^e de M. being at liberty to keep her appointment with *me* at 12 at Noon, she was *en route* at *ten* in the morning for France! A Note, most | *unwelcomely*, came in her stead. I must now only look back to the wonderful circumstance of my having had this blessing at all! —— and look back with the utmost thankfulness. ——

1226   [11 Bolton Street], 21–22 January 1820

To Mrs. Locke

L., copy, excerpt in hand of CFBt (Diary MSS. viii. 7230-[1], Berg), 21-22 Jan. 1820

Double sheet 4to   2 pp.   (Pages 2, 3, & 4 have L., copy in hand of CFBt, FBA to the same, 17 Feb. 1820.)

To Mrs Lock. Elliott Vale

21. Jany 1820

—— And while this alarm for Alex's health has been undermining my acquired cheerfulness by nameless terrours, & doubts whether to be guided by or to brave them,—News has reached me of the dangerous illness of my dear sister in law Mrs Rishton—[1] followed Even now—by the sad tidings that she is no more—we had not met for I believe 17 years —But absence that is not voluntary can make no change in affection—& I am very—very sorry for her loss—though not sorry now as I should have been while happier—because, as our sweet Amelia most penetratingly discerned on the departure of the Queen, Sorrow is but a *wonted Guest* with me at present.—Yet, at Elliot Vale,[2] I found power to mix her with comfort, nay, pleasure. How do I regret that the loved Friend—Friends—who still retain such influence over my feelings are so rarely within my reach!—even now to pour forth my immediate disturbance to your kind & faithful Ear solaces me—& I am somewhat less heavily burthened. With my Alex I always struggle against affliction — — he reads to me whenever his Evenings are not engaged—& though my attention frequently wanders—I contrive that he shall not find out its deviations.

Jany 22—In addition to the melancholy loss I heard of in my sister in law Mrs Rishton,—I am now informed of the deprivation of another old Friend—not equally valued, certainly, yet much esteemed, & long & faithfully attached, Mrs Holroyd[3]—sister of Lord Sheffield—and ᒷ a woman of singular character & merit.

1226. [1] Elder daughter of CB's second wife Elizabeth Allen *née* Allen of King's Lynn, Maria (i, p. lxxiv) had in 1772 married in Ypres without family consent the young Norfolk squire Martin Folkes Rishton (*c.* 1747-1820), an elopement described in *ED* i. 115. The marriage, seemingly happy enough when FB spent the summer of 1773 with the couple in Devonshire (see 'Tingmouth Journal', *ED* i. 228-61), had become intolerable to Maria by the summer of 1792 as FB was to learn when she visited them at their home in Thornham (i. 229, 256-9). In the years 1797-8 FBA had been the recipient of Maria's long confidential letters on her marital troubles and her plans for a separation (see iii, L. 222 n. 10), plans eventually carried out in a migration to Chelsea College (under CB's protection), after which she set up housekeeping in Bury St. Edmunds (iv, L. 304 n. 14). That the couple had reunited, however, is indicated in a letter of 12 December 1807, in which William Windham records having 'passed two nights with Mr. and Mrs. Rishton and attended the Ball at Lynn' (*Windham Papers*, ii. 335). The couple appear together on a memorial tablet in the parish church of Hillington.

FB and the lively-spirited Maria had been close friends since girlhood, though the relationship had been overclouded in 1814 by Maria's resentment at what she took to be CB's unfair treatment of JB in his will (see ix, L. 1077 nn. 1-4).

[2] FBA's long-planned visit to Eliot Vale had taken place in the week 13-21 December 1819 (Diary), when Mrs. Locke entertained AA as well.

[3] Martha Holroyd had died at Bath on 12 January 1820 (*GM* xc^1. 94).

[11 Bolton Street],
25 January 1820

To William Wilberforce

A.L.S. draft (Osborn), 25 Jan. 1820
Single sheet 4to   1 p.   written on address page of A.L.S. William
Wilberforce to FBA incomplete [*franked*:] London. May twenty 1818
/ W free Wilberforce [*addressed*:] Madame D Arblay / Bath   Single
sheet 4to   1 p.   *pmk* FREE 20 MY 1818
  Docketed in pencil: Fanny Burney
  Edited by FBA, *who annotated* p. 1 *of her draft*: Answer to Lett^r
2^d. Not written till afterwards, upon occasion of the Marriage of Y^g
Wilberforce   [*and* p. 2 *of her draft*:] Letter 2. continued / NB. The
Answer on the / Reverse—
  Also L.S., copy of complete A.L.S. Wilberforce to FBA, as above, in
hand of CFBt (Diary MSS. viii. 7104, Berg)   single sheet 4to   2 pp.
  Also copy of FBA to Wilberforce, as above, in hand of CFBt (Diary
MSS. viii. 7234–5, Berg)   single sheet 4to   2 pp.   numbered 5
  These letters were printed *DL* (1842–6), vii. 346–8.

Nearly on the commencement of the dread visitation which
on the 3^d of May, 1818, tore up by the root my Earthly happiness, Mr Wilberforce, ever watchfully alive to promote the
Calls of Religion, & soothe himself in soothing others, had
the kindness to send me a pious tract,[1] as tender as it is energetic, to aid me to support a blow the weight of which he is
amongst the very few that I believe capable of even conceiving; for my bereavement can only be fairly judged by such as
have some criterion by which to know what is (human) excellence. No insensibility to your kindness occasioned my
silence; on the contrary, it was balsamic to me; but I —— ——
had no spirit to tell you so! I could not urge myself to write:
& afterwards, when better able, I was distressed how to make
my tardy apology.

1227. [1] William Wilberforce, after calling on FBA in May 1818, had sent her
a note of condolence (copy, Berg, dated 20 May) begging to put into her hands
'a sweet little piece', written by the Revd. Richard Cecil (1748–1810), *A Friendly
Visit to the House of Mourning* (1792). In reply to FBA's tardy but appreciative
comments on the tract, Wilberforce was to write solicitously (10 February 1820,
Berg) urging her 'acceptance of my own religious publication', probably *A Practical View of the Prevailing Religious System . . .* (1797), which would run through
40 editions before 1826. See Furneaux, pp. 144–51, and further, L. 1280A.

Is it not Now more tardy still? you will ask. Yes; but Extremes are so ever prone to meet, that your Felicity[2] at this moment seems offering its hand to my Sorrow: & I cannot recollect how you felt for my Affliction, without experiencing a kindred feeling for what, I hope, is your Joy. Forgive then, ¦ I entreat, both my long taciturnity & its abrupt cessation, & accept my cordial wishes that this young lady may merit the high distinction of being brought under Such a paternal roof—et *c'est tout dire*—& believe me, Dear Sir, with the truest sentiments of esteem

your &c
F d A.

25ʰ Janʸ 1820

1228   [11 Bolton Street],
17 February 1820

To Mrs. Locke

L., copy in hand of CFBt (Diary MSS. viii. 72[31]-[3], Berg), 17 Feb. 1820

Double sheet 4to   3 pp.   (Pages 1-2 have L., copy in hand of CFBt, FBA to the same, 21-22 Jan. 1820)

To Mʳˢ Lock. Elliot Vale

17. Febʸ 1820

No one, my dearest Friend, can live—and breathe—and think; and dare lament that the so good, so pious, so amiable, & so exemplary *George the Third* should be gone to his great reward[1] — — should be relieved from those trammels of

---

[2] The marriage of Wilberforce's eldest son William (1798-1879) to Mary Frances (*c.* 1800-80), daughter of the Revd. John Owen (1766-1822), Rector of Paglesham, Essex, Minister of Park Chapel, Chelsea, and Secretary (1804-22) to the British and Foreign Bible Society, had taken place on 19 January.

1228. [1] King George III had died at Windsor on 29 January in the eighty-second year of his life and the sixtieth of his reign; and the subjects of the blind old king,

151

Earthly machinery that were no longer informed by the
faculties that for so many years guided him to all that was
Right—should have his soul liberated from the malady of his
Brain & freed to enjoy the salubrity of those Regions for
which it was fitted, — — nevertheless, no one could have
known him as I have known him, in all the private excellencies
of his domestic benevolences,[2]—& have shared as well as witnessed them—without feelings of depression & sadness that
such a Man is now no more!—I do not therefore marvel at
myself that I have been extremely affected by his death —
— and I grieve for my sweet Princesses! they will feel it
most sensibly, however religiously;—& not a little lament
that all hope is now extinct that the filial piety with which
they have hovered in his vicinity—abided in the gloomy
Castle to which he was consigned & never once *All* for a single
night quitted its precincts will ever reach his mortal Ear, or
draw forth from his benign lips the approbation that would
have paid them, by one smile, the exertions & the privations
of years. The so unexpected & quick death of the Duke of
Kent had been a very severe shock to them all,[3]—& the succeeding real & dangerous illness of the new King has filled
them with alarm.[4]—Of course, there has been no *correspon-*

in numbers far surpassing those attending the funerals of either Queen Charlotte
or the Princess Charlotte, made their way in streams to the Castle, where, admitted
at the grand entrance to the Upper Ward, they passed through halls, chambers,
and ante-chambers, draped in sable and lit by candles, to the Presence Chamber,
where the King lay in state. In the rush 'many persons were thrown down and
trampled upon', and for the funeral on the evening of 15 February as much as 50
guineas was offered for 'a single ticket of admission to the north aisle' of St.
George's Chapel. See *AR* lxii[2] (1820), 692-714.

[2] For FB's encounters with the King when for almost five years (1786-91) she
served as Keeper of the Robes to Queen Charlotte, see *DL* ii, iii, and iv *passim*.
For the famous pursuit in Kew Gardens, *DL* iv. 242-50, and for his kindness to
the d'Arblays on their visit to Windsor in 1791, see 'Windsoriana', iii. 175-7,
190-3.

[3] Edward Augustus, Duke of Kent and Strathearn, had died at Sidmouth on
23 January 1820, in the fifty-third year of his life, having succumbed to a cold,
from which, as it was put at the time, half the kingdom recovered with impunity.
The *AR*, op. cit., 680-91, describes the order and itinerary of the funeral procession from Sidmouth to Windsor and the obsequies on the evening of Saturday
28 January.

[4] Very ill even then with pleurisy or pneumonia, the Prince Regent was pro-
claimed King at noon on Monday 31 January at Carlton House. The gun-salute
from St. James's Park, the trumpeters, 'habited in splendid gold lace dresses', the
arrival of the royal dukes, and the burst of brilliant sunshine at the crucial point

dence at such a period—but I have had a few lines from Lady Charlotte Wynn Belasyse,[5] written by the kind commands of the Duchess of Gloucester, to remove my *expressed* apprehensions for H.R.H. precious health.

M[r] George Locke will I hope indulge Alex & me with the reading his Sermon upon my ever dear & honoured King. Alex means to request it. M[r] Matthews[6] gave one that was excellent on the first Sunday, & M[r] Repton another yesterday.[7] I was disappointed, nevertheless, not to hear my favourite D[r] Andrews,[8] but I conclude he was at his Deanery.

How dreadful this assassination of the Duke de Berry![9] Alex just now enters with the news, | which he has heard from M[r] John Angerstein!—

What Monsters are these that prowl about the Earth!—

in the ceremony, all contributed to the general effect. 'The crowd in Pall Mall by half past 11 became immense, but all proceeded with the utmost tranquillity' (*AR*, op. cit., 'Chronicle', 23–38).

Critically ill, the King was not to recover in time to attend, as chief mourner, his father's funeral on 15 February ('Court Circular', *AR*, op. cit., 38). On the evening of the 15th, therefore, the new King was convalescing at Brighton when by the light of torches, flambeaux, and tapers the old King was carried from the Castle to interment in St. George's Chapel. The bells tolled all over London and at Windsor bugles sounded the last call over Great Park as the long reign of 60 years and the long illness ended.

[5] Daughter of the 3rd Earl of Fauconberg of Newborough, Charlotte Belasyse (1767–1825), Lady of the Bed Chamber to Queen Charlotte, and now lady-in-waiting to the Duchess of Gloucester (Stuart, *Dtrs. Geo. III*, p. 248). In 1801 she had married Thomas Edward Wynn (*fl.* 1801–26), *later* Belasyse (iv, L. 255 n. 8). Her letter is missing.

[6] Conjecturally, the Revd. George Mathew (*c.* 1768–1833), vicar of the parish of St. Alfege, Greenwich, for 20 years.

[7] Son of Humphry Repton (1752–1818), the Revd. Edward (*c.* 1783–1860) was perpetual curate (1820) at St. Philip's, Regent Street, canon of Westminster (1838), chaplain of the House of Commons, and finally vicar of Shoreham, Kent (1843).

[8] Of the four preacher-authors mentioned here, only the Revd. Gerrard Andrewes (L. 1203 n. 2) is listed under George III, sermons on, in the Catalogue in the British Library.

[9] Charles-Ferdinand d'Artois (1778–1820), duc de Berry, had been fatally stabbed at the Opera House in Paris on the evening of 13 February, his assassin, the political fanatic Pierre-Louis Louvel (1783–1820), whose object was to put an end to the Bourbon dynasty.

poor Kotzebue scarcely yet cold![10]—& M[r] Perceval still in every one's Memory![11]

1229

11 Bolton Street,
24 April 1820

To Thomas Payne

A.L.S. 3rd person (Osborn), 24 Apr. 1820
Facsimile (7 X 4.4″) of what seems to have been originally a double sheet 8vo. The conjugate leaves were separated and a segment (see facsimile, 1.5 X 3.7″) was apparently cut from the second leaf and perhaps pasted to the blank *verso* of the first leaf.
Addressed: Mr. Payne, / Pall Mall.

Madame d'Arblay troubles Mr. Payne with a few Books which, from some accident, had been omitted to be placed in the Bags of which M[r] Payne was so good as to take the direction last June. M[me] d'A. will think herself extremely obliged to Mr. Payne if he can spare time to look over the Catalogue which she now sends of the many very valuable Books which were conveyed to Calais in 1815, by the late General;[1] & if

---

[10] The dramatist August Friedrich Ferdinand von Kotzebue (1761–1819) had been stabbed on 23 March 1819 by the radical student Karl Ludwig Sand, who immediately thereafter fatally stabbed himself.
[11] Spencer Perceval (1762-1812), Prime Minister (1809), was shot in the lobby of the House of Commons on 11 May 1812 by John Bellingham (hanged on 18 May 1812), a man with a grievance.

1229. [1] Books left by the d'Arblays in storage in Calais in the autumn of 1815 were brought to London in the autumn of 1819, as may be seen in FBA's Account Books (Berg) for that year: storage, £5. 10s. 0d. and carriage ('Trunk Books from Calais — — 3. 10. 0'). See also entries of 13 October and 11 November 1819 (Diary).
The Catalogue, doubtless the careful work of the General, was verified by Alexander, who on his travels of the summer of 1819 had stopped in Calais from 5 to 15 August for that purpose. By 4 April 1820 FBA has recorded as a duty the preparation of 'the Calais Books for Sale!' and on the 9th, having sent the 'Calais Books to Mr. Payne!!' that is, to the booksellers Payne and Foss, of Pall Mall, with whom she had been in negotiation since 16 June 1819, on which date the elder Payne himself had called at 11 Bolton Street to examine the 'Books destined for Sale!!' For the Catalogue compiled by Payne & Foss, the sale, and the cash receipts, see L. 1237 n. 3.

Mr. Payne will favour her with his skilful & experienced advice what best she can do to avoid their confiscation, —— —— or her own ruin!—from the enormous Charges to which they are liable. They were all examined & verified in August last year, 1819, by her son, who took the enclosed Catalogue.

11. Bolton Street Berkeley Square
24th April 1820.

1230   [11 Bolton Street],
                          10–12 May 1820

To Esther (Burney) Burney

A.L. (rejected Diary MSS. 7240-[3], Berg), 10-12 May 1820
Double sheet 4to   4 pp.   *pmk* 12 ⟨M⟩Y   black seal
Addressed: Mrs. Burney / at Mrs. Locke's, / Quay, / Minehead / Somersetshire.
Endorsed by EBB: 1820 Rec^d May 14— / answered / June 12
Edited by CFBt. *See* Textual Notes

May 10, 1820

How kind—how Very kind, my dear Hetty, to write me such interesting intelligence, so soon, as that of your arrival at the sea side,[1]—& without ever—in the phrase of Merlin[2] —the hint of a reproach, though it is your third Letter unearned. Most heartily I thank you, for very anxious I have been for this experiment for both you & my dear Cecilia,— & eager I shall be to hear of its success.

You will be doubly glad you were so indulgent to my silence, when you hear I have been very ill—much more seriously in my own ideas & expectations than I made known, while still uncertain whether my opinion might not be

1230. [1] It was apparently in May that EBB had taken her ailing daughter Cecilia (L. 1191 n. 1) to Minehead.
   [2] Joseph Merlin (1735-1804), the inventor (i, L. 3 n. 117), whose early attempts to speak English had provided the Burneys with phrases they never seemed to forget. For some of his inventions, see Scholes, ii. 203-9; and for the Merlin Table owned by CB, ii. 271.

erroneous. To you, Charlotte, Mrs. Lock & Mme de Maisoneuve I most particularly wished to keep off the knowledge of my *physical* ill state, while it hung in suspence, because I had no means of satisfying the kind solicitude I thought I should awaken—for I could not write—the oppression upon my breast was so severe—& Alex absolutely *detests* writing, whether pledinly or *Vittily*. He is insufferable on that head —& has so often given me the most poignant pangs by mal-apropos taciturnity, in our absences, that Maria must at least not *wonder*, whether she can forgive him or not. He is on this point absolutely impenetrable. And he calmly says it is his intention to go through life that way!—& when people know it, he pretends they will take it all in good part, & like him just the same:—*particularly Maria & Sophy*, he says, for they know his humour of old,—& *They Three* shall always be above common forms. He says these things with a gravity & a *bonhommie* that combat all my efforts to make him more reasonable. *Time*, I doubt not, will do it—I have only to pray the period may not ¹ be precipitated by *Misfortune* —i.e. affronting his best acquaintances, & losing his best friend & favourites.³ He never alas—sees danger of any kind, & therefore never prepares against it. *My* foresight is, thence, doubly keen, & doubly uneasy.—*Basta!*—

I am charmed your Journey was so beautiful, & that you have walks & views within reach so delightful to you. I know no one to whom the loveliness of Nature in her rural Varieties dispences more pleasure. I know nothing of Minehead, but I shall seek it in my English Atlas. Your account of Mrs. Locke,

---

³ The patron who was to prove most useful to Alex was his mother's early friend, the Revd. George Owen Cambridge (L. 1190 n. 2), who, in a letter (Berg) of 30 April [1820] had commended AA's recent performance at Twickenham Chapel: 'It would not be doing justice to my own feelings or to the success of my excellent young Friend, if I were to allow him to return to you without taking with him a *Certificate* of my entire satisfaction at the manner in which he now reads the service of the Church. which I may now venture to say can hardly be done with more feeling, judgment & piety. . . . The next step in the Temple is into the Pulpit. . . .' 'Indeed, indeed My dear good *Friend*', Sarah Baker (L. 1205 n. 7) added in an accompanying note (Berg), 'the Delivery was an improvement on the engaging modest Delivery heretofore—so distinct, so energetic, so en-forcing!'

& Mr. William Lock[4] answered all your kind purpose, in making me smile repeatedly, & drawing from Charlotte, to whom I read it, a hearty laugh. The coincidence of the Names with the contrast of the Characters, had an effect most comically burlesque. Charlotte is in town for about a week,[5] & with me daily—but I have no room—helas—to return her Richmond *Nightly* hospitality: nor can I wish it, as it is only obtained by my losing my *non-descript*, who, with all his tantarems, is the support of my existence. I want more, not less, of interest, near interest, in life. I have spent far, far the greater part of these last two melancholy years in utter solitude. My long given promise, however, for opening or quitting my Cell I am now beginning to perform. My progress is slow—but I will not again suffer it to retrograde.

I do not talk to you of the particulars of my late illness, because they would fill up all my Letter,—& I am now so well recovered, that yesterday I walked out: & to day I have *encored the same*. I was forced, by a sudden fit of apprehension in Alex, to call in advice: for where Alex is not all apparent indifference even to apathy, he awakes all at once to sensations of acutest anguish. He thought me in danger of a decline,—I thought so, too,—so thought, also, James:—& his *agony* rather than *entreaties*, till I consented to see a medical man I quite affrighted me. James's Powders, however, had already removed the Fever ere I called in *Mr. Chilver*,[6] a pupil

---

[4] EBB had apparently written in humorous vein to FBA about a family at Minehead with the surname Locke and Christian names corresponding to those of the 'exquisite' Lockes of Norbury Park. As the estate rentals and parish registers show, there was indeed a William Locke (*fl.* 1819-32), 'tenant of an unspecified piece of property at Minehead between 1819-24', who shows also in county records of 1832 by reason of his 'arrears' in payments on a house 'on the Quay at Minehead', the house in which, as the address (*supra*) shows, EBB and her daughters were lodging in 1820. Like William Locke II, who married the beautiful Elizabeth Jennings (iv. 434), this William also had a wife Elizabeth (*c.* 1755-1831), and there may have been others with corresponding names but contrasting manners, Mary Locke (*fl.* 1793), for instance.

The editors are most grateful to the County Archivist, the Somerset Record Office, Taunton, for his examination of parish records and other documents establishing the above family.

[5] Daily from 7 to 20 May (except for the 15th) CBFB had paid long visits to FBA, usually for tea in the evening (Diary).

[6] Samuel Chilver (d. 16 February 1824) of 14 New Burlington Street, surgeon,

of Sir Walter Farquar,[6] & an admirable physician. He has astonishingly penetrated into my complaints, & put me on the road to their amelioration. Poor Charlotte has been very ill herself. She is still weak & languid. I hope she will go to the sea side ere long. She returns you her affectionate thanks for your kind message, & her own kindest Love. I have not seen our dear James very lately, but he is well, & Alex was with him on Sunday Evening at Sr Joseph Banks.[7]

You have asked me if I would not see L^y Banks.[7] I have seen *nobody*, except quite intimate old friends, or I would have said *yes*; but now, that I mean to comply with Alex's vehement desire, I shall be glad if we should meet. I have seen nothing of Sarah-Harriet this age. She has been mu[ch] a sufferer from pains of various sorts: but I hope this [cut] weather will re-instate her. Charlotte Barrett always comes to me when she can, & always is lively, lovely, & interesting. She is looking much better, & recovering back her beauty. You will be glad to hear I am now writing to you from my Drawing Room—which I have at length begun to inhabit. More reasons than I will write, as they are all mournful, have made this little removal difficult to me. But, it is over, now, as Alex has seized the smaller room for his distinct study, & the reception of his own friends.—Mrs. Lock—not of Minehead—has also been very ill, but is reviving. She always warmly mentions you in her Letters. Mrs. Angerstein is now in town, to my great satisfaction, for her society, when I can get it, is truly a cordial to me. She has brought her eldest Daughter, Caroline,[8] to town, to be presented at the first Drawing Room. I was very glad to hear of your old friends & admirers coming ǀ to Bath. I perfectly remember the adoration of Miss

who had given the name Farquhar to his son Thomas Farquhar Chilver (1805–75), L.S.A. (1826), F.R.S.C. (1852). Sir Walter Farquhar (1738–1819), M.D. (1796), Bt. (1796), was for years CB's physician (iii *passim*).

[7] Still President of the Royal Society, Sir Joseph Banks (L. 1185 n. 5), long a friend to CB and to JB, and his wife Dorothea *née* Weston-Hugessen (1758–1828), FBA and EBB had known for a long time. In ill health for some years, Sir Joseph was to die at Spring Grove (his house in Heston) on 19 June 1820. See Hector Charles Cameron, *Sir Joseph Banks* (1966).

[8] Caroline Angerstein (b. 25 March 1802) must have been presented at the King's first Drawing Room, 15 June (see *The Times*, 16 June).

Yates,[9] as well as the imperious, or derisive haughtiness, or irony, with which you received her worship. I have a vague recollection of 3 or 4 young damsels of more riches than wit, who fell in Love with you, & were treated with the same rigour. I am glad Miss Glover remembers me with Kindness. She was amongst your adorers who met with affability; but she had more sense than enthusiasm, & therefore did not excite wicked sport. Nevertheless it is *your* wish about my Writing that I answer. Alas, my dear Hetty—I am all un-nerved!—However, the very Letter to which I allude, that spoke of Miss Glover,[10] determined me, if again I recovered, for I was very ill indeed when I received it, to renew my attempt: not, in truth, as yet, to *write*, but to arrange & search & select materials. I had worked at this even labori-ously at Ilfracomb—but since then, never looked at a Paper of our dear Father's till since *Miss Glover's* exhortation. I am now once more surrounded with the old hoards—diminish-ing them daily, but selecting what I can for future preserva-tion.[11] I will begin upon this subject another time, for I have no room now beyond stating this *opening reformation*, which I know you will approve. I have not seen poor Mr.

[9] The only child and heiress of Joseph Yates (d. 9 May 1820) of 68 Park Street, Commissioner of Bankrupts, Charlotte Louisa Elizabeth (*c.* 1788-1836) was the granddaughter of Chief Justice Sir Joseph Yates (1722-70) and on the maternal side, of John, Lord St. John of Bletso (1725-67). In a will (PRO/PROB/ 11/1480/433, dated 19 January 1804) her grandmother Dame Elizabeth Yates (d. 1808) had bequeathed her £1,000, but in a codicil dated 1 August 1807 had, in view of the 'very great and almost unexpected affluence' of her son Joseph, and with his 'entire approbation', replaced that trifling sum by a 'diamond pin as a mark of my love to her'. The loss 'would not be felt but might cause trouble'.

Presumably in her London youth a pupil of EBB or her husband, Charlotte had married in December 1820 George Wigley Perrott (*c.* 1786-1831) of Cra-combe House, Worcester, and was the mother eventually of five children. Her M.I. can be seen in the church of Fladbury, Worcester.

[10] Only child and heiress of Robert Glover (d. 1813) of Barwick House, Nor-folk, Anne (*c.* 1759-1835) had married in 1787 Sir William Hoste (*c.* 1753-1824). FBA, who tends to refer to these former acquaintances by their maiden names, mentions in L. 1267 this same Ann Hoste as 'the ci-devant Miss Glover of Queen Square'. This was the part of London apparently adopted in the 18th century by many residents of King's Lynn including CB's second wife, who found a house for the Burneys there in 1778 (*HFB*, p. 35).

[11] The strenuous editorial work FBA had undertaken on papers fallen to her care, she described in some detail in her Diary, 12 July 1818 (x. 955-6). See fur-ther L. 1238, and for the temptation to relinquish 'the wasteful and laborious task', L. 1243 and xii, L. 1397.

Sansom[12] since my illness: my voice is still so husky & nervous, & my respiration so short &, still, *nearly* painful, that I engage as little in *talk* as I can help. This, however, will soon, I fancy, be over.

My love to stout Amelia, who seems to be your Body Guard. You cannot have a better mental Companion than Cecy—but I wish her more Corporeal. I am sorry poor Sophy is so miserably thin—Alex is less so—He has discovered a *Cause* we hope to remove: *worms.* I am vexed the Sandfords have taken a new House [in Worces]ter,[13] instead of Bath or London.

Kiss me, my dear ⟨God child⟩ adieu dearest Etty—
11th May 1820 |

I wish Cecy would try Liquorice Tea. i.e. a Lump of Spanish liquorice broke into morsels, & then disolved in a Cup of boiling Water, with a tea-spoon brim full of brown sugar, & a quarter of a spoon full of Powder of Nitre. This has done good to my late cough beyond all else— |

I open this, May 12. to tell my dear Hetty I had last night James, Mrs. B. & *Sallera*[14] to meet Charlotte to Tea—

1231   [11 Bolton Street],
7 June 1820

To Mrs. Locke

L., an excerpt copy in hand of CFBt (Diary MSS. viii. 7244, Berg), 7 June 1820

Single sheet 4to   1 p.   sewn to small single sheet 4to, on which is a draft of an editorial note in the hand of CFBt, *see* Textual Notes.
Edited by CFBt.

[12] This aged and humble relative FBA had got into the habit of receiving frequently (see L. 1191 n. 16, and Diary for these months).
[13] At Rainbow Hill, near Worcester (see L. 1210 n. 27).
[14] JB's daughter Sarah, now aged 24.

To Mrs Locke

Wednesday—7 June 1820

— — All London now is wild about the newly arrived Royal Traveller.[1] As she is in this neighbourhood our part of the Town is surprized & startled every other hour with some new Groupe of the curious rushing on with all transport of unlimited curiosity to see Her & her 'Squire the Alderman, at their Balcony. Her 'Squire, also, now never comes forth unattended with a vociferous shouting multitude. I suppose Augusta who is still nearer to the Dame, & the 'Squire of Dames, is recreated in this lively way yet more forcibly.

The 15th of this month is to be kept as *King's Birthday* at Court.[2] *Orders* have been issued to the Princesses to that effect & to tell them they must appear entirely out of mourning. They had already made up dresses for *half mourning*, of white & black. I should not marvel if the Royal Traveller should chuse to enter the Apartments & offer her Congratulations upon the Festival.

<hr>

1231. [1] Having landed at Dover on 5 June, Queen Caroline had entered London late in the afternoon of the 6th, and at about 7 p.m., the centre of a cheering mob, hubbub, clatter, and loud huzzas, she concluded her progress at Alderman Wood's house on 77 South Audley Street, not far from Bolton Street and nearer still, as FBA says, to Lady Martin on 8 Hertford Street. 'For a mile and more round South Audley Street', wrote Joanna Richardson, *Disastrous Marriage*, pp. 134-5, 'rose the mutter and growl of threats and brawls, and the crash and tinkle of shivering window panes' as the London crowds evinced the allegiance they were to sustain for a year and a day to the 'Queen of England'. See also Farington, ii. 251-3.

Whether or not FBA saw, heard, or merely heard of the noisy entrance to Mayfair, she was well apprised of the events by the next day.

[2] Although George IV had celebrated his birthday 'with the usual demonstrations of rejoicing' on 24 April (*The Times*, 25 April), the 'Birthday' Drawing Room was held on the traditional date, 15 June. In addition to dispensing with the hoops that had made 'court dresses' curious anomalies throughout the regency, the King announced that 'no person would be admitted in black or mourning to the Drawing Room, it being for the celebration of his birthday' (*The Times*, 16 June).

[11 Bolton Street,
3 July 1820]

To Mrs. Waddington

A.L.S. (Berg), n.d.
A single sheet and a double sheet 4to   6 pp.   *pmk* 3 JY. 820
seal
Addressed: Mrs. Waddington / Llanover House / near / Abergavenny

———

Docketed: circa 1820 / W

I had not answered your preceding Letter, my dearest
Mary, because I feared to disappoint you by my apathy
respecting the Work of Mme Neckar,[1] of which—almost exclusively—it treated. I have not yet seen it, though I have
always, on Your account, intended to exert myself to its
perusal. But I have so lost all pleasure in reading that the
purpose was a labour to me, & therefore put bye.[2]—Indeed,
except with Alexander,—or For him—or for his sake,
Books are to me become mere blank paper: they give me no
ideas,—the words pass before my Eyes without entering
into my understanding.

⌣

You will be kindly sorry, I am sure, to hear of this melancholy change since Books—could they catch my attention;
might beguile me, transiently, of my rooted depression—.
At present, Alexander,—& some social intercourse, which
I am beginning to accept, alone draw me back to this life.
—But I shall never be locked up from any disturbance of
your's, my ever dear Friend—Such will always awaken my
dormant old sympathies. But with what *wonderful* partiality
you exaggerate my powers,[3] even when they were sustained

———

1232. [1] Possibly *Ésprit de Mme Neckar, extrait des cinq volumes des Mélanges
tirés de ses manuscrits, publiés en 1798 et en 1801* (1808). For earlier editions,
see v, L. 459 n. 3.

[2] In the months preceding, however, FBA was steadily perusing her manuscript collections, including Dr. Burney's pocketbooks and 'Memoirs', and she had
read three or four of Sir Walter Scott's novels (Diary).

[3] Mrs. Waddington had apparently suggested that FBA edit Mrs. Delany's
manuscripts and letters, on which by 1792 FB had already done some editorial

by Health, Happiness & public favour, to imagine any scales could be found in which they could weigh against £2000!—Nevertheless, ¹ my dislike to decline any desire of Your's was urging me to compliance, however reluctantly,—till an interrogation occurred that stopt me — — i.e. with what propriety could *I* make the attempt,—I, who,—but for my annihilating miseries, should ere this have published a selection of the Correspondence, with Memoirs of the Life of my dearest Father—a task delegated to me by my family—& accepted as a *devoir*;—a *Tribute* to his honoured Memory.⁴

Most completely I join with you in the horrour you express of *making money* by revealing the secret effusions of unsuspecting Friends, who have unbosomed their thoughts to each other in the firm confidence of scrupulous discretion & inviolate honour—& the thousands of Letters which I have committed—or shall commit to the flames, would prove, could their embers reach you, with any discernable traces of what they had been, how truly, here, we are actuated by a fellow-feeling. But — — of the Letters in question I know absolutely nothing. I do not recollect even who *Mrs. F. Hamilton* was.⁵ How could she be Mr. Dewes' Mother?—was there a 2ᵈ marriage? So utterly in the dark, how can I judge, much less presume to direct Mr. D[ewes]? What cause can be gained by a pleader ignorant alike what there is to urge ¹ & what to repel? If there be any chance against this £2000, it can only lie in your own representations, my dear Mary—& if you make them with the same energy & distress you have written them to me, how will he help being moved by them? — — Yet, with regard to what you say of the *wishes* of my revered Mrs. Delany, no one would hold more sacred any

work (see i, L. 18 and n. 4). The papers, edited in six volumes in 1861-2 (see i, p. lxiii) by Mrs. Waddington's daughter Augusta, later Lady Llanover, included acrimonious attacks on FBA. Though later resentful, Mrs. Waddington apparently trusted FBA at this time.

⁴ In the year 1832 FBA was to fulfil this obligation by the publication of *Memoirs of Doctor Burney* (3 vols.).

⁵ Frances (d. 1819), the daughter of the Revd. Franciş Hamilton (1700-46) of Dublin and his wife Dorothy *née* Forth (d. 1820), was a friend not only of Mrs. Delany but of her sister Ann Dewes *née* Granville (1707-61), mother of the Dewes brothers (see below). The *Letters from Mrs. Delany to Mrs. Frances Hamilton, 1779-1788* (1820) were edited anonymously, perhaps by Mrs. Waddington herself. FBA was reading that book on Sunday 23 July (Diary).

effort to fulfil them; but on this point, I do not think they were irreversible, or unconquerable. They were only, I believe, guided by her modesty;—by a timid idea that she was not worthy—& not that she was averse that her name should be found amongst the Records of those who had not lived to die unremembered.

I have strong reasons for this opinion.

Nevertheless, You,—so much nearer, You, her adopted Child, have an indubitable claim to be heard, as well as to speak.—Yet, if your repugnance is insuperable — — tranquilize your spirits, my dearest Mary—I see no great danger any way: £2000! — — Who will give it, Now, faded, or fading away are all those to whom the excellencies & attractions of my venerated Friend were known.

It seems, also, as far as I can devellop a chaos into which I have no clue for finding my way, that Mr. Dewes himself has relinquished,[6] perhaps forgotten his own design, as the Bookseller says that Years have passed since he saw *the gentleman, whom he concludes to be dead.* If so, to address Mr. D. upon the subject, may give him a notion that Rumours are abroad, & that Expectations are awakened, that may stimulate rather than slacken *his* hopes of success. What if you seek some new documents upon the state of the affair, from your good sister Hariet,[6] or from Mrs. Stratton,[6] previous to any measure whatsoever?

Had these papers fallen into any other hands, I should completely have shared as well as have felt for your uneasiness & chagrin: but Mr. Dewes will certainly take care that nothing secret, nothing of family matters, nothing that could do mischief, shall be left unerazed — — & then, what can come from the pen of Mrs. Delany that will not do honour to

[6] Of the sons of John Dewes (*c.* 1695-1780), GMAPW's uncles, it was Court (1742-93) who had published in 1793 a biography of Mrs. Delany (i, L. 18 n. 4). At his death the papers would have been handed down, in all probability, to his brother Bernard (1743-1822) and thus to Bernard's son Court (1779-1848) or his daughter Anne (1778-1861), who became in 1805 the wife of George Frederick Stratton (1779-*c.* 1833), of Tew Park, Oxfordshire—the Mrs. Stratton, certainly, whom FBA mentions here. Harriet Port (L. 1223 n. 4) was Mrs. Waddington's sister.

herself, & to her sex? Should the Writing be unimportant, the censure can only fall on the Publisher. The *Editor*, I mean: *She*, who did not write for the press, can never be satirized that she did not prepare for it. Her Letters to Dean Swift had general approbation, for their elegance, good taste, & simplicity.[7] Let this, in all events, be your consolation.

Adieu, dearest Mary — — — I began this one day after your's arrived—but I was seized with a dimness of sight at the end of the first page, that made me unable to go on till today. Pray let me know how you arrange your measures— or your mind—& how your Fanny does—& her Child, or Children,[8]—& how my dear Augusta goes on, & what are her pursuits & employments. My *non-descript* Alex always looks back to her as one of his first favourites.[9] I conclude I have told you he was ordained Deacon by our old—& my faithful & most servicable friend, I the BP. of Salisbury?[10]—&, since, Priest, by the BP of Carlile.[10] But he neither has, nor seeks, any thing *permanent* yet, wishing first to feel his wings— which a Curacy or Rectorship must pinion. What he covets, is a Lecturship in London[11]—but that I believe is very difficult of attainment. Mean while, he gently & gradually *prepares* for his future career, by doing duty now & then at Portland Chapel, & by the study of Theology.[12] He continues as thin as ever, but is well, & my few remaining friends have no

[7] Six or seven of Mrs. Delany's letters to Swift had appeared in the edition (n. 3 *supra*).

[8] For the Baroness Bunsen, her marriage and children, see L. 1224 n. 2.

[9] For AA's friendship with the Waddington sisters, their visits to Bath and his to Llanover, see vii–ix *passim.*

[10] AA was ordained deacon on 27 September 1818 by Dr. John Fisher (L. 1180 nn. 3, 4), whom FB and GMAPW had known as Canon of Windsor (*DL* iii *passim*); and priest on Easter Sunday, 11 April 1819, by the Bishop of Chester (L. 1203 n. 2). 'Carlile' is a slip of the pen.

[11] Cf. Southey on this subject, L. 1210 n. 9.

[12] Portland Chapel, later, St. Paul Church, Great Portland Street, 'was erected in 1766 on the site of what had been a reservoir for supplying water to that part of London, but . . . for many years disused . . . was not consecrated till 31 Dec. 1831'. See George Hennessy, *Novum Repertorium Ecclesiasticum Parochiale Londinense* (1898), p. 328.

Alex had nevertheless read morning service there on 22, 24, and 26 March 1820 (Diary), probably at the invitation of the Revd. John Croft (*c.* 1792-1869), Fellow (1816-39) of Christ's College, Cambridge, 'a good man of business', who, as the holder of various college offices, often acted for Bishop Kaye, Master of Christ's. Croft was to be appointed P.C. of Portland Chapel on 6 January 1822, and there on 1 October 1820 Alex was to preach his first London sermon.

bounds in their kindness towards him, to aid his not suffering from my seclusion.—which, however, his impetuous exhortations are now breaking into, *malgre moi.*

My dear Fanny Raper was with me yesterday, looking blooming & sweetly. Poor Mrs. Maltby,[13] greatly changed, has spent some Weeks in town to consult Dr. Baily.[14] She is now at Cheltenham. Adieu once more—Pray let me hear how you are,—& whether you Vanquish—or Yield.— Heaven bless—& preserve you!—

My ever dear Friend—My love to Augusta.

F d Ay [1]

What a Mess! I have just with great dismay, seen I had written on a half sheet, & gone on on a mistaken turn over!— I beg your pardon sincerely—but feel *you* will forgive my not rectifying it by another & a Copied Letter—which my Eyes at this moment would not permit—

How terrible to pay a double Letter for such a scrawl!—& not one word of Her of whom alone every one else writes or talks![15]—

1233   [11 Bolton Street,
                                         3 August 1820]

To Esther (Burney) Burney

A.L. (Berg), n.d.
Double sheet 4to 4 pp. p. 1, three lines of cross-writing, and marginal writing (pp. 1, 2, 3, 4) connected by signs (a), (B), (C), (D), E) and continued without signs *pmk* 3 AU black seal
Addressed: Mrs. Burney, / at Mr. Lock's, / Minehead

[13] On 2, 18, 22, 24, and 26 June (Diary) FBA had received or visited her Bath friend Harriet Maltby (1763–1852), now on a visit to London. See also ix, L. 967 n. 8, and for her sister Elizabeth and her brother-in-law, the Bishop of Lincoln, ix, L. 979 n. 3.
[14] Probably Matthew Baillie (1761–1823), F.R.S., one of the most eminent physicians of the time (see also ix, L. 988 n. 21).
[15] Queen Caroline (L. 1231 n. 1).

Endorsed by EBB: august. 5th 1820 / received / answered / August
21st
Scribbled numbers, p. 4.

True Comfort—I may add, with truth, also, pleasure—
rarely as That can reach me—I received in the most welcome
& agreeable surprize of a new & un-earned Letter from Minehead;[1] my dearest Etty—such news of my sweet God Child
revived me—& still less for Her, or for myself, than for her
dear deserving Mother, whose office as Nurse, when so requiring to be Nursed, continually grieved me. Cecy's recovery
seems to brighten the Past as well as the Present & Future—
for what toil, what alarm is not overpaid by success?—I am
infinitely glad you resolved to prolong your stay by the sea-
side. I would it could be till Autumn. Though your own
health—to me the most precious, you do not mention! —
— Fie!—*fie*! I yet conclude the salubrious breezes are insensibly recruiting it, at the same time that they restore that
of Cecilia: & even the fair Porter of the Family, Amelia—&
so fair a Porter was perhaps never exhibited before,—may
become still more sturdy & robust, & better fitted for the
Winter's campaign, by remaining a while longer in braving
Winds, Waves, Rocks, & Pebbles. And, by the description in
all your accounts of Minehead, I should suppose August to be
the very month in the year for seeing it to the most advantage. Your own sweet situation in Lark Hall place will be in
highest beauty in October.—Besides, the expence of the
apartments is *all* you can have of difference on the score of
œconomy; as live, Eat, & *Quaff*, you must all Three do every
where: & equip yourselves to boot; therefore, one Journey
being over, & the *other equally costly Now as by & bye*, |
all your Calculations must be confined to the subject of
Health: and then. Qy—Whether the sea air 6 weeks longer
may not be full as cheap as the apothecariy's Bills in consequence of your quitting it 6 weeks sooner, i.e. before re-
establishment.

⌒⟶

1233. [1] The letter is missing, but for EBB's sojourn in Minehead, see L. 1230 n. 1.

My health is almost incredibly better than it was, since that spasmodic attack which I have always regarded, *bodily*, as critical. That crisis, too, led me to listen to Alexander's impetuous demands of asking medical advice, & Mr. Chilver[2] has done me infinite good by his sagacious prescriptions. He was pupil & aid to Sr Walter Farquaur,[2] & is now nearly as fashionable. It was Mrs. Angerstein who recommended him. Indeed all my friends here, our James at their head, were almost persecuting to induce me to consult some physician. I was very ill.

That good James was here yesterday, with his good Wife, both looking well.—&. *happy*: their harmony & chearfulness & sociability is such as it never was till now from the even dawn of their Union. Their looks have lost all the *wear & tear* that so often & so long disfigured them of discontent, gloom, care & discomfort. Never have I seen so pleasant a change. The accident of poor James was frightful: A trap door was left open, by a careless servant, in the passage, ready for unloading a chaldron of coals: James, not knowing this, came from the front parlour, & fell; one foot descending into the opening,—had the other followed, he must have been maimed for life, if not killed, as the Cellar is 10 foot deep from the Ceiling!—but there is an Iron Bar across the aperture, & on that he was saved: but his fall upon it was so rough & violent, that he felt demolished, | &, unable to move, lest he should plunge downward; he called aloud for help. Martin, Sally, Mr. Ayrton,[3] & Alexander were in the front Parlour, & flew to his succour. Mr. Ayrton, who happens to be as strong as he is adroit, lifted our dear Brother up, & carried him, in his arms, aided by Martin, to the front Parlour; but there, the violence of the bruise in his side from the Iron Bar, joined to the shake of his frame, & a feeling of dislocation, cast him into what Martin called a trance; it was a violent fainting fit, in

---

[2] For the physicians Chilver and Farquhar, see L. 1230 n. 6.

[3] Among the whist players who used to assemble at Captain Burney's house on 26 James Street, Buckingham Gate, was Edmund Ayrton (1734-1808), musician, and master of the children of the Chapel Royal (Manwaring, pp. 228, 240), and, in later years, his son William (1777-1858), F.R.S., music critic and impressario (*DNB*). See also Lamb's invitation (*Letters*, ii. 219) to 'keep *our Thursday*'.

which his Children both had the horrour to believe him dead!
Mrs. Burney was out—but returned during this dreadful
interval. She knocked at the door repeatedly, in vain—&
heard the screams & convulsive sobs of Sally, who was flung
⟨into⟩ a state of despondence & sorrow the most terrible,—
while Martin called out, to the Maid, 'You have killed my
Father! you beast! you wretch! you monster! You have killed
my Father!' & buffetted her out the room in a rage almost
insane:—somebody, at length, opened the door to Mrs. Burney—whose good sense did not forsake her, & while they
said 'Let Mr. Thomas be sent for!'[4] she flew out herself to
the neighbouring Hospital,[5] & seized upon a surgeon, &
brought him back with her. By him, & Mess.rs Ayrton & Martin, our poor James was carried up to his Chamber, undressed,
put to Bed, & examined; but still senseless. Alex, at the name
of Mr. Thomas, flew off to Leicester Fields, & entering the
house—darted into the study of its Master, exclaiming 'Mr.
Thomas!—come with me to my ⎮ uncle directly!' Mr. Thomas
saw a wild affright in him to which he, wisely & humanely,
yielded, & set off instantly: for Alex was incapable of speech,
not only from terrour, but from breathless haste. Mr. Thomas
has owned he feared he had run himself into some immediate
danger, & walked back half way silent, to give him time to
recover, before he demanded particulars. our James was recovered when they arrived, & had 12 leeches applied to his
side: which, with abstemious diet, & proper medicines, have
so averted all ill effects, that Mr. Thomas has declared he
never had experienced so speedy, & certain, a recovery from
so dangerous a blow. Let us Thank Heaven together, my dear
Esther. He is now even particularly well. Charlotte & her
Namesake are at Brighton, & prosperously. Sea air does the
former astonishing service. Yield then to dear Cecilia—& the
more so, as I have forgotten to mention before, that £10. of
our running account I deduct for *her* share of the Minehead
residence.[6] You would refuse it for yourself, but you have *no*

---

[4] Honoratus Leigh Thomas (vii, L. 676 n. 2), surgeon, with experience in the
army and navy, F.R.S. (1806). Apprenticed to the famous anatomist John Hunter
(1728-93), he was also a pupil of William Cumberland Cruikshank (1745-1800),
anatomist, succeeding in his practice in Leicester Fields.

[5] In all probability, Westminster Hospital.

[6] Recorded in FBA's Diary for 14 August is the gift, £10.

right to refuse for my god child to her God Mother. It must long since have been spent, but you must remember that only £.20 remain between *you & me* for future instalments, which are not to commence these 2 years, as we settled before. This money I can spare perfectly being all a kind of Windfall, i.e. a debt I never expected to be re-paid, & owe wholly to the noble exertions of Mme de Maisonneuve. Oh how I regret her departure! I am sorry you thought I was *writing* —— —— I am but *reading* the MSS. are so long & innumerable: but I work at them daily.[7] [How can] I have written so much & not have mentioned Q. Caroline! Nothing else is mentioned here: & expectation for the 17th.[8] is quite sick with Impatience. Heaven keep all quiet! *Justice* must be done Now to Both parties. Poor Alex is still under worm discipline. Mrs. Lock always is most affectionately anxious about you. I am very glad of your correspondences: They keep Life alive. Adieu, dearest Etty—Your kind Letter & excellent tidings have done me good. very sincerely. Sarah Harriet yet at Cheltenham.[9] O yes—Death is dreadfully busy![10] the BP. of Winchester & Archdeacon I lament. All people miss Sir Joseph Banks as a public loss. I am glad you wrote to y^r good old friend.[11]

[7] For a day-to-day account of the manuscripts read, see Diary for the year.

[8] 17 August was the opening date for the debate in the House of Lords on the Bill of Pains and Penalties.

[9] The novelist had now time and means for a holiday. Her *Country Neighbours; or The Secret* (2 vols.), Colburn had published in the first week of the year, advertising as early as 15 January a second edition of it. By 8 February he was offering a second edition of the complete 3-volume set of *Tales of Fancy*, which included the work above and *The Shipwreck* (first published in 1816). He also offered second editions of *Clarentine* (3 vols., 1796) and of *Traits of Nature* (5 vols., 1812).

[10] How 'busy' death had been among old friends and supporters of the Burneys may be seen in the obituaries of the *AR* lxii[1] (1820), 569–89. Keenly felt by EBB must have been the death on 12 July of the Rt. Hon. Brownlow North (i, L. 33 n. 10), Lord Bishop of Winchester for nearly forty years, the generous patron of her son and of the Worcester Burneys generally.

EBB and FB had known from their early years Arthur Young (*ED* i *passim*), Secretary to the Board of Agriculture, who had died on 29 April; and on 19 June died at his house near Hounslow, Sir Joseph Banks (iii, v *passim*), long a friend of CB and of JB.

At Bath the deaths of 1820 included on 12 January, aged 81, Sarah Martha Holroyd (ix, x *passim*) and on 28 May, CB Jr.'s friend the Revd. Venerable Josiah Thomas, 'officiating minister at Christ Church, and archdeacon of Bath'.

[11] Sir Joseph's widow (L. 1230 n. 7).

Give my Comp^ts I beg, to Mrs. O'Kelly[12]—a very good judge thought her very amiable!! I hope she is very sorry for me?

I am very glad Sophy is better & at Brightwells & that Maria keeps in health & beauty. I am charmed with your good Butcher—at least with his Poney.

1234

[11 Bolton Street],
15–[16] August 1820

To Mrs. Locke

L., copy in hand of CFBt (Diary MSS. viii. 7246–8, Berg), 15 Aug. 1820
Double sheet 4to   4 pp.
Edited at the Press. *See* Textual Notes

To Mrs Lock. Elliot Vale

Augt 15. 1820
London

How long it seems —— ——
—"Seems, Madam! nay it is![1] —" —
since I have heard from my most loved Friend!—I have had, however, I thank Heaven, news of her, and cheering news, though I have lost sight of both her dear Daughters: but a few days ago I learnt from Lady Templetown[2] that she was well, & with her one of the best & most prized substitutes for her Amelia and Augusta that the 'Fates—the Sisters three, & such small branches of learning'[3] have been able to

[12] In 1802 General d'Arblay accompanied Jean Charles O'Kelly (v, Ll. 479–80) and his wife on their return to France, joining them at Greenwich, where he and FBA were visiting CB Jr. FBA saw Mrs. O'Kelly briefly from a window as on 15 February the party set off for Dover.

1234. [1] *Hamlet*, I. i. 76.
[2] FBA had paid visits to Lady Templetown (L. 1222 n. 9), at 65 Portland Place, on 30 June, 24, 27 July, and again on 10 August, while later in the month reciprocal visits became more frequent.
[3] *Merchant of Venice*, II. ii. 66. For the friendship of Mrs. Locke and Sophia Upton (L. 1222 n. 4), see letter of the former (Barrett, Eg. 3697, ff. 202–3b), [13 August 1819].

provide for her occasional accomodation—namely, her Grand favourite, Sophia Upton.[3]—This intelligence gave me pleasure more ways than one—

. . . We are all, & of all Classes, all opinions, all Ages, & all parties, absolutely *absorbed* by the expectation of Thursday.[4] the Q. has passed the bottom of our street *twice* this afternoon in an open carriage, with Lady Ann[5] and —— —— Alderman Wood![6]—How very inconceivable that among so many adherents, she can find that only Esquire!—And *why* she I should have *any*, in her own Carriage and in London, it is not easy to say. There is a universal alarm for Thursday: The Letter to the King breathes Battle direct to Both Houses of Parliament as much as to His Majesty.[7] Mr Wilberforce is

[4] Thursday 17 August, the opening of the debate in the House of Lords on the bill to degrade and dissolve the marriage of the King.

[5] Daughter of Archibald, 9th Duke of Hamilton (1740–1819), Lady Anne (1766–1846) had served as lady-in-waiting to the Princess of Wales before she left England, and on her return had joined her on 28 May at Monthard near Dijon (*AR*, op. cit., 196). She later published *The Authentic Records of the Court of England, for the last seventy years* (1832).

[6] Matthew Wood (1768–1843), Lord Mayor of London (1815–17), Alderman (1817 ff.), M.P. (1817–43), 'one of the chief friends and counsellors of Queen Caroline' (*DNB*). Like Lady Anne (*supra*) he had gone to meet the Queen at Monthard, accompanied her to England, and 'at the entry into London on 6 June 1820 sat by her side in an open landau' as they proceeded to his house No. 77 South Audley Street.

[7] Queen Caroline's letter of 7 August to the King (printed, *The Times*, 14 August) was written, it is said (*DNB*), by the radical reformer William Cobbett (1762–1835), whose *Political Register* since 10 June was devoted almost exclusively to Queen Caroline and her wrongs. Delivered on the 8th to the King, who refused to receive it, the letter was the ostensible reproach of a 'dutiful, faithful, and injured wife' and an afflicted mother 'suddenly bereft of the best and most affectionate and only daughters'. 'Every being with a heart of humanity in its bosom will drop a tear in sympathy with me.' As for the separation, that was the act of the King 'without any cause assigned, other than that of [his] own inclinations, which, as your Majesty was pleased to allege, were not under your control'.

A bid for sympathy, the letter was an attack on the King, the Court, and both Houses of Parliament. 'When to calumniate, revile, and betray me, became the sure path to honour and riches, it would have been strange indeed if calumniators, revilers, and traitors, had not abounded. Your Court became much less a scene of polished manners and refined intercourse than of low intrigue and scurrility. Spies, Bacchanalian tale-bearers, and foul conspirators, swarmed in those places which had before been the resort of sobriety, virtue, and honour.'

As for the Parliament, its proceedings 'are such as to convince every one that no justice is intended me'. Nor, indeed, could it be expected from the Lords or from the Commons, where the majority 'is composed of persons placed in it by the Peers and by your Majesty's Treasury'.

called upon,[8] & looked up to, as the only Man in the Dominions to whom an arbitration should belong. Lord John Russel[8] positively asserts that it is not with Lord Castlereagh[9] & the Ministers that conciliation or non-conciliation hang, but with Mr Wilberforce & his Circle. If I dared hope such was the case, how much less should I be troubled by the expectance awakened for *tomorrow*—it is now *Wednesday* that I finish my poor shabby billet. Tremendous is the general alarm at this moment; for the *Accused* turns *Accuser*, public & avowed, of King, Lords, & Commons, declaring she will submit to no award of any of them.

What would she say should Evidence be imperfect or wanting, & they should *acquit* her?

It is, however, open War, & very dreadful. She really invokes a Revolution in every ⏐ paragraph of her Letter to her Sovereign Lord and Husband.

I know not what sort of conjugal rule will be looked for by the hitherto Lords & Masters of the World, if this conduct is abetted by them.

Lord K[eith] being past seventy,[10] is exempt from the *appel*; but though fearful of the heat & crowd, he will stay the 2 first days to prove his loyalty, if necessary; & at all

---

[8] For Wilberforce's attempt (24 June) to effect a compromise between the stands taken by the Queen and by Parliament on the inclusion of her name in the liturgy, see Furneaux, op. cit., pp. 384–92. Appeals to Wilberforce came from all sides. William Lamb (the future Lord Melbourne) wrote to him privately; and William Cobbett, publicly, in *Cobbett's Weekly Political Register*, xxxvi, No. 16 (1 July 1820), 1105–40; while Lord John Russel (1792–1878), Whig statesman, exponent of parliamentary and electoral reform, in a petition to the King, printed in *The Times* (5 August), to 'prorogue the Parliament' and thus put an end to the proceedings against the Queen, appended a public letter of appeal to Wilberforce, 'a man on whom much depends'. 'I believe you capable of doing at this moment a great benefit to your country.'

[9] Robert Stewart (1769–1822), 2nd Marquess of Londonderry (1821), better known as Viscount Castlereagh, Foreign Secretary in the years 1812–22, was manager of the House. In June 1820 he had attempted to persuade Queen Caroline to quit the country and on her refusal, it was generally believed, instituted the Bill of Pains and Penalties (L. 1233 n. 8), with a clause providing for the divorce desired by the King.

[10] On 17 August 'the peers of the three realms have to be in Parliament at 10 o'clock in the morning, under pain of imprisonment in the Tower, or of a fine of 5000 guineas a day. Only septuagenarians are excused . . .' was the order. See Joanna Richardson, *Disastrous Marriage*, p. 150. Lord Keith (L. 1193 n. 8) was now 74 years of age, and his intentions FBA had probably learned from Lady Keith, who had called on 12 August (Diary).

events, to fulfill his duty as a Peer in attending the opening of this great & frightful cause: & then retire to his magnificent new building in Scotland.[11]

The Heroine passed by the bottom of our street yesterday, in full pomp & surrounded with Shouters & vociferous Admirers. She now dresses superbly every day & has always six Horses: & an *open* carriage: to shew her dear Aldermans *favour* & *constancy*!—What amazing Conduct! She seems to think now she has no chance but from Insurrection, & therefore all her harangues invite it. Oh Dr Parr![12]—how my poor | Brother would have blushed for him! he makes these orations with the aid of Cobbett![13]—and the Coun-

[11] At Tulliallan or Tullyallan in Fifeshire. For a description and a Plate showing the Castle, see Hyde, pp. 319-23.

[12] As it was the unwelcome task of the government in power, i.e. the Tories, to establish the guilt of the Queen and to dissolve the marriage, the Whigs, including Dr. Parr, came forth strongly in her favour. When on 12 February 1820 the Privy Council at the insistence of the King had ordered that the Queen's name be excluded from the liturgy, Dr. Parr, perpetual curate at Hatton, had found means to circumvent the order by the substitution in his church of 'the bidding prayer', from which the councillors had forgotten to expunge the mention of the Queen ('. . . not having read any order to omit the name of Queen Caroline in the Bidding Prayer I have introduced it and shall continue to introduce it before the sermon'). See Warren Derry, *Dr. Parr* . . . (1966), pp. 316-18. Dr. Parr's action thus far FBA could have learned from his godson, her nephew, Charles Parr Burney.

In mid-June Dr. Parr, at the age of 73, made his way in person to London to offer every 'assistance that could be derived from his support, talents and weight of character, whenever she [Caroline] might think proper to call for his services'. Acquiring 'an acknowledged position' among the Queen's close counsellors, he was able to supply the Defence with a classical analogue to the King's behaviour (Nero's treatment of his wife Octavia), which in that classically oriented age was to serve only too admirably to discomfit the King, whose resentment at the comparison was vented for years on the Advocate who had long to wait in his stuff gown for silk. See Derry, op. cit., pp. 319-24; and *AR* lxii[2] (1820), 'Chronicle', 32-3.

[13] With 'the aid', that is, with the implements, usages, spirit, not to say sedition of the ranting radical William Cobbett (1762-1835), whose defences of the Queen, with complementary attacks on the King and his ministers, Parliament, the Army, the Courts of Law, the Church and its 'Parsons', had filled the weekly leaflets of his *Political Register* since 10 June 1820. In his comprehensive censures of the 'parsons' he exempted, among a few others (see his sixpenny number of 23 September), Dr. Parr, who had found mention also (12 August) as a seconder of the resolutions embodied in the Address to the Queen from the freeholders of Middlesex, an Address approved in orations by Samuel Charles Whitbread, Sir Francis Burdett, Alderman Wood, J. C. Hobhouse, and others, in a noisy meeting in the Mermaid Tavern in Hackney.

Sympathizers in the cause of the Queen, Dr. Parr and Cobbett had met only

cil,[14] I suppose. Of course, like Croaker in "the Goodnatured Man" I must finish with "I wish we may all be well this Day three months![15]—

1235   [11 Bolton Street,
                 c. 3 September]–25 October 1820

To Esther (Burney) Burney

A.L. (rejected Diary MSS. [7250-3], the foliation 7252 marked in red p. 3, Berg), ⟨2⟩0-24-25 Oct. 1820
Double sheet 4to   4 pp.   marginal writing on pp. 1, 2   *pmk* 2⟨5⟩
[O]ct [1]8⟨2⟩[0]   wafer
Addressed: Mrs. Burney, / Lark Hall place, / near / Bath.
Endorsed by EBB: answered by favor of / Miss Poilleux—Oct. 30
Edited by CFBt, *who conjecturally emended the date* p. 1 [7250] *top margin from* Oct [2]0 *to* Oct 30; [*a date presumably derived from the endorsement*]. *See* Textual Notes.

Oct. [2]0 1820

My Letter-Conscience, my dearest Hetty, though the hardest—& I try to persuade myself the only hard part of my conscience, will not struggle against the exertion of taking a pen, to you, when an opportunity proves debonnaire,—for the kindness with which you always yield to that excitement for my good always touches me. *Sarah-Harriet* told me, on Sunday,[1] that an acquaintance of hers would convey any Letters to Bath towards the end of this Week—so here, as our James says, Here Goes.—

once, however, and that in September 1807 when on his annual ramble Dr. Parr rode over from Ealing 'to spend a day with Cobbett on his farm at Botley' (Derry, p. 249).
   [14] Henry Peter Brougham (1778-1868), later Lord Chancellor (*DNB*), and Thomas Denman (1779-1854), M.P. (1818-26, 1830-2), the Queen's Solicitor-General. See Roger Fulford, *The Trial of Queen Caroline, passim.*
   [15] See Oliver Goldsmith, *The Good-Natured Man*, Act V: 'Well, now I see content in every face; but heaven send we be all better this day three months!'

1235. [1] On Sunday 3 September, when SHB spent the morning with her half-sister (Diary).

The contents of your last Letter were extremely comfortable to me with respect to dear Cecy,——dear to me, not alone for herself——though that might be enough,——nor yet alone for *you*, earnestly as I wish her to add to your consolations, not——& dreadfully——to diminish them,——but yet for a third motive, united with the two others, that is involved in my heart's core, the extreme partiality with which she was loved by our Susan[2]——that sweet *Mammy-Pilly*, who would have been highly satisfied to have made the adoption serious, as well as playful, through the medium of poor Norbury, had no viper's venom been dashed on the mo⟨st d⟩istant——idea of such a desire. I am by no means, however, equally contented upon a yet deeper interest, your *own* prosperity, my dear Esther, at this Minehead. I know the situation well, for it is not, I believe, much above 20 miles from Ilfracomb——where I spent an anxious——but Oh how I deem it, Now, a happy summer 3 years ago.[3] It was so Northern & cold a Coast, that I had frequently recourse to Fires, from the Chill of the mornings & Evenings, though we were in nearly the most pleasant Lodgings in the place, at the house of my good Eliza Ramsay's Father.[4] The Country around very much resembled what you describe of Minehead, & the town of Ilfracomb itself was *equally agreeable*. There was, however, what they called a Circulating Library,[5] though no one read there, & its outward promise exhibited only Toys & Fruit. |

Fortunately I had not placed the *date* when I began this Letter, for Alex went to Twickenham, & put off his Chelsea intention of being convoy for this Letter, & other matters, as arranged with Sarah, till the occasion was gone by, & till, now, the lady is gone by also, for Sarah, I hear, is at Brighton.[6]

---

[2] For the delight that both Mrs. Phillips and Mrs. Locke took in the infant Cecilia when she was placed out to nurse in Mickleham in 1789 and 1790, see iii. 35. Norbury Phillips would have been about 3 years old at the time. The 'Viper' was the 'cruel Major' Molesworth Phillips (iv *passim*), who had evidently crushed his wife's desire to adopt the child, and as FBA firmly believed, had in time crushed out SBP's very life as well.

[3] From 1 July to *c.* 4 October 1817 (x. 690–714).

[4] Robert Ramsay (*c.* 1753–1843). See x, L. 1095 n. 10.

[5] Mary Hooper's circulating library (x, L. 1095 n. 16).

[6] In a letter (Berg) of 1 November 1820 to CFBt, SHB mentions having stayed for some time that summer in a 'Boarding-House at Brighton' ('my late frolics have made me agog for more').

So I will Date Now at This present moment;—for you are not a friend to Letters on the stocks,—This is 24th Octr 1820.

I have had no intelligence, my dear Esther, of your return to Bath, or certainty of your quitting Minehead, though I cannot doubt either: but, as our quaint worthy friend observes,[7] in speaking to me on this matter the other day, "one rather loves to be at a certainty than the contrary—" & therefore, he told me, he had made enquiry high & low on this interesting topick of whether that deserving—& he was tempted to say meritorious lady was yet safe lodged upon her own premises — — Therefore, my dear Esther, pray give me this solution as early as you can conveniently. I have had another most furious attack of the spasmodic species—but it is past, & I am again getting, bodily!—well. Alex is going through a regular course of worm medicines, & therefore not fatter!— but otherwise better, & with a complection much cleared, & a more healthy appearance.

I well know I shall give a solid pleasure to your kind feelings when I tell you I am more satisfied & easy about this object of ceaseless solicitude than I have yet been since I have lost all aid in his guidance; he has now taken to the real study of his destined *chosen* & decided profession, with a steadiness of application the most honourable, & an ardour of zeal that renders its pursuit a delight to him. You will be surprized— & ¹ surely pleased, for, till he suddenly betook to it voluntarily, he had disheartened himself into a sort of disgust of Theology, as a *study*, & believed it a science of pious dullness!—He is now, on the contrary, seeking Texts, investigating various readings, & working at Discourses of his own, not only for whole Hours, but whole Days, & I have as much difficulty to get him to his Meals from the Scriptures, as I used to have from the Mathematicks, or from Poetry. These two last are now wholly set aside!—*Extremes* are by no means desirable; but where a character is excentrick & difficult, we must always be grateful & content that the excess leans to the Right side. He began by reading Prayers at Twickenham

---

[7] James Sansom (L. 1191 n. 16), who, like his uncle James Sleepe (see *HFB*, pp. 4, 216), was evidently given to the comic malapropisms and formal circumlocutions that used in times past to delight the young Burneys.

Chapel, & then at Portland Chapel: & he has now Twice Preached at the former,[8] & once at the latter. My old Friends —Those who remain! who are all ready nay eager to come around me, & serve me through him, (as his noble & tender Father foretold me, in counselling me, in his last days, to approach them) inform me That they can propose nothing for his advancement till he is known as a good Preacher, from the great encrease of ecclesiastical Candidates since the Peace, which has chaced such innumerable bodies of young men from the Army, the Navy; Diplomacy, & other War callings. *Diplomacy* may sound like an occupation of Peace; but its ramifications in time of War, from Treaties, alliances, leagus, &c are multiplied, both in quantity & in requiring abilities, Three fold, & more, in periods of active Hostility, to what they are in the season when arms give place to Civil life.

This is a subject to me of such deep interest, & I have so much suffered & so much apprehended from my Alex.'s long *inertion*, that I make no apology for giving up my Letter to it. I *am* sure that what comes Home to My Business & Bosom will find its I Way to yours.—I am truly impatient for news of the final result of the sea-side excusion to your precious health & that of sweet Cecy. I shall expect news of the Belvederians from Fanny, when she returns from Brightwell —or rather to give her *relation* of Brightwell,[9] since Edward has acquainted me she left if for Rams-Gate. And Amelia I make a point of considering the prop of the House. Poor James has been very unwell, lately, though not seriously,— for last night he played his Chek-mate with my young student—who will far sooner for That quit his Bureau than for his mutton chop. Can I have written all this, & not have mentioned The House of Lords?[10] You have no conception what a relief it is to Think, Speak, or Write upon any thing else. What an horrible, at once, & Endless Trial!—James kindly

---

[8] AA had preached the 'First Sermon—of His own entire composition at the Archdeacon Cambridge's Chapel at Twickenham' on Sunday 18 June (see Diary).

[9] The usual inquiries for EBB's children Maria Bourdois and Sophia Burney at 5 Ainslie's Belvedere, Bath. The governess Frances (L. 1191 n. 4) had evidently visited her brother the Revd. Richard Allen Burney, Rector of Rimpton and stipendiary curate of Brightwell, of which in the absence of the rector, the Revd. William Garnier (L. 1180 n. 18), he occupied the rectory.

[10] For the voting, see L. 1237 n. 2.

gave me your very entertaining Letter to read. Believe me I have always communicated to him parts of your Letters to me; his enquiries were not from non-information, but non-attention, for he is absent beyond all folks, save Alexander! who of absence is King. 'Tis better, however, than being so, just now, of England!—I rejoice Cecy will Winter under the immediate skill of the good Mr. Sand[for]^d a man you have well, & long, made me love: & his charming Wife renewed all my early partiality to her manners & character in my little sad-deplorable sight of her at Bath.[11] She is as full of feeling as of vivacity. I am disappointed that neither London, for Edward & myself, nor Bath, for you & Belvedere, have profitted by the change of Dwelling. You will be glad to hear that Alex has made me, at length, see various old Friends, & that by 4 I have been drawn from my solitary Evening fireside to quiet Tea-society.[12] How is the poor Hand *actually*? I am glad you have not named the clumsy Esquire who *helped* you so unwisely across the Brook. I hope the death of the good B^P of W[inchester] will not hurt the situation of the Revd Richard?[13]

A certain Mary Marshall visits me to say she longs to return to y^r service alias, Mary Buckingham——[14]

Sweet Mrs. Lock has charged me never to write to you without adding her kindest remembrance. cross circumstances have prevented my visit to Eliot [Vale] but I shall still go

[11] For the Sandfords, see i, p. lxxv.

[12] The frequency of FBA's visits to the Princess Augusta (14 occasions since 23 June, sometimes on consecutive days, Diary) suggests short periods of waiting or service, conjecturally when the Princess's ladies-in-waiting were on holiday. At Buckingham House on 11 September she saw H.R.H. the Duke of Clarence and on the 13th, the Hon. Mrs. Damer and the Duke of York. In this active social summer she paid a round of visits: three, to a former acquaintance at the court Miss Gomm (L. 1238 n. 26); one to Sophia Hoare *née* Thrale (L. 1238 n. 22); and seven to Lady Templetown (L. 1222 n. 9) at Portland Place, who on one gala day (26 August) invited her to drive to Eliot Vale, Blackheath, to see their mutual friend Mrs. Locke (Diary).

[13] The Revd. Richard Allen Burney, in spite of the death of his patron the Hon. Brownlow North (L. 1233 n. 10), was to retain the stipendiary curateship of Brightwell until 1831, when the rector, the Revd. William Garnier (*supra*), son-in-law of the Bishop, decided to give up the living (one of the several he held) in lieu of a stall in Winchester Cathedral (see 'Worcester Journal').

[14] Mary Marshall *née* Buckingham (*fl.* 1816–20), formerly one of EBB's servants but now a 'poor match woman' and mendicant, to whom FBA frequently donated articles of clothing and small sums of money (Diary).

I am laboriously at work in reading our dear Father's Letters, memoirs, papers, &c, as much as my poor Eyes will permit

25th Octr I am just informed the Trial must end within a Week—or less—

I have left no room for concluding so must Here say— God bless my dearest Esther for ever—

1236
[11 Bolton Street, 6 November 1820]

To Mrs. Barrett

A.L.S. (Berg), n.d.
Double sheet 8vo   2 pp.   *pmks* Piccadilly 7 NO 1820 7 NO 1820 wafer
Addressed: Mrs. Barrett, / at Henry Barretts Esq / Richmond / Surry — / With haste.

I trouble you I hope & trust for nothing, my dearest Charlotte but as there is no hope without Fear, I do not trouble you the less. Alexander I expected last night, though not positively—yet uneasily;—& he is not returned to day—

Monday—at 5 o'clock—& he has engaged Mr. Jacob to Tea[1]—& I know not Mr. Jacob's address to put him off — —

I hope & trust, I repeat, that my Etourdie will be here presently; but I write lest I am disappointed, to entreat a line by return of post with news Why he is detained—if detained—

F. d A |

He left me on Saturday by the 4 o'clock Coach—meaning to dine at the Meadows—& to accept the kind Archdeacon's kind offer to mount his pulpit on Sunday—He had no *project* of staying beyond Dinner yesterday[2]—

1236. [1] At Ilfracombe in the summer of 1817 (x *passim*) FBA had got to know Edward Jacob (L. 1185 n. 7), AA's tutor, who having been called to the bar on 28 June, had begun a successful, though short career in law. For his publications, see ix, L. 956 n. 5. Occasionally, as on Monday evening 6 November (Diary), he came to 11 Bolton Street 'to tea'.

[2] On 28 December AA was to return 'from Cambridge very unwell' (Diary).

I meant this for my dear sister but fear to startle her—
I know my *other* dear Charlotte's *firm* nerves when she can
aid or comfort those she loves—I have tried them for this
same naughty Etourdie—

1237   [11 Bolton Street,
                                   7–12 November 1820]
To Mrs. Broome

A.L.S. (Berg), n.d.
Double sheet 8vo   3 pp.   wafer
Addressed: Mrs. Broome, / Ormond Row, / Richmond / Surry.—
Endorsed by CBFB: Sister d'Arblay / 1820

How sorry I am to have made known my disturbance to my
dearest Charlotte's twain! but it was necessary not to risk losing
a Second day, if any mischief or mischance had occasioned
the non-return of my truly *non-mi-recordo* Alex, who had
quite forgotten the expectation he had left me under — —
    Your note is this moment arrived—& a most kind one, on
another subject from my good & faithful Mrs. Baker.[1]—The
Bill has passed for a 2ᵈ readᵍ—with the Lords far more
quietly than was thought possible.[2] It is now believed all will
be ׀ gone through so gradually, that the poor *mis*informed or
uninformed Many will have time for cure of their disease
before the finishing of the business. But I shall always keep
your *refuge* in view with satisfaction & alacrity.

1237. [1] CBFB's letter is missing as is that of Sarah Baker (L. 1205 n. 7).
    [2] The vote on the second reading of the Bill of Pains and Penalties, taken on
6 November, yielded 123 'Contents' and 95 'non Contents'; and on the third
reading (10 November) the majority was reduced to 9. The Queen was judged to
be guilty, therefore, but since Lord Liverpool, anticipating defeat in the Lower
House, dropped the Bill, the King failed to secure the divorce he desired. The
Queen's supporters felt they were the victors, and the illuminations encouraged
by the Lord Mayor for the nights of the 10th, 11th, and 13th, were continued on
the 14th 'in some quarters of the town' (*The Times*, 10–15 November). In defer-
ence to the window-breaking propensities of the mob, most citizens, like FBA and
even the Duke of Gloucester and the Princess Sophia, lighted their windows,
though in proportion to their enthusiasm for the cause (*Star*, 11 November).

I cannot yet fix for my possession of it—our Books[3]—our poor mismanaged Book-sale begins to day—& into to-morrow God bless my dearest Charlottes twain—

I cannot write *Notes* twain at this moment—so let this serve for *twain* from their affect

⟨F. d'A'y⟩ ∣

P.S. This Letter, written 6 days ago, was by a mistake, not taken to the post—I pop it off however, now not to waste such elgant Paper & Writing. ∣

2^d & last P.S.

All is quiet in this street at present—but an Illumination is *expected*—& on Monday will be *ordered*. I shall obey, as meanly as possible, but I shall obey, & therefore be under no uneasiness, for I should dread to leave my dear Pictures, &c to the care of others, if there must be a lighting up to announce that the frail fair one has been dubbed guilty, but is not to be pursued by punishment, though her Sposo is dubbed what is sung by the May Bird so merrily.

---

[3] The books in the Burney-d'Arblay library (Ll. 1194, 1229 and n. 1) would seem to have been incorporated in *Catalogue of Books now on sale . . . by Payne and Foss, Pall Mall* [1820], 8,014 titles in all, with prices. A section 'Livres Français' (pp. 97–128), items 2119–3086, includes authors like Alexandre Lenoir well known to General d'Arblay and works compatible with his interests (a treatise on minerals and a high incidence of Voyages).

The English section includes works constantly cited or quoted by FBA from her earliest years and books of peculiar interest to her, such as G. O. Cambridge's life of his father (1803). For sale also were editions of *Cecilia* (1809, 1820) and of *The Wanderer* (1814).

In cash receipts for 1821 (Account Books, Berg) is the record 'Payne & Foss for our Books! — — 39. 9. 10.'

The residue of FBA's library was to be sold in 1883 after the death of her godson and residuary legatee the Revd. Richard Arthur Francis Barrett (1812–81). See *Catalogue* [*including*] *Miscellaneous Books from the Library of Madame d'Arblay* . . . , to be sold at auction by Messrs Sotheby, Wilkinson, & Hodge, 12–14 January 1883.

11 Bolton Street,
[25]–28 November [1820]

To Esther (Burney) Burney

A.L.S. (Barrett, Eg. 3690, ff. 128–35b), –28 Nov.
Four double sheets 4to   16 pp.   paged 1–16
Edited by FBA, p. 1. *annotated and dated: written sometime* in
Nov. 1820
See Textual Notes.

11. Bolton Street
Berkeley Square.

How kind is my *dear Etty* to so liberally encourage my poor *retardy* pen!—Fanny, who has just left me,[1] says she shall soon be under her maternal roof, & I will begin at once a packet of thanks, & of many &c-s.

And first, I am sadly disappointed Minehead has done so little to ameliorate your health—it seems as if its only benefit is by *reflecting influence*, in the good it did to our dear Cecy. And even to her, I imagine a more southern clime might have been more salubrious. I know that Ilfracomb, which is not far distant, & has equally a Northern Aspect, was far from genial to me, except in sultry weather. It was then delicious. But my Ramsay tells me all its Natives are either very strong & stout, or die of Consumptions. Should you seek the sea breezes another year, my dear Esther, I hope it will be due south. As to Brighton, I am informed it is become so dear, since it is a decided Court Residence, that it is Now the last place to chuse for social life. I cannot, therefore, wish you should *settle* there, as air & sea breeze are not sufficient in themselves, save for stated periods, & for recruit to enable us to live elsewhere. Charlotte, however, is an experienced Judge, & therefore more worth consulting. The *texture* of your house vexes me,[2]—& vexes more than it surprises, as *we*—alas!—*we* feared from the first view of it that as a Winter's Abode it would be both | bleak & damp.—What you say of Bath in general it is not for me to mitigate! — —

1238. [1] Frances Burney had visited her aunt on 25 November (Diary).
[2] No. 5 Lark Hall Place, Batheaston.

— too fatal has been my own disappointment there! Though I am well aware it might have been the same any where else. —however, *you* have a too near & too dear Claim, & Solace, still left in that spot to make it fair for me to dilate upon these ideas.—I would, indeed, you were more within *my* reach, my dearest Hetty,—& often, often lament our so long distance; — — especially as I have found so abortive my expectations respecting Charlotte. — — Yet I see *her tolerably* frequently—& am always within reach of a short summons—whereas Bath is an Age asunder. — — The final settlement of Alexander is so entirely as yet in the clouds, that it keeps *my* final settlement (*Earthly* one, I mean,) still uncertain. Charlotte & I always *mean* to approximate our Dwellings, when our Males are well *F*emaled—If, then, it might be so arranged as to form a *Trio* by my dear Hetty! — —

You see I support myself better, by this gleam of Castle Building.—But let me now, that I may send a double Letter, perform my promise of detail with respect to the manuscripts of our dear Father.[3]

I am, & have been for some months past, as I told you, elaborately engaged with them: but not in *writing myself*, far from it.—It is in *reading*, in decyfering. The enormous load of Letters, Memoirs, documents, Mss: Collections, Copies of his own Letters, scraps of authorship, old pocket Bookes ǀ filled with personal & business memorandums, & fragments relative to the History of Musick, are countless, fathomless! I shall difficultly come to the conclusion. I entirely think with you that I have lost the time for *pecuniary* publication; —but I lost it from circumstances as unavoidable as they were melancholy. I had scarcely been put in possession of these papers by poor Charles, who had wholly to himself the first over-looking & regulating of them all, & through whose hands alone they any of them came into mine, ere my own embarrassments & distresses, & subsequent accidents, Flights, illnesses, or *nursings* in illnesses ten thousand times more terrible to me, absorbed all my faculties—&, with but short

---

[3] This letter includes the most complete account ever given by FBA of her editorial work on her father's papers. A day-by-day account of it entered in her Diary for 1826 shows her alphabetical progress through letters *to* her father.

intermissions, have nearly continued so to do till within the last few months, that I am—faintly—endeavouring to recover some use of my mind & intellects. Nevertheless, I could not think myself authorized to transfer the business, as I have very long known that my Father *designed* & *wished* & *bespoke* me for his Editor. From the time of the death of my Mother-in-Law,[4] he put the Key of his Bureau of private Letters & papers into my hand, & began employing me to examine, read, preserve, or destroy his long accumulation. This was our constant occupation, *I* reading, & he listening, during the fortnight or 3 weeks I spent with Him at that time: & when I left him for dear—dear Westhumble, he told me I should renew it every visit I made;—& so I did, in the few ι intervals in which we were tête à tête from that period before my departure for France. But they were rare, & our joint rummage did not extend, I think, beyond his early Letters:—& he never, I have reason to believe, went on with the investigation himself, further than with his Correspondence with my Mother in Law, & all her Letters & papers, & those of Bengal Richard; of all of which I never found a single vestige.[4] All else, he amused himself in sorting & arranging, but destroyed not a line; not even an invitation to dinner. During my absence on the Continent, he had decided, in case I had not returned, to put Charles into my post, conceiving him, next to myself, most acquainted with his literary habits, intentions, & wishes. Charles, however, gave up *that* with a very good grace, upon my re-appearance, considering the very erroneous ideas he had formed & nourished of the *value* of that post; I mean the *pecuniary* value: for he had concluded the *Memoirs* were such as they would have been if written at the time & in the style of the Italian & German Tours;[5] & had judged of the

---

[4] On 20 October 1796. In the years 1796-7 when CB destroyed 500 of his wife's letters with an equal number of his own to her (i, p. xxii, n. 2) he had probably, out of consideration for her, if she had not herself done so, destroyed all letters relating to their son Richard Thomas Burney (1768-1808), who, as a result of some scrape, the details of which are lost with these very letters, had sailed at the age of 19 to India never to return. The only comments bearing on the event were those left by an oversight in the Journals of SBP (see i. 203 n.).

[5] *The Present State of Music in France and Italy* . . . (1771) and *The Present State of Music in Germany* . . . (2 vols., 1773), recent editions of which were edited by Percy A. Scholes, *Dr. Burney's Musical Tours in Europe* (2 vols., 1959); and by H. Edward Poole, *Music, Men, and Manners in France and Italy 1770* (1969).

185

Letters from the high Names of many of the Writers, without knowing their Contents. I, also, at that time, thought the same, & therefore was induced, & with true sisterly satisfaction, to engage to my dear Esther to share with Her, as joint Residuary Legatee, when the expences of Copyists, paper, &c were deducted, the profits of the Publication. I had an affectionate pleasure in this *perspective*, as the labour would be all my own; but I also thought it just, as this trust was not mentioned in the Will—an omission that has often astonished me, considering the unexamined ¹ state of his private memorandums, & the various papers that could not have been spread, even in a general Family review, without causing pain, or Confusion, or mischief. —— When I again was at Chelsea, on my first return from Paris, he again put his Key into my hands, & pointed to the Pigeon holes in which were the packets he bid me read to him. We went through the Letters of Mr. Greville,⁶ from the commencement of that early intercourse,—all of which were clever, but many disputative, quarrelsome, & highly disagreeable. He did not preserve above 3 or 4. What else we revised, my recollection does not, at this moment, call to mind. The chief of our private time was given to his poetry, & to bits & scraps of his Memoirs, pointed out by himself—& which, taken separately, & selected, & apropos to some current subject, or person, read agreeably,—when read by Himself, & consequently intermixt with anecdotes & recollections that rendered them interesting—as was every thing he ever related.—He meant

---

⁶ Fulke Greville (*c.* 1716-1806), of Wilbury House, Wiltshire, CB's early patron (see *Memoirs*, i. 109-17). The quarrel was monetary, arising from the £300 with which Greville had purchased the indentures that bound CB for a term of seven years (from 1744) to the musician Thomas Arne (Lonsdale, pp. 8-23, 232). Later, embarrassed for money, Greville requested Burney to reimburse him. The bitterness of the quarrel and Greville's 'returning kindness' emerge in CB's verses entitled 'To Fulk Greville Esqʳ upon the termination of a long contested difference'.

> Long had our hearts, O Greville! felt his pow'r,
> Till discord seiz'd their strings, in evil hour,
> Destroy'd their tone, proclaiming mental war
> Nor ere wᵈ let them vibrate, but to jar!—
> —From Reminiscence let me blot those times
> Nor keep the painful records in my rhymes—
>
> .   .   .   .
>
> Long may this harmony of soul remain—

186

I should go through his whole stores, *to* him, & *with* him; I meant & wished it also, most sincerely; but he had no sleeping room for me at the College; our Evenings, therefore, were necessarily very short,—& I lived more at Charles's & with Charlotte than at the College; & my own work, promised to the publick, by Longman, at a stated period, without my consent,—through some mistake—entangled my time so dreadfully that the progress of our manuscript researches was slow & scarcely perceptible.[7] It was at this epoch he told me he had promised all the Letters of Mr. Twining to Charles,[8] who had asked them of him. Consequently, all that Charles had not found, & rightfully taken possession of in his own immediate rummage, I collected afterwards, & I left for him at Richmond, in a sealed packet, with Charlotte.

At the moment we lost our dear Father, I was in too much affliction for any authorship faculties or calculations; but my internal opinion & expectation were That I had nothing to do but to revise & somewhat abridge his own Memoirs, which I thought would contain 3 Volumes in Octavo; & to select his Correspondence to the amount of 3 more, which would rapidly sell the whole, in chusing them from the Names of Garrick, Diderot, Rousseau, Dr. Warton, Dr. Johnson, Mr. Mason, Horace Walpole. Lord Mornington, Mr. Crisp, Mr. Greville, Mrs Greville Lady Crewe, Mr. Bewley, Mr. Griffith, Mr. Cutler, M^rs Le Noir Lord Macartney, Lord Lonsdale. Duke of Portland, Mr. Canning. Mr. Windham. Mr. Wesley. Mr. La Trobe. Mr. Walker.—Mr. Burke. Mr. Malone. Sr J. Reynolds. Mr Seward. Kit Smart. Mrs. Piozzi.[9]

Can any one read such names, & not conclude that the Press would cover them with Gold?—It was not till I came to Ilfracomb that I was completely undeceived, for it was not till then that I had been able to go seriously to work at my always melancholy task — — though Then how *bright* to

---

[7] For FBA's changes of residence in the years 1812–14 and the production of *The Wanderer* (5 vols., 1814), see vii *passim.*

[8] For the letters of the Revd. Thomas Twining (1734–1804), now being edited by Professor R. S. Walker, see *Catalogue.*

[9] With the exceptions of Rousseau, Dr. Warton, Mrs. Lenoir, Lord Macartney, and the Duke of Portland, one or more letters written *to* CB by the correspondents listed survive as well as his to most of those named including the five above (*Catalogue*).

what any has been since!—Doubts, & strong ones, had, indeed, occurred, from my occasional view of the state of the Repository, in hunting for some secret Letters & papers of Mr. Broome, which Charlotte most earnestly claimed from me, & helped me to seek: but it was at Ilfracomb, in 1817. that my definitive disappointment took place. In reading the Memoirs *de suite*, with a red pencil in my hand, for little erasures & curtailings, I soon, unhappily, discovered that they really were so unlike all that their honoured writer had ever produced to the Publick, that not only they would not have kept ǀ up his Credit & fair Name in the literary World, if brought to light, but would certainly have left a cloud upon its parting ray—attended by a storm of disapprobation, if not invective, upon the Editor who,—for a fortnight's quick profit from his earlier established Celebrity, had exhibited her faded Father's faded talents.—A fortnight, I say; because, the first curiosity satisfied, the Memoirs would have sunk to Waste, & have been heard of no more.

All the juvenile Voluminous Mss. are filled with *literal* Nurse's tales,—such as, narrated by himself, were truly amusing, as his vivacity & quickness & ready Wit rendered every thing that passed his lips: but on paper, & *read*, not *recited*, they were trivial to poverty, & dull to sleepiness. What respected his family, mean while, was utterly unpleasant[10]—

[10] Of Irish descent (Scholes, i. 1–3) James MacBurney III (1678–1749), of Hanwood, Shropshire, CB's father, FBA's grandfather, the first to discard the 'Mac', was a musician, painter, and actor whose theatrical career in London in 1718, 1729–31, can be followed in *The London Stage* (11 vols., 1956–8), now that, most usefully, it is indexed (1979). At Goodman's Fields in these years he acted in such plays as Congreve's *Love for Love* (1695) and *The Old Batchelor* (1692), played the part of Sir Avarice in Henry Fielding's *The Temple Bar* (1730), and at Bartholomew Fair (31 August 1730), Goody Tyler in the droll *Wat Tyler and Jack Straw*. In 1729 his 2nd wife Ann *née* Cooper (*c.* 1690–1775), of Shrewsbury, conjecturally accompanying him to London, consigned her young sons, Charles, aged 3, and Richard, aged 6, to a 'nurse' in Condover, thereby incurring, it may be assumed, FBA's epithet 'unnatural'. See *Memoirs*, i. 3–5; and Professor Slava Klima, editor of the fragmented 'Memoirs', frags. 1. 2, who has identified the nurse.

CB's 'Eldest half-brother' Thomas (b. 1707, 'Worcester Journal') was the son of James III (*supra*) and his first wife Rebecca *née* Ellis (*c.* 1681–*pre* 1720), an actress. Thomas was a dancer, performing in the years 1726–32 at Lincoln's Inn fields, Drury Lane, and Goodman's Fields as Punch or Pierrot or Harlequin (*The Amours of Harlequin*) or in pastorals such as *The Shepherd's Holiday* or in 'new' Dutch, Turkish, or Indian dances. In the 1730s he ran a dancing school in Fetter

& quite useless to be kept alive. The dissipated facility &
negligence of his Witty & accomplished, but careless Father;
the niggardly unfeelingness of his nearly unnatural Mother;
the parsimonious authority & exactions of his Eldest half
Brother; the lordly tyranny of his elder own Brother; the
selfish assumingness of his Eldest sister,—& the unaffec-
tionate & Worldly total indifference of every other branch of
the numerous race to even the existence of each other,—
poor good Aunt Rebecca excepted—all these furnish matter
of detail long, tedious, unnecessary,—& opening to the publick view a species of Family degradation to which the Name
of Burney Now gives no similitude. |

In coming to the epoch of Manhood, I had hoped to find
some interesting details, & descriptions, relative to our dear &
lovely own Mother:[11] but—from whatsoever Cause, he is
here laconic almost to silence. 3 or 4 lines include all the history of his admiration & its effects. Whether these were
recollections too melancholy for his Nerves, or whether the

Lane, offered his half-brother Richard employment in it on his arrival in London,
but seems by 1743 to have migrated to the Carolinas ('Worcester Journal').

CB's 'elder own Brother' Richard *supra* (1723-92), of Barborne Lodge, Worcester, was a violinist, dancing master, and a collector of prints and paintings, who
appears in a hospitable and amiable light in the Early Diaries and Letters of CB's
children (*ED* ii. 161-70), though 'Daddy' Crisp's letters of 1777 (*ED* ii. 159-61)
reflect current Burney exprobration of the 'Lordly uncle' for his resistance to
plans advantageous to his son Edward (1760-1848), the artist, in a migration to
London. He died in 1792, the victim, apparently, of a mugging in Covent Garden
('Worcester Journal').

CB's 'Eldest sister' Ann (1722-94) was to the young Burneys in the 1770s
'good Aunt Nanny . . . the best nurse in England, tender, careful, and affectionate'
who nursed nieces and nephews through illnesses, visited Charles at the Charterhouse, and came in from York Street to tea in the evening 'in hopes that she
should *meet with no foreigner*' (*ED* i, pp. lxxx, lxxxvii, 26, 41). Indulgent to
youth, as was her sister Rebecca (1725-1809), she shared in the secret or the
'frolic' of the anonymous publication of *Evelina*, taking 'no denial to my reading
it to *them*, in order to mark errata' (*DL* i. 22-7).

By 1786 the sisters were living in Kingston (*DL* iii. 92), by 1791, in Richmond
(i. 69 n.), where CB visited them, providing for them apparently in rents from his
house in York Street, Covent Garden.

The versatile and talented Burneys were dancers, singers, actors, artists, musicians, novelists, and journalists, that is to say, entertainers, who as such held no
high place in eighteenth-century society but need not now be decried—nor was it
necessary even in the 1820s, one would think, to destroy the records of their
colourful activities.

[11] For an idealized picture of Esther Sleepe (1723-62), see *Memoirs*, i. 61-82;
also *HFB*, pp. 4-6.

intensity with which he had once felt on this subject had blunted his remnant sensibility, I cannot determine—but he gives his whole paper at this time to enormous long paragraphs & endless folio pages, upon the City electioneering for organs & Concerts, & Stanley's rivalry, & Frasi,[12] & local interests of the day, now sunk from every memory, & containing Nothing that could either benefit or amuse a single Reader by remaining on record.

Then follow various Cahiers on Norfolk & Lynn, with some more agreeable style of Writing,—but still upon people not generally known, nor ever described with circumstances that may create a running interest for them. All is detached, vague, & unknit into any consistence.

At last comes London; & Then all the great Names I have mentioned to you begin to occur: & here I had the full expectation of detail, anecdote, description, & conversation, such as to manifest these characters in the brilliant light of their own Fame, & to shew our dear Father the Carressed, sought, honoured & admired Friend of such a constellation: for such he was, & as much loved & esteemed as if he had been the Universal Patron of them all.— |

But alas, what a falling off ensues!—He contents himself with *Naming* all these people, saying where they met, mentioning the first day he made acquaintance with them; where they dined together—the Day, the Week—the Month, the Year—& then stops short, to go to some other date for some other such encounter. There is little more than Copying the minutes of engagements from his Pocket Books, made at the time his Memory was full & gay, & when he purposed dilating upon every Name & circumstance in his Memoirs, as he did, on the moment, in his discourse to his family or friends.

This is the General History of the Memoirs, 12 Volumes in

---

[12] The loss of such details has been lamented as a possible loss to the history of music in London. Through the influence of such friends as Sir Joseph Hankey (d. 28 May 1769) CB had obtained in 'the electioneering' of 1761 the post of organist at St. Dionis's Backchurch and had gained as well the place of John Stanley (1714–86), the blind composer and organist, who had directed a series of fashionable concerts at the Swan Tavern and later at the King's Arms. For this post and the importance of it in Burney's career, see Lonsdale, pp. 23–4 and CB's MSS. 'Memoirs' therein cited. 'Among his scholars' at this time, Lonsdale goes on to say, Burney was soon able to count 'two of Handel's leading singers', Giulia Frasi (*fl.* 1742–72) and Gaetano Guadagni (1725–92).

number, through which I have been Wading, painfully, laboriously wading;—for the hand is small sometimes to illegibility, & the Abbreviations are continual, & sometimes very obscure. Some of the Volumes I have read over 4 times, from different Copies, now of his own, & now of some Copyist. When the latter has been *Sarah*, the *writing* is flowing & easy. But— most elaborately, the dear indefatigable author wrote frequently the whole of every Cahier 3 times over him self: & my fear of missing any thing that might be recorded in one, & not in another, & my desire to ascertain whether there were any difference in the narrations, & any choice to be taken, induced me to hold it right not to destroy a line unexamined. |

There are, you will be sure, many exceptions to this general *anathema*, but they are partial, & of so little Volume, compared with what is hopeless, that I have not stopt to enumerate, though I shall carefully preserve them.[13]

So much for the Memoirs, which I have now perused through-out, with the most sedulous attention, & have gone over a second time, in marking & separating every leaf, or passage, that may be usefully, or ornamentally, Biographical. While all that I thought utterly irrelevant, or any way mischievous, I have committed to the Flames. Whatever admits of any doubt, or demands any Enquiry, I have set apart.

Thus, you see, my dear Esther, I have, at length, made a great advance—though to produce, I fear, but little purpose. However, it is not nothing to *me*, in the present state of my health, spirits, & life, to have dissected this multifarious Work, & to have removed all that appeared to me peccant parts, that might have bred fevers, caused infectious ill-will, or have excited morbid criticism or ridicule.

My Mind has been considerably easier since I have attained thus far, because, in doing it, I have seen how much evil might have accrued from its falling into other hands, less aware of various allusions, &c than myself.

Besides, I am firmly persuaded my dear Father would have

[13] Saved from this process of dismemberment, cutting, culling, and burning, are the remnants of the MSS of CB's Memoirs (Berg Collection of the NYPL), with a few fragments also in the Osborn Collection and the British Museum (Add. MS. 48435, etc.). See Intro. to *Dr. Burney's Memoirs*, ed. S. Klima *et al.*

made all these omissions himself, had he written these memoirs while still living in the World.——And Then——he would have given to what remained the Zest of observation, Conversation, & ⎮ Anecdote.

I am now occupied, in like manner, in going through the Correspondence—which is fatiguing, in general, past all description, for my dear Father has kept, unaccountably, All his Letters, however uninteresting, ceremonious, momentary, or unmeaning. The Few I find that are not fit to light Candles, even from the greatest Names, is nearly incredible. They are Chiefly invitations, or arrangements of *rendez-vous*. I speak of the Letters of the Great in Rank; those of *Friends* I have not yet begun. Those of great Authours, are concise, & upon some accidental occasion. Letters upon Literary subjects, such as our dear Father was so qualified to write with excellence, very rarely occur, as his time was swallowed up by business or his musical researches. Upon this last subject, I find innumerable Epistles; but the pith of them has been woven into the History of Musick.

I hope you will have selected me something sprightly & entertaining from the very original Mr. Cutler?[14] Yet, with all their *agrémens*, & all their excentricities, you will be able *a little* to judge of the toil of reading through Bag after Bag of Collections made without choice thus, by Wholesail.

However, speed the Plough! my Eyes are better, though still cruelly weakened——Who can Wonder?——but I go on as industriously as they will permit me; &, I conclude by surmizing that about 3 years hard reading, for myself, will finally produce about 3 quarter's of an hour's reading to my Lecturers. Such, however, as the poor little Book may one

---

[14] This 'most excentric of queer Epistolary Men' was Samuel Cutler (*c.* 1727-98), a native of Dantzic, but lately of Worcester and 'formerly in the banking-house of Sir George Colebrooke and Co.' (*GM* lxviii. 999). Distinguished, according to his obituary, by 'urbanity and elegance of manners', knowledge of 'polite literature', and a 'total seclusion' of late from the world, he seemed, like the recluse Samuel Crisp, to be attracted to the lively and out-going Burneys. Of the 'vast volume' of his letters to CB, FBA preserved three (of the years 1783, 1787, see *Catalogue*), which, with his letter (Berg) of 22 March [1777] to herself, indicate in a fine secretarial hand cultivated interests in music as well as French literature. His crest, as seen in these letters, was three dragons' heads erased. See also i. 104, and *Memoirs*, i. 340-1.

Day be,[15] should I live, at last, to write / edit / it, its Net profit shall most scrupulously ⎸ be shared between the Residuary Legatees. But—if it were not, as it is, a business of Conscience, there is no advantage I would not gladly relinquish to get rid of so toilsome, perplexing, unwieldy & harrassing an occupation. It has long hung upon me, heavily & uncomfortably—Yet I ought never to regret that the whole is not Now in the hands of Charles Parr—on whom, had I returned home a little later, it would by this time have devolved. It is not that I doubt either his honour or his delicacy; but he *could* not have found time, & *would* not have found patience, for such a revisal as would have kept to his own breast the innumerable memorandums, &c that might most grotesquly, from one secretary or amanuensis to another, have got dancing about in the World.

This is quite a pamphlet, my dear Esther,—but I know you are anxious upon the subject, & I know you have no common right to be informed exactly how it is stated. I fear I may have been wearisome, but I wished to make you completely *au fait*; & though I am very sorry to think how disheartening you will find this estimate, no good could have been gained by a longer suspence, & you seem to have had the judgment to prepare yourself for considering the time to be gone by for any emolument. The fact is, I think there was *never* wherewithal to obtain emolument in materials so diffuse &, in general, so uninteresting. For You, I am sorry, & for Alex;—as to myself, my feelings on these matters, —authorship & emolument—are at this moment very obtuse!—blunted, utterly, into a sort of sad Apathy, rather than philosophy.

Now, then, to present topics. — — —

⎸ I think you will have the happiness to see Fanny looking much better, & very pretty, to boot. I fear she will give you a very pitiful account of my hospitality! But I am not up to *incidental* Dinner giving. Ramsay is an excellent Creature, but a Vile Cook, & a still worse *server*. If I bid her add oil to the

---

[15] For the set-back in plans to publish CB's correspondence, see xii, L. 1397 n. 10, L. 1398 n. 5.

cruets, she forgets salt & pepper; if I tell her to bring up more plates, she is sure to produce fewer Knives & Forks. She was not brought up to serve, or Cook, or Wait, & my retired life, & easy *temperature* as to food, keeps off any progress: so that, in fact, I am ashamed to exhibit my little Nothings on 2 *plates of Delph*, even where the Nothings themselves might be well received. And—in fact, I have not yet regained the sort of strength of powers to be really equal to so long a visit as a Dinner requires, unless from You & Charlotte—or Mʳˢ Lock:—I can exert tolerably well for about 3 hours,—but beyond that, my Soul sighs for some Vent, some Nature— such as it can only find in those with whom I may break forth, occasionally, upon the subject to which it is constantly yearning. I have no such claim upon Fanny—& she knows but slightly how greatly I want it.—Yet I begin to take more to Fanny, & I feel as if I should love her more if she came more in my way, for I think her manners grow milder & more genial. I have Always admired her, for her talents, parts, understanding, & acquirements: but her *laugh*, since my Misery, has been *poignant* to me. We meet better, however, now, for I am more chearful, & *She* is more gentle. I hope we shall grow better Friends & better;—'tis so pleasing, where-ever it is possible, to cultivate affection.—

I am much charmed with that which you experience for Miss Hayes.[16] Do not fear to indulge it, for I hear from many good Judges that she merits the highest regard. I thank you for your account of your society. Remember me, I I beg, to Mrs. Beckford & the Miss Hayes, & poor Mrs. Thomas.[16]— How great a loss is her's! & all, I am told, from an imprudent dinner, which broke into the required regimen of the poor Worthy & lamented Archdeacon.[17] Alexander has twice preached at Twickenham Chapel, since the little history I wrote in my last, &, as Archdeacon Cambridge writes me word, with great success! Peculiar circumstances have kept me in Town all Summer & Autumn[18]—but Seasons have at

[16] For EBB's friends Mrs. Beckford, the Hayes sisters, and the widowed Mrs. Thomas, see L. 1189 nn. 20, 21 and L. 1200 n. 11, respectively.

[17] See L. 1233 n. 10.

[18] FBA may have been in effect 'on call' (see L. 1235 n. 12) as she was to be the following summer when the Princess Sophia's ladies-in-waiting were on holiday (Diary and Ll. 1267, 1270).

present lost their charms in their changes with me! & I shall go to Eliot Vale, & to Richmond, in Winter, full as contentedly!

⌐⎯⎯⟶

I am sorry you should have lost neighbours you so highly appreciated as the de Beauforts.[19] I am not likely to meet with them *promiscussly*, as I make no visits but of settled privacy. Alexander spent the day, lately, at Charles Parr's, to meet a Burney party, & there he saw, for the first time, Caroline, sister to the generous Richard of whom I wrote you the history.[20] It seems she is a very lovely Girl, & well brought up & pleasing. Her Complection a little Indian, but her features very pretty. Fanny Raper is to bring her to me some morning. I send you a little Box of acidulated Lozenges, such as I find remarkably good to hold in the mouth when dry & sleepless. Try them for my sake. I send you also the admirable Socks, made for me by Mrs. Parker, poor Miss Cambridge's faithful attendant.[21] If you can bear to wear shoes large enough for them, in the Cold Weather, as I do, you will find them of the greatest comfort. I have plenty, therefore do not spare them. Our good James is tolerably well; but alas, my dear Esther, by no means as flourishing as last year: I think him changed, & broken; he is weak, & stoops cruelly; but, at times, he retains all his wonted powers of wit & humour, & his parts & understanding are brighter, I think, than ever. God preserve him!——his Wife & Son & Daughter are remarkably well & prosperous. |

I purpose going to our dear Charlotte when Alex visits Cambridge. We cannot be at her house together, as she has only one spare room, & that, also, is only *spare* when Clement is from home. Charlotte was here last week, & looking amazeingly well; quite young & pretty.

[19] For the Beaufort family, see L. 1189 n. 16.

[20] Caroline Jane Burney (1802–71), daughter of FBA's half-brother Richard Thomas Burney (n. 4, *supra*) and sister of Richard Burney (L. 1184 n. 11), with whom she lived in later years at 1 Cunningham Place (St. John's Wood), London.

[21] Mary Parker (*c.* 1755–1839), of Kew Horse Road, Richmond, for many years housekeeper at Cambridge House and mentioned in the will of Richard Owen Cambridge (PRO/PROB/11/1382/808, pr. 3 November 1802). Of late she was apparently acting as nurse or companion to Charlotte Owen Cambridge (*c.* 1746–1823), the victim since 1806 of some mental or nervous derangement. See L. 1305 n. 1 and A.L.S. (Berg) from CFBt to FBA, *pmk* 1 AP 1823.

I wish extremely to know where Mrs. Piozzi is, & how I can direct to her. Will you be so kind as to enquire? Her Daughters, my constant friends, are all far away in the Country.[22] Fanny gives me a very lively account of your two little GrandChildren, Henry & Clara.[23] I wish I could give you a similar one of mine!—I am earnest to see Alexander established—but how difficult to find a Wife that will suit such an Excentric Husband!—I have not seen Edward this age.[24] He has been twice ill—but is now, I am assured, quite well. How unfortunate that *he* never married, who is so made for domestic life! I am always vexed when I think of the excellent Sandfords neither at Bath nor in London.[25] You ask me after Miss Gomm; we meet when we can, but she has had a gay new connexion in her house, by the marriage of her Nephew & Heir, Sir William Gomm, & that has made me shy of visiting her.[26] However, she calls here pretty often: & lately she almost compelled me to meet the New Couple, by telling me her Nephew wished to make acquaintance with Alexander. *So we went together*; it was rather an effort, but went off better than I expected.—

[22] HLTP's address, Penzance, Cornwall, is shown in the headnote of L. 1242. FBA was in touch directly or indirectly with all four daughters: Lady Keith (L. 1193 n. 8) of Tulliallan Castle, Fifeshire; Susanna Arabella Thrale (1770-1858), who lived at Ashgrove, Knockholt, near Sevenoaks, Kent; Sophia (1771-1824), the wife since 1807 of the banker Henry Merrik Hoare (1770-1856) of 31 York Place, Portman Square; and Cecilia Margaretta (1777-1857, widow of John Meredith Mostyn (1775-1807), who in these years lived abroad (Hyde, p. 304 *passim*).

[23] Henry (1814-93) and Clara (1818-59), children of the Revd. Richard Allen Burney (i, p. lxix).

[24] Edward Francesco Burney (L. 1189 n. 12), the artist.

[25] The Sandfords had moved to Rainbow Hill, near Worcester (L. 1210 n. 27).

[26] Jane Gomm (*c.* 1753-1822), formerly governess to the younger princesses (i, L. 7 n. 5), and now living at 38 Hill Street, Berkeley Square, who had called at Bolton Street at least five times during the year and whom FBA had visited by invitation to tea, on 14 August, a visit returned the next day (Diary). The visits continued as did the polite calls of Sir William Maynard Gomm (1784-1875), G.C.B., a nephew whom Miss Gomm had brought up. He had married in October 1818 Sophia Penn (d. 1827), daughter of Granville Penn (1761-1844) and great-granddaughter of William Penn (1644-1718), founder of Pennsylvania (*DNB*). FBA and AA had spent the evening of 4 September with this family and their visit had been returned by Granville Penn on the 5th, Lady and Miss Gomm on the 6th.

Sir William's tribute to his aunt is expressed at length in a M.I. in the Abbey, Bath.

Adieu, dearest Etty—give my love to Amelia & at the Belvedere, & believe me most affectionately

& faithfully your F. d'A. ǀ

NB. Pray do not take any Notice of what I have said of my Brother when you write to James Street—it would affect him painfully. To *me* You may say any & every thing, as I never put a Letter out of my own hands, though I read sundry parts often,—& sometimes the whole.

Tuesday, Novr 28th I finish This long Epistle to send to Fanny, who will quit this troubled City in the midst of its turbulence to-morrow morning. It is now said that Addresses are projecting in every part of the Kingdom, not as absolute counter-addresses, because they are not to Name the Queen nor the Trial; but as protestations against revolutionary principles or any sort of Insurrection. Cambridge University is to begin.[27] I think the plan admirable because it *ought* to meet the wishes of *Both* hostile parties, since it will not be *personal* against *either*. Heaven keep us from public Contention! —This unhappy Process seems to have brought all Dangers to a Crisis.

It is full 3 Years, my dear Hetty, since I have written so long a Letter—& Then, in October 1820,[28] by an opportunity I sent off such a one to Paris! — — ! —

Adieu, my dear Esther, adieu — — — Love to Amelia & the Belvedere—

I have been twice, lately, to Eliot Vale for the Day, carried by L^y Templetown,[29] but I have not yet made my lengthened visit—peculiar circumstances have kept me in town—too long now for entering upon — — I enclose a sweet Letter from that sweetest M^rs. Locke for You.

[27] As a counter-blast to the rush of Addresses to the Queen, Addresses to the King began to appear, and among them, the Cambridge Address received by the King on 7 December (see *The Times*, 8 December 1820). Though the Duke of Gloucester, Chancellor of the University, was not present, the deputation of 229 members included the Vice-Chancellor, the Bishop of Ely, and the Archbishop of Canterbury.

[28] This was FBA's letter of vi, L. 595, comprising 12 quarto pages dated *c*. 22 March–June 1812, in which she described her mastectomy of 30 September 1811.

[29] These drives to Blackheath had occurred on 26 August and 30 October (Dairy).

197

1239   11 Bolton Street,
                                  15 December 1820

To Mrs. Piozzi

A.L.S. (Diary MSS. vii. 7254-[7], Berg), 15 Dec. 1820
Double sheet 4to   4 pp.   p. 4 torn by seal   *pmks* Piccadilly
15 DE 1820 15 DE .820   black seal
Addressed: Mrs. Piozzi, / Penzance, / Post Office, / Cornwall.,
Edited by FBA, p. 1 (7254), *annotated*: Nᵒ (7.) [*and foliated*]
13, 14
Edited also by CFBt *and the* Press. *See* Textual Notes.

                                      Bolton Street,
                                     15. Decʳ 1820.

At last ⟨time⟩ is it, Dear Madam, that Now, at last with a
real pen I venture to answer your kind acceptance of my
Bath Leave-taking address,[1] of a date I would wish you to
forget—& I ⟨would wish to cover⟩ with oblivion, but ⟨now⟩
the Letter is before me, & has no other word I should like to
relinquish. But more of *grief*—at the consequence of my
silence, namely your own, hangs upon the circumstance than
shame, for I have been so every way unwell,—unhinged,
shattered, & unfitted for any Correspondence that could
have a chance of reciprocating pleasure, that perhaps I ought
rather to demand your Thanks than your Pardon for this long
delay. I will demand, however, which you please, so you will
but tell me which you will grant, for then I shall hear from
you again.

I must, nevertheless, mention, that my first intention,
upon reading the Letter with which you favoured me was to
forward to you the verses on October, of my dear Father,
which you honoured with so much approbation; | but I have
never been able to find them, unless you mean the ode,

1239. [1] For FBA's letter of 13 October 1818, acquainting HLTP that she had
left Bath and inviting her when in town to call at her new address 11 Bolton
Street, where there dwells 'an old Friend who with ⌐ever⌐ invariable attachment
sincerely signs herself', see L. 1183 and n. 1. HLTP's 'speedy' response of [*pre* 17
October 1818] FBA had found 'strange & fantastic' (Diary, 17 October) and had
only now set about a reply. For HLTP's request for verses CB had written on
October, see *DL* vi. 388-9 (where the letter is incorrectly dated and placed).

198

written in that Month, on the anniversary of his marriage with my Mother-in-Law, beginning

> Hail, Eldest offspring of the circling Year,
> October! bountiful, benign, & clear,
> Whose gentle reign, from all excesses free,
> Gave birth to Stella,—happiness to me.—&c

If it be this, I will Copy it out with the greatest alacrity, for the first opportunity of conveyance.

So here, again, like the dun of a Dinner card, I entitle myself to subjoin 'An Answer is required.'

And Now, I must—& will add, that I was very far from insensible to the known approach of your last Birth-Day,[2] fully purposing to take that occasion for making my peace-offering, with my most sincere felicitations, & warmest wishes for your happiness;—&, mentally, I prepared at least twenty Letters for that Day:—but they were commonly composed in the Night, when no substantial Pen was in the way, & though the broad light faded nothing of my intentions, it ¹ withered their expression, & a general dimness of general dejection made me feel quite unequal to coming forward at an epoch of Joy, when faint phrases might have seemed cold, & rather have damped than exhilarated the spirits required for the Fête,—and which, my Nieces write word, had the effect of exciting them all around.

You enquire if I ever see any of the Friends we used [*tear*] to live amongst:—almost none.—but [*tear*] I may resume some of those old ties this Winter, from the ardent desire of my son. I have till very lately been so utterly incapable to enjoy society, that I have held it as much kindness to others as to myself to keep wholly out of its way. I am now, in health, much better, & consequently more able to controll the murmuring propensities that were alienating me from the purposes of life while yet living,—This Letter, indeed, will shew that I am restored to the wish, at least, of solace,

---

[2] Mrs. Piozzi had celebrated her 'eightieth birthday' on the day that 'she would be 79 years old' (see Hyde, pp. 309–13; Clifford, pp. 450–1), that is, at the beginning of her eightieth year, 27 January 1820, on which date 'A company of over six hundred persons gathered at the Assembly rooms [at Bath] for a concert, ball, and supper. After her health was drunk to a round of cheers, Mrs. Piozzi opened the ball with Sir John Salusbury, and danced with astonishing elasticity until early in the morning'.

& that the native chearfulness of my temperament is bursting an opening from the weight of sadness by which I had
long believed it utterly demolished. But Time —— 'uncall'd,
unheeded, unawares,'³— ¹ works as secretly upon our spirits as
upon our Years, & gives us as little foresight into what we can
endure, as into how long we shall exist.—I am sure you will
have been very sorry, & very sorry was I, for him whom you call
'The only Friend we now have in common—' Archdeacon
Thomas.⁴ And I am told his valuable life was lost through
a neglect of attention to the regimen prescribed by Dr.
Gibbes,⁵—to whose prescriptions I, for one, should always
be ready to bow down. I think he has much of that sort of
sagacity that so charmed us in our favourite Sir Richᵈ Jebb.⁶
Yet I only saw him once; but that was in a tête à tête, alter-
nized with a trio by my son, that lasted a whole afternoon.
I am told by Mrs. H. Bowdler,⁷ that S[ophie] S[treatfeild]⁸
now resides in Queen Street May-Fair;—but I have not seen
her, nor Sʳ W. W. Pepys,⁹ though the latter made sundry kind
efforts to break the spell of my obscurity on my first arrival
in Bolton Street. Lʸ Keith¹⁰ is *over the hills & far away*¹¹—
she almost lives in Scotland, & Miss Susan in Kent¹²—much
to my loss: but I saw Mʳˢ M. Hoare¹² for a moment Yesterday, & from her I learnt the address I now so tardily make
use of—*tardily* but not with wilful insensibility, believe me,
Dear—& ever d[ear Ma]dam, as faithfully I sign myself—
Your ob[liged & eve]r affectionate

F. d'Arblay.

My son is at Ca[mbridge]—far, alas—from robust,—but
fr[e from co]mplaint.

---

³ From Mrs. Piozzi's best-known poem 'The Three Warnings', published in
1766 (see *DNB*). ⁴ See L. 1233 n. 10. ⁵ See L. 1181 n. 4.
⁶ Sir Richard Jebb (1729–87), M.D. (1751), F.R.S. (1765), the physician in
attendance in former days at Streatham (see Clifford *passim*).
⁷ Harriet (or Henrietta) Bowdler (L. 1210 n. 23), who at times wrote to FBA
and visited her at Bolton Street (Diary).
⁸ Sophia Streatfeild (1754–1835), the beautiful Greek scholar and siren of the
Streatham days (see Hayward, ii. 329–33).
⁹ Sir William Weller Pepys (1740/1–1825), a member of the literary coteries
of the 1780s (see i, L. 12 n. 11; *DL* i, ii, v *passim*), whom FBA was later to receive
in Bolton Street. ¹⁰ See L. 1193 n. 8 and L. 1234 n. 11.
¹¹ A song, *The Beggar's Opera*, I. xiii.
¹² See L. 1238 n. 22, and further, L. 1294 n. 6.

1240   [11 Bolton Street,
                                    22 December 1820]

To M. de Lally-Tolendal

A.L.S. draft (Berg), n.d. written on address page single sheet 4to of
a letter addressed to: Madame d'arblay / Bolton Street, / Piccadilly /
London *pmk* 1820 RICHMOND 2 DE 1820   red seal
  Single sheet 4to   2 pp.   showing obliterations and overwritings
characteristic of a draft.

O M. de Lally! dear, excellent, benevolent & faithful Friend
—Friend to the Gone! the Absent, the so often forgotten!
—I am almost blinded by reading your Letter to M. de Caze,[1]
which has only Now been imparted to me by my much loved
Mme de Maisonneuve, but I would sooner be quite blinded,
than have lost so noble a testimony of Honour to the Manes
of Him who little foresaw—yet who so dearly would have
valued, this flattering personal proof of the justice of his
Appretiation of that Eloquence which He always enthusiasti-
cally admired in The Cicero of France, as He ever called
M. de Lally. If my Eyes, however, are swollen, 'tis from
tenderness & gratitude now mingled with grief; my Heart,
therefore, is ¹ lightened, for pleasure—a guest of late so rare
to it! steals into it's melancholy recesses, & bids them make
room for other feelings than anguish & sorrow—in reflecting upon the delight & pride with which my dear Partner in
All would have learnt —— And perhaps May learn!—such
a mark as this of the still loving Friendship of M. de Lally,
& M. Victor de La Tour Maubourg, Addressed publicly to

1240. ¹ On 20 December (Diary) FBA had received a letter, now missing, from
the ministre de la Guerre, Victor de Latour-Maubourg (L. 1225 n. 1), and on the
21st, a letter from Lally-Tolendal (L. 1195 n. 8), of which there survives only the
2nd leaf 4to (utilized by FBA for the draft of her reply, *supra*). These French
friends were attempting to obtain for her the 'honorarium' or 'customary offering made to the married survivor of a General officer' (viii. 531-2). Their letters
she answered (see Diary) on 23 and 22 December respectively.
  Missing, unfortunately, are the letters of Madame de Maisonneuve for the latter
half of the year 1820, one of which, FBA says, had informed her of the interces-
sion of the two friends above with Élie, duc Decazes (1780-1860), the King's
friend and adviser and favourite, ministre de la Police (1815) and president of the
ministry of 1819.

His King, in favour of his Wife.[2] This Idea is so cheering, that it sooths the sadness of that to which it owes its birth. Nevertheless, should the whole Fail, you must not vex; the Tribute, the intention, & the exertion will always have afforded the greatest of consolations to dear M. de Lally's

most obliged & affectionate

Friend & servant

F. d'Arblay.

1241   [11 Bolton Street,

27 January 1821]

To James Burney

A.L.S. (PML, Autog. Cor. bound), n.d.

Double sheet 4to 4 pp. trimmed *pmks* T. P. / Piccadilly 27 JA 18⟨ ⟩ wafer

Addressed in hand of AA: Captain Burney, / R.N. F.R.S. / 26 James Street, / Westm^r

Dated in pencil, p. 1: Jan 27 1821

Docketed, p. 4: Cara. M^de D. A——

My dear Brother will think I have been very long in answering his kind enquiries, & his interesting document;[1] but I have

---

[2] Nothing seems to have come of this well-meant attempt. See x, Appendix.

1241. [1] The 'document' evidently meant for the Duke of Clarence is missing, but it was probably a request for the Duke's support to the petition (P.R.O. ADM. 1. 5233) that James had addressed to the King in Council on 6 October 1820. In this memorial James again pointed out that far from benefiting from the Order in Council of 19 December 1804 he 'has been continued now nearly sixteen years . . . on the retired Captain's List, in which time thirty officers junior to him in the Service, have been appointed Super annuated Rear Admirals, as entitled by the Order, with a difference in Pension in their Favour which at this time amounts to £2900'.

This complaint, with the relation of his service at sea from 1760–85, his voyages of discovery with the circumnavigator Captain Cooke, and his own successul convoy of a Fleet of East Indiamen to Madras, was not new (cf. L. 1210 n. 7). What was new in the petition, what in point of time it was now possible to allude to, and what conceivably allowed the Duke and/or the King to act, was the mention, modestly enough made, of his important scientific, historical, and geographical publications. 'Your Majesty's Memorialist has made his Profession as a Marinear his Constant Study through a long life up to the present Hour, and

been very unwell—which added to my watchful Nursing has kept all pen & Ink aloof from me to this moment. I am now much better. And my dear Nursery is going on as well as I *ought* to expect, after so severe an attack of Cold & Fever, fastening upon prior evils. I thank Heaven I see no Call for a *consultation*, without which I could not dismiss Mr. Chilvers for Mr. Thomas,[2] highly as I think of the latter. Mr. Chilvers, too, has recovered me from the far more serious malady which, last year, threatened to deprive my poor Alex of his vigilant *garde malade*. Mr. Chilvers has been also very encouraging for the future result of *amended health & strength*, if the Patient persevers in rejecting all heating aliment, & in taking *constant* exercise, when the weather, & his restoration, will permit. Mrs. Angerstein recommended Mr. Chilvers as a second Sir Walter Farquhar,[2] of whom he was the favourite pupil, & the successor. She always has him for herself & her Children, & has ˡ the same consideration for him, & high opinion of his sagacity, that my Father had of his Master. I trust, therefore, we are in very good hands. He lives, also, so near, that Ramsay can herself go to him in 5 minutes— which she has twice done, *very* late, & *very* early, when I was frightened for my poor Alex.

Now to the Document.

In the first place, *I like it.*

So much for *my opinion*, in brief.

But you demand my *critique*, also.

Well, I would not ask the '*interest*' of a Prince of the Blood, now so very near the Throne. They are not used to that term, which seems like belonging to electioneering canvassing amongst our equals. I would beg either his *Protection*, or his *powerful recommendation.*

---

besides devoting his time and Labour, has expended more than £2000 in Maritime Publications within the last 20 years, to which Expence he submitted from unwillingness that the Experience he had gained should be wholly useless.'

Whatever the support lent in Council by the Duke of Clarence, JB's representations, now partly based on his literary efforts, were not likely to go unheeded by that great patron of Arts and Letters, George IV, and it is probable that James, like his father and sister before, won his way at last with his pen.

[2] For the physicians Samuel Chilver, Sir Walter Farquhar, and Honoratus Leigh Thomas, see L. 1230 n. 6 and L. 1233 n. 4.

After the Word *Publications*, I earnestly wish a marginal reference to a brief list of your really meritorious labours, or at least the mention of the *South Sea Voyages*, in quarto,— *with Charts of your own.*

This I think really essential to constitute your ǀ claims on this head—which to me appear well founded & just.

This is all, my dear Brother, I have to offer, except praise, on your moderate, manly, yet modest appeal.

Alex charges me to say how much he also likes the Address.

He has been very naughty in insisting upon going out, the other day, for *air & exercise*! in the midst of the heavy fog! — — he came back half dead, & is now forced to see he must wait brighter skies before he again runs away from his Nure & Nursery.

I sincerely hope you go on amending, & that your dear Wife keeps you Company in so doing. And with my love to Sally,[3] pray tell her I have just been making, & with success, an imitation of the excellent Gloucester Jelly[4] she so kindly ǀ prepared for me last year. God bless you my own Brother

F d'A

I have had comfortable Letters from Hetty & Charlotte lately.

[3] For the members of JB's family, see L. 1180 n. 2.

[4] The recipe is given by Richard Dolby, *The Cook's Dictionary, / and / House-Keeper's Directory; / a / New Family Manual / of / Cookery and Confectionary* . . . (1830): 'Jelly, *Gloucester*.—Take an ounce of rice, the same of sago, pearl-barley, hartshorn-shavings, and eringo root; simmer with three pints of water, till reduced to one pint, strain it. When cold it will be a jelly; when you use it, serve dissolved in wine, milk or broth.'

1242 11 Bolton Street,
6 February 1821

To Mrs. Piozzi

A.L.S. (Diary MSS. vii. 7262-[5], Berg), 6 Feb. 1821
Double sheet 4to   4 pp.   *pmk* 8 FE .821   black seal
Addressed: Mrs. Piozzi, / Post Office. Penzance. / Cornwall.
Edited by FBA, p. 1 (7262), *annotated, top margin*: N° (9) [*paged*:]
17 [p. 3 (7264):] 18
Edited also by CFBt *and the* Press. *See* Textual Notes.

11. Bolton Street
Berkeley Square
6. Feby 1821.

You would be re-paid, Dear Madam, if I still, as I believe,
know You, for the great kindness of your prompt answer to
so tardy a reclamation, had you witnessed the satisfaction
with which it was received;[1] even at a time of New—and
dreadful solicitude; for my son returned from Cambridge unwell, &, in a few days after his arrival at home was seized
with a feverish Cold which threatened to fasten upon the
whole system of his existence—not with immediate danger,
but with a perspective to leave but small openings to any
future view of Health, strength, or longevity. I will not dwell
upon this period—its horrour will be but too easily conceived—I will briefly say, it seems passed over. He is now,
I thank Heaven, Daily reviving, & from looking like—not
a walking, but a creeping spectre,—he is gaining force, spirit,
& flesh visibly, & almost hour by hour. Still, however, he
requires the utmost attention, & the more from the extreme
insouciance, from being always absorbed in some mental
combinations, with which he utterly neglects himself. I am

1242. [1] To FBA's long delayed L. 1239, dated 15 December 1820, but completed
only on 27 December (Diary), HLTP had sent a prompt, pleasant, and obliging
reply, dated 18 January 1821 (printed in *DL* vi. 392-4).
The loss of her old abundant energies and the 'list of dead acquaintance' that
had 'lowered my spirits cruelly' was an omen of her own death, now but a few
months away. In any case her letter of 18 January, in its adaptations to FBA's
mood and the kind and flattering recollections of far-away days, is the nearest
thing to returning 'kindness' on HLTP's part that this editor has seen; and FBA,
thankfully seizing on its kinder tone, replied (as above) without undue delay.

therefore wholly devoted to watching him, & to the care of his Nutriment; upon which his recovery depends; as Mr. Chilver, successor to Sr Walter Farquar,[2] the medical man I I have consulted, & trusted,—from personal experience of his sagacity,—assures me to be the case, the seat of his complaints being the stomach. This accords, also, with the nearly general system of Sir George Gibbes. I was glad to find that tribute of honour had been paid to the worthy Doctor.[3] I live so out of the World that I only heard it from your Letter, in which it was one of many things that gave me pleasure.—I am quite vexed not to find the right October.[4] However, I do not yet despair, for in the multitude of MSS. that have fallen to my mournfully surviving lot to select, or destroy, &c, *Chaos seems come again*; & though I have worked at them during the last year so as to obtain a little light, it is scarcely more than *Darkness visible.*[5] To all the vast mass left to my direction by my dear Father, who burnt nothing,—not even an invitation to dinner; are added not merely those that devolved to me by fatal necessity in 1818, but also all the papers, possessed from her Childhood to her decease, of that sister you so well, Dear Madam, know to have been my Heart's earliest darling—& with whose Hair you so kindly wove your own for me in a Locket that travels with me whithersoever I go. When on this pile are heaped the countless hoards which my own now long life has gathered together, of my personal property, such as it is, & the correspondence I of my Family & my Friends, & innumerable incidental Windfalls, the Whole forms a body that might make a Bonfire to illuminate me nearly from hence to Penzance.[6] And such a Bonfire might perhaps be not only the shortest, but the wisest way to dispose of such materials. This enormous accumulation has been chiefly owing to a long unsettled home, joined to a mind too deeply occupied by immediate affairs & feelings to have the

---

[2] Once again the physicians Chilver and Farquhar (L. 1230 n. 6).

[3] George Smith Gibbes (L. 1181 n. 4), whom HLTP referred to as 'Sir George Gibbes'. Physician-in-ordinary to her late Majesty Queen Charlotte, he had been knighted on 10 May 1820.

[4] See CB's verses on his marriage on October 1767, transcribed in part by FBA, see L. 1239.

[5] *Paradise Lost*, I. 63.

[6] Some 10,000 of these items have been listed in *Catalogue* (1971), to which over 300 letters can now be added.

intellect at liberty for retrospective investigations, even though on subjects so near to 'my business & bosom.'

What a long detail!—I know not what has urged me to write it—yet I feel as if you would take in it some interest; & an instinct of that flattering sort is always pleasant, though far from always infallible. And, in truth, in This case, Bolton Street offers not much more choice of subject than Penzance; for if You have Nobody to see, I see Nobody, which amounts to the same thing. It is not that my intentions are changed from those I mentioned in my last, of seeking revival, in some measure, to social life for the remaining Acts of my Worldly Drama; my quick acceptance of the assistance to that purpose for which I called from Penzance, & which has been accorded me with such generous vivacity, may shew my steadiness, as well I as my Gratitude: but I had not taken into my self-Bargain this illness of my son. However, as he gets better, I shall do better.

———

I am much obliged by Dr. Whalley's kind remembrance;[7] he often called upon me, but never till my doors were shut to all occasional visitors, alas — — — I shall soon be very glad to see Sir Wm Pepys,[8] who has a constancy in his attachments as rare as it is honourable. The 'once charming S S'[9] I have never met with since I last saw her under the roof where first we made acquaintance. I hope the Pitches[10] have been more fortunate than the Tattersalls.[11] Oh yes!—well do you say,

[7] FBA and HLTP had lost many friends but among their mutual acquaintances still living was the Revd. Thomas Sedgwick Whalley (1746-1828) of Bath, D.D. (1808), at one time, according to HLTP, FB's 'constant admirer'. He 'keeps *his* tall figure and high head above water, spite of many efforts to hold him down' (*DL* vi. 392-4; also *DL* i *passim*, and for his marriages of later years, ix. 38-9 n.

[8] Sir William Weller Pepys (L. 1239 n. 9) FBA was next to see on 6 April when she records a visit 'From . . . my very old friend, & the last of the original Blue Stock[ing] club—'. See further, L. 1248.

[9] Sophia Streatfeild (L. 1239 n. 8).

[10] The family of Sir Abraham Pitches (*c.* 1733-92) of Streatham comprised several young ladies, one of whom was poisoned by lead of mercury absorbed from cosmetics (skin bleach). See *Thraliana*, i. 200 *passim*; and the account HLTP gave of the family in her reply of 15 March, *DL* vi. 398.

[11] At Streatham some forty years ago HLTP had introduced FB to the 'Tatter-salls' (*DL* i. 66), that is, the Revd. James Tattersall (1712-84), rector of St. Leonard's, Streatham, and of St. Paul's, Covent Garden, his 2nd wife Elizabeth

for my serious consolation, a sorrow such as that son has given makes *any* other lighter!——Edifying, however, as well as satisfactory, is the contrasted termination of the Two Servants[12] whose lives merited such equally exemplary Justice.

Adieu Dear Madam, & believe me, with faithful attachment your obliged, affec[te] & obed[t]. s[t.]

F d'Ay[13]

née Critchlow (*c.* 1723–1803), and among his children by his first wife Dorothy *née* de Chair (d. 1764), his 3rd daughter Frances (*c.* 1755–1840), who had married 4 September 1784 the brewer Sir John Davis (d. 9 November 1817), of Hawkhurst, Kent, and Albemarle Street, London, kt. (28 September 1778), captain of the West Kent militia and the 'first militia captain who had the honour of mounting the King's Guard' (Snow).

In the newspapers, as HLTP had seen (*DL* vi. 392–3), and at length in the *AR* lxii[1] (1820), 'Chronicle', 99–103, were accounts of the misdeeds and prison escape of their elder son John Henry Davis (*fl.* 1804–35), lately a lieutenant of the Yeomen of the Guards (a commission that had cost his father £5,000) and formerly (1811) captain of the 1st Regiment of Life Guards. He had lost his patrimony of £20,000 at the gaming-tables and, driven to desperation by gambling debts still unpaid, he had forged for £6,000. Detected and committed to the 'Giltspur compter' to await hearings, he made a spectacular escape in a suit of livery similar to that of his servant who, allowed daily visits, had supplied the spare clothes.

Whatever his subsequent career, he would not seem by 1835, if one may judge from relevant clauses of his mother's will PRO/PROB/11/1936/756, dated 9 December 1835, pr. 21 November 1840, to have gained appreciably in trustworthiness. By this will Lady Davis provided £1,000 to be held in trust for him by his younger brother (the principal legatee), but to be paid only 'at such time or times' as the 'trustees shall in their discretion think proper but so and in such manner as that the same may not be subject to his debts engagements liabilities or forfeiture nor be charged or subject by him or by any art or default of his in any manner howsoever'. In the account of the Davis family in Burke's *Family Records* (1897) his name is omitted.

[12] For these servants, see HLTP's letter of 18 January 1821 (*supra*).

[13] This letter, with HLTP's reply of 15 March 1821 (*DL* vi. 397–9) was the last exchange, as far as the editors know, between the former friends. Mrs. Piozzi was to die on 2 May 1821 and in a Memorandum Book, now missing, FBA ruminated on her character, comparing her for brilliance with Mme de Staël. This study was transcribed by FBA's editor and niece Charlotte Barrett, who printed it with deletions and emendations (e.g., *terror* for *disgrace*) in *DL* (1842–6), vii. 363–5 (see also *DL supra*). Anxious to suppress records of a rift much deplored by the Francis family, to make the most of returning kindness, and to present both ladies in the best light, CFBt deleted the adverse criticisms, with which FBA had balanced her account. 'She was in truth a most wonderful character, for Talents & Eccentricity, for Wit, Genius, Generosity, Spirit, & powers superlative of entertainment, ⌐which would have rendered her a phenomenon', FBA had written, 'had not want of judgement, carelessness of veracity, & passions unguarded & uncontrolled, perversely and ruinously sunk her from the fair height to which she was elevated by her charming qualities . . .'.¬

⌐'Both [Mme de Staël and HLTP] were kind, charitable, & munificent, &

I hope this will arrive before the Clifton Primroses lose its direction. I have not been able to receive Mrs. M. Hoare from total confinement—L^y K[eith] & Miss T[hrale]¹⁴ are constantly out of town.

1243A   11 Bolton Street,
                          10–12 February 1821

To Esther (Burney) Burney

A.L.S. (Berg), 10–12 Feb. 1821
Double sheet 4to   4 pp.   *pmk* 12 FE .812   black seal
Addressed: Mrs. Burney / Lark Hall Place, / near / Bath.
Endorsed by EBB: answered / Feb.——1821

Bolton Street.
10th Feby 1821—

Great pain has—I am sure—been spared my dear Esther by her non-reception of Letters or news from Bolton Street during this my last silence—Oh my dear Hetty—I need not —& will not tell you what has been the state of my mind to see my poor Alexander seized with a Fever & Cold, from

therefore beloved; both were sarcastic, careless, & daring, & therefore feared: both were admired alike for first-rate understandings, & censured in the same manner for suffering their passions to triumph over their Reason.⌉ The morality of Mad^e de Staël was by far the most faulty, but so was the society to which she belonged, so were the general manners of those by whom she was encircled. ⌈Their native propensities were equally ungovernable; for while Mad^e de Staël, more licentiously, betrayed her conjugal duty for an adored lover, Mrs Piozzi, only & literally took out a licence to desert her maternal duties for a similar indulgence of passion.
    I cannot help sincerely, nay with affliction regretting, Mrs Piozzi, with all her failings; from the fond, the unbounded friendship she formerly cherished for me, & which I truly returned: my approbation, indeed, was lost, & my esteem was terribly undermined, but as much affection, as can subsist without those ingredients, hung & still hangs about my heart, for her regard for me which had no limits either in tenderness or good opinion, had tied me to her with such warmth & grateful, and gratified feelings, before the cruel & unjustifiable desertion of her children, that the twinings have twisted themselves about my sensations so as to adhere to them almost whether I will or no.—'⌉
¹⁴ For HLTP's daughters, see L. 1238 n. 22 and further, L. 1294 n. 6.

which the recovery seemed more affrighting than the disease[1]
—He is now, I bless Heaven! really better,—& walking, at
this moment, in the Park. The seizure was in the 2[d] week of
January, immediately upon his return from Cambridge, where
he had spent some time, without the faithful Flapper[2] so unfortunately essential to his well doing, in care of his health—
which his eternal negligences, & his very insalubrious hours,
when left to himself, always endanger.—I called in Mr. Chilver, successor to Sir Walter Farquar, who last year succeeded
in saving me from menaces very serious; & he has been equally
prosperous with one to whom Life is every way far more
worth preserving. The Attack in itself would have been nothing, had not its consequences threatened—Oh my dear Hetty!
—total dissolution!—Faded, pallid, emaciated, enfeebled,
he seemed drooping before my Eyes, with a skin that literally
covered fleshless bones—

I had better stop, for both our sakes—you will join in my
thanks to the Almighty dispencer that I see before me now
rational Hope of his re-establishment. He still lives by severe
rules; allowed meat, & that boiled, but twice a week, while
Gruels, Jellies, Apples, light Fish, & Vegetables make his
constant food. ⎮

My absolutely Sole employment Now, from Morning to
something more than Night, is watching my dear excentric &
little manageable Patient, & inventing & executing quaint
modes of Diet to somewhat save him from the satiety so

1243A. [1] EBB, whose daughter Cecilia was to die at Rainbow Hill, Worcester, on
3 April of 'consumptive complaints', could yet sympathize with FBA in her
anxieties about AA: 'And *shocked I am* to think of poor dear Alex—having had
so alarming a relapse—My poor Fanny—What you have suffered! and have to
suffer from the delicacy of that sweet youth's frame & Constitution, pains me to
the heart—for I find the heart can find room for many pangs at the same time.—'
See A.L.S. (Eg. 3690, ff. 140–1b), 4 April 1821.

To her favourite nephew Charles Parr Burney EBB wrote in a slightly different
strain: 'What the effects may be to my poor Sister—should his Malady terminate
fatally—I tremble to think of! resignation to an inevitable misfortune, tho' sent
by the Will & hand of God,—will, I *fear* not be Conspicuous in her.' See A.L.S.
(Osborn) 8 May 1821.

[2] In a footnote to *The Wanderer* . . . (5 vols., 1814), iii. 253, FBA acknowledged her source for the term flapper as 'Swift's Laputa'. See *Gulliver's Travels*,
III, chap. 2; also her letters of 1814 to AA (e.g. vii, L, 822; ix, L. 983).

wearisome of his ordered privations. His Study—for we have now left his Chamber, is my apothecary's & Cook's shop. 'Tis my first appearance in this Character, for hitherto I have had Agents far superiour to such a principal: but my poor Ramsay, though in many points a treasure to me, as a Servant is none in any. But as, in his weak state, he cannot receive any Company, my occupation is so far cheering as that any thing manual is better than every thing mental at such seasons. I am truly glad your kind heart has been spared the useless anxiety of knowing all this during its suspensive state—his Cousins, too would I am sure have sincerely felt it for him. I trust it is now over. He returned from his Walk while I was writing, much refreshed. Poor Charlotte has been fruitlessly afflicted, & sent the Richmond Carrier 3 times a Week to save me from Writing by verbal messages. Mrs. Lock & Mrs. Angerstein have been other Sisters in their apprehen⟨sions⟩ for us. —our dear James, far from well himself! has not been able to come to us, nor I to go to him. This has been grievous— but all seems now coming right. The trial has been the more awful, as Hope no longer, with me, will ever take such a lead as to blind me—even in the midst of all the anguish of Fear & Sorrow—from Despair!—That is over for-ever! — —

12ᵗʰ Febʸ. I will now go on—I can never, Now, write a long Letter *de suite*,—& you are not the worse for that, though my Letters are the longer upon the stocks. But *de suite* always leads me to Melancholy!—I thank God My Alex is visibly gaining ground at this moment. I would you could tell me just such words of our dear Cecy!—But Now to your Letters—

Never in your life, my dear Esther, Though I do not believe you ever passed by an occasion of doing a good office, have you had more reason to be satisfied with that genial instinct which leads you to such deeds than when you liberated me from the tie I I had imposed upon myself of reciprocating the intended Publication,³ & so affectionately left me sole judge of its appearance or non-appearance. The Thought of my

---

³ For long it had been FBA's intention to publish her father's correspondence with a biographical Preface (see x, J. 1170.859 and further, xii, Ll. 1397–8).

Engagement to you[4] has alone kept me to this wasteful & laborious task from the time I saw what were my materials at Ilfracomb. Yet I never hesitated, nor meant to draw back, from the fear you had formed, in the absence of proof, a different view of the subject, & that therefore I might inflict upon you a disappointment—& that, my dearest Esther, would at any time cut me to the heart. But to see you so cordially, so unsolicited, so unexpectedly, pronounce upon my massy Budget the very sentence of my own painful, but most deliberate opinion, is a relief to my mind nearly amounting to a Cordial. When I read to Alexander, who has long murmured at this unpromising toil, & wished for its annihilation, some of your liberating phrases, he clapt his hand upon the table with enthusiastic rapture, calling out: 'Oh Mama! a Bonfire! a Bonfire! This very moment a Bonfire!' — — And when I read to him your kind words of joining in my contentment that this Pile, alltogether, had fallen into the hands, however fruitlessly, for which it had most peculiarly been destined, he actually rose to shake hands with me in congratulation at such an *affidavit*, saying 'Bravo, Aunt Hetty!—'

I have made, however, no Bonfire as yet; I have not even seen one of the mass many weeks; Papers are changed with me for Gruels, mineral waters, apple & Lemonade drinks, & little cup puddings. But I shall not by & bye be slack in blazing forth my concurrence in your decree. Meanwhile, I am certainly well 'disposed' to reserve any thing for *your* sight & consideration, that you may wish; so if any thing occurs to you, pray say. And indeed, I mean to withhold from the Flames all such *morceaux* as may have any interest in them, & yet be *innoxious*, both of the Memoirs & of the Correspondence.

From the time of my last Letter to the terrifying attack of Alex, I had only had power to read the Letters of Mr. Bewley[5]

---

[4] EBB, as one of the residuary legatees, was entitled to half the proceeds accruing from the publication of her father's papers.

[5] William Bewley (1726–83), originally of North Shields, Northamptonshire, a 'hard-working country surgeon' of Great Massingham, Norfolk, and one of CB's

—as bulky in size as those of Mr. Cutler;[6] though highly superiour in sterling worth. Nevertheless, though they are equally shared between I Wit & Urbanity, as was the Character of their Writer; they are so local, & their charm hangs so much upon the *aprospos* of the Moment, that there are not above 2 or 3 that could entertain any one out of our family. With respect to Mr. Cutler, I think, in judging by 3 or 4 loose Letters that were accidentally left out of the Collection in your hands, I am persuaded that what you have written upon them would be precisely what would be the Verdict in all the best Reviews. Therefore, dear Etty, dispose of them completely as you list. I feel just as easy within me as if I had read them myself, only so much the less fatigued.——How much more I could say to you on this fertile subject, were my paper not already filled! But *Basta* for this *bout*. I am very glad you concur with me in poor Fanny's improvement in gentler manners.[7] Her mind has much in it of your own generous texture, or she would not have mentioned my desire, or rather insistance upon being her Banker in any sudden Call, or temporary embarrassment. I well know she might be trusted with much higher privileges, could I accord them, & that I have only her *Scruples* to fear. I join with you in certain regrets; & I will surely be on the Watch for any occasion to effect the change of System we equally think adviseable.

You have given me Very great pleasure indeed by your assurances that upon the whole, the sea breezes have done you good. I am, also, very glad you go to the Concerts! I think Musick might be soothing to *me* could I get within its harmonious spell without dress or Ceremony. I have another matter to discuss with you when I write next.——but I have

earliest and most helpful literary friends (see both Scholes and Lonsdale, *passim*), had died at CB's house in St. Martin's Street on 5 September 1783 (*ED* i. 317-18 n.). Noted for his learning in many branches, including music, he had 'for more than twenty years' (see *DNB*) supplied the *Monthly Review* 'with an examination in innumerable works in science and articles of foreign literature, written with a force, spirit, candour, and . . . humour, not often found in critical discussions' (see also *Memoirs*, i. 105-7, 265-7; ii. 347-53). For the letters surviving, see *Catalogue*. See also Roger Lonsdale, 'William Bewley and the *Monthly Review*: A Problem of Attribution', *PBSA*, iv (1961), 309-18; and Garry Bowers, 'The Letters of William Bewley to Charles Burney, Mus. Doc.', unpublished dissertation, McGill University.

[6] See L. 1238 n. 14.   [7] Cf. FBA's remarks, L. 1238.

now *20* unanswered Letters in my Writing Box. That is, *19* when this is on the road.——

I have this moment much better News of our dear James, who has 3^{ce} taken the air.—— Adieu—& God bless my dearest Esther—prays her ⟨truly⟩

F. d'Ay

Pray pay Mr. Hervé for me[8]—'tis so small a sum for so Great a purpose. I can *settle the balance* with Fanny, or Edward. I have had a very charming Letter lately from Mrs. Piozzi, written with the hand, & spirit, of 25.[9]——

I will have a true Margland discretion.[10]——

Finished 12th Feb^y

1243B

[11 Bolton Street],
12 February 1821

To James Burney

A.L.S. (BL, MSS 43,688 f. 157), 12 Feb. 1821
Single sheet 4to   1 p.   seal
Addressed: Captain Burney, / 26. / James Street, / Westm^t
Docketed: D'Arblay Feb. 12. 1821

How are you, my dear Brother? pray let my two messengers bring me word, & bring me good news. Alex goes on amending, but very slowly. He walks out every fair day, & that would tempt me to accompany him as far as to your Fireside, but that I see he always requires rest after every excursion, & therefore I have procured him an easy chair,

---

[8] A miniaturist of 'no mean celebrity' and of a family of miniaturists working in London in the years 1800–58, Peter Hervé (d. 6 June 1827 in France) had exhibited at the Royal Academy from 1802 to 1820. He had formed the Hervé Charity in Bath in 1811, and it was to this institution, later absorbed in the National Benevolent Institution, that FBA wished to send her contribution. See Rowland Mainwaring, *Annals of Bath* (1838), pp. 104–5; Edward Evelyn Barron, *The National Benevolent Institution, 1812–1936. A short account of its rise and progress extracted from the minutes* (1936); and *GM* xcvii[2] (1827), 190.

[9] This is Mrs. Piozzi's letter of 18 January 1821 (see *DL* vi. 392–4).

[10] Mrs. Margland is the grim governess in *Camilla* (1796).

upon which he reposes at least half an hour on his return from the Green Park. We may soon, however, hope for more strength——& our first use of it will carry us to James Street. I am much better myself, though not quite of the boastful train.

I want to know whether you have sent your Letter to your *Brother Officer*.

I beg you will be so good as to request Mrs. Burney, with my kind love, to deliver the enclosed to Mr. Sansom when she next sees him. I give the commission to Mrs. Burney, because —— —— Will you know why? —— because I should almost as soon trust it to the remembrance of Alexander as of his Uncle. I would he were as like that said dear Uncle in demonstrative activity of mind as he is in absence & absorption.

I have heard lately from Hetty & from Charlotte, & both are pretty well. So now you have news of 3 of your sisters at a stroke —— —— of the pen—

witness yr^s truly. F. d'A.

12th Feby 1821
I send back your Seal—in hopes you will let me see its impression ere long.

1244 [11 Bolton Street,
16 February, 1821]

To Mrs. Broome

A.L. (Berg), Friday
Double sheet 8vo   4 pp.   *pmks* 1821 PICCADILLY   To be Delivered / by 10 Sund Morn   seal
Addressed: Mrs. Broome / Ormond Row / Richmond / Surry.— / near Dorking
Endorsed by CBFB: Sister d'Arblay / 1821

Friday

I well know how my dearest Charlotte & Charlottina— have sympathized with me in this terrible season—& I have grieved not to write details—but my time has been so

215

exclusively devoted to my very very unwell——& very very
unmanageable Invalid that I could never, with safety, quit
him a moment——I thank God he is now, apparently, once
more better: but there have been continual draw backs——
& my spirits have had as much & as difficult employment as
my strength & thoughts. I must not tell——but *en passant*——
how dreadful at times have been his looks & my fears! —— ——
one morning, a summons the most condescending, written by
her own hand from our Eldest Royal Sister,[1] took me to her
palace in the Park——where I spent 3 hours very deliciously——
but alas——though I had left my Patient remarkably well, &
promising to take a walk in the Park, the morning being the
most beautiful imaginable —— —— I found ⏐ him——at my return——pale, altered, thinner than ever, & wholly abstracted
& absent lost in mathematical researches!——& so he had past
the 3 hours——& he has never been as well as the day before
that day, till This very one on which I am writing, when——
once again——his looks are less livid——& his Cough is entirely
gone——But for his affrighting thinness I should be at peace——

Mr. Chilver had taken leave——but I was forced to call him
back again——but he has taken leave *encore*, & has been very
comforting for *summer*——but charged me with innumerable
injunctions till that balmy season——

I look forward to the 2 Reposing *Boudoirs* with true hope
& pleasure,[2] my dearest Charlotte——so does he——I pray God
we may meet!——

But oh be careful how you remove——spare *meat & drink*
rather than ⏐ Coals & wood——or fatal effects will make me
rue the removal——

I hope Marianne joins me in this idea, & will enforce it by
her active zeal——I am sure Charlottina will abet me——

God bless you, my dearest kindest Charlotte——I have felt
quite unhappy not to write but my nerves have been dolour-
ously shaken——

1244. [1] This is the A.L.S. (Berg), dated Buckingham House, 6 February 1821,
from the Princess Augusta: My Dear Madame d'Arblay / Will you kindly come to
me tomorrow Morning at *ten* oClock. I am only in London for three days and
I should be very sorry to miss the pleasure of seeing You. I hope *You* and *Alex*
are well / Ever your affectionate friend / AUGUSTA

[2] Mrs. Broome was about to move apparently from Ormond Row, Richmond,
to 3 Under the Hill. See headnote, L. 1248.

I thank God our dear James is recovered—I had very good news of him 2 days ago. He has taken the air 3^{ce} & I have good accounts from Bath of our dear Esther—But poor Cecilia is far far from a state of serenity![3]—

Adieu—Adieu—

You will let me know the probabilities when you know them yourself of yr kind plan—that I will endeavour to accord to it as I wish—

Heaven bless you— |

Have I thanked my kind Charlottina for her excellent receipts?—

1245   11 Bolton Street,
                                            2 April 1821

To Charles Parr Burney

A.L.S. (Osborn), 2 Apr. 1821
Double sheet 8vo   3 pp.
Addressed: Revd Charles Parr Burney, / Greenwich, / Kent.
Annotated in pencil: 65—

Bolton St.
Berkeley Square
2^d April.1821.

My dear Charles,

The sight of my hand—at last!—will lead you to fatal fears for our dear suffering lovely—expiring Favourite;[1] but nothing final is arrived—though Hope seems extinct. 'Tis on *business* for her poor Mother—far more than for myself,

---

[3] About this time EBB had left her home in Bath for Rainbow Hill, near Worcester, to help nurse her daughter Cecilia, whose recovery was despaired of by the surgeon William Sandford (L. 1210 n. 27) and 'two other *eminent* medical men here', so EBB was to report to FBA in her letters of 25 and 28 February, and her heart-broken letter of 4 April marked the end (Eg. 3690, ff. 136–41b).

1245. [1] Cecilia Charlotte Esther Burney (i, p. lxix) had taken 'to her Room' on 22 February, the very day on which her mother arrived ('Worcester Journal').

that I now write—for alas, my dear Charles, to give you *pleasure* I have no Pen!—The Case will open for itself by your perusing *N⁰ 1.* which produced *N⁰ 2.* which generated N⁰ 3. which has brought forth This morning N⁰ 4.[2]

⌒

Now, supposing you to have read them, you will see that this poor little minikin affair must fall into your hands, or fall to the Ground. I am very sorry you should have any trouble about such a trifle; were it something of importance it would be, I am certain, a satisfaction rather than a toil to you; I I have no Probate—& to send to Bath would be useless, while my poor Sister is at Worcester. I can see no other way than your trusting yours to Mr. Sansom, to shew to these soliciters, who will shew it to the Master, accompanied with a written signature of your hereditary—Alas!—claim to act as Executer.[2]

If this should be the mode, I entreat you, at the same time, to beg these Gentlemen to deduct at once the fees & expences from the sum due.

If you see any better mode, you will of course adopt it: if the whole should prove inconvenient, or disagreeable, to you, the loss in result, when divided, & with its deductions, will be too insignificant for serious vexation.

I have been nearly absorbed, during this last week, in affliction for the dreadful blow just struck upon my most dear Mrs. Angerstein—& her family;[3] I tremble for its effect upon her delicate health; my dear I Mrs. Lock has fixed herself at Woodlands to watch & console her—

[2] The documents cited are missing, but the legal matter here, presumably a small legacy chargeable to CB's estate, seemed to concern his residuary legatees (FBA and EBB) and their relative James Sansom (L. 1191 n. 16), responsibility for whom CPB had inherited from his father CB Jr., who until his death in 1817 had Sansom in his employment or under his protection.

[3] Henry Frederick Angerstein, aged 17, a pupil at Eton, while rowing alone in a small skiff on the Thames on 27 March, lost an oar, and, reaching for it, fell into the water and drowned. Mrs. Locke wrote to FBA (A.L., Barrett, Eg. 3697, ff. 207–8b), 'You have, perhaps, heard The circumstances of this sad affliction— Their dear excellent Child Henry at Eton went alone on a boat! — — It was not till within this hour that . . . his poor remains [were] found.' See *AR* lxiii (1821), 234; and for FBA's letter of condolence, Diary, 21 April; 'To *Amine* on poor Harry's loss.' A mural tablet to his memory may be seen in the church of St. Alfege, Greenwich.

Alexander dined out yesterday, for the first time—& the difficulty of saying No to the goods of the Table is obviously & cruelly apparent in his heated breath & quickened pulse today! — — From 5 Relapses, owing to equally trivial causes, he has been *recovered:* but when I shall see & consider him as *established*—ah, that is a happiness of which I know not the date! — — —

I beg to be very kindly remembered to Mrs. Burney,[4]—& do not let Mrs. Bicknel forget me.[5] My best wishes await all your fine Children—though I am so utterly unknown to them that a message from me would appear to them as out of the way as one from the Man in the Moon.

Adieu, my dear Charles,

ever most sincerely yours

F. d'Arblay.

1246   [11 Bolton Street],
7 April 1821

To Mrs. Broome

A.L. (Berg), 7 Apr. 1821
Double sheet 8vo   4 pp.   *pmk* ⟨Ma⟩y Fair ⟨1821⟩
Addressed: Mrs. Broome, / 3 under the Hill, / Richmond / Surry.

Friday Morn^g.
7th. April 1821.

I was just going to execute the melancholy Commission I received yesterday from Worcester—when my dearest Charlotte's Letter arrives — —

---

[4] Frances Bentley *née* Young (*c.* 1792-1878), whose eldest child Frances Anne was about 9 years old. There were by this time five younger children (i, p. lxxii).

[5] Sabrina Bicknell (i, L. 7 n. 18; v, L. 426 n. 2), CB Jr.'s housekeeper, who on his death had remained with CPB and his family. To Frances Anne (*supra*) she was in 1837 'dear old Mrs. Bicknell ("Bicky") . . . much changed' and in June 1841, 'dear old Mrs. Bicknell (a very old friend indeed)'. See *A Great Niece's Journals*, pp. 123, 327; and Roger Lonsdale, '. . . Sabrina', *Evidence in Literary Scholarship*, ed. René Wellek and Alvaro Ribeiro (1979), pp. 281-308.

Surely I will come to you—*I* in the dual number—as fast as possible.—

But—have you had no intimation of the dangerous illness of poor sweet Cecilia?—the *hopeless* illness, as it has now long been?—

Yesterday the news of the fatal catastrophe was sent me —[1] with the desire I would reveal the sad tidings to you & to my other Charlotte—to our Brother—&c Fanny Burney & Edward are to take the mournful office for Chelsea— Fanny Raper—Charles Parr—

The sweet girl has been visibly & rapidly declining 15 or 16 months, in the Eyes of our poor Sister. It is thought she never recovered the long & afflicting nursing & sufferings of her adored maternal aunt, the excellent M[rs.] Hawkins[2]— They lasted 6 months, during which period the grateful adopted niece devoted her heart & mind still more than her strength & cares to the tenderest assiduity of fond watchfulness—

Her own exit was perfectly serene & quiet—she was quite unsuspicious of her immediate danger—& so innocent, so good, so dutiful, & so pious in her nature, & in the conduct of her whole life, that my poor sister & M[rs] Sandford thought it unnecessary to risk the impression of the awful declaration of her approaching departure.—

There are many opinions upon this subject—but surely we may hope *All* that are *strictly* followed up, according to a *religious* & *conscientious* deliberation, will be pardonable, if wrong, in the sight of God, & meet the merciful mediation of our Redeemer.

Our poor sister is resigned in the most exemplary manner,

1246. [1] News of the death on 3 April of Cecilia Margaret Burney, aged 33, had reached Bolton Street in EBB's letter (Barrett, Eg. 3690, ff. 140-1b), dated Rainbow Hill, 4 April 1821: 'To *you* my Dearest Fanny deeply grieved & Heartstricken as I am at this moment—I *will* write myself: tho' to no one else—we have lost our sweet & beloved Cecy! . . . her dear remains are to be deposited with those of her beloved Aunt Hawkins. by her own desire (expressed long ago—'

Of all EBB's daughters perhaps the most talented and most loved, Cecilia is memorialized in the 'Worcester Journal' for her compositions, her poetry and music, 'elegant little songs' written in her 13th year, and for the 'taste, neatness & expression' of her 'Pianoforte playing'. The Houghton Library, Harvard, has some of her compositions.

[2] For the death of Ann Hawkins, see L. 1191 nn. 1, 3.

for the sight of the hopeless lingering sufferings of the poor Patient made all wish of lengthened ᛁ existence seem selfish to her — —

She was not fed with those false hopes that paint future health succeeding to actual torment! — — —

Therefore she is resigned—but heart-stricken, & deeply, dreadfully afflicted—she sends you her kind love—& to my other Charlotte—Marianne you will include & add my love also.—Clement of course.

My Alex goes on amending—even *rapidly*, when prudent —but alas the smallest deviation is akin to quick relapse!— his diet—his beverage—his exercise—his studies—his recreation—his sleep, his *humours*—All, all must be measured not to be dangerous! And with a carelessness & forgetfulness such as his, how is this to be effected? I am in constant anxiety — — !! —

It will do us *both* good to accept your most tender invitation—& we will come forthwith[3]—but only for a *Week* at first—for reasons I will detail when we meet—

Let me only know what is *your* outward mourning for this sweet departed—stuff or silk that I may accommodate mine —as we ought [to be] alike—& I will be fixed by you— ᛁ & the day that brings me your answer, shall carry back my day, or rather hour, as I wish to be with you immediately. Entreat your dear & *too* hospitable housekeeper to have the *plainest* food, possible—all else being inimical—

I went yesterday to our dear Brother—my first Visit— nay, first absence from my fireside, since the middle of December last—save for 2 Hours one sole morning.

adieu, for a very short time, my own dearest Charlotte— I revive in the sweet prospect of our really meeting— ᛁ

P.S. I wish to arrive by the latest coach—Pray tell me how to do to be *snuggest*.

---

[3] FBA and AA were to set out for Richmond on Tuesday 10 April (Diary).

[3 Under the Hill,
Richmond],
14 April 1821

To Sarah Burney

L.S., printed in G. E. Manwaring, *My Friend the Admiral* (1931), pp. 265–6.

For the Fair Bride of this Morning, 14th of April, 1821.[1]

My Dearest Sarah,

Accept my warmest and kindest wishes in writing—since I cannot give you them verbally—that you, your happy partner, and your excellent parents, may meet every anniversary of this day by rejoicing in the event with which it will commence.[2]

1247. [1] On 12 April FBA had received a letter from 'the Bride Elect, *Sarah Burney*', and to her response of the 13th, a reply of the 14th from 'the Bride—Sarah Payne' (Diary). Of the letters sent from Richmond on this occasion, only the first letter above survives.

[2] The Wedding Breakfast at 26 James Street, Buckingham Gate, on 14 April 1821 is immortalized in Charles Lamb's essay 'The Wedding', wherein much is made of the father of the bride and his withholding permission until she should have reached the age of 25. Sarah (b. 17 November 1796) was 24, and tricked out, according to her cousin Fanny Raper, in a 'beautiful Bonnet of transparent figured thicke gauze with a plume of White feathers', a 'Gros de Naples Spencer and a nosegay of Myrtle and Roses', she had married on Saturday morning 14 April her cousin John Thomas Payne (*c.* 1796-1880), the natural son of Thomas Payne (L. 1192 n. 5), the bookseller, which business he was to take over in 1825. After the breakfast Sarah 'put on a purple silk Gown and Spencer and Bonnet and took leave separately of all present. Uncle James handed her into the carriage and John Payne followed, they smiled out of the Window and drove off like a very happy couple the people looked a little blank for a minute or two and Miss Lamb and two Little Girls cried a little but they all soon began to chirp and chatter and in about half an hour we all dispersed.' See Fanny Raper's letter (Berg) to CFBt, 21 April [1821]; also Joyce Hemlow, 'Lamb Recreates a Burney Wedding', *The Evidence of the Imagination*, ed. Donald H. Reiman *et al.* (1978), pp. 178-94.

Sally's marriage to the natural son of a *tradesman*, howbeit celebrated by Charles Lamb and blessed by Madame d'Arblay, was not such, in EBB's opinion, as to '*raise* her consequence in the Eye of the World' (Eg. 3690, ff. 138-9b). From Chelsea College SHB wrote dourly of the 'great probability of [her] losing cast by the union'. 'I am perplexed', she confided to CFBt in a letter of 17 February 1821 (Berg), 'as to the class of society to which she will henceforth find herself restricted. Admired & liked as she is, will *her pill* be swallowed in consideration of the sweetness she can administer with it?—How will your Richmond folk stand affected on this subject? . . . The proud militaires here, I grieve to think, will all hold aloof.' Poor Sall, she might have done better if wanted, was the

Most affectionately yours, my dear Girl, ever,

F. D'arblay.

All that are now within my reach desire to join their names in hearty concurrence with this benediction.

(Signed)   Charlotte Ann Broome
            Charlotte Barrett
            A. P. D'Arblay
            Henry Barrett [Sr]
            Marianne Francis
            Julia Barrett
            Henry Barrett [Jr]
            Arthur Barrett, his mark X
            Hetty Barrett
            R. Barrett

1248   [11 Bolton Street,
                                23 APRIL 1821]

To Mrs. Broome

A.L.S. (Berg), n.d.
Double sheet 4to   4 pp.   *pmks* T.P. / Piccadilly 24 AP 1821
black seal
    Addressed: Mrs. Broome / 3 Under the Hill, / Richmond / Surry.
    Endorsed by CBFB: Sister d'arblay / April 1821

I ought to have written to my dearest Charlotte sooner[1]—
I wished to have written immediately—but the difficulty of
arrangement with Alex, relative to our return to your dear &

general verdict. FBA, however, who 'praised Mr J Ps manners as being gentlemanly
& elegant', CBFB, and CFBt, were determined to make the best of 'poor Johnny'.
'Poor dear Sall! I hope she will be happy, & she is such a clever & good tempered
girl, & has such good sense withal, that I think she will not miss of it.' See the
letter (Eg. 3706D, ff. 20b–22b) from CFBt to SHB, 5 October [1821].

1248. [1] After a visit of about 10 days to Mrs. Broome FBA had returned to
Bolton Street on 18 April (Dairy).

hospitable roof, kept me silent, rather than send you a *bilumi-nary* incomprehensibility, of yea & nay, to & again, half promising on, half wheeling off, till you could know no more what to expect than I could what to undertake. But when your Letter came to day, I took a decicive measure—

But first to our arrival hither.

We had not been landed half an hour, ere an invitation came for Alex to Dine on Easter Sunday with your old acquaintance, & my very old Friend, Sir William Wellere Pepys:[2] This he eagerly accepted, happy in the prospect of making himself a nook in some future good old Blue party; for if any stockings of that colour are still extant, they are worn at his house; he is the last *male* of the *original Blue Stocking Literature.*ˡ

—I have been interrupted, & must therefore come to the point, or lose today's post — —

Yesterday I first lost my face ache—And to day, as soon as I got your Letter, I felt courage to sally forth, to consult upon our visit with our good Brother. Dian & I proceeded therefore to James Street, where I found him much better than report had painted him—from the comfort & revival of a very chearing Letter from his darling Sarah—I impressed him with your kind wish to see him, & his good Partner— who well merits inclusion — — & told him Alex & I meant to accept a similar affectionate call for This Week or the Next, but I offered *him* the choice, as Clement's rooms could not quite accommodate an establishment of 4.—He was excessively good humoured, & professed himself much pleased you were so kind as to wish & press his visit while you had still our so *all-dear* Charlottina—ˡ and, after various considerations & deliberations, *he* fixed for *next Week*—but not his *day*—the promise however is *made*, & very pleasantly, & with perfect satisfaction in its *seasonable* demand,[3]

He had purposed drinking tea with me this Evening, but we now settled—since I feel so much better, that Alex & I should take that beverage with *him* to-morrow[4]—

---

[2] At 11 Gloucester Place, Portman Square (L. 1239 n. 9).

[3] This was on 23 April. The Paynes had gone to Italy on their wedding tour. The Barretts would set off for Ghent in mid-May. The visit of JB and his wife to Mrs. Broome was not to take place until 5-15 May (Manwaring, p. 278): 'They [CBFB and the Barretts] gave me and Mrs. B. ten days good nursing, and both of us came to town the better for it.' [4] On Tuesday 24 April (Diary).

And—on Wednesday we hope & mean to quaff it from your own dear hand, by your own fire side.[5]

At the same time as before.

And I beg my dear Marian will not dress again, nor sit up, but meet us at the Breakfast table next morning, Thursday. I cannot bear to discompose her, unless I could see her by no other condition.

Thursday Morn. I shall embrace again my other so very dear Charlotte—I hope for good tidings of my dear Godboy[6] —I had not heard the sweet Cecilia's affectionate arrangement.[7] She was not a Parent, nor a Guardian, & therefore is blameless for listening to her heart's yearnings—*otherwise*, poor Fanny must have stood first—but I she had a *natural* right to expect to out-live all of them! sweet thing! She must have had a strong feeling of inward decay!—I grieve for her early loss—she was truly amiable —— ——

God bless—& long long preserve my dearest Charlotte & her beloved namesake—& all her's—

prays devoutly your
most aff^{ect}

F d'A

[5] FBA was to resume her visit at Richmond on 26 April but to return to Bolton Street within three days to make room for JB and his wife, whose visit was, however, deferred (See L. 1249).

[6] Richard Arthur Francis Barrett, aged 9, too unwell temporarily to accompany his parents abroad, was to be left in the care of Mrs. James Burney (see L. 1253) until August, when he was to travel unaccompanied to join them, though met by his father at Ostend. 'I hope Dicky will be sick & safe in the cabin instead of climbing about the masts', his mother would remark in a letter (Barrett, Eg. 3702, ff. 130-1b) to CBFB, 31 July-[3 August 1821]. A younger son Henry was left in a school in Richmond. For Richmond schools, see ix, L. 993 n. 13.

[7] With the exception of small legacies (£10 each to surviving brothers and sisters), Ann Hawkins (L. 1180 n. 15) had in a will (PRO/PROB/11/1613/73, pr. 27 February 1819) bequeathed all her real and personal estates to her niece Cecilia, together with the Hop Kiln ('all that Messuage or Tenement adjoining the vicarage Garden at Halstead'), which was to be sold to her advantage. Cecilia had in her turn therefore money to bestow, and in a will (PRO/PROB/11/1642/249, dated 29 April 1820, pr. 2 May 1821) she bequeathed the interest on her funds in the 4 per cents to her sisters Maria Bourdois and Sophia E. Burney and to her uncle Edward Francesco Burney (i, pp. lxix, lxxv). 'I feel myself under particular obligation to him and trust he will consider this little remembrance as of a proof of my dutiful regard for him.' After his demise the interest was to go to her niece Clara Burney, now only 3 years old.

It was probably the omission of her mother and her sister Amelia that caused the comment.

I will certainly bring the old Journal—We cannot stay beyond a few days, & we shall take the precaution you so sagely suggested with respect to *Church & State*; messages or Invitations:—nothing *else* or *less*, shall draw us *abruptly* away.[8]

I am quite sorry our poor dear Esther cannot come James was much pleased with your Letter & ⟨truly⟩ with Hetty's acct.

1249   [11 Bolton Street,
                              1 MAY 1821]

To Mrs. Broome

A.L. (Berg), n.d.
Double sheet 4to   4 pp.   *pmks* T.P. / Piccadilly 2 MY 1821
2 MY 1821
Addressed: Mrs, Broome / 3 Under the Hill, / Richmond, / Surry.—

My Charlotte—my dearest Charlotte how I regret to have lost so much time from you, as our Brother cannot benefit from my absence!—I went to him yesterday morning,[1] & found he had made arrangements that impeded his little journey till Friday, *after Dinner*; he wrote to you while I stayed, —& therefore I had not meant to take the Pen on this point: but it has since occurred to me that it is possible he may *forget to send the Letter to the Post*; such things have happenned: but should that not now be the case, do not betray my *calumny*.

I send poor Mrs. Cooke's Letter,[2] which you will keep for

---

[8] An oblique reference perhaps to a possible summons from one of the princesses. The extant Diary for March and April 1821 records no less than twelve pourboires to 'Cocher de la P^sse', or 'Domestique de la p^sse' or 'Laquey La p^sse'.

1249. [1] On 30 April. For visits of FBA and JB and his wife to CBFB at Richmond, see L. 1248 nn. 3, 5.
[2] The Revd. Samuel Cooke (iii. 2–3), for fifty-two years the vicar of Great Bookham (see L. 1182 n. 6), had died on 29 March 1820, in the 80th year of his age (M.I. in the Church of St. Nicholas, Great Bookham).

me till we meet, inserting, when you write, the kindest of messages & concern in my name, with your own.

I paid my Royal Visit[3]—& more sweetly gracious than ever were the honours—as well as comforts it afforded me. How would the generous mind of my *Partner in all* have glowed with noble pleasure, had he foreseen that to *him* I should owe added favours! to *his* honoured Name, & his Sovereign's sense of his services!—The kindness, the goodness, the condescendsion of my sweet Princesses are all their own, all instinctive, native—but the power to shew it publicly, without too much partiality, I I have the great, the unspeakable satisfaction to believe to be *his* gift—for the date of that publicity has been from the period of his restoration to his military rank; & it has not, of course, diminished, from his King's conferring on him the title of comte, in his Mission to Treves, nor from his (the King's) elevating him to the military rank of Lieutenant General when he (the King) put him on the half pay list, at the peace. Sunday Evening the Princess Augusta & the Duchess of Gloucester made me walk with them, *en trio*, for two hours in the Queen's Gardens of Buckingham Palace—& the Princess Augusta then sent me home in her own Carriage. If they knew the secret source of delight which their sweetness gives me—it would but double their benevolent pleasure in the gratitude they excite—for they are truly, truly made up of the *Milk of human kindness*—

I have now a word for my second dear Charlotte[4] which I beg you to let her read in your own room.—Should Alex take advantage of his uncle's delay to stay on another day,—what good you will do him, my dear Charlot*t*a, & consequently to *me*, if you will *inveigle* him to get the better of his *dread* of figuring in a little dance, I though it is now *prescribed* for him! If you can ensnare him into doing the figure

[3] On Sunday 29 April FBA was received by the Duchess of Gloucester and the Princess Augusta at Buckingham House, and when all three went strolling in the garden, FBA seized on the opportunity to speak of her brother James, his health, his works presumably, and the letter he had recently sent to the Duke of Clarence about his promotion (see L. 1241 n. 1; L. 1256 n. 3; L. 1257 nn. 1, 3; and Manwaring, p. 284).

[4] Charlotte Barrett and her daughters Julia and Henrietta (i, pp. lxxii–iii), now 13 and 10 years of age, respectively; Alex was 26.

of right & left with you & your little loves,[4] & then to *hay* with them, while you push him to & fro, you will be his best Doctor: but it must all be spontaneous!—It will become a medicine at once, if a Doctor's orders are hinted at. It must be a sudden jerk of the moment;—a literal hop, skip, & jump without apparent plan, or cause; it must not be *asked*;—for it would be *denied*:—it must not be *entreated*, for it would be *resisted*: it must be done by *surprize*,—as a mere whim of your own,—a Capricio—or Capericcio, wholly extemporaneous. When he once finds how easy that is which he now thinks so formidable, his light figure, & remarkably well-formed instep will make him fond of the elasticity of the movement, and then — — Nymphs, have at ye all![5]—he will be a *made man* in youthful female groups. I the more wish it, because if he does not begin *now*, he will want to do it at fifty. You, my dear Charlo*tta*, who can do what you will with him, *do this*, which I doubt that any other can perform. But, to keep *me* out of the plot, which else will be *marred*, if he stays, make him write me a ׀ line, to prevent Expectation. or *you*, my dear *first* Charlotte, will be kind enough to pen him down to a slip of paper, & tell him two words will suffice.

Should he, by chance, already be set out when this Letter arrives, let my scheme fade away—& vanish into annihilation in the flames of your next fire.

I have announced the *Brighton* plan[6] to dear James—who much approves it.—*I* approve any change of place, that will save your so pretty house from a character of melancholy by so abrupt a difference—. I have had a long Letter from Sarah Harriet, written in sprightly spirits, & very interesting. I find she is *already* at her new Friends[7]—I had no idea the affair

[5] Cf. *Bucks, Have at ye all; or The Picture of a Playhouse* (1784), a farce by David Garrick.

[6] On the departure of the Barretts for the Continent in May, Mrs. Broome had intended to go to Brighton for her health, but was prevented by the unexpected return of her son Clement Francis from the Continent (see L. 1253 n. 1).

[7] In a long letter (Eg. 3698, ff. 84-5b) of 7 December 1820 SHB had announced her intention of giving up her apartments in Chelsea College, where she had lived since CB's death in 1814. Among other 'stupifying properties', she found the air 'moist and relaxing' and 'the society miserably confined'. 'The climax of all its abominations is, its distance from my family & many of my best friends, & the difficulty (without giving a day's previous notice) of procuring any sort of conveyance to Town.'

At this date, SHB was already established at 26 Upper Cadogan Place, as com-

was actually finished. I would something similar could offer for poor F[anny] B[urney][8]—I am certainly better for my little excursion to you, my dearest Charlotte—& I hope this autumn we shall be together much longer.—& await the return of our so loved—so justly valued—so sweetly amiable Traveller.[9]—I shall not expect you to write while you still possess her.—I hope my dear Dick is quite recovered.— make Alex give me a *word*, unless he is coming directly.

Adieu & Heaven bless you, my *both dear Charlottes*—

1250   [11 Bolton Street,
14 May 1821]

To Mrs. Barrett

A.L. (Berg), n.d.
Originally a double sheet 8vo, of which the second leaf has evidently been torn away   2 pp.
Docketed in pencil p. 1: n. date

How I thank my dearest Charlotta for her very welcome lines—& her capering attempts at so hurried a moment. They were truly unseasonable for all but You, to whom the service, or pleasure of others always makes your own.

I now write to beg a word of the Day when you will be in

panion to Charlotte Anne Gregor (1800-25), only child of the Revd. William Gregor (1761-1817) of Trewarthenick, Cornwall, chemist, mineralogist, and landscape painter (see *DNB*) and his wife Charlotte Anne *née* Gwatkin (d. 11 Sept. 1819). An orphan at this time, therefore, and, as a codicil in her own will shows, an epileptic, Charlotte was chaperoned by Jane *née* Urquhart (*c.* 1770-1854), the widow of her uncle Francis Gregor (1760-1815). Mrs. Gregor, as SHB reported in her letter (Eg. 3698, ff. 88-9b), had travelled much, had resided in Italy, and was 'fond of books, painting, music'. The niece, deprived by ill health 'of all the amusements of the gay world', was to remove to 'the country' when she came of age in June 1821, apparently residing thereafter at Stanley Grove, King's Road, Chelsea. The pathetic story unfolds in the Gregor wills (PRO/PROB/11/1597/ 519, pr. 15 October 1817; PRO/PROB/11/1697/198, pr. 2 April 1825; and the Admon. PRO/PROB/6/196, Cornwall, 14 September 1820).

[8] For Fanny Burney's career as governess, see L. 1191 n. 4.

[9] For the travels of Charlotte and her family to Ghent, where it cost less to live and where masters could be procured for moderate sums, see L. 1250 and notes.

town,[1] that I may keep it sacred & at liberty for the hope of seeing you. If to *lunch* I shall be charmed—I dare not ask Mr. Barrett to Dinner—I am so ill provided with materials— from never dining but tete à tete—or with so kind a 3ᵈ as your indulgent Mother. I have nothing here of my own. I came hither caring for nothing— ¹ & now, that I would try to care a little for others, my proprietor will listen to no amendments.—

Fanny Raper has come in & stops my further Episterorly— My tender love to my dearest Elder Charlotte & I will ⟨inscribe⟩ to Lʸ Bedingfelt[2] by post—

Alex has a morning engagement in town for Monday

1251   [11 Bolton Street, *post* 19 May] 1821

To Mrs. Locke

L., copy in hand of CFBt (Diary MSS. viii, 7240-1, Berg), 1821
Single sheet 4to   2 pp.
Edited at the Press. *See* Textual Notes.

To Mʳˢ Locke

1821

How is my beloved Friend? and how *doing*? I want news —& I have missed it most vexatiously. The sweet Amine &

1250. ¹ Charlotte Barrett paid her farewell visit on 16 May (Diary).

² Living in or near Ghent at this time were Sir Richard Bedingfeld (1767- 1829) of Oxburgh Hall, Norfolk, 5th baronet, and his wife Charlotte Georgiana (1770-1854), whom FBA had met in Bath (see ix, L. 967 nn. 9, 10 and *passim*). Lady Bedingfeld was the daughter of Sir William Jerningham (1736-1809) of Cossey, Norfolk, 6th baronet, and his wife the Hon. Frances *née* Dillon (1747- 1825), who was living at this time at 13 Bolton Row with her third son Charles William Edward (1774-1822), barrister-at-law, and his wife Emily *née* Middleton (*c.* 1788-1822), the mother of four young children. FBA's letter and Lady Bedingfeld's reply to it (see L. 1253 n. 4) were to initiate a train of associative references to family events of the next five years. It was this Edward Jerningham who proved the relationship of the Jerninghams to the Viscount Stafford (Lodge, 1845), beheaded in 1680 for treason, and had the attainder lifted. For all these matters, Lady Bedingfeld, and her family, see *The Jerningham Papers*.

her dear Sister both came hither the only morning I have been forth *visiting*.[1] A long requisite etiquette took me to Portman Square to Ly H[arcourt][2] and thence kindlier movements took me elsewhere—& none so salutary to me as were called forth in Portland Place, where I had the happiness of passing an hour & half with your dear & *all accomplished*, as my dearest Father called her, Lady Templetown.[3] Our talk —always to me interesting both from manner & matter— was nearly confined to *you* & *yours*, subjects that even always, & even yet exhilarate as well as delight me.

And yet—oh my dearest Friend—The *spirit of enjoyment* is gone!—gone!—though the *animal* spirits still, at times, are revived by social exertions. From all this, wholly different & distinct is the operation of *Alex* upon my feelings. He gives me an *interest* in ¹ life unspeakable—utterly, utterly indescribable—but it is never the *spirit of enjoyment*!—alas no! My fears, my alarm, my doubts, keep continually at Work every pulse with such living anxiety, about him, alike mentally & corporeally, that while he spares me that dread dead calm in my existence caused by my deplored privation—he shakes the whole frail machine—material & immaterial—by an alternation that is like a Whirl, of Apprehension & Hope.

His health demands such unattainable caution;—his character is so singular & excentric, mixt up of a sensibility in some points the most piercing, & an Apathy in others the most impenetrable—that to what to look forward for his future welfare in this nether World, is as formidable to my foresight as to my wishes—when he shall have lost the maternal Friend—*Flapper,*[4] Steward, Guardian, & confidant, that has hitherto helped on his incurable inexperience

---

1251. [1] On 19 May (Diary).

[2] Wife of the 3rd Earl Harcourt, Mary *née* Danby (*c.* 1750–1833), confidential friend of Queen Charlotte (see ix, L. 1051 n. 2; x, L. 1176), had called on FBA on 15 May (Diary). FBA returned the call on the 19th.

[3] Lady Templetown (L. 1234 n. 2), on whom FBA called on the 18th and 19th (Diary).

[4] Cf. L. 1243 n. 2.

[11 Bolton Street],
21 July 1821

To Charles Wesley

A.L.S. third person, two drafts (Berg), 21 July 1821 written on pp. 2 & 3 of a ds. 8vo of A.L.S. third person from Charles Wesley[1] to FBA, *dated* York Buildings N⁰ 2, New Road, near Gloucester Place, Marylebone, 19 July 1821, 1p.

Annotated by FBA: The Answer on the other side.

The 2nd draft is here printed. The actual letter was sent on the 26th (Diary).

Answer.

Mad^e d'Arblay regrets her inability to aid the friendly wishes of Mr. C. Westley in the service of Mrs. Cosway,[1] to whom she would gladly have been of any use; but Miss Burney of Chelsea has been mistaken with regard to the Executership. Mad^e d'A. has been left, conjointly with her eldest sister, Mrs. Burney *Residuary Legatee*; the *Executers* were Capt. Burney & Dr Charles Burney: the latter alone acted; & the Residuary Legatees passively *Received* from Him what He judged to be their Right, & in the same manner implicitly *answered* every claim which he judged to be just. Every thing passed through His hands, & He assured them that not a Call remained unsettled. Mad^e d'A. nevertheless, has sought amongst the papers of her revered Father that have fallen to her care, but vainly, for any memorandum of any subscription due to Mrs Cosway, or to any other subscriber, for the Creation of Haydn: she finds no Note on the subject. & she herself never possessed any Copy of that immortal Work. ǀ

[Complimentary paragraph at the end of the first draft:]

1252. [1] Charles Wesley (1757-1834), a musician, son of the musician and hymn-writer Charles Wesley (1707-88) by his wife Sarah *née* Gwynne (1726-1822), had written to FBA on behalf of Maria Louisa Catherine Cecilia *née* Hadfield (1759-1838), miniature painter (see *DNB*), the widow of Richard Cosway (1740-4 July 1821), miniaturist, who averred that though she had subscribed through CB to the publication of Haydn's *Creation* in 1800 (see Lonsdale, p. 401), she had not yet received her copy of it.

Made d'A. returns her Compts to Mr. Mrs. & particularly Miss Westley,[2] with every good wish for their health & happiness.

21st July. 1821.

1253   [11 Bolton Street],
30 July 1821

To Mrs. Broome

A.L.S. (Berg), 30 July 1821
Double sheet 8vo   4 pp.   black seal

Monday Evening
30th. July, 1821.

I am so sorry for this melancholy termination of poor Clement's travels,[1] that I am almost ashamed to tell my dearest Charlotte how disappointed I am at this unexpected & abrupt stoppage of our so earnestly desired & so long delayed re-union. But I really ought not to talk about it, the cause is so much more important. Pray tell dear Clement I feel sincerely for such a sorrowful blow to his favourite friends[2]—& not a word of my personal share in the catastrophe. It could only uselessly vex his kind heart. I shall immediately—*nearly*—let Mrs Lock know I can accept *her* hospitable friendship sooner than I had intended; but I must defer it a few days;—it is easier to be ready for a dear sister than for even the dearest of Friends—& such she is—who

---

[2] 'Mr. Mrs. & particularly Miss Wesley', that is, Charles, his mother (*supra*), and his sister Sarah (1760-1828).

1253. [1] Clement Francis, finding the hardships of travel in Germany beyond his strength, had returned to his mother at Richmond (see further, L. 1256).
[2] The death in Paris on 2 July 1821 of Rose Tunno, daughter of John Tunno (*c.* 1746-1819) of Devonshire Place, London, and sister of Edward Rose Tunno (*c.* 1795-1863), formerly Clement's pupil, who graduating from Trinity College, Cambridge, B.A. (1818), M.A. (1822), had later read law and was M.P. for Bossiney (1826-32).

has other connections, & consequently some forms of *etiquette* which require some preparation.[3]

Let me tell you, however, my dearest Charlotte, something that will please & gratify you, as it has myself. I have just received a Letter from Lady Bedingfeld,[4] answering mine by our Charlotta, full of the most elegant praise of that loved person, &, far from making any merit of complying with my request of admitting her to L^y B's select society, she *thanks me* for giving her the opportunity of being the first to introduce her.——A clause however, follows, that will make my dear Charlotte smile —— —— she broadly hints that a *return of favours* would be but equitable, & tells me her *Mother* & a *Brother* & *Sister* live in Bolton Row, whom she cannot but wish I should acquaintance with!——

If Mrs. Lock's spare room is luckily in possession of its name, I shall probably go thither ere the end of the week: but always direct to Bolton Street, I when you can write, for my Letters are always safe, & always follow immediately.

⟨Dash⟩, now, has full time to be purified for his espousals.
——

I have had two bits of Letters from Alex——one of them from Dover, the 2^d· from Calais.[5] This is an attention essen-

---

[3] Visits to Mrs. Locke entailed visits to and from the Angersteins of Woodlands, the Revd. George Locke and his family, Lady Martin and Sir George, the Vansittarts (L. 1270 n. 23) and others (Diary), and consequently more formal dress.

[4] In a reply (Berg) of 3 July to FBA's letter of introduction (see L. 1250 n. 2), Lady Bedingfeld wrote in praise of CFBt 'here is Talent and good breeding, and travelled Experience, and all Sorts of Virtues, full blown and blowing'. And in letters of May (see copies made by MF, Berg) CFBt in her turn told how Lady Bedingfeld, 'eminent for active kindness', had sent on the evening of the arrival of the Barretts to invite them to tea, had devoted the whole of the next morning to finding a suitable school and a pianoforte for the girls, acting as guide to the Public Library, Botanical Gardens, and other parts of Ghent. 'She is . . . a very intelligent & charming woman' and 'the being known to her is a sort of passport into all the english families here'. On 28 May the Barretts dined at Sir Richard's and as a result 'we have been most hospitably received & visited &c by some very delightful people——'.

To FBA Lady Bedingfeld spoke of her 'Valuable Mother', the dowager Lady Jerningham, now living near FBA in Bolton Row, who in the past had enjoyed FB's novels; 'how much would she like to make a personal acquaintance with You! & I think you would find her's a pleasant House, she never goes out in an Evening, and is glad to see any body that calls. I have a Clever agreeable Brother, who with a delightful wife, & Children, live with her' (L. 1250 n. 2).

[5] AA had set off on 23 July with plans to join his friends Charles Babbage

tially good to me. I dare not flatter myself with further news for an Age.

I hope the dear Archdeacon & his Cornelia are at Twicken-ham—I know how greatly *that* will contribute to chear Clement—but how he will miss our Charlotte—Marianne will do all she can, but who has two sisters cannot be content with halving such a commodity. The *Mère*, however, here; the dear dear *Mother* will afford such a son more solace & solid comfort than all the rest of the world put together. I hope what the World reports is not true of this sweet Rosebud[2]— tis' quite enough for Clement's affectionate heart to ¦ grieve for his *friends*. Yet—if the World has been right—what a *blessing* in the midst of sorrow that a nearer connexion had not ten thousand fold embittered the loss! Our dear James was here last week, looking well—& I drank tea with him & his good wife last Friday—very sociably & pleasantly. Edward & Fanny were with me the day before to the same beverage, & well. The news from Bath is rather better. Fanny Raper & her sposo were with me on Sunday after Church: *she* still a Hebe of freshness & beauty—*he* ever more her adorer, & therefore happy. I long to know whether Maule[6] is a constant friend, or only an incidental flatterer. Pray tell me.

Mrs. Burney charged me to mention that she would take the utmost care of our noble Dick, in every point.[7] And begged you would be quite easy about him & his little com-panion. It has rained all day, or I had had hopes of seeing them, which I much wished.

Adieu, my beloved Charlotte,

My Love to Clement & to Marianne—

ever tenderly your

F. d.'Ay.

(L. 1185 n. 6) and John Frederick Herschel (L. 1185 n. 8) in Paris for a tour of Switzerland. Letters he had sent from Dover and Calais respectively had reached his mother on 25 and 27 July.

[6] Possibly William Maule (*c.* 1775–1851) of 185 Piccadilly, and later, of 19 Saville Row, appointed in this year aurist to His Majesty. See further, xii, L. 1361.

[7] See L. 1248 n. 6.

To Mrs. Waddington

L. printed, 'A Burney Friendship II', *Monthly Review*, ix (Oct. 1902), 151-3.

It was indeed a sad length of time that had elapsed—in your own words, since you had written to me, when *in December* I received a letter in answer to my last in July 1820; though in July I, even I, with my poor, tardy, and reluctant pen, had written twice *by return of post* to two letters that expressed urgency; notwithstanding *till* July *not one word*, in that whole 1820[1]—and for how long I remember not of 1819—had reached me from my erst, most kind, most anxious, most tender, and most indulgent correspondent. The change, indeed, has been in unison with the period, melancholy, uncongenial!—I deem it attributable—according to your own confession from Rome—to my not burning or returning all your letters[2]—and from that avowal, which robbed their profusion of its charm, I mentally relinquished them—and have only waited for opportunity to collect in order to destroy or restore them.

Should you ask why I did not quiet your mind by this assurance, I answer, that *to quiet your mind*, from the lamented period of its first and early distresses, as far as I have had the power, has ever been a soothing and favourite object to my own; but to give you this promise prematurely I thought would produce the contrary effect; for to say I would *collect* your letters, was to inform you that they were dispersed; and would that have given you quiet? No, my dear anxious friend, no, to have known they were, some at Calais, with our books from the Custom-house; some at Paris, with our remaining chattels, some, nay most, at Richmond, with Mrs. Broome—and the rest in sundry trunks and

---

1254. [1] FBA had written to GMAPW on 3 July 1820 (L. 1232) and again on the 15th and the 18th (both letters missing) and had received a reply on the 17th.
    [2] For GMAPW's request in the summer of 1816 that FBA return her letters, and the promise FBA then gave, see i, p. xxii; ix, L. 1010; x, L. 1109 and *passim.*

packages, with my other goods[3]—to have known this would have harassed you trebly, and plunged your affrighted imagination into every magazine, newspaper and gossiping pamphlet for at least a quarter of the present century. Yet was this a dispersion that imperious and cruel circumstances had rendered unavoidable, and such as had involved them in the same intricacies that encircled my own manuscripts that I held most sacred. Now, however, that I can give you a solemn assurance *That All Are Collected*, and safe, and under my own immediate Lock and Key, I take once more my pen, to give you this only comfort it is in my power to bestow.

Do not, however, infer, my forever dear—though I *think* estranged Mary! that I have done nothing consonant to your wishes till I could comply with them wholly; on the contrary, I took the most solid and essential measures to obviate any future mischief or disturbance to you upon the arrival of that epoch which takes your manuscripts from my care and protection[4]—and I will now copy the paragraph which proves my real attention to your wishes, and which, in case of accidents—as every day is uncertain of its morrow, will keep a satisfactory claim in your hands.

Copy.

'Extract from the Will of Frances Burney, Widow!! of Lieutenant-General Comte Alexander Jean Baptist Piochard D'Arblay. . . . In like manner, I desire my son to return to my dear, early, partial friend, Georgiana Mary Ann Waddington, Great-niece of my venerated Mrs. Delany, All and Every Letter or Paper in her handwriting that may be found in my possession after my decease unread and unexamined. They are endorsed, For Mrs. Waddington. I beg my son will deliver them to her, or her Commission immediately after my Funeral.

'Witness my Hand,
'Frances D'Arblay.'

To write this was among the first *devoirs* I compelled myself to fulfil, when able to fulfil any, after the dread laceration

---

[3] For the vicissitudes of the d'Arblay possessions left in Paris and the trunks stored in Calais, see FBA's Diary and Account Books and Ll. 1189 n. 5; 1229 n. 1.

[4] For the final disposition of the Burney manuscripts in the possession of FBA, see her will (PRO/PROB/11/1922/88, pr. 17 February 1840), printed in xii, Appendix, or i, pp. xliii–xliv.

that tore from my tortured heart its Companion, its Confidant, its Partner in all, on whose unsullied Honour, Delicacy and Sympathy I had implicitly relied, for the just disposition of whatever might remain of mine, in case, by sudden dissolution, I had been called away first. But the First Call has been His, and every moment of my solitary leisure, in the absence of my son, that my poor care and grief-worn eyes will permit, has, from that desolating 18th of May,[5] been invariably consigned to the examination, arrangement, selection or destruction of Letters, Documents and Manuscripts of every description in my possession. But the hoards are so immense, and my interruptions are so long, from my enfeebled and aching sight, and weakened and wearied spirits, joined to the frequently disabling effect of one line—one word, in stopping my investigations, that my progress is still but small on the *whole*, though the *parts* that I have done with are countless! for it is not only all my own letters from my many friends, or written by myself, and fallen back to me by deathful rights, conjugal, filial, or sisterly—with all my own innumerable personal manuscripts, but all of every sort that belonged to the most honoured of Partners, the most revered of Parents, and the most darling of Sisters—making altogether four collections[6] of such enormous magnitude that even were I much younger and much healthier than I am, I could not expect to go through with them. But I have completed a general list of them, and I am taking in succession from that list those I regard as most sacred, or those concerning which I have confidential reasons for being most anxious. *Yours* are included under this last class, and I am *now* reading, and as well as I can, sorting them for *you*, or for the *Flames*. They are indescribably interesting, even yet! and so touchingly tender, and so fondly trusting, that, oh my dear Mary!—you can never look over them, I *think*, without a recurrence to those feelings which made you for so

[5] Possibly an error in the printed source (*supra*) for 13 May, General d'Arblay's birthday, or 3 May (his death).

[6] The four collections of papers, letters, and Journals, in the order of their acquisition would have been those of SBP (Mrs. Phillips died in 1800), the Memoirs and letters of CB (d. 1814), General d'Arblay's papers, and finally her own.

many years hold to your heart's core as the dearest of your Friends

Your ever truly affectionate,
F. D'Arblay.

P.S.—You know now that your letters are safe, and are your own, but do not, therefore, dearest Mary, 'die,' but rather live 'in peace'—with me especially I entreat.

1255   3 Under the Hill, Richmond,
7 August 1821

To Edward Foss

A.L.S. (Berg), 7 Aug. 1821
Double sheet 8vo   black edged   1 p.   *pmk* 13 AU 1821   black seal
   Addressed: Edward Foss Esqr, / 36 / Essex Street / Strand.
   Also a typescript copy (Berg) 1 p.   4to.

Madame d'Arblay would be ungrateful not to acknowledge the considerate attention of Mr. E. Foss, though the communication it conveys fills her with true concern,[1]—as well as with great anxiety for her poor Nephew.[2]

Mad^e d'Arblay begs Mr. E. Foss to accept her Compliments & Thanks.

7th August. 1821.
Richmond
3 Under the Hill.

1255. [1] 'Rosette' (b. 1759), CB Jr.'s widow (i, p. lxxi), had died on 2 August. Edward Smith Foss (*c.* 1756–1830), solicitor, having married on 17 August 1780 Anne *née* Rose (d. 26 May 1808), was 'Rosette''s brother-in-law.
   [2] Charles Parr Burney (1785–1864), only child of CB Jr. and 'Rosette' (*supra*).

[Twickenham Meadows *and*
3 Under The Hill, Richmond],
10 August 1821

To Charles Parr Burney

A.L.S. (Osborn), 10 Aug. 1821
Double sheet 8vo   black edged   4 pp.

I am sure I need not tell you, my dear Charles, how sincerely I feel for the afflicting loss you have just sustained;—
I could not so intimately know the many excellent qualities
of the dear Departed & not cordially appreciate them;—I
could not view her as the so invariably loved Wife of my dear
—dear Brother & not as such doubly respect her,—& I was
not likely to be conscious of the excessive, the boundless
partiality she so long & ardently cherished for myself without being touched by Gratitude as well as Affection: & though
all immediate intercourse has of late, from distance, absence,
—&, recently, alas—from our joint misfortunes, been
broken, the remembrance of her ╎ fond early friendship
revives warmly at this awful separation to give fresh force to
my regret. Mr. Ed[ward] Foss, who wrote me the melancholy tidings, says you were on a Journey—What a comfortless call back to You, my poor Charles, & how truly do I
compassionate it! It is not that this is a blow that could
hardly ever have met you utterly unprepared—so deplorably
precarious has the poor sufferer's health been for many years;
but I conceive it at the present moment to have been unexpected, & I am certain it will have been severe.—Your
little ones, my dear Charles, & your amiable Wife—these
indeed are Consolers.—

Alexander set out on the 23ᵈ of July for Switzerland.[1] He
wrote to me from Dover, & again from Calais; & I flattered
myself he meant to keep me comfortably & cheeringly *au
courant* ╎ as to his travels & proceedings; however, I have not
had one word from him since; though probably he may have
at this moment 3 or 4 Letters to me envelloped in his problems

1256. [1] Cf. L. 1253 n. 5.

& *conjurations* in his Port Folio: for such was the case during
his Continental excursion 2 years ago, when he brought me
—the day after his return, about half a dozen long & detailed
Letters of his adventures, which he delivered with own hand,
very composedly telling me that he had always forgotten to
put them to the Post.

I have had news of him, nevertheless, from Paris, through
my Friend Mad^e de Maisonneuve,[2] sister to our late French
Ambassadour. He accompanies two of his Cantab. *camarades,*
famous for Science, & capable of *turning* his *tour,* if he is not
too wild & absent to attend to them, to much excellent instruction; Herschal & Babbage.

Your Uncle is tolerably well; but the Coronation has not
yet smiled[3]—as we had hoped, upon his promotion. The
accounts from Bath are not bad:—I am sorry to say ⎮ that
poor Clement is returned from Germany in very ill health, &
cruelly altered. You would no longer announce him as the
Producible young Man you styled him on his appearance at
your family meeting. He is now, however, under regular
medical discipline; & will, I hope, ere long recover both
within & without. His good Mother is his constant & tender
Nurse.[4] The Barretts are still at Ghent. The Rapers, Edward,
& Fanny B[urney] all well. I now write from Mrs. Broome's

[2] This is Madame de Maisonneuve's letter (Berg) of 1-5 August 1821, which,
sent in the diplomatic bag, had reached FBA on the 7th (Diary). Of the letter,
two double sheets are extant, but the closing pages presumably containing the
matter that FBA reports in this letter and in Ll. 1257 and 1258 are missing.

[3] The coronation of George IV on 19 July 1821, the date that, notwithstanding the delay, was to appear on JB's commission as rear-admiral (see L. 1257 n. 1).
The brevet (extant in the PML) refers to Orders in Council of earlier dates wherein
it was directed that 'such Captains in the Navy who notwithstanding their Seniority
had been . . . set aside by the promotion of Flag Officers should be appointed by
Commissions Rear Admirals in general terms without expressing any Squadron or
Division of Colours used in the Fleet and that they should be esteemed as superannuated Sea Officers and placed for the rest of their lives on the ordinary estimate of the Navy with a pension equal to the Half Pay of a Rear Admiral.

'And whereas you have applied to Us for such Commission and Pension We do
in pursuance of the aforesaid Orders in Council hereby constitute and appoint
you to the Rank of a Rear Admiral in his Majestys Fleet accordingly.'

[4] 'I fancy Clement likes nursing when he can get it', his sister CFBt confided
in a letter (Eg. 3706D, ff. 20b-22b) to SHB, 5 October, 'for he always takes a
poorly fit when he goes home, and sets Mama cooking and coddling & cooing over
him— . . . However, I should not seek his merits to disclose, for I do just the
same thing, & save up all my head aches & pains in my chest for Mama, because
I know she will believe in them and pity me more than anybody—'

at Richmond⁵—& am charged with her Love & Clement's & Marianne's. Mine pray give to Mrs. Burney, & my kind Compliments to Mrs. Bicknell.

Adieu, my dear Charles, & God bless you!—

F.d'Ay

10ᵗʰ Augˢᵗ 1821.

Poor Clement begs me to add a few words for himself in particular, as he has so much personal reason for regret at this event; for his aunt had ever treated him with peculiar kindness.⁶ *Peculiar*, however, her other Nephews would not call it, for she was *gratefully* loved by them all.

1257   [Twickenham Meadows,
post 14 August 1821]

To James *and* Mrs. Burney

A.L.S. & A.L.S. (PML, Autog. Cor. bound), n.d.
Double sheet 4to   3 pp.   trimmed
Addressed: To / Admiral Burney,¹ / 26. James Street, / Westminster / Middlesex—
Dated incorrectly in pencil, p. 1: (?20. July) 1821

⁵ For explanation of the change of plan from Eliot Vale to Richmond and Twickenham Meadows, see L. 1258.

⁶ Clement Francis had been a pupil at CB Jr.'s school at Greenwich.

1257. ¹ FBA had been apprised of her brother's promotion in a letter (Berg) from his wife Sarah, dated 14 August 1821: 'My dear Sister & most kind friend / we have just received from the Admiralty notice that a commission is signed bearing date the 19ᵗʰ of last month appointing James Burney Esqʳᵉ Admiral on the Retired List. And now be assured of my happy thanks to you, my dear & ever steady friend—for it is all, all, owing to *you*. and I know the Joy my dear sister Broome, &c will feel on this occasion. . . . / Ever My Dear Sister / Yʳ truly affecᵗ & grateful / S. Burney.'

For FBA's rôle in the appointment (Sunday, 29 April), see L. 1249 n. 3; also Mrs. Burney's letter to her daughter (Manwaring, p. 284); and the cryptic entries for 23 and 26 June (Diary): 'my dear James D. Clar.', 'my dear James Pˢˢ A.'

JB on his part wished to give assurance of his good conduct on the occasion. 'I was tolerably diligent for me. I received notice of the good intended, from the Admiralty on Tuesday evening [14 August] at or after 8 oclock, and before I went to the Admiralty, at 11 oclock next forenoon, was at the Duke of Clarence's door, but he was gone, and I was told, to remain some months in the country, and had not been gone above two hours. There I was out of luck as well as out of time; all I could do was to leave a letter and a card.' See A.L.S. (Berg), 17 August 1821.

My dear Admiral![1]—
My noble Admiral!
My admirable Admiral!—

I cannot say—it is quite impossible—the joy that has burst upon my wounded soul in this welcome News[1]—*Nothing* now on Earth can happen that would give me equal pleasure, except seeing *Alex* a Dean, or a Bishop.

Nothing else can bear any competition with the happiness This intelligence has imparted to me.

Your Letter of yesterday had kept my hopes alive—for never have they been crushed, though often agitated, since that expressive smile of my sweet Princess Augusta[1] when I talked of the Letter of my *Brother officer Framed & Glazed* — —

She is so feeling & so good, that I knew *her* brow would be clouded instantly if she did not foresee sunshine to mine. I have never mistaken her *looks*; & *speech* she denies herself about Armies & Navies.

The *19th*!—how agreeable that! And how I rejoice the *Coronation* went off so gloriously—'twas a good omen. I shall always Hail the Day.—I assure you I can ǀ hardly breathe, or write, from my impatience to Direct!—I hope to be the First to set the Post Man a staring—

I will surely write to my great Favourite Pacchierotti,[2] but I cannot till I return to town, & look out his Letters, both to my dear Father & myself, to recollect the topics that may give him interest. By *Post* a few lines at random would not be worth their *age*. But I will not fail to write, nor to let him know fully that it is our dear Sarah who charged me so to do & to thank him for his kindness & amiability to herself. I shall have now to add the title of her pappy—

As to Alex—I have not had a line from him since that long Epistle I read you from Calais[3]—But, I have heard *of* him from Madame de Maisonneuve,[4] who had not *seen* him, though he carried her my Letters,—but he left it for her, &

---

[2] JB's daughter Sarah Payne, having reached Padua on her wedding tour, had sent a note in English to the old friend and idol of the Burneys (*DL* i *passim*), the castrato singer Gasparo Pacchierotti (1740-1821). For the welcome he gave to this representative of 'the House of Burney', see L. 1270 n. 19, and for his letters of the 1780s to FB, 14 of which survive, see *Catalogue*.

[3] Received on 27 July (Diary).   [4] See L. 1256 n. 2.

she gathered from others that he had met his *Camarades*, & had left Paris on his way to Geneva on the 1st of August. Since that, I have again heard *of* him, by Mrs. Babbage,[5] who has kindly addressed me a line to say that, in case he had not written, she had had a Letter from her husband, who mentioned that he was well, with Herschall & himself, & at Dijon the 4th of August.

And now adieu, my dear Admiral, Joy! Good spirits, Good Health, & Long Life to you!

Yr ever affecte
F. d'A

For Mrs. Admiral Burney.

How kind is the Letter of my dear sister & constant Friend! —I read it with the first sensation of real *Joy* I have known for more than 3 years — — it was so new to me as almost to be overpowering. Luckily I found it at our dear Sister's,[6] & Charlotte alone was with me. We embraced like the two Kings in the Rehearsal,[7] again & again—after I had thanked God with fervent thanksgiving—for I have long feared a *disappointment* would be seriously prejudicial to the Health & Longevity of my dear Brother, first from its injustice, & next from the Hopes I had myself of late so warmly encouraged & partaken. How delightful a termination to his toils! how honourable, gratifying, & exhilarating!—

My dear Charlotte congratulates you with all her heart & soul — — so will Clement & Marianne when I can catch them—

But I cannot write another moment without trying to

[5] The letter from Mrs. Babbage (L. 1185 n. 6) had arrived on the 16th (Diary). On the 19th and 21st FBA was to learn from AA himself that the travellers had reached Geneva by the 10th, Yverdun, by the 21st.

[6] On disruption of plans to visit Mrs. Locke at Eliot Vale (see Ll. 1258-9), FBA had instead spent the fortnight (9-22 August) with the Cambridges at Twickenham Meadows and from there crossed the bridge daily to call on CBFB at 3 Under the Hill, Richmond, where she had found Mrs. Burney's letter (n. 1).

[7] George Villiers (1628-87), 2nd Duke of Buckingham, *The Rehearsal* (1671). In Act II, Scene ii, the two right kings of Brentford enter 'hand in hand' and in V. i, they dance. Embraces and other comic stage business could easily have been inserted by the actors in a play the Burneys had seen many times in their younger days (*ED* i. 163-4; ii. 280).

Catch First of All the Right of the New Address. Adieu, my dear sister & Friend—

Hail to the *19*th!

ever Affect^{ly} Yours
F. d'Arblay.

What delight to the Bride! I congratulate Martin.

1258   Twickenham Meadows,
20 August 1821

To Alexander d'Arblay

A.L. (rejected Diary MSS. 7276-[9], Berg), 20 Aug. 1821.
Double sheet 4to   very thin paper   4 pp.   *pmks* RICHMOND/2 P.P.P. RICHMOND/22 AU ⟨   ⟩ F 21/298   wafer
Addressed: La Suisse. | Monsieur | Monsieur d'Arblay | à | Yverdun | Poste | Restante
Docketed: le 5e 7bre / 1821
Edited by CFBt. *See* Textual Notes.

Twickenham Meadows
20, Augst 1821.

I must set aside alike Disappointment at your long silence, & pleasure at its cessation,[1] to desire you to doff your Hat, & Wave it in the air on the Mountains—in the Vallies, with a loud Huzza! Houra! Huzza!—to the tune of bright joy, begging your kind Companions to eccho it,—till, hoarse by vociferation, you All call for the Nectar of the nearest pellucid stream that you can catch gushing through the friendly aperture of some stately Rock, and Then quaff it, my dear Alex, to the tune of Health to Admiral Burney! — — Your two Companions will pledge you, I feel sure. This happy termination to the many Reclamations took place the other Day. It is to be dated from the period of the Coronation. The arrears are relinquished, & all the long contested &c eras— but the admiral's half-pay, the retired Admiral's Rank are his

1258. [1] On 19 August (Diary) FBA had received AA's letter of the 10th, dated Geneva.

own: & the delight of all the Family, & of all his many Friends, with his own honest glee, are truly exhilarating. He sent me the News hither, & I can hear none with equal interest till some Good Preferment is offered *You*, which you gratefully accept, *or* till some fair, prudent, *Spirituelle*, & amiable Damsel charms both our hearts by frankly accepting *You*.——I ought to have added to my requisites *well-portioned.*

Apropos——I am told that since M. A's departure a certain lady is very much dejected, & looks wretchedly. There has surely been some misunderstanding, rather than essential cause of separation.

And now let me answer your long — — wished for, & most welcome Letter.[1] I am glad you saw good M. Le Noir,[2] & rejoiced you witnessed again the excellence of Talma,[3] especially in his greatest part, Manlius, & I am enchanted you have been presented to La Place:[4] but I am vexed past all description that you missed Mme de Maisoneuve & the Chev^r sans peur et sans reproche, M. V. de La T[our] Maubourg[5]— Edmond Beauvau[6]—Maxime[5]—& All our French Friends & Favourites. They are all non-compos.——or at least deem *You* so, at such bad contrivance. Upon your return, if you only Enter to Exit, you must do so, or be renounced. If you are en *dissabille*, you must demand an interview *in private*; Mme

[2] For personal effects left with M. Lenoir by General d'Arblay and other business entrusted to him, see L. 1189 n. 5; L. 1229 n. 1; and for the legacy of £50 that the general left to him and his gratitude for it, see M. Lenoir's letter to FBA (Berg) of 24 Sept. 1822 (part of which is quoted in L. 1194 n. 1).

[3] François-Joseph Talma (1763-1826) had played in the title role of *Manlius Capitolinus* (1698) by Antoine de La Fosse d'Aubigny (1653-1708) at the Théâtre-Français on 31 July 1821. AA and his father had called on Talma in London on 19 June 1817 (see ix, L. 1083 n. 3).

[4] Pierre-Simon La Place (1749-1827), mathematician and astronomer, founding member of the French Academy, known for his kindness to foreign visitors and to younger men in his own fields of study (*Encl. Brit.*).

[5] For Madame de Maisonneuve and her brother, now ministre de la Guerre, see L. 1192 n. 6; L. 1195 n. 4; for her son 'Maxime', L. 1195 n. 6, and vii *passim.*

[6] Edmond-Henri-Étienne-Victurien de Beauvau (1795-1861), a cavalry officer, and about AA's age, was the 2nd son of Marc-Étienne-Gabriel (1773-1849), prince de Beauvau Craon, with whose family General d'Arblay had been on intimate terms (v–x *passim*).

de M[aisonneuve] or Mme Victor will *either* of them ^| receive you with open arms, if you seek them in the most tattered fragments of your Brier torn, or Rock cut, or Lake besplashed Garments, so you go to them *at all*. But they are really hurt & offended that you can know their long friendship, & have received such kind marks of it, not only in Childhood, but at past 20 when they were in England, & pass, nevertheless, several days in Paris, without finding a moment to embrace them. Mme de M[aisonneuve] writes me this,[7] thankful that, at least, you did not carry my Letter, also, to the Mountains of Swisserland. Edmond de Beauvau says he can only forgive you in throwing his arms round your Neck, which, in defiance of his wrath, he is eager to do, from a thousand kind remembrances of yourself & your noble Father.

You don't tell me whether M. Le Noir settled anything with you relative to our affairs?[2]—I am dying to arrange *mine* finally with *him*, in discharging my commissioned Legacy. Give me one line upon this subject in your next, previous to my again addressing him.

⸺

I received your Letter from Dover, & your 4 words from Calais—& 400 from any where else would not have caused me as much satisfaction. It is true you left them to do their office a sufficient length of time without any reinforcement! — — but *Boy eddy dood Boy*! so no more of that. Nevertheless, but for Mme de M[aisonneuve]'s Letter from Paris, which shewed me you had been there, as it answered mine to that dear friend; & but for a little intimation from Dijon through Mrs. Babbage, I should have been in a state of desperate uneasiness—Be dood Boy, dear Alex! — — & I will always give you homeward News when you inform me where to direct.

How sorry I am for poor Miss Wilson's Letter![8] but you

[7] The source of this information about AA's sojourn in Paris may have been the missing sheets of Madame de Maisonneuve's letter (Berg) of 1-5 August (L. 1256 n. 2).

[8] Harriet Wilson (L. 1180 n. 12), with whose penniless plight FBA seemed to sympathize, had removed apparently from Bath to London, and on 16, 21, and 24 July she had spent whole mornings at Bolton Street and was there for tea on the 28th (Diary). For the progress of the lawsuit in which she was engaged, see L. 1304 n. 10 and L. 1332.

did perfectly right to annonce the misfortune, that I may prevent her from believing her business done.

I regret your Letter for Berne, if you have not recovered it —& surely Mrs. Goldsmidt[9] will not spare you for such negligence of her favours— I I hope you have not been equally unlucky with the Epîtres of Mme du Thon?[10]

And Now let me give you some history of *ourselves at Westminster.*[11] According to my promise, I prepared to begin my summer *campaign* with your dear Aunt Broome, & I was packed & *ready* on Monday to set off on Tuesday—when Just as I *was* setting off, arrived an Express to tell me Clement was suddenly returned! He had been taken ill, in consequence, he thinks, of unaired sheets & shirts, &c used while he was taking medicine for rheumatic pains, & which utterly disabled him from travelling. I need not say how much more sorry for the Cause I was even than for the effect. He is still very indifferent, & confined to his house, & his tender mother's care; which, *after* all his rambling, he finds, he says, balsamic.

This plan frustrated, I wrote to Eliot Vale—but lo & behold! Lady Martin called the same day, to tell me she & Sir George

[9] Probably Isabel *née* Goldsmid (1788–1860), wife of Sir Isaac Lyon Goldsmid (1778–1859), whose daughter Anna Maria (1805–89) AA seemed to know. For the history, with genealogical tables, of the distinguished and immensely wealthy Goldsmid families, see Chaim Bermant, *The Cousinhood. The Anglo-Jewish Gentry* (1971).

[10] Mme Adèle du Thon (*fl.* 1819–27), author of *Histoire de la secte des Amis, suivie d'une notice sur Madame Fry et la prison de Newgate* (1821) and *An Account of the principal charitable institutions of the Parish of St. Mary-le-Bone* (1823). In a letter (in the possession of the Society of Friends, Euston Road) to the Quakeress Priscilla Gurney (1785–1821), dated Paris 13 July 1819, Mme du Thon speaks of visiting prisons such as Newgate and of committees recently formed in Paris for a similar purpose. Indicative of her interests also are her *Lettres à Isabelle . . . sur l'éducation et la société* (1823) and her *Notice* (1827) of the famous Swiss educational reformer Johann Heinrich Pestalozzi (1746–1827). A friend of Amelia Opie as well as the Gurneys, she seems to have spent some years in London. (See further, x, L. 1365.)

[11] An ancient phrase, used by the sovereigns of England in referring to themselves as the seat of government. For FBA's previous use of the phrase, see iii. 82 and v. 445.

were going to summer it at Eliot Vale, as I had always said *I* could not go thither till Autumn! —— Well, This second *contretems* has produced an effect that will give you pleasure; for when the Archd^n & Mrs. Cambridge heard of it, they wrote me so pressing an invitation to make their house my *Hotel*, whence I might visit, or receive, my sister at will; & urged my acceptance with such affectionate warmth, that I had not the heart to refuse their kindness—& Here, at Twickenham Meadows, I am at this moment,[12] They are all indulgence to my propensity to retirement, & I pass great part of every day with Aunt Broome & Marianne, & Clement, who is recovering, but slowly. |

How dangerous was your flight up & down the Jura Mountain I supplicate you, my dear Alex, to think more of the value of your life at least to me. Miss Acland[13] was presented at the Great Court Drawing Room that preceded the Coronation; but neither her Brother nor Sister nor any of the Hoares were there. I have heard nothing more. L^y K[eith] is always in Scotland, & Mrs. M. Hoare is at Malvern.[14]

I am extremely obliged by the feeling & kindness of Mrs. Babbage in giving me communication of your safe arrival at Dijon. It was truly amiable. Pray tell it to Mr. Babbage Always direct to me *11 Bolton Street*, as cross posts are precarious, & Ramsay takes greater care of my Letters than of any thing else.—Clement says he came home stronger & better from Swisserland than from any other tour, but charges you to beware you go no where without a Guide, & above all that you do not run before him! The 2 Eldest Jelfs[15] charge me

---

[12] FBA had gone to Twickenham Meadows 'fetched by Archdeacon Cambridge' on 9 August, returning to Bolton Street on the 22nd (Diary). For the house and its site, see Plate, *DL* ii. 238.

[13] Daughter of Sir Thomas Dyke Acland (d. 17 May 1794), 9th Baronet, Elizabeth Lucy Theresa (*c.* 1794-1857) was presented at the Great Court Drawing Room on Thursday 26 July (*The Times*, 27 July). She was to marry in 1823 Captain Henry Jenkinson (1790-1868), Admiral (1862). The brother and sister [in-law] whom FBA mentions would have been Sir Thomas (1787-1871), 10th Baronet, and his wife Lydia Elizabeth *née* Hoare (*c.* 1787-1856), only daughter of Henry Hoare (*c.* 1756-1828) of Mitcham Grove, Surrey. For her four brothers see Burke's *Landed Gentry*.

[14] Lady Keith (L. 1193 n. 8) and her sister Mrs. Hoare (L. 1238 n. 22).

[15] The two eldest Jelfs were George (1796-1859), barrister-at-law, and Richard William (1798-1871), M.A. (Oxon. 1823), D.D. (1839), 'a most eminent scholar

with kind compliments. The Archdⁿ & Mrs. Cambridge & Mrs. Baker[16] with Love—Marianne & Clement with d^o Charlotte Barret will soon go to Bologne sur Mer. Did you recollect our voiture there?[17] I have been invited to dinner at the B^p of London's,[18] but was not well enough to accompany the Archdⁿ. Young Sheridan[19] is returned, & intends visiting us. Miss Ogle[19] is going to settle in London. God bless you my Alex—Give my comp^{ts} & *don't forget* to your companions—*Pray* write soon. Your Letters are my solace.

1259   [Twickenham Meadows],
         21 August 1821

To Mrs. Barrett

A.L.S. (Berg), 21 Aug. 1821
Double sheet 4to 4 pp. wafer
Addressed: À Madame / Madame Barrett, / Gand.

and learned divine', appointed in 1826 tutor to Prince George of Cumberland, and in 1844, Principal of King's College, London.

The Jelfs were Gloucestershire connections of the elder Cambridge, Richard Owen (1717-1802), and visiting Twickenham Meadows at this time was (?)their mother, Mary *née* Kidman (*c.* 1773-1850), the wife since 1792 of Sir James Jelf (1763-1842), a banker at Gloucester, mayor of the town in 1814, who had 'received the honour of knighthood on presenting an address to the throne'. See Cobbett, *Memorials of Twickenham*, pp. 53-4.

[16] See L. 1205 n. 7.

[17] The d'Arblays were in Boulogne in 1814 (viii. 34).

[18] William Howley (1766-1848), Bishop of London (1813-28), Archbishop of Canterbury (1828). See further, L. 1304 nn. 4, 7.

[19] Charles Brinsley Sheridan (*c.* 1796-1843), son of the dramatist (1751-1816) by his 2nd wife Hester Jane *née* Ogle (*c.* 1771-1817). She was the youngest daughter of the Revd. Newton Ogle (1726-1804), Dean of Winchester (1769), and his wife Susannah *née* Thomas (*c.* 1734-1820), a family the Burneys had known in their younger days (see *ED* ii. 298-9 *passim*), and Mrs. Ogle FBA had found again in Bath in the years 1816-18 (ix, x, *passim*). The 'Miss Ogle' would have been the eldest daughter Susanna (1762-1825).

The Ogle sisters live in CAB's Journals by virtue of their embarrassed rendering in St. Martin's Street in [1784?] of 'Drink to me only with thine eyes' and the line on the rose and its 'smells', at which they stopped short. ' "Why don't you go on?" cried Mr. Ogle. "Why the rest is nothing but about *stinks*", answered Miss Ogle. "Never mind, *if* it was the Black joke and I desired you to sing it, you ought" ', and they perforce sang on.

21st Augst 1821.

This is truly my Charlotte—my Charlotte herself—
This second Letter without even an allusion to the debt incurred by the first.—And yet—see how soon, at all times,
all seasons, all ages, we are facile to spoil!—I am half tempted
to be aware I am my own Enemy in this acknowledgement,
for, erst, Three Letters were agreed upon as the industrious
premium for one *tardy return* — — So now, upon this
recollection, as tardy as my spirit of response, were I one
whit less averse to writing, I should begin all over again, omitting paragraph the First.

I am highly gratified, & highly obliged by all you say of
Lady Bedingfeld,[1] & still more by a charming Letter she has
been so good as to bestow upon me. When we came to Bath,
we soon found her, to our joint tastes, one of its first attractions—in so much that, when she left it, I remember severely
reproaching her for having been so attaching. — — Alas,
had she remained, I knew not then that She, like all things
else, would so quickly afterwards have lost all power not
merely to charm but to solace.—for all became irksome to
me, for a while, & a long while! save Alexander & Solitude.
—Your gentle & feeling intercourse, like that of your tender
Mother, I might have borne even immediately—but neither
were attainable !

I quite regret not having shewn you the charming Design
of Lady B[edingfeld] *The poor Soldier*;—but I have so little
been in the habit, of late, of seeking any species of enjoyment, that its possession occurred not to my deadened
Memory. You will hoard it now in Your's, still all alive.—I
am, however, struggling actively to perform my long given
promises—ill performed from failing health as much as
courage,—of changing my life of seclusion to one approaching more nearly to sociality. *Witness*, I now write to you
from Twickenham Meadows. As soon as Alexander left me,
upon his Swiss Expedition, I accepted your dear Mother's
long invitation to pass the time of his absence at Richmond:
—& I was packed & prepared on Monday to set off on Tuesday—When poor Clement returned suddenly,—his tour

1259. [1] See L. 1250 n. 2; L. 1253 n. 4.

broken up by the death of one of the Tunnos;[2] & took my destined apartment; & happily, for his kind heart, without any suspicion of the successor he superseded. I turned, however, now, my acceptance round to Eliot Vale—to which sweet place I had received incessant invitations—but lo & behold! before my Letter could reach Mrs. Lock, Lady Martin called to ask me if I had any message for Eliot Vale, whither she & Sir George were going to spend some Weeks if not Months. Quick! Presto! begone! cried I, to a Letter of recantation. But, meanwhile I there came so urgent a request from the Archd^n & Mrs Cambridge that—since prepared to leave home—I would make their house my *Hotel*, for seeing, thence, at pleasure, your dear Mother,—a request which she herself, & Clement, came to Bolton Street to enforce, that I would no longer resist its kindness—which for more than 3 years I have impulsively done—& therefore, Here I am. — — And any thing more amiable, more kind, better bred, or more pleasing than both Host & Hostess to their Guest, cannot be even imagined. And so fond are they of my sweet Charlotte, that I wish she would more frequently *shew* her sense of their goodness by personally naming them[3] in her charming Letters to her Mother & Marianne—parts of which are read at every meeting, though by the former sometimes only a sentence, for you know her scrupulous discretion. This hint, of course, you will not allude to, save to me. But that I know your real value for these valuable people, I should not have given it: for I would not for the world mar the very charm of your Letters that makes me love them, by any sort of *constraint*, the essence of their merit consisting in their being perfectly natural. I won't tell you that *natural* stands alone, unaided by spirit, or archness, or tenderness, or observation—but I *will* tell you that, without that natural, all those 4 so essential & high ingredients, would to me be null in their composition.

---

[2] Rose Tunno (L. 1253 n. 2).

[3] To this reproachful hint CFBt would offer in her reply of 28th September (Barrett, Eg. 3706D, ff. 19-20) a defence, explaining that she had given her mother 'a *list* of friends & a graduated scale of loves & greetings suited to them all—in hopes she will supply my messages from her own recollection when an opportunity called for it & so that I might have more room in my letters for other matters'.

You will certainly have been much struck with the sudden, &, in such a state of mind, & Conduct, dreadful Death of Queen Caroline:[4] how unfortunate that the poor Prince of W[ales] who required a Wife that should have been a Model, should not have heard as a warning voice those voices of which you detail the sounds of just Wonder at his choice in Marriage! He is the only Prince of his Race who has been thus deceived. The 3 new Duchesses, his Sisters in Law, Clarence, Kent & Cambridge,[5] are as exemplary in their lives, as far as they are called into action, as was his august & virtuous Mother. Even Cumberland,[6] since her marriage, has been faultless — — to him, ⏐ therefore, Information must have been banefully wanting, or Foresight unnaturally blinded, or Chance cruelly at enmity; for, far from studying to reform him, she acted with as little delicacy, prudence, or propriety before she was accused of guilt, as with shame, forbearance, or Penitence after Conviction. For convicted she stands, here on Earth, as far as her trial proceeded:[7]—& that it was not carried on to its sentence was but from the Fright given to the Administration by Clamour, & to her own dexterity in calling the stopt proceedings by the name of Acquital. Believe nothing that you read of her last days, as no account has yet been published that has not been contradicted. All that is clear is that she has pronounced William Austin her decided Heir[8]—whence I conclude him to merit the other little word

---

[4] Queen Caroline had died at Brandenburg House on 7 August.

[5] For the marriages of the royal dukes, Cambridge, Kent, and Clarence on 2 May, 29 May, and 11 July 1818 respectively, see G. E. Cokayne, *Complete Peerage* . . . (1887); and for the arranged marriage of the Prince of Wales on 8 April 1795, Joanna Richardson, *The Disastrous Marriage*, chap. 3.

[6] Daughter of Charles Louis Frederick (1741-1816), Duke of Mecklenburg-Strelitz, the Princess Frederica Caroline Louisa Sophia Alexandrina (1778-1841) had married as her third husband on 29 May 1815 her cousin, the Duke of Cumberland. For the marriage and previous scandals, see Anthony Bird, *The Damnable Duke of Cumberland* (1966), pp. 120-41.

[7] The Bill of Pains and Penalties was passed in the House of Lords on its third reading (10 November 1820) by a majority of 9.

[8] FBA could have seen in *The Times* (13 August 1821) that Queen Caroline's chief beneficiary was one William Austin, the circumstances of whose birth had been investigated by the 'lords of the council' in 1806. In spite of widespread suspicion that he might have been born to the Princess he was found to be 'born in the Brownlow-street Hospital, on the 11th day of July, 1802, of the body of Sophia Austin, and was first brought to the princess's house in the month of November following'. See *AR* lxiii (1821), 641; for the unhappy life, insanity,

of 3 Letters that commonly precedes that important one of 4: why, else, for Him is set aside All her Relations, Friends, & Connexions?

How much more genial a theme had been your dear & deserving uncle's final success?[9]——But my sister begged to forward that intelligence; & I can only Give & Call for our mutual Congratulations, in which I am sure Mr. Barrett will most heartily join. Alexander left me the 3d week of July for a tour to Swisserland. I heard of him from Dijon the 4th of Augst quite well & in gay spirits. He travels with 2 *Cantab.* Friends of great celebrity in Science & ingenuity, Herschel & Babbage. I was sure how my Princess Augusta must delight whoever saw her[10]——I would you had happened to be of the Number. I can have no surprize that Julia so much pleases; & Hetty will not fail to take her turn. But give them Both your mammy's prescription of *Beauty Sleep*, that their bloom, already a little faded, may be forth coming when they shall be coming forth themselves. For That most winning attraction of Beauty you cannot call back the season, if you pass it over. —— —— Tell Mr. B[arrett] this, in my name. adieu, my sweet Charlotte—may they but [wi]thout & within remind of their fair Mother. Their & Her truly affecte

F. d'Arblay

I have particular pleasure in telling you that Marianne, who

and death of William Austin in Chelsea in 1849, see Joanna Richardson, op. cit., pp. 61, 245; and for his letter to CB Jr. and one from Anne Hayman (1753-1847) to CPB concerning his education in the school at Greenwich, see *Catalogue.*

[9] JB's promotion to the rank of rear-admiral (L. 1256 n. 3; L. 1257 n. 1).

[10] On Saturday 28 July (see *The Times*, 30 July) the Princess Augusta had left Buckingham House to proceed *via* Ramsgate and Cuxhaven to Germany, where she was to pay visits to her brother the Duke of Cambridge at Hanover and to her two elder sisters, the Queen of Würtemberg (1766-1828) and Elizabeth (1770-1840), Landgravine of Hesse Homburg. For an account of her travels, see her letters to Lady Harcourt (L. 1251 n. 1), *Harcourt Papers*, vi. 227-32.

'I went to Frankfort to fetch Augusta on the 6th of August', wrote Princess Elizabeth on 22 September (Berg) to FBA, '& you may believe my extreme heartfelt joy at bringing her back to my own house.—She has witnessed the excellence & perfection of my perfect better half.' Tuesday 14 September, when the Princess Augusta departed for Stuttgart, 'was a *bleak* day . . . you well know how delightful she is'. The Princess was not to return to England until 4 December.

is well & in good looks & spirits, seems a little recovering her social amiability.

[I] am sure you are sorry for poor Rosette,[11] who had many good qualities—

1260   [11 Bolton Street,
                                       c. 25 August 1821]

To James Burney

A.L.S. (PML, Autog. Cor. bound), n.d.
Double sheet 8vo   2 pp.   trimmed   cover missing

My dear Brother,

If your present run of uniform expences would make so small a *modicum* as £15. of any use,[1] I trust you will not refuse to be my Banker for it—nor to let me *double it the middle of next month*, if it will be of the smallest convenience: I shall want £30 for a particular purpose about next May, & keep it for the same—therefore you see my offer is only of what, till then, will be but dead money to me. Ergo, then, my dear Brother, give me this little pleasure, & don't be too proud because you are an Admiral,—for I am as proud as You, on that score, in being, very affect^{ly}

an Admiral's Sister
F d'Ay

Besides, If you were only a Midshipman, I should write the same.

Turn over |

2^d Besides.

And if a similar matter should ever be of the least convenience to *me* from *You*, I should not hestitate a moment in sisterly acceptance.

---

[11] Sarah 'Rosette' Burney (L. 1255 n. 1).

1260. [1] The sum is recorded in FBA's Account Book (Berg) for the year 1821: 'Lent my dear dear Brother—Rear Admiral James Burney £15. 0. 0 (Repaid by his son Martin)'.

Result.

Shall I draw an order, in whatever Name you will, on Hoare, for the 1ˢᵗ 15.

or

Shall I get the Rhino myself & wait upon you with idem?

N.B. The favour of an answer is desired.

2ᵈ N.B.
At your leisure.

1261
11 Bolton Street,
26 August 1821

To Charles Parr Burney

A.L.S. (Osborn), 26 Aug. 1821
Double sheet 8vo   4 pp.

Augˢᵗ 26ʰ 1821.
11. Bolton Street
Berkeley Square.

My wish, my dear Charles, is *Your's*, now I see so clearly what that is, & hear assigned so filial, so right, so tender a reason as your *certainty it would be her's*. I beg to receive the destined melancholy Memorial.[1] I shall only, therefore, desire, in accepting the choice you kindly give me, that it may not be so deeply black as to be wearable only a few months, & then be seen no more; but with a ray of that mourning dye between two of plain Gold, & encircled, in the usual manner, with the Name that gives the tribute its value, & that I then may make it one of my things of general wear. ᛁ I explain this that you may be so good as to give the order yourself. I have no heart for seeing a messenger upon such an errand.

I knew you would delight for our noble Admiral.

1261. [1] The favour of a mourning ring for 'Rosette', CB Jr.'s widow, who had died on 2 August at Greenwich.

I am but just returned to town.[2] I left Clement very slowly recovering,[3] & his Mother panting for the sea air at Brighton,[4] which she means to enhale as soon as he is re-fitted for Cambridge.

How terrible are the rites with which the Faction think they honour the manes of *Their* departed Sovereign![5] Characteristic they may be, indeed—but not from that reason less unseemly. There appears to | be much of mystery wrapt up in certain circumstances relative to her departure: though one mystery, with which, for 16 or 17 years she has been envelloped, is generally deemed to be now wholly cleared away, —namely, the Birth of William Austin:[6] for he, in her last hours, was so predominantly her first & dearest thought, that

[2] On 22 August (Diary).

[3] Fellow of Christ's College (1820-9), ordained deacon (1820), priest (1821), the Revd. Clement Francis held the college offices of Dean (1821-2), Bursar (1827-8). The last eight years of his life were to be a losing struggle with tuberculosis of the lungs.

[4] Mrs. Broome managed to go to Brighton in October (see L. 1269).

[5] According to the plans and wishes of the Government the funeral procession of Queen Caroline was to proceed from Brandenburg House through Hammersmith to the Kensington gravel pits, where it was to turn north to the Bayswater Road, thence along a new route from Paddington to Islington, and so on to Colchester and Harwich, and there to embark for Brunswick, where the Queen was to be interred. See Roger Fulford, *George the Fourth* (1935), pp. 236-8; and *AR* lxiii (1821), 'Chronicle', 124-8. It was further ordered by the Government that the funeral cortège was to have an escort of troops (on the first lap of the journey, the Oxford Blues) and this in defiance of the strong objections of the Queen's friends who represented to Lord Liverpool that since in her lifetime the Queen had never been granted a military escort, preferring in any case to trust to the love and good will of her subjects, such an escort would now provoke the suspicions and resentment of the mob as would the diversion of the route from the city. This proved to be the case.

To prevent the turn at the gravel pits, the crowds 'tore up the pavements, and threw down trees, which they placed across the road, . . . resolved that the procession should go through Hyde-park corner gate'. Turning through the park at a fast clip, however, the cortège reached Cumberland Gate, where it was again stopped. Rain fell heavily, stones and mud 'flew about in all directions, and the Horse Guards fired upon the mob', killing two men, but the procession was forced down Edgeware Road, and, headed off at Tottenham Court Road, was herded into Drury Lane, entering the City at Temple Bar, where the Mayor placed his carriage at its head. It was then allowed to pass quietly through White Chapel and on to Romford, from there to Chelmsford, and on out to the coast.

These scenes, as much as the Queen in life might have enjoyed them, 'were the most disgraceful, the most degrading to conventional decency', remarks Fulford, op. cit., 'and the most discreditable to Government of all the turbulent incidents connected with her name'.

[6] See L. 1259 and n. 8.

in mentioning him then as her Heir, without any authenticating of his race, or origin, she invites belief that he must be her Son, also. I am the more inclined to this opinion from knowing her resistless taste for talents, celebrity, & amusement; while I have always heard that this chosen object ' was without parts, sport, or attraction. However, as her most trusted Confident is already wrangling with her selected Executer,[7] it is not *quite* impossible but that the delicacy of Both may so far give way to their animosity, as to throw some light upon secret transactions that in hands of more forbearing faithfulness, might for ever have been involved in their proper darkness.

I am not at present quite well, though not ill; but as soon as I am recruited from my recent exertions, I shall again go out of town, & probably not return, to abide, till I come to meet my dear Traveller, *now*, I believe, at Yverdun. I shall *then* hope you will speed me a visit—but I sh[d] be vexed you should waste a call

Remember me kindly to Mrs. B[urney]—& give my Comp[ts] to Mrs. Bicknell,[8] & get strong again, & stout, my dear Charles.

Yours most sincerely

F. d'Ay

[7] The animosity between Alderman Wood (L. 1234 n. 6) and Stephen Lushington (1782–1873), M.P. (1806–8, 1820–41). On 26 October 1820 the latter had defended the Queen in a 'masterly speech' (see *DNB*), had been present at her death on 7 August 1821 and, as one of her executors, had arranged for the removal of her body from Brandenburg House to Brunswick.

FBA could have seen Alderman Wood's letter to the Editor (*The Times*, 22 August), wherein he expressed his resentment at having been excluded officially from the funeral procession as arranged by Lushington. Feeling 'this treatment most severely', Wood made his own way to Brunswick 'to follow to the grave the remains of our neglected and injured Queen'. In subsequent accounts of the funeral, a distinction is consistently made between the official party and Alderman Wood's group.

[8] See L. 1245 n. 5.

1262   11 Bolton Street,
                                        28 August 1821

To James Burney

A.L.S. (PML, Autog. Cor. bound), 28 Aug. 1821
Double sheet 8vo and single sheet 4to   5 pp.   *pmks* T.P / Piccadilly 30 AU 1821   wafer
Addressed: Admiral Burney, / 26 James Street, / Westminster.

> 11. Bolton Street,
> 28th *August*
> 1821.

What is your opinion, my dear Brother, of all this Rain? Here am I in Town, in August, & alone, & anxious to see you again—yet cannot get to you, because, forsooth,

> The Rain it raineth every day.[1]—

Do pray tell me, upon your serious word & Conscience, what is your opinion upon this point, & if you really think such Weather as this in the midst of Summer, is shewing a proper respect for the sister of an Admiral? That's the point.

You might just as well, for aught I see, have continued a Captain.

However, as I know not when the better conduct of the Elements will bring us together, I write to you now to enforce my request ⎸ that you will not let my Law-narrative[2] transpire—especially not to such as Correspond with our Esther, namely Edward—Charles Parr—Mrs. Sansom, Fanny Burney—for my intended hoax will lose all its zest, if she knows what is to come ere she arrives at its Climax; — — and, besides the loss of a laugh—no small loss to our dear lively Hetty,—it may cost me a *Frown*—at least an *apology*,

---

1262. [1] *Twelfth Night*, V. i.

[2] First narrated in JB's house for his amusement (see L. 1270) was FBA's farcical account (L. 1264) of her timorous appearance in the Court of Chancery and her apprehensions of the costs of collecting a legacy of 5 guineas, which had been bequeathed to her father CB in a codicil, dated 15 February 1798, to the will (PRO/PROB/11/1352/42, pr. 31 January 1801) of one John Devaynes (c. 1726-1801), apothecary, Spring Gardens: 'I give to my very good friend Dr Burney of Chelsea . . . a ring and Five Guineas'. As residuary legatees EBB and FBA would have been entitled to this part of their father's estate.

for letting her own affairs travel to her by Agents or Accident, instead of from the strait-forward Principal.

And the reasons I have not yet written are — — in Mr. Vellum's phrase, two-fold;[3] First, I do not like to tell the tale till I can finish it by saying I have placed her *moity* in the hands | of her honourable Steward, Edward: which I cannot do till I have negociated the Note, which I defer till next Week, on account of other business I shall then have to transact at the same time. And, Secondly, Hetty owes *me* a Letter, which puts my Conscience quite at ease for not writing till that debt is paid, & I think you will understand, as well as most men, my dear Brother, that where there is any excuse for procrastination in Letter Writing, one is very apt not to pass it by.

Pray communicate all this to my dear Mrs. Admiral.

'So much for Buckingham!'[4]

And Now let me add, it is my fixed resolve to drink tea with you again before I go again out of Town.[5] So do not attempt to dissuade me. | But I shall wait to the last,—i.e. to the end of the ensuing week, to see if the Weather will, at last, shew any bowels, & suffer Diane, Ramsay, & the Admiral's Sister, to make their accustomed triplet to your dwelling: but, if it still prove obdurate, it shall gain nothing by its spite,—for I shall not let Mess[rs] Clayton Scott & Clayton[6] make me Rich for Nothing, but find my way to you in a manner fitting & becoming for an Admiral's Sister, even though it should Rain—as Alex says it does upon the Jura Mountains of Switzerland,—Cats & Dogs.—

I have heard no more from that wayward Traveller since I saw you: but I will not forget to bring you his one long Letter. How I wish he would have imitated your Bridal Correspondent! |[7]

---

[3] The systematic enumerations characteristic of Vellum, the steward in Addison's *The Drummer*.

[4] *Richard III*, IV. iii, as altered by Colley Cibber (1671–1757).

[5] FBA was to pay an evening visit to JB and his family on 10 September (Diary).

[6] Solicitors, Lincoln's Inn, 6 New Square, on whom FBA called on 25 August (Diary) to collect, as she reported, '9. 11. 0'.

[7] JB's daughter Sarah Payne, now on her wedding tour in Italy (L. 1247 n. 2 and L. 1257 n. 2).

Adieu, my dear Brother—my dear Admiral, Adieu.—I am sure you will not be sorry to see that the first poor *spirt* of a little returning power of pleasantry has been given to my so long shattered—dormant spirits by the true satisfaction with which I glow in signing myself

Most affect^ly—an Admiral's Sister—

F. d Ay

I have many kind Compliments of congratulation for you from Mrs. Lock, who called to hurry me to her Country villa last Monday.[8] I hope you & Mrs. Admiral are all the better for your rustic ramble,[9] & that you stayed out while the Season was Seasonable, & got to your quarters just before this new Winter's usurpation. I remember, many years ago, upon a similar elementary Jumble of January with July, Hetty very gravely wrote me word she thought it so unjust, that she was meditating an application to Lord Mansfield,[10] to demand whether such *swopping* were Legal.—

1263   11 Bolton Street,
                    3 September 1821

To Alexander d'Arblay

A.L. (rejected Diary MSS. 7302-[5], Berg), 3 Sept. 1821
Double sheet 4to   4 pp.   *pmk* F 21/232   wafer
Addressed: A Monsieur / Monsieur d'Arblay. / à / Yverdun, / La Suisse. / Poste / *Restante.* / 3 Set^re 1821.
Docketed: 17. 7bre
Edited by CFBt. *See* Textual Notes.

Always Write, Long or Short,
—when you can,—pray—

[8] Mrs. Locke was to call on the 29th and 30th but the visit to Eliot Vale was deferred until 8 November.
[9] Possibly on visits to the Rickmans (L. 1264 n. 5) at Epsom.
[10] William Murray (1705–93), 1st Earl of Mansfield, Lord Chief Justice of the King's Bench (1756), Lord High Chancellor (1757, 1767).

3^d Septr 1821.

Always/Direct: 11. Bolton Street,

Piccadilly

You have forgotten to give me any Address, my dear Alex, but I am too much pleased with your new Letter not to risk Franking *The Reply Courteous*,[1] in the hope it may reach you. Your Last is dated the very Day, *21. Augst* I wrote mine to you at *Yverdun*.[1]—as you give no new Direction, I suppose the same will be most likely to be sought by You, or ordered to send on elsewhere. Yet to Berne & Basle you go for *de l'Argent*[2]—though you only mention the *Post* for Yverdun. I am much puzzled. In future put your address at the End of every Letter.

To begin with the Essential; Certainly, my dearest Alex, I can be your Banker if your means fall short of completing your plan comfortably. But you must enquire *how* I can supply you, & let me know both *sum* & *moyen*. I leave wholly to your own prudence the *First*, & the *Second* to that of your money dealers.

I am quite charmed, quite exhilarated by your adventures hitherto in Switzerland. But for Heaven's sake do not be as poetical when solo on the Mountains as to the fair Ladies in their Villas! If you repeat on those summits 3 or 400 lines of DeLille,[3] or 3 or 4 odes of Le Brun,[3] your Enthusiasm may make you bound too high or leap too low for your Equilibrium, which will by no means be safe in your charge if, upon such precipices, or over such abysses, you put it in the power of your Imagination. I am really not quite easy at your Wandering thus alone. I would your *Camarades* had participated in the *pleasure* & the *danger* of this tour with

---

1263. [1] *As You Like It*, V. iv. 75. FBA's L. 1258. AA's letters of these years are missing.

    [2] Recorded in FBA's Account Book (Berg) for 1821 are:

A Draft upon Berne	Oct^r	20. 0. 0
A Draft upon Paris	Nov^r	30. 0. 0
2^d Draft upon Paris	Dec^r	30. 0. 0

    [3] The French poets Jacques Delille (1738–1813) and Ponce-Denis-*Écouchard* Le Brun (1729–1807).

you: though I am ⎮ delighted & edified by the development
you mention of the astonishing & unexpected powers of
Exertion with which your self-dependent situation has invested you. I long to relate them to our Archdeacon, who
avers—not knowing this foretaste of your skill,—that as
soon as you take a *Responsibility personal*, of *Your own*
fixing, you will become exactness & punctuality personified
in the execution of your Duties; & experience a new pleasure
& a New Life in the Reputation you will acquire.

Apropos: I hope I told you I have passed a fortnight with
this excellent Friend,[4] & his amiable Partner, & my faithful
Mrs. Baker, at Twickenham Meadows. It was a violent effort
to me—but I am certainly better for it, every way—though
I needed, & need repose to my so long secluded Faculties in
consequence. Did I tell you my invitation to the B^p of London[5]—which I was not strong enough to accept?—but
which I hope I may hear repeated when I am fitter for such
a sort of honour, & perhaps when I have you to urge me.
Since then, another B^p has sent to propose me a visit —— ——
This I hope to be well enough to accept. 'Tis your friend &
patron of Bristol.[6] Thus, my dear Alex, if Honours could
heal a wounded Mind—an afflicted Heart—they are granted
me *here*, &, to my great amazement, offered me, I find
through your Letters, even amidst the beautiful sceneries of
Switserland. All you said on that ⎮ was touchingly pleasing to
me—& Mrs. Lock—a *bit of a Swiss herself*, by her Mother,
Lady Schaub,[7] is *en extase*. How kindly she interests herself
in all your proceedings, & longs for our joint visit to Eliot
Vale to detail them minutely. Sweet Amine is not returned
from Spa:[8] but amends in her precious health. L^y Martin &
Sr Geo.[9] are just set off for Paris, for 2 months. Nothing has
reached me of Brides or no Brides—& I have not seen regu-
lar News-papers, so that I am as much in the dark as if I were

[4] From 9–22 August (Diary) with the Cambridges and Sarah Baker (cf. L.
1258).

[5] William Howley (L. 1258 n. 18).

[6] John Kaye (L. 1181 n. 2), Bishop of Bristol (1820).

[7] Marguerite *née* de Ligonier du Buisson (iii, L. 122 n. 6), widow of Sir Luke
Schaub (1690–1758).

[8] For the Angersteins and their previous visit to Spa, see L. 1218 n. 1.

[9] FBA's friends the Martins (L. 1191 n. 15), Lady Keith (L. 1193 n. 8), and
Sophia Hoare (L. 1238 n. 22).

making a Tour in Swiss——myself. L^y Keith does not name the fair person in her Letters. Mrs. M. Hoare is at Malvern.[9] How charmed you must have been at the Admiralship! you ought to write a Line, if no more, on the occasion, with the happy Direction, Rear Admiral Burney. The James St. Bride & BrideGroom[10] are now, also, at Paris: But only for a Week. In 9 Days they are to be at Home.——

How I like Mad^e la Baronne at Nyon!——But how could you suggest so dangerous a plan as walking round the Lake in so short a time? it was enough to Kill your body, & to starve your Mind——for what could you see well in so fatiguing a course, your Eyes dazzled & your feet aching? I see no skill in striding, as if for a wager, over Ground of such beauty & scenery as to merit the creeping reluctantly on, so as not to overtake a snail. Mais, chacun à son gout. Your adventure & repast behind the mountains of Chillon delighted me. I see near Berne a place call[ed] Thun——[11] |

I have got a little commission to give you for Paris, which I beg you to execute delicately. It is to order me a New Black coat of superfine cloth, best make & Fashion. I mean it for a Birth Day Cadeau of 1820, Dec. 18th And a Gillet for a Xmas Box same period, of the newest cut: & an Indispensable for a New Year's Gift of 1821; I desire they may all be elegant, because I destine them for Conquest, & for a Jeune Monsieur très comme il faut, who will not favour me with accepting them if they are not *du dernier Goût*. So pray be upon your guard not to disgrace my offering. And, for the better preserving them from seizure, I must beg you will take the precaution of putting them on once or twice, or thrice, when you see our Victor, & Edmond, & Maxime,[12] that they may tell me if they are perfectly the pink of the mode. Pray do me this courtesie, & trust me for it till your return. or deduct it from our account in the New Loan we are to open. But, above all, pray take care to have them such as to stimulate my destined Wearer to Greet me in them with a Paris Bow & an English Embrace. I confide myself to y^r taste.

[10] John and Sally Payne (L. 1247 n. 2).

[11] An ancient and picturesque town 16 miles SSE. of Berne.

[12] The usual admonition to call on members of the Latour-Maubourg and Beauvau families (L. 1195 nn. 4, 6; L. 1205 n. 2; L. 1258 n. 6), and the General's faithful friend Marie-Alexandre Lenoir (L. 1189 n. 5).

Adieu, my dearest Alex—write me more such Letters, for they do me infinite Good. Remember me, at Paris, to my dear Ambass^r Ambass^ress & dearest Mme de M[aisonneuve] most tenderly & to M. Le Noir most kindly.[12] You tell me nothing of what *Business* passed with him—nor of Evelina nor M. de Narbonne[13]—nor of his & M. Norry's Books[14]— Execute something of all this when you see him again. Do ⟨not o⟩ver fatigue yourself—& you will retu[rn Cha]^s Parr says, all health & Vigour.

Beautiful young William L[ocke] was among the Officers knocked from his Horse by the dreadful Rabble.[15] He is still unrefitted,—2^ce bled—&c—

[13] FBA wished her son to rescue from the impending sale of books and prints in Paris such treasures perhaps as Edward Burney's illustrations for *Evelina* and a portrait of the comte de Narbonne (ii, pp. xiv-xv), which, handed down in the Barrett-Wauchope family, was offered at auction by Sotheby (*Catalogue*, December 1960, No. 296).

[14] Books probably promised to Charles Norry (L. 1194 n. 6).

[15] William Locke III (L. 1195 n. 16), an 'Adonis' and said to be 'the handsomest man in London', perhaps the William Locke who, according to the Army Records, had acquired a sub-lieutenancy in the 1st regiment of Life Guards. So hated by the mob were the Life Guards or 'Piccadilly Butchers' 'that pamphlets were printed and circulated, suggesting that iron balls with sharpened spikes should be scattered about the streets so as to maim the horses, and that every man should carry a knife so as to stab, or at all events cut the reins and thus render them unmanageable'. See Lord William Pitt Lennox, *My Recollections, 1806 to 1873* (2 vols., 1874), i. 71-5, who describes his command of a squadron of the Blues 'during the riots which took place in London, from the time Queen Caroline first landed in England, up to the day of her funeral'. The Blues, however, were less hated than the Life Guards, who 'were denounced by the mob, pelted, and insulted on every occasion'. Emily de Viry, a partisan of Queen Caroline, rejoiced that her cousin William Locke 'would not be on duty with his regiment on the day of the funeral' (*Locks of Norbury*, p. 309): ' "what a comfort . . . to think that the Mob did not see his lovely face employed in contradiction to their wishes" '. If not on the day of the funeral, then on a day soon after, it is evident that his 'lovely face' had indeed been pelted.

[11 Bolton Street],
3 September 1821

To Esther (Burney) Burney

A.L. (rejected Diary MSS. 7280-8, Berg), 3 Sept. 1821
Two double sheets 4to   8 pp.   paged 1, 4, 5.,
Edited by CFBt. *See* Textual Notes.

Begin 3^d Septr 1821.

If I read with peculiar satisfaction, which most truly was the case, your approbation, my dearest Esther, of my legal proceedings in our financial concerns with the venerable Master in Chancery, Mr. Stephens,[1] & with Messrs Clayton, Scott, & Clayton, Soliciters of Lincoln's Inn; as well as with Mr. Charles Wesley, & Mrs. Cosway;[1]—You may imagine that it will not be with absolute indifference I shall await your acquittal of my conduct upon a new occasion, in which, as I have not been able, with all my willingness, to keep you from being involved, with myself, in some expence, I shall be anxious to know that you exonerate me from any unnecessary extravagance in our joint concern. The sum, indeed, when divided, is not alarming, (though it may be rather inconvenient) considering it is to pay the costs of a Chancery suit—but being taken quite by surprize, I knew not how to make any reclamation in our favour. I never had the smallest business of the kind upon my hands before, & to be summoned—& peremptorily—which I have been, to Lincoln's Inn, filled me with perturbation. A short time ago I could not have answered such a Call, whatever might have been the consequence of my Refusal: but I must tell you by what fortuitous circumstances I was able to obey the Citation—& you will soon rejoice as much as myself that I conquered my repugnance to appearing, because, as it turned out, had I not gone in person, our loss upon the occasion would have been *more* than trebled. I mention this to console you before hand. for the impending claim upon your poor purse, & to prepare you ǀ from being frightened out of the favourable hearing

1264. [1] James Stephen (1758-1832), Master in Chancery (1811). For these legal matters, see L. 1262 n. 2.

I wish to obtain for the path in the affair which I really knew not how to avoid taking without subjecting us both to a charge of meanness—a quality so very far from Your character, that you must not wonder, my dear Hetty, I did not care to bear the odium of letting it all fall upon mine.

This preface is terribly tedious: so must be the detail of the circumstances by which I have been drawn in to this suit —for it is only by tracing them minutely I can let you see how utterly impossible it was I should foresee the Costs before it was too late to recede from their payment. It appears to me, at this instant, almost incredible that any thing should have produced the effect of involving me in a Chancery suit. Take, however, the history in its progress, & candidly—I am sure you will *kindly*—consider as you read that if I did not foresee the end in time to avert it, I did not, as You will do, ponder over probabilities & dangers composedly over my writing Table,—I was hurried into action *tout d'un coup*, without a soul with whom to consult, or even a *minute* for deliberation, & obliged to present myself, thus unprepared, For the First time in my long life, in a Court of Law—the most imposing, every way, in the Kingdom, where to abide by what I heard, & to acquiesce in what I was bid *do, sign*, & *pay*, seemed the only Business that brought me There, & made me, in my embarrassment, amazement, & apprehension There to find myself, happy things were no worse, & thankful to get away.—All I beg is that you will not mention the matter to Charles Parr, till I can soften off a little my share in it—for he ¹ will so exult in his prognostications when he hears of our *costs*, as he charged me to get out of the scrape *coûte qui coûte*, for if once we entered a Court of Chancery, the costs would treble the Legacy. However, I can truly aver that, in this latter part of the affair, I have been no Volunteer.

To the point.—Just after my return from Twickenham Meadows, I was setting out, (prepared so to do, I mean,) for the Honour of a royal visit to Kensington Palace, when a counter-command arrived from Her R.H. the Princess Sophia to change my day: at the same instant a Letter came by the post, returned to me after some delay, from Richmond, whither it had been sent by mistake, to Charlotte's: what was my surprize to read a Summons from Mess.ʳˢ Clayton Scott &

Clayton, to attend in person at Lincoln's Inn, to receive Mr.
Devayne's Legacy,[2] before 2.o'clock, on forfeiture of the
same!—It was now one!—I had not a moment to ponder, or
ask advice; I thought of Charles Parr—& I knew your disaffec-
tion to Law & all its chicaneries: these Mess[rs] also, had written me positive word that the demise of the acting Executer
without a Will rendered the legacy null. What could this
change mean?—*Brief*, I was fortunately equipped, & determined to assume courage to enquire ere I relinquished. I
made Ramsay bedizen hastily for my companion; I took
Diane for my Esquire; & ordering a King's Chariot, I bid the
postilion gallop with all speed to the Court of Chancery.
I resolved, as I drove on, to ask frankly for the costs, &,
should I find them such as Cha[s] Parr represented, to withdraw, formally, our claim. I am sure of your approveance for
this prudence. And I set myself above the ridicule of not
being conducted, as is usual, by a Lawyer, & made Ramsay,
who had been there before, lead the way to Mess[rs] Clayton.
We alighted in Lincoln's Inn, & had to parade sundry courts,
avenues, passages, arch-ways, & squares, most of them
formed of stone structures of awful & gloomy grandeur, &
wearing the desolate appearance of being nearly uninhabited,
except by sundry busy clerks, & here & there some perambu-
lating Advocates or Attorneys, with Briefs, parchments, Vel-
lums, & written Documents, hanging over their arms. But—
as if all this was not enough to impress me, Ramsay presently
called out 'O look, ma'am! there's the Lord Chancellor!'[3]
and, crossing a small court to gain an open Corridor, the Lord
Chancellor, in his Robes & enormous wig, was just before us.

We then traversed various passages & stair cases, till I met
with a Clerk, who pointed to me the door of Mess[rs] Clayton
Scott & Clayton's Chambers. I No one asked my Name, nor
offered to conduct me. I felt a little queer, but would not be
discouraged. My greatest difficulty was how I should make

---

[2] John Devaynes (L. 1262 n. 2) had named as sole Executor of his will his
brother William Devaynes (*c.* 1730-1809), a wealthy government contractor.

[3] At this date John Scott (1751-1838), 1st Earl of Eldon (1821), Lord High
Chancellor (1801-27).

known who I was; & that, all at once shewed me the propriety
of a client's being accompanied by a Lawyer. However, this
occured too late for any change, all my alarm being lest the
Clock should strike 2 ere I was in presence. This fear helped
me to exertion; & leaving Ramsay & Diane in the anti room,
when I found no one came forth to receive or announce or
introduce me, I entered the inner & larger room, of which the
door was open, & determined *to behave like a man*—being
my first appearance in that Character. A Gentleman in Black
was looking over papers at a Desk, standing, & with an Air of
arranging them for being gone; & a Clerk was Writing at
another Desk in a corner. He had very much the air of a
Gentleman, though he was so intently occupied, that he
neither looked towards me, nor seemed to perceive that any
one had appeared. This was rather awkward. I stood still a
minute or two, & then, not willing to risk interrupting some
calculation, yet not thoroughly satisfied with this mode of
waiting his leisure, I quietly looked for the handsomest Chair
in the room, & composedly took possession of it. Upon this,
he raised his Eyes. I then presented him my Letter, saying
'Mr. Clayton, I suppose?'—He Bowed, took it, offered me
another seat, proposed shutting the Window if I feared the air
& gave me the pleasure of finding that I retain, what my dear
Father often loved to call it, *An Honest Face*; for he made no
sort of enquiry, demanded no manner of identification, but
went to his Documents, my Letter in his hand, with as firm
a conviction that *I* was *I*, as if he had known me all his life,
& all my Parentage & Kin. Gaining courage by this, I now
began to conn over in my mind a little discreet interrogatory
as to Fees & Expences. But while waiting till he should no
longer seem too busy for interruption—without impertinence,
all on ¹ the sudden he darted to me, with a pen ready dipt in
Jet, in his hand, & placing a paper on a Table before me, with
a manner & look gravely polite, but in a voice that spoke him
accustomed to dispence with any reply, he gave me the Pen,
& pointed to a spot on which he desired me to write my
Name. Put off my guard by the suddenness & authority of
this proceeding — — Would you believe it? I actually signed
my Name incontinently! But recovering, as soon as it was
done, my recollection, though I could not my signature,

I determined at least not to act for *you* till I knew better
what I was about, & in *your* name, as absent, to enquire
about the Fees, before I would take upon me the double
responsibility. However, those who think they may do what
they list, & say what they wist, to a money'd Man of Business
in a Court of Law, have had less experience than *I* have, Now
—or, a great deal more; for the haste of Motion, & the
brevity of Words, are such, that an unpracticed Client has not
the smallest chance to catch a moment for any thing but surprized submission to orders: for just as I thought, while he
took up my signature to throw some sand over it, that I had
formed a phrase with sufficient Laconism to catch his attention without importunity,—before my lips could possibly
part to utter it, my soliciter, clapping my paper into a small
port folio, which he grasped in his left hand, & clapping
abruptly his Hat upon his head, uttered these alarming words
'Please to go with me, Now, ma'am, to the Accomptant
General.'— I

The Accomptant General? thought I; what kind of a *Badinage* is this for a *modicum* of only 5 Guineas, without the
partition? & then, Taxes—Deductions—Fees!!!—Then I
reflected upon the prognostics of Charles Parr—Then, upon
the sick feels of my Esther already on the very opening of
this business;—& I became so much discomposed, that I
hesitated whether I should comply;—but he led the way,
quitting the room with a quick pace even while speaking.—
If I go not, however, thought I, I may be fined for Contempt
of Court!—This suggestion forced me forward. The moment
I reached the stair case, which my Lawyer was already descending, out rushed Diane, bursting from the vainly con-
trolling hands of Ramsay, who had in charge to keep her out
of the way. Delighted to find me safe, in a strange place,
where she had been, Ramsay says, in deep dismay at the
separation, she now would not quit me. I therefore told Ramsay to come also, & down we all three followed Master Soliciter.—At the foot of the stair case, he had the courtesie to
stop for me, & from thence to walk by my side, my rustic
Damsel & my Canine Esquire obsequiously keeping behind
—except that the latter, when not called to order by the
Damsel, chose to Caper friskily round his mistress, or Bark

furiously round her Soliciter.——I now hoped I should obtain an opportunity for my long intended harangue, by his entering into some conversation: but his politeness extended no further than in adopting my pace; for mouth opened he not. This was as new to me as all the rest, having never, that I remember, in my life, begun an attack;—having Always myself been addressed, or I remained silent: but I was Now upon Ground where, probably, a word & a Fee are one! I did not, however, think of that till this moment; but soon finding I had nothing to gain by my taciturnity but it's reciprocity, I resolved to put an end to it. Which I did, by begging leave to enquire who was the Accomptant General? 'Sir John Campbell;'[4] he answered. 'O——I have not the pleasure to know him,' quoth I. But not a syllable further uttered my Guide. This won't do! thought I; I must come to the point more plumply. 'Give me leave, Sir, I cried, to ask, whether my signature will be accepted, or hold good, for my absent sister, Mrs. Burney, who resides at Bath, & could not, for such a trifle be brought to Town?'—'Perfectly, ma'am.'——he replied. 'But I have written only for myself, sir, without naming her; & she is joint residuary Legatee.'—'Your signature is all that is requisite, ma'am.'—Is This a hoax? thought I; or what does it mean? Total silence, however, ensued; till, seeing, by numerous persons passing & re-passing into a handsome stone building, that we were approaching our place of destination, I again assailed him, & more pointedly; growing really anxious to know whether there were not some errour in the whole matter. 'I have been seldom, sir,' I said, 'more surprized than by your Letter, for I had received one, many Months ago, to tell me that the Executor having died intestate, the legacy became null.'—'And such, Madam,' he now replied, 'is the legal fact. The Legacy is lapsed: but as it is for so small a sum, no advantage has been taken of that accident, & I am directed to pay it You.'—I now became a little comforted; but I was dying to ask *by whom* directed; as there appeared, in the all together of the affair, something mysterious. I had I no sooner, however, answered eagerly 'That is very generous,—& I feel very much obliged,—& who ever

---

[4] Sir John Campbell (1767–1834), Master in Chancery (1801–20), Accomptant-General (1819–26).

complains of the Law, & of Lawyers, *I* must stand forth to praise & laud them,——' than he quite unbent his Chancery Brow, & said, with a smile——'Ma'am, your Legacy will now amount to nine pounds Eleven shillings, as interest upon interest has very nearly doubled it.' A greater surprise I think never came upon me than this speech produced: & if it had not been for my suspence as to costs & Fees & deductions,—— I should have mocked Chas Par's prognostics, & have thought I had a very good cordial for my dear Esther's sick feels. However, we entered——mounted the stairs,——& saw there the Accomptant General, seated at an immense Table, with Clerks & Writer under his command in great abundance, & several clients in waiting, & new ones entering every moment: yet all so silent, so orderly, so awfully under subjection, that the accomptant's voice alone was heard in the vast chamber, every reply being made in humble whispering. Mr. Clayton went up to him; what passed no one could hear but the Accomptant: Mr. Clayton, however, soon made me a motion to approach; I advanced: a paper again was placed before me to sign: After which, the Accomptant put into my hand a Draft on the East India House for 9.11.0.——Mr. Clayton asked me whether I had 4^s & sixpence? I said yes. 'Give it me, then, ma'am, & I will save you the trouble to call again to pay your costs. They amount to 4^s & 6^d——' I stared—— really not believing my Ears: but Mr. Clayton abruptly disappeared. I looked at the Draft, & could not forbear ejaculating 'I am very much surprised, indeed——& very much obliged——though I do not know to whom!' The Accomptant turned quick round to look at me, with a pleased laugh; all the rest smiled——& Ramsay. Diane & I *gracefully* retired. Thus, my dear Esther, I have incurred you a Debt of 2^s & 3^d which I shall, meanly deduct from your £4: 15: & 6^d in paying only 4.13.3. to your steward, Edward.

Since I have written this, I find I have left too small a space for enclosing one sheet in another, & therefore I have been forced to defer sending my long detail in waiting for a Frank: but our Admiral, to whom I had communicated the whole history just as it stands here, has kindly offered to carry this for me to Epsom, whither he is going to-morrow Morning, & there, in the course of a day or two, to get it franked by his Friend Mr Rickman.[5] To procure this with good grace, I have found it requisite to make a, partial, lecture of the business—& his concern at the sum I have, innocently, involved you in paying is much such as I suspect will be your own— |

Mrs. Maling[6] will be very glad you will mention her love when you write again to Miss Sayre[6] |

If Envy of a Cotemporary's Good looks will kill you—Die in thinking of Mrs. Maling's—Meanwhile she lives in thinking of you with unabating kind remembrance. She looks astonishingly Well

Mrs. Lock comes to me whenever she can—She is sweetly well—& loves your messages tenderly. poor Mrs. A[ngerstein] still at Spa[7]—

I am glad you hear from Mme de Pougens[6]—Will you remember me to her when you write next I hope her amiable & accomplished Chevalier is in better health than when I left France |

My Letters from my Alex are very rare—but written in high spirits—in his last he was going to Berne |

Fanny I understand is in Norfolk.[8] I have not seen Ed-[war]^d this age—

---

[5] One of JB's friends, John Rickman (1771-1840), statistician, F.R.S. (1815), and clerk assistant or Secretary to the Speaker in the House of Commons (1820). 'A perfect man', according to Lamb, he had married in 1805 Susannah Postlethwaite (*c.* 1771-1836), a tall, good-natured woman, 'prank'd out' on visits, it was said, 'like a Queen of the May'. The couple entertained JB and his wife at their country place near Epsom and, in later years, the widowed Mrs. Burney in a house near Portsmouth. See Orlo Williams, *Lamb's Friend the Census-Taker. Life and Letters of John Rickman* (1912); Manwaring, p. 215 and *passim*; and for a vivid description of Rickman, Southey's letter of 9 February 1809 to Landor.

[6] The daughter of John Sheeles (*fl.* 1731-74) and his second wife Anne Elizabeth Irwin (*fl.* 1735-62), who ran a school for girls in Queen Square (see *HFB*, pp. 11, 15), Martha Sophia (1748-1832) married in 1769 as his second wife Christopher Thompson Maling (1741-1810) of Hendon Lodge, West Herrington, co. Durham. For their children, see L. 1282 n. 15 and xii, L. 1374 n. 5.

Related apparently to Mrs. Maling was Frances Julia Sayer (v, L. 451 n. 10), the wife since 1805 (see vi, L. 570 n. 8) of the distinguished Marie-Charles-Joseph de Pougens (v, L. 546 n. 12), blind bookseller in Paris and member of the Institut.

[7] Cf. L. 1263 n. 8.

[8] At Barwick House (see L. 1230 n. 10).

I am very glad Emily[9] looks ruddier—Tell me do, of the two others—my love to all three— ǀ

Poor Miss Eliz. Hays! poor Mrs. Beckford! poor Miss Hays! I know not which to feel for most of the 3.[10] ǀ

I like very much your account of Miss Reid,[11] & am very glad you have her Correspondence.

---

[9] EBB's youngest daughter Amelia Maria (i, p. lxix).

[10] For the Hayes family, see L. 1189 n. 21; for Mrs. Beckford, L. 1189 n. 20; and for Elizabeth Hay, L. 1208 n. 4.

[11] Eldest daughter of the Revd. William Reid (*c.* 1732-78) and his wife Elizabeth *née* Pickering (d. 28 October 1810) of the parish of St. James's, Westminster (see ix, L. 974 n. 3), Elizabeth Pickering Reid (1761-1834) had long been known to EBB, who had described her at some length in her letter (Berg) of 31 August [1821]:

> ——do you ever recollect to have seen a Miss Reid, with whom *our* house were very intimate?—Mrs Reid had 4 Daughters: her Husband *many* years since, put an end to his own life—she had had *100 Thousand* p^d to her fortune—nevertheless, from some circumstances with wch I am not clearly acquainted, —this fortune was *manshed* away—and for some years back Mrs R. & family have appeared rather going *down* the Hill—in respect to style & manner of living:—Miss R. took Lessons of my poor Mr B.—and was at that period, a lively, loud talking, shewy & flaunting sort of a Miss,—not without sense—or humour.—but being herself in person far from pleasing;—tho' she shewed us great partiality—I was not fond of her—still her conversation was entaining—but in too prominent a style to please me—she *ever* shewed the greatest partiality to my D^r Mr. B. myself & family—and courted our society as did the family in general. . . . Miss Reid found . . . that *WE* were resident in the vicinity of Bath.—and commenced a Correspondance with me—I really wish you could see, some of her Letters.—She seems herself a much improved Character—& her Letters contain so much of attachment, of affectionate recollection of former times (when we lived in Titchfield St.—and previous to that time) with such excellent remarks,—and *Just* sentiments—that I cannot speak too highly of them—they really prove a source of entertainment to me, —after having lain by, for Months & years.

The details above are substantiated by the baptismal registers of St. James's, Piccadilly, and by the wills of the Revd. William Reid (PRO/PROB/11/1044/299, dated 8 November 1774, pr. 15 July 1778) and that of his daughter Elizabeth (PRO/PROB/11/1846/256, dated Guildford Street, Russell Square, 18 August 1834, pr. 7 April 1835). For her work on Botany, see xii, L. 1373 n. 3.

11 Bolton Street,
4 September 1821

To James Burney

A.L.S. (PML, Autog. Cor. bound), 4 Sept. [1821]
Double sheet 8vo   4 pp.   trimmed   cover missing

4th Septr Tuesday Night,
11. Bolton S^t.

My dear Admiral,

If This is not provokuss, I know not what is! I am appointed
for Thursday Evening[1] — — & so appointed that, vexed as
I am at the delay of James Street Tea-Age, I should be graceless—

unnatural,
or affected

to say I am vexed at the appointment itself.

But what is the Worst in This; I can Name no other Day till
this engagement is over, lest I should again have to set it aside.

But the perverse part of the business is This—

I have never a *morning* to give at present for Love or
Money;[1]—It is not that all my mornings are positively be-
spoken; but they are all in requisition, so that I keep them
blank.

And what is provokuss also is a Note from Sarah-Harriet to
offer to come to me to-morrow: & receive her I cannot—nor
all the Week—*at least.*

But—I have no reason to expect any *Evening* will be in

1265. [1] To the Princess Sophia (1777–1848), in the absence of whose ladies-in-
waiting (see L. 1270 n. 11), FBA in these months received frequent summonses.
As explained at length in Ll. 1267, 1270, the Princess was sitting at this time to
John Linnell (1792–1882), whose miniature of the Princess is extant (Frame 7,
No. 4, dated 1821) in the Collection of H.M. the Queen, as the editor was kindly
informed by Mr. G. Reynolds, Keeper of the Department of Prints and Drawings
and Paintings. 'I ventured to make my pictures to look really like them, though
as favourable as truth would admit', commented the miniaturist, 'and I calculate
it was on that account I had no more from that connection'. See A. T. Story,
Life of John Linnell (2 vols., 1892).

On 6, 7, 8, 13, and 14 September (Diary) FBA was called to Kensington
Palace, and on the 7th she was to walk with the Princess in Regent's Park.

requisition after Thursday; & if not, I shall give You & Mrs Admiral Carte blanche to name your own time for my Tea-Age——

I have had no Letter from Turin—not a word,—sly ¦ nor simple. I hope it will come. I shall be very sorry indeed to lose one from my dear Sarah—I thank dear Mrs. Admiral cordially for her loan,——[2]

I trust you will not be *sharp* upon a Bride for wanting a Cooing shed with her love——? as to the Slyness—'tis neither more nor less than an anxiety to avoid seeming to oppose any plan or wish of yours—joined to —— —— What?—out with it!—a private resolution *to have her own way!*—But *pappys*, as well as *mammys* must allow for the spoilt indulgencies in all their fancies usually accorded to the Bridal first year. Don't shorten its Charm. ¦

Adieu, Noble Admiral——

Do what you will, & say what you will, I shall never mince the matter in calling you by your title. What a dickens? have I not been wishing for it long enough? And Now that it is come, shall I throw it away?

I have looked at the List in which you will be enrolled next year, & I find you in such good company that instead of being discomfitted by your Yellow-ship;[3] I see none of the Blues nor the Reds in better society.—And, Therefore, with as much pleasure as Affection, I persist to sign myself, in partaking of your dignity,

An Admiral's Sister
F d A

² The loan of Sarah Payne's letters from abroad (Manwaring, pp. 274 ff.). Mrs. Burney's offer survives in a fragment (Berg): 'Should you My Dear sister feel yourself disposed to be a little idle I enclose two letters for your perusal which are not sly ones.' The letters are missing.

³ 'Admiral of the Yellow' was the colloquial term for a superannuated Rear Admiral who had attained that rank and pension through an ascent in the seniority lists rather than in active service at sea, where flag-officers were promoted in the order Admiral of the Red, White, or Blue Squadron.

FBA may have seen the coronation lists published in *The Times*, 21 July 1821 or those appearing in the *London Gazette* of 17 July.

276

I told my P^ss Sophia your History, because I heard the Duke & Duchess of Clarence⁴ were to pass through Town from Bognor to Bushy, & might call on H.R.H.

1266   [11 Bolton Street,
                                         12 September 1821]

To Charles Parr Burney

A.L. (Osborn), n.d.
Single sheet 4to with large wafer tear 1 p.   *pmks* T.P.P.U. / May Fair 12 SP 1821
Addressed: To the Rev^d / Charles Par Burney, / Greenwich, / —Kent—

Alex—to my great regret, is alone—his companions decided upon going on immediately to Italy—& visiting the Alps with their instruments of unheard of exactness;¹—I doubt

---

⁴ The Princess Adelaide Louisa Theresa Caroline Amelia (1792-1849) of Saxe Meiningen, whom the Duke of Clarence had married on 11 July 1818 (Burke). See also Philip Ziegler, *King William IV* (1971), pp. 121-6, and for his acquiring Bushy House, pp. 82-3 *passim*.

1266. ¹ In the year following the tour of Switzerland, Papers by AA's 'scientific' friends would appear in the first volume of *Memoirs of the Astronomical Society of London* (1822), i. 144-5, 309-14, and in this year Babbage was awarded a gold medal by that Society for the invention of 'an engine' for astronomical calculations. In *Phil. Trans.*, 114 (1824), pt. iii. 1-403, Herschel and James South would publish 'Observations of the apparent distances and reactions of 380 double and triple Stars, made in the years, 1821, 1822, and 1823'.

It was, however, the romantic rather than the scientific aspects of nature that commanded d'Arblay's attention and efforts, as may be seen in the MSS (Berg) of his 'Dithyrambe écrit au pied du Mont Blanc à la vue des aiguilles de Chamonix en août 1821', of which three versions, some 18 stanzas in all are extant:

> Toi dont la cime se colore
> Des premiers rayons de l'aurore,
> Et du jour expirant reçoit les derniers traits;
> Toi, qui semble toucher le Ciel qui t'environne
> Qui porte dans les airs les Neiges pour couronne
> · · · · · · · ·
> Ah! puissai-je long-tems conserver en mon Ame
> Ces transports, ces élans, ces traits de vive flamme
> Qu'inspirent de ces lieux les sombres majestés;
> Et puiser en ton sein, adorable Nature,
> Cette volupté pure
> Qu' ignorera toujours le luxe des Cités!

277

not they will make a scientific Tour that will not be confined to their own observations—Alex had neither project nor means for this *extension* of *measures*:—he contents himself with La Suisse. His last Letter is from Geneva, of which he had made the Circle on Foot in 7 days—out of which he deducts one for rest at Lausanne—where he met Mrs. Siddons[2] — —

1267   11 Bolton Street,
                                  17 September 1821

To Mrs. Broome

A.L.S. (rejected Diary MSS. 7290-[3], Berg), 17 Sept. 1821
Double sheet 4to (8.8 × 7.2")   4 pp.   [*may once have had a cover*]
Edited by CFBt. *See* Textual Notes.

Monday Even^g Septr 17th—1821.
Bolton Street.

At length, my best & dearest Charlotte, I think I have got a quiet moment—i.e. Hour or two—to confab with you as I love, namely with leisure as well as Confidence & Affection. I hope, imprimis, your Nose pinches have been productive of more effect than you were prepared to expect; you must be very cautious not to repeat too rapidly or too frequently the operation. After 3 pinches, a Week should ensue ere another attempt is made, as the *produce* is sometimes very sluggish in beginning, & very active where it is thought at an end. I know not whether our Bride has brought the supply, having forgotten to enquire: but should this depart the place before I meet the fair Honey Moon again,[1] I shall enclose another 3 *dozes* for security that you are not longer kept waiting.

[2] In the summer of 1821 Sarah Siddons (1755–1831) had paid a visit to her brother John Kemble (1757–1823) at Lausanne and 'found him living in a beautiful retirement, near the borders of the Leman Lake'. See Thomas Campbell, *Life of Mrs. Siddons* (2 vols., 1834).

1267. [1] On 8 September John Payne (L. 1192 n. 5) had called on FBA and on the 9th and 13th, Sarah as well (Diary).

I have been much gratified by hearing, from Sarah Harriet, that Clement is going on most prosperously.[2] Give him my love & congratulation. I hope dear Marianne is well,—& that she has not forgotten her *half promise* to shew Twickenham Meadows *fair play*, & not desert them at the same time their old friend has taken her flight.

I long eagerly for new tidings of our Charlotte:[3] I am sure you will indulge me with a full account when you write. |

My life, eventful even yet, in defiance of its obscurity as well as its dejection, has taken, for the present, a quite new turn. I left Twickenham hospitable Meadows, & my dear Charlotte's so prized vicinity, for an intended complete seclusion, to repair & refit my poor faculties & spirits, previously to giving them their best exertion at Eliot Vale, in the service of Mrs. Lock, whose sweetness would recompence every effort, or pardon every failure: but lo!—neither to Eliot Vale have I travelled, nor in this purposed seclusion have I reposed — — by a strange coincidence of circumstances,[4] on the very day after my return I received a billet from Her Royal Highness the Princess Sophia, to visit her at Kensington Palace, where the King her Brother has made her mistress of a charming suite of apartments, This was utterly unexpected, for I had not received any summons from H.R.H. since last December—or January—when I had been compelled, with whatever reluctance, to decline accepting the honour of an invitation, on account of the illness of Alexander. This was a motive to add pleasure to the present call, as I knew my refusal was a sort of thing unheard of in Courts, & that I should have risked mortal displeasure with any royal personage of a less liberal disposition, or | possessing less sweetness of Character. I had the happiness to find her in much amended health, & to be fully assured she had not taken ill my uncourtly *Maternity*. She was sitting, at this period, though not on this day, for her Picture, to an eminent Miniature

---

[2] For CF, see L. 1261 n. 3.

[3] The Barretts, still at Ghent (L. 1253 n. 4), were to return *c.* 20 October.

[4] See L. 1265 n. 1. FBA had been received at Kensington Palace at least five times in 1820 (19 September–19 December) and, in the period August–October (1821) inclusive, at least on eighteen occasions. It was on 7 September (Diary) that she 'walked with Princess Sophia in the Garden of The Regent's Park'.

Painter.[5] She permitted me to attend at the next sitting; &, to cut my narration shorter, she next invited me to be present upon every subsequent occasion of the sort. I told her of my approaching engagement to Mrs. Lock, but faithfully assured her how thankfully I should postpone it for the Honour offered me: she accepted the little tribute of grateful respect, with infinite sweetness, & Mrs. Lock—who came to hasten me the following day, immediately gave up her present claim with even delight at the Princess's request. Since this, I have been entirely at H.R.H[ness] devotion; for not only I have gone to every sitting[4]—which always last two or 3 Hours,—but I have had the gratification of passing several Evenings tête à tête with her—& once of being taken, most condescendingly, by her fair self to see the Regent's Park— which I had never beheld—& which, but for this flattering incident, I had most contentedly left life without seeing! for all curiosity, all pleasure in sights, or excursions, is dead in me!—I receive none but through the medium of *participation*, & when any thing is presented to me *so*,—a something bordering upon former sensations arises once more to animate my spirits. I I know my dearest Charlotte will like this little history, & rejoice, rather than lament, like Mrs. Lock, that, for such an occasion, I should try the air of Bolton Street instead of Eliot Vale. These frequent meetings give an encrease of intimacy that shews Her Royal Highness in a fairer & fairer point of view—& I always think the time I spend with her short, be it extended how it may.

I have had another long & very comfortable Letter from my Alex, though *one* more only.[6] It is from Geneva, like the former one, at the end of the Walk round the Lake he had projected, & which he has happily executed. He was then going to Chamounix & thence to Berne. Pray make my most affectionate remembrances to my dear Friends at the Meadows, & to Mrs. Baker. My visit to Eliot Vale is to take place as soon as the Picture is finished. Our Admiral enjoys his Honours with philosophy of manner, but with real & great internal satisfaction. So do I for him, God knows. He is now at Epsom, on a visit to the Rickmans.[7] The Bride is returned

[5] John Linnell (L. 1265 n. 1).
[6] AA's letters of this time are missing.   [7] See L. 1264 n. 5.

improved in looks, & in all sort of amiability, The *Groom* conducts himself with [r]eal good sense & propriety. They are seeking a Dwelling in this neighbourhood. My last Letter from dear Esther is tolerably chearful. Fanny Burney is at the *ci-devant* Miss Glover's of Queen Square—now Mrs. Hoste of Norfolk.[8] Edward I expect to Tea by appointment tomorrow Evening. Fanny Raper I have not seen. Nor Sarah Harriet: I can make *no* morning appointment at present.

Pray do not lose sight of the fitting time for Brighton. I always build upon it as the best harbinger of remitted health & vigour & spirits, for the winter's campaign. As to me, my Eliot Vale not yet begun—I certainly could not come to you till late in the Season.

Do Clement's friends, the Tunnos,[9] incline to the Villa pointed out by the Archdeacon? Poor Mrs. Angerstein is returned from Spa,[10] in better health, & rather renovated spirits. She is a pattern of resignation to the Will of Heaven in all things.[11] When your plans are formed, give me an *'int*, privately, that I may try to fashion mine by them. Are we to wear our Mourning 3 months?[12]—adieu, my dearest Charlotte. Put me a Letter on the stocks, as formerly.

Yours completely—ever & ay—
F d'A.

1268   11 Bolton Street,
2⟨6⟩ September 1821

To Charles Parr Burney

A.L.S. (Osborn), 2⟨6⟩ Sept. 1821
Double sheet 8vo   3 pp.   *pmks* Piccadilly 27 SP 1821   black seal
Addressed: Revd Charles Parr Burney, / Greenwich, / Kent.
Docketed in pencil, p. 1: (82)
See Textual Notes.

[8] See L. 1230 n. 10.   [9] See L. 1253 n. 2.
[10] For Spa, see L. 1218 n. 1.
[11] For the accidental drowning of Henry Angerstein, see L. 1245 n. 3.
[12] Mourning for their sister-in-law 'Rosette' Burney (L. 1255 n. 1), who had died on 2 August.

2⟨6⟩th Septr 1821.
11, Bolton Street,

My dear Charles,

I am very sorry I missed seeing you this morning—though I hope you do not think I merely write to say what your own sagacity & Affection must already—I trust,—have said for me: No,—I write to say that I *must* be in town till the End of This Week, and therefore that I *will* be here for the beginning of the next. I shall hope, consequently, that the honour you have indicated to me will not be missed. I must hope, also, that you have never betrayed any doubt as to my *capabilities* of reception, as there never can have been any as to my *readiness*—or rather wishes to make personal acquaintance with Bishop Kaye.[1] I say *Bishop Kaye*, because Bishop of ǀ *Bristol* may mean any such dignitary for the last 1700 years—(or *thereabouts*—we won't be particular for a century or so;)—or any such for the time to come, when a *translation* may make me confused myself as to the *Original*. Indeed, I regret that Bishops do not always sign & mark themselves rather by their Family Name, which may carry them down to posterity, rather than by that name which, however sacred its source, they are only known by in the Nursery. Now however quick, & however high the beginning, I have no notion that Bishop Bristol will be the ending of Bishop Kaye.—

⎯⎯⎯⎯

I had a Letter 2 days ago from Alexander, dated Yverdun. He is so considerably, he says, improved in strength, that he has walked, on an average, during this last fortnight, 30 miles a day!—There can be little doubt, therefore, ǀ that he means to favour the public [with] accurate observations on the laws, customs, manners, temper, character, and societies of Switzerland.—He tells me to direct next to Bâle, where he

1268. [1] On 2 October (Diary) FBA had duly received John Kaye (1783-1853), D.D. (1815), one of CB Jr.'s most distinguished pupils, who as Master of Christ's College, Cambridge (1814), had befriended AA for his uncle's sake (ix, x *passim*). Vice-Chancellor of his University (1815-16), Regius Professor of Divinity (1816-27), Bishop of Bristol (1820), he was to be translated to the see of Lincoln (1827).

means, he says, to *take the Rhine*,—for how long or short
a course I know not.

Adieu, Dear Charles — — —

I am not merry—but I do beguile *The Thing I am*[2] by
seeming otherwise The peculiar circumstances at which I have
hinted, which detain me in town, call forth from me an exertion that begins somewhat more to habituate me—will I, Nill
I, to the things & intercourse of this nether sphere—that to
you, will long, I trust, my dear Charles, be as sprightly in
Fact as in semblance.

Yours &c
F d Ay

1269

[11 Bolton Street],
24 October 1821

To Mrs. Barrett

A.L. (Berg), 24 Oct. 1821
Double sheet 8vo   4 pp.

24th Octr 1821

I am so pleased at your return, my dearest Charlotta, that
I cannot lose a moment in giving you my cordial & tender
Welcome back to Old England and
                    '*Your Fireside.*—'

But I am truly chagrined for *both* that you miss—& are
missed by your fond Mother on the instant of your return.[1]
It was all from *shilly shally*;—one party could not make up
his mind whether to *sea* it at all or not prior to the ensuing

---

[2] *Othello*, II. i: 'I am not merry, but I do beguile / The thing I am by seeming
otherwise.'

1269. [1] After about five months in Ghent the Barretts had returned to Richmond *c.* 20 October, only to find that Clement Francis had departed for Cambridge and Mrs. Broome for Brighton. See CFBt's letter of 19 September (Eg.
3706D, ff. 15–16b) to CF and CBFB's letter (Eg. 3693, ff. 93–4b), 27 November–
1 December [1821] to FBA.

Dogmaticmal Dignity; & the other will always make any the greatest self sacrifice, rather than press a favourite to make the smallest. Yet you must not let her yielding Heart know all your Disappointment till you *meet*; & if you have done it, in the first effusions of its force, you will do ⎮ well, & like yourself—excuse that tautology—to write her a *quietizer* out of hand—& assure her you have so much to do, you shall enjoy her society trebly for her being absent while material bustle occupies you: otherwise, though the œconomy of the Journey will induce her to stay her stated time, the breezes from which she has so often reaped benefit will only turn noxious, & she will come back not braced, but shattered.

To resist Lady Bedingfeld[2]—and you is beyond all power of repugnance: though the idea of either declining her already pressed suit, or of complying by *presenting myself* to a *New acquaintance*, has hitherto made me silent to her charming Letter—But I am Now, by such a picture of her kindness to my Charlotte, painted on the canvas of my long admiration & ⎮ esteem, more than vanquished—for I will write to her within a Week, & on my return from Eliot Vale, I will obey her injunctions with all the alacrity I can assume, & with Gratitude, *sans* assumption, that she holds me worthy to receive such, with their concomitant implications.

I think, too, frankly, from much I have heard, that,—the *abord* over—! my compliance may procure pleasure & satisfaction to myself — — *Mais* — —

My Alex wrote to me last from *Berne*. He meant to visit Lucerne, Schaffouse—Basle—& then a sale upon the Rhine —& then Paris. He was quite well. I am—& have been—kept in Town by extra-causes ever since I left Twickenham:—but so peculiarly as to be able to make no engagements either *at home or abroad*: I have shut up House, therefore, & am a — — no, not *quite* a Princess—but a *Person* in disguise, not ⎮ avowing I am not—(where, but for these peculiar circumstances I *should* be)—at Eliot Vale—& Thither I am packed for going the very instant my call away—which however is

---

[2] Lady Bedingfeld had suggested (L. 1253 n. 3) that FBA call on her mother the Dowager Lady Jerningham (L. 1250 n. 2), who was living with her son Edward and his family at 13 Bolton Row, but untoward circumstances soon to occur prevented the visit.

a very agreeable one to me—ceases:[3] Nurse therefore your cold, which I am grieved to hear of, & do not waste a visit at this fruitless moment on one who will with such true open arms & Heart, fold you when you can, at her return, give her the always bright & beaming invitation of your kind approach. —I have been forced, very reluctantly, to keep aloof dear aunt Sarah—for these, now, nameless reasons; & I have not seen our dear Fanny this age. I am constantly in expectation of departing: & it is only to the Admiral I can ever be visible; & that, as he is so near, is, at odd times of security, feasible as well as agreeable.

My Love to the dear Children, & to my dear Marianne— I hope she remembers her engagement to *keep up* the renewal with the excellent Archdeacon & Mrs Cambridge. My best Regards to them & to Mr. Barrett, & Miss Baker.

God bless my dearest Charlotta. |

My visit to my dear Archd^n & Mrs. C[ambridge] did me indescribable good with respect to bringing me round to some *power* of social exertion—

1270 [11 Bolton Street]
and continued at Eliot Vale
21 October–[*post* 8] November 1821

To Esther (Burney) Burney

A.L. incomplete (Diary MSS. vii, not numbered, Berg), 21 Oct.– [Nov.] 1821
Two double sheets 4to   8 pp.   [*A third sheet, with the conclusion is missing*]
Docketed p. 5, 11–14: replied To
Edited by the Press*. See* Textual Notes.

(Begun) Octr 21st 1821.

Your *mind*, my dearest Esther, was always equal to literary

---

[3] Still in the service of the Princess Sophia (see L. 1267 n. 4 and Diary), FBA was not to set out for Eliot Vale until 8 November.

pursuits, though your *Time* seems only now to let you enjoy them. I have often thought that had our excellent & extraordinary own Mother[1] been allowed longer life, she would have continued to make you sensible of this sooner—I do not mean in a common way; for *that* has never failed, but in an uncommon one; I mean in one striking & distinguished: for she very early indeed began to form your taste for reading, & delighted to find time, amidst all her cares & calls, to guide you, in your most tender years, to the best authours, & to read them with you, commenting, & pointing out passages Worthy to be got by heart. I perfectly recollect, Child as I was, & never of the party, this part of your education. At that very juvenile period, the difference even of *Months* makes a marked distinction in bestowing and receiving instruction. I, also, was so peculiarly backward that even our Susan stood before me. She could read when I knew not my Letters. But though so sluggish to learn, I was always observant; —— —— do you remember Mr. Seton's[2] denominating me, at 15, *The silent observant Miss Fanny?* Well, I recollect your reading with our dear Mother all Pope's Works, & Pitt's Aeneid.[3] I recollect, also, your spouting passages from Pope, that I learnt from hearing you recite them, before—many *years* before I read them Myself. For it was not till I was 15 a taste of that sort came upon Me. But after You lost, so young! that admirable, that incomparable Guide—you had none

1270. [1] Esther would have been 13, Fanny 10, and Susanna 7, when their 'own' mother Esther *née* Sleepe died in Poland Street in 1762.

[2] Alexander Seton (1743–1801), with whom FB, aged 16, had 'the first real conversation I ever had in my life', was the third son of Sir Henry Seton (1703–51), 3rd Baronet of Abercorn, brewer, of Edinburgh, who had married in 1726 Barbara Wemyss (d. 1770). See Sir Bruce Gordon Seton: *The House of Seton: A Study of Lost Causes* (Edinburgh, 2 vols., 1939), ii. 520–3. In London in 1768–70 he attended, with other members of his family, youthful parties in Poland Street, playing havoc in the heart of EBB, then aged 19. 'Poor Hetty passed an uneasy night, racked with uncertainty about this Seton, this eternal destroyer of her peace!' But, as did '*the silent observant Miss Fanny*', she perceived him at last as fickle and 'artful'. '*Were* he sincere, she owned she could be happier in a union with him than with any man breathing:—indeed, he deserves her not;—but the next morning, when she had considered well of every thing, she declared were he to make her the most solemn offer of his hand she would refuse him,—and half added—*accept of Charles!*' See *ED* i. 33–98 *passim*.

[3] Christopher Pitt (1699–1748), whose translation of the *Aeneid* appeared in 1738. An edition (2 vols., 1784) was in CB's library in 1814 (see Sale *Catalogue*, op. cit.).

left: our dear Father was always Abroad, ⎮ usefully, or ornamentally; but, ultimately, always for serious advantage: but,
after giving you a year in Paris, with the best Masters that
could be procured, you came home at 15 or 16, to be exclusively occupied by musical studies—save for the interludes
that were 'sacred to Dress and Beauty's pleasing cares'[4]—for
so well you played, & so lovely you looked, that admiration
followed alike your Fingers & your Smiles,—& the Piano
Forte & The World divided your first Youth,—which, had
that exemplary Guide been spared us, I am fully persuaded
would have left some further testimony of its passage than
barely my old Journals written to myself, which celebrate
your Wit & talents as highly as your beauty. And I judge I
was not mistaken by all in which you have had opportunity
to shew your mental faculties, i.e. your Letters; which have
always been strikingly good & agreeable, & evidently un-
studied.

When Alex comes home, I will try to get Crabbe:[5] & try
to hear it with pleasure. The two lines you have quoted are
very touching. I have read nothing of his but his first, admirable, poem—the something *Curate*, I forget the title: but our
poor Charles once read to me some of his fugitive short pieces
that I thought highly beautiful.

⌣⎯⎯⎯,

Thus much, my dear Etty, I wrote on the Day I received
your last: but —— —— &c. &c. &c.——

November—I write now from Elliot Vale,[6] under the kind
& elegant roof of sweet Mrs. Lock, who loves & prizes you
sincerely, & charges me with her most affectionate remembrances. Perhaps I may meet here with your favourite Crabbe;
as I subscribe to no *Library*, I know not how, else, I shall get
at his. I am sure you will *All* rejoice that I have just had a
Letter from *Paris*, where my Alex was just arrived; I think he

---

[4] The toilette of Venus, Pope's *Iliad*, xiv. 192.
[5] FBA may have been thinking of the Curate in *The Borough* (1810). EBB's
quotation is missing, along with her letter.
[6] FBA had arrived on 8 November, 'fetch^d by my dearest Friend Mrs. Lock,
to solace the absence of my Alexander in her soft & dear society' (Diary).

will pass a fortnight there,[7] & then ⎮ join me, by special invitation, at Eliot Vale. He has been scampering 3 months—nearly 4—over the Mountains of Switzerland, when he only purposed an excursion of 6 weeks. But he says his strength is greatly encreased, by early hours, & much exercise in the open air; *both* always agreed with him, but always have been of difficult attainment when not excited by something extraordinary.

I thank you 1000 times for the good *bulletin* of your health, my dearest Esther, & I know how kindly you will reciprocate my satisfaction when I tell you mine is inconceivably ameliorated, *moyenant* great & watchful care: & Alex keeps me to that with the high hand of peremtory insistance—according to the taste of the times; for the 'rising Generation,'[8] as my good old Baronet would observe, *expect* just as much obedience to orders as they *withhold*. If you were to hear the young Gentleman, delivering *to me* his Lectures on Health, & dilating upon Air, Exercise, Social intercourse, & gay spirits, you would be forced to seek a Magnifying Glass to believe that your Eyes did not deceive you, but that it was really your Nephew haranguing his Mother. However, we must pass by the exhorting impetuosity in favour of the zealous anxiety that fires it up in his animated breast. He has written me several Letters that have been very delightful to me, with full accounts of whom as well as what he has seen. This has given me a comfort, & done me a good, quite inexpressible.

Sweet Mrs. Angerstein is returned from Spa[9] greatly amended in her health, & restored in her spirits, though her's was a tragedy never to be quite got over. She trudges across the dirty & rugged heath, in all Weathers but hard rain, *every*

---

[7] AA was not to return until April 1822.

[8] Sir Hugh Tyrold in FBA's *Camilla*, book I, chap. i: '. . . by what I hear, the rising generation's got to a much greater pitch since my time.'

[9] See L. 1245 n. 3; and L. 1267 nn. 10, 11; and for these visits 8-23 November (Diary).

day to see her adored Mother. Lady Martin is now at Woodlands, & also calls daily.——I have not heard whether Fanny is
returned from Norfolk.[10] I was kept in town by a particular
circumstance—I might say, like the Play Bills, By | *particular
Desire*, for it was a fair Royal personage who condescended
to ask me to remit my visit to Eliot Vale, that I might attend
her Sittings for her Picture, her 2 Ladies being at that time
absent on *congée.*[11] You may believe how much I was gratified by the honour, *because* you know my sincere & truly
warm attachment for all those loved & gracious personages:
but you may be surprized your poor Sister could now be
pitched upon—where so much choice must *always* be at
hand—for whiling away the tediousness of what she, the
P^ss—calls the *odious occupation* of sitting still for this exhi-
bition: but the fact is I was able to fulfil her views better
than most people could do in defiance of my altered spirits
& depressed faculties, by having recourse simply to my
Memory, in relating things I saw, or heard, or did, during the
long Ten years, & the eventful added one more, that I spent
abroad. Only to name Buonaparte, in any positive trait that
I had witnessed, or known, even without either embellish-
ment or admiration, was sufficient to make her open her fine

[10] From Barwick House (L. 1230 n. 10).

[11] Absent temporarily from their posts at Kensington Palace were Lady John
Thynne (*c.* 1778-1863) and Georgiana Anne Vyse (1781-1857), Lady of the Bedchamber and Woman of the Bedchamber, respectively, to the Princess Sophia.

Mary Ann *née* Master, the wife since 18 June 1801 of Lord John Thynne
(*c.* 1772-1849), 3rd and youngest son of the 1st Marquess of Bath (1734-96),
was formerly Lady of the Bedchamber to Princess Charlotte and one of the first
to be aware (see Farington, viii. 152) of the unexpected death of the Princess in
childbirth. Later Lady Carteret, when in 1838 Lord John succeeded his brother as
Baron Carteret of Hawnes, she was a sister-in-law of Lady Isabella Thynne (1768-
1835), who had been appointed in 1812 as Lady of the Bedchamber to the
Princess Mary.

Niece of Dr. William Vyse (L. 1304 n. 20) of Lichfield and daughter of
General Richard Vyse (1746-1825), who in 1780 had married as his second wife
Anne (d. 1784), daughter of Sir George Howard (1720-96), K.B., of Bookham,
Surrey, and of Stoke Place, Stoke Poges, Bucks., Georgiana Anne lived, as did her
brother, in Stoke Poges, apparently dying, however, at 36 Brunswick Terrace,
Brighton. Her will (PRO/PROB/11/2255/588, pr. 1 July 1857) reflects her years
of service to the Royal Family and their regard for her as shown in gifts or
remembrances, for instance, 'a pearl hoop ring . . . given to me by Her Late
Majesty Queen Charlotte'.

For the identifications of the Princess Sophia's ladies, the editors are indebted
to Miss Olwen Hedley, author of *Queen Charlotte* (1975).

Eyes in a manner extremely advantageous to the Painter; who himself was so enchanted to be in the room with any one who had seen Buonaparte, that in his envy of my great happiness, he evidently began to look upon me himself as a personage eminently extraordinary. This affair, however, over, you may imagine with what eagerness I wished to come, at length, to my dear Mrs. Lock: but lo & behold! poor Ramsay got a hurt upon her breast that threatened the most dreadful consequences, & I could not endure to leave her, in so critical a situation,—& one I knew so fatally both how to feel for, & how to aid. I stayed, therefore, till by good management, & proper means, the danger passed away, & on the 8th of This month I reached Eliot Vale, after an absence from it of 2 years, from various impediments; save of mere ¦ morning visits, in our airings, occasionally, with Lady Templetown.[12] I find this sweet soul all herself, in every mental perfection, —but no longer, alas, wholly unchanged in her beautiful outward appearance. A very bad illness she has lately had, has now, for the first time, shewed the mortal power of Time & Malady on that Face which, till within these last few Months, seemed as if destined, even here on Earth, to be immortal as her Soul. It is still, however, most sweet, nay lovely,—but no longer unfaded & unimpaired in Beauty, as, till now, it has so wonderfully continued. This attack was an acute rheumatism, with fever. It is over, I thank God, & she is fast recovering, though much slower & heavier in her movements. But her spirits & conversation & manners retain all their original charm & bewitchment. And you are a never-failing favourite subject with her.

I spent one Morning, & drank tea one Evening with dear Admiral James immediately before I left town.[13] He shewed me sundry old family Letters, written by my dear Father, & all of us round, to poor dear *Miss Young*,[14] which, upon her death, had been sent to him by Mr. Ste[phen] Allen.[15] I can-

---

[12] For FBA's visit of December 1819, see L. 1226 n. 3; for drives with Lady Templetown, L. 1235 n. 12.

[13] FBA had visited JB on 5 November and on the evening of the 6th (Diary).

[14] Dorothy Young (iii *passim*) of King's Lynn, a life-long friend of CB and of both his 1st and 2nd wife (*Memoirs* i. 97–9; iii. 340; and Lonsdale, p. 456). For her correspondence with the Burneys, see *Catalogue*.

[15] The Revd. Stephen Allen (1755–1847) of King's Lynn, son of the 2nd Mrs.

not tell you he looks well in health—on the contrary, he
declines sensibly, but Not rapidly, I trust, nor irremediably;
& I have always hoped his long sought promotion would
lengthen as well as sweeten his life. I took an interest in it
indiscribable—& in more ways than one—for it really appeared to me that he affixed to it an importance that would
have made its failure nearly produce his own. God be praised
it has been obtained! He is to get me this franked for you by
Mr. Rickman,[16] on my sending it enclosed to James Street.
It was his promise of that aid-conveyance that occasioned my,
erst, writing you That Full & Fine Account of my appearance, conversation ǀ and Behaviour, on my first Summons to
a Court of Justice.[17] The truth is, I drank tea with him on
the Evening of that very Day, &, as he had heard of the
Legacy in its previous state, I sought to amuse, yet alarm
him, by recounting the whole long story in all its circumstances: & I succeeded so well, that, in full expectation every
moment I was coming upon Taxes, Stamps, & our Costs, he
grew breathless & open mouthed with eagerness, so that
when I came, with due solemnity, to our Divided expences of
Two shillings & sixpence each, for a Chancery suit — — the
surprize & pleasure produced so hearty a Horse Laugh,—
ecchoed back by Mrs. B[urney] that I took courage & patience
& Time to go through the same meanders for my dear Esther,
in hopes of the same result. And I was promised a Frank, on
condition I went & read the whole over to him again, on the
return of his Bride. 'Tis the only Letter I ever *wrote* that I
ever *read* before. And every tittle of my own anxiety, &c is
literally true. I am still at a loss to know *how* we escaped said
Stamps & Taxes.

The *Bride* is returned well & I hope happy.[18] The *Groom*,
for the very little *I* have seen of him, behaves with a propriety that marks sense & modesty. I earnestly wish her well;
she is the delight of the very soul of our dear James. How
charmed I have been, & how pleased you will be, to hear that

Burney by her first marriage. In St. Margaret's, King's Lynn, there is a large
memorial tablet recording his life-long services to the church.

[16] John Rickman (L. 1264 n. 5).

[17] L. 1264.

[18] For the calls of John Payne and his bride at Bolton Street, see L. 1267 n. 1
or (Diary).

Pacchierotti is living,[19] & spending his latter days in splendour, yet rationally, elegantly, & benevolently, in Padua, where Sarah P[ayne] saw him. She wrote him a Note in English, to claim his notice by her birth & connections; he received her instantly, & with an urbanity & pleasure that have enchanted her. He spoke of our dear Father with enthusiasm of kind remembrance—& he spoke of his former Correspondent & early mistress of English, in terms that warmed my heart to a thousand pleasing & grateful recollections. I had thought him dead,—& ¹ having heard, & believed a report that asserted his departure, I had grieved for him sincerely, & never had heard the assertion contradicted, as I had never made any enquiry, from having no doubt of its truth. He expressed to Sarah P. the most animated nay fervant desire to renew our correspondence;—It was not easy to me to so do, after a chasm of so many years, which had included, on my part a bereavement of such unutterable & never never ending sorrow—but still, the pleasure of his remembrance, & the thoughts of his many excellencies, & sincere friendship, conquered my difficulties, & I wrote him a very long, explanatory, melancholy, yet very cordial Letter: He returned me an Answer immediately, written by his Nephew,[19] but signed by his well known hand. It is in English, & very refined English, poetical & elevated, such as he had imbibed from the lessons of his first Master, the Poet Mason,[20] who esteemed his character as much as he admired his talents. This Nephew, who is his adopted Son, was brought up in England, whither he was sent a Boy, by his Uncle, in gratitude, he told Sarah P. for the spot where he had passed his happiest days. He had

[19] Gasparo Pacchierotti (L. 1257 n. 2) had died on 25 October 1821 but the letter of 10 October that he had had his nephew write to FBA is extant (Osborn): 'What I had the happiness of saying about you to your amiable Niece and to her good husband was but a faint expression of what I feel and not one half of what was passing in my mind, which the presence of so near a relation of the house of Burney roused to a kind of delitious rapture, in spite of the cold and heavy overflow of Hydropsy—under which I was labouring. The visit of your Niece seemed to have restored to me my spirits, and even my health, which since that day has continually improved. . . .'

The nephew may have been Giuseppe Cecchini Pacchierotti (*fl.* 1820–44), who was probably speaking of himself in the affectionately grateful close of the memoirs *Ai Culturi ed Amatori* / *della musica vocale* / *cenni Biografici* /*intorno* / *a Gasparo Pacchierotti* (Padua, 1844).

[20] William Mason (1724–97).

meant him for *Charles*—who would have been very proud of the distinction; but it was at the time of the blockading of Buonaparte, & none of his Letters to Greenwich arrived—or I should have heard of them even rapturously from poor Charles—& therefore none were answered, &, uncertain whether our dear Charles were alive or dead, Pacchierotti trusted the youth to some one who placed him according to his own fancy, or interest, & I can tell you of no particulars: but the young man seems deserving the adoption, by his chearful & most assiduous devotion to his parental Uncle. What a long history!—but it will ˡ travel to you through Mr. Rickman, & the subject interests me, &, I think, will you. His health—there's the other side of the picture!—his health is miserable! he has some dropsical complaint of the extremest suffering—which he bears with a patient resignation & fortitude truly affecting, as his good Nephew told Sarah P. He receives every Evening in Padua all that is most elegant & literary of society.—

Do not be *frightened*, my dear Hetty, in supposing *you* are to be called to a Court of Chancery, should you soon receive a *Free* from the Chancellor of the Exchequer, with a packet; & do not be *elated* non plus, in supposing some snug Sinecure insinuating itself into the Frank: but know the previous purport: my dear Mrs. Lock offered me some seeds of Italian Flowers, having had more imported by Mrs. Chaˢ Lock[21] than her Gardiener or Garden requires: I told her I had neither place, knowledge, nor spirits for meriting the donation; but that *You* had not only 2 Gardens, & a great love of Flora, but also a Friend who was versed in such lore, Mrs. Beckford,[22] who would delight to aid their cultivation. She quite coloured with her beautiful heightened pink Cheeks, in saying 'O—if I can do any thing that will be agreeable to my dear Mrs. Burney it will give me very great pleasure indeed, & I will watch a moment for a Frank from Mr. Vansittart, who has privileges quite peculiar; only, that she may open it carefully, give her notice.' Both Mr. V. & his worthy sister[23] have very politely

[21] Cecilia Margaret *née* Ogilvie (L. 1192 n. 9; L. 1193 n. 3), who, returning from Italy via Paris, had reached England in May (*Locks of Norbury*, p. 306).
[22] See L. 1189 n. 20.
[23] Nicholas Vansittart (v, L. 425 n. 1), M.P. (1796-1823), Chancellor of the Exchequer (1812-23), and his sister Sophia (*c.* 1768-1836).

renewed acquaintance with me since I have been here: though my kind Mrs. Lock, at my earnest request, never *calls* me to any of her visitors. These 2 came while I was in the Drawing Room. This is not often the case in the Mornings: but in the Evenings we are inseparable, for Then not a soul ever enters. The situation of Eliot Vale [*remainder missing*]

1271 [Eliot Vale, Blackheath, 19 November 1821]

To Mrs. James Burney
and Sarah Payne

A.L. & A.L. (PML, Autog. Cor. bound), n.d.
Two single sheets 4to 3 pp. trimmed *pmk* 19 NO 1821 wafer
Addressed: Mrs. J. T. Payne / ⌐ Stratton Street ⌐ / 26. James Street / Westminster.
Docketed, p. 4: Madame D'Arblay / 1821.

Oh what a stroke![1]—my Brother—my dear Brother— Good God—my dear Mrs. Burney—my Sister—my Friend

1271. [1] James Burney had died at half past 8 o'clock on Saturday morning (17 November) after what seemed a heart attack. Among the obituaries appearing in the newspapers on Monday, that written by William Ayrton (L. 1233 n. 3) for the *Morning Chronicle* was summarized in the *AR* lxiii (1821), 'Appendix to Chronicle', 246: 'At his house, St. James's-street, Buckingham-gate, suddenly of apoplexy, in his 72nd year, rear-admiral Burney, F.R.S. eldest son of the learned and elegant historian of music. The admiral had the honour of accompanying captain Cook, in the two last of his enterprising and important voyages. He was one of the most scientific geographers of this country, as is evident from his valuable and laborious work, the history of "Voyages of Discovery," his account of the "Eastern Navigation of the Russians," &c. As an officer and as a man, his conduct was uniformly engaging, humane, disinterested, honest and affectionate.' See also *GM* xci (November 1821), 469–70.
      The lament of the whist players appears in Lamb's letter to Wordsworth (*Letters*, ii. 319): 'There's Capt. Burney gone!—what fun has whist now? what matters it what you lead, if you can no longer fancy him looking over you?' And a typical family lament appears in Charlotte Barrett's 'Pink Letter Book' (Barrett, Eg. 3706D, ff. 24b–25b): 'This year has taken from us my dear Uncle, Admiral Burney, who had claimed that title in vain, during forty years, & was an old Post Captain till the Coronation, when his long desired & deserved honours were granted him, & we trusted they would help to lengthen as well as sweeten his days —but his days were full, & he was taken—May God pardon & accept him, for His sake in whom alone the best & the wisest can be accepted.'

—how unexpectedly a dreadful sudden Blow is this! — —
to *me*, at least—for your sake, I must rather hope you were
not without some preparation—Charles Parr I know has
thought him declining these two years—yet *This* End—
Apoplexy, has nothing to do with declining—'tis what I
should least of expected for this dear Brother—though for
the other[2] it was my constant apprehension from the time of
my return to England. How chearful he was the last Evening
I spent with you!—my dear dear Brother!—

I have been so unhappy—*you* will not wonder—that Mrs.
Lock will not suffer me to quit her, though I am shut up in
my Bed Room—till my change of dress must make it necessary—I write not alone to tell you—what you cannot doubt
—my true & affectionate feeling for *You*, my dear Mrs. Burney, but to beg you will go to Bolton Street, if you wish to
be ׀ quite quiet for a week or fortnight & I entreat you, in
that case, to take possession of the Room of Alexander. I
name that in preference to my own, that my return may not
drive you away, but rather induce you to stay on with so true
a sympathizer in your loss. I shall write by this same post to
Ramsay, & bid her call for your directions, & prepare the
apartment. Alexander is at Paris, & well, & ignorant of this
terrible event!—& I do not expect him this fortnight. You
will excuse, in this tragical moment, my hoping you will use
my room, which is large & airy, for your sitting & Eating
room, till I arrive, as I have unfortunately—or rather unavoidably—the Key here of my paper & picture room, & the
little library. I shall charge her to keep good fires in both
apartments. Oh my dear Mrs. Burney! heavy heavy is my
heart at this severe stroke! He took—by accident, an uncommonly affectionate leave of me in his Embrace on my quitting you all[3]—so little aware I should see you *All* never more
—on Earth! My kind love to poor Martin[4]— ׀

[2] CB Jr. had died in apoplectic fits on 28 December 1817 (x, Ll. 1141-3 and
notes). For a more particular account of JB's last day, see a letter (Berg) from
Fanny Raper to FBA, 21 November 1821, part of which FBA quotes in L. 1272.

[3] On 6 November (Diary).

[4] Martin Charles Burney (L. 1180 n. 2), now aged 33, an attorney, but little, it
would seem, in demand, had married on 18 April 1816 Rebecca Norton, then
a minor, and according to H. Crabb Robinson, 'a low person'. See Phyllis G. Mann,
'The Marriage of Martin Charles Burney', *C.L.S. Bulletin*, 139 (November 1959),

Oh My poor dear Sarah — — — my very dear Sarah— even my own affliction surrenders to what I know your warm overpowering filial grief must be!—newer & fresher to misfortune, this, your first *real* trial, I should pity from the bottom of my heart even if its Cause were unknown to me—but —oh my dear Sarah—my own severe affliction doubles my compassion—Greater Worth—Honour Integrity, Kindness & Goodness of Heart never fell to mortal lot than what we are now so suddenly—so abruptly deprived of — — —

Mrs. Lock tells me she has written hersel[f] to Mr. J. Payne, & I beg you to add my thanks for his & your dear Mother's considerate feeling for me at such a period—Mrs. L. has also, she says, the mournful tidings through your desire by Mrs. Whilly[5]—those are attentions to lessen the shock to the *nerves*—but the grief to the heart sinks beyond their reach —Take the utmost care of your health, dearest Sarah—your kind Partner will be your best physician. My kind love to poor Martin—

1272
11 Bolton Street,
23 November 1821

To Esther (Burney) Burney

A.L. (rejected Diary MSS. 7294-7, Berg), 23 Nov. 1821
Double sheet 4to   4 pp.   *pmk* 24 NO .821   wafer
Addressed: Mrs Burney / Lark Hall Place / near / Bath—
Endorsed by EBB: Nov. 24. 1821 / *answered* / Dec[r] 9 /
Annotated with a reminder: Mrs. F. Bowdler's / message
Edited by CFBt. *See* Textual Notes.

175-6; and Manwaring, pp. 284-5. This marriage was the 'Thorn' referred to by Mrs. Burney in the otherwise joyful days of JB's promotion. The biographers (*supra*) affirm that Martin 'was not upon good terms' with his father, and this, if so, explains the excess, from painful regret as well as loss, of his suffering now. See further, L. 1287.

[5] Mrs. Locke's housekeeper, in all probability, or her personal maid, was conjecturally one of the Williters of Mickleham, among whom the parish registers afford among many possibilities one Ann Williter, who died in 1835, aged 82.

Friday—23^d Novr 1821,
11. Bolton Street,

I cannot—My dear—& alas more than ever dear Esther—
read your Letter & do any thing till I have answered it[1]—I
would, indeed, have written sooner, but from incertitude
how, or whether you were apprised of this our new & most
irreperable misfortune—for whatever he had that was imperfect was nothing nothing in the scale of his good & excellent qualities. I hardly know how to begin, or what to write,
I feel so completely your want to hear *all*, & my head is so
confused, with nervous pain that visits it in patches, & my
heart is so saddened by this sudden loss, that I am incapable
to arrange & concentrate what I would communicate clearly.
However, any way that is quick you will take, I know, kindly.
I have a long Letter by me, that I *began* immediately after
reading your last but This, & it was to have been sent a by
a Frank that our poor James was to have procured me![2]—
it is now so malapropos, that it would rather teize than
gratify you, & I shall only send it if I should hear of a parcel
when so engaged that I can not write afresh.

You ask me if I had seen him shortly before this blow?—
yes, I thank God, & seen him something *more* than as kind,
cordial & affectionate as heretofore. We have been, for some
months now, in continual intercourse, by meetings or billets.
But I was at Elliot Vale[3] when this afflicting stroke cut him
off from us all. Of his last days, therefore, I can tell you
nothing.—I am but just come back—nor should have returned now, but for mourning! for, acording to those injunctions by which, in all things possible, I regulate my life, I had,
—at length,—left off Black—for just 10 Days—Mrs. Lock,

1272. [1] In a letter (Berg) of 20 November EBB had begged to know particulars
about the death of 'this dear & good Brother'. 'He was ever kind & affectionate
towards me & mine, and possessed a *heart* of the most generous Nature!—' 'My
dear Fanny will, I hope when her present feelings have a little subsided, give me
some particulars respecting the latter days of this Dear Brother, for she may believe
I must be anxious to be made acquainted with something more than merely that
he is lost to me! . . . it will be Charity my Dear *when you can* to write me a few
lines—' FBA's long Ll. 1272 and 1275 are her response to this plea.

[2] From John Rickman (L. 1264 n. 5). This is L. 1270.

[3] From 8–23 November. FBA had returned to Bolton Street on the day of the
funeral.

who had fetched, also brought me home—with what different sensations I need not say. The first thing I saw on entering my room was your Letter—just arrived before me: & nothing could be ¹ more congenial, or well timed, for to write on this subject where there is such true sympathy is all I am fit for: My Alex is at Paris—he will be truly grieved, for he loved this dear uncle to his inmost heart, & in return — — O, it is difficult to describe the partial fondness & high estimation with which that uncle honoured him.⁴ It was quite as a child, & a favourite child that he loved Alex, delighting in his sight, brightening at his praise & never tired with making him the theme of his discourse.

I have not yet seen poor Mrs. B[urney] nor Martin nor Sarah—but I learn, from Ramsay, they are all together. I would have persuaded poor Mrs. B. to take Alex.'s apartment for a few days, or a week—but she had declined leaving her home. Sarah has a Dwelling in Stratton Street: but I find they are *all*, at present, united in poor James Street. —I shall write to them to-morrow, & see them whenever they may wish it.⁵ To Day—alas,—was the last above Ground of our poor Lamented Brother⁶ — — I have no

---

⁴ Out of his limited estate JB had bequeathed to his nephew Alexander d'Arblay fifty guineas (PRO/PROB/11/1653/56, pr. 6 February 1822; and Manwaring, p. 286). Devoted to his uncle (ix, x *passim*), AA had recently recommended to his friend Charles Babbage JB's work *An Essay, by Way of Lecture, on the Game of Whist* (1821), republished in 1823 and 1848 under slightly different titles (Scholes, ii. 353).

⁵ FBA had written to Mrs. Burney on 19 November (L. 1271), and she was to make her painful visit to James Street on the 27th (Diary).

⁶ The funeral (on 23 November), according to JB's wishes, was to be 'plain and quiet', Mrs. Burney informed FBA in a letter (Berg) of 22 November: 'a hearse & four, a Coach & Pair, containing four persons', two representatives of the family (Charles Parr Burney and John Payne), John Rickman, representing friends, and Molesworth Phillips, 'representative of one branch of the family & a fellow mariner'.

'My father [Phillips] is *very much* with them in James Street', Fanny Raper had observed in her letter to FBA of 21 November, op. cit., 'and is to be one of the *very* small number who attend my uncle's funeral—The arrangement is I suppose needful but I acknowledge my regret at so strict a limitation of numbers— but Mrs. Burney seems not inclined to make any alteration.' One of the four official mourners, then, Phillips also arranged for the cast of the face and the bust, later collecting the costs (see further, L. 1296 n. 1). It was shipmate Molesworth again who attested to JB's handwriting in a codicil to his will and who was finally to be buried at his own request in JB's grave (Manwaring, p. 282) in St. Margaret's Churchyard.

account to give you of the previous days—for I have not heard any: but I believe there was no illness whatever. But I will copy for you a deeply interesting paragraph out of a Letter Fanny Raper has written to me on this subject.[7]

'On Friday Evening he had a small party of Friends, & was in particular good spirits. Sarah & her husband had dined there, which, as the event proved, was desirable & providential for poor Mrs. Burney, who would otherwise have been still more distracted in the first instance, & still more desolate when all was over. When the Company was gone, my Uncle said he should smoke a little before he went to Bed, & desired to have two pipes left for him. The family then retired to rest; but, at about half past one, Mrs. Burney—who is always anxious about the Candles when she leave him up—went down, & as she was descending the last stairs—she heard him fall!—it was a mercy that I she was moved to go down stairs when she did, for it would have been an infinite aggravation of their affliction had he lain for an unknown time unassisted. Mrs. B. found him on the Ground, insensible—he had been very sick; & they suppose that the exertion had broken a vessel of the Brain, as the Medical Men who have attended, declare that it was *not* Apoplexy. They say that by the constant & too great working of his Brain he has produced an ossification of part of it, and, in Age, this becomes brittle: & similar effects have been known before. They sent immediately to the Westminster Hospital, whence assistance can be procured at any hour of the Night. One of the surgeons came instantly, & bled him. After some time, the Blood flowed, though slowly. They applied two blisters, but they had no effect. They were round his Couch all Night. He had rattles in his throat, & breathed loudly, as in a sound sleep'

She tells me afterwards, that as this seizure happened down stairs, & was so speedily fatal—at 1/2 past 8 o'clock—the

---

[7] A favourite at James Street, as her father was and her mother SBP had been in former days, Fanny Raper had been one of the guests at 'a small party' there on the evening preceding her uncle's death and was thus able to give the details that FBA here transcribed for EBB.

dear soul was not removed, but extended in his usual place, in the Parlour — ! — Fanny Raper—who has so much reason to love & honour & regret him, desired to look at him, on the Tuesday—& says 'my poor dear Uncle is very little altered, & has a very sweet, calm, & benignant expression on his countenance, & looks as if he only slept'.

I am sure my dearest Hetty will like—as I did—to hear this. It gave kind pleasure also to our Mrs. Lock—who has had a melancholy visit from poor me!—but her soothing sweetness supported me, & she indulgently permitted my living wholly in my own room, after these mournful tidings arrived, till the Evening, when I went down to tea, & was sure to find her quite alone. The shock this news ⁱ occasioned me would, I think, have been quite baneful to me, had I heard it, & had to sustain it, here! so alone! so sequestered!—But Mʳˢ L[ock] was truly balsamic. And she charged me to express her sincere sympathy for you. I shall go back for a fortnight when Alex returns. When That may be, I never know. To conclude—our dear Brother had died in charity & Good humour with All the World—esteemed, loved, & lamented by All who knew him. His promotion had softened his Heart & his Temper, & given him a peace of mind, & a pleasantness of Spirits, that have caused me the most delight I have experienced since 1818—All his prejudices of every sort were shading off, & his generous Nature was struggling to find vent for its pleased feelings. He had long suffered me to name our dear Father without reserve, & with the tenderness I have ever felt for him; but he now, occasionally, mentioned him, & with respect & affection, himself, & he made me look at the place, by the Fire side, where the portrait of that dear Parent was pendant between two of his Friends, Mr. Crisp & Mʳ Windham.[8] I had had the happiness of finding an ancient

---

[8] Possibly one of the three copies by Edward Francesco Burney of the Reynolds portrait of CB (for present locations, see ix, L. 990 n. 1). The original, purchased by CB Jr. in the Streatham Sale of 1816, is in the National Portrait Gallery (see ix, L. 990 n. 1).

Edward Burney's portrait of Samuel Crisp (1703-83), painted at Chessington Hall in 1782 (see *HFB*, p. 154, and shown ibid., *facing* p. 16), was bequeathed in the will of Papilian Catherine or 'Kitty' Cook (*c.* 1731-97) to FBA (iii, L. 247 n. 17), who had recently given it to James (see Diary, 28 August and 19 September 1820).

The portrait of the family friend of the Burneys William Windham (i *passim*),

confidential Letter,[9] written to me at the time of the projected marriage of Charles with Rosette, in which he declares
that his principles decide his giving only Education & Profession to his *Sons*, & all he could hoard of Money to his Daughters. This, by making clear there had been no latent resentment
in the Disposition of the Will, banished for-ever every angry
passion—& I do not believe a heart could be more filled with
unmixt goodwill towards all mankind than that which beat
in his honest breast till one o'clock last Saturday morning —
— for *me*, & *my* comfort, you will be kindly glad to know
I have the consolation, in my great sorrow, to be assured by
Mrs. B. & by Sarah, he believed I had been instrumental to
the justice at last done to him.[10] Accident had turned out

not known to have been an original nor yet a copy made by Edward Burney, may
have been one of the large engravings of portraits of him painted through the
years by Sir Joshua Reynolds, John Hoppner, or Sir Thomas Lawrence, prints of
which were made available in the years 1791, 1792, 1798, 1803, 1804, 1816. On
sale in Norwich in 1804, for instance, was a print of a Windham by Hoppner
(24 × 15½").

[9] This statement the editors have not seen, but among the fragments of CB's
'Memoirs' (Folder vi, Berg) is an account of JB's early education:

'My eldest son had been entered on board a man of war, the princess Amelia,
Capt. Montagu in Octr 1760 where there was a regular school for younkers to
pursue their naval studies and go on wth their education. When he returned from
this voyage I placed him in an academy to proceed in mathematics.

'One of the first houses at which I attended properously after settling again in
London, was that of the Honble Col. afterwards General Carey, brother to Lord
Falkland, . . . and when the Colonel found I had a son destined for the sea, he
offered to get him a birth on board a Frigate commanded by Sir Thos Adams,
Bar^t. . . . I now had the honour to present my son to Col. Carey, after which he
quit his naval academy, & was rec'd by Sir Thos Adams on board his ship the
Boston in 1762, and afterwards in the Niger, where he was rated and perfectly
well treated till Feby 1765.'

' "The cockpit of a man of war, among young gentlemen . . . is to the navy
what a public school is to those who move in civil society" ', observed Gavin
Kennedy, *The Death of Captain Cook* (1978), p. 1. Cook had enjoyed no such
advantages, though Nelson had. For an appraisal of the early education CB had
procured for JB, see also ix, L. 1077 n. 3.

Charles (1757–1817), the 2nd son and future Greek scholar, was sent to the
Charterhouse in 1768. This CB accomplished with the help of Lord Holdernesse
(Lonsdale, pp. 15–16, 55), whom, as part of the entourage of his early patron
Fulke Greville, he had met in Bath in 1746.

[10] Cf. Mrs. Burney's letter to her daughter Sarah about JB's promotion (Man-
waring, p. 284): 'This did not come unexpectedly or by surprise upon us; your
Father wrote to the Duke of Clarence soliciting his interest, which he immediately
granted, your father says knowing his desert from his Geographical works; but
I must add to it some interest obtained by your very kind and affectionate Aunt
D'Arblay with the Princess Augusta.'

truly favourable in giving me an opportunity to make his case better known to the D[uke] of C[larence]—I must stop now to express my extreme satisfaction in the proposition of Indian Richard.[11] I beseech you not to hesitate. She is a sweet Girl, body & mind, & will not only be a sweet companion to Emily, but to yourself, for there is an innocent gaity in her pleasing manners, that cannot but interest & engage & attach you. How seasonable too, on the opening of this melancholy winter is an occupation so endearing!

adieu, my Hetty—my dear Hetty
& God preserve you!—

Love to y^r trio & pray—to y^r 4th

1273
[11 Bolton Street,
26 November 1821]

To Mrs. James Burney

A.L.S. (PML, Autog. Cor. bound), n.d.
Double sheet 8vo   black edged   4 pp.   *pmks* T.P / Piccadilly
26 NO 1821   black seal
Addressed: Mrs. Burney / James Street / 26 / Westminster—

I will be with you certainly my dear Mrs Burney to-morrow[1] —I believe you are right to see the most deeply affected Mourners—after yourselves—that can come in your way, immediately. It is not that I do not resign myself to This loss far more submissively & composedly than I was able to do to the *4 Blows* which were struck *First*[2] — — for I am now tamed by Grief, & my feelings are under the awe of resignation.—Happiness once Gone—sorrow cannot give the same blight as when it had That to fasten on—but still, the wound

---

[11] Richard Burney (L. 1184 n. 11) had apparently arranged that his sister Caroline Jane, aged about 18 and recently arrived from India, should stay with her aunt EBB in Bath for the winter.

1273. [1] The visit was made on 27 November (Diary).
     [2] The '*4 Blows*' refer to the deaths of SBP (6 January 1800), CB (11 April 1814), CB Jr. (28 December 1817), General d'Arblay (3 May 1818).

is piercing—& will rankle at my heart to ᛁ the remnant of my days—with greatly, cruelly diminished comfort & pleasure during their passage — — And to enter That House! — — 'Tis best, however, to be done at once especially as I shall return to Eliot Vale myself as soon as I have received—& prepared—my poor Alexander, who will then accompany me thither.

Pray let me find you quite alone—in your room, if any body is below.

I perfectly comprehend *your* not shutting *his* Doors, that were open ever to his friends—

I desire to see my dear Sarah before I quit the house,— pray ᛁ tell her so, with my kind love, & thanks for her Letter. I would not have that meeting hang on either of our minds for so long an interval as my return to town.

I would I could also have seen poor Martin—tell him I truly grieve for him—& will receive him as soon as he is able & disposed to come to me after I am again in London.

I do not think I shall be with you before 3 o'clock *Certainly* not till after 2.—I am extremely pleased you & my dear Sarah will go to Epsom—And I honour—nay *love* Mr. Rickman for this unfeigned & warm proof of his solid regard for my dear Brother,[3] & respect to his Memery ᛁ for rare indeed is it to wish for the association of mourners in their first affliction.

Heaven bless you my dear sister & Friend!—prays y^r affe^te

F. d'A.

[3] It was William Ayrton (L. 1233 n. 3), as FBA was later to learn (L. 1275), and not John Rickman (L. 1264 n. 5) who wrote the obituary of JB that appeared first in the *Morning Chronicle* (L. 1271 n. 1). For the print-offs, see L. 1275 n. 3; and it was Rickman, with his wife, who took JB's widow and daughter for change of scene to their country home in Epsom. For the family friends John Rickman and his wife, see L. 1264 n. 5.

11 Bolton Street,
11 December 1821

To Mrs. Broome

A.L. (rejected Diary MSS. 7306-9, Berg), 11 Dec. 1821
Double sheet 4to   black edged   4 pp.   *pmks* T.P.P. / Piccadilly
12 DE 1821   black seal
Addressed: Mrs. Broome, / Richmond / under the Hill, / Surry.
Endorsed by CBFB: Sister d'arblay / Dec[r] 1821 / ans[d]

11th Dec[r] 1821
Bolton Street—

Ah, take care of Yourself, my dearest Charlotte! take care
—more than ever—of your dear & precious life! This New
sorrow has fallen heavily upon me —— for though our dear
Brother has been visibly declining in health,[1] or rather in
strength, for these last two years, I thought it but a sudden
dropping into old age, which comes so variously on different
constitutions, but which often brings not Death for many
a long year afterwards. That was my idea; that he would have
a lengthened, but, I hoped, a chearful & agreeable long old
life. I believed he would find it extended beyond my dear
Father's, because I thought he would avoid the gloomy retirement & seclusion into which that dear Father fell, & which
embittered & harrassed & depressed many *years* of the existence that might else, like that of Mrs. Delany,[2] have been
lent him for his own comfort, & the delight of all his Friends.
—You, my dear Charlotte, with your large & rising family,
& Hetty, with her's, are in no danger of falling into this im-
poisoning mistake—

For myself—I must now, indeed, struggle to avoid it—&
bear—with what resignation I can acquire, the inflictions of
Heaven so as to make them—please God—preparatory for
a better World—without suffering | their ascendence to
deprive me of the use of such comforts as yet remain in *This*,

1274. [1] Cf. Manwaring, p. 285.
    [2] Mrs. Delany was already 82 years of age when in January 1783 she allowed
Mrs. Chapone to present FB to her, and she was 88 when she died at Windsor,
where for the last few years FB saw her almost daily. See *DL* ii. 193-202.

for the rest of my broken career. This blow sinks deep—yet what is it but a natural fore-runner — — I will not grieve my affectionate Sister by going on, but cheer Her by what supports myself, a stronger & stronger inward conviction of a blessed Re-union that makes all separations but temporary.

It was well—I may say providential for me that I was with my kind—kind Mrs. Locke at the first of this event. She communicated it with gradual openings that prepared me— as gently as the nature of such an event would allow, for the ill hanging over me — —

I will not till we meet enter into further details. I left her when it was necessary I should return to the outward Black I had only 10 days left off ever since the 18th of May 1818! —By *injunction* I was to have done it at the end of the usual time—which I, of course, made 2 years—but at that period, & ever since, either our Family or ǀ the Royal Family have kept me to the hue that most reluctantly I had laid aside— for 10 days only![3]—

I should delight to come to you, my Charlotte—but I am in waiting for my Alex, & have, *therefore*, declined all Mrs. L[ocke]'s earnest entreaties I would finish my promised month with her.

You were most considerate & comfortable—as is your way to be, in sending me kind Clem's reply—But Alex *purposes* coming home, & I can stir in no direction till he arrives, or writes more explicitly. I know, through my dear Mad^e de Maisonneuve, he has learnt our affliction[4]—& I hear it has quite changed him! — — He dearly loved that dear Uncle. He had come to Paris wonderfully invigorated & strengthened by his Swiss tour. You would be charmed for us *both*, so would his loving Cousins, to see what Mme de Maisonneuve writes of the opinions of his *hereditary* kind Friends of him before this grief — —

I would not now hurry him home—I would rather he prolonged his stay, since all here must be so sad—do & plan what I may—& I plan every thing I can devize to make his

[3] There was a long public mourning for King George III (d. 29 January 1820) and in the Burney family, three months for a sister-in-law 'Rosette' (d. 2 August 1821).

[4] An announcement of JB's death had appeared in *Le Journal des débats* (25 November 1821). See further, L. 1279 n. 8.

Home, for the Future, more chearing to him. How well Mr. Chilvers[5] judged of the necessity of removing ˡ him completely from all his studies, &c. —— —— The success seems to have brought him to more health & strength than he has known for a long, long time, indeed. 'Tis therefore I now wish him to stay at Paris, till my powers agree better with my wishes in my manner—or project—for receiving him. But I wait his answer. I had poor Sarah Payne with me yesterday,[6] for the 1st. time—a Morning visit—which lasted in Melancholy conference, from 11. to 5.— ! —for she came at the first hour, & stayed till her husband fetched her on the last. I felt soothed & pleased, to try to soothe & please her, poor girl, I went to poor Mrs. B.—*Mrs. Admiral Burney*![7]—as soon as she liked to receive me, & could engage being alone—but indeed the entrance into the house I had so lately quitted with my dear Brother's kindly accompanying me out & warmly embracing me, as I was going next day to Mrs. Locks—made me ill, quite ill, for some days—she was very grieved, *truly*, but very composed; & she has been at Mr. Rickman's ever since—& is there now—

Sarah herself is but just returned from Mr Rickman's[8] The kindness of Mr. & Mrs. R to them both is a *very* great pleasure to me. I fear our other dear Sarah is by no means well. This is not a stroke to heal her![9] poor Sarah!—I have Letters full of feeling from our Esther—& her distance made me write to her all I knew, through Fanny Raper's very kind communications.[10] *My* health is again recruiting. Mrs. Lock certainly saved me from an illness—

My kind love to Charlotte & Marianne—

adieu my beloved Charlotte—& kind remembrance to Mr Barrett. I am sure Twic[kenham] Meadows will be very sorry for us— ˡ

How completely I join in all you say of that unworthy or

[5] See L. 1230 n. 6.

[6] On 10 December (Diary).

[7] On 19 November (Diary).

[8] See L. 1264 n. 5; and L. 1273 n. 3.

[9] For the years (1798–1803) that Sarah Harriet Burney lived with her half-brother JB, see iv *passim* and vi, L. 570 n. 10.

[10] See L. 1272 n. 1. By this time FBA had received EBB's letters of 24 November and 11 December 1821, to which a lost letter of 27 November (Diary) and L. 1275 are the replies.

rather worthless character!¹¹ I never will remain under the roof with him.

1275   11 Bolton Street,
12–14 December 1821

To Esther (Burney) Burney

A.L.S. (Berg), 12–14 Dec. 1821
Double and single sheet 4to   6 pp.   wafer
Addressed: Mrs. Burney / Lark Hall Place / near Bath,
Endorsed by EBB: replied to *in part* / Dec. 25th / This I replied to
—by Fanny / Jan—
Docketed incorrectly: 1822

12—Decem^r 1821.
Bolton Street,

Your Letter has found me still here, my dearest Esther, for my Alex is still at Paris. Instead of hastening him back, since this unhappy event, I desire him to remain a little longer. Mr. Chilvers¹ has so imbued me with his representations that Alex must neither study nor meditate till fixed in his health re-establishment, that I feel, *à plus forte raison*, he must not be chilled with sorrow and solitude: yet it is not precipitately or *tout d'un coup* I can separate myself from either. I will do what I can, & as soon as I can,—but it is not a blow like This that can *expedite* chearfulness!—Mrs. Lock is earnest with me to return to her; but I will not let Alex come home to an

¹¹ In a letter (Barrett, Eg. 3693, ff. 93–4b) of 27 November–1 December [1821] CBFB had expressed regret at the constant presence in James Street of Molesworth Phillips (1755–1832), whom the sisters had never ceased to blame in bitterest grief for his unfeeling treatment and the death (even) of SBP (see iv *passim*). 'We are all shocked', wrote Mrs. Broome, '& concerned at hearing of that unfeeling wretch Philips's continual presence in James St:—weakened by affliction as her poor mind must be, if she lets him transact her affairs, he may run her over head & ears in debt— . . . I cannot help rejoicing that sweet Mrs Locke would not let you go to town—the agitation in James Street—the to, and fro— & the gloom of your home, without dear Alex, must have almost killed you—and then, that wretch being there, what could you have done!—'

1275. ¹ See L. 1230 n. 6.

empty house, even for a night: & indeed I shall be glad of a few hours tête à tête with him.[2]

I, also, now, have been told Mr. Ayrton was the Writer of that quickly produced & heart-dictated panygeric of our dear James. It has given very general satisfaction, I hear: I had concluded it to be by Mr. Rickman: but Mr. Rickman, also, was so much pleased with it, that he made his Printer, Hansard, throw off 20 or 30 on separate small sheets.[3] I have one myself which was sent me, at Eliot Vale, by Mr. Angerstein, *l'ainé*.[4] I could have wished for more, but was much gratified by all there was. Certainly, great as were his peculiarities, & ill-judged as were some ⎸ of his actions, from his excentric idea he might hold himself above the controul of opinion, or Custom, he yet had a Heart of the noblest Nature, formed for even tender kindness, & earnest zeal for those he loved. The coolness my dear Father's Will had, alone, ever created between us,[5] gave way to Reflexion, & to Justice, & he had become more than ever attached to me. For no one else, they all tell me, did he ever leave his pen, & I never visited him in a morning that he did not lengthen our meeting by accompanying me home. He had taken, also, to the kind, & quite new habit of frequently writing to me, little occasional billets, & exciting mine in return.[6] All this is soothing to me—yet all this, my dear Hetty, adds to the sadness of my loss. Your distant residence certainly makes your's less personal, though not less affectionate. It is not *very* long since he said to me 'I think of taking a peep at Bath again, to shake hands with Hetty.——' He spent 10 days, last summer, or spring, with Charlotte,[7] in high spirits visiting with her wherever she

[2] Alex was not to return from Paris, however, until April 1822.

[3] For the obituary supplied to the *Morning Chronicle* by JB's neighbour William Ayrton (L. 1233 n. 3), see L. 1271 n. 1. Extant in the Scrapbook (Berg), 'Fanny Burney and Family, 1652-1890', are two leaves (4.8 X 7″), 3 pp. of text, printed by Luke Hansard (1752-1828) and Sons (see *DNB*), printers to the House of Commons. The printing was probably arranged by JB's friend Rickman (L. 1264 n. 5), Secretary to the Speaker.

[4] John Julius Angerstein (L. 1209 n. 9), now aged 86.

[5] For JB's feeling that as the eldest son he was disinherited by his father's will, and for his refusal to act as executor, see vii, Ll. 769, 773, and 777.

[6] Few of JB's missives survive (see *Catalogue*). An example of his style can be seen in what Clement Francis in his boyish days thought a fine 'piece of Capt[n] Burney's Poetry'. See *HFB*, p. 417, and CF's letter (JRL) of 1810 to HLTP.

[7] From 5-15 May (see Manwaring, p. 278; and L. 1248 n. 6).

pleased. He was grown fond of Company, &, *for him*, very attentive to dress, wearing the best things, though not always put on in the best manner. He had the happiness to see his dear Daughter safe returned, but he was anxious & disappointed at the long stay of Alex, & fondly made me read him all his Letters. He died, as he lived, adoring that Daughter with the strongest possible paternal affection. I will see of her all I can, in remembrance of the high pleasure that ever glistened in his Eyes when—in our last meeting but one, I told him I would be a good neighbour to her. Her back windows & mine, face each other.[8] I I have seen her yet but once—but 'twas a Morning visit of 6 hours—for she came at 11. & stayed till her husband came for her at 5.—I was very much worn—though soothed, & pleased. I have not been well enough to see Mr. J[ohn] Payne, nor, indeed, any one, except her; & I have only once been out since my return, which was to M*rs* *Ad^l Burney*,[9] & that I held to be a duty—but to drag myself to James Street was a very severe one. — — Shall I never quit this subject?—I hear poor Sarah Harriet is very unwell —her grief must be very great! I pity poor Mr. Sansom very much.[10] 'Tis to him a loss in every way important & grievous. I will send him your commission immediately—& it shall urge me, sooner than I might otherwise have done, to see him. It is a great satisfaction to me to hear that Mrs. *Ad^l B.* will receive the Pension without difficulty arising from the promotion.[11] Our dear Brother had expressed his hope & comfort in that immediately on its taking place. I have heard nothing of the Will, but that it is All that is equitable & good, like it's former. Something, nevertheless, is, it seems, defective as to Law,[12] which Martin will rectify when recovered

[8] The Paynes had settled for a time on Stratton Street. Sarah had last visited her aunt on 10 December (Diary).

[9] On 27 November (Diary).

[10] FBA was to write to JB's pensioneer and indigent relative James Sansom (L. 1191 n. 16) on the 13th and again on the 18th and to receive him for tea on that day (Diary).

[11] 'The widow's pension of a superannuated Rear-Admiral was £100 a year', Manwaring informs us (p. 287 n. 2), and 'Mrs. Burney's petition for a pension is in the PRO Admiralty 6 / 369'.

[12] The difficulty was that a codicil to JB's will (PRO/PROB/11/1653/56, pr. 6 February 1822) with bequests to the servants Mary More and her daughter Mary Waters or Standhal was neither witnessed nor signed. It was necessary, therefore, to have the handwriting attested. Manwaring explains (pp. 286–7) how, therefore,

from a very severe illness — — Poor Martin! depth & bitterness of grief have been his, I understand, beyond all comparison with any other.[13]—Can I never have done?—

Pray let me know, when you have leisure, whether my short view of Caroline has been just, or too flattering; where there is so much of Beauty, one is apt to be partial: but I hope as well as believe the beauty is internal as well as outward. You will find her worshipping her Brother,—no wonder! what a Brother has he been to her, & is still continuing! —I liked Sarah also; she is not handsome, but looks clever & observing. I shall be quite anxious to know that your fair little companion gives you pleasure, & such as to counterbalance care & exertion.[14] I am sure Emily will like her. I I am quite charmed with the Rickmans,[15] though I never saw them, but their goodness to my dear Brother's Memory is edifying; they took Mrs. Burney & Sarah to their Country Villa 3 days after the last rites—& they have kept Mrs. B[urney] there ever since

This is *Friday*, 14th & I have had a long visit from Fanny, who is eager to set off for Lark Hall place—& Belvedere—& tells me I must send my packet off *sharp*, or she may be gone. I am glad I was already so far prepared. Thanks, my Esther, for your enquiries, my health is now pretty well re-settled— but my poor head has been in a state rather alarming as well as painful, such strange partial pains & throbbings, & an impossibility to put it on the Pillow even for a moment except on one side. I have not again sent for Mr. Chilvers,[16] as this time I have not had any fever; but I have sent his prescription for the *head* to the Chymist, & am under its regulations with much amendment. I was ill indeed in James Street!—I had

'Molesworth Phillips, "of Brook Street West Square, in the parish of St. Mary Lambeth, Lieutenant of Marines," appeared personally, also "Charles Lamb of the East India House, gentleman, and made oath that . . . they verily believe the codicil to be in his handwriting".'

[13] Suffering from remorse as well as sorrow, Martin now exerted himself in expiatory deeds, including the erection in St. Margaret's Churchyard of a memorial to his father (see L. 1271 n. 4, L. 1276). And to FBA's pleasure he was soon to call in Bolton Street to repay a voluntary loan (an advance on a uniform, L. 1301), of which she had kept no account and which she had intended to forget.

[14] Caroline Jane Burney, her brother Richard, and her sister Sarah Ross, see L. 1184 n. 11.

[15] See L. 1264 n. 5; and L. 1273 n. 3.   [16] See L. 1230 n. 6.

spent a very unhappy week, though softened by our sweet Mrs. Lock as much as possible—but re-entering James Street —which I had quitted so lately with my dear Brother by my side—was truly afflicting. Mrs. Ad^l B. received me in the Drawing room, which was some relief—she purposes residing there, if she continues in the House, which, *I believe* was left her for life, if the Survivor, by the Will of Mr. Hayes.[17] But I am not sure. I will enquire about Mrs Humphries[18] when I write to Mrs. Lock: & Miss ⟨   ⟩. Dear Charlotte presses me to Richmond—but I must await Alex, or news of his decided longer stay at Paris, where, he has been since the 4th of November. He arrived there quite a new man, so strengthened & invigorated—but since he has known of this event, *il est tout changé*, Mme de Maisoneuve writes me word.[19] What reason had he to love & honour his dear Uncle!—My dear Friends, & his, in Paris *fête* him most cordially. He has a constant *couvert* at the Hotel of the Minister de La Guerre,[20] our late Ambassadour, the Marquis de La Tour Maubourg, & Tickets from Son Excellence to go to the Chamber of Peers to hear the Debates—& of Deputies—& he frequents the Institutes, & has been presented to LaPlace, the *living* Newton of France[21]

I am quite sorry poor *Dr.* Richard[22] is so ill; his noble conduct, in early prosperity, to his family, raises him so highly in my esteem, that I like to cultivate his intimacy with Alexander, & have pleasure in inviting him, from time to time, to tea in the Evening.

[17] John Hayes (*c.* 1708–92), reputed to be the son of Sir Robert Walpole (1676–1745), and an old friend of CB, gave and devised by a will made on 7 January (PRO/PROB/11/1225/56, pr. 13 November 1792) 'unto Captain James Burney of the Navy Son of Dr Burney all that my freehold Messuage or Tenement with the outbuildings and appurtenances thereto belonging situate in James Street . . . to the use of the said James Burney his heirs and assigns for ever [subject only to an annuity of 10 pounds annually to a maid servant]'.

[18] EBB had inquired about a Mrs. Humphreys, perhaps some connection of the Worcester Burneys (*ED* ii. 171 and *passim*), who, she believed, lived in Blackheath and who FBA thought might have been known to the Revd. George Locke (L. 1188 n. 3), rector of St. Margaret's, Lee (see further, L. 1279). No likely identification, however, appears in the parish registers.

[19] See L. 1274 n. 4.

[20] Victor de Latour-Maubourg (L. 1192 n. 6; L. 1225 n. 1).

[21] See L. 1258 n. 4.

[22] Presumably Richard Burney (n. 14), whose success in his studies and all walks of life had perhaps tempted EBB to give him an honorary or prophetic appellation.

My billet with your commission went to Mr. Sansom; & I
have asked him here for Tuesday Evening. I am quite full of
compassion for that poor Man, who has always—or *long*, at
least, dreaded out-living my poor Brother. That dear Brother
dined & spent the Day on the Wednesday with his Daughter,
in Stretton Street,—& sent thence here to enquire tidings of
Alex—whom he almost pined to see, so much he loved him.
He pressed me often to urge him home: but the consequence
would have been an added excitement to resume his tour
next year, *if* my solicitation had been successful: but why
should *I* alone expect an influence so *gone by* now adays?—
Indeed, I do not think, seriously, I *ought* to go beyond *counsel* to a young man at his time of life: *exhortation* should be
reserved only for evil, or danger.

At *all times* I beg you to direct to Bolton Street, as my
Letters carefully follow me when I am absent; & my absences
are so rare, alltogether, & so short, that there is more risk
than speed in their travelling by cross posts.

I have seen nothing of dear Charlotte Barrett & her's since
their return to England, but rejoice, doubly, she is here, for
poor Charlotte's sake. How sorry I am to hear of your Cough,
& expectoration! Liquorice Tea always does best for me— I
the famous Baron Larrey[23] told me there was more healing
virtue in it than in all the Lozenges of the World. Cut it in
small slices or bits, dissolve it, with a little Nitre as much as
will cover a Sixpenc[e,] Boiling Water, poured over in small
drops, repeatedly, & then add sugar, & *sip* it very frequently.
not [d]rink it.

What quantities I have written to you! Adieu, my dearest
Esther—

ever & aye most truly & affec^ly yours
F. d'Ay

How I am thankful our poor James had given up his continental plan![24] He very frequently talked of you when we met,

---

[23] Dominique-Jean Larrey (L. 1190 n. 3), the famous army surgeon, who had
operated on FBA in 1811 (vi, L. 595).

[24] See JB's letter to his daughter (Manwaring, p. 280): 'I am reading . . . *The
Diary of an Invalid* [1820] with a wish to learn where the severity of a winter can
be best evaded; but what with the want of fire places, and with marble or stone

always in his old style of true & hearty affection. How hurt I felt that the hard-hearted, & impenitent Author of our first dread Family calamity should have been one out of only Four selected for the last personal tribute![25]—Charlotte is equally shocked. But his art & skill had kept a hold there of which he was more than undeserving. That dear Brother had ideas of Hospitality generous & noble, yet exaggerated & erroneous, for he was guided by the old Adage, *Open Locks whoever Knocks.*[26] Rest his dear Soul! for Good & Kind were his *intentions* always!

Pray distribute my remembrances—Fanny is returned in excellent good looks[27]—& seems every way pleased with her autumnal excursion, which much rejoices me.

This is the only real Letter—The others are offerings to some odd moments of *Ennui.*

1276   [11 Bolton Street,
                        25 November–18 December]

To Alexander d'Arblay

A.L. (rejected Diary MSS. 7298-[301], Berg), n.d.
Double sheet 4to   4 pp.   *pmk* F 21/295 2⟨1⟩ ⟨Decembre⟩ 1821 black wafer
Addressed: La France / À Monsieur / Monsieur Al[r] Piochard— / Grande Hotel de Tours— / place des Victoires / À Paris.
Edited by CFBt. *See* Textual Notes.

You know, then, my poor Alex, the fatal blow that has been struck to our Family happiness—My last Letter to my dear Mme de Maisonneuve, with one enclosed for you, parted from this house almost on the very hour that one arrived from

floors, the author [Henry Matthews] makes the south of Europe less comfortable than England!'
[25] Molesworth Phillips (see L. 1272 n. 6).   [26] *Macbeth*, IV. i. 46.
[27] Fanny Burney, at her return from Barwick House (L. 1270 n. 10).

Her[1] — — not you!—tenderly condoling upon my great loss; & informing me that you had heard the ill tidings chez la p^{sse} d'Henin. To *Her*, my Mme de Maisoneuve, I had already written them, that she might be prepared, should they travel to France, to save you at least any suspence, as well as to obviate any unnecessary *uneasiness* as to my exertions for supporting them. But to *you* I only have a preparatory hint, just to spare you a sudden shock, both in that billet, & another a *fortnight after* that I again enclosed. I had been willing to save you such evil news while in the pursuit of *pleasure & knowledge*, after the attainment of *health & strength*, from all 4 of which I flatter myself to see you *spring* forth, this spring, a new man, conscious of new powers from such an aggregate of new exertions, bodily & intellectual, eager to cast off the old habits that annulled all *use* of your faculties, & buoyant with the thought of so appearing, so exhibiting yourself, & so enjoying at once & augmenting your improvements, as to merit, & obtain, the happy result of pleasing some distinguished Fair one with whom you are yourself more than pleased, & becoming a delighted *member* of that state for which I think you—Thank Heaven!—eminently formed, when your Excentricities & Impetuosities are softened off, to Receive & to Bestow Felicity. Amen! |

Thank God! I say, & repeat: for you must have not only a Mate, but one Loved & Loving; such a one as to draw you to regular habits of Society, from the pleasure of *giving* pleasure to one dear to you. You have no other means to Live & Keep your Faculties: for, left to yourself, even your Mathematicks would not flourish, though they might, occasionally, sparkle. For if you have not at your *Home* a kind yet spirited *Flapper*,[2] you would dwindle into incurable Languor from Supine Self-indulgence & inertion; or your Brains would boil over with effervescence from over-heated & intense application.

Realize then, my dear Alex, *my* wishes & *your* Welfare. Come Home to me fraught with health Corporeal & mental &

1276. [1] This was Madame de Maisonneuve's letter (Berg) of 29 November (L. 1274), which FBA had received on the 30th, having written to her friend on the 25th (Diary). A letter from the princesse d'Hénin (ii–viii *passim*) had arrived on 3 December (Diary). [2] Cf. L. 1243 n. 2.

imbued with those fair purposes & diligent plans for which you have bespoke my aid *with all my might & main*; lively, industrious, sociable and amiable—& look me out a fair Belle Fille who may gently be my Friend, as well as delightingly yours, & fix permanently your Happiness, your Character, & your Fame.

N.B. To give you some encouragement—I have been told that a young lady of excellent connexions has declared she thought you the most pleasing Converser in the World! — — There, Monsieur!—

It is not The Eliza—nor any one you ever named to me, *I think*, but one who has been in your Company at some time, no doubt, to your advantage? ¹

I will make the loan certainly, my dear Alex, but cannot apply to Mr. Shaw,³ as nothing of the annuity kind is ever paid but to direct Receipts & Principals, or acredited Certificates of Life. I shall lend you, however, only £20.—Because why?—This Day is your Birth Day,—the 18ᵗʰ of December 1821 — — And therefore, anticipating & amalgamating This Day with the Day of Xmas & the Day of the ensuing New Year, I mean, instead of some cadeaux here, to make my offering in one, of *Ten pounds*, for as far as it will procure my dearest Alex the safe arrival of his Books.

So God bless & preserve you thereupon, my Alexander. But I shall write instantly to Mr. Hoare to forward the £30. all in one.⁴

But pray let me immediately hear when you have touched the Rhino, on account of my own affairs with the said Messʳˢ Inserting at the same time your projects as to returning, & other matters *agreeable*.

Alas, I greatly need them! I am grieved to the very Soul! Your excellent Uncle was at the Royal Society on the Thursday Night⁵—& surrounded by heartily congratulating

---

³ Presumably the Revd. Joseph Shaw (1786-1859), Fellow of Christ's College (1807-49), who was to hold a number of administrative offices at his College (see Venn) and to whom as his former tutor (ix, L. 1050 n. 4 and *passim*) AA apparently thought he could apply for advances in his emolument as Fellow.

⁴ FBA's remittances show in Hoares' Ledgers for 1821: 11 Apr. (£45), 1 Dec. (£30); for 1822: 29 Jan. (£30).

⁵ On 15 November JB, elected to the Royal Society in 1809, took notice of the honour only in 1815. See ix, L. 988 n. 8 and Beverley Hooper, *With Captain*

members F. R. S. *Babbage*, who has called here yesterday
with enquiries after you, & condoleances for me, told Ramsay he was amongst them.[6] Every body rejoiced in his promotion, & there has been much sincere grief at his so sudden
departure. —— My dear Mrs. Lock softened the blow to
me as much as was in her power, & suffered severely herself
in the task of revealing it. Martin has been ill ever since. He
has felt it, more keenly, & more permanently than any one.
He reproaches himself for every word or look that was not
expressive of duty & affection, & Now says he thinks there
exists not ¹ so firm & high a character. He is making a memorial
for a Tablet, which he means to finish with the line of Pope

An Honest Man's the noblest work of God.[7]——

Your Aunt Sarah is quite overwhelmed with grief, & still very
ill. A Liver complaint has menaced: but Dr. Paris[8] says the
danger is now over. Poor thing! 'tis the *most* severe stroke to
Her, she avows, that misfortune has ever inflicted. Clement is
recovered, & at Cambridge. Dear Charlotte Barrett & her's are
at Richmond, consoling my poor sister Broome. Poor Richard[9]
is laid up with a *savage* rheumatism, he calls it, at Cambridge.
Caroline is going to Bath, to winter with your Aunt Hetty, by
an arrangement the most liberal of her truly liberal Brother.
Our dear Amine is *tolerably* well, & *superlatively* kind &
good, & yours most constantly, & her tender Mother has
bespoke us for your return. I would not stay longer without
the repose of total retirement, after such a blow.

You don't answer one word of Business—I will not re-write,
but I *earnestly request* you will re-read my last Letters, & not
come home doing nothing in our affairs, with good M. Le
Noir:[10] M. Norry,[11] Mme de la Gallissonière,[12] M. d'Essards,[13]

James Cook in the Antarctic and Pacific. The private Journal of James Burney ...
(1975), Intro., p. 16. Charles Babbage had called on FBA on 18 December (Diary).

  [6] See L. 1271 n. 4; and L. 1275 n. 13.

  [7] Pope's *Essay on Man*, iv. 248.

  [8] John Ayrton Paris (1785–1856), M.D. (1813).

  [9] Richard Burney and his sister Caroline (L. 1184 n. 11).

  [10] See L. 1189 n. 5; L. 1200 n. 8; and L. 1229 n. 1.

  [11] See L. 1194 n. 6.

  [12] Marie-Pierre Sonnerat (L. 1194 n. 7), whom the d'Arblays knew as Mme de
Grandmaison (v, L. 514 n. 21 and *passim*), had married thirdly, on 9 February
1818, Alexandre-Paul-Augustin-Félix-Élisabeth Barrin, comte de la Gallissonière
(1757–1828).   [13] See L. 1194 n. 7.

Mr *Narbonne* & *Evelina*[14]—la Voiture & above all let me know whether M. le Noir has finished all his share of his long & laborious & most kind exertions. I cannot else present the 50 so long in waiting. I am pleased indeed about M. Ampère[15] —pray tell him so. I long to see, but will not hurry you. Diane is well.

Tell my dearest Mad^e de Maisonneuve I have received her charming last Letter of le 3 Dec^bre[16] but cannot write by the poste feuille in less than 15 days. I long for you to see Maxime, & am charmed at all you say of Edmond— I

I hope my dear Mme de Maisoneuve has received my 2 Long packets per post feuille.

I have no way to hear of the duty on Books—'twould be here a sore & offensive subject—you must enquire of the Bookseller Wurz[17]—in Paris. You gain nothing, I believe, by bringing them yourself, & better give a fair Commission. Have you paid M. Le Noir? See all you can of Mme de Mais. & the Ambass[ador] & M. de Maub[ourg] & l'aîné They Love you surprisingly & Mme de Tracy.[18] Read my other Lett^rs
Speak for me to my dear Ambassadeurs most tenderly.

---

[14] See L. 1263 n. 13.

[15] According to Mme de Maisonneuve's letter (Berg) of 15 February 1822 (L. 1282 n. 12) Alex had been befriended by his father's acquaintance (ix, L. 943; x, L. 1111 and n. 2), the mathematician and physicist André-Marie Ampère (1775–1836), member of the Institut (1814), who on 18 September 1820 had read a paper opening up the 'whole field' of electromagnetism (his name today being a household word for units of electricity). Alex also made friends with Ampère's son Jean-Jacques-Antoine (1800–64), later a distinguished philologist and man of letters (x, L. 1111 n. 6), but like AA in these years neglecting mathematics for poetry, on which AA made playful parodies. See further, L. 1280 n. 12, L. 1282 n. 12, and Louis de Launay, *Un amoureux de Madame Récamier . . .* (1927).

[16] Perhaps the letter FBA had received on 8 December (Diary).

[17] Johann Gottfried Würz (vi, L. 594 n. 13), a bookseller in Paris.

[18] The friends FBA hoped her son would see included Edmond de Beauvau (L. 1258 n. 6), Mme de Maisonneuve, her son 'Maxime' (L. 1195 n. 6), her brothers the Latour-Maubourgs, and such friends of former days as the princesse d'Hénin, Lally-Tolendal, and Émilie-Pérette-Antonie *née* Durfort de Civrac (v, L. 526 n. 21), the wife of the philosophical writer Antoine-Louis-Claude Destutt de Tracy (1754–1836).

Tell them to *return*! & to Mme dHenin & M. de Lally—& M. de La Fayette & M. Gallois. & M. Ampere & M. Le Noir & M. Norry. Edmond & Maxime surtout[18]

1277 [11 Bolton Street], 25 December 1821

To Sarah Harriet Burney

L. printed by G. E. Manwaring, *My Friend The Admiral*, p. 289

'. . . Are you surprised I say Mrs. Admiral Burney! My dear Sarah, it is a consolation to me to be able to do it, and it always a *little* smooths remembrance; for had that promotion, so long deserved and so long delayed, not finally taken place, or rather, had it ever finally been refused, I should always have believed that such a disgraceful and injurious and unjust disappointment had caused the blow which has robbed us of that dear Brother.

I saw him so frequently, latterly, both here and in James Street, that I had conceived a real terror of a failure, from observing how his whole soul and all his thoughts were occupied almost exclusively upon that point. And the pleasure he received from his success, the constant good humour it excited, the universal benevolence it occasioned and the complete extinguisher it proved to all hostile passions or ill will, civil, religious, or political, smoothed and cheered his latter days, and made his last four months four of the gentlest and most contented he ever passed. I can tell you many instances of his recovery from ungenial prejudices, and I feel a blest conviction that he died at peace and harmony with himself and all the world.'

Eliot Vale, Blackheath *and*
11 Bolton Street,
[late December 1821]–27 January [1822]

To Mrs. Broome

A.L.S. (Berg), –27 Jan.
Double sheet 8vo   4 pp. and single sheet 4to   2 pp.   *pmks* Picca-
dilly 31 JA [182]2 31 JA 1822   black seal
Addressed: Mrs. Broome / Under the Hill / Richmond / Surry.
Dated in pencil, p. 1: Jan 27. 1822

Eliot Vale.

How vexed I am, my dearest Charlotte, thus, at last, to
miss you!——but I would not write that I came hither, lest
that might prevent your hieing to Bolton Street in case of
renewed floods: & I left linnen & orders with Ramsay, for your
reception, & a charge she would keep my Bed & Room in constant readiness: I can now only lament that the so long delayed
visits take place just as I must miss their kind participation.
I was lead to listen to the kind voice of [1] Mrs. Lock in returning hither,[1] by her giving me directions by which Alex, should
he return to England during my sejour here, would be apprized
on the road where to find me; as Eliot Vale is but a few yards
out of the high Dover Road, & all the Diligences stop at an
Inn hard by. I was, besides, certain he would not quit Paris
on the opening of a New Year, since he had stayed there to
that period,——for the New Year there is a call to every sort
of Hospitality——& Gaiety——as Christmas, in old Times, was
on This side the Water.——And indeed

Bolton Street, Jany 27th!!

I began this the moment a note from Ramsay, inclosing
your Letter, [1] apprized me of my ill luck——but an interruption was followed by so many Imitators——that Here I am
returned, & Weeks have elapsed, & this miserable small sheet
remains still away from the kind Eyes it is filling to meet!——

1278. [1] FBA's visit of November 1821 to Mrs. Locke had been interrupted by
news of JB's death and the present visit of January 1822 was to be cut short by
the vain expectation of AA's return from Paris. AA would return only in April.

I am so overwhelmed with Letters[2]—truly welcome to *arrive*, but truly fatiguing to *answer*—of condoleance—that I am really hand-heavy with scrawling—& head-heavier still with never emptying it of such work. —— I am gratified, at the same time, very truly by the interest announced thus in our family calamity, & by the honour it reflects on our dear Brother's memory:—& I can never I reply without enlarging upon the subject that I may do what justice I can to his Worth —& to our loss.—Alex comes not!—I now returned in full expectation of his arrival, in consequence of what he intimated in his last Letter of his designs, dated 4th Jany Paris: —but I have neither him— I nor News—I think incessantly on his habitual incertitude, to keep off *positive* uneasiness— & I have never written to press his haste: I would not do it while I felt too unconquerably sad to receive him with chearfulness, because I am well aware his health & Character & spirits demand invigorating, not depressing: so he has no fault but in not *writing*: & That—he will not correct.—

I am flattered that the amiable & exemplary L^y Pembroke honours me with I her remembrance:[3] if Marianne sees her again, tell her, with my kind Love, I beg her to say so.

I hope you have now Clement with you comfortably.

Do you know that Charles Parr is gone to Oxford to take his Doctor's degree?[4]—How painful to me it will be to hear

---

[2] For the extant letters of condolence on JB's death, see *Catalogue*.

[3] FBA had met the dowager Lady Pembroke (1737–1831), Lady of the Bedchamber to Queen Charlotte (1783–1818), at Brighton in 1779, at Court, and again at Mrs. Crewe's at Hampstead in 1802 (v, L. 502a n. 13).

[4] On 17 January 1822 Charles Parr Burney (1785–1864) had supplicated the Congregation at Oxford for a grace to take the degree B.D., arguing that he had fulfilled most of the requirements. He had spent seven years since he became M.A. (1811) in the study of Theology, had attended the lectures of the Professor of Theology, had once responded and twice opposed in disputation in the school of Theology, and had delivered a Latin sermon in the University Church of St. Mary the Virgin. As, among details of the procedures, he had failed to give notice, as required, of the 'quaestiones', that is, the questions for discussion in the disputation, he had had to apply for a dispensation. The grace was granted and he was admitted B.D. on 17 January 1822.

On 18 January he supplicated for his doctorate, stating in his supplicat that he had done all that was necessary for the degree. He had applied himself to studies in the faculty of Theology for the time required. He had attended the lectures of the Professor of Theology and he had given six solemn lectures and three cursory lectures in the school of Theology. A cursory lecture, as the editors are kindly informed by Mr. T. H. Aston, Keeper of the Archives, University of Oxford, was a formal lecture giving an exposition of a particular point or question. A cursory

announced Dr. Burney—& see neither my dear Father nor dear Charles but in melancholy Memory!—However, it ought to be; & I believe him very worthy of following the title 3^{d} in Generation. He has spoken to me of it with great modesty & feeling, as if willing to prepare me for the Sound — —

I am grieved poor Sarah mends so slowly—but comforted she is with so tender & excellent a Friend & Protectress as she describes Mrs Gregor.[5]

Esther writes me word she is quite delighted with the lovely Caroline,[6] who is the admiration of all Eyes, & gives active employment to the mind & attentions of our dear Sister, who assures me she is herself, except her Cough, well. She retains all her excellent powers of exertion, & would not listen to *your croakings* about *weakness & infirmities*, & *time of life* —she would think you urged them to hoax her!—

What a pretty snuff Box you have given a most unworthy snuff person, as snuff I never take: but I will guard it for I you with as many thanks as if I exhibited it with curved finger & Thumb, the former garnished with a diamond Ring that the dark powder might shew to more advantage.

How I pity you for the illness & its termination, of your poor Cook! I approve much more your remedy of soap snifting that of snuff snifting.

When Alex comes, I have promised to finish my twice broken visit at Eliot Vale,—Richmond, then, will take its long procrastinated turn by the First opportunity. How are the excellent Cambridges? & Miss Baker?—I hope Charlotta & Babes go on flourishingly: I wish to know whether Charlotte ever received a Letter in which I detailed some requests relative to young Mr. Bedingfeld.[7] I have never yet been in spirits adequate to writing to L^{y} B[edingfeld] & beginning

lecture consisted of reading through a book, perhaps translating it and making short comments on the matter. As notice of the lectures had not been given as required, Charles Parr had had to apply for a dispensation. The grace was granted and he was admitted D.D. on 18 January 1822.

[5] Jane Gregor (L. 1249 n. 7).
[6] Caroline Jane Burney (L. 1272 n. 11).
[7] Possibly Lady Bedingfeld's eldest son Henry Richard (1800–62), who was briefly in England at this time (*Jerningham Letters*, ii. 217, 254), or possibly her third son Edward Richard (b. 1805), the midshipman (see further, L. 1345 n. 11).

a new acquaintance with her Mother & Sister in Law—but I hope I shall ere long—I am but too conscious of the mischief to my poor nerves of this perpetual seclusion!—I got considerably better at Eliot Vale. God bless you, my dearest Charlotte & preserve you!—

Ever & ever truly & tenderly yours

F d Ay

Kind Love to Charlotte Marianne & Clement & kindest regards at the Meadows.[8]

1279 [11 Bolton Street],
25 January 1822

To Esther (Burney) Burney

A.L. (Berg), 25 Jan. 1822
Double sheet 4to   4 pp.   *pmk* FREE 2⟨5⟩ JA 182⟨2⟩   black seal   *franked*: *N. Vansittart* / London Jan^ry twenty five 1822
Addressed: Mrs. Burney / Lark Hall Place / Bath
Endorsed by EBB: answered / almost immediately
Scribbling, p. 4

25. Jany. 1822— ! —

Would you not have been a little astonished, my Etty, had you received this cover from The Chancellor of the Exchequer unprepared?[1]—Mrs. Lock has been so kind as to send it to me for a few *words*—which, once begun, to *you*—never fail to be many *lines*—& though I had decided to write no more under 10 Letters of return—the *bulk* of my late Epistles having been trebled from common commerce, & therefore demanding adequate interest, I yet am quite pleased at this fair occasion to draw me from my usury—for I really longed to thank you at once for your last, so gratified I was—that the pretty, pleasing, innocent, engaging Caroline had appeared to *you* as to *me*. ⎮

[8] Twickenham Meadows, the home of the Cambridges (L. 1205 n. 6).

1279. [1] The franked cover procured from Nicholas Vansittart (L. 1270 n. 23).

I had quitted, as I told you, Eliot Vale when it was necessary to shew the outward Respect that my inner heart waited
no time for displaying—& I then meant to remain in Bolton
Street till the arrival of Alex:—but no Alex came—& on the
approach of the New Year, I was Sure of a Fortnight's longer
absence, from my experienced acquaintance with France on
the opening of every New *année*—Therefore Mrs. Lock came
again to fetch me to her peaceful & elegant little Villa: for
Alex has Still at Paris such Friends & Connexions as would
pay to Him the courtesies & hospitalities erst & in happier
times paid to his honoured Father—and, for Eleven years, to
his favoured Mother: — — I judged right, for he came not
—but, the fortnight over, a Letter arri[ved] | that prepared
me for something more substantial — — shadows of shades,
however, are all that my poor aching Eyes have dancing before them — — while every postman's Knock raps at my
heart, & every stopping Coach in the Neighbourhood lights
up hopes that momentarily *rajeunir* me:—only, however to
oldify me *davantage.*

I ward off, however, uneasiness—*positive* uneasiness, by
concluding he has listened to the invitation of a part of the
excellent de Maubourg's family, who have a country seat near
Calais.[2] [*T*]*here* I should be *glad* he should abide awhile —
— Would he but write to *say* that there he is!—

Well!—as Baretti used to say by a bad throw at Back-
Gammon, as he tossed the dice | on the Board '*We mun ave
dem as dey are!*—'[3] Alex *will not* accord himself to the
usage of the World, nor the wishes of his Friends—*hors* that
— — he is certainly not insufferable. But the most hopeless
part of the business is that he says *He is sure the World will
think as well of him & his friends will love him as dearly*, in
going on his own Way, as in *torturing* himself into theirs,
when once they all see he is unalterable!!! provided they
notice,—he has the grace to add,—that he loves them *always*

---

[2] 'La maison dite le Petit Lys à Farcy' near Calais was acquired in 1809 by the
wife of General Victor de Latour-Maubourg (L. 1195 n. 4) and Mme de Maisonneuve. From 1850-69 it was occupied by 'Maxime', son of the latter (L. 1195
n. 6). See Archives départementales, Melun.
[3] Giuseppe Marc Antonio Baretti (v. 264), Italian critic, who used to call at
St. Martin's Street and whom FB would have met at Streatham as well. See *ED,
DL* (ii), and *Thraliana, passim.*

the same as if he wrote Letters & made Visits all day long: *two bores*, he declares, that he will go through life in escaping!!!

What think you of This? Don't *spread* such reasoning, I beg.——dear——horrid——oddity!—— ˡ

I am glad of what you tell me of Miss Ashton's *vardy*[4] of my Non-Descript——he had named her to me as both pretty & agreeable——& she had spoken to him highly of Fanny.——I enquired for your poor Mrs. Humphries at Eliot Vale——[5] Mrs. Lock had never heard of her; but Mr. George, the Rev[d] told me she was one of his very respectable Parishioners—— but that he had not observed her at Church for some time, & feared she must be very unwell. You will delight to hear, as I to tell, that sweet Mrs. Lock has *recovered* her angel skin, her *perenial* bloom, now that she has quite conquered her late stomach attack, which had been very alarmingly severe. We are to go back to her *together*, when my Traveller has done, for the present, at least, with the Continent. I flatter myself you are having, or have had, or are soon to have, the great regale of seeing your deservedly great favourite, Charles Parr——I was highly gratified by the ˡ manner in which I saw him estimated in his own neighbourhood.[6] There is one voice only for his commendation. He finds time, they say, for *every thing*, & *every body*, where he can be useful.——sweet Mrs. Angerstein likes him particularly. I am charged by her, her sister, & more than all her darling Mother, with the kindest remembrances to you. We rarely meet that you are not a principal & a First subject of enquiry & discourse. I had

---

[4] There seemed to be no Ashtons living at Bath at this time, but resident at 12 Johnstone Street in the years 1819-29 (Bath Directories) were William Assheton (1758-1833) of Downham Hall and Cuerdale, high sheriff of Lancashire, and his wife Letitia or Lettice (d. 1834), the 2nd daughter of Sir Richard Brooke, 4th Baronet, of Norton Priory, Cheshire. The younger ladies in this family included a daughter Mary (1790-1871), who had married on 2 October 1818 John Armytage (1792-1836), son of Sir George Armytage (1761-1836) of Kirklees, Yorkshire; and a daughter-in-law Annabella *née* Cockayne (d. 25 July 1835), wife since 1816 of the younger William Assheton (1788-1858).

[5] See also L. 1275 n. 18.

[6] CPB lived at Croom's Hill, Grenwich (see Fanny Anne Burney, *A Great-Niece's Journals*, Plate *facing* p. 304), in the parish of St. Alfege. In the affairs of this church as in plans for building the daughter church of St. Mary's (see L. 1308 n. 8) CPB served on committees along with John Angerstein and Nicholas Vansittart, Chancellor of the Exchequer (L. 1270 n. 23), and other substantial citizens. See also L. 1297 n. 4.

known nothing of Mr. Ayrton but I am pleased to find that his Character of our dear lamented Brother is universally approved, & very popular.[7] Even in Paris Alex read it—& was so contented with it as to say he sighed to give me the melancholy pleasure of seeing, There, such notice done to his dear Uncle[8]—whom he truly loved.——You will be sorry, I know, if I do not mention myself—My dearest Hetty— I have had again spasmodic warnings, that have now operated in making me *take what care I can* to avoid as *abrupt* an exit as our two dear Brothers have experienced. I go out, there- fore, daily, for exercise in open air—& I do other things of which I have no space to speak—but which you would kindly like to hear, to try to a little unsadden my waning career.

God bless you, my very dear Hetty—

All well in my last news of Richmond— |

Poor Sarah is still ⟨confined⟩—She is deeply grieved—&c

J 25. yours comes *this Moment* ⟨per⟩ 2^d post

Jan 25
1822

[7] See L. 1271 n. 1.
[8] An obituary following closely that in the *Times* of 19 November (though adding an allusion to FBA) appeared in the *Journal des débats* (25 November 1821): 'Il étoit un des meilleurs et des plus savans géographes que ce pays-ci ait produits, ainsi que le prouvent abondamment sa volumineuse et correcte histoire des voyages de découvertes, sa relation de la navigation des Russes dans l'est, et d'autres ouvrages non moins estimés. Dans sa profession, ainsi que dans la vie sociale, il se distinguoit par son humanité envers ses inférieurs, son désintéresse- ment, son incorruptible intégrité, et par une sincère hospitalité.'

[11 Bolton Street],
4 February 1822

To Alexander d'Arblay

A.L. (rejected Diary MSS, 7310-[13], Berg), 4 Feb. 1822
Double sheet 4to   4 pp.   black seal
Addressed: à Monsieur / Monsieur d'Arblay— / Hotel de Tours.
Edited by CFBt. *See* Textual Notes.

So the Letter from *Mr. Tit*—which I concluded would certainly bring an answer from *Mr. Tat*, has produced no Reply, because, I presume, it was written on the very day, 4th Jany that the most idle of all human Correspondents had already written? But you forget that Mr. Tit demanded a Categorical Yea or Nay to receiving or discarding the packet of £3:7.-0 p^r post? Another came since, while I was yet at Eliot Vale, & Ramsay, wisely, refused it, first having had no orders to take a *packet per post*—of 10^s 6^{d1}—& next—having no Rhino. The First of these must by this time be forfeited: the second you may yet save, if you arrive ere the given month's Law be past. But I now Write—in defiance of my intention to wait your arrival, or at least fresh News, in silence, merely to beg you will send *nothing* here unaccompanied by a Letter, or preceded by one; so many hoax's & impositions being abroad, that every body to whom I have named it, assure me there is every reason to suspect so preposterous a way of extravagant carriage could never have been *meant* by you.

Since, however, my Pen is in hand, I have not the heart to send off my paper with only this dry business. When am I to see you, my Truant? Are you *en route*? how happy shall I be to beg Mme de Mais[onneuve] to destroy this if you have left Paris!¹ Yet I do not write to make any reproach at your stay, nor even now to press your return: all I reproach is your *silence*—& bringing me to my solitary Dwelling, from the balm of my Mrs. Lock & Amelia, in expecting what never

---

1280A. ¹ FBA's Paris letters were sent in the Ambassador's bag and through the kindness of Victor de Latour-Maubourg (L. 1192 n. 6), gouverneur des Invalides (1821), delivered to his sister Madame de Maisonneuve (L. 1195 n. 4), who seems to have taken in charge letters to AA.

arrives. I assure you, my poor Alex,—let me soften this off as I will, in declaring I have never interfered about your lengthened sojourn, our joint friends here take in very ill part my continual *ignorance* of your intentions & plans, & my *unnecessary* seclusion from Eliot Vale or Richmond in consequence of your writing that you had only to Buy a Box for your Bookes, see Mme de Grandmaison[2] & Chastel,[3] purchase some Dress elegancies, & return.—

Why write this on the 4. of Jan^y—& Now on the 4th of Feby neither be arrived nor write again?

In the joy of seeing you again, all will be forgiven by *me*: but do not make yourself so easy a Conscience as to let my perpetual watchings & disappointments be as readily forgiven by *yourself*. ׀

You give me, also, no clue as to what detains you. Your Letters from Paris are sterile in the extreme. Those from Switzerland are charming. I can form no Conjecture what thus delays you. And you tell me nothing of *affairs*—M. Le Noir[4]—M. Benier[5]—&c. I will not re-write—but *Pray look over* all my *Business matters*, if they are still undone.

Now do it at once.

Come—shall I have the complaisance to talk to you a little of *Things as they are*?—Well, in hopes of their being merited by & bye, when Boy will be dood Boy, after the *nasty wet*—here goes

———

[2] See L. 1276 n. 12.

[3] Presumably Nicolas-Charles Chastel (1749–1822), seigneur de Moyenpal, or his wife (v, L. 517 n. 12). [4] See L. 1189 n. 5.

[5] Grégoire Benier (1777–1845), who served in a succession of posts in the Ministry of War and in 1820–3, as adjoint à l'agent special chargé de la manutention de Paris. As arrears due on the *retraite* of the late General d'Arblay, he was to remit in this year £40, as may be seen both in the Ledgers preserved by Messrs Hoare, bankers, and in FBA's Account Books (Berg): 'Rec^d from M. Benier, p^r La Guerre! 40: 0: 0'.

This sum was the 1,000 fr. (roughly £40) that had been deducted from M. d'A's *retraite* on grounds of non-residence from *une trimestre* and *une semestre* when he had in fact been at the necessary dates on French soil. A copy (in FBA's hand) of his paper to this effect in his Private Diary for 1818 (Berg) shows that he had made the claim without success but was advised by Victor de Latour-Maubourg that it was *en règle* and should be pursued. If one third was wrongly deducted from his *retraite* of 4,000 fr. in respect of three quarters, he would have been entitled to 1,000 fr. or *c.* £40. See x, Appendix.

The lovely Cecilia Lock is to be married next month.[6] To the Grandson of an Earl on one side, & the son of a Peeress in her own right on the other; yet much time was taken ere consent was obtained, as the Income was thought incompetent. It is now, however, made out to be 1000 a year, & will hereafter be 3^ce that. They are to retire into Wales, on a small estate in present possession, & only be in or near town on visits to his high Relations.

The Archdeacon is still your warmest Friend & ready Patron,[7] though vexed at your long abode in foreign parts when your excursion was over. You are sure of his kind interest, & *he* is Sure, he pretends, you will aid it by some good clerical Composition, which will smooth his interference, & of which he is persuaded you are highly capable. With this I will not meddle, my dear Alex: *hasten*, or *postpone* or even *decline* all Clerical promotion; exactly at your own Will. *Vous avez vingt ans*, said your Noble Father, in his Affecting representation of your situation, & therefore, he thought,

---

[6] Georgina Cecilia (1798-1867), 2nd daughter of Charles Locke (1769-1804), was to marry on 25 April 1822 the Hon. Robert Fulke Greville, Jr. (1800-67), called 'Murray' Greville, grandson of Francis Greville (1719-73), 8th baron, 1st Earl Brooke (1746) and son of Louisa *née* Cathcart (1758-1843), *sub jure* Countess of Mansfield. Printed in the *Locks of Norbury* (pp. 311-14) is the bride's delightful account of the part of her honeymoon spent at Kenwood, as the guest of the 3rd Earl (half-brother of the groom). 'This is the most beautiful place, quite a princely abode, and the style of living perfect, so magnificent and yet comfortable at the same time. I was too late for prayers this morning, which Lord Mansfield always reads to the family at a quarter before ten o'clock. I like this custom especially where there are such thousands of servants: I reckoned twelve men servants waiting at dinner. The house is very large and the grounds appear too beautiful.'

Cecilia's grandfather, the redoubtable Mr. Ogilvie (*c.* 1740-1832), 2nd husband of the Duchess of Leinster (iii, iv *passim*), had probably noted, as had his daughter Mrs. Charles Locke (L. 1192 n. 9), that all was 'easy on the money side'. 'The estate in Wales was entailed on him ['Murray'] and never brought in less than 5,000 a year, and there was other property besides. . . . "During their lives their parents will allow him £1,000 a year, which with a house rent and tax free, and the run of theirs in town and at Richmond with everything found such as carriages, etc., certainly equals £2,000 and I think is very handsome. He is not extravagant, Cissy very saving, so I have no fears on that head." ' (*Locks of Norbury*, op. cit.).

What was to be feared could hardly have been foreseen, the derangement of the young husband.

[7] For practice in the Twickenham chapel (L. 1190 n. 2) AA was already indebted to the Revd. G. O. Cambridge, who was to be influential in 1824 in his obtaining a curacy.

you ought to *decide* for yourself, when he gave you his *opinions*: shall I forget, or not emulate, such generous indulgence?—God forbid. All I have done is This; to prevent offence, I have openly said To the Archd[n], & to Bishop Kaye,[8] that you only desire to *begin* your career, whenever it may begin, in *Town*: that all Country promotion would be unacceptable till you have seen more of the World, & engaged a Partner—& a Family—to enliven & endear Clerical, Literary & scientific Retirement.

Thus stated, openly & explicitedly nobody finds this wrong.

And yet—I sigh when I think—& feel—a connection of the first rate, for every thing personal, elegant, high bred, pure & amiable, *might,* I perchance, have given to your life, & your pursuits, that delicious partnership that would have heightened every enjoyment, & mitigated every disappointment, had you earlier had that *regular* occupation that constitutes a citizen, i.e. a post in which, if only a Curacy, there was Responsibility & order:—such as give zest to leisure, & industry to avoid the inertness by which Those who hang desultorily upon themselves, rapidly lose half their existence, to procure for the other half those rapturous moments that Waste while they delight. You know, I believe, our good friend Lady Keith's maxim[9]—That no Man can make a happy Wife who is not forced into some Business by his situation, for some part of every day: for that, she says, gives a consequence & dignity to his Character that makes his other pursuits, be they what they may, never thought trifling or *déplacée*: & prevents his always hanging upon his poor Wife to guard him from *ennui*.

I have great reason to believe—though no conviction, that this was the reasoning that occasioned the *change* you observed *quoique part*, & that gave the preferment to the ⟨Cousin⟩. Kingman I am told, has now carried the day.[10] What's done, however, can't be undone &c. & to other times.

[8] A preference that FBA may have intimated to John Kaye (L. 1181 n. 2), Bishop of Bristol (1820), on the occasion of his visit to Bolton Street on 2 October 1821 (Diary).

[9] See L. 1193 n. 8.

[10] Possibly William Kingman (*c.* 1784-1839) of Walcot Street, Bath, son of William Kingman (*c.* 1739-1811) by his wife Ann (*c.* 1750-1814). His marriage to one of AA's acquaintances has not been established.

Mr. J[ohn] Ang[erstein][11] is persuaded you will come home a complete Senator, to *tip him a touch*, he says, of the speeches & voice & manner of all the orators of the two Chambers. And, seriously, my dear Mme de M[aisonneuve] says she will write me nothing of political events, as you understand & can expound them in a way that will be highly interesting to *me*, & in *you* even admirable. Her partial kindness is all my support in your taciturnity.[12]—But—having Now had such ample means to see & study & know all Paris & its &c.s—even *She*, & even *all* your French Friends, are *surprized* you can spare from *Waning Youth* so much Time where you have no *useful pursuit*, nor *ostensible cause* for abandoning your Home.

Give me, then, something to say to Them All, Here, & There, as well as to myself: or — — Come & Tell your Travels, & shew your Improvements—

[11] See ix, L. 962 n. 1 and iv. 326.

[12] In a letter of 22 January (Berg) Mme de Maisonneuve had commented on AA's immersion of the time in poetry: 'son goût pour la Poésie absorbe tous les autres, les froids calculs des Mathématiques ne peuvent plus plaire à une imagination toute remplie d'images de descriptions poëtiques toute parlant a l'ame et au coeur; tout en admirant son talent, son imagination, sa mémoire, son esprit, et les sentimens parfaits que peignent ses vers, je suis fachée de le voir passionée pour la poësie, toute passion est nuisible, et entraine malgré soi,—Ce goût pr Talma, les ressources que trouve à Paris celui qui cherche a alimenter son talent, vont, je crains, l'absorber, et l'ont déjà retenu trop long-tems a Paris, il me semble, pour votre satisfaction et votre fortune; il a été fort frappé cependant de voir dans votre dernière lettre que vous étiez revenus l'attendre a Londres, il a dit qu'il ne seroit plus a Paris que pour une semaine. Toutes les fois que je le vois depuis les mois je le conjure d'aller chez Mr Benier il en prend la résolution, mais il n'y a pas encore été parce qu'il est tout entier dans la poésie, la lecture ou la composition. il nous a dit qu'il vouloit encore deux ans de liberté, avant de prendre un Bénéfice, j'ai entendue cela avec peine; je suis persuadée qu'étant avec vous, toutes ses impressions seront modifiées par votre ascendant sur lui, et votre influence; aussi je le voudrois a Bolton Street au lieu de l'hôtel de Tours. . . . ⟨le⟩ moment il n'a je suis sur pas autre chose dans le coeur et l'esprit que l'envie de partir pour Londres. mais il faut s'attendre que son imagination inalteré ne s'apperçoit pas des intervalles et les semaines et les mois s'écoulent avec encore plus de rapidité que pour tout autre personne. je lui ai envoyé un billet pour assister a une séance de la chambre des députés, je me flatte que cela le ramènera un peu sur la terre . . . il s'appercevra qu'il n'est ni au milieu des anges, ni dans l'olimpe, je voudrois qu'en sortant il fut ⟨arreter⟩ une place dans une voiture qui lui conduit de Paris a Londres. outre le plaisir de le revoir, quel intérêt aura pour vous sa conversation, et ses récits sur les Evénements qui touchent votre seconde Patrie, et tant de personnes que vous honorez de votre souvenir et de votre interêt;—personne ne pourra vous rendre un compte plus intéressant de tout ce qui se passe depuis 3 mois qu'alex, qui parle aussi bien en prose qu'en vers.—'

Meanwhile, to encourage you, I have formed the positive plan to relinquish my too dear—too sacred seclusion—&—*gently*—to come into all your wishes, *pas à pas*, as much as my health & strength will permit.

Yes, your excellent uncle received your Letter from Berne —& instantly in his kindness, said He would come to me to open it before me!—It ˡ gave him great pleasure. But he was very uneasy at your staying so long abroad, & said often, 'Young men throw away their Youth before they find out its Value: he should give himself a rank in society, as one of its Citizens first—& amuse himself afterwards.' The young married Pair go on very well, I believe.[13] Caroline Burney is at Lark Hall place with Aunt Hetty—Maria is wholly affronted with you.—I was just going to conclude when I heard a very surprising piece of News, which I do not know what to think of—nor whether to tell you, or not—but yes, suspence is so disagreeable I will not excite your curiosity only to create it: the Marriage I had heard was over, with the Cornish Knight, is broken off[14]—why or wherefore or How I know not: but it was told me by good authority, Namely The Aunt—& without assigning any reason—so that I know not whether the lady *rejected* at last, or threw Cold Water on the advances so as to stop the declaration!—but 'tis odd!—The *other* match is with a youth than whom the fair Bride elect is 3 years older.[15] Well—Come over, if you can—or *write* if you cannot, my dear Truant—

---

[13] Sarah and John Payne (L. 1247 n. 2).

[14] Possibly an allusion to Lucy Locke (1801–93), youngest daughter of Charles Locke (L. 1192 n. 9), FBA's informants being his sister Lady Martin or Amelia Angerstein. Lucy was to marry Captain Alexander Ellice (1791–1858).

[15] Obviously Cecilia Locke and 'Murray' Greville (n. 6).

11 Bolton Street,
                                4 February 1822

To William Wilberforce

A.L.S. (Bodleian), 4 Feb. 1822
Single sheet 4to   2 pp.   bound

I have long almost *yearned*, Dear Sir, to return You my
sincerest acknowledgments for your kind, acceptable, &
seasonable present, & to tell You how I valued—how I have
studied—& how—I humbly hope—I have profitted from
it;[1] but the fear of taking up time that already must be so
inadequate to the triple interests of Religious, Patriotic, &
Family calls merely to offer such poor thanks & trite praise
as benevolence like Yours must bring perpetually to Your
Ears, kept my Pen to myself—though not my Gratitude, for
that has gone forth by every opening that has offered it a
vent. But the silence of Respect must run no risk of being
mistaken for that of Insensibility—& what other could keep
me wholly quiet when I know Mr. Wilberforce to be himself
afflicted by the same awful doom that moved so generously
his compassion for me in 1818?

Alas, Sir—we little Then foresaw that the same pious
Tract You so kindly, at that fatal period, sent to ǀ Me, would
so soon be yet more immediately applied to yourself![2]—To
offer You consolation—who on Earth shall presume? but to
express to You Sympathy—who is invested with a right

1280B. [1] This was Cecil's *A Friendly Visit to the House of Mourning* (L. 1227
n. 1), from which, as Wilberforce mentioned in recommending it to FBA (20 May
1818, Berg), the late Archbishop of Canterbury himself had derived comfort.
[2] Wilberforce's elder daughter Barbara had died on 30 December 1821, aged
21. In his reply of 14 February (Osborn) Wilberforce was to speak of the 'severe
trial' in 'the loss of a grown-up Daughter, justly very dear to her Parents'. 'But,
blessed be God, we have been enabled, on good grounds, to entertain a firm persuasion that our dear Child is gone to that World where she is *Safe*, & will be
happy for ever.' 'We are left with a fresh incentive to tread in the path in which
our dear Daughter walked, that we may at length . . . have an entrance into the
same ever-lasting Kingdom.'
    The letter was written by an amanuensis ('A complaint in my Eyes, which is
now become almost habitual to me, compels me to write to you by another
hand'). 'I hope to be in London however ere long, & to have the honor of paying
my respects to you.'

more entirely emanating from yourself than I am?—Nor am I amongst those who conclude that the ability of giving lessons to others in Sorrow, in Pain, or in distress, includes the power of bearing similar trials unmoved;—No,—I believe your own heart to be tenderly susceptible of woe, personal as well as collateral, though your principles resist its desponding effects, & seek to receive it as the Harbinger of Mercy & Bliss.—That your Health, therefore, may support the inevitable struggle against your feelings, & that the comfort You are called upon to dispence to your poor Partner & your Children, may reflect back its genial warmth upon your own future existence is most sincerely & cordially the wish of her who is, with the deepest esteem & consideration,

Dear Sir,

Your most obliged & obedient servant,

F. d'Arblay

4th Feby 1822.—
11. Bolton Street,

1281   11 Bolton Street,
                                       14 February 1822

To Charles Parr Burney

A.L.S. (Osborn), 14 Feb. 1822
Double sheet 8vo   4 pp.
Docketed in pencil, p. 1: 1822

Not very gaily I have to request you will be so kind, my dear Charles, as to make known to Mr. Foss that Alexander is still in Paris.[1] — — —

Not for his missing the Club Dinner, even of loved Family respectability, am I concerned at his absence; for *all professed*

1281. [1] Probably Henry Foss (L. 1191 n. 8), a former pupil, as was d'Arblay, at the Greenwich School, who was evidently issuing invitations to one of the dinners held four times a year since April 1805 by the Burney Club. For the formation of the club, see vii, L. 652 n. 3; for the eminence of some of CB Jr.'s graduates, x, L. 1150 n. 6; and for the meeting of April 1824, L. 1334 n. 2.

Dinners have, hitherto, been inimical to him: & I wish him with all my heart to keep out of their way; he has no immediate warning of their mischief, for his *head* is not attacked; on the contrary, he can There bear wine & good living without any sensible effect: but it is his *whole system* that is disordered by them the ensuing night, & following day, | or days —manifested by feverish heat, faded complexion, general *inertia*, & sleepless restlessness.

On This subject, therefore, with all my true good wishes to the Club of his *Mother's* Family, I am not grieved he should remain about the Family & Friends—more immediately his own, of his honoured *Father*: yet I think the absence very— very long!—

Receive, my dear Charles, my sincere congratulations upon your new Honour.[2] May you wear as you have won it, by the general worth that has secured to you general approbation!—

When my dear Brother took the title of Doctor, I begged him always to Me to announce himself as the | *Reverend Dr. Burney*, or as Dr. *Charles* Burney, that so my reception might be to *himself*, & consequently with a pleasure unallayed by any latent regret: he complied—as what would he have refused me?—and the effect was always chearful: You, now, must go a step further to save, at once, & gratify my feelings: You must announce yourself as the Reverend Dr. Charles Parr Burney—by which appellation, while you spare me needless & painful retrospections, you assure yourself, thus Individualized, the cordial welcome due to *you* by yourself *you*.—

Pray give my kindest compliments to your engaging Wife,[3] & believe me my dear Charles, most sincerely yours

F.d'Ay

I would always be remembered to Mrs. Bicknell.[4] Your little Boy[5] made a Conquest of my dear Mrs. Locke.

11 Bolton Street
14th Feby 1822. |

[2] See L. 1278 n. 4.   [3] See L. 1245 n. 4.   [4] See L. 1245 n. 5.
[5] Probably CPB's elder son Charles Edward, aged 7. Edward Kaye, the 2nd son, was 5 years of age (i, p. lxxii).

1282   11 Bolton Street,
                        29 January–13 March 1822

To Esther (Burney) Burney

A.J.L.S. (rejected Diary MSS. 7314-[25], Berg), 29 Jan.-13 Mar.
1822
    Three double sheets 4to   12 pp.   numbered 1-12
    Endorsed by EBB, p. 12 [7825]: This Packet replied to / April 2 by
Mr Twining
    Edited by CFBt. *See* Textual Notes.

                        Bolton Street 29th Jany 1822.

I so delight in your plan,[1] my dearest Esther—it will give
me such true & tender Joy to see & embrace you—that I
stop short at the end of your first page & 6 lines, to Write
this, before I can go on—Welcome—welcome to my expectations is the project!—And when you know any thing more
precisely of Times & Seasons, communicate immediately that
I may arrange quietly being certainly in town every instant
you can spend in it:—*quietly*, I say, for arrange it I *will*,
even if with a thousand difficulties. And—should it happen
during any absence of Alex, how shall I rejoice in having you
next room to me!—but as to your *3 times* a week—that,
I trust, is meant for *fudge*,—since if you give me not *every*
moment in your power,—you will not only disappoint, you
will wound me. Basta!—you would not do that, I am sure!
— — You, & Charlotte, only, alas!. I have now strength &
spirits to wish under my roof—for *the whole day*,—my
faculties weary, & my spirits sink, with every long visit from
any one else. A short visit revives me, & I cheer & animate so
as to surprize myself, after the *first* meeting is past: but I
never *begin* gaily, because I am always *found* ungay!—Oh
how changed! how changed!—But with *you* I feel that every
Hour will only make me long for another. So complete is our
mutual confidence, that the interest of life & existence is
exhilarated by our intercourse.—My dear Mrs. Lock ought
to have been placed a *third*, for she is balm itself, & ever open
to sympathy in grief, as well as to the highest enjoyment of

1282. ¹ EBB's visit to London was to take place in early July (see Ll. 1288-9).

every *spirt* of vivacity that brings me back——occasionally, to old times.——Come, my dearest Esther!——& if in Summer for me it will be better, as more likely to give me the joy of possessing you entirely: though for your sake, as well as Alex's I ought not to wish his absence on ǀ some new excursion——

I have now finished, & will answer your very interesting Letter.

March——

Things impossible, & indeed useless, to trace, broke in upon me at the top of this page, & my fast purpose of waiting *fair play* for my repeated pen-fagging earnings, have made me contentedly bear the interruption, till your's of March 1st arrived, with the resistless intimation of a Frank opportunity which I always accept with glee, for it takes from me all scrupulosity both as to *manner* & *matter*, & casts my Pen at random, with no thought but of *Quantity*. So here——as our poor dear——dear James used to say, *here goes.*——

I am really charmed by your accounts of Caroline,[2] & quite delighted she has so won your good graces. It has been intimated to me, also, that she is far from ungrateful——or rather, that she is quite the reverse. If you see her wild, bear with it as a proof that you see her happy, & have set her at ease: for she *can* be composed, silent, & decorous, so as not to utter a word that is not drawn from her, nor to make a movement that is not called for by obliging attention. Such was her deportment in her single visit to me, & it shewed a sense of propriety that at once interested me in her favour, & the more, as I perceived, by the brightening Eye, & ready smile, when she was addressed, joined to the quick, though ǀ gentle voice of native vivacity, that her heart was instinctively gay, though her demeanour, from mingled feeling & respect, had caught the seriousness of mine. She filled me with kind thoughts, & so did her Sister,[2] who though neither so pretty, nor so engaging, nor so lively, has a look of intelligence & observance that invites investigation, & promises to repay it. That Caroline is not *deep* I easily conceive, yet I would not judge her to be *shallow* merely from her delight in admiration.

[2] For members of 'India' Richard's family, at this time in England, see i, pp. lxxiii–iv; L. 1184 n. 11; L. 1272 n. 11; and L. 1275 n. 14.

'Tis so natural, however little wise, that she seems but to 'Warble her native wood notes wild,'[3] like all the Birds in the Air, in jocundly chorussing 'Oh how pleasing 'tis to please![4] —— —' But, let me also whisper in your Ear, my dear Esther, that, besides the general blyth enchantment from being an object of praise & pleasure, Caroline may have a latent joy in it that may be neither frivolous nor vain, namely a secret hope of some happy establishment that may keep her in this Country. I am told she loves it quite passionately; & therefore the prospect of quitting it, & perhaps for ever, may give double zest to every opening that beams upon her youthful expectation with a perspective of remaining. This is quite for ourselves. I would not have her suppose such a wish is conjectured, because, then, failure would add *Mortification* to Disappointment. Her Brother, who, while he tenderly loves, is also proud of her, would be most happy to see her, properly & prosperously, settled in England; though, otherwise, he is fully prepared for standing to the great expence of fitting her out, & paying all the charges of returning her to India with Nabob views. Of all this, however, the less *said* the better; but I know the subject must now have great interest to you, & make no apology, therefore, for letting it nearly fill my Letter.

Not *quite*, nevertheless; I must not let you dedicate your meditations all to a *Niece*, while there is a nephew who goes so near to engaging all mine:—No Alex yet returned!—& as I left Eliot Vale from *given* expectation to meet him—so, after my vain waiting, & again quitting town, to solace myself with our good Charlotte, have I left Richmond, also, on a Letter of appointment, (so understood, at least) only to come hither once more to Solitude & Abortion! And, in addition to my general—though long restrained yearning for his sight & society, I have now a very serious Necessity for his help, his abilities, his calculations, & his concurrence, from the new, & I fear heavy change in our joint Income from this unexpected tax upon our funded property in the 5 p^r C^{ts} I am anxious to know whether I You, my dearest Esther, escape the mischiefs of his new regulation,[5] so good to the

[3] Milton, 'L'Allegro'.   [4] Addision, *Rosamond*, III. iii.
[5] A new regulation, designed to 'diminish permanently the charge of the

Public at large, & so severe upon the Individual in private? Our dear & sagacious James had counselled me, 2 years ago, to sell out from the Fives, & buy into the 4. Luckily, *half* my fives had so been placed by Him whose judgment had seen good reason for it almost immediately upon our settling again in England: but the reasons which opposed the further Change suggested by dear James, were such that, though too long for a Letter, appeared to him so sufficient for running the risk, that he finished by agreeing to them, with the Words, 'Well, then, let them bide where they be.'

I have now no sort of real or natural money adviser; & I have never, in my long life, had the experience of managing my money transactions myself: but the only Two persons with whom I have at all consulted, have given me an opinion that I think right to mention to you, in the Case that either Yóu, or Maria, or Richard, or Amelia are still 5 pᴿ Centers: which I hope, at the same time, you are not.

Mr. Barrett, who is saved the personal inconvenience by being in other funds, has nevertheless bustled about very much to get lights & information, & was actively obliging in imparting them to me: & their result was, that, not having, unhappily, taken any measures for selling out while stocks were higher, it was Now ˡ more likely to be advantageous to leave the property untouched, & trust to the good faith of

public debt' as explained in the *AR* lxiv (1822), chap. vii, was 'the reduction of the interest on the Navy 5 per cents to 4 per cent'. For this purpose the Chancellor of the Exchequer submitted a plan to the proprietors of that stock proposing that a 'new stock . . . be created, bearing interest at the rate of four per cent per annum, payable on the fifth of January, and the fifth of July in each year; and not to be paid off until the fifth of January, 1829'.

'All holders of five per cents, who should not signify their dissent, were to have, for every 100*l.* five per cent annuities, 105*l.* in the new four per cent stock, on which the first dividend was to be payable on the fifth of January, 1823.'

As shown in the Ledgers preserved by the bankers Messrs. Hoare of 37 Fleet Street, FBA had an investment of £2,421. 16*s.* 8*d.* in Navy 5 per cents, which in the years 1818–21 had yielded £121. 1*s.* 10*d.* per annum (see also her own Account Book, Berg). Converted in 1823 to the New 4 per cents, the sum yielded in 1824, for instance, £101. 4*s.* 4*d.* By the conversion she would seem to have lost in income about £20 per year.

In addition she had had since 1817 an investment of £2,862. 12*s.* 4*d.* in [the old] 4 per cents, which continued to yield £114. 10*s.* 0*d.* annually; and appearing in her portfolio for 1823 was an investment of £778. 8*s.* 10*d.* in 3 per cent Consuls, an investment that she augmented annually until it reached in 1833, for instance, £1,283.

Government in the new 4.s——in which, though unavoidably losers, the 5. stockholder would be *less* so than in selling out to buy in the 3ˢ.

As soon as I came from Richmond, I had a visit from our sweet Mrs. Lock, & I laid my position before her. She has nothing herself in this Fand, but her Son Mr. George has his *all* there: she therefore consulted with *him*, & has most kindly sent me his opinion, & its causes, in the advice of two Bankers, Messʳˢ Coutts & Messʳˢ Martin,[6] which coincide completely with the advice of Mr. Barrett.

I am assured that public Approbation in this *manœuvre*, notwithstanding its personal severity, is nearly universal, & that *we losers* shall, finally, *in our Successors*, at least, be recompensed for our present diminished lustre, by a lessening of taxation, & generally encreased cheapness in all the requisite articles of living.

Amen!——I must be patriotic enough, for one, to accept this comfort. And indeed I think so highly of the character of Mr. Vansittart,[7] that I am well disposed not to murmur,—— though it is a little difficult to rejoice. especially as a better & stronger foresight might have saved me this fleecing.——

I left dear Charlotte, her lovely Namesake, & Marian all well. Clement is by no means recovered: I am not absolutely alarmed for him——but I am far from seeing him in a state of security. Though not without his foibles—— ǀ but who is?—— he is really a very worthy creature, & always well intentioned, obliging & good-natured. I fervently hope he will be re-established. He means to go only to the sea Coast this summer, instead of Greece, Egypt, & Constantinople, & his tender Mother will accompany him thither. I conclude Brighton, though no place is yet fixed.

We earnestly desire, when you know them yourself, to have speedy intelligence of your times & seasons, my dearest Esther. *I* am fixed to accord myself to them be they what they may: but still I shall be glad so to do it as least to disconcert or disappoint certain kind Expectants. Do not imagine

---

[6] Consulted by the Revd. George Locke were members of the firms Thomas Coutts (1735–1822), banker, of 59 The Strand; and Martin & Co., of 68 Lombard Street, a bank founded in the time of Queen Elizabeth I.

[7] The Chancellor of the Exchequer (L. 1270 n. 23).

by this I want you to tell me what your own affairs, & perceptions of futurity, have not yet devellopped to yourself!
—no, no; only when *you* see Day-light into your movements, don't keep *me* in twilight. That's all.

Sarah Harriet is wonderfully recovered, I am truly rejoiced to have heard, & to relate. I have not yet been able to see her, which I much regret: but till lately she *declined* the offer of my visit, fearing, she said, in her weak & precarious state, the melancholy of our meeting, after a loss to *me* so Severe—& to *her* the most heart-piercing she has ever endured.[8] But now, when I shall be able, she invites my approach. I have returned from Richmond with a hurt, from a gravel stone, that indented itself into my foot on Richmond Hill, & has taken off my walking faculty ever since, till this very ׀ Day, which is the First, since the accident, that has seen me shod, just as if Miss Footibuss had some secret *inkling* of the kind affections of Her to whom I wrote, & would not let her hear of The Cripple but as a *ci-devant*. While writing this long *Epître*, I have had a very kind Note from Mrs. Admiral!! Burney, to propose coming to tea with me to Night, & bringing Martin—whom I have not seen since his heavy, & I verily believe heavily & truly felt loss of his dear Father: but I have put them off to Friday,[9] that I may devote all the time my poor weak & worn Eyes can serve me in to you, my dear Hetty. You would be sorry to know how inadequate I am to *continue* writing, even to *you*, to whom it is but thinking on paper, from the harrassed Nerves of my over-worked (Mr. Chilver says)[10] head, which now cries aloud for rest after every hour's bending downwards—a position that, I suppose, sends the blood too *thick* to the Brain. After dinner—slight & frugal as is my repast, I have, of late, been compelled to give up writing or examination of hand-writing, *completely* till after Tea: I am going, now directly, to begin a new system of regimen in trying if the poor Pate will be bettered by wholly leaving off *Tea*: which I love in rivalry with any washwoman of the United Kingdoms: but I love the power of occupation beyond all else. *Evening Society* is what I most

---

[8] The death of JB, with whom SHB had lived in the years 1798–1803 (iv, L. 295 n. 1 and *passim*).
[9] See further, Ll. 1298, 1301. [10] See L. 1230 n. 6.

require; & in London—in my quiet retirement, it is what is most difficult to arrange. However, when *Alex* comes I shall have—now & then, at least, a Companion. I am much pleased by Chas Parr's kindness to the Revd Rich^d I have not seen the new Doctor!^11 but Mrs. Chas Parr made me a visit not long since. I hope poor Mr. Sansom is better. I pity him truly. ^1

Wednesday *Morn^g 13. March.*

I have seen nothing of Edward, nor of Fanny, This Age. I had great pleasure in thinking the latter looked in much amended health & strength when I last revised her face & complexion. You will easily believe how these disturbances in Paris redouble my desire for the return of my tardy Traveller. His dread of sea sickness, *hereditary* on my side, may be the cause of his *late* procrastination, as those continual storms render the passage, however short, doubly suffering. My kind Mme de Maisoneuve alone makes me support his *absence* & *silence*;^12 for she writes to me often, whole Letters full of him, & all consolatory & flattering. He has been viewed by his hereditary connections in the fairest light, & is only, I fear, too much carressed & considered!—I *mean* for his

---

^11 For CPB's D.D. (Oxon.), see L. 1278 n. 4.

^12 In letters of 15 February and 19 March (Berg) Mme de Maisonneuve obligingly reported what she could learn of Alex's activities. According to 'la maitresse de la maison' at the Hôtel de Tours, whom she had consulted, Alex departed for the day about 9 a.m. to attend courses of lectures on poetry and drama, and a great deal of his time seemed to be spent in writing 'exercises' suggested by the courses. At such times he stayed for whole days in his room writing, taking no care for a fire or food. 'Il travailloit beaucoup' and 'ne pronoit jamais garde a ce qu'on faisoit dans sa chambre'.

He saw a great deal of the Ampères, 'Pere et fils', the former, 'un fameux Mathématicien . . . en relation avec tous les savans de l'Europe', who had given him the task of translating a 'Gros Mémoire en anglois bien savant et bien ennuyeux'. For the son, Alex 'a fait une Parodie d'une longue Tragédie pour faire appercevoir au jeune poète les deffauts de sa pièce'. Such scientific persons no less impious than learned were little likely to encourage Alex, opined his mother's friend, in 'le gout de la profession qu'il a choisie'.

Of his compositions, Mme de Maisonneuve considered his verses on Mont Blanc by far the best. There wrapt in the wild and 'extactic wonder' experienced and described by Shelley in his letter of 22 July 1816 to Peacock (see Kenneth N. Cameron, 'Mont Blanc', *Shelley. The Golden Years* (1974), pp. 243–51), Alex too wrote an 'Ode on Mont Blanc' (dated September 1821) and three versions of a 'Dithyrambe on Mont-Blanc', some 50 pages (Berg).

In the end his mother's friends procured him a place in the diligence, which amiably, as was his wont, he accepted, and as may be seen in his mother's letter of L. 1285 he was home again by April, after an absence of nine months.

re-settlement here. I was much gratified by what you told me of the observations of your friends Mrs. & Miss Ashtons[13] when they met him in public: for in private only can I make any myself.

The last Bride of the family is really a charming young woman,[14] but yet, near as she is to me, I can see her but seldom, as it is only alone she can give me any comfort by her society; & I would not for the World hurt her husband by asking often the separation. Yet a *stranger*, of any sort, is a mere *gêne* to me; or a cause of such effort as is become unnatural.

Poor Mrs. Maling has lost a very dear Daughter, Mrs. Ward,[15] who lived at the top of this street. She had just before written me a kind condolence in the loss of our dear Brother! I shall go to her, when I am uncrippled enough to make so distant a walk: *Cadogan place*: & then, if possible, on to Sarah Harriet & to Fanny Raper.[16] 'Twill be a complete Country airing for Ramsay & Diane, & myself. |

Pray tell me if you know any thing—& *what*—of Mr. Twining: his Life & Correspondence of his charming Brother was promised 5 years ago?[17] Has it appeared during my *total* seclusion?—

You are *certainly* Right that my poor Traveller mistakes greatly in believing he may rule the world as to indulging his

[13] See L. 1279 n. 4.

[14] Sarah Payne *née* Burney (L. 1247 nn. 1, 2).

[15] Mrs. Maling (L. 1264 n. 6), whom the Burneys had known in their childhoods at Queen Square, had recently lost her 3rd daughter Catherine Julia (1772-1822), the wife of Robert Plumer Ward (1765-1846), novelist and politician (*DNB*). She had died at 3 Bolton Row on 28 January (*AR* lxiv, 'Chronicle', 268).

[16] At Stanley Grove, King's Road, Chelsea, and Field Cottage, King's Road, respectively.

[17] Richard Twining (1749-1824), a director of the East India Company and head of the famous firm of tea merchants on the Strand (*DNB*), had suffered a paralytic stroke in 1818 (see his account of it, x, L. 1162 n. 4), and in the years 1818-24 paid occasional visits to Bath offering at times to carry letters from FBA to EBB. In 1816 FBA had honoured his request for the return of the letters that his half-brother, the Revd. Thomas Twining (1734-1804), classical scholar and critic, had written to CB (see ix, L. 978 n. 9) and now after five years, as she says, she was looking for their appearance in print.

The editorial work was left, however, to the 3rd Richard Twining (1807-1906), who would publish a selection of the letters in *Recreations and Studies of a Country Clergyman of the Eighteenth Century* (1882) and *Selections from Papers of the Twining Family* . . . (1887). A new edition of the letters (see *Catalogue*) has been undertaken by Professor R. S. Walker.

utter hatred of Letter-writing & visiting, except as they suit his humour of the moment. In order to bear my own share of this excentricity, I am always forced to be enacting my own Sir Hugh & exclaim: The Rising Generation's come to quite a new pitch![18]—

How pleased I feel the *china Rose Bush* has still bloomed![19] — — Oh bloom for-ever—beyond mortal fragrance, its planter! — — Mrs. Lock is much pleased at your kind acceptance of her flowery Gift.

How exactly could I re-*write*, as well as re-read all you say of dear happy, happiest Chesington![20] ere Care, Fear, or even Hope disturbed us, for There all was positive enjoyment!—

You delight me with what dear generous affectionate James has done[21]—a *hint* has been given me, by a bye road, of something of that nature meant, eventually, to revert to my Alex—but Wills & I and Alex have been so unfortunate, I hope he will not hear of it unless by *fruition*. I preach aloud to every body to keep their testamentary intentions to themselves,—then may they make what changes they will without injustice—I am, nevertheless, surprised by what you intimate about Sophy—I had always thought Fanny the least well off pecuniarily, from my belief in the *avowed* intentions of Maria for Sophy [XXXXX 2 *words*].[22] ⎮

You will be charmed to hear what I am charmed to write that our sweet Mrs. Lock has recovered all her *beauty* as well as *health*. Her *youth, only* is gone! She is a sight of Wonder & Admiration for retaining *beauty* after its flight. Poor Lady Templetown—her earliest friend, is in a very declining state, & has been thought dying frequently; but she is suddenly enough better to revive hope of recovery. To *Her* I sometimes go out to *tea*, because she gives it me tête à tête in her Bed room—& her Daughter, Miss Upton,[23] fetches & brings me

[18] Sir Hugh Tyrold in *Camilla*, I, 1.   [19] See L. 1270.

[20] See *ED passim* or *HFB*, pp. 17–18.

[21] In a codicil to his will (PRO/PROB/11/1653/56, pr. 6 February 1822), JB had bequeathed to EBB the dividends of his 4 per cents (Manwaring, p. 286); and to AA, 50 guineas (L. 1272 n. 4). FBA is probably recollecting the expectations for AA that Antoine Bourdois had apparently led her to entertain (vi. 535, 542), and it is hinted that CB Jr.'s failure to make a will was also a disappointment (see x, L. 1143).

[22] A reference to the beneficiaries of Cecilia Burney's will (L. 1248 n. 7).

[23] See L. 1222 n. 9.

home, taking the interval to make some visit, or to take an opera or Concert, which her filial duty forbids when her Mother is *sola*. This is equally good for *me*, as my Evenings are now pernicious to me in solitude, from the state of my Eyes & Head.

Shall I never have done?——Dearest Esther, is it not *converse* to take my pen to *you*? —— ——

You are most kind to speak so comfortingly of your precious health.

I like much your regulation of your Dwelling. How pretty it is!—Does Caroline love the Country?

I am sorry you lose Miss Hayes[24]—

I cannot make out the history of the Child at Mary bone[25] —perhaps the He was written hurryingly for *She*.

I hope all are well at Brightwell & at Worcester. |

I enclose you, my dearest Esther, two precious manuscripts, your own property, & which you will press to your lips & your heart with reverence & tenderness —— —— I have come to them but since my abode here, or should have restored them long ago. How they were left amongst our dear Father's hoards I have no means to say: but they had neither direction nor cover: They are from our own excellent & extraordinary Mother.[26] What would I not give I had a line of her's addressed to myself! It seems plain she had written to me—but I have no Letter nor its remembrance.

I enclose you, also, a Letter of the famous Cha[s] Em[l] Bach,[27] as you are named in it—& will prize his hand-writing: & I enclose you a very characteristic note of Mrs. North,[28] to amuse you.

God bless you, my ever dear Etty!——

yours ever & ever

F. d Ay

My Love to all your fair ones. & remembrances to those I know that you consort with—Mrs Thomas—Mrs. Beckford

---

[24] Anna Maria Hayes (L. 1189 n. 21) was soon to marry George Eyre (1772-1837) of the Warrens, Bramshaw, Hants.

[25] An allusion lost with EBB's letter.

[26] Esther *née* Sleepe (1723-62), whose letters are missing.

[27] Carl Philipp Emanuel Bach (1714-88). Of his letters to the Burneys, only that of 1 September 1776 (Osborn) to CB is known.

[28] See i, L. 3 n. 10 and iv, L. 324 n. 7.

—Miss Hayes—&c &c &c &c & *Miss Wood* particularly. I am charmed she so more than keeps her high favour with you.[29] I am very sorry, all ways, for the Ash's[30]—though I did not know them. They were universally esteemed.

1283   [11 Bolton Street,
                               25] March 1822

To Mrs. Barrett

A.L. (Berg), Mar. 1822
Double sheet 4to   4 pp.   red seal
Addressed: Mrs. Barrett, / Richmond.
Docketed, p. 4; C. 18

March 1822

No Alex — — I avail myself therefore of your offer, my kind Charlotte, & enclose a Letter[1] for him through my kind Mme de Maisonneuve, which you will re-enclose to kind Mr. Penn.[2] I have still too much hope he is *en route* to risk my Spur to the discussion of an Hôtel Garni[3]—& Mme de

---

[29] For EBB's Bath friends, see L. 1200 n. 11; L. 1189 nn. 20, 21; and L. 1200 n. 10, respectively.

[30] For the financial failure of the Bath Subscription Concerts, since 1810 under the management of Andrew Ashe (*c.* 1759-1838), violinist and flautist, his wife Mary *née* Comer (bapt. 13 April 1777), vocalist, and their numerous family (ix, L. 1052 n. 25). The *Bath Chronicle* of 10 January 1822 announced the last concert (5 February) given by the Ashes in Bath, and the same newspaper (28 March) gave notice of Mrs. Ashe's last benefit. The d'Arblays, all three, had attended her benefit of 7 April 1817 (Diary).

1283. [1] The letter or 'Spur' may have been L. 1284 or some similar missive of inquiry, reproach, or admonition.

[2] Known for some years to Marianne Francis and Charlotte Barrett were the sons and daughters of Richard Penn (1735-1811) and his wife Mary *née* Masters (d. 1830) of Philadelphia. Deputy Governor of Pennsylvania (1771-3), Richard had returned to England in 1775 and, entering politics, was elected M.P. for the years 1784-91, 1796-1806, dying in his house in Richmond on 27 May 1811.

Of his two sons (see *DNB*), it was probably Richard (1784-1863), F.R.S. (1824) of Richmond, who, connected with the Colonial Office, was able to aid the d'Arblays at this time. 'Rose' or Mary Penn (1785-1863) CFBt was shortly to introduce to FBA (see L. 1298 n. 2).

[3] See L. 1284 n. 4.

M[aisonneuve] will most religiously burn it should it—to my unspeakable satisfaction, arrive too late.

I must now, my sweet Charlotte, say a word in *answer* to a word that dropt from you relative to the Elegy on L^y Coventry,[4] which I have regretted not having been struck with as demanding a little elucidation more immediately: but I hardly at first entered into its meaning, from a hurry to comply with any request of yours within my power; & afterwards, from the hurry of spirits which the little, but now very unusual exertion occasioned; & lastly, from the hurry of package, & leave-taking, which put the whole matter from my thoughts: but it no sooner recurred to them than I felt, & feel that I ought not to leave you under a mistake as to my notions upon the subject.

I had understood you, my dear Girl, to ask me to repeat to you that Elegy as a poem with which you were unacquainted. It was under that persuasion that I had recovered by studious recollection, in a sleepless Night, the parts of it I had forgotten; & these beautiful verses had again, as many a time before, the power to soothe my restlessness: but it was to you only I had purposed to recite them, though I could not *object* to Julia—how could I?—on ¦ the contrary, I could wish to have Both your dear & amiable Girls with & about me continually—I mean were my Time—which it is not—in my own hands: —— but if, as I afterwards conceived, you had the flattering to *me*, idea that for Julia to listen would be to Julia a lesson, I must explicitly declare that had such been

---

[4] William Mason (L. 1270 n. 20), parson and poet, 'Elegy IV, On the Death of a Lady' (1760). Of the two Gunning sisters famed for surpassing beauty, Maria (1733-60) had married on 5 March 1752 George William (1722-1809), 6th Earl of Coventry. After a brilliant but flitting career, she was 'attacked by consumption' dying on 1 October 1760 in her twenty-eighth year. 'Ten thousand persons were present at her funeral', states Horace Bleackley, in his biography of her sister *The Beautiful Duchess . . . Elizabeth Gunning, Duchess of Hamilton and Argyll* (1907), pp. 85-9.

This was the occasion of Mason's famous elegy ('The midnight clock has toll'd'), which Bleackley says 'remained a favourite classic in young ladies' seminaries, being recited by such celebrities as Fanny Burney'.

> Yes [Coventry] is dead. Attend the strain,
> Daughters of Albion! Ye that, light as air,
> So oft have tript in her fantastic train,
> With hearts as gay, and faces half as fair:
> For she was fair beyond your brightest bloom . . .

my intention, I should have repeated the Elegy in a very different manner, i.e., *simply* & *plainly.*

I think *Taught* Declamation belongs only to an Actress.

If you ask whether I practiced this rule with Alex,—I answer, No; nor would I, were he within my reach, with Dick. To a *male*, whatever gives courage, & helps Address, encreases his Consequence in Society, & his ease & happiness in himself. I have no time, till we meet, to say what I think upon this part of *education* for a *Female*. For myself, *si je me suis laissée allée* it was not from any *Study*—or *Design* —or *Imitation*—but from having read the poem with warm admiration till I had it by heart, & then repeating it, in the dead of sleepless Nights, so often, so collectedly, so *all to myself*, that I believe I must have caught every possible meaning of the Poet, not only in every sentiment, but in the appropriation of every word, so as to enable me to pronounce as I conceive him to have thought. This, namely entering into the Poem as if it had been the production of my own brain, gives to me an energy in repeating it that nearly electrifies me from the strong sense with which I enter into ˡ every line:— &, in reciting, by accident, all the latter part of it lately to Mrs. Lock, I saw her nearly transfixed by deep attention, joined to surprise & admiration, as this charming Elegy was quite new to her. I know you so susceptible of the same sensations, from your glowing delight in literary excellence, that I felt happy in the accidental power to give you pleasure. I am still awake to it myself, when Alexander recites some poetry that is new to me: & the more his energy, the more I enter into the spirit of his Authour,—& the more happily, for awhile, fall into forgetfulness of myself.—

Monday

I have much more to add to make this—I fear—Clear— but no faculty to go on, from the enormous weight of Letter writing now on my hands—& from not being, *egarée* by the continued absence & silence of Alex during these insurrections in France & storms on the sea—

So, put your own good head to work to *make* out all I *leave*

out, & you will be no loser, while I, in time, shall be a gainer.
& kiss your 4 Loves for me—& give my kind Comp^ts to Mr B.

Adieu, dearest Charlotte— ı

I have this moment been vexed by hearing that Mr. Barrett
has called—& would not wait to send up his name—O fie—

1284   [11 Bolton Street],
                                          25 March 1822

To Alexander d'Arblay

A.L. (Berg), 25 Mar. 1822
Double sheet 8vo   3 pp.   wafer
Addressed: a Monsieur / Monsieur Alexandre Piochard d'Arblay.
Edited by CFBt. *See* Textual Notes.

25th March. 1822
!!

Still no *Alex*!
And no *Letter*!—

What upon Earth is become of you? M. de Thuisy[1] offers
to carry Letters for me—I will once more enclose a few lines
to Mme de M[aisonneuve].

M. de Th. concluded you in England—so does Mme de
Maurville[2]—& La P^ss d'Henin & all send me politely kind reproaches for your not calling to take leave!—

Talma[3] scarcely could give a start more theatric than M. de

1284. [1] Jean-Baptiste-Charles de Goujon, 4th marquis de Thuisy (1751–1834),
who had married in 1780 Catherine-Philiberte-Françoise de Bérule (b. *c.* 1760),
by whom he had six children (see vii, L. 764 n. 8). Living in Richmond since their
emigration in 1792, the family was to return to France in 1825.

[2] The friend found so useful in Brussels in 1815 (see viii *passim*), Henriette-
Marguerite *née* Guinot de Soulignac (iii, L. 237 n. 9) was the widow of Jean-
Louis-Bernard Bidé de Maurville, an *émigré*, who, dying in London, was buried in
the parish of St. Pancras on 2 August 1796. He was related to the princesse
d'Hénin (v, L. 446 n. 23; and portrait, vi, *facing* p. 532).

[3] According to Madame de Maisonneuve's current letters (L. 1280 n. 12 and
L. 1282 n. 12), it was AA's enthusiasm for the arts, the theatre, poetry [and perhaps the freedom to write] that kept him in Paris through the winter.

Th. when he heard you were only at l'Hotel de Tours.[4] Oh Alex! what a waste, a wanton waste, of Present endearment of friendship—& of obviating Future endurance of ill will! for *be sure* if you go on thus *braving the World*, a time will come when Resentment will find its vent, in pouncing upon either your *Reputation*, your ¹ *happiness*, or your *Fame*— according to the openings your progress in life may make for the workings it may have you exposed to of *Scandal*, or *ill will*, or *criticism*.

But This mundane view apart, what pleasure, what enjoyment you lose in slighting kindness, & offending affection!

There is quite a cry against you in *Paris*: & *Here* it is only kept under by *my* assumed resignation! —— ——

Awake, awake, my Alex! *come*! or *Write*!

But beware of your *Sinecure*! The visitations of all monies that go unearned is now so severe that every old foundation is menaced by them: & *Residence* out of the country is a theme calling for ¹ Taxation among the Reformers in many a present cabal.

Some think you have entered into Politics, & are annoyed, if not detained—

others believe you to have lost your heart to some unattainable object, But most suppose you immersed in the oblivious Hocus Pocus ship of Mathematics.—

We are all here upon the Reduced system, from the stocks. Why do you neither come nor write your notions of things upon so important a crisis to us?—

If to Stay, *coute qui coute* be from any unknown cause essential to your Happiness, I will not interfere—

I point but the attendant dangers: If it be mere inertia, or unthinkingness—Rouse, Rouse! awake! awake!

And Come to your best Friend—

At all events w⟨rite⟩ for I am almost spent—

---

[4] *Le Nouveau Condocteur de l'Etranger à Paris en 1829* (15th edn., 1829) lists under *Hôtels garnis* (p. 12) le Grand Hôtel de Tours, 32, Notre-Dame-des-Victoires, a travel or coaching centre according to Hillairet, which must have been noisy and alive with its 'service de transports sur tous les points de France et des pays voisins'. Convenient for travellers, FBA may have thought, but in point of elegance and gentlemanly exclusiveness comparable to the gare du Nord or the Grand Centrals of the railway age.

1285   [11 Bolton Street,
                                        12] April 1822

To Lady Bedingfeld

L.S., printed in *The Jerningham Letters (1780-1843), being Excerpts from the Correspondence and Diaries of the Honourable Lady Jerningham and of her Daughter Lady Bedingfeld*, ed. Egerton Castle (2 vols., 1896), ii. 235-8.

Dear Madam,

Your Ladyship's so kind mention of me to my Niece[1] at so afflicting a period, gives me a spur irresistible to express at once my acknowledgements and my commiseration. Alas! how restless is woe! and That chiefly which is irremediable. But that every new deprivation is a new signal for new Preparation to Follow as it Leads—how could our Hearts endure unbroken,—or even our Heads underanged—such fatal blows to our earthly felicity?—I have felt very unwell with myself for not answering, long since, the charming Letter with which your ladyship honoured me on the subject of my amiable Charlotte; but I fancied my most acceptable answer would be waiting upon Lady Jerningham. And for that exertion I was spiriting myself up, when a new stroke to my peace, in the very sudden loss of my last Brother, Admiral Burney, checked all new efforts at social intercourse, and even deadened old ones. In a different class, and way of life, I might nearly repeat of this dear Brother what so eloquently your Ladyship

1285. [1] This is Lady Bedingfeld's reply (see L. 1253 n. 4) of 3 July 1821 to the letter (now lost) that FBA had sent her in May introducing CFBt, who was to set out with her family to Ghent for the summer. In this letter (Berg) Lady Bedingfeld had lamented the death 'in the prime of Life' of her brother William Charles Jerningham (1772-1820), 'the favorite playmate of my childhood the gay companion of my youth, & the friend of my riper years!' It is to these references to a lost brother that FBA, referring to the losses of her own brothers, CB Jr. and JB, draws from their best qualities 'amalgamated' a modest parallel.

The 'deeper . . . than brotherly privation' suffered by Lady Bedingfeld would have been the death in childbirth on 29 or 30 January 1822 of her eldest daughter Frances Charlotte (1796-1822), the wife since 2 June 1815 of William Henry Francis Petre (1793-1850), 11th Baron Petre.

For these deaths and the burial of William Charles Jerningham in the vault of the beautiful Roman Catholic Chapel attached to the Hall at Cossey, Norfolk, see the *Jerningham Letters*, ii. 175-9, 226-33.

writes of your own;[1] or, rather, to meet that character, so impressively drawn, I must *amalgamate* the best qualities of the two Brothers that within the last sad 4 years have gone before me. The yet deeper, however, than brotherly privation by which Your Ladyship has recently been wounded, had made me fear I had passed by the time for compliance, and that my projected visit would no longer be opportune: Charlotte however, filled with gratitude for your Ladyship's goodness to her, and partially persuaded of its extension to her Aunt, loves to suggest that Lady Jerningham may rather more than less require new attentions from new calamity. And if She can suppose that any from me would be seasonable, who can wonder she should desire I should hasten to mark my own Sense of obligation to your ladyship in seconding her? More fit, too, am I—and more ready to go to the house of mourning than of joy:—though I would struggle hard not to suffer that species of congeniality to mar your ladyship's filial design, in leading me to sadden, instead of seeking to chear, the Parent I see so dear to you. Such, therefore, as I now am, my *health* being no longer an obstacle, I cast wholly upon your Ladyship's decision, whether or not it be now too late to shew my willingness to avail myself of your encouragement and my vicinity. We could not want subjects of mutual interest while one to her so precious, and to me so animating, would always be at hand: and while my grateful recollections of the Chevalier Jerningham at Paris,[2] and of Mr. Edward Jerningham, the Poet, in England,[2] might afford many amusing details: and a source of conversation would always be open upon the Good, the Wise, the eloquent M. de Lally,[3] who, with a partiality the most flattering in copying for us his Cossey Album, indulgently inserted an

---

[2] Lady Bedingfeld's uncle Charles Jerningham (1742-1814), chevalier de Barfort, maréchal de camp (1784), chevalier de Malte and de St. Louis, a general in the French service, FBA had met in Paris (v, L. 529 n. 8 and pp. 368-9). His brother Edward (1727-1812), the poet, she had met in 1780 in Bath 'looking the gentlest of all dying Corydons' as he sang to his own accompaniment on the harp (*DL* i. 350-2); and in 1794 he had sent her his tragedy *The Siege of Berwick* (iii. 79). For his letters to his niece, see *Jerningham Letters, passim.*

[3] Related to the Dillons (see *Jerningham Letters*, i. 57, 221), Lally-Tolendal (i-viii *passim*) had spent the first period of his emigration with Sir William Jerningham (1736-1809) and his wife the Hon. Frances *née* Dillon (L. 1250 n. 2) at Cossey.

Envoi for Bookham. My Son, who is just returned from Paris, has frequently seen this excellent Statesman and accomplished Orator, who is now in peculiar good health; and he has enclosed for me, in a Letter written with all the warmth of heart that so singularly endears as well as embellishes his Genius, sundry of his latest and truly admirable Speeches. Alexander has made a tour in Switzerland last Summer and Autumn that has been equally, I think, beneficial to his health and his Mind. He has been so enchanted with the scenery, so regaled with the clear pure air, and so delighted by his intercourse with the Inhabitants, that he is returned an enthusiastic Mountaineer.

I beg leave to present my best compliments to Sir Richard, and have the honour to be, Dear Madam,

Your Ladyship's most obliged and Obed^t

F: d'Arblay.

April 1822.

1286   [11 Bolton Street,

post 28 April 1822]

To Mrs. Barrett

A.L.S. (Berg), Saturday
Double sheet 4to   4 pp.
Addressed: Mrs. Barrett
Dated in pencil, p. 1: 1822 (?)
Scribbling: p. 4.

Sat^y Night.

The kind attention of the excellent Archdeacon, & of dear amiable Mrs. Cambridge would draw from me another Letter to themselves but that I see their appreciation so like my own of the Interpretess they have chosen. Tell them, then, for me, my dear Charlotte, how sensibly I feel their saving me from any suspense or uneasiness upon this critical journey,[1] which

1286. [1] Possibly the journey of the Barretts to Boulogne for the summer, a clear statement on the causes and circumstances of which appears in L. 1287 and n. 2.

seems to me arranged in the best manner possible, & even so as to be—perchance—eventually productive of the greatest benefit. Supposing the local motives out of the question, I should still have believed such an experiment well worth trying. A note this evening from your dear Mother confirms the opening good account; & I feel persuaded that some how, or other how, my very true Friends will let me be informed of the arrival, & its result. How fervently I hope, & am inclined to believe it will be prosperous I can not—& I need not say.

My dear sister's kind solicitude that Alexander should make one in her Monday's party will certainly bring him to her. He is quite well enough for *that*, though the remains of his Cold are still too strong ! to make it prudent he should work at his discourse. And yet, though he is heated, & his nostrils are restlessly troublesome, & though the feverish part of his attack displays its exit upon his lips, Nose, & Chin, his recovery from the assault has been so rapid as to comfort me with the perfect assurance of his really & established renovated health. He caught this mischief by casting himself upon the Grass in Hyde Park, after a very long walk; &, forgetting he was not breathing the pure æther of the Mountains of Switzerland, permitting himself to drop asleep.—The seizure on the same Night was quite violent: it was moaned through, without a moment's respite for repose: & the next morning his pulse were above 100.—I prevailed with him, happily, to try James's powders—so often in earlier days his preservers —&, by small dozes every 4 Hours, he was not *better*, but *cured* on the second day. I mean as to *Fever*: but the *cold*, in various forms, lasts still, though without any symptom but that of demanding lengthened care. He is well enough, however, not to resist an invitation from my very old Friend, Sir William Pepys,[2] for dinner to-morrow. Pray tell my dear Marianne that that same good old friend made very kind enquiries about her when I last saw him. !

The Wedding re union of the two families to which Alex was invited was *previous* to the Ceremony. It was at Mrs. Angerstein's, where the Murray Grevilles & Lockes were

---

[2] FBA's old 'Blue' friend (L. 1239 n. 9), who resided at 11 Gloucester Place, Portman Square.

assembled *en masse.*[3] *After* the Ceremony, all parties separated. But—what is this hint of Weddings, & Wedding Plumes at Richmond?[4] my dearest Charlotte!—is there any hope of such an event as you glance at? If so, give me a small sketch of the outlines of Expectation,—it will much amuse & interest me to Colour & fill them up in the interval of incertitude.

How earnestly I hope those fears about the Mines may prove false!—yet — — *mine* join with the idea, in taking in the *whole* of this most unexpected change. So good they are, so wise, so piously philosophic, that, at all events, they will meet so as to counter-act any evil that is merely mundane. With Mr. Proby you have enamoured me.[5]—But — — give not too large Draughts of such praise to those who swallow it without any suspicion of its intoxicating qualities! *Your* praise, my Charlotta, is so sweet to Al[ex] that you must bestow it in small & measured dozes, not to make it enebriating. Kindness of encouragement is always good; but all beyond is precarious—& dangerous. The first pleasure over, & confidence confirmed—how soon does Arrogance & self-sufficiency mar any further improvement, from creating a reliance that no further effort is wanting, or labour worth while!—It is best to keep within the modesty of doubt, if only to preserve to Approbation its power of giving delight. From *me*, nevertheless, withhold nothing that marks the world's indulgence to him: to *me* it ˡ not only can do no harm, but it is warmth & Life.

Thank my dearest sister for her Note, which I have answered in my first page:—except, that I am far more *fit*, as well as *willing*, to come to her dear roof when she is only surrounded by her own, than when her circle is enlarged.

[3] The Lockes and the Grevilles (see L. 1280 n. 6 and *Locks of Norbury*, pp. 311–14).

[4] An allusion, conjecturally relating to MF, but lost with CFBt's letter.

[5] Doubtless the Revd. Charles Proby (*c.* 1771–1859), who had filled posts as chaplain to his cousin John Joshua Proby (1751–1828), 1st Earl of Carysfort (1789), ambassador to Berlin (1800), and later to George Spencer (1766–1840), 5th Duke of Marlborough, and also to the Baroness Seaforth (*c.* 1755–1829). Canon of Windsor (1814), he had held in addition three or four livings and had been appointed on 30 January 1818 as vicar of the New Church at Twickenham, where he was to remain for 41 years (Cobbett, *Memorials of Twickenham, passim*).

I shall send this by the earliest Monday's post, that my dear sister may know her favoured Godson will surely attend her.

God bless you, my dearest Charlotta—

ever yours most affec^{ly}

F d'Ay—

My love to my dear little Girls—I hope to see a blooming proof of their early hours written on their Cheeks on my next visit. Best Regards to Mr. Barrett.

May I request my kind Charlotta to make Alex *take a place* for one o'clock on Tuesday—as he has a 5 o'clock Dinner for the play in Gloucester place[6]—2 miles hence? he will else return on foot, with his Cold, inflamed anew. He is engaged to Mrs. M. Hoare & a dress party at 5.[7]—

Your intimation about Dr. Andrews,[8] &c—involves all my best views & wishes.—

1287 [11 Bolton Street],
7 May 1822

To Esther (Burney) Burney

A.L.S. (Berg), 7 May 1822
Double sheet 4to   4 pp.   *pmk* 9 MY .822   red seal
Addressed: Mrs. Burney, / Lark Hall Place, / near Bath.
Endorsed by EBB: May 11th 1822
Docketed: S. 817

1822. 7th May.

O Yes—my dear*est* Esther, the very idea of again so soon

---

[6] Probably private theatricals (cf. n. 2) at the home of W. W. Pepys.
[7] At the home of Merrik Hoare, 31 York Place, for which see Hyde, Plate *facing* p. 174.
[8] The Revd. Gerrard Andrewes (L. 1203 n. 2), formerly rector at Mickleham (v. 16, 201), collated to St. James's, Piccadilly (1802), was to serve for one year (1820-1) as vicar of Great Bookham, succeeding the d'Arblays' old friend the Revd. Samuel Cooke (L. 1182 n. 6), who had died on 29 March 1820. Mural tablets to both clergymen are to be seen in the parish church of St. Nicholas, Great Bookham. See further, L. 1363 and n. 7.

embracing you fills me with tender joy.[1] I am glad you will write again as to the exact period, first, that I may be free from all entanglements, even of the kindest Friendship, & 2dly that my true welcome may escape that hurry of surprize that—for so long a time—utterly disorders me. Charlotte only is discomfitted, in the fear she shall be gone, or going to Brighton, as her time is at the disposal of poor Clement, who is still far from well, & purposes passing his next vacation at the sea side. However, she flatters herself she may find you at her return. The Barretts—malheureusement—spend their summers abroad, & will go the very instant they can let their House at Richmond. 'Tis a new speculation which they have adopted, to make their Rent pay for their travels. It succeeded last year, & they think will this.[2] Oh how shall we both miss the cordial pleasure with which our James would have seen us once more re-united!—M^{rs} Ad^l [Burney], at first hearing your plan, earnestly hoped you would spend a week or so with Her: but now—she is employed in repairing her house, & is forced to sleep herself in an attic. Our Mrs. Lock, I cannot doubt, will make a point of seeing you at Eliot Vale, if her Grand Children are not occupying her single Spare *Room*

1287. [1] EBB was to arrive at the end of June (see L. 1288).

[2] Involved in these expedients were doubtless reports from the lessee of Barrett's sugar plantations in Jamaica (see ix, L. 993 n. 9), just such a letter as that of 12 July 1824 (Eg. 3708), wherein the tenant promised a bill of exchange for 'the balance so long due to you for last year's rent'. To meet these arrears he had shipped '10 Hogsheads of my best sugar' but had to plead indulgence for 'the present year's rent', 'for such has been my miserable crop, and the state of the sugar market, that the common expences of the estate will not be defrayed but of its proceeds'. See further, Mrs. Broome's letter (Eg. 3693, ff. 99–100b) of a few years later [*post* 4 May 1826): 'Barrett does not receive his remittances from the West Indies—& cannot get any employment in England, so he says.' In 1829 there was still nothing but 'bad Jamaica news' (see CFBt's letter, of 12 April to CBFB, Eg. 3702A, ff. 188–9b): 'I shall no doubt be able to meet with some little girls to educate to make out our income. Mrs. Cambridge has some inquiries on foot.'

Barrett's situation was not unique. See ix, L. 993 n. 9 and S. H. Romilly, *Letters to 'Ivy' from the first Earl of Dudley* (1905), p. 347. In a letter of [19 February 1830] the Earl spoke of 'complete ruin' in the West Indies. One of his friends 'who in one good year netted ninety thousand pounds, will hardly pay his expenses'.

In the face of these difficulties Barrett preferred to rent or sub-let his dwelling in Richmond and reside abroad, where living expenses were less. An additional advantage with a growing family was the relative cheapness on the Continent of masters in languages, music, drawing, painting, and dancing. CFBt herself took lessons in painting at Ghent (see her notebooks, Eg. 3706D).

& *Closet*, And why do you not number *Greenwich*[3] with your nomenclature of Richmond, London & Brightwell?[3]— I wish you to make the most chearing *Voyage* possible. I think it may essentially benefit, as well as affectionately re-create you. And to *me* it will do a good that comes warm to my heart every time I look forward to it. I have so many things to answer in your ǀ late *generous* Letters, that I know not with which to begin—*Caroline* I have not seen—though I invited her & her Sister to accompany the Brother hither to tea at any time they would appoint.[4] He told me he was going to take Caroline to Cambridge—but would bring her before the sea voyage. I must reserve till we meet this too long subject of discourse & discussion & narration.

———

I grieve sincerely for poor Sansom[5]—who would have been *in heaven* to have seen you!—He never recovered the loss of our Brother: he seemed to regard it as his *End*, & to struggle no longer for life. His faithful & devoted wife, & good son,[5] were his never failing aids, Comforters, & consolers: but they were quite inadequate to revive the desire of living. Existence had literally lost all charm for him.—

Poor Sarah Payne is fallen into a dreadful state of ill health, lately, & is under the immediate direction of Mr. Thomas & Dr. Bailey.[6] Her stomach has some serious & unknown seizure, that is replete with suffering, & demands incessant attention, or menaces fatal consequences!—Poor Girl—I am truly sorry—not only that she was my Brother's darling, but that she is really, in all I see of her, as amiable as she is cultivated & *spirituelle*. A more improved young person I never saw— & to me she shews an enthusiasm of affection that must be winning were she otherwise.

---

[3] At Croom's Hill, Greenwich, home of CPB; and the rectory, Brightwell, Berkshire, where EBB's son the Revd. Richard Allen Burney (L. 1180 n. 18) and his family resided, along with two of his aunts.

[4] See L. 1282 n. 2.

[5] James Sansom (L. 1191 n. 16). The Computer File Index shows a James Sansom bapt. 21 October 1803 at St. Andrew, Holborn, possibly the son.

[6] The surgeon Honoratus Leigh Thomas (L. 1233 n. 4) and Matthew Baillie (L. 1232 n. 14), M.D.

Your history of Martin makes me shudder[7]—The tale—not exactly such as you write—had been communicated to me, *whether I would or not,* by a side wind, by Mr. Sansom, 2 years ago: but not so absolutely as to impede some hope it was a rumour: I never heard it again named till since the Death of our dear James—& then by Cha[s] Parr—who concluded I knew it—but charged me not to divulge his having acted from that persuasion. I have no inclination, God knows, to propagate so fearful a history! The young man himself, the Mother, & the Sister, evidently & earnestly desire I should not be informed of it. They not only avoid all allusion to any such event, but take the utmost pains to keep all that might lead to the subject far afield. Alas—this accounts too well for the excess of poor Martin's grief—which was nearly frantic—& threw him into a severe illness—from which he is not yet recovered.

I am quite ashamed that my Alex should join in this unacountable perversity & negligence you so justly censure in Richard of India. Was it from foresight & anticipation I conceived those dolourous complaints & *wonderments* of my poor Sir Hugh upon the new ways of the Rising Generation?[8] I struggle in vain to procure any amendment. All those attentions, they say, are gone bye—quite fogrum—& rather the marks of a debasing obsequiousness, than of a general polish! —I have the less chance of reform, because, such as he is, Alexander is admired, courted, sought, carressed, in a manner that is almost incredible!—

I shall be heartily glad of some tydings from you of our sister Sarah Harriet;[9] not a line has she written me from Cheltenham, though I had begged earnestly some news of her health. She has her share of this rising generation, for she likes to write or to let it alone; to visit, or to drop the Ceremony, as well from impulse & the humour of the day, as her

---

[7] For Martin Burney's secret marriage, see L. 1271 n. 4.

[8] See *Camilla,* I. i.

[9] SHB had accompanied her charge Charlotte Ann Gregor (L. 1249 n. 7), who had been ordered by Dr. Paris (L. 1276 n. 8) to Cheltenham for her health. See SHB's letter (Barrett, Eg. 3700A, ff. 146-7) to Mrs. Broome, 17 March 1822.

dutiful nephews & nieces. Through Miss Wilbraham,[10] however, I have heard she is pretty well, & I was as glad as if she
had been *gooder*, though I not so thankful. If you see her, tell
her that her very pleasing pupil could not, by her manners,
have done more honour to Mme de Genlis.[11]

I thank God my dear Alex's health is amazingly invigorated:
& in the midst of his absences & deficiencies & excentricities,
he has made, & preached, a sermon, at Twickenham, that
won all hearts, & sent a new & eager congregation thither the
following Sunday in the hope to hear him.[12]—I, also, am
proud of your Mitred visit.[13] Have you lost Miss Hayes?[14]—
I am sorry Richard the Reverend did not close with Charles
Parr —— How true is all you say of Chesington![15] 'twas
indeed a Paradise to us All. Our incomparable Daddy Crisp
could not have loved a progeny of his own more zealously.—
I am glad you will bring *Emily*,[16] who deserves a frolic, &

[10] Anna Wilbraham (L. 1191 n. 7), a friend SHB had made 'for life' when in
the years 1805–7 she served as governess at Delamere Lodge, Cheshire.

[11] FB had met the famous governess at the Court of Queen Charlotte in 1785
(*DL* ii. 288–9, and *passim*) and had read many of her well-known works on education. See also i. 158 and *passim*.

[12] At Twickenham Chapel (L. 1190 n. 2) at the invitation of Archdeacon
Cambridge (L. 1190 n. 2), whose approbation of AA's preaching was conveyed
to FBA's old friend, John Fisher (L. 1180 n. 3), Bishop of Salisbury, in the manner described by CFBt in an undated letter (Barrett, Eg. 3702A ff. 43–6) to FBA:

The other day I drank tea at Twickenham & met the Bishop of Salisbury
—the Archdeacon said 'Mrs. Barrett will join with me in thanking your Lordship for the kindness you have shown to Mr d'Arblay—Ah, said the Bishop in
a tone of great pleasure, 'is he a relation of yours—he is very well, he was
with us last sunday'—The Archdeacon said that Alexander had preached
several times lately, for him, & that he handled his subjects in so striking &
fine a manner, & wrote with such force & precision as w^d make him a very
eminent & popular & useful preacher if he were to obtain a lectureship in one
of the London churches— . . .' 'He has had no employment yet I believe?'
asked the Bishop—'I have mentioned him to the Bishop of London'—'Aye'
said the Archdeacon I know you have, & Madame d'Arblay & I are very much
obliged to you for it. he will do honour to your recommendation I will answer
for it'—'and so on, & so on, & so on.'

Two years were yet to pass, however, before 'employment' was at length found.

[13] Evidently, as it later appears (L. 1293), a visit from Shute Barrington (1734–
1826), Bishop of Llandaff (1769), of Salisbury (1782), of Durham (1791), a
friend both of CB and CB Jr.

[14] Anna Maria Eyre *formerly* Hayes (L. 1282 n. 24).

[15] See *HFB*, pp. 17–18 and *passim*.

[16] EBB's youngest daughter Amelia (i, p. lxix), now aged 30.

will, I hope, encrease your comfort, as *two* can go any where. —*Certainly* I have had Sarah P[ayne]'s Husband with her to Tea here, & *twice*: but Sarah herself many times more, for, as I know him not, & have no *ready-mounted* spirits, it is a great exertion to me to admit him. I hope he is a good & tender husband. I have found the 2ᵈ Letter from our sweet Mother.[17]

Lady Templetown—after nearly a year of hopeless illness & entire confinement to her Room & her Bed Gown—This morning made me a visit!—& last week I drank tea with Her & Mrs. Lock *en trio*![18] So never Despair of Recovery while there is yet Life. All you say of caution about Caroline, &c, I so entirely coincide in, that I am now going—reluctantly to Burn all your Letters about her! Is that heroic? Heaven bless you, my dear*est* Esther! Yours most affec^ly

F d'Ay ⌐

All you say of Miss Wood *replies* to the lovely promise of her lovely Countenance.[19] I wish you would send me better news of poor Sophy.

1288   [11 Bolton Street, 24–25 June 1822]

To Mrs. Barrett

A.L. (Berg), —Tuesday
Double sheet 4to   3 pp.   *pmks* Piccadilly 25 JU 1822   wafer
Addressed: Mrs. Barrett, / Henry Barrett's Esq. / Richmond / Surry.

To resist so kind a proposal of dear Mrs. Cambridge, & that with the full persuasion of the Good as well as pleasure that would accrue from accepting it, is *pas mal* severe—
But my sweet Charlotte will feel & therefore will explain

---

[17] See also L. 1282, n. 26.

[18] Of Lady Templetown's undated social notes and invitations, FBA had saved twenty-four (Berg) but, lacking dates, they furnish little confirmation of fixed events.

[19] See L. 1200 n. 10.

for me, that to take 4 days from a poor 14 arranged for me by my dear sister Burney,[1] who deferred to the last her visit to *town* on my account, would so counter act all comfort, from a sense of apparent *mismanagement* at least, that neither the cherished society nor balmy air of Twickenham, & its salubrious vicinity, could either brace or heal an Invalid who should thus be mentally ill at ease. —— ——

Speak all this for me, with my best thanks & Regrets, I entreat—& take them, & *spread* them to my dear Sister most sincerely.

It would be entirely convenient to me to receive at this moment of my sister's stay the little Girl of 13[2] who is recommended by you & Marianne for *one Week* from the day she can come, i.e. to-morrow, or as soon as possible afterwards.

I shall feed—pay journées—a 2^s & 6^d for the week *certain*—n'est ce pas? |

How sorry I am—how truly sorry for poor Lady Bedingfeld! What accumulated misfortunes![3]—When I conceive her to be visible, if I am only tolerably able, I shall endeavour to *tell* her my deep concern—as she is now so nearly my neighbour. —

I am very considerably better—& taking much asses milk very successfully—

1288. [1] EBB's long-planned visit to Bolton Street and to Richmond was to take place in early July (Ll. 1289, 1293). At this time CFBt found her 'Aunt Burney', now 72 years of age, 'in excellent health & spirits, takes long walks without fatigue, puns & jokes, & enters into all our little intrigues, & is as Mama says, one of the youngest in our party'. 'Amelia is all gentle placidity—& plays beautifully on the piano forte'. See letter of [July or August 1822] to FBA (Barrett, Eg. 3702, ff. 43-6).

[2] The little servant girl of 13 sent by CFBt from Richmond in the absence presumably of Elizabeth Ramsay or her under-servant and denominated by FBA (L. 1289) Ann 'Shipeley' is probably the 'little Stapley' who, 'very quiet, civil, and slow as a snail' was later employed by Mrs. Broome. See CFBt's letter (Berg) of 16 January [1825] to her husband. Ann may have been Marianne (b. 21 October 1810), daughter of Samuel Stapley (*c.* 1768-1838) and his wife Phyllis (*c.* 1773-1825), who emerge in the parish registers of Richmond.

[3] In addition to the loss of her brother William Charles Jerningham and of her eldest daughter Lady Petre (L. 1285 n. 1), Lady Bedingfeld had now to mourn the untimely deaths of a second brother Edward (L. 1250 n. 2), who had died on 29 May, and as well, his wife Emily *née* Middleton (ibid.), who survived him by a month. The deaths were caused by erysipelas, which the wife first contracted, communicating it to her husband and to a nurse, both of whom died before she succumbed. For Lady Bedingfeld's return to the house of mourning on Bolton Row, see *Jerningham Letters*, ii. 242-54.

Thank my dear Archdeacon for his extreme kindness & goodness to his *Pupil,*[4] who recorded it all with such beaming pleasure!—

I thought I had *never* seen Clement wear a better *mine*—so great an improvement of looks since I had last parted from him I have rarely witnessed. ⟨*Much*⟩ I wish Mrs. *Disney* may be definitive?[5] There *was* a Mrs. Disney of Ireland that my darling sister Phillips loved to her heart[6]—Is this likely to be *Her*?—

God bless you my sweet girl—

I have *no news* yet from Poor Ramsay—& am much astonished—Her 6 weeks furlough will end the 5th I think of July—How happy should she have yielded to my representations to her Father![7]—yet I fear her silence—& this last weakening illness shews me more than ever | her insufficiency against such attacks, with all my real & great regard for her & her true attachment—

Tuesday morning

Pray tell dr Mrs Cambridge I am really & truly very sorry—though much *less* than if she were alone—i.e. earlier—But I *would* have accepted, *neanmoins*, had I been able.

[4] Presumably AA, whom Archdeacon Cambridge invited to conduct services in Twickenham Chapel (L. 1190 n. 2) and probably advised or instructed as well.

[5] Conjecturally Sophia *née* Disney-Ffytche, who on 22 September 1802 had married her cousin german John Disney of the Hyde (1779–1857), of Ingatestone, Essex, barrister-at-law. Having added to an inherited collection of classical antiquities, he catalogued them (see *DNB*) and later bequeathed them to the University of Cambridge, where they now form 'one of the principal sections of the Fitzwilliam Museum'. Their son Edgar (b. 22 December 1810) was of the age to require a tutor, a post that Clement, according to CFBt, was hopeful of obtaining.

[6] The name Disney recalled to FBA Jane *née* Brabazon (iii, L. 222 n. 20 and iv *passim*) of Mornington, Co. Meath, who had married on 22 November 1798 the Revd. Robert Disney (*c.* 1769–1832), curate of St. Mark's, Dublin (1807), of Glasnevin (1809), and Prebendary of Cloyne (1809). See also *FB & the Burneys, passim.*

[7] Robert Ramsay (*c.* 1753–1843) of Ilfracombe (L. 1182 n. 3 and x *passim*).

1289   [11 Bolton Street,
                                             4 July 1822]
To Mrs. Barrett

A.L.S. (Berg), Thursday
Double sheet 8vo   4 pp.   *pmks* Piccadilly 4 JY 1822   wafer
Addressed: Mrs. Barrett / at Henry Barrett's Esq / Richmond / Surry.

                                             Thursday—
Very vexed am I to miss you, my sweet Charlotta,[1]—yet
the ascertained 3 Months go further to lighten an always
heavy Heart than could have been effected by most things.
Few things, indeed, are even equally precious to me with my
dear Charlotta's society.

Alex is almost *non compos* that preparations unavoidable
for a visit to the Baronness de Rothe,[2] near Dorking, which is
to take place to-morrow morning, impede his doing his best
to impede *you* in your own preparations to day: but chancing
to have left his arrangements to the last moment, he is compelled to leave *your's* unobstructed:—& this he laments the
more as such a circumstance never before occurred to him.
Only yesterday, he was sure he could bring Richmond into
his calculations — — but I finding that, by some odd accident, he had not a single article ready for his excursion, nor
any appointments fixt with the ladies he is to accompany, he
is forced, at this instant, to be flying from Holbourn to Portland Place, & from Fleet Street to Dorset Square, for Commands from the Fair, & purchases from the — — not *Foul*,
but, probably, *Brown*. And you can conceive nothing like his
indignation that all this did not *come done*, nor his astonishment that it cuts I short his real & most genuine intention &
wish to shake hands with his delightful & dearest Cousin—

Prosperous be your expedition, my sweet Charlotta—in
the autumn I hope to join you & your beloved Mother—

1289. [1] The Barretts were to leave shortly for the Continent, their address for
the summer and autumn, No. 93, Place d'Alton, Boulogne.
    [2] Charlotte Julia *née* Campbell (*c.* 1770-1846), who had married in 1798
as his second wife George William Evelyn-Leslie (1768-1817), 11th Earl of
Rothes (1810), whose residence was Juniper Hill (iv *passim*), on the outskirts of
Mickleham. See also L. 1218 n. 1.

whom I now earnestly desire should be of your Boulogne
party, escorted by Clement—

My kindest remembrance to Mr. Barrett—Marianne &
Julia & Hetty—God bless you my Charlotta—

I mean—when able to go forth, to make personal enquiries
after poor L^y Bedingfeld, should she still be my neighbour
— —

The little ann Shipeley[3] did very well I I sent a Note to my
dear Sister by her this afternoon—My sister Burney is well,
& full of engagements[4]—With *Hope* I look forward to your
return, my affectionate dear Girl—tenderly I love you—

F. d'Ay

1290   11 Bolton Street,
                              15 August 1822

To Lady Anne Murray

A.L.S. draft (Brigham Young University Library), 15 Aug. 1822
Single sheet 8vo   1 p.   [*the cover is missing*]
Docketed, p. 1: ⌈ Fanny Burney ⌉

I have long been internally persuaded that to personal kindness, & a wish to procure me pleasure, I have owed the representations of my friends that Lady Murray desired to renew
an Acquaintance of her Ladyship's Childhood,[1] with one yet

---

[3] See L. 1288 n. 2.   [4] Cf. L. 1288 n. 1.

1290. [1] Anne Elizabeth Cholmley Phipps (1788–1848), the daughter of Constan-
tine John Phipps (1744–92), 2nd Baron Mulgrave (I. 1775), and his 2nd wife
(1787) Anne Elizabeth *née* Cholmley (1769–88), who had died at the age of 20
after giving birth to this her first child. The death of the young wife in childbirth
had made something of a stir at the time and great sympathy was felt not only for
Lord Mulgrave, her husband, but also for her father Nathaniel Cholmley (1721–
91), M.P. (1756–74), and for her stepmother Cholmley's 3rd wife, Anne Jesse
(b. *c.* 1750), the daughter of Leonard Smelt (1719–1800), Sub-Governor to the
Princes (i *passim*; and *DL* ii *passim*). A favourite with the Smelts, FB, after leaving the Court, had visited Mr. Smelt and his daughter at Kew in 1791 (i. 94),
when the orphaned child in question was only 3 years old but seems not to have
seen her since.

In 1807, at the age of 19, Miss Phipps had married Sir John Murray (1768–
1827), 8th Baronet (1811), and was living on Wimpole Street. For the renewal
of these old associations, see further, L. 1295.

more changed by Unhappiness even than by Years, since the period in which she witnessed the dawning promise of all that might be expected from the Daughter of the late Lady Mulgrave: I must not enlarge here upon what I have been told of the fruition of that opening; I must only beg that if my friends have not been mistaken, & if that kind desire still subsists, I may cast wholly upon Lady Murray an appointment that will give me an opportunity of offering my very sincere acknowledgements for such long & persevering partiality.

F. B. d'Arblay.

15. Aug^st 1822—
11. Bolton St. Berkely Square

1291   11 Bolton Street,
                                              21 August 1822

To Mrs. Broome & Marianne Francis

A.L.S. (Berg), 21 Aug. 1822
Double sheet 8vo   4 pp.   *pmks* P.P. / Piccadilly 22 AU 1822
wafer
Addressed: Mrs. Broome / under the Hill / Richmond / Surry. / or Miss Francis.

Bolton St
21st Aug^st 1822.

I am very uneasy now for News of my dearest Sister—or rather of poor Clement—which is Her & Him in one at this moment.[1] I write to beg intelligence, & entreat my dear Marianne to bestow it upon me, if—as I hope,—the Brighton excursion has at last taken place.

I was much obliged by the recommendation of the tidy

1291. [1] According to CFBt, Mrs. Broome had given up her comfortable house in Richmond 'to fall in with Clement's plans and was now spending £50 a year for Sea Lodging in Brighton'; and MF agreed that the care of the semi-invalid was 'hard on Mama'. See CFBt's letters of 1821 in the Pink Letter Book, Eg. 7306D.

& pretty young Jane. I only regret she could not stay till I was settled. I have taken a Damsel from next door now to remain with me till that period.

Alex has heard twice & most kindly from the good Archdeacon, & once from Mrs. Baker, since Twickenham Meadows were relinquished.[2] |

Till I know where you are, & how dear Clement goes on, I will add no more, except in answer to your kind solicitude for my health, to assure you I am as well as I have any reason ever to expect being in this World. My Cough is gone, my breast is healed & quiet, & my head free, just now, from those alarming attacks that threatened frightful abruptness of assault. I walk out constantly, & admit old friends. | I must finish with a line of what I have much at heart to my dear Marianne: I had begged her to spare me the chagrin of a visit from Mr. Wilberforce in my *absence*:[3] but not to impede his visit on my *return*: nevertheless he has never called—

Tell me, dear Girl, has there been some misunderstanding? & may I hope for the comfort & honour & happiness of seeing him yet?—some affairs keep m[e] at this time in town: I shall go to *Mrs* Lock when at liberty. Alex is well, & busy | just now in some mathematical — — labours, I was going to say, but pleasures would be his own word. I have a kind Letter from dearest Charlotta from Boulogne—adieu —dear Sister.

> dear Niece—
> ever y^{rs}
> F d Ay

Sarah Harriet is going to Cheshire to Crewe Hall[4] — — Sister Burney & her's are well & returned to Bath.

---

[2] FBA's visit, relinquished in late June (L. 1289).

[3] From 1813 MF was often a guest for weeks at a time in the home of the Wilberforces at Kensington Gore, where to attend the Bible Society, to read religious tracts, and to engage actively in all possible charities made the order of the day. There she had met, among other members of the Clapham sect, Hannah More, 'who is the greatest darling I ever knew. Fat, & in mourning: eyes, more brilliant & penetrating than any I ever saw—quiet & full of humility, but lively & energetic, & warm in all her feelings & expressions of them; kind, sweet, & encouraging in her manners to a very attractive degree' (MF to CFBt, 2 July 1813, Eg. 3704A, ff. 97–8b).

[4] This seemed to be the forerunner of 'great news' concerning SHB. As Fanny

[11 Bolton Street,
c. 21 August 1822]

To Mrs. Locke

A.L. (Berg), Monday
Double sheet 8vo   4 pp.

Will This billet also meet a shake hand on the road—from that dear hand whose every scrap I welcome?—I should not, however, now write again, but that you desire to know my *hour* of arrival, & that I am just able to give it. —— —

We are to start from Kensington Palace at one[1]—& the Princess says the drive will be an hour, & that Her Carriage will call for me at 4—to bring me to my own door, with her august self, by 5, here to deposit me.

Could I, my dearest Friend, propose remaining, & leaving *her to her Carriage*, when most flatteringly she talks of our two Tête à Tête ǀ *Chatteries* in our to & fro' excursion?

I could not have done so by Lady Templetown, on any of the occasions when she has proposed giving me this indulgence.[2]

Raper would inform CFBt, 'Lord Crewe had been desirous of Miss Burney's taking charge of his grandchildren who are wards in Chancery, & the Master, Mr Courtney has nominated her to the care of them. She is to have a house in Park Street kept up for her, they are placed under her control quite independently of Lord Crewe & they are to have a Swiss governess who is to be under her direction & who will undertake all the drudgery of education, walk out with them, &c. The salary for Aunt Sarah . . . will be 300£ a year. . . .

'I am truly rejoiced at so comfortable & happy a prospect for this poor soul & consider it as quite providential in her present situation. She is at this moment on a visit at Crewe Hall, making acquaintance with her young charges. If she does not tire of the job & quarrel with the children it will be a provision for life because an annuity would certainly be settled on her after they grow up.' See CFBt's copy of her letter of 14 September [1822] to her mother (CBFB) in the Pink Letter Book (Eg. 3706D, ff. 42-4b; and for a copy of her reply to her informant, ibid., ff. 45-8b): 'The present prospects of poor dear Aunt Sarah [are] better than any she has ever had. . . . Having a french bonne under her direction & being placed with these young people on so independent a footing I think she will preserve her liking for them & with it her good humour & all the charms of manner & conversation which make her so pleasing when pleased.'

1292. [1] In a note (Berg) of [Wednesday] 21 August [1822] the Princess Sophia had proposed an excursion to Blackheath. 'Is Mrs Locke at Eliot Vale & w^d you like visiting her to morrow? Thursday? If so I will send the Carriage to fetch you & bring you ⟨here⟩ by one o'clock.'
[2] For a recent drive to Eliot Vale with Lady Templetown, see L. 1287.

I should think it copying my own Mr. Brangton,[3] in making *some use of a Lord's acquaintance* if one borrows his Coach'.

I hope, therefore, my sweet Amine will entice you back again to Woodlands till the further day in the week that you will name for my residence. And if my dearest Friend will not be fatigued with so many billets too much to write me one word—

Month
    or   at a *spell* |
Fortnight

it would accommodate some of my arrangements to know the same to-morrow—

& be really & truly

to me of equal convenience, & since I should not *lose* a day either way, of equal Agreeability—

Shall I close this Note without telling you the wonderful news that the King has lately made mention of me, *kind* mention? and desired I might be told the same? Tell my Amine to store this for obtaining another dear Evening visit during my stay.——

And if the Enquiry be not sufficient—she may, *Then* add That *His M.* added he would have M^e d'A know he had not forgotten her, for he considered her as a most agreeable Creature! —— ——

If This won't do for *2 Evenings*, I think my | Amine must be *extravagant*, for if she tells it half in half, œconomically, it will surely be irresistible.

Seriously, though, however I am amazed, & led to smile, I am really grateful, & *very* grateful to find all parts of the Family so favourably disposed to one whose devoirs, while in place, were exclusively consecrated to *one* of it. It is, *in serious*, a comfort & an Honour—and—&—A Hope— hereafter, for my Alex—

Monday Morn^g

[3] 'Goodness, then,' cried young Branghton, [since 'Miss has danced with a Lord'] 'if I was Miss, if I would not make free with his Lordship's coach to take me to town.'

'Why ay,' said the father, 'there would be some sense in that; that would be making some use of a Lord's acquaintance, for it would save us coach-hire.'

'Lord, Miss,' cried Polly, 'I wish you would, for I should like of all things to ride in a coronet coach' (*Evalina*, ii, Letter xxiii).

1293 [11 Bolton Street,
28 August]–7 September 1822

To Esther (Burney) Burney

A.L.S. (Berg), —7 Sept. 1822
Double sheet 4to 4 pp. *pmk* 7 SE .822 wafer
Addressed: Mrs. Burney, / Lark Hall place, / near Bath.
Endorsed by EBB: answered by a parcel / Sep—13—1822—and
an certificate / of the burial of / the Genl d'Arblay
Scribbling, p. 4
Edited, possibly by CFBt. *See* Textual Notes.

Long I thought your silence, my dearest Esther, but that
was *nothing* at this time, since I was under no doubts or uneasiness, as various means found me out to tell me of your
general health & proceedings—nothing, therefore, was the
silence, compared with my loss of my dear Hetty's sight &
society, so chearing & so endearing to me. But how shall I
thank you enough for the last words of your Letter?—that
you do not despair of renewing to me—& to yourself &
others—that gratification I have found so beneficial as well
as *recreative?*—for I know the pleasure I shall impart to you
when I say that I missed you so much, & not alone for all I
saw of you,—which I thought but scanty,—but for the enlivening feel of daily *expecting*, daily knowing I *might* perhaps welcome you, that upon your departure I found my
seclusion, in the absences of my Alexander, had lost its
absorbing powers, & I began to *require*, & even *wish* for
social intercourse: so that it seems as if your regretted 'aimable et douce violence' had operated according to your desire
magnetically:—& since I lost you, I have so far put ajar my
almost hermetically closed doors, as to see some one, either
Morning or Evening, nearly every day. The approbation of
Alexander you need not doubt, nor his readiness to under-
write your sentence That 'I *might as well go to Fetter Lane
as*' &c.—I will give you an account of the persons this new
effort has put on my little list when I have done ¹ with more
interesting family matters,—if then room remain. To begin
with what is uppermost with me, & much uppermost at this

369

moment, Mrs. Sandford,[1]—I am truly anxious for a more calming account of her, & I beg you, my dear Esther, to let me have some news of that valuable & super-amiable person, as soon as conveniently you can — — unless, indeed, which God forbid! there is any thing of an alarming & critical nature, which would put me into a painful suspense too afflicting to hear without frequent communication—which I could not exact in such a case, where every one would have still more to tremble for the event than myself, sincerely & even heavily as I should feel it—for round & around we may all look ere we see so sweet a Character; & I only place you all before me because you are within her immediate spell; for I doubt who—except Mr. Sandford himself,[1]—would have loved her more, had she been within my reach.

If this part of your Letter filled me with concern & uneasiness, another part acted the very reverse by me; your account of my Lord BP. of Durham is the most exhilarating that I ever read.[2] There, indeed, is Age desirable, There, where it is healthy, benevolent, & chearful, as well as honourable & venerable. Such was it, erst, with my revered Mrs. Delany,[2] whom I have heard Mr. Burke call the *Pattern* to shew us what was high breeding & Goodness in former times. Your Bishop must be her Companion as the Male Model for the same representation. I very sincerely am sorry at the internal documents you are forced to darken your Picture with, which, else, would be All of a congratulatory description for our dear Divine. I was pleased to see his name coupled to a very good Subscription, for a Country Church, in favour of the famished Irish.[3]

1293. [1] This is the cousin Rebecca or 'Becky' (*ED* ii *passim*), whose kindness along with the helpfulness of her husband the surgeon William Sandford (i, p. lxxv) of Worcester are constant factors in the life-histories of EBB and her family.

[2] Shute Barrington (L. 1287 n. 13); and for FBA's recollections of the attractive old age of Mrs. Delany, and Burke's references to her, see *Memoirs* ii. 300–15, 367–76, 396–8; iii. 45–57, 103–5.

[3] With the heavy and incessant rains of the year 1821 potato crops had rotted in the ground in Ireland and before May 1822 whole provinces were 'in a state of actual starvation'. Relief included collections made in parish churches throughout England and long lists of contributors, printed by *The Times*, included for 9 July, Brightwell, Berks., 'per Rev. R. Burney £10. 0. 0; for the 13th', Twickenham

‹———›

Since I began this Letter—now 10 days are passed, & I hope no news is good of dear Mrs. Sandford, whom I will now conclude recovering. I have had a visit *pour prendre Cogée* of Fanny, previously to her sea side expedition with Mr. & Mrs. H. Russel.[4] She no longer looks so bright & plump as at her first return from Norfolk, neither so wan nor meagre as ere it took place. Her spirits seem never failing.

‹———›

My latest account of poor Bridal Sarah are again ameliorated. The *Groom* called, & told me he had just left her at Sand place,[5] & better: & I grieve to see much hesitation in removing her to the Continent, whither Mrs. Burney alone ought to accompany her, since her state is so precarious, & so alarmingly menaced by 3 medical men: but as she is now better, *convenience* is listened to, which is all against the excursion —— —— alas, how may its utmost power be unavailing for consolation should the poor thing be the victim to non-observance of medical advice! I uttered this aloud—but the young man said *another year* he might be able to go himself: I told him this was dangerous procrastination—&c—he

Chapel, Rev. Archdeacon Cambridge, £30. 11. 0; St. Martin-in-the-Fields, Rev. Archdeacon Pott £378. 15. 10; and for the 29th, Great Bookham £36. 13. 9. Comparatively speaking, Richard's parishioners did well.

    4 Fanny Burney, the governess, had been employed in the family of the Rt. Hon. Sir Henry Russell (1751-1836), Chief Justice at Bengal (1807), Baronet (1812), who had retired in 1813 with a pension of £2,000 a year (*DNB*). He had married on 23 July 1782 as his 2nd wife Anne Barbara Whitworth (d. 1814), a sister of Charles, Earl Whitworth (1752-1825), the diplomat (see *DNB* and v *passim*). Of the eleven children of this marriage, five were daughters, and the 4th daughter Henrietta (b. 7 December 1795) had married in 1820 Thomas Greene (1794-1872) of Slyne, Lancashire, M.P. (1824-57). In 1823-4 (see Ll. 1321, 1329) the governess was to pay long visits to her former pupil Mrs. Greene in Lancaster, and it must have been this Mrs. Greene and her husband, though within the range of possibility, the 2nd Baronet Henry Russell (1783-1852) and his 2nd wife (1816) Marie Clotilde *née* de la Motte et de la Fontaine (d. 31 January 1872), whom Fanny was to accompany at this time to the sea coast.

    5 Not Sand Place (iv, L. 399 n. 1) near Dorking but Sandgate, which seaside place Sarah Payne and her mother (JB's widow) finding very 'dull' and Hastings 'vulgar', had left, asking CFBt to find them lodgings near her in Boulogne. See A.L.S. (Barrett, Eg. 3706D, ff. 34b-36), 26 August 1822. Observable now in FBA's letters are such slips in the writing of proper names, e.g. perhaps Russells for Greenes *supra*, and certainly here. On 13 June she had reached the age of 70.

371

listened with embarrassment—but whether from defect of rational answer, or from vexation at not being let go his own way without a representation that predicted its likely evil, I cannot say.

———

Another Sarah has made me a visit of which I doubt not you have had a Letter of contents: but in case that has not arrived yet, I will summarily mention I hope she has a present call that will finish all her necessary exertions for a comfortable competence. She was going, the next Day, to Crewe Hall, with Lady Crewe's ¹ GrandChildren, who are put under her entire care,⁶ in a manner similar to the charge of Mlle Woranzof to Miss Jardine.⁷ I am much pleased with the future prospect, though the present care & responsibility are arduous: I give no particulars, concluding they would be repetition.

———

Certainly, that *small* part of my disappointment from Maria⁸ which you mention, would be *null*, were it *as you*

⁶ See L. 1291 n. 4 for SHB's post as governess to the granddaughters of the 1st Baron Crewe (1742-1829), the wards in Chancery, Henrietta Maria Hungerford Offley Crewe (1808-79) and Annabella Hungerford Crewe (1814-74), whose mother Henrietta Maria *née* Hungerford Keates had died on 14 January 1820, at the age of 48. Their father John Crewe (iv, L. 266 n. 4; and *passim*), 2nd Baron (1829), spent most of his life on the Continent, dying in 1835. The 1st Baron Crewe, the grandfather now making the arrangements, was the husband of CB's life-long friend, the famous beauty and wit Frances Ann *née* Greville (i–vii *passim*), and would have seen much of the Burney family in his wife's lifetime (she had died in 1818).

⁷ Daughter of Alexander Jardine (d. 1799), Lt. Col. (1793) in the Royal Invalid Artillery (i, L. 7 n. 16), Joanne (*c.* 1769-1830), known to the Burneys as early as 1781 and much approved for her talents in music, had become companion-governess to Catherine Woronzow (1783-1856), the motherless daughter of Simon, Count Woronzow (1744-1832), Russian Ambassador to the Court of St. James (1785-1806) and resident in England from 1809 to the end of his life. See *AR* lxxiv (1832), 208-9. On 25 January 1808 Catherine had married George Augustus Herbert (1759-1827), 11th Earl of Pembroke. Long service with such responsibilities in the education of orphaned daughters was usually recompensed with a good salary, in SHB's case, £300 per annum, and an annuity for life.

⁸ For FBA's affection for the first-born of her nieces and nephews, see *ED* ii. 164, 171-9; for the part the d'Arblays played in arranging her prosperous marriage, iv. 422 ff.; for FBA's care and solicitude in Paris in the early weeks of her widowhood, vi *passim*; and for the alienation and the reconciliation, Ll. 1338, 1341.

conceive; but *all* would be null, that were only of trivial or passing neglect or omission: the wound she has given to my belief in an attachment I had thought sincere as my own, is of a deeper nature: & deeply has it sunk into my mind. But why will my dear ever affectionate & feeling Hetty enter again upon a subject I do my best to forget, as well as forgive? Maria is happy, I presume, in her *own* approbation of her conduct to me, since she has never demonstrated the least regret at the violence with which she has torn away mine. Oh my dear Hetty, let not *our* correspondence, which is one of my few remaining real comforts, be disturbed by painful discussions.[8]

I have told our dearest Mrs. Lock that perhaps the most unallayed pleasure you tasted in your excursion was at Eliot Vale: she joins me in rejoicing at your dear hint of repetition. I leave L^y Murray,[9] whom I *have* seen, to next Letter, & all else, save good news just this morning brought me from Boulogne sur Mer, that poor Sarah is *There*, with Charlotte Barrett & M^rs Ad^l & seems better.[10] Charlotte writes me word she & her's return in November. Charlotte *l'ainée* is at Brighton with poor Clement, still *far* from recovered. It is Dick Barrett who brings my Letters from Boulogne.[11] Always direct Here, though I hope next week Alex & I shall be at Eliot Vale—

God bless you, my dearest Esther,

Love to Emily, & believe me, most truly y^rs

F. d'Ay

7th Septr 1822.

[9] See L. 1290 n. 1.

[10] This letter is missing but in CFBt's letters of 4, 9, 14, 22 September, 21 October, etc. (Eg. 3706D, ff. 36b–49 *passim*) there are accounts of Sarah Payne and her mother at Boulogne. 'We have found them a lodging exactly opposite to our own, in the same street & it greatly enlivens & impoves our walks & evenings to have them so near us.' Sally, much improved in health, 'takes italian lessons every day, & dancing lessons'. The bookseller John had 'behaved in all matters most nobly, generously & affectionately—I quite forgive him for being a bookseller—& wish Sally may like him—he doats upon her & sends the tenderest letters, full of money'.

[11] Richard Barrett (i, p. lxxiii), FBA's godson, to whom returning by himself to school via London his mother entrusted letters. For Dick's boyish adventures, e.g. at Dessein's Hotel, see CFBt's letter of 2 August 1822 (Eg. 3706D, ff. 32–3b).

I am forced to make a change of my funded property in the Bank[12]—which is refused without a Certificate of the same melancholy nature that Maria has 2^{ce} procured for Alexander from the Rector of Walcot Church![13] may I ask my dear Hetty to obtain & enclose one? it is not in a hurry! — |

A Letter came to you by 2^d post a day after your departure—I imagine it may wait for an opportunity. Neither Edward nor Fanny know the handwriting. The seal is black; the motto *A Vous*—but I am named Mad^m. d'A.—which is not very *recherchée*, in the direction.[14]

1294   Eliot Vale, Blackheath,
                              10 October 1822

To Alexander d'Arblay

A.L. (rejected Diary MSS. 7326–[9], Berg), 10 Oct. 1822
Double sheet small 4to (8.9 × 7.3″)   4 pp.   *pmks* 12 OC 1822
12 OC .822 ⟨ ? ⟩
Addressed: Revd A. P. d'Arblay, / Nash's Library,[1] / Tunbridge Wells, / Kent.
Edited by CFBt. *See* Textual Notes.

[12] Some of FBA's stocks were evidently registered as owned jointly with her husband (deceased, 1818) and the bankers found it necessary to correct the now incorrect registration. Cf. FBA's entry 6 August 1823 (Diary): 'To Messrs Hoare's Affidavit for 3 p^r c^{ts}.'
[13] The General was buried on 9 May 1818 in the old cemetery on Walcot Street in a plot to the right of the burial chapel. The rector at this time was the Revd. Charles Abel Moysey (1780–1859), M.A. (Oxford, 1805), D.D., and Bampton Lecturer (1818), rector of Walcot, Bath (1817–39), archdeacon of Bath (1820–39), prebendary of Wells (1826–39).
[14] For Mary Cole's letter to EBB, see L. 1295 n. 6.

1294. [1] Founded by John Nash (*c.* 1776–1837), said to be related to 'Beau' Nash of Bath, the circulating library is described in J. Clifford's *Descriptive Guide* . . . (1822) as 'a most agreeable lounge, . . . a desirable resort for intellectual and colloquial recreation', to which subscriptions were received 'by the week, month, quarter, half-year, or year, . . . monthly reviews, magazines, . . . daily London and provincial papers, . . . also an extensive assortment of stationary, &c. constantly on sale'. Here, according to J. Sprange, *The Tunbridge Wells Guide* (1817), 'divines and philosophers, deists and christians, wigs and tories, Scotch and English,

Eliot Vale, 10th Oct^r.
Blackheath—1822

Why my Alex!—why how is *This here?* you are turning
the most amiable Correspondent *du monde*. Vive, Tunbridge!
if the very odour of its beverage produces effects so salubrious.
I am very glad you have written to Mr. Jones:[2] there is no
welcome so comfortable as that of being expected & desired:
added to which, there may perhaps be 'a Lady in the case'—
& then sudden intrusion is *no go*, in your own elegant phrase.
Our own Amine is returned brightened in Eyes & in spirits
& strength by her Spa excursion:[3] though the dreadful Catastrophe at Boulogne has shaken all the family.[4] Not, however,

debate without anger, dispute with politeness, and judge with candour; while
every one has an opportunity to display the excellency of his taste, the depth
of his erudition, and the greatness of his capacity, in all kinds of polite literature,
and in every branch of human knowledge.'
    The place seemed a natural for young d'Arblay.
    [2] AA's Welsh friend the Revd. Richard Jones (viii, L. 840 n. 5; ix, x *passim*),
the economist, would marry in Brighton on 23 January 1823 Charlotte Attree.
His father, Richard Jones, an 'eminent soliciter', had practised in Tunbridge, Kent,
from 1789-1815 (see Law Lists) but according to Whewell (*below*), he later
moved to Brighton, perhaps retiring to one of the livings in Sussex (x, L. 1125
n. 11) held by his famous son. A biographical sketch of the economist is provided
by William Whewell, ed. *Literary Remains, . . . / Lectures and Tracts / on / Political Economy, / of the late / Rev. Richard Jones . . .* (1859); and for a vivid and
amusing depiction and a portrait of the colourful person and sermons of 'Professor Jones', see Frederick C. Danvers *et al., Memorials / of / Old Haileybury College* (1894), pp. 173-80.
    [3] Spa (L. 1218 n. 1) was at the height of its popularity in the autumn.
    [4] The catastrophe at Boulogne was the fatal street accident suffered by Mrs.
Charles Locke's eldest daughter Emily Frederica, the wife since 1817 of Giorgio,
conte de Viry (L. 1193 n. 3) and the mother of three children, the third having
been born at Boulogne on 23 August. The Duchess of Sermoneta, who tells of
the conte's ill-temper and the terrified depression of the wife ('I wish I was a
virago, an independent!, masculine character, to make myself *dreaded!*'), was con-
fessedly unable to reconstruct the fatal accident (see *Locks of Norbury*, p. 314),
the circumstances of which, however, CFBt (at that time at Boulogne) records in
her Pink Letter Book (Barrett, Eg. 3706D, ff. 45-8b): 'The Countess Viri . . .
went out for the first time after her lying in—they put her on a donkey for safety,
with a little french boy to lead it. She saw a run away horse & cart coming furiously down the street & went under an archway. the poor little french boy placed
himself before her to keep the donkey quiet & it seems that this very archway led
to the horses stable so he dashed furiously into it, threw them down, killed the
poor boy instantly & the Countess only lived long enough to be carried to a warm
bath & expired soon after they placed her in it. She was only 26 years old.'
    Mrs. Charles Locke, her daughter ('the beautiful Cecilia') and her husband
'Murray' Greville were 'all walking with her when the terrible event took place',

as it would have done before the *Marriage*, which had appeared to rob life of its charms to the poor victim. You had judged *Cecy* quite well in her high character: she is now quite mindless of the bloom of a Bride, & all its concomitants, & devoted in tender pity to her miserable Mother. They are all gone, a party of woe, to Paris, to *la belle mère*.

Caroline is much better,[5] & can walk, a little, & ride a good deal; but Dancing is forbidden for months yet to come. 'Tis odd the two fair Cousins should thus be stopt by the heel, so nearly one to the other, & for the same length of privation. Will she, also, ¦ meet with a Lame Lover to soothe her by sympathy into those bonds which sympathy only can make genial?

I am quite pleased that Clarissa has made you discover you have not yet a heart of Stone: though the *yet*, & the blythe *ça viendra*, seem to shew that your ambition of obtaining that point of perfection is still of the Marble sort. Had the last vol. of Clarissa failed to move you, you might certainly have set yourself down as invulnerable; for it has the deepest tragic powers that the pen can address to the heart. The Mourners, it is true, except the Mother & Anna Howe, have so thoroughly merited punishment, that Pity, at first, stands aloof from their sufferings: but one soon finds them so exquisitely wretched, that the feelings of *vain* remorse which heighten their grief, produces, ere long, its just effect, of rendering them only more excruciatingly objects of compassion

Should Miss Thrale be within your reach, pray make her a visit.[6] I am sure you will be well received, & you may there

and in Boulogne also at this time, according to Barrett, was another member of the Locke family, 'the Beauty of the World', Mr. William Locke Jun[r].

[5] Caroline Angerstein, now aged 20, whose disability was similar, FBA says, to that suffered a few years previously by her cousin Cecilia Locke (L. 1192 n. 9), who, 'chained to her bed or a sofa by her bad knee', was carried downstairs daily by Woodyear, 'the old servant in whose arms her father had died' (*Locks of Norbury*, p. 289).

[6] Since 1807 Susanna Arabella Thrale (L. 1238 n. 22) was living at Ashgrove in the village of Knockholt near Sevenoaks, Kent. See Hyde, Plates, pp. 276-9. Alex, who presumably made the visit suggested to him at this time, was to return there in 1827, 1828, 1836, and probably on other occasions.

According to the present owner of the beautiful property, Mr. Derek Chittock, Miss Thrale had come into possession of it in 1828, and it was some time 'after 1813', he thinks, that she brought there from Streatham 'Dr. Johnson's summerhouse'. See letter to *TLS* (24 January 1975), p. 38; also Hyde, p. 335n.

hear some tidings relative to quickening or slackening your intended improvement from hints drawn from Edgworth on Education.[7]— I do not, however, go late in the day, as if you were prowling for a Dinner! nor yet *stay* late, as if you were snifting its inviting approach with a Culinary Nasal perspicacity: that sort of tardiness, either in coming or Going, is rarely attributed to Absence, either by the Hungry, who are kept from their Dinner, or the Cook, who is scolded for bringing it burnt & dry. Better work hard again at your own famishing shoulder of Mutton!—But do not let this Houshold precaution impede your seeking my dear Miss Thrale; I am sure she will be glad to see you, if you send up your Card before you have had a denial as a stranger: & she is one of my most faithful friends, & full of high, generous, & disinterested notions. These alone have kept her, with all her Fortune, Wit, & Beauty, single; she could not form an engagement that satisfied her mind, & she would not form any other. If you talk to her of her almost idolized sister Hoare, you will see her best smiles; I believe her capable of being a real & feeling & Zealous Friend in any *difficulty*, or emergency, as well as in Sun-shine.

To *Her*, & to Mrs *Jones*,[2] fail not to go.

You will be glad to know that your favourite Babbage is the only Executor named by Sr Wm Herschal to act with his Wife & Son:[8] the latter is returned: & I fancy entirely, for the present, at Slough.

You have not yet mentioned Knowl?[9]

No answer being arrived from Ly Templetown about Mr. I Benson,[10] we fear she is again relapsed! I am grieved at the thought, for, besides the warm friendship she has most

[7] Perhaps Richard Lovell Edgeworth, *Professional Education* (1808).

[8] Sir William Herschel (1738–1822), the astronomer, had died at Slough on 25 August (*DNB*). Named as Executors of his will were his wife Mary *née* Baldwin (*c.* 1751–1832), his distinguished son John Frederick William (ix, L. 940 n. 8), and Charles Babbage (L. 1185 n. 6), AA's friend, and possibly FBA's informant on the details mentioned.

[9] See the Hon. Victoria Mary Sackville-West, *Knole and the Sackvilles* (1922); also *DL* i. 270–2.

[10] Conjecturally the Revd. Christopher Benson (1789–1868), B.A. (1809), M.A. (1815), Trinity College, Cambridge, in 1817 elected preacher before the university, and in 1820–2, Hulsean lecturer (*DNB*). A noted preacher whose published discourses went through several editions, he had in these years the kind of career that apparently AA would have liked and perhaps aspired to.

partially conceived for me, she is certainly, Intellectually, one of the most charming of Women.

I am glad you are fallen, *for a while*, into all that desultory reading—*seeing* there is much occasion of increased general minor knowledge: but pray neither Forget nor Neglect Mr. ⟨G. Br——⟩[11] force yourself to a *serious beginning*, if it be *possible*; & if you find it otherwise, to a quick *renunciation*. I believe, & have reason to *believe*, that the Relict is *impatient*; but that our indulgent Friend will not hurry you, because he conceives you to have some excellent *ulterior* plan. Above all, be finically careful no mischief comes to borrowed Bookes that have the *non-replaceable* charm of being Gifts from Authors & Friends. I worry you, because every day adds to the ill Grace of renunciation—& *that* is what I expect for the termination!——

Your Letters—free, easy, natural, are all that I like.

You will give me a hint when I must write no more—my Letters not being calculated pro bono publico! I hope poor Miss White is better.[12]

I delight in your health, &c —— ——

God bless!

Your writing so often makes you very Popular here: you will be most affectionately *embraced* by our Mrs. Lock. Sweet Amine comes daily—& is sweeter & sweeter.

---

[11] Initials only given but evidently the sponsor of some literary undertaking contemplated by AA.

[12] Daughter of Stephen White (d. *pre* 1798) of Miskin, Glamorgan, sister of Anne Bassett Saunderson, presently living in Tunbridge (see below), and heiress to the Bassett Estates, Lydia Rogers White (*c.* 1763-1827) was a well-known socialite, London hostess, and wit. She emerges in many Memoirs of the time, being known for instance, to Lady Holland, op. cit., pp. 17, 18, and to Samuel Rogers, see P. M. Clayden, *The Early Life of Samuel Rogers* (1887), p. 348, who in a letter of 1798 mentioned her wit and talents, the 'admiration of the Pump Room'. She is said to be the 'Miss Diddle' of Lord Byron's 'The Blues. A Literary Epilogue' and to her Caroline Lamb dedicated her tale *Ada Reis* . . . (1823). She had acquired, according to Rogers, the house built by Sir Joshua Reynolds on Richmond Hill (see Plate, *DL* ii, *facing* 89), a house that CB and FB visited in June 1782.

In her will (PRO/PROB/11/1722/127, pr. 26 February 1827) Miss White mentions her sister Anne Bassett (d. 1845), wife of Francis Saunderson (1754-1827) of Castle Saunderson, co. Cavan, who was then residing in Tunbridge, Kent.

Eliot Vale, Blackheath,
14–17 October 1822

To Esther (Burney) Burney

A.L.S. (Berg), 14–17 Oct. 1822
Double sheet 4to   4 pp.   *pmks* 18 OC .822 18 OC 1822   black
seal
Addressed: Mrs. Burney, / Lark Hall Place, / near Bath,
Endorsed by EBB: Answered by a / friend—Nov. 18.—1822

Eliot Vale
Blackheath
14.Octr 1822.

Has my dear Hetty thought me lost?—Lost, she will perhaps say, I *ought* to be, as the least excuse admissable for not
answering her last Letter — — Well, then, suppose the matter so, to cut short tiresome explanations, & only receive Me,
in my Letter, as *found*. Eh?—my Hetty?—how do you like
this *ratiocination?*—If it is not very rational, 'tis at least very
convenient, so on to other matters.

I came to this sweet small Paradise, & its ever lovely, even
as an ever-Green, but ever *unfallen* Eve about 10 days ago,
fetched by Her from my just finished confinement to Bolton
Street, whence Carpenters & Painters, & such like Geer, were
hardly banished before me. Alex was a *week old* at Tunbridge
Wells. I believe you do not think him many months more of
age *any* where. His excursion, after its due duration, is to
finish here: but I cannot make him say the *when*; & so much
the better, perhaps, for 'tis a million to one if, having eased
his Conscience in pronouncing the Day, he did not afterwards
ease his Memory from the trouble of remembering it. He is
certainly, as Merlin called Sir Christopher something, '*a singu-
lier Particulier:*'[1] so do not try any more not to love him, for
the so doing will not lead you into the scrape of loving *such
like*, no resemblance to him, that I know of, being *ici bas*.

How sorry you will have been for the dreadful sudden
death of poor worthy Mrs. Wilbraham![2]—& how concerned

1295. [1] Joseph Merlin (L. 1230 n. 2), the inventor.
[2] Described in *AR* lxiv (1822), 'Chronicle', 291; and by CFBt 'Pink Letter

for our Mrs. Lock by an equally abrupt fatality to her Grand Daughter ǀ Madame de Very, 2ᵈ Child of Mr. Charles Lock,[3] at Boulogne sur Mer. As I conclude you will have seen it in the Papers I will not recapitulate the tragic story. Mrs. Angerstein took her Mother to Woodlands, & kept her there till I was at liberty to come with such poor consolation as I can now offer: I have, however, exerted myself *out* of myself to my best ability, from the spur of such a motive, to such a friend; & not without success. She charges me with her kindest remembrance to you. The other day, pointing to the pretty Cottage at the foot of her Grounds, which you must have remarked from the Bed Room, *jadis* your's, which I now inhabit, she said 'The new tenant of that sweet spot, Lady Dowager Roslyn,[4] made me a visit last week: she is very sensible & agreeable — — but how much should I have preferred for so near a neighbour dear Mrs. Burney!—' This exquisite Friend is almost as much obliged to you as I am myself, my dear Hetty, for your having said you do not despair of making such another excursion. How I wish I might hear of any thing to propose that could facilitate such an event! I am always upon the Watch, as far as my little opportunity allows.

Caroline's Letter is edifying.[5] I know not how you can thank her enough for so much intelligence & entertainment, joined to the marked condescendsion of such a *proof* she had not

Book', Eg. 3706D, ff. 48b–49b, is the road accident that caused the death of Maria *née* Harvey (d. 11 September 1822), the widow of George Wilbraham (L. 1191 n. 7), mother of SHB's friend and former pupil. 'Poor Mʳˢ Wilbraham . . . was taking an airing with her daughter in a low four wheeled carriage drawn by one horse & driven by her footman — — in short, the safest possible equipage to human apprehensions but a jolt threw the footman from his seat this frightened the horse who set off at full speed & threw out both the ladies. Miss Wilbraham is recovering but her poor Mother who was fat & heavy was taken up insensible & died very shortly afterwards—'

[3] Not the 2nd, but the 1st child of Charles Locke (1769–1804), whom FBA must have remembered as an infant at Norbury Park (iii. 269), the first of the Locke grandchildren (b. 12 December 1796). For the fatal accident, see L. 1294 n. 4.

[4] Charlotte *née* Courtenay (1751–1826), widow of Alexander Wedderburn (1733–1805), Baron Loughborough (1780), Earl of Rosslyn (1801), Lord Chancellor (1793–1801).

[5] Caroline Jane Burney (i, p. lxxiv), who lived with EBB during the winter (L. 1272 n. 11).

forgotten you. You were right to give me a specimen, also, of the blank paper respect.

⟿

I have opened, as you desired, the Letter with the seal *à Vous* —& find it signed M. Cole;[6] it is very affectionate, & filled with apologies for certain deficiencies of Writing, & warm expressions of regard. The date is Widcomb Crescent, July 30. It is a Letter of much kindness, & anxiety to hear from you. |

Right, my dear Esther, & wise & kind is your *non-delay* of my melancholy Commission—for though I want it not Now, I am ignorant of the moment it may be demanded—& it spares me the heavy necessity of fresh mentioning the request —Did you happen to notice a Head—a noble head, antique, on a Screen in *our* room at Eliot Vale?—it bears a resemblance so strong to the constant Image on my heart, that my indulgent Mrs. Lock will suffer me to take it Home & not for all else she could offer would I change it — — I trust I shall shew it you.—You will be glad to hear that *Emily* pleased here very much, & that Mr. & Mrs. George Lock never cease to talk of her charming musical talents.[7] Tell her so, with my kind Love. I conclude that Maria & Sophy remain at Rainbow Hill to enjoy the recovery, after sharing the alarm for her safety, with Mr. Sandford, of his sweet Rebecca.[8]—

I am extremely glad of your *addenda* to your account of the Bishop of Durham,[9] as in the 1st narrative I was not mentioned: but I shall surprize you by *my addenda*, i.e. that I have no recollection of ever seeing his lordship!—though similar messages have been communicated to me, *jadis*, from poor Charles; &, particularly, warm congratulations on

[6] Mary *née* Hunter (*fl.* 1789-1822) was the widow of the Revd. Charles Cole (d. 28 August 1821), formerly of Twickenham, where at least one of their sons is buried (Cobbett, *Memorials of Twickenham*, p. 73). Since 1809 the family seems to have resided at 4 Widcombe Crescent, Bath.

[7] EBB's daughter Amelia Maria (i, p. lxix).

[8] See i, L. 1191 n. 1.

[9] For the jolly nonagenarian Bishop, Shute Barrington, see L. 1287 n. 13. His brother Daines Barrington (1727-1800), barrister-at-law, F.R.S. (1767), was one of CB's correspondents (see *Catalogue*; Lonsdale, pp. 152, 282; Scholes, i. 136, 268). The nephew mentioned was one of FB's friends at Court in the 1780s, namely William Price (1749-1817), equerry (1782-7) to King George III, with offices later in the Queen's Household (i, L. 16 n. 12), and a friend of the Worcester Burneys.

my return from France. I can only attribute this to his having borne some other title than Durham at the time of our meeting. His Brother, Daines Barrington, I remember well, & his Nephew, Major Price, was one of my first favourites[9]—as he was of almost all who knew him: particularly of the *Barbonites*, whom he frequently mentioned to me, & always with praise & regard.

———

Nothing yet opens for Alex, though we have now a new string to our long Bow—for my real Friend, Miss Maltby,[10] has been *talking him over, con amore*, to her Brother in Law, the new Bishop of Winchester. |

Octr 17th I am just returned from reading your delightful account of the B^P. of Durham to Mrs. Lock: but I must not go on further without coming to L^y Murray.[11] Hearing nothing from her, after your departure, I began to conjecture she had meant, by desiring you to *prepare* the way for our meeting, that I should take some measure myself; & fearing she might, in that case, be unpleasantly astonished at my insensibility to her condescending perseverence in seeking to renew our acquaintance, I took the arm of Alex, & called, & left a card in Wimpole Street,[11] with a note explanatory of my gratitude & *better health*—This she answered by coming next day: but, not expecting such vivacity, she was not received: she then wrote a very kind answer & proposed an appointment, which I accepted, & have much rejoiced so to have done, for I think her all you say of her, & find every trace her Childhood had presented now drawn out. She made me a long visit, which appeared very short, from the much of old recollections brought forward to both. She spoke of you *warmly*, as a charming Person, & said your spirits were quite exhilarating, & promised, she hoped, future visits, & long continuance. She is going to Holland till next spring, when we are to *renew our renewal.*—I have not heard *from* Sarah Harriet since she has been in Cheshire,[12] but *of* her variously,

[10] Harriet Maltby (L. 1232 n. 13), sister-in-law of George Pretyman-Tomline (1750–1827), Bishop of Winchester (1820).

[11] See L. 1290 n. 1.

[12] See L. 1291 n. 4; L. 1293 n. 6.

& always of her great contentment in her new abode. Fanny called P.P.C. before going to the Russels:[13] & Edward once drank Tea with me. Sarah Payne I have the pleasure to hear is better. She is at Boulogne, with her Mother, whence the Barretts are soon expected. Our poor Charlotte, in my last accounts, was still nursing Clement at Brighton. Fanny Raper is well; Martin, invisible. |

Always direct *Bolton* S[t] whence my Letters always follow. Let me know whom you associate with. Adieu, my dearest Esther—ever yours with true affection

F d Ay

Mrs. Angerstein is returned much better for Spa.

1296

Eliot Vale, Blackheath,
and 11 Bolton Street,
11–24 December 1822

To Esther (Burney) Burney

A.L.S. (Berg), 11-24 Dec. 1822
Double sheet 4to   4 pp.   *pmk* 26 DE .822   wafer
Addressed: Mrs. Burney, / Lark Hall Place, / near / Bath.
Endorsed by EBB: Dec. 24 / 1822, / answered Jan—5th / 1822.

11. Dec[er]
1822 Eliot Vale,

I have so much to say to my dear Esther, that I will begin at once, & go on as I can: for this is destined to be conveyed by Alexander on the *27th*—

In order the quicker to have done with what is merely painful, I pounce upon your embarrassment relative to the *Bust.*[1]

---

[13] See L. 1293 n. 4.

1296. [1] Fanny Raper (daughter of Molesworth Phillips and SBP) in her account of 21 November (Berg) of JB's death had mentioned that on Sunday morning (18 November) 'a cast ha[d] been taken from his face by the head person from Nollekens'. Phillips, who had probably made the arrangements, now set himself to collect the costs from the Admiral's sisters. FBA's payment is recorded in her

—I am very sorry for your disturbance, my dear Hetty—& feel for you all the contrariety of your wish to display your Respect & Affection for Him who so truly deserved them, with your inability to find a place, & your indignancy at the unauthorised force meant to be put upon you by one whose every obtrusion must be revolting while Memory holds her Seat,[2] & retains the loved Image of the injured Saint he immolated—for whose immolation not one moment's penitence has ever appeared to soften off his crime, or plead for his forgiveness. *Therefore* is it that I hold against him my inalterable horrour. He has never been presented to me in any light of appeasement—a 2^d wife deserted—Children by a 2^d Bed abandoned—a mistress openly kept — — & the possession of spirits triumphant in boldness! — — oh my dear Esther —was That the lot of the most delicate, as well as purest & most excellent of human beings?—

Account Book (Berg) for 1822: 'Bust of my dear Brother, Admiral Burney! — — 2: 7: 0'. See also CFBt in a letter of 22 September [1822] (Eg. 3706D, p. 101): 'Mrs. B[urney] says she did not order the busts to be sent . . . It is all Col. Phillips's doing through officiousness.'

² That Phillips was always Phillips (iv *passim*) is indicated by an anecdote related by CBFB in a letter (Berg) of 29 July 1817 to CFBt:

Col. Phillips was visiting in James St. & on his opening the St[reet] door a Man desired to know if Col. Phillips was there, the latter I understood smoaked he was a Bailiff & told him he w^d find the Col. at 12 o'clock—intending to be off—but the maid being ignorant of the matter let him in soon after, & pointed thro' the Glass door wch was Col. Phillips — — He was immediately arrested, I think for £27. or 37—& y^r poor Uncle forgetting at the moment of distress all other circumstances only remembered that it was his Old shipmate, & was bast for the debt—but it did not ans^r for there was another Writ out against him & it is understood He is now in prison — — the James St arrest was for House rent for his Wife, wch he had tried to elude by telling the creditors that she was not his wife, only a sham Marriage, & the Landlord was on the point of turning her out of doors, only she brought them certificates of the marriage, & now it is thought they will let her remain for a time — — in her distress she sent the Bailiffs to James St. so y^r poor uncle has had it to pay — — — 'tis pity it did not happen at Mr FitzGeralds, for he c^d have afforded it better, tho' He is at a loss for he lost £5000. by his Tenants last year, & has been obliged to sell his yacht—Phillips owes him about £500 — — but Mr Fitz is a man of fortune.

Gavin Kennedy, *The Death of Captain Cook* (1978), pp. 64 ff., offers a reassessment of the part played by Lieutenant Phillips and his undisciplined Marines in the fatal attack in the Sandwich Islands in 1779. They fired once and ran, it would seem, and the heroism commonly attributed to Phillips (*DNB* and i, ii *passim*) is now in question.

I quitted my pen,—Grief-disordered—but I will now finish this painful subject, by saying that the dear Representation was sent to me, also, with a Bill of £2 - 7^d but no message whatever, & I concluded it to come from Martin, and therefore instantly paid & placed it—not consulting my *immediate* convenience, but wondering *Martin* I should send it without notice or enquiry—till I heard afterwards, by Mr. J[ohn] Payne, that *Martin* had had no share in the order, & was very uneasy that such a liberty should have been taken—& even *You* have never been named to me upon the subject—nor has it since been started; but as I am *prepared*, should it occur, depend upon my response being such as I think you would approve. As to Alex, he joins me in the *Cry* you mention of his Cousins, & says he should have given the same advice. I have seen *Mrs. Admiral!!* Burney but twice since her return from Boulogne & Hastings, &c.[3] She looks very considerably better & is occupied most industriously & carefully in refitting her house—which I understand has been completely repaired, generally new furnished, painted, papered, & improved. My first visit to it will be but the more melancholy, from recollections—but I am extremely glad they have been able to accomplish such a change, & I believe their plan to be as wise as it is comfortable, for by all living together, Mother, Son, & married Daughter & her husband, the united purses will render the expence easy to All, & the enjoyment as safe as it will be desireable. The I *private* history has never once been hinted to me:[4] & as it has only been told me with charges of not divulging from whom I heard it, I avoid every avenue to its disclosure, that I may learn it—if unavoidable —*according to form*. I am certainly in no haste!—

And now, shall I speak to you of my health?—I may as well, for you must needs hear something has been wrong— & I would not name it in a short *Post* Letter. But first, let me say how I am concerned your own has suffered so cruelly from the rheumatism in your Gums, for such I conceive, from your description, must have been your complaint. I long to hear of your relief—& very especially that you may

---

[3] Mrs. James Burney and her daughter Sarah had returned from Boulogne with the Barretts in November but had gone on to Hastings.

[4] Martin Burney's unacknowledged marriage (L. 1271 n. 4).

escape any injury from the *Dentist* to whom certainly [you]
have owed the most *agreeable* goo[d.] But, before I arr[ive
a]t what is always so difficult to [*tear*] as *Self*, let me not
fail to mention how glad I am the valuable Mr. Sandford is
better[5]—though, till your manner of describing your own
satisfaction struck me, I had not conceived his illness of so
dangerous a Nature, nor do I now at all understand what the
complaint may be. I thought they both looked in exceeding
good health when I saw them in Bolton Street—but that was
not *yesterday*.—Alex still adheres to his intention of visiting
Bath at Xmas. He went to Cambridge, to vote for Lord Hervey, who is Grandson to Lady Templetown,[6] & at Cambridge
he got a *heated Cold* which is still hanging upon him, & which
does not much delight me, especially away from Home, as
the strictest temperence alone brings him right, & *that* is impossible, where an elegant table is seconded by a lively taste
for its merits.—My poor Alex. requires for perfect Health a
Constant Attention—& *that* is truly *son moindre defaut*!— ǀ

2⟨4⟩ Dec^r—Bolton Street—Alas my dear Esther—this
Letter, begun at sweet Eliot Vale just after my arrival, & continued occasionally, with intent to form a packet for Alexander's Belvidere Visit—is now finished abruptly, to be sent
off by post, that I may claim a few lines of intelligence of
poor worthy Mr. Sandford[5]—& yet more eagerly to learn
how his dear fond Wife supports her *health* — — of all
things else I ask nothing! while she is in exertion she can

[5] The progress of the surgeon's illness, beginning on 7 August 1822, is detailed
in the 'Worcester Journal'. On 30 October he had set forth with his wife Rebecca
née Burney (i, p. lxxv), Maria Bourdois, and Sophy Burney for Bath, where he
spent a fortnight at 5 Ainslie's Belvedere without improvement, and returning to
Rainbow Hill was to die there on 26 January 1823.

[6] An election for a representative in Parliament for the University had been
held on 26–7 November to supply the vacancy occasioned by the death of John
Henry Smyth (1780–1822) of Trinity College, M.P. for the University for the last
ten years. See C. H. Cooper, *Annals of Cambridge* (5 vols., Cambridge, 1842–53),
iv. 539. The candidates, all of Trinity College, were: William John Bankes (*c.*
1787–1855), traveller, friend of Byron, the successful candidate (*DNB*); James
Scarlett (1769–1844), M.P. for Peterborough (1819–30); and Lord Frederick William Hervey (1800–64), later M.P. for Bury St. Edmunds (1826–59). Hervey was
the son of the 5th Earl of Bristol (1803), who in 1798 had married Elizabeth
Albana Upton (iv, L. 269 n. 11), eldest daughter of Lady Templetown, who in
a letter (Berg) of 28 November had conveyed the thanks of the family to Alex
and the 'amiable Madame d'Arblay [who] have been most kind & active in our
service, & have I believe, procured several Votes'.

hardly herself know—Sophy's Letter holds out no hope—
How for You, especially, do I grieve, my poor Hetty, who
have so long looked up to him as your Medical Apollo, as
well as so dearly valued friend!—& for Maria I grieve too, for
she has loved & been loved by him from a Child—& I grieve
for All who knew him—I returned yesterday, & to day Alex
left me for the Vicarage of Horsham, whither he is gone to
keep Xmas with a fellow Clergyman, a Cantab, who has just
got a House of his own, to which he invites his favourite
friends, & — — his Father & Mother—to embellish his
Vicarage Warming.[7] How old-fashioned & amiable!—our
Charlotte is at Brighton with poor Clement, now wholly lame
of one arm from acute rheumatism!—I have a Letter from
Sarah-Harriet, who is in high Spirits & Feather at Crewe Hall.
Mrs. Lock loves & admires you with warmth & constancy.
Mrs. *Ad^l* Burney!—& Sarah Payne called on me this morn.
while I was taking my ordered doze of exercise. I have something to say that will please you from that quarter, in my
next—As also of Alex—but can only now add adieu, & for
God's sake [& *m*]*ine*, as well as &c — — try to sustain this
sa[dnes]s with fortitude—you^{rs} ever most affectionately my
dear Esther & truly

F d Ay ⏐

I heartily hope poor Miss El. Hay is better.[8]

---

[7] This was AA's friend Hugh James Rose (ix, L. 956 n. 10), 14th Wrangler
(1817), medallist, Select Preacher, and future Principal of King's College, London,
who in 1821 had been presented to the living of Horsham, Sussex. He had married
on 24 June 1819 Anna Cuyler *née* Mair (*c.* 1796-1855) and among the guests expected at the Christmas party at the vicarage were his father, the Revd. William
Rose (1763-1844), F.R.S. (1786), vicar of Glynde, Sussex and his wife Susannah
(*c.* 1763-1839). See *AR* lxxxi (1839), 334; and xcvii (1855), 264.

[8] See L. 1208 n. 4.

11 Bolton Street,
28 December 1822

To Mrs. Locke

A.L.S. (Barrett, Eg. 3695, ff. 95–6b), 28 Dec. 1822
Double sheet 4to   4 pp.   *pmks* P.P. / May Fair   30 DE ⟨   ⟩
red seal
    Addressed: Mrs. Lock, / Eliot Vale / Blackheath / Kent,—
    Endorsed by Mrs. Locke: ans 1ˢᵗ Jan / 1823
    Docketed in pencil, p. 1: 1823

Bolton Street. 11.
28 Decʳ 1822.

Indeed, my dearest Friend, this is too much[1]—why mingle pain with powers so uncontested of giving pleasure as your's over me?—*Angry?*—Oh How?—I feel all your kindness, & all its tenderness—but why make me *Sorry?*—I speak out, that such *Loans* may not occur again. *Loans, quoth* 'a?. Why if *This* Loan had been my own device, I should be more shrewd at making a Bargain than Messʳˢ Baring, Taylor, Roth-child[2]—or any, the richest money-mongers of the Day. Loan?—How a Loan? am I to *Borrow* it during the severity of the Winter, when it will bestow upon me warmth & com-fort, yet demand neither care nor Attention; & then *Return* it to you in the heat of Summer, when it will *give* you noth-ing at all, except plenty of plague & Watching; yet demand from you abundant Nourishment, of Tallow, Pepper, or Camphor; &, if you should be a Niggard in your supply, Hostilly venge itself, by pouring upon you a Host of fat mag-gots, rolling one ǀ over the other, like the Boys & Girls on your neighbouring Hill on Whit Monday, gnawing every tip-pet & muff in your Wardrobe, & bidding you, if you are cold,

1297. [1] This is Mrs. Locke's gift of a 'Foot Basket'. See her letter (Berg) of 26 December 1822 to FBA: 'The Weather is become so cold that my dearly loved Friend must not be angry if I send her a Foot Basket & remember how necessary to the poor dear *Head* it is, that the Feet shou'd *never* be cold—It is *a Loan*'.
    [2] The eminent financiers Alexander Baring (1774–1848), M.P. (1806–35), cr. Baron Ashburton (1835), trained in his father's financial house (*DNB*); pos-sibly William Taylor (d. 1819) of the great exporting house, Norwich; and Nathan Meyer Rothschild (1777–1836), head of the English branch of the house of Rothschild.

blow your own fingers for your pains——? accompanied by
a swarm of revelling Moths, that won't leave you a morsel of
flannel for your rheumatism, nor a Blanket thicker than a
Cobweb to cover your poor Limbs at the next fall of snow?
—If these are to be the Conditions of your Loan, you really
lift me up higher, by many pegs, than I have yet been lifted,
in Business, Speculation, & Foot-Jobbing.

But *seriously* & very seriously, my dearest Friend, let me
not have this sort of remonstrance to make again. If I dared
act for Alex—I should almost exhort equally my dear
Augusta.—but, for this one time—Alex will be too delighted
to hear of my *pribbles & Prabbles*.

My dear Plant, however, thrives—

And my beautiful Bouquet is still fragrant; & my elegant
little *Bonnet* wants only a skilful Pinch to be *my* tip of the
Mode. I like it, however, so much, that I shall trust it to no
Milliner under a G. C. Knight's Lady.[3]

I had really a delightful Evening with dear Charming Lady
Templetown—yet she had one painful spasm—but it soon
passed away, & she was all herself—I could almost say her
best self, it is so difficult to conceive her more agreeable.
I wish You could have been regaled & *rejoui* with her cordial
amusement in hearing I had nearly mounted to the Belfray
in my short-sighted commotion, when I wanted to run away
from all observation—but my own—at Lee Church.[4] But

---

[3] The *Triennal Directory* for the years 1817–24 and *Robson's improved London Directory* . . . (1820) show an establishment at 6 Great Portland Street, Marylebone, under the names E. H. Knight, milliner, and H. Knight, milliner and dress-maker.

[4] AA's performance in Lee Church at the invitation of the Revd. George Locke on a Sunday in the late autumn when FBA was visiting Mrs. Locke and the showers of felicitations offered on his sermon by the Lockes, the Angersteins, the Martins, and their friend Nicholas Vansittart (L. 1270 n. 23) had made 'the *far* happiest Hour' that FBA had had 'since May 1818'. See her letter to EBB (L. 1301).

Mrs. Locke had heard from her son that CPB also had 'expressed himself with warmest terms of approbation & delight of our dᴿ Alex—saying, "that he had been astonished at his powers, and that his eloquence was of the sort best suited to his profession, & that he had employed it exactly as cou'd be wished that he cou'd not fail of being a distinguished Preacher"—my dear George repeated this to me with great pleasure, adding that "it was a very joint opinion & that he thought Dᴿ P. Bs judgement to be depended on as sound and acute". How I love to collect these tributes so justly due and present them to my beloved Friend— our dear Alexs "*Mammy Locke*" has a truly maternal gratification in them—'. For CPB, see further, L. 1299.

how kindly have you prejudiced her for my Alex!—& what a dear Xmas Box did you greet me with on Xmas Day!—& how agreeable a one again by my kind Augusta!—Ah, my dear Friend—had pleasure—in possession & in perspective —such as this, been accorded me 4 Years & 4 Months ago— would not my heart have been too full? would it not have burst its earthly machine?—I think so.—This, however, as it now stands, is the highest Consolation, nay delight, I am capable to receive. To see Alex so approved by Those whose Approbation is dearest to me!—That burst upon me of felicitation—that kind burst, on the first Sunday—never shall I forget—It made L^y Templetown absolutely *greet* when I detailed it to her—& I omitted not the marked & speaking expression of Mr. Vansittart's smile. She was pleased, too, at what I told her of my firm conviction that not only the family so loved, & its circle, but also the general Congregation were led, at first to favour Alex by the air of kind at once & deep attention with which the Rector himself listened. It was, to me, truly encouraging.[4] |

So you were determined, *poz.* to make us Dine as well as Lunch from Eliot Vale?—What usage we are obliged to put up with!—But I have a terrible Crow to pick with Mrs. Cooke[5]—She put two such hard mouthfuls into my Sandwich, that I conceive she meant to Choak me. I was very near demanding a Coroner's Inquest—in which case she would have been cast Nem[ini] Con[tradicenti] I think she takes bad lessons. Example, they say, prevails, where precept fails: now while *you* give the one, who can wonder that the other, which *I* give, is effectless?—Alex went on Tuesday, with Mr. Wheevil[6]—or some such name: but how was I pleased at a Letter from Mr. Rose, the new Vicar, to Alex, proposing, if he had any difficulties of arrangement for the Journey, that he should join his—(Mr. R.s) *Father & Mother*, who

[5] Possibly Sarah Cooke (*c.* 1763-1837), a servant who may have been recruited at Great Bookham, Surrey, where her burial is recorded in the parish registers, 22 May 1837, aged 74. In a will (PRO/PROB/11/1809/763, dated 17 April 1827, pr. 1 December 1832) Mrs. Locke bequeathed to her 'good servant Sarah Cooke for and during her life . . . the interest and dividends of £750' and besides the annuity, £50 to be paid immediately.

[6] William Whewell (1794-1866), at this time fellow of Trinity College. For his career and his concern for AA, see ix, L. 1064 n. 12, and x *passim*.

were to come to Horsham at this 1ˢᵗ Vicarage Warming.[7] What an old fashioned amiability!—I take all the care in my power of my Evenings, my dear—tender Friend—& with tolerable success. Monday I go again to Lʸ T. After that I shall expect Alex till he arrives. No Letters from Bath or Worcester; I hope therefore, though but *faintly* Mr. Sandford is amending.[8] My dear Diane is a very cheering Evening Companion. I walk every Morning, stoutly & steadily, & Diane capers round me. I have sent a very long Letter to dear M. de Lally,[9] & finished it to Mᵐᵉ de Maurville.[10] I said much of Eliot Vale & the 2 A-s. I long to hear my sweet Amine continues at least *tolerably*, & that dear Caroline is re-established. I thought Augusta [looked] charmingly. God bless my most dear Friend!

F d Ay [1]

My best Compᵗˢ I entreat, to *Sir*—& *Mr.* & *Mrs. George*: & Mr. J.A.[11]

1298   11 Bolton Street,
                                    30 December 1822

To Mrs. Barrett

A.L.S. (Berg), 30 Dec. 1822
Double sheet 4to   4 pp.

11. Bolton Street
Berkeley Square.
30. Decʳ 1822

I am glad of this resistless spur not to let the year conclude in dull & dim—though never willing—silence to my sweet Charlotte: — — Alexander returned with me from Eliot

---

[7] See L. 1296 n. 7.   [8] See L. 1296 n. 5.
[9] Lally-Tolendal was a great favourite in former days at Norbury Park (iv *passim*).   [10] See L. 1294 n. 2.
[11] Sir George Martin (L. 1191 n. 15), the Revd. George Locke (L. 1188 n. 3), his wife Harriet Poulett *née* Thomson (*c.* 1783–1837), and John Angerstein (L. 1195 n. 14).

Vale on the 22^d—only to quit me on the Eve of Xmas, to pass the Holydays (do you know of any *other* days that fall to his share?) with his Cantab. Friend, Mr. Hugh Rose.[1] In setting off, he asked me to open such Letters as might require immediate attention—& I judged my dear Charlotte's might be of that description—& lo & behold, by the enclosed, whether I judged rightly. The ticket was fortunately in my care & I know how happy he will be to have it change hands to lodge in yours. I will not wait his return, though I expect him this Week, as *Wednesday* is the only day; & the ensuing may perhaps be more convenient to you & Mrs. Paynter[2] than a later.—Besides—I have owed you a Letter[3] — — ought I to speak *au pluriel*? so long, that I look upon this inviting opportunity as a farewell Compliment to the Old Year not to be neglected.

New sadness, Alas, threatens the opening of the New One, to all the Worcester & Bath Branches, & to all to whom He was known through-out the family, in the approaching loss of Mr. Sandford,[4]—who is so desperately ill, that not a hope remains—How do I pity poor amiable—feeling—affectionate Mrs. Sandford, who has been amongst the select of Wives in conjugal perfect happiness! |

I have not seen Sarah Payne since this my last return from Eliot Vale, but I had very great pleasure from her sight after her long absence, as it was so completely in unison with the

[1] See L. 1296 n. 7 and L. 1297 n. 7.

[2] Second daughter of Richard Penn (L. 1283 n. 2), Rose or Mary (1785-1863) had married on 14 June 1821 as his second wife Samuel Paynter (1774-1844). Attesting to the friendship between the Penns and the Barretts is a letter (Barrett, Eg. 3705, f. 184) from Richard Penn (1784-1863) acquainting CFBt of a bequest made to her by his sister (Mrs. Paynter) of parts of the proceeds of a 'leasehold estate in Augusta Street'.

[3] This is the letter (Berg), dated 93, Place d'Alton, Boulogne, 4 September 1822, a copy of which CFBt had made in her Pink Letter Book (Barrett, Eg. 3706D, f. 37b). The original (Berg) CFBt had sent from Boulogne by her son Richard, a 10 year-old returning to school. 'This letter must contain no secrets of State as it is to occupy a most precarious situation in Dicky's pocket. But I would not quite lose the chance of his presenting or sending it, though I am half afraid of his taking his own little person to London in safety. he is going alone, but we have no other means of sending him & must therefore trust to Providence, which after all is the best resource though one is so apt to make it the *last*.'

[4] See L. 1296 n. 5.

comforting account of her amended looks which you had imparted from Boulogne.[5] Yet I tremble for the Winter!—what a risk does it present, & what an experiment is that of her husband & her Mother! either the most eminent men in Surgery & in Medicine must wholly have mistaken her case, or we shall all have to grieve at the temerity with which their opinions have been braved. God grant they may make us all a set of *Molierists,*[6] & as merry at the Expence of Physicians, as the Physicians, hitherto, have been merry at our's.

Poor dear Clement! may he but be one of our party!

If my dear Sister means to continue at Brighton, I will write to her thither shortly: if not, I will hope for a peep at her loved face ere long in Bolton Street.

Where does the dear Archdeacon pass his X^mas? Mr. Hemming[7] gave hopes to Alex that his next abode, in leaving Ely, would be London: what an inexpressible acquisition to me! —especially now, that I am peremtorily commanded to abstain from all my too—too dear—& most sacred written hoards always in the Evening.—I feel too imperiously the justness of the prohibition to rebel—but ǀ the difficulties annexed to it are unspeakable.—

Who is Mrs. Kingston?[8] I did not think Mr. Barrett had

[5] CFBt had reported the recent arrival (*c.* 4 September) at Boulogne of 'Mrs Ad^l Burney & Sarah Payne (Eg. 3706D, ff. 37b–39): 'Mrs B. . . . seems very happy, nursing & indulging Sarah, who has quite recovered her good looks, is very pleasant & . . . thinks she shall not be obliged to winter abroad.'

[6] FBA knew *Médecin malgré lui* (1666) and probably also *Docteur amoureux* (1658) and *L'Amour médecin* (1665).

[7] A Revd. Samuel Hemming (1724–85), a resident of Twickenham since 1760, had been 'Minister of Twickenham Chapel' from 1761 until his death; his nephew the Revd. Samuel Hemming (1767–1828), D.D. (Oxon., 1801), rector of East Lavant (1805), in the years 1790–1805, when he was succeeded by the Revd. G. O. Cambridge (see L. 1190 n. 2 and Cobbett, *Memorials of Twickenham*).

[8] Elder daughter of Sir Giles Rooke (1743–1808), Judge in the Court of Common Pleas, Harriet Ann (d. *post* 1860) had married in 1812 as his 2nd wife John Kingston (*c.* 1782–1860) of Clarence Terrace, Regent's Park, and had at least six children.

John Kingston's first wife was not Henry Barrett's sister Julia (who had married a Harvey) but her illegitimate daughter Julia by Sir Peter Nugent (d. 1799) of Donore, Westmeath. See *GM* 1799². 724. Born in March 1783, this daughter is referred to in Sir Peter's will (see extracts, Berg) as Julia Barrett or Harvey or Mary Harvey or Lily Barrett or Harvey. At the time the will was made she was living with her father. Educated in France and generously provided for (see various documents, settlements, indentures, copies of will, etc., in a wooden box, Berg), she had married on 21 March 1804 John Kingston (*supra*), gave birth (25

a sister living. I wish to see & embrace my dear little Big Girls, & my bold noble *God Boy*;—I shall keep that name for him, from pleasant remembrances, till he remonstrates with me in person upon its little decorum, *vu* his growth, height, & old years.——My dear Charlotte!——I could not but feel entirely in harmony with your sensations, avowed & implied, relative to the Pedagogical munificence.[9] I believe we have a good deal of the same sort of stuff running in our veins.——Yet I both love, esteem, & admire the *Ped.* sincerely. So, I little doubt, do *you*: but there are certain things one loves to avoid *avec qui que ce soit.*

I am extremely glad at what you tell me of our poor Sarah Payne's brightening destiny in the generous proofs of attachment so handsomely lavished by her kind-hearted Sposo.

I have had one visit—at length, from Martin—I could not see him—even after so long a period—without strong emotion: but I am happy to tell you he came on a most honourable errand, & entirely *de son chef*—to repay a small sum I had prevailed on my dear lamented James to suffer me to advance for his *uniform*!![10]—I had refused any memorandum, & had never mentioned it to the family; but Martin found it recorded—& came to do it honour. We will not *affront* him by being surprized—*but* there is nothing derogatory in saying the World is not absolutely overstocked with such sort of delicate probity.[10] |

I have seen as yet nothing of our dear Fanny. Is my good Mrs. Baker on the Hill?—I could give you a little recent detail of Alex that would not only make your partial constancy to him exult, but greatly gratify the spirit of applause with which Mr. Barrett has encouraged his opening career —— but I have no room left—However, lest you should wish all that has preceded at the bottom of the Thames, for taking its place, I will just intimate that he has preached at Lee

September 1805) to Peter Nugent Kingston (xii, L. 1436 n. 5), M.D., and died on 9 February 1809. This date and perhaps some fragments of the story had apparently clung to FBA's memory, prompting her present query.

[9] This matter is lost with CFBt's letter, but perhaps some allusion to taking pupils as a means of augmenting the family income. See further, xii, L. 1396 n. 3.

[10] For Martin Burney's expiatory deeds, see L. 1275 n. 13 and L. 1276.

Church,[11] for Mr. George Lock, with such general approbation, that I could hardly bear the burst of felicitation with which I was overwhelmed when the Service was over. I had seated myself, as at Twickenham, in a separate pew—neither to constrain others, in case of disappointment, nor myself, in case I had reason to augur success — — & the Rector's Pew opened upon me, one by one, with speechifications the most dulcet that could reach my Ears. I found him, indeed, amazingly improved since I had heard him last. His First, Kindest & most effective Preaching Friend, the Archdeacon, would greatly have been pleased at such a result to his many hints, remonstrances, & spurs.—

Adieu, my dearest Charlotte—Give my kind love to Marianne, & many thanks for her two most welcome little visits, with my wish for their repetition, & best Comp[ts] to M[r] B[arrett] & Kiss for me my dear little Girls, & *put them to Bed & pull them out therefrom* as early as may be possible at Night & at Morn.

ever yours with warm love & interest,
F. d'Ay.

What a *Prodige* is that poor Miss Biffin with her Lip-Needle & Pencil![12]

---

[11] See L. 1297 n. 4 and further, L. 1301.

[12] Sarah Biffin or Beffin (1784–1850), who, born without arms, hands, or legs, became a miniature painter of some distinction (see *DNB*). CFBt had seen her 'among other exhibitions' at Boulogne. 'This poor soul used to be exhibited at Ham Fair for sixpence a visitor & astonished their weak minds by threading a needle with her lips. She has now been studying *painting* at Brussels, and actually paints portraits in miniature in a very tolerable style, & takes very strong likenesses. . . . The painting brush is pinned on a little puff at the top of her gown, where her shoulder ought to be, & she turns her head on one side & guides the brush by taking one end of the stick between her lips. It is admirable & horrible to see her at work. Her landlady says she is married to a handsome young man [a Mr. Wright] who takes care of her money & lifts her about, but she preserves her first name, like Madame de Stahl, because it is the most celebrated.' Two samples of her work, including a self-portrait, are shown by Daphne Foskett, F.R.S.A., *Collecting Miniatures* (1979), Plates 70E and 70G.

11 Bolton Street,
5 January 1823

To Charles Parr Burney

A.L.S. (Osborn), 3 Jan. 1823
Double sheet 8vo   4 pp.
Docketed in pencil, p. 1: 1823

Bolton Street
5th Jan^y—
1823—

My dear Charles,

I could answer for Alex no sooner, as only last Night, too late for the post, he returned from Horsham[1]

You cannot doubt his pleased acceptance with your invitation.

As to me, You have answered for me in the very terms of your invite.[2] You *Both* understand me too well to experience either surprise or disappointment that I beg my '*Representative*' may profit by the Bed & Board offered to his Mother. I have no spirit of exertion but what springs from *occasion*: to that, I am still awake—but the *intentional* effort belonging to a settled Dinner-Party has long forsaken me.—Should it return—you, my dear Charles, & your amiable & Agreeable Partner shall have news of its arrival. |

As to the Preacher—how much I could Say that I care not to write! I could not but see *Your* opinions in your Silence when we met—& I thank you for absenting yourself at that critical moment from the warm & almost fascinated Friends who were assembled at the Rectory.[3] To have damped Them would have been to damp Him, who wants encouragement to rouse him to action, as much as he wants a 'kind & experienced Friend' to keep his energies, when once animated, from running Wild as the Wind. Practice will calm, & Time will soberize him—& then, with a voice capable of every

1299. [1] See L. 1296 n. 7.   [2] Received 3 January (Diary).
[3] The rectory at Lee, Blackheath, where after his sermon AA was congratulated by his mother's friends (the Lockes, Martins, Angersteins) and their guest Nicholas Vansittart (see L. 1297 n. 4 and L. 1301).

species of inflexion, ⏐ & the dauntless courage which—to my utter astonishment—he says takes possession of him the moment he enters the Pulpit—I cannot fear, I frankly own, the failure of your kind prophesy; or that he will not become —in the words of Mr. Vansittart, a powerful Preacher.[3]

After I had read to him your Letter, he charged me to tell you he was much gratified by your approbation.

You will not think it a bad sign if I add, that, after ruminating some time upon your expressions, he declared that—knowing how severe you were, & how sincere—they gave him more pleasure than all the unqualified, unlimited, enthusiastic praise that most indulgently had been poured upon him by his too partial Friends. ⏐

I conclude your whooping Coughers are all expelled to their own Fire Sides. But I am concerned that *you* do not yourself take the recreation of change of Scene, & give it to Mrs. Burney.[4] You can hardly, I think, more deserve than require that relaxation. Remember me very kindly to your pretty 'little lady'[4]—Every body, I am told by Alexander, was struck with her beauty at Woodlands.

Remember me also, kindly, to Mrs. Bicknel,[5] whose soft & meaning Eyes spoke much of remembrance to *me*!—

Yours ever, my dear Charles,

affec^ly

F. d'A.—

1300 [11 Bolton Street, 23 January 1823]

To Mrs. Locke

A.L. (Berg), n.d.
Double sheet 8vo   4 pp.
Docketed: in pencil, p. 1: To Mrs. Locke?

[4] See L. 1245 n. 4; L. 1210 n. 18.
[5] See L. 1245 n. 5.

In waiting & waiting for opportunity—by which I mean not only time but spirits—to write to my dearest Friend as I *love* to write, namely all that is most upon my mind, or in my affairs, when I hold the Pen to her, I am so continually in arrears, that half what I tardily at last offer is in a waste of explanation—A *waste*, I say, for however delay may make it necessary, it is not more *ennuyant* to scribble than to read. Now ¦ I am thinking, my dearest Friend, since this occurs so often, & from the same subsisting situation must still so often occur—whether it were not better we should go back—in this one thing, in which we *can* go back!—to old times, & give & receive a weekly kind word, under all the chances of writing that kind word *only*, but wholly & mutually absolved *d'avance* from either murmur or alarm in writing no more?—

What instigates this proposition is my growing impatience for news of the entire ¦ departure of the Cold, & for some information of our sweet Amine, who was not quite as well as usual, even, when the *Kind* Augusta wrote her most amiable answer to Alex. I had the pleasure to see Sir Geo. in one of my prescribed stamps round Berkeley Square, with my dear little Diane—& I only wish you could all *be* as well as he looks. I have spent a most endearing Evening with L^y T[emple-town][1]—but I cannot go to her a q^{rtr} as much as I wish—or as she urges—for my dear Alex has scarcely any fixed *appointments* ¦ at present,—& he is really very busily occupied in his 3 pursuits

Poor Mr. Sandford still lingers rather than lives[2]—My sister Burney is pretty well, & always supports her incomparable spirits: my poor Charlotte is still anxious for Clement, who never recovers, though he amends: Sarah writes very gaily from Crew Hall. My *Niece* Sarah *braves the Doctors*, & is returned to winter in London.[3] I earnestly hope she is not too presumptuous: she is a charming young Creature, for intellect, manners, & all accomplishments. Pray embrace *for me* my sweet Amine—& eke Augusta—

1300. [1] On 15 January (Diary).   [2] See L. 1296 n. 5.
[3] JB's daughter 'Sally' Payne (L. 1247 nn. 1, 2).

[11 Bolton Street],
—19–27 January 1823

To Esther (Burney) Burney

A.L.S. (Berg), —19-27 Jan. 1823
Two single sheets 4to   4 pp.   *pmks* 28 JA 1823   red seal
Addressed: Mrs. Burney, / Lark Hall Place / near Bath.
Endorsed by EBB: answered Feb. 27. 1823

Finished 27. Jany 1823.

My dear Esther,

Our good & dear Edward will have accounted for my silence
last week, as he told me he was to write himself; & I am aware
his account of what has excited your kind solicitude as to my
health will be of a satisfactory nature, for I am, indeed, at
present, more recovered, *corporeally*, than the wisest of
human Aesculapius's could have made me, by any prediction,
believe. And *before* last week, I had dropt all intention of
writing upon the subject, from the daily apprehension of receiving news from yourself of so melancholy a nature as to
make a history of dangers apparently *past* utterly uninteresting. Sophy's Letter to Alex had powerfully alarmed me for
poor amiable *Rebecca,*[1] & grieved me for you all, & for myself—but as the blow has so long been suspended — —
perhaps the fine Constitution & skilful management of this
excellent man may conquer the disease — — what a joy
should that be allowed!—Do they ever try Iceland Moss?[2] it

1301. [1] Rebecca *née* Burney (i, p. lxxv), whose husband William Sandford (L. 1296
n. 5), the surgeon, was to die on the 26th. An account of his death with tributes
to his work in the Infirmary at Worcester is to be found in the 'Worcester Journal'.
  [2] Prescribed for membranous classes of consumption of the lungs, Icelandic
Moss was a bitter aromatic plant, whose foremost advocate seemed to be Richard
Reece (1776-1831), who in 1803 published *Observations on the Anti-phthisical
properties of the Lichen Islandicus, or Icelandic Moss*, recommending it as well in
his *Domestic Medical Guide* . . . (1803), pp. 171-2, and in his popular Medical
Guides, some seventeen editions of which appeared in the years 1803-51.
  Washed in cold water to remove little sticks and green bits, re-dried in a gently
heated oven, the moss was then ground and sieved. The resulting powder could be
boiled in milk or distilled water or made into a jelly or porridge. Its beneficial
properties were thought to reside in its bitterness and in its 'mucilage' or nutri-
tious elements.
  'So prevalent and destructive' was consumption in Great Britain, Reece

is now prepared in Jelly, & Conserves, so as to mix up in a moment with hot water & milk. I am longing to send a pot of it—but dare not, unless I could be assured it would not rather sadden them—by so recent recollections,—than be serviceable. You can judge far better than I can, & I will abide by your opinion. It is very possible they have it not in that form at Worcester. Savary prepares it;[3] & I am giving it now to Alex, for a Cold—& for his extreme thinness; & it *evidently* & *palpably* nourishes him. He is not *ill, au contraire*, he is remarkably *well*, except in those 2 afore named particulars.

But now to my explanations: First, as it will be shortest; for James Street.—Eh bien; Martin, whom I had not seen since our loss of his much & ever lamented Father, came to me, about ˡ a week before my last Letter, accompanying his Mother, to pay me the £15 my dear James had kindly permitted me to lend him upon making his Admiral's Uniform! This was not *only Right*, but something beyond that; it was Conscientous & delicate; as I had never claimed or even *mentioned* the loan, & as I had not any knowledge that my poor Brother had left any memorandum of its existence. Martin, however, had found it recorded in his Father's account Book.[4]

I know you will be glad, for many reasons, of this—& I rejoice to tell it you, first for Martin's sake, & next to completely set at ease all pressure on another score, to which this has no analogy, save in the similar kindness & true affection it evinced to me. But This was a real matter of business,

remarked, 'that it is calculated to destroy no less than sixty thousand of its inhabitants annually, the majority of which is supposed to be under twenty-five years of age'.

[3] A socialite and man about town, a patron of the arts, the theatre, and the opera, and occasionally a guest at the Pavilion, Brighton, the chemist Thomas Field Savory (1776-1847) would be appointed by King William IV on 13 February 1832 Gentleman of His Most Honourable Privy Chamber in Ordinary. His portrait painted by Lawrence is still in the family.

The inventor of seidlitz powders (patent no. 3954, 23 August 1815), he was a member of the firm Paytherus, Savory, & Moore, chemists of New Bond Street, who in 1806 were dispensing prescriptions to the Prince Regent and the Royal Family. The firm Savory, Moore, and Davidson, still very much existing at 143 New Bond Street and other addresses, prepared the coronation oil for Queen Elizabeth II.

Thomas Field Savory was succeeded by his nephew John (1800-71), who, certified as an apothecary on 19 March 1828, was to become in 1844 President of the Pharmaceutical Society.

[4] See L. 1260 n. 1.

emanating not from a private & separate store of my own, but from A[lex]'s & my current income; & it had a peculiar destination, which it now fulfils. For the *other*, which you disappoint me in mentioning, no Note can ever be found, as it was a separate store—& I would I dared beg you to cancel even its remembrance.[5]

⌐—,

Jany 19—I mark well your *calumny!*—but I did not plot to Tantalize You:—I really began my Eliot Vale Exordium with full intent to devote 3 sheets to my 3 Notices: as my Franker was so soon to be so nearly your Guest. I now see that, with a few *currencies*, I can merely execute *two* of my projects that which is before you, & — — either myself or my Alex — — Well, I cannot be *answered* which you would chuse First,—but I think I shall best suit your taste in taking that which is *Still present*, my tale of Alex, than that which is, apparently, of no immediate interest, myself—for I am so much better that my account of what is *past* I may more quietly wait a future opportunity than what regards such a Will o' th' Wisp of the moment as Alex — — Thus, therefore, stands the matter. Upon our last invitation to E[liot] V[ale] Mr. G[eorge] Lock insisted that Alex should preach at Lee Church, in his, Mr. G. L.'s Pulpit. Alex—nothing loath—consented, & went hard to work to make his best preparations. He was not ready till 11. on Saturday Even^g And then—on shewing me his Sermon, I saw it of such a preposterous length, that I feared it might put all his Congregation asleep. There was, however, no time for altering properly,—& I persuaded him to resign this laborious performance, & take another that he had already preached at Twickenham, but which he had much changed & amended since. He could not bring himself to agree—& I was very uneasy—but on the morning, at the instant we were all setting out, he relented. I was much troubled at all this, & not sufficiently mistress of myself to bear accompanying my dear Mrs. Lock, who was buoyant in kind expectation, to sit in the pew, as usual, with the Wife & Daughters of the Rector,

[5] A sum of £40 offered to EBB at the time of her husband's death (L. 1219 n. 4).

Mrs. G[eorge] & the Miss G. Lockes, to whom were joined
S^r G[eorge] & Lady Martin—&, in the next pew, Mr. Mrs. &
the two Miss Angersteins, with the younger Sons.⁶ I thought
I must constrain their civility, or subdue my fears into an unnatural composure. I escaped them all, & the more as I was
informed that the Chancellor of the Exchequer, I then on a
visit to Miss Vansittart on Blackheath,⁷ had been invited by
Mr. J[ohn] Angerstein *to hear Alex.* Mr. G. Locke *smiled*,
but made his Clerk shew me to a private & empty Pew. Alex
partook not my tremors! his congregation only animated
him, & so great an improvement from the time I had heard
him, 2 or 3 years ago, in Portland Chapel, I really never witnessed. His voice is penetrating, & full of variety—his manner is energetic, & his Sermon was deeply impressive. You
see, my dear Esther, I disguise not my approbation: but what
is that to what Was poured upon me! S^r G[eorge] M[artin]
came to me first, crying 'I hope you'll never be nervous for
him again!' L^y M. followed, with 'I hope you are proud of
your Alex!' Then Mr. J. Angerstein 'He has given us the most
eloquent discourse I ever heard.' Then Mrs Locke, her sweet
Eyes red with her own emotion 'How admirable he has been!'
Then Mrs. Angerstein, tears of sensibility running down her
cheek, 'Oh how I have longed to be by your side to congratulate You!'—And Then. Mr. Vansittart, to say 'I think him
full of promise to become a *most powerful Preacher*'. And
Mr. G. L. to tell me he knew not whether he had most approved
his manner or his matter — — Was this flattering enough?
it was truly the *far* happiest Hour I have known since May
1818!—You will be glad I am sure, my dearest Hetty for
your affect

F d A I

Pray tell me as soon as you can you are in your own hands,
dearest Etty—but why *Mr. Phinn?*⁸ Where is Mr. Hay?⁸

⁶ For the Angerstein family, see L. 1195 n. 14.
⁷ See L. 1270 n. 23.
⁸ Thomas Phinn (*c.* 1782–1837), apothecary, 3 Prince's Buildings, Bath, was
in partnership with George Edmund Hay (L. 1180 n. 19; and ix, L. 1059 n. 19).

1302   11 Bolton Street,
                              —29–30 January 1823

To Mrs. Broome

A.L.S. (Berg), —29–30 Jan. 1823
Double sheet 4to   4 pp.   *pmks* 31 ⟨J⟩A 1823 31 JA 1823   red seal
Addressed: Mrs. Broome— / To the care of / Mrs. Barrett, / at Henry Barrett's Esq; / Richmond—*Surry*.

Bolton Street. 11.
29. Jan^y
1823.

I hope you are now safe landed in your Winter's quarters, my dearest Charlotte? Your other half,—in Nature as in Name—was expecting you when she wrote to me last,[1]— yet a blank feel always rests on the mind where there is any possible uncertainty. Let me hear from you, then, my dearest Charlotte—but not as I now write to you!—by a melancholy commission, from Edward—who gave it me through Fanny—& received it from worthy Blue[2]—I need not be more explicit to be understood.—Poor Mrs. Sandford lost her beloved & admirable husband the 26th.

The good & feeling Edward set out instantly for Worcester, in the midst of the thick snow, & on the Eve of its succeeding floods—though he was carefully *entreated* by Blue not to risk the Journey,[2] & its great expense & loss to him, on so mournful an errand. But Edward is one of the rare beings, who never listens to a call of pleasure that would separate him ǀ from any Devoir—& never is deaf to a Call of Devoir,

1302. [1] A letter received on 1 January (Diary).

[2] Elizabeth Warren Burney (1755–1832), who according to the 'Worcester Journal' had come from Brightwell to Rainbow Hill, Worcester, on 29 November 1822 at the express wish of Mr. Sandford and to 'the great relief of her unhappy sister'. It was she who would have commissioned her brother Edward the artist, of Clipstone Street, London, to inform FBA of the surgeon's death (26 January), a letter delivered to FBA (see Diary) by their niece Fanny Burney (i, p. lxix), the governess.

Edward (*supra*) had reached 'Rainbow Villa' on 28 January and the Revd. Richard Allen Burney (L. 1180 n. 18) of Brightwell, on the 29th. The funeral took place on 4 February at Claines Church ('Worcester Journal').

though it should separate him from every pleasure in life. He is indeed exemplary.

We know no detail relative to poor Mrs. S[andford]—but I conclude she will go to reside at Bath. Her Rainbow-Hill house will be too expensive, &, Now, too melancholy;[3] at Bath she has all she most loves, except Edward—& except Blue,—but the former is only *one*, though that one is a Host; & the latter is but a Day's Journey, away from her, & so situated as to invite frequent intercourse.

I wish to hear that dear Clement is stronger, & more his own man—I suppose he will not be with you again till Easter. Yesterday Alex begged me to receive his early friend, Mr. Jones,[4] who requested the introduction, & had every claim to it that my esteem could give him. I could not but be pleased with him, though ⎹ the meeting was far from cheering to me, or, consequently, pleasant to himself. He stirred up recollections so tender! He had been known to my best Friend, & they had reciprocated great liking. However, at another period I shall see him more chearfully.

⌣⟶

I am waiting the movements of this eternally procrastinating & forgetful Alex to answer—or make him answer, *our* Charlotte's last billet. Every day he promises the *next* shall be effective, but — — but — — but — — the *next* is never the *present*!—I am disappointed not to have my dear Archdeacon & his truly amiable Cornelia for my *neighbours*, as they half engaged themselves to become this winter. I tremble lest there is some change. Pray tell me. And good Mrs. Baker —have you seen her?[5]

Sarah Payne keeps wholly at home, but goes on astonishingly well—she has had 2 parties to open the new decked house,[6]

[3] FBA's conjecture proved correct. Mrs. Sandford leased 'Rainbow Villa' and, with her sister Miss E. W. Burney, removed to Worcester on 17 March, where they remained during the 'sale of the furniture'. On the 25th they went to visit relatives in Bath and on 9 May moved to the rectory at Brightwell, 'where Mrs. S. being invited by her nephew R. A. Burney [fixed] her future abode' ('Worcester Journal').

[4] FBA had received AA's friend, the future political economist (L. 1294 n. 2), on Sunday 26 January (Diary). For General d'Arblay's regard for Jones, see viii, L. 840.

[5] Formerly an inseparable friend of Charlotte Cambridge (i. 2, 81). See further, L. 1305.　　　　　　　　　　　　　[6] See also L. 1301 and n. 3.

& presided very pleasingly. Mrs. B[urney] is recovering. Let our Charlotte acquaint ¹ you with the upright conduct of Martin. He has since been to drink tea with us by appointment, & I never saw him so unassuming in his opinions, or so free from extravagant maxims. I was extremely glad to observe this amendment, & I have cordially invited a repetition of his visit in consequence of it. I am quite sorry Sarah is so out of my reach. S[arah] *Harriet* writes in very good spirits from Crewe Hall: I hope they will be steady. The situation ought to be of *permanent* advantage to pay for its enterprize & its &c, &cs, according to *my* way of seeing life. She comes to town at the end of February.

I have this moment a fresh note from Fanny to say that Blue writes word that her Sister wishes to avoid all Letters of condolence, that she may escape answering—or even reading the[m] — — In grief like hers, her own feelings & wishes should alone be studied & complied with.[7]

I have seen poor good Mrs. Sansom, for herself, & on the part of the two poor Sleepes.[8]

Often as I put off—unwillingly always, though so ⟨for you⟩ frequently, writing to my dearest Charlotte, I yet never take the Pen that I can close till my paper is gone—so much I have to say, & so naturally subject follows subject—God bless you, my love—& *give* my Love, the kindest, to your dear namesake—& remember me very affect^{ly} to Marianne [and] best Comp^{ts} to Mr. Barrett. Yours for ever & aye

most truly

F d'A

Alex is well.

[7] For the Worcester Burneys, see nn. 2, 3. EBB's daughter 'Fanny' (i, p. lxix) was their niece.

[8] Elizabeth Margaret *née* Wood, widow of James Sansom (L. 1191 n. 16), indigent relative of the Burneys and Sleepes, had called on FBA on 22 January (Diary), receiving in all probability the annual pension of £4. 0s. 0d. (as recorded under Expenditure in FBA's Account Book, Berg). On the same day FBA wrote to Esther Sleepe (L. 1191 n. 17) and on the 24th to Frances Sleepe (Diary), doubtless remitting to them as well £4. 0s. 0d. (see her Account Book, Berg, paid to the 'Sleepes').

This instant, late at night, I have a line from L^y Martin to inform me of the death of Mr. Angerstein[9] |

How concerned I was at hearing of the Fire—but how grateful 'twas at *noon*—

[30 January]

Thursday—This Letter, written last Night in the dark, only wanted sealing, directing & Signing when Mr. Barrett called, & made me a *très aimable* visit—adieu encore, my Charlotte

1303   [11 Bolton Street, *post* 18 February 1823]

To Mrs. Locke

A.L.S. (Berg), n.d.
Double sheet 8vo   4 pp.

I have obeyed the injunctions of the sweetest of Enjoiners as long as seems to me good & fitting — — & not because my *weekly bulletin* would have hurt me—but because I know my indulgent Friend loves not to leave me unanswered, & because while it is judged by that dear Enjoiner that writing would be injurious, it's consequent avoidance must fall upon *Her*, my poor Amine herself—And could I be so selfish as to even *wish* for a line that should come from that overwhelmed hand — — & not hand alone, but Heart, & Head?—No,— while the ever | kind Augusta[1] can satisfy both my tender Friends of *my* health, &c, I will surely accept the same Ambassadress between the two Parties for the statement of

[9] John Julius Angerstein (iv, L. 334 n. 4) of Pall Mall had died at Woodlands, Blackheath, on 29 January. Born in St. Petersburg in the year 1735, he 'came to England, under the patronage of the late Andrew Thomson, esq. an opulent Russian merchant', in whose counting-house he remained until, introduced by his patron to Lloyd's, he 'quickly became celebrated as a broker and underwriter', eventually reaching 'the summit of commercial fame and prosperity' (*AR* lxv. 189–90).

1303. [1] Lady Martin and Sir George had called on Sunday 16 February (Diary).

Their's—& wait till all is tranquilly—& I hope far more serenely & happily than heretofore—arranged in affairs, & restored in Health. I write this only therefore, in the mean time, to shew I acquiesce in my Amine's injunctions, & to say that I am myself considerably better, & even astonishingly repaid for my strict observance of ordained privations, as my poor head is no longer so laboriously & painfully pinioned down I to one side, & one spot, for the night's *manqué* rest. I have entirely taken leave of medical consultation, & go on *all by myself*, according to circumstances.

But I have wholly—perforce!—renounced all my dear commerce with my *sacred* Papers at Night.[2]

Alex is much with me—& I have 3 houses to which I resort occasionally to Tea in his absence[3]—& some few come to *me*—And when none, I have opened a new resource in examining lighter & slighter MSS.—yet all *necessary* to my repose for passing through my hands, ere they are selected for the Rectory, or destined to the flames.

Ever & Ever & Aye
My dearest of Friends
Yours truly
F. d'A

No Reply—but through Augusta. I

I passed the Evening with dear dear Lady Templetown on Tuesday[4] & she was not well!—but cheered—& brightened ere we parted—

She had just finished her beautiful Bag for her inestimable Friend—she had wrought me one also that I long to frame & Glaze — —

I omit all that might lead to reply, my dearly loved Friend —all — — — — — — — — —.

but I neither think nor feel nor yearn the less — —

No Reply!—none— ! —

as yet.

---

[2] By January of this year FBA had arranged her materials and had begun to write the biographical sketch of her father intended as an introduction to an edition of his letters. See plans for the opening sections (Diary, 1 January): 'Sketch to Death of lovely & loved Esther', etc.

[3] To Lady Templetown, the Duchess of Gloucester, and the Princess Sophia (Diary).   [4] On 18 February (Diary).

To Esther (Burney) Burney

A.L.S. (Diary MSS. vii, not numbered, Berg), 29 Feb.–10 Mar. 1823
Three double sheets 4to   12 pp.   foliated 1–12   II of which the
franked cover is missing
   Endorsed by EBB, p. 9, *at top*: Answered April 18—1823 [*at the
bottom*:]   this packet—partly answered March 25—1823 finally
Answered / April 18—1823
   Edited by ?FBA, *top margin annotated*: Head seizures. papers Streat-
field. Vyse
   Edited also by ?CFBt. *See* Textual Notes.

29. Feby 1823

I must needs hope I shall never live to hear of a *Frank* for
writing to *You*,[1] my dear Hetty, that I do not *honour*, for
wofully must I be altered, either in force or in feeling, in
capacity, or in *heart*, ere that can be the case. Any alteration
in the *latter*, I humbly trust, is out of all question. I will *begin* therefore, Now directly, as per date—& go on as I can,
by leave of my head, & by chances of leisure uninterrupted,
till the destined day for Departure from Mr. Twining. And
First, my dearest Esther, let me thank you for your Letter,
which I had thought uncommonly long on its route—especially as I was aware of that little Sly inuendo upon the
latitude accorded me by my Correspondents!

⌒⟶

As you say I may send a packet, my purpose is to collect for
you some of the loved Letters of our darling Susan,[2] that I
had put apart to read to you, when we met:—but I will not
wait, as by that time I may find many more to communicate.
I shall also take this opportunity to put into your safe & kind

1304. [1] The offer of the family friend Richard Twining (L. 1282 n. 17) to carry
letters on his periodic visits to Bath for his health allowed FBA to compose and
send this long letter (12 pp. 4to) and as well a document (n. 3) without extra
postal costs to the recipient. EBB's letter, with its queries, often referred to here,
is missing.
   [2] For SBP's letters and journals, see iv. 447–8, 477; and *Catalogue*.

custody a melancholy *Affidavit,*[3] that was prepared for Alexander to carry last Decr to Mr. Hay, whom he was to beg to
accompany him to the Chief Magistrate, & there sign it. Mr.
Hay well knew the honoured Object both in France & England! As Alex's journey is delayed, & as I always dread his
losing any document, I shall be more easy to have it lodged
by this means with my dear Esther, who is as careful where
business is concerned, & as zealous where Friendship is to be
enacted, as if she had I never known, from her Youth upwards, what it is to be gay, light-hearted, sportive or skittish
in all her born days—whereas Deponent here avereth, that
she never knew nobody more oftener display those qualities
aforesaid than the said Esther B whether as Spinster or Wife
—whence the Deponent under-named is ready to affirm on
Oath, if required, that it is her, said Deponent's, belief, that
what is Solid & what is Airy may be amalgamated in the same
Composition, so as not to make it necessarily implied that a
Person who can be prudent, steady, & useful, must of course
be as dull as an Owl, or as heavy as a Brick bat, or as stupid as
a Post.   F. d'A.   witness.

These elegant similes having presented themselves, un-
sought, to my Imagination, I indulged them with insertion,
persuaded you would be well pleased to see my Fancy once
more invoking the flowery luxuriance of the Poetic lingo.

Thanks for that kind *jump* of Joy for the success of Alex
at Lee, & for my hopes from St. Paul's.[4] You ask who named
him *Preacher for the 5th Sunday in Lent*—How could I omit
telling you 'twas The Bishop of London himself?[5]—This has
been brought about by a detail too long for Paper—but the
Name of your Nephew is at this moment inscribed amongst
the Lent Preachers at St. Paul's, by the side of the choir, in

[3] Needed apparently in applications for General d'Arblay's *retraite* was a certificate or affadavit of his death (see also L. 1210 n. 15). In September 1817 the
General had conducted apothecary Hay on a guided tour of Paris (x, L. 1127).

[4] AA had been invited by the Bishop of London to preach in St. Paul's Cathedral on Passion Sunday 16 March (L. 1307).

[5] For the conversation between FBA's friends the Bishop of Salisbury and the
Archdeacon of Middlesex on AA's abilities and career, see L. 1287 n. 12.

the Cathedral itself. I have been there twice, *to look at the Pulpit*, &c & There I saw my dear dear cherished Name, mixed with that of 6 Divines for the 5 other days & Easter. Our hopes, however, on this appointment are merely of the Castle Building tribe, for Alex has never been presented to the Bishop. ꟾ 'Tis chiefly to my faithful old friend, Bishop Fisher of Salisbury, & partly to my other faithful adherent, the Archdeacon of Midlesex,[5] We owe this mark of attention; which, also,—for wheel within wheel has long been at work, —has been accellerated by the friendship of Mrs. Maltby,[6] who recommended Alex strongly to the Secretary of the Bishop of London, Mr. Hodgson, who is also Secretary to her *Beau Frere*, the present Bishop of Winchester, & with whom she is intimately acquainted.[6] I have reason, also, to believe that *yet another wheel* has revolved in the same circle—so that should all these mountains produce no Mouse, I shall be down among the dead Men. Things might, *perhaps*, have been sooner forwarded, but for an unfortunate circumstance that compelled me to damp intended favour to myself from the Bishop of London & his Lady, Mrs. Hooley.[7]—About 2 years ago, they heard of my being at Twickenham, & they came over to invite me to accompany the Archd[n] & Mrs. Cambridge in a party to Fulham Palace, for a Dinner already arranged there — — I felt their goodness,—felt it sincerely —& its possible consequences—but some of my most poignant recollections hung upon Fulham Palace, whither General d'Arblay had pursued my Brother Charles on an

[6] Harriet Maltby (L. 1232 n. 13), whom FBA had cultivated in Bath (ix, x *passim*) and visited in 1820 in London, was a sister-in-law of the Bishop of Winchester (1820). Christopher Hodgson (L. 1180 n. 9) served as secretary from time to time to a number of Bishops, including the Bishop of London.

[7] Mary Frances *née* Belli (*c.* 1783–1860), wife since 1805 of William Howley (L. 1258 n. 18), at this time Bishop of London, Archbishop of Canterbury (1828). It was in August 1819 when FBA was visiting Twickenham Meadows that the Bishop and his Lady called inviting the Cambridges and FBA as well to dine at the Bishop's Palace (Fulham). And it was five years previous to that (October 1814) that General d'Arblay arriving from France to find Alex in difficulties at Cambridge (see vii, Ll. 827–9) had followed CB Jr. to Fulham to enlist his influence and urge his intervention with the master of Caius. The proximity to Richmond, where the d'Arblays were living at the time, the recollection of events involving the Palace and persons now deceased (both husband and brother) had proved to FBA overpowering. Now she would be more resilient. The first step is the one that costs, she observed, quoting for a second time Mme de Deffand's famous witticism on the steps taken by the decapitated saint (ix, L. 1016 n. 3).

occasion of deep & piercing interest respecting Alex:—& the sudden invitation brought the circumstances so powerfully to my Mind, that an overwhelming grief surprized me off all guard, & I felt incapable of accepting their obliging proposal, or even of seeing them, to make my excuses, as Mrs. Cambridge urged, & so begin an Acquaintance—alas, I was disolved in tender & painful rushes of memory: could I have seen them to apologize, I could equally have seen them to ¹ pay my visit at Fulham Palace. *Ce n'est que le premier pas qui coûte.* I was quite disordered all the rest of the day with the strong emotions this unexpected overture awakened, & with my great regret I had not been able, for Alex's sake, to conquer them. But I have always held it right, for my Friends as well as for myself, to resist society, unless I could appear in it with chearfulness. *Sorrow & seclusion* should go hand in hand,—except on those rare occasions where *sympathy* takes the place of the latter. And you, my dearest Esther, with all your Native vivacity, have found the way to take that place with me in my bitterest moments of existence

⌐⎯⎯⌐

Mrs. Lock is nearly recovered. I have just got a few lines from her of a cheering nature.[8] The Angersteins will, I fancy, come to town earlier this year than usual. There are 2 young ladies to bring out.[9] Have you seen the Name of poor Miss Wilson in a Law Suit?[10] It is to have a New trial, as, from a blunder in her advocates, she has been non suited.

⌐⎯⎯⌐

You still ask about my health, &c—I thought the good result would have sufficed. But thus stands the detail. I was packing up a sacred hoard of papers, to carry with me for my private hours to Richmond, many months now ago & employed above an Hour in the arrangement, stooping my head over the trunk,—& on my knees—when—upon meaning to rise, I was seized with a giddiness, a swimming of the head,

[8] On 2 March (Diary).

[9] Caroline and Elizabeth Julia, now aged 21 and 17, respectively (L. 1195 n. 14).

[10] For Harriet Wilson and her action against her half-brother Joseph for non-support, see L. 1180 n. 12. She had visited FBA on 2 March (Diary).

a glare of false & fiery sparks before my Eyes, & a torturing partial pain on one side of my head, that nearly disabled me from quitting my posture, & ˡ that was followed, when at last I rose, by an inability to stand or walk—I tottered to a chair near at hand, & sank upon it, without force to reach out my hand to ring the Bell; but by the time that force returned, all was over,—my head was free from pain, my strength was restored, & I felt as if I had nothing the matter — — save an awful opinion that I had been upon the point of an apopletic fit. I had now gently recourse to such regimen as I remembered used to Mr. Thrale,[11] & I was wholly without any similar seizure till towards the beginning of November: but my *head* has long been in a most unnatural state, refusing to let me ever repose but upon one Ear, under penalty of hearing a tremendous *crack*, nervous no doubt, but horrible in its sensation, & seeming to menace a burst of all the interiour Vessels:—my second *threat* of seizure was at Eliot Vale, while Alex was at Tunbridge. It was in the Evening, & while I was stooping over some of my MSS, & erasing *passages* of *Letters* that I wished not *wholly* to destroy,[12] but leave for Alexander's *Children*. It was after a rich Dinner, for *me*, & I was talking with my dear Mrs. Lock, who was at work—& after about half an hour, when I raised my poor Pate, the same giddiness assailed me, accompanied with extreme faintness & sickness. I got out of the room as well as I could, & gained my own apartment—where, to be brief, the faintness, sickness, & alarming *malaise* of Tête continued till past 2 o'Clock in the morning—when I fearfully ventured to my *side-repose* in Bed, & persuaded Mrs. Locke to ˡ retire—though most reluctantly, to hers; leaving however, her excellent Sarah Cooke,[13] my old friend at Norbury Park, to sleep on a small Bed in Watch. I declined sending for any one, as there was no body I knew—& as I had no fear of immediate danger—though much of danger hovering.

The next day I was quite well again. Yet when I came to town, I put myself under Medical care—but to avoid long

---

[11] For Henry Thrale (1728/9–81) and the series of apoplectic fits to which he succumbed on 4 April 1781, see Clifford, pp. 175–99; and *DL* i *passim*).

[12] A sample of a manuscript so treated may be seen in the facsimile, i, Plate I.

[13] Sarah Cooke (L. 1297 n. 5).

details of what is past, to give the results: I have been suddenly taken a *third* time, in the middle of the Night, & with a seizure as if 100. wind mills were turning round in my head, which I held with both my hands, & which *seemed* as if Gun-powder worked the mills, which prepared for an explosion that would operate like a pistol shot into my Ear. This, again, dissipated —but my head was more confined than ever to the small part that could bear to be pressed upon the Pillow,—& I now went to Bed in the dread of a stroke that would bereave me of speech & perhaps sense, if I moved an inch in the Night. I had a horrour of going to rest — — —

In short,—I had now recourse to serious Medical help— &, finally, I have been Cupped in the Nape of the Neck, & prescribed a new Regimen, & a very severe one, & sundry medicines — — &, to come to the sum total, I am now so much better, that I pass my Night without any of those awful expectations, & believe myself to be merely ǀ on the common road of such gentle gradual decay as—I humbly trust, I have been prepared to meet with highest hope—though with deepest awe—for now many years back — —

The chief changes, or *reforms*, from which I reap benefit are *1*st *Totally renouncing* for the *Even*ing! all revision or indulgence in pouring over those Letters & papers that hold contents that come nearest to my heart, & work upon its bleeding regrets: *next*, transferring to the *Evening*, as far as in my power, all of sociality, with Alex, or my few remaining friends, or the few *he* will present to me of new ones— And when, as most ordinarily, I am, nevertheless, alone, I confine my reading & researches to gay old juvenile memorials or collections,[14] that amuse me in the amusement they enable me to prepare for my Grand Children. 3d *Constantly* going out every Day—either in brisk walks in the Morning in my neighbourhood, or in brisk jumbles in the carriage of one of my 3 friends who admit, & send for me, to a tête à tête *Tea-converse*. 4th strict attention to diet by my own daily experience.

Is here, at length, enough, my dear Hetty?

[14] This material, much mutilated, was edited by Annie Raine Ellis, *The Early Diary of Frances Burney, 1768–1778* (2 vols., 1889) and is now being re-edited by Lars Troide of McGill University.

Now to *you.* I feel vexed at your disappointment in your pretty house,[15] but not *surprised,* as I always feared it was too remote for a *winter* residence, though for summer beautiful. I am sorry, also, for the young proprietoress; but what can be kinder than your concessions to her advantage. As to its being *worth while,* or *not* to make the experiment, I I should hold *not* to do it a species of Suicide,—for why are Observation & Experience accorded us, if not in using the first to direct us in combining circumstances that may guide us for the *future,* & the second, in recollecting & weighing mistakes that had led us to judge wrongly in the *past?* Certainly, at our time of life we cannot have such a mass of *Superfluous* health as to make us indifferent to guarding or losing any part of that commodity. For myself, my present most earnest struggle in *active* life, is for so much exertion as may spare me from becoming a bodily burthen to my own existence, &, consequently, to the attentions of my Friends.

I ought to have told you the medical sentence pronounced, upon which I act in my present General Regimen—These were the words *You have a Head over-worked,* & *a Heart over-loaded.* — — The *product* of this is a disposition to a fullness in both that causes stagnation—&c—with a consequent want of circulation, at the extremities, that keeps them cold & aching.

Knowing this, I now act upon it as warily as I am able.

The worst of all in difficulty for my relief, is that I have lost—totally lost my pleasure in reading! Except Alex is my lecturer, for whose sake my faculties are still alive to what—*erst*! gave them their greatest delight. But alone — — I have no longer that resource! I have scarcely looked over a single sentence, but some *word* of it brings to my mind some mournful recollection, or acute regret, & takes from me all attention—my Eyes thence glance vainly over pages that awaken no ideas.—This is melancholy in the extreme. Yet I have tried

---

[15] No. 5 Lark Hall Place, into which CRB, EBB, and their family had settled in May or June 1817 (see ix, L. 1074 n. 7). As the LTA (Walcot parish) shows 'Burney' both as 'proprietor' and 'occupier', it is possible that he may have bought the newly-built house and that at this time EBB was trying to rent or sell it. See further, xii, L. 1363 n. 10. The 'young proprietoress' is probably EBB's daughter Amelia, who in due course, as things stood, was likely to inherit the property, and out of her legacy (see vii, L. 716 n. 12) may have helped pay for it.

every species of writing, & Writer—but all pass by me mechanically, ⏐ instead of instructing, or entertaining, me intellectually.

But for this sad deprivation of my original taste, my Evenings might always be pleasing & reviving — — but alas! — —

Whither is it my dearest Etty means to make her next essay? Not a hint is dropt on that subject. Still as high as the Belvedere? or more away from the Winds & storms?—Pray let me know. All, too, seems *en l'air* as to poor Mrs. Sandford.[16] Edward & Fanny drank tea with us yesterday, (This *actual date* is 10—March)—& I obtained no intelligence. I wonder not she is yet unable to decide definitely. Your idea for her of in or near London I should meet & greet with true satisfaction,—with more, indeed, than I will permit myself to dwell upon without some encouragement of probability. Castle building—were I still airy enough for such construction, might animate yet *nearer* & *dearer* hopes — — — but I keep myself in order, for I have no need of the repression of new Disappointments.

After all my long projects with respect to our dear Charlotte, I am more in the clouds than ever as to our approximation—! The Barretts plan the continent—& Charlottina anxiously wishes her mother to accompany them!—& who could reason, or try to persuade a Mother to resist so tender a filial desire? — — on the whole, I keep myself in order as well as I can, & wait events. *one* plan is in agitation that would save at least the *Seas* from separating us, i.e. the Barretts accepting an offer of the good & generous Archd^n Cambridge to inhabit his prebendary house at Ely[17]—during *10* Months in the Year, as their own: — — but even then, while I anxiously long for this scheme, *I* should lose sight & converse with them completely!—Sarah Payne, also, means to go abroad next Summer—& she ⏐ is so wonderfully improved, so agreeable, so cultivated, so good a discourser, & is become so even fondly affectionate to me, that her pleasing society, joined to her partial attachment, will make her loss severely

[16] See L. 1302 n. 3.

[17] For the summer of 1823 the Barretts accepted an offer (arranged apparently by G. O. Cambridge, Prebendary of Ely) of a vacant prebendary house in Ely, that of Henry Thomas Dampier (1791–1831), vicar of West Wratting, Cambs. (1821–9), prebendary of Ely (1821).

felt——& the more, as she is ever ready to come to me in an
Evening,——And my Mornings have so much at hand they can
always take care of themselves.——Mrs. *Admiral*! Burney has
been very unwell, but is recovered. Your own News from
Sarah *Hariet* is of later date than mine, & I am extremely glad
it is so good. I expect to hear of her in town every day[18]——
I see Fanny Raper very rarely, as she scarcely ever comes to
town from want of an *escort.* She was with me Sunday week,
with her husband, & was still in blooming beauty.——I thought
both my Guests of last night looked well. Edward does not
open at all about Mrs. S[andford] either because he is fearful
of indulging his wishes of her approaching his residence, or
because he is *trusted,* & consequently bound to silence.——I
have seen Martin no more since I wrote, but I am told he is
growing social & *aimable* —— —— Perhaps he has pensioned off
his ill-taken Rib,[19] as the Rev^d Mr. Vyse did a parelel connection formed in a luckless hour, & repented ever after, & never
made known but by the provisions of his *Will,* as he survived
her![20]——*He* was the object with whom the accomplished &
beautiful Miss Streatfield was so desperately enamoured, in
ignorance of his chains, that she demonstrated her unguarded
& resistless passion to *him* & *all she met.* She still lives, but
had pined away her health & spirits & beauty & happiness, &
power of forming any other connexion, many, many years
ago. I dare say you have heard me, formerly, speak of the
SS.? Sir William & Sir Lucas Pepys,[21] who alone of all the

---

[18] At 29 Park Street, Grosvenor Square, the house provided by Lord Crewe
(L. 1291 n. 4) for his granddaughters and their governesses.

[19] Rebecca *née* Norton (L. 1271 n. 4).

[20] This was the learned William Vyse (1741-1816), of Lichfield, D.C.L. (Oxon.
1774), F.R.S. (1781), canon residentiary of Lichfield (1772), rector of St. Mary,
Lambeth, and of Sundridge, Kent (1777), who had inspired the life-long devotion
of Sophia Streatfeild (1754-1835), the beautiful Greek scholar, who, with her
beauty and ability to cry at will, had wreaked such havoc in the hearts of the
Streatham circle, not excluding CB. See Clifford, p. 158; Hayward, ii. 329-34; *DL*
ii. 176 and *passim*; *Thraliana passim.*

In his will (PRO/PROB/11/1581/342, dated Tunbridge, Kent, 26 May 1812,
pr. 12 June 1816) there is no mention of his wife, but out of an estate of about
£3,000 (bequeathed for the most part to relatives), he gave 'to Sophia Streatfeild
now living in Queen Street May Fair London . . . the sum of five hundred pounds
which I hope she will accept for a Ring and in testimony of my sincere regard'.

[21] Sir William Weller Pepys (L. 1239 n. 9) and his brother Sir Lucas (i. 93; *DL*
i, ii *passim*), the physician, had called at Bolton Street on 6 April and 5 June
1821, respectively (Diary). FBA's Diary for the year 1822 is missing.

Streatham set have lived, & found me out in Bolton Street, except the 3 daughters of the House, Lady Keith, Mrs. Meyrick Hoare, & Miss Susan Thrale, now & then ǀ give me the pleasure of an Hour's social recollections of old time, that is interesting to us all.

How is poor Mrs. Beckford?[22]—How Miss Hay?—how the Brother?[23] Did the scheme prosper for bringing Miss Reid to Bath?[24] How is Mrs. Blagden?[25]—Mrs. Daly?[26]—are they as agreeable as ever? Do you ever see poor Mrs. Thomas?[27] Lady Murray did *not* go to Holland at last;[28] she heard, I suppose, that you held the Dutch but low in your estimation, so changed her plan, & passed the Winter at Brighton.

I send Mrs. Cole's Letter.[29]

And a dear dear small one from our dear exquisite Mother[30]—

Your recommendation of a good sturdy woman about 40, with strong nerves, & a large stock of Patience, is a portrait the most judicious possible for my *belle-fille*—Alex shouted aloud, & said 'O pray Keep that Letter of Aunt Hetty! — —'

I wish you could as easily reform as you can entertain him! He has not yet begun his *work* for the 16th!—I am kept in boiling water with the fear he will reduce himself to a toil of *night & day* at the last, so as to *mount the rostrum* half dead![4]

[22] See L. 1189 n. 20.

[23] Elizabeth Hay (L. 1208 n. 4) and her brother George Edmund (L. 1180 n. 19).

[24] See further, L. 1372 n. 3.

[25] Probably Mary Blagden (d. *c.* 1825 or *pre* June 1826), who appears in Larkhall Place. According to the Bath Directories (1819-24) she resided at 2 Grosvenor Place.

[26] Elizabeth Daly (*c.* 1754-1829) of 13 Lambridge Place, who according to her obituary (*Bath Chronicle*, 11 June) was the widow of 'Major Peter Daly, of Lisinore co. Galway', probably the second wife of Peter Daly 'of Lismore', who died 3 March 1803, at the age of 79 (see burials, All Saints, Weston). Living at 2 Lambridge Place was a Miss Ann Daly (*c.* 1767-1832), possibly his daughter by a first marriage, who, dying *c.* 5 November 1832, at the age of 65 (*Bath Chronicle*, 15 November), acknowledged in her will (PRO/PROB/11/1815/285, pr. 4 May 1833), a legacy of £1,000 'left me by the will of the late M[rs] Elizabeth Daly' and also an annuity of '£50 left by Miss Ellen Daly'. The burial of a Miss Ellen Daly (*c.* 1804-26) of 13 Lambridge Place is recorded in the Walcot burial registers (22 February).

[27] See L. 1200 n. 11; and ix *passim*.

[28] See L. 1290 n. 1.   [29] See L. 1295 n. 6.

[30] Esther *née* Sleepe (i, p. lxix), whose letters mentioned in L. 1282 and elsewhere are missing.

Do not let this spread, especially to Mrs. Maltby,[6] I entreat; it may make a laugh, but it is a serious dismay to me.

I have been 3 times to the great Temple, to view the scene of *Diction*—I wish it over — — — *well* c-à-dire !

adieu my dearest Esther—remember me kindly to all who kindly remember *me*—if such after this long absence be found.—Fanny read us parts of a charming Letter from You, & a pleasing & lively one from Emily, last night—with a *noble* trait of a fair Eliza[31]—which, to complete its dignity, went formally through my hands—that the munificence might be more widely *diffused*.

I am recommended not to *seal*, nor fold, for reasons of State by Fanny, who was very gay & agreeable—

God bless you ever, prays your ever affect[e]

& faithful F d'Ay

10 March 1823.

I hope you will not be as tired with reading as I am at this moment with writing, though, as usual, when Franked at my ease, I know not how to leave off to my dear Etty.

You ask about my poor Ramsay[32]—I am filled with regret in parting with her *personally*, from the devoted attachment that our 4 years *inmateshipness* has encreased rather than abated. Could I keep Three, she should be my Favourite, my Companion in my Walks, & my Trust in all my Money trans-actions, & my faithful confidant in all my current intentions — — but she is far too high, in every point of view, to have any one placed above her; & not at all equal, to guiding one below her,—she could only be a *non descript*, & I have Already an Inmate of that Nature!!—

---

[31] An allusion lost with Amelia Burney's letter.
[32] For the history of Elizabeth Ramsay of Ilfracombe, see L. 1182 n. 3.

[11 Bolton Street,
c. 3 April 1823]

To Mrs. Barrett

A.L.S. (Berg), n.d.
Double sheet 4to   4 pp.   red seal
Addressed: Mrs. Barrett, / at Henry Barrett's, Esq., / Richmond, / Surry. / By favor / of the first / Messenger / that happens to / pass — — Not by / Express—

My dear sweet Charlotte,

Poor—excellent Mrs. C[harlotte] Cambridge! to Heaven indeed, as you say, do I believe her translated.[1] Grief for Her is out of all question—& Grief for Myself—took its hold, & its vent, in 1812—when I returned to England, & found her not! then, indeed, with bitter tears I missed her. How would she have welcomed my return!—how should I have rejoiced in her welcome!—But Now—there could be as little sense, or feeling, as Religion to grieve that the conscious Soul is awaked while the poor morbid body sleeps eternally.

The Brother who so loved her, & who beyond all things Mortal was by her beloved, will have many sad feelings of regret:—but I am by no means surprised that you found them as rational & resigned as they may be many years hence.

1305. [1] This is FBA's reply to a missing letter from CFBt apparently containing news of the death in Gloucestershire of Charlotte Owen Cambridge (i, L. 1 n. 6); who was to be buried on 3 April 1823 by her own request in the parish of St. Mary the Virgin in Twickenham. See CFBt's letter (Berg), *pmk* 1 AP 1823; and Cobbett, *Memorials of Twickenham*, p. 77.

Having suffered *pre* 1812 some nervous or mental breakdown, Charlotte Cambridge had been cared for in Gloucestershire, either by her brother Charles Owen (1754-1847) of Whitminster or by Lady Jelf (ibid.). 'This week', CFBt was to inform her aunt, 'the Funeral procession will come from Lady Jelfs in Gloucestershire, and about Thursday next, they are expected to arrive here', and expected with the cortège were Lady Jelf herself and Mary Parker (L. 1238 n. 21), formerly housekeeper at Cambridge House, who had probably served in recent years as nurse or companion to Charlotte.

To be counted among the mourners was 'poor dear Mrs Baker' (L. 1302 n. 5) of Richmond, who, according to CFBt, 'bears her shock with the resignation which the circumstances seem so peculiarly to enjoin but, she is, if possible, even the most grieved of the three dear mourners. The Archdeacon feels & sees as you do. And Mrs Cambridge always sees with his eyes—but I think Mrs Baker, like myself, had cherished some hope of a return, a recovery, and this utter disappointment afflicts her the more.'

She was so good, so excellent, so affectionate, she must forever be missed by those whom she marked out for her friendship—& ¹ my poor dear Mrs. Baker will—I greatly fear—suffer severely. Tell her, when you may see her, my dear Girl, that were she either alone, or with any Companions but just those who are now under her roof, I should write to her more directly,—but what could *I* say *she* has not heard from those who want *her* consolation as much as she does their's?—Give her my very kindest love—my love truly sympathetic.

And if you can gather any thing of good nay admirable Mrs. Parker, pray let me know, when next you revive me with some account of my beloved Sister²—for She now is the subject on which my thoughts & anxieties most hang—& will continue to lurk & linger, till I can be informed she has dismissed her Medical adviser. That she should be with her darling Charlotte—I could almost say with mine—is indeed a satisfaction ¹ to obviate all of uneasiness that does not cling to illness under any auspices:—and for you, my love, it is an equally happy circumstance, since you would be almost torn to pieces with the *to & fro's*—of any separation. I know how assiduous would be Marianne, but I know, also, you could no more content yourself to forego your own share of watching so dear a Parent, than that Parent could forego the endearing attentions of Both. Clement I conclude to be at Cambridge, &, I hope, spared this inquietude.

Alex is a *smile out of pocket* by the wish relative to the Bᵖˢ & the Archys.—but he is not well; he has had a *feverette*,³ & is now under its discipline, but getting better, I trust, very fast. This has stopt his going to the Minor Canon concerning his school sermon,⁴ & has vexed us both—*me* at

---

² In a reply (Berg) *pmk* 1 AP 1823 CFBt was to gratify FBA with a detailed account of Mrs. Broome's recovery: 'With what joyful and thankful alacrity I obey your injunction to write as soon as I had good news to give you—My dearest Mother left her room yesterday . . . but was not the worse for this exertion.'

³ CFBt's wish is lost with the missing letter, but in the letter (*supra*) she expressed the hope that 'our dear Alexander's feverette is disappearing & I trust that when my Dicks holidays are over, & his nest vacant, we shall be able to persuade Alex to try change of air hither'.

⁴ This was the Revd. Henry John Knapp (1779-1850), D.D. (1840), minor canon of St. Paul's (1817) and vicar of Willesden, Middlesex, who had invited AA to preach a sermon on Easter Day at his charity school in Leadenhall Street, an invitation that AA was able to accept on Sunday 11 May (Diary).

least—lest it should occasion some other *officiant*. Alex has just heard, from ⏐ an author who is coming out with a work on that subject, that all *spinal fears* demand *Exercise* much more than the fashionable *costume* of *posture*.[5] Dancing is its first prescription. Tell this to my dear Julia & Hetty, & let them caper together, à *qui* music *mieux*.

My very tenderest love to my very dear Sister—& when you are able, another line will much contribute to my peace, if it be such as *you* will write with alacrity. My best comp^{ts} to Mr. Barrett. I have written to Mrs. Cambridge by this same post. Most affec^{ly} yours,

my dear Girl, ever,

F d'Ay

I have very long been in the hope of a promised interview with my sister—but must now patiently wait her recovery — ⏐

How dear a plan is the Ely![6] & how dear an archd^{n} & Mrs. Cambridge. to have your fine Boys brought up so near first rate rising *Branches of Learning* will make them early friends of the utmost use—& Mr. B[arrett]'s well bred—& *your*, my Charlotta fascinating manners will attract all of best promise for future service—

[5] As may be seen in a letter (Eg. 3706D, ff. 12-13b) of 20 September [1821] to MF, CFBt was concerned for her daughter Julia, whose backbone was growing 'awry'. The cure consistently recommended in those days was inaction, and though CFBt had made Julia lie down for an hour a day, she saw no amendment. AA had evidently known of a forthcoming and a very important work by John Shaw (1792-1827), surgeon and anatomist, *On the nature and treatment of the distortions to which the spine and the bones of the chest are subject . . .* (1823), a treatise extended in 1825 in *Further Observations on the lateral or serpentine curvature of the spine . . . (With an inquiry into the effects of various exercises, and other means which are used to prevent or cure these deformities . . .).* Illustrated by a fine series of plates, many of which were engraved by Landseer, the first work 'is quoted to the present day as an authority on orthopaedic surgery' (*DNB*).

[6] That is, the occupancy of prebendary Dampier's house in Ely (L. 1304 n. 17) in place of the usual flight to the Continent to save expenses in living. 'The *Ely plan* is indeed one which I contemplate with the utmost gratitude', CFBt was to state in her letter (*supra*). 'It prevents my leaving England, & Mama, & all I love best—therefore I try not to think that I am leaving Richmond & many friends whom I love much—but I should not see as much as I ought of the *brightest* side of the matter. for there are no very broad lights in life—at least none near which the shadows do not take their full space.'

To Mrs. Barrett

A.L. (Berg), n.d.
Originally a double sheet 4to, of which the first leaf is torn away.
1 p.   *pmks* Piccadilly ⟨22 AP 1823⟩
Addressed: Mrs. Barrett, / Henry Barrett's Esq, / Richmond, /
Surry.—

. . . staying till Monday, we shall arrive at Night,[1] & bring tea
tackle for our supper, some stale bread & unstale Butter—&
milk of the latter cast.

What is my confidence in my Charlottina's love to make
me bold to thus puzzle & perplex & occupy her, yet hope
that to give me the comfort of passing some time with her
will *make amends*?

Well—who & what has created that confidence?—why—
Wou[ld] you know?—hereditary fidelity of never varying
manifestation of affection—

My tenderest love to my dear Sister—

                                        adieu my dearest Girl.

Mrs. C[ambridge] has just left me,[2] & is enchanted with
the success of the Ely scheme—whence the arch^dn augurs
many kind *romances in real life.*

1306. [1] For AA's health, as FBA is to explain in L. 1307, she had taken lodgings
in Richmond for the week 24–30 April, exchanging visits daily in that time with
members of the Broome, Francis, and Barrett families (Diary).

  [2] Cornelia Cambridge (L. 1205 n. 6) had called at Bolton Street on 22 April
(Diary).

1307 [11 Bolton Street,
5 May 1823]

To Esther (Burney) Burney

A.L.S. (Berg), n.d.
Double sheet 4to   4 pp.   *pmk* 6 MY 1823   wafer
Addressed: Mrs. Burney, / Lark Hall Place / near Bath.
Endorsed by EBB: received / May 9th 1823 / replied to / *May 14—*
/ by favour of Mrs / Ashe— / a Second reply— / made—June 17th

Heartily as I thank you, my kind Esther, for your generous
Seconda, I *am bold to confess* it was not quite unexpected.
And I the more readily make this avowal, because I shan't
take it ill if you look upon it as a gentle hint that This very
identical paper Now in your hands stands good for Two more
ere we shall be squares. Lady Keith tells a comical story, very
apropos to this *inuendo*, that, while, upon some occasion, she
was on board her Lord's ship, she heard an honest Jack Tar
say to a poor French Prisoner—'Lookee, Mounseer, all in
this here place is "change & bargain; so if you'll larn me
French, d'y see, I'll larn you English. — —' Thus, if I give
you 3 sheets, whether together or successively, 'tis in the true
spirit of *'change & bargain*, to have as good as I bring.

Both your Letters are replete with matters that 'come
home to my business & feelings'—sometimes very painfully,
but always with a true sense of your affection, & a deep
regret I cannot avail myself of it as unreservedly as of old—
but the times now are such as to make all correspondence in
some degree circumspect, or in a great degree dangerous &
imprudent. Our hearts would most willingly & mutually open
to each other as frankly by pen as by speech — — but past
is the period & Gone—when we used to scribble with no
other thought or care but of one to the other, with that
'abandon' of confidence that did not merely leave prudence
& foresight out of the question, but that knew not even of
the existence of ǀ those horrible logs to free, spontaneous,
heart-glowing intercourse. Such was the careless, idle, but

423

dear stuff of our early Letters,[1] both to ourselves & to our
Mr. Crisp[1]—O! what striking proofs of this pass now daily
before my Eyes in my Letters from our adored Susan! & in
mine, all sedulously preserved & restored to me, to herself!
They, at present, are what are in review for my solitary hours
—& how few dare I keep from the flames! for the very
charm of their unbounded their fearless openness, which gave
them their principal delight, has cast around them dangers &
risks that, should they fall into any hands not immediately
our own, might make them parents to mischief, rancour, &
ill will incalculable! Yet was our Susan amongst the most
lenient & benevolent of human Judges: but her understanding was too excellent to be imposed upon by Fraud or Folly;
& her sentiments were too noble to let her view without
aversion ill-conduct & unworthiness; while her taste was so
exquisite that she could not be blind to any imperfection,
though she could readily be silent; & her sensibility was so
disinterested, that she could never be tame or indifferent to
the wrongs suffered by others, however patiently & like an
Angel she endured what were inflicted on herself. Oh what
a Character, my Hetty, was our Susan![2] — — — Yet these
were the feelings, & the perceptions, that made her judge-
ments, where she wrote from their unbiassed dictates, contain, from the very simplicity of their *truth*, a poignancy
fitted only for private & sacred *conversation*, spoken—or

1307. [1] The passages left free or unobliterated were published by Annie Raine
Ellis (L. 1304 n. 14). For Mr. Crisp, see *HFB*, pp. 16-17 and *passim*; also *Burford
Papers*.
[2] To these recollections, EBB in a letter of 13 May (Barrett, Eg. 3690 f. 142)
was to make a feeling reply:

what a sweet and striking picture have you drawn of our lost Angel!—if ever
perfection could or did inhabit the bosom of a mortal being, surely it dwelt in
hers.—believe me my Dearest F. I sympathise with you in all y^r feelings on
her dear subject—and at times lament with *fresh* sorrow our irreparable loss
in her! and all that tends to console me—is the *certainty* that she would never
have enjoyed peace had she been spared to us.—and that so many years of
Actual misery must have been her portion:—her dear & confidential Letters
—after repeated readings and lamentations over them,—I have with a repugnance indescribable thought unsafe to keep—and many have I been compelled
from common prudence to sacrifice! a *few* I have picked out—as being free
from any dangerous matter, . . . if you—my Dear F. will promise to be the
Survivor I will leave a pacquet of them to you—but to no one else—and such
as I have preserved of your own—shall be sealed up for YOU.—

For a list of SPB's surviving letters and journals, see *Catalogue*.

written | with fearless openness, heard with reciprocated con-
fidence, & kept from all Eyes, save Those that sent, & Those
that received with almost holy scrupulosity. —— —— But how
am I letting this fond subject fill up my paper!—'tis to Both
of us so dear, that I have run on as if speaking; but I now
stop short, to *answer* to those things you desire, & chiefly, as
well as imprimis, Alex. His sermon was somewhat elaborate,
& not without design, as it was meant for the Canons &
Minor Canons, more than for the Congregation;[3] not being
given at the hour when the City Grandees visit the Cathedral,
but on the ca[nonical se]rvice, where the Dignitaries of the
Churc[h] almost al[l as]semble, except those who can spare
no other ti[me. T]hese last, therefore, could be but little edified; however, there was no other alternative than that of
Writing for the one *or* the other: & his business, in having
only one occasion to be heard was certainly to answer as well
as he could the purpose for which he had been summoned,
namely, to please the Judges who would probably name him
to the Bishop. *Otherwise*, his Duty would have been to
preach to his Flock; *Here*, however, he was excusable, as he
was not their *Pastor*, but an accidental & passing Shepherd.
I mention this, as I am persuaded Fanny, who was zealous
in kindness & curiosity enough to go & hear him, disapproved
his discourse, on, a Ground that fully, but for this explica-
tion, justified her disapprobation; that of not seeking to be
most intelligible to the poorer & more ignorant hearers. I
very much *honour* Fanny for the sincerity she shewed by her
Silence. However, you, my dearest Esther,—& *she*, too,—
will be glad to know that what he aimed at he obtained. The
canon residentiary, the Hon. & Rev^d Dr. Wellesley,[4] *thanked
him for his excellent discourse*, & invited him to Dinner at
the Cathedral Table: & Mr. Knap,[5] a Minor Canon, took him
thence to tea with himself & his wife, & asked a touch of *his
powerful eloquence* for a charity School in Leadenhall Street.
This was accorded with great satisfaction: but, almost immediately after, Alex was taken ill with this Influenza,—&

[3] Delivered at St. Paul's on Sunday 16 March. See also L. 1304.
[4] The Revd. Gerald Valerian Wellesley (1770-1848), D.D. (1810), prebendary
and Canon of St. Paul's (1809), brother of the Duke of Wellington.
[5] The Revd. Henry John Knapp (L. 1305 n. 4) and his wife Elizabeth *née* Jen-
kins (*c.* 1780-1856). See *GM* xlv (1856), 1, 215.

confined to the house, & unable to go & thank Mr. Hodgson,[6] or to inform the Bp. of Salisbury of what was passed; or make any attempt at seeing the Bp. of London—&c &c—& he relapsed so often in his convalescence, that I at length resolved to go with him to Richmond, to *Lodgings*, where I could superintend his *food* & his *hours* & yet let him enjoy the society of his Aunt & Cousins & the Cambridges, *between meals*, as well as partake that enjoyment myself. We *have* been, & had good success: but a Letter from Mr. Knap has called us thence, for the Charity Sermon is to be preached next Sunday.[7] His Name was given out in Church to that effect yesterday.

You ask how I bore the Cathedral exertion: why very well, though much fatigued. But I was by no means as well pleased, personally, as I had been at Lee: & for the reasons I have already assigned. I mean to go to the City. And to-morrow, by appointment, I am to be received by Mrs. Fisher, &, probably, the Bp. of Salisbury.[8] Therefore —— if the present promise of recovery be not again blighted, I really think something may at length be done for my excentric companion—who has a *general* apathy upon the Subject quite astonishing, when contrasted with the *particular* energy even to torture that seizes him for a few moments, from time to time.[9]

Mrs. Lock is much better. Mrs. Angerstein was here just now;[10] she is come for a month or two—sadly altered! in all

---

[6] Secretary to the Bishop of London (L. 1180 n. 9), who with Dr. Fisher (L. 1287 n. 12) and William Howley (L. 1258 n. 18) may have been instrumental in obtaining for AA the opportunity to preach at St. Paul's.

[7] On 11 May (see L. 1305 n. 4).

[8] John Fisher and his wife Dorothea *née* Scrivener, friends of long standing (L. 1180 n. 4). The visit took place on 6 May (Diary).

[9] 'Dear Alex—has numerous friends—surely some good will be derived from his own merits and their zeal', his aunt EBB was to remark in her letter of 13 May, op. cit., but as to his 'apathy', that could not be excused 'upon a subject so serious, and important—it is to be much deplored—however—I sh^d hope—if his friends do serve him—it will be absorbed, and better feelings will arise spontaneously—but—after all is it to be wondered at? who could expect anything but Apathy from a Child of yours?'

[10] On 5 May (Diary). In her reply, op. cit., EBB was to lament Amelia Angerstein's 'being *again* sadly altered—her complaints seem to baffle all medical skill

but exquisite sweetness & goodness!—I have 1000 more things to say, but no space—yet nothing must intervene with my assuring you I this moment Burn the Letter you judge— too truly—fit only for Writer & Reader. I am now making such sacrifices daily—always with regret—!—alas! I have resigned my poor Ramsay & with much reluctance[11]—How was I touched, & pleased at once by All you tell me of sweet Beckey & faithful excellent Blue![12] Would they came nearer this way!—Bath to me, my Hetty, may not be! —— but London, to *you*, I trust will always be a *Jaunt* at least. God bless you, my dearest Esther—I could run over 3 sheets again if I had Franks Adieu—en attendant ever & ever

affec.y F D'A [1]

My Head continues quite cured, my kind Sister, *quite* & most amazingly. You make me love Mrs. Adams.[13] Blagden & Daly[14]—I delight in them for you —— —

—I fear she labours under . . . an atrophy'. The sisters forbore to mention, if indeed they knew of the corroding worries and fears caused in these years by Amelia's eldest son, John Julius William Angerstein, now about 23, whose gambling debts by 1822 were higher than his father could or his grandfather *would* pay. ' "He . . . must . . . be an outcast and a wanderer on the face of the globe forever! He can never show his face in this country any more, is the cry!" ' His ruinous career was eventually halted by the threat of disinheritance. Thus Amelia to her brother William in the 1830s: 'I have agreed to join in a deed by which he will incur the penalty of disinheritance if he raises money or otherwise runs into debt, after having now been completely cleared. Even this his father has only consented to do at my request.' See *Locks of Norbury*, pp. 312, 358, and *passim*.

[11] Elizabeth Ramsay (L. 1182 n. 3 and L. 1304).

[12] The sisters Rebecca Sandford and Elizabeth Warren Burney or 'Blue' (L. 1302 nn. 2, 3) were to spend their remaining days with their nephew the Revd. Richard Allen Burney (L. 1180 n. 18) at the rectory in Brightwell or that in Rimpton, where in the parish church mural tablets preserve their memories.

[13] Possibly Amelia Sophia *née* MacPherson (*fl.* 1796–1823), of Philadelphia, the wife since 1796 of Edward Hamlin Adams (b. 30 April 1777 in Kingston, Jamaica), of Middleton Hall, Carmarthen, and M.P. for the county (1833–4). He was on the jury lists for the tithing of Easton and Catherine (1822–4) and according to Bath Directories, lived for these years at Bailbrook House, Batheaston, not far from EBB at Lark Hall Place. In 1837 he had a house in Bath (No. 25 Circus). He died in Carmarthen on 30 May 1842 (*GM* n.s. xviii. 110).

[14] Mary Blagdon and Elizabeth Daly (L. 1304 nn. 25, 26).

[11 Bolton Street],
21 June 1823

To Esther (Burney) Burney

A.L. (Berg), 21 June 1823
Double sheet 4to   4 pp.   *pmk* 26 JU 1823   red seal
Addressed: Mrs. Burney, / Lark Hall Place, / near Bath,
Endorsed by EBB: answered July 5 / 1823
Emended by FBA. *See* Textual Notes.

21ˢᵗ June, 1823.

What a regale, my dearest Esther![1] I am *at* your Concert,
I hear once more the nearly unrivalled charm of Expression
with which you were wont to play——I see your 'little Fingers'
kissed, & am almost ready to kiss the enchanted Kisser; and
I witness the heroick rapture of the burlesque prostation, half
real gratitude, while the other half only is comick exaggeration. Far from wondering at the enthusiasm of Mrs. Adams,[2]
I conceive it—independent of my dear Hetty & Emily, a
realy touching sight, to behold a Mother & Daughter confabu-
lating thus together in sweet Melody, speaking, replying, re-
joining, in 'Concord of sweet sounds'[3]—the one with all the
fire & vigour of instructed Youth & Talent, the other with all
the taste & feeling of experienced and inborn excellence. The
little detail has animated *me* —— & I thank you for it with
all my heart. Neither, I am very sure, can ever appear to such
advantage, or excite such interest, as thus in drawing out
mutually the gifted powers of each other.

I was just preparing to write to you—how differently!——
You have cut short my Commission, in a manner that will
delight my Commissioner. Lady Murray,[4] a day or two ago,
after enquiring with great zeal about your health, & your
hand, begged me to acquaint you that a cure of a *crooked
Finger* —— not such a one as Mrs. Adams carressed so be-
witchingly—has just been performed under her own Eye, as

1308. [1] EBB's letter had arrived on 21 June (Diary).
  [2] See L. 1307 n. 13.   [3] *The Merchant of Venice*, v. i.
  [4] Lady Murray (L. 1290 n. 1) and FBA had exchanged visits on 30 May and
8 June (Diary).

it was for her own favourite Maid, by Steam: and I have to add, that every Menace ¹ of my own hand,—I instantly *boil* away from a small tin Tea Kettle, whence I pour water from on high on the threatened part, over a large Bason: after which, I rub in opodeldoc, put on a warm Glove, & —— am always not alone relieved, but delivered from the evil. I wish Richard would make the essay. I described the process to Fanny when I last saw her, & begged she would send it on to Brightwell.⁵

You do not tell me *who's* was the Duet? I conclude it was of the ever dear & good best Friend to both performers.

I am very sorry for poor Mrs. Beckford & Miss Hay,⁶—but alas, I am trembling still & far nearer home! Clement is in so debilitated a state, that he has now 2 professional Nurses, to alternate attendance, under our poor Sister! —— They are at Brighton; & Mrs. Barrett has kindly spared her lovely Julia⁷ to be with her Grand Mother, to whom she is a first rate darling; & with justice, as she inherits her Mother's sweetness, activity to serve, & delight in obliging: though I do not think she *equally* inherits that mother's extraordinary talents. She has, however, very good sense, & a truly blyth juvenile love of humour: & she is such a favourite with our poor Charlotte, that her own Name sake alone, perhaps, could be equally serviceable to her. Julia, *en outre*, writes all her Letters for her!—even to me & to Richmond. God grant our poor dear Charlotte may yet be spared so dreadful a blow!—

I have hopes poor Mrs. Charles Parr is rather better— Charles invited Alex to dinner & to see the Ceremony, & to walk in the procession, of laying the first stone of a new Church at Greenwhich, at which Princess Sophia of Gloucester presided:⁸ but, most unfortunately, he was too

---

⁵ EBB's son and daughter (i, p. lxix).
⁶ See L. 1189 n. 20; L. 1208 n. 4.   ⁷ Now aged 15 (i, p. lxxii).
⁸ To relieve overcrowding in the old parish church of St. Alfege, Greenwich, plans had been formed in 1821 by a committee including the Revd. George Mathew (L. 1228 n. 6), Charles Parr Burney, John Laurens Bicknell (i, L. 7 n. 18), and Richard Smith (see xii, L. 1465 n. 1), for the building of the daughter church of St. Mary's. The trustees included the vicar and CPB again, the Hon. Nicholas Vansittart (L. 1270 n. 23), and John Angerstein of Woodlands (L. 1195 n. 14). The architect was George Basevi (1794-1845), a cousin of Disraeli. See *DNB* and

indisposed to accept the invitation. ⎟ I do not alarm myself, I thank the Almighty. nor see reason so to do, seriously for my Alex — — yet he keeps me in eternal inquietude, for his stomach is become so weak that he is now never well but in living upon Grain, Vegetable, Fruits, & *boiled* Meat or Fish! And as some temptation frequently comes in the way, *irresistibly*, to vary this diet, he has relapses continually, from an approaching re-establishment of health!—I have besought Mrs Angerstein, Mrs. Lock, Lady Martin, & all that I *know* of his Dinner Friends, to invite him only for the Evening. — — but circumstances often overturn my care, & therefore my anxiety has rarely a long release.—He is to preach again Next Sunday at St. Paul's[9]—by order of the Bishop of London — — whom he has never yet seen,—but to whom the Bishop of Salisbury has promised me to present him. If This sessions passes without some Curacy, at least, I shall be terribly disheartened. From the time the Parliament breaks up, the Bishops are dispersed, & no hope remains till the Houses call them together again. A short time, therefore, now, will end my Suspense, at least, till next year! — — This is tedious, as well as precarious.—

I can never fail to give your messages to our dear Mrs. Lock,[10] & in best manner, namely in your own words, for we scarcely ever meet & rarely even write, without its being cordially *question de vous* — — she is deliciously well, & in

Transactions of the Greenwich and Lewisham Antiquarian Society, iv, no. 1 (1936), 36–43.

The foundation stone was laid on 17 June 1823 by H.R.H. the Princess Sophia Matilda of Gloucester (1773–1844), who, appointed in 1816 Ranger of Greenwich Park, lived in the Ranger's Lodge there; and the church was consecrated on 25 June 1825 by the Lord Bishop of Oxford, the Rt. Revd. Edward Legge (1767–1827). Closed in 1919, it was demolished in April 1936 (*Transactions, supra*). For a Plate showing the church, a description, and other matters relating to it, see Henry S. Richardson, *Greenwich: its History, Antiquities, Improvements, and Public Buildings* . . . (1834), pp. 107–12.

[9] FBA was to record the event in her Diary, Sunday 29 June: 'St. Paul's Cathedral Alex's 2[d] Sermon There'.

[10] 'I feel greatly for Mrs. Locke', EBB had written in her letter of 13 May, op. cit., 'make my *tender & loving* respects to that sweet friend for—friend she is,—in despight of all that Worldly circumstances may tend to distance us.—I wish you had seen her reception of me on my late visit to her at Eliotvale.—how she almost sprang in to my arms. and folded me in hers; I shall never forget it—*or* the unceasing instances of affectionate regard with which she gratified and Charmed both Emily and me—during our stay.—'

quite restored beauty!—but poor Lady Martin is very ill, of spasmodic complaints, & reduced to a shadow! Mrs. Lock is at Lady Templetown's purposely to see her daily. The Physicians declare there is no *danger*—yet I shall bless God when I see her well again! And Apropos to Health & Life—I know you will truly rejoice, my dearest Hetty, that my poor but amended Head still ceases to give me any menaces of that sudden deprivation of faculty, if not existence, which so lately made all my Friends within reach uneasy, & my affectionate Charlotte quite ¹ wretched;—*that* is passed—I think —— —— Nevertheless, all is so uncertain, even where youth & vigour remain, that you will not, my ever dear Hetty, be moved if I say I earnestly desire to run no risk for my incurably inexperienced Alex; & therefore—that I am often ill at ease, in silent hours, in reflecting upon what Messrs Hoare have sent me word, namely that should any thing happen to me before the change of disposition at the Bank takes place, it may cost infinite difficulty to Alex to prove his rights, from the circumstance, so continually perplexing, of the 2 Countries to which he belongs, the one, *his real Family*, the other, the place of *his Nativity*, England. *The sooner therefore the better*, they told me, should the fatal document be legalized. At that moment, as Alex thought of going straight to Bath, he was himself to arrange the affidavit with *Mr. Hay*, who *alone* knew his honoured Father both in France & in England, & who has most obligingly & feelingly offered his services to us upon any such occasion.¹¹ Now—much as I dislike to involve *You* to make this melancholy request to the friendship of Mr. Hay, the retards of the Journey of Alex, & the hazards of mortal duration, make me almost wish my dear sister could speak or Write to Mr. Hay, & shew him the Affidavit, with Alex's & my own best Compliments, & apologies, but trust in his kindness, to see it executed; & permit *you* to be my Banker for its costs. I did not mean to do this when I *began* my Letter—but the much of illness in it urges me so to *conclude*; & my faithful confidence that to save me—though it may be but 3 weeks of awful fear, will be a payment to your kind Heart for the trouble & exertion. I do not name *3 weeks* in the name of Alex—whose changes, &c, determine me never

¹¹ See also L. 1304 n. 3.

to answer for him; but I know it is his entire & sincere intention, at This moment, to set off for Bath when his Ecclesiastical hopes are either frustrated or confirmed; because, at all events, he expects no *Possession* beyond a *Promise* for some months to come. [*seal*] pardone this worry, my dearest Esther ˡ & believe me nothing but general caution induces this desire, for I am really & truly in *bodily* health amazingly renovated, & greatly more composed *mentally*——& yours ever & ever with truest affection.

I saw Fanny quite well on Thursday——she & Edward drink Tea here next Sunday.[12]

I long to hear you have secured yourself warm——and *Social*. ——apartments for the next *Winter*

I hope Mrs. Daly was of your grand party——& Mrs. Blagdon? & Thomas?[13] ˡ

Poor Lady Templetown is very ill *always*. I spend many Evenings with her, as she can send for me & return me without difficulty.

I had been told that Sophy was qu[ite] recovered, & Maria quite well,——but your accᵗ is not so flourishing. ˡ

Let me not fail to mention that, in looking over my eternal MSS. I make it a rule to *Leave* no single paper [or] Letter on which is written '*Burn this*.' I should think it culpable.

I am very glad for Richard & Blue that sweet Mʳˢ Sandford stays at Brightwell: Not so for Edward & myself. ˡ

I saw Sarah Harriet the other day, happy & healthy —— —— but not her Pupils.[14]

Pray return my thanks to Lʸ Trimbles*ton* for her kind remembrance.[15]

---

[12] Or on Wednesday 18 June (Diary). Edward had called on the 29th.

[13] For these friends of EBB, see L. 1304 nn. 26, 25; and L. 1200 n. 11.

[14] Henrietta and Annabella Crewe (see L. 1293 n. 6) of Crewe Hall, Cheshire, aged respectively 15 and 9.

[15] Maria Theresa *née* Kirwan (*c.* 1764–1824), the wife since 1793 of John Thomas Barnewall (iv. 128n.), 15th Baron Trimlestown. FB had known her since 1784 (see *ED* ii. 314).

1309

To Mrs. Locke

A.L. cut up and pasted to (A.L.S., FBA to CBFB, 17 Sept. 1821, rejected Diary MSS. 7290-[3], Berg), n.d.

Originally a double sheet or perhaps 2 double sheets 8vo (7? X 4.3″), 23 cuttings from which were taken by CFBt as Pasteovers for the letter L. 1267 as above.

Edited by CFBt. *See* Textual Notes.

[*top of page missing*]

⟨was a⟩
of my Alex—
sympathy
Alex is wild to persuade me those
Waters would, to me also, be of similar
salubrity[1]—but Oh. they would want
double, treble their qualities to *undo*
in me the deadly mischief of crossing
the Sea,[2] before they could be called into
action to *do* any thing ulteriorly
[good. And yet, that bodily suffering
would be nothing[2]—absolutely] nothing
compared with what would pass mentally
in crossing again the Sea! — — I hardly
think their united influence could
do less than demolish me.—But my
poor Alex sees me only at the Spring
that Spring that so revives the
loved Amine— & the ways & means
& various difficulties of getting there
escape his calculations. Alas—'tis so
often Sorrow only, or Misfortune, that

1309. [1] Evidently the Angersteins had suggested that FBA and AA accompany them on their customary visit to Spa. See L. 1218 n. 1 and L. 1311. Amelia was to take leave of FBA on Saturday 19 July (Diary).

[2] FBA had suffered violent sea-sickness in her crossing in 1802 (v. 225-7), in 1812 (vi, p. 726), and in 1814 (viii, L. 837).

teaches forethought & prudence that I

[top of page missing, probably a continuation of the last line on the page]

hardly can regret he has that lesson
still to learn! though often, often
I lament that Nature has left out
of his composition that species of
intuitive perception that foreruns
experience, & rescues us from the
weight of its calamities by serving as
a spying Glass to discern their approach

[2? lines cut out]

since ⟨s⟩
worrying *I know not whats* that are
always coming in ones way—
[Ale]x says the concert was the most
delightful he ever heard—&, could you
believe it Miss Upton brought him
home at 3 o 'clock in the morning
though she had *2 Ladies* to make place
for in her carriage. How very amiable.
I spent that Evening with her *all but* incom-
-parable Mother, whom I found very unwell
indeed, though she cheered & grew bright as the
Evening advanced & between whiles was all
her charming self. Adieu, my beloved Friend—
I long to have Augusta again under your care—
for I think, with respect to her health, she

To Mrs. Broome

A.L.S. (Berg), 2–3 July
Double sheet 4to   4 pp.   *pmk* ⟨3⟩ 1823   wafer
Addressed: Mrs. Broome, / 50. King's Road, / Brighton.
Endorsed by CBFB: Sister d'Arblay / 1823

No Answer. And No Hurry. Read at leisure.

2^d July, Bolton Street—

I begin my Letter with those emphatic—& generous Words, that my dear harrassed Charlotte may read it with tranquility; for I know—too well!—by saddest experience, how much the pleasure of receiving a Letter, even from those dearest to us, is crushed by the thought of the time & exertion to which its Reply lays claim. I here, therefore, give notice, that I will accept no return but by the Pen of dear Julia: not even *dictated* by you! a *message*, merely, must come in your Name, but be written by her own unguided Pen; & that over, I trust to her kindness for adding a few paragraphs relative to your way of life, & her dear Uncle's situation, & her own manner of passing her time, & any other matters that may occur to her, unprompted; for nothing can she say that will not be interesting to me, from the love I bear herself, as well as the tenderer love still she knows I bear to her beloved Grandmama.

This premised, you will read the rest at any odd moment.

I will not enter upon my concern at the slow progress to recovery of my dear Clement, nor speak of what I feel for your lengthened cares & solicitude — — you know it all! —& I have only forborne writing because I understood *answering* was painful to you: but now that I apply to my dear Julia for that part, I will abstain no longer; for indeed it has seemed most unnatural to me to go on week after week without any *direct* intercourse with a Sister—Friend— *Crony* & Favourite like my Charlotte. Let the spell be broken, & let Julia be the magician whose Wand shall break it. She

435

must write quite naturally, & without study or formality or *fear*—I was going to say or *Wit*—but I leave ⎸ that last article to her own management, provided it comes tout bonnement into her Pen,—without putting herself to the fatigue or trouble of belabouring her pretty pate, like the Man in the epigram, who says

I knock my head, & tell the Wit to come! — —
Thump as I will, there's Nobody at home![1]—

Alexander & I go on as usual, well & ill alternately; never long enough the first to feel fearlessly established; nor yet long enough the last for serious alarm. The seat of his A's draw back from health is decidedly the stomach, for when he lives strictly by regimen, he is stout, gay, & hearty; but the moment he deviates, or neglects his rules, he is feverish, restless, thinned, & disordered. 'Tis dreadful, really dreadful to me to see how much he requires a constant watcher for his health, as well as Flapper[2] for his proceedings. Without the one, he is for-ever indisposed; & without the other, he forgets all he has to do! so that, with parts that plant him rather above than below all his immediate cotemporaries, he is constantly behind every one of them in whatever ought to be progressive. How earnestly do I wish I could see him united with an amiable companion, partial enough to bear with his eccentricities, as well as to value the qualities & talents that might reward her patience! ⎸

But before I proceed with any other subject, let me hasten, lest I forget it, to mention the continued appeasement of the nervous or spasmodic attacks of my head; I really have them no more to my ceaseless surprise. Neither want of sleep nor even anxiety bring them back, except of strong, or of sudden emotion—*then* they shew me they are still at hand, if I neglect the prescriptions that have sent them aloof. This morsel is for an example to my dearest Charlotte, that she will tell her Julia to imitate it. But pray do not give her your Richmond Ink: & if you have taken [it] to Brighton, do me the favour to cast it into the Sea. Not that it absolutely

1310. [1] Alexander Pope, An Epigram, 'The Empty House'.
[2] See L. 1243 n. 2.

requires the ocean to make it vanish, for it would not discolour Water in an empty Walnut shell. When you send it 'tis hardly legible; but a week or two faints it away into so fair a White, that I took up one of your last Letters for a sheet of blank paper, & had very nearly sent it you back with my own scrawl run over it.

This Moment, 3ᵈ July—I receive from Marianne an answer to a request made to Charlotta for your address[3]—& I find you have that dear—invaluable Creature now with you—& her two sweet Girls. God grant my dear Clement may be well enough to enjoy seeing them! What comfort to you, my Charlotte, will their society then give!—Mrs. Lock is now in town, to help nursing her eldest Daughter, Lady Martin, who has long been alarmingly ill, but, at this instant, is better, thank Heaven. Alex preached, for the 2ᵈ time, last Sunday at the Great Cathedral,[4] &, I hope, well —— —— but, he has delayed from Day to Day waiting ⎮ upon the Bishop of Salisbury, who had promised to present him to the Bishop of London, till —— —— going only *yesterday*, he heard he was a fortnight too late! the BP. & whole family having left town till next Sessions! I am inexpressibly vexed & disappointed. There is now no longer any hope of promotion till another year has passed over his head.—He, mean while, is as careless & indifferent about it as if he had no interest in the matter. He is particularly happy, also, now, & occupied, by the arrival from France of a family which, next to the de La Tour Maubourg's, was our most intimate, most loved, & most esteemed, & admired: 'tis the whole House de Beauvau,[5]—the Prince, the Princess, the eldest son with his wife,

---

[3] MF's letter is missing but FBA had answered it on Friday 4 July (Diary).

[4] Cf. L. 1307 and n. 9.

[5] For General d'Arblay's friends, the family of Marc-Étienne-Gabriel de Beauvau (1773–1849), prince de Beauvau-Craon (1793), and his wife Nathalie-Henriette-Victurnienne *née* Mortemart (1774–1854), see v, viii *passim*. Their eldest son François-Victurnien-*Charles*-Just (1793–1864) had married in 1815 Lucie-Virginie de Choiseul-Praslin (1795–1834); their elder daughter, Nathalie-Irène-Marie-Victurnienne (*c.* 1798–1852), on 5 February 1820, Auguste-François-Joseph Le Lièvre (1780–1826), chevalier de la Grange (F. E. 1800). Unmarried still were the 2nd son *Edmond*-Henri-Étienne-Victurnien (1795–1851), who, near AA's age, was said to be a handsome model of a young *militaire*; and the younger daughter

the eldest Daughter with her husband, & the youngest single
son & single Daughter. They are all as beautiful as they are
amiable. I have seen them all, but the Eldest & the most
youthful; & their sight caused me extreme emotion,—for
well they appreciated Him who had brought us together!—
Alex is with them almost from Morning till Night.

our dear Sister Burney writes me very pleasant accounts of
herself Maria & Sophy are better; but poor Richard is a
Cripple with acute & dreadful Rheumatism—Sarah Harriet
is prosperous every way, Fanny Raper is ever blooming—
Minette, getting well. Fanny Burney is in good looks. Edward,
in good spirits—Mʳ J. Payne promises me a visit from his
belle mere as soon as she returns to town. Do not let our
Charlottina plague herself to write—as Mrs. B[urney] is
coming, I will wait patiently for her news.[6] So plague not
yourself, my own dear Charlotte, just now, to answer even by
proxy: but Love as you are Loved by your faithful

F. d'Ay |

Kindest Wishes & Love to dear Clement, And to All.

Henriette-*Gabrielle*-Apolline (*c.* 1801-69), who would marry in February 1824
Dennis-Mathieu-Omer, vicomte Talon (1783-1853).

The princesse de Beauvau and her son Edmond had called on FBA on 30 June,
and recorded in FBA's calendar of the next three weeks are nine visits from Prince
Edmond and from other members of the family.

[6] Mrs. Burney (the Admiral's widow) would call on FBA on 10 July (Diary).
It was about this time that her daughter Sarah, having recovered her health in the
previous summer in Boulogne, was to set out with her husband John Payne (L.
1192 n. 5) for Italy. Sarah was to write her aunt 'a mountainous letter' (Berg),
dated MILANO, 7 Aug. 1823, in which giving short shift to Paris, Dijon, Geneva,
Lausanne, and other cities, she dwelt at length on the splendours of Mont Blanc
('his triple head glittering in the Sun'), a violent thunderstorm on Lake Como, and
another near Geneva, where, employing boatmen formerly employed by Lord
Byron, they heard of his preference for 'stirring weather', when the lake was unsafe, and his always 'taking pistols where there was no danger'. Passing over the
Simplon, the travellers reached Milan on 30 July, and after visiting Venice and
Florence, they were to return early in 1824 (see L. 1332).

FBA was to receive this letter on 22 August (Diary), a day when, as Sarah
envisaged, her mother would have been summoned to hear it read (Diary). 'Would
you give my tender love to my dear Mother, if you please when you may happen
to see her, my dearest Aunt.'

[11 Bolton Street,
pre 29 July 1823]

To Mrs. Locke

A.L. unfinished (Berg), n.d.
Double sheet 8vo   4 pp.

I will not wait to the end of the Week to write my *Bulletin*
to my dearest Friend, when I can give her so much satisfaction at the beginning, by telling her I have again seen our dear
Lady Templetown—& seen her—once more—all herself!
—She was up,—at first,—though she threw herself immediately afterwards on her Bed,—but she was in quite revived
spirits, & renovated faculties—far better, & more cheering, &
more self-possessed, than for the last *two* times, before the
3ᵈ & latest time, when I saw her so deplorably suffering &
feeble that I could pass with her but 10 minutes, by the
opinion of her own surrounding family. Now, however, easier
about her, they were all absent, ⏐ happy in knowing that,
from her excessive kindness to me, they might all, for the
moment, be spared. She told me she had begun a Letter to
you, herself,—& oh! how we talked of you, my ever dear
Friend! 'Tis our constant theme of union. — —

I was again invited into the mansion of your Royal Neighbour,[1] & received with the utmost cou[r]tesie: & I did not
again say to the Footman, when asked to alight, 'I thank you,
but I had rather not.—' Yet I again made my lowest obei-
sance to one of the attendant Ladies—as she came forward
to meet me. She had the good sense to find it out, I am sure,
as,—after my ceremonies were over with the '*railly princess*',
she smiled & made me a fresh inclination of civility, that said
'*I* am *I* — — & not therefore unwilling to know you, though
I am not *She*.' This passed in the expression of her countenance. ⏐ I know not her Name, but it began with a C. I think.
The Princess asked much after You, & more after Amine—
but just properly & feelingly of both. My return home was
cheerful & interesting with my dear Princess Sophia, in spite

1311. [1] For the Household of the Princess Sophia at Kensington Palace, see
L. 1270 n. 11.

of Rain, slush, & mud, which we waded through without intermission during this our rural search of enjoying the country air.

My dear Alex is in Heaven!—His satisfied & rational expectation of now soon becoming what he calls a Member of the community, seems to have regenerated him, so much better is his health, & so much better are his looks. The Bishop of London mentioned him *again* to the Archdeacon, in quitting town for Weymouth, saying '*I take great interest in Mr. d'Arblay.* — —' Imagine what a Text is this for a young Candidate in orders!—He now forgives my so earnest pleading against Spa,[2] which would have put him out of the way of this fair opening to All his hopes in Life.— ¹ Thrown out, however, from that favourite plan, he is less in haste for what excursion may re-place it,—Brighton—Hastings—Wales—Cheltenham—&c so we are still for a while together, as he has begun a new composition, that absorbs him entirely, almost, & is meant to be shewn to the B^P—by the advice of the Archd^n And he has time before him, as the B^P. is gone for 3 months.[3]

He has charged me to tell you those good last words of his Lo^d ship. I read the Letter, &c to L^y Templetown & her kind Eyes glistened for me with pleasure.—Alex was charmed at the cordial congratulations I repeated to him of Mr. George, though he said he felt *sure* of them. Indeed the encouragement he received through-out at Lee has been a spur to him ever since.[4]

When he leaves me, I am not without thoughts of listening to the earnest desire of my Sister Broome in passing a fortnight with her by the seaside.[5] Poor Clement is *rather* better. My other sister, & her's, are all well. I long—almost inexpressibly—for

---

[2] Cf. L. 1309.

[3] Eventually sent to the Bishop of London was one of the sermons that AA had preached at St. Paul's (16 March or 29 June). See further, L. 1314.

[4] See Ll. 1297–9, 1301.

[5] That Mrs. Broome and son had come to town, probably for medical advice, is indicated by FBA's visits of 30 July and 1, 2, 5, 6, 7 August to 'my dear Charlotte & Poor Clement' (Diary).

[11 Bolton Street],
8 August 1823

To Mrs. Locke

L., incomplete copy in the hand of CFBt (Diary MSS. viii. 7330-2, Berg), 8 Aug. 1823
Double sheet 4to   3 pp.

To Mrs Locke

Augt 8. 1823.

— — I have spent two evenings, since I wrote last, with dear Lady Templetown,[1] whose kindness towards me really passes words;—it sometimes almost distresses me, in the midst of the true pleasure as well as gratitude it inspires: but it causes my necessary resistance to her endearing propositions of more frequent intercourse to give me real pain; so strongly I feel her goodness & wish to shew my sense of it. And it cannot be—no arrangement is in my power, with propriety, for indulging myself oftener in Portland Place — — though most true it is, I never am there without wishing the Evening had double its length, or that I could renew it on the following.—Little indeed is there of intercourse such as L^y T. can give when, added to her rare powers and ǀ high accomplishments, is taken in Partiality so engaging as that with which she both charms & honours me. We have so much, also, such endless themes to talk of in common, & to love in Union—that we never cease reciprocating our regrets that we never met with this confidential intimacy sooner.—Alas, my dearest Friend, she will not suffer me to hope it may now last long!—Yet, how forbear?—Unless, indeed, I *left* her as reduced in strength, voice, energy, & spirits as I now generally, find her. — — *Then*, indeed, the view of her even eager resignation to finish her earthly career might reconcile me to a quicker deprivation. But her mind & faculties have a power over her frame really marvellous, &, after a little *forced* exertion, she revives into the *natural* exertion that makes the charm of her conversation. I do not beg pardon for saying so

1312. [1] On 29 July and 4 August (Diary).

much of *L*^y *T.* to *you*, my dearest Friend, for I never beg it when I make *you* my Theme to *Her.*

My meeting with Mr Wilberforce[2]—after a *ten years* chasm, following one single interview, would swallow up all my paper were I to enter upon ‖ it—and you would like a detail that would double & treble that paper.—*Therefore* I shall leave it to our own meeting, only saying I found him charming, and of the First, the Old, & I *fear* (for Alex's sake) the Best school for Conversation-powers. He and Lady Temple-town are remnants of that bright school that, even in its zenith, must have been amongst its most distinguished Ornaments. On the main point, & that towards which he is always bend-ing, I certainly do not meet the tenets of Mr Wilberforce— I might be much happier if I did; for certainly if I believed such sort of privations &c, as his favourite authors recom-mend would lead to Rewards such as they promise, I should think their practice a *badinage* rather than a sacrifice: but where my Reason resists, my Faith will not be complaisant, & to *Opinions* my Reason will not be subservient, though to *Mysteries* it bows down with awful faith. Mr Wilberforce seems to comprehend this, for he flies me not:—in the five last days he spent in Town he accorded me *three* visits[2]— each of them longer & more amiable than the other — — —

1313   [11 Bolton Street,
                             c. 19] August 1823

To Esther (Burney) Burney

The first part of the letter ('What an interesting letter . . . pilferers.'), of which the manuscript is missing, was printed in *Diary and Letters of Madame d'Arblay*, edited by Charlotte Barrett (1842-6), VII. 372-3, August 1823.

The second part is extant (Berg):
Single sheet 4to   2 pp.   *pmk*   FREE 22 A⟨U⟩ 1823   red seal
[*franked*:] A Upton / London August twenty two / 1823

[2] On 27, 28, and 31 July (Diary). FBA had first met Wilberforce at Sandgate on 19 June 1813 (vii, L. 723).

Addressed: Mrs. Burney / Lark Hall Place / Bath
Endorsed by EBB: answered— / Sepr 2^d 1823

August, 1823.

What an interesting letter is this last, my truly dear Hetty;[1] 'tis a real sister's letter, and such a one as I am at this time frequently looking over of old times! For the rest of my life I shall take charge and save my own executor the discretionary labours that with myself are almost endless; for I now regularly destroy all letters that either may eventually do mischief, however clever, or that contain nothing of instruction or entertainment, however innocent. This, which I announce to all my correspondents who write confidentially, occasions my receiving letters that are real conversations — — Were I younger I should consent to this condition with great reluctance—or perhaps resist it: but such innumerable papers, letters, documents, and memorandums have now passed through my hands, and, for reasons prudent, or kind, or conscientious, have been committed to the flames, that I should hold it wrong to make over to any other judgment than my own, the danger or the innoxiousness of any and every manuscript that has been cast into my power. To you, therefore, I may now safely copy a charge delivered to me by our dear vehement Mr. Crisp,[2] at the opening of my juvenile correspondence with him.—'Harkee, you little monkey!—dash away whatever comes uppermost; if you stop to consider either what you say, or what may be said of you, I would not give one fig for your letters.'—How little, in those days, did either he or I fear, or even dream of the press! What became of letters, *jadis*, I know not; but they were certainly both written and received with as little fear as wit. Now, every body seems obliged to take as much care of their writing desks as of their trinkets or purses,—for thieves be abroad of more descriptions than belong to the penniless pilferers.

Most fortunately—& by a chance that never occurred before, I was with Miss Upton when she was making up covers

1313. [1] This letter, now lost, FBA had received on 15 August (Diary).
  [2] Samuel Crisp (*HFB*, pp. 16–18 and *passim*). For his warnings against 'studied letters', see *ED* i. 268.

for her Brother, General Upton, to Frank[3]—& she *begged leave* to add a Direction for *me*—which, as you see, I graciously accorded. *This Letter was already a quarter* written—or I could not have gotten so much ready,—though I begged my date to be 2 *days later than the* night it was franked. It was at poor—admirable—suffering L.y Templetown's.

Mrs. Admiral—Burney drank tea with us last Night.[4] She is recovered to 10 years *youngerness* in her appearance. Sarah Payne is at Milan, whence I had a very chearful Letter from her yesterday: & I sent to invite her fond Mother to hear it over the tea table. Sarah P[ayne] seems happy, & I hope will so continue. Her sposo quite adores her, & she rules with no *rod of Iron*, for one of Feathers suffices. Mrs. B[urney] has made arrangements for their all living together that are very rational, & keep her with her best affections upon terms of mutual œconomy. Martin is Head of the House, though John is head of the table. They seem to go on in perfect amity all together, & nothing is ever hinted at of any 5.th person.[5] I imagine the same plan has been adopted as that I mentioned to you of Dr. Vyse.[6] Adieu, my dearest Esther—O!—this moment I have a Letter from Marianne Francis, with the excellent news that poor Clement is *much better*! Living in the air, & throwing away all physic, seems I to agree better than Apothecaries' Hall. How happy this makes me! The sea breezes, now, may again reinstate our good Charlotte.

Pray take to the *Flamy System* you recommend, my dearest Etty—

Sarah Harriet is at Crewe Hall: but has written to none of us in these parts since she left town.

I have no room left to talk of M.me Campan,[7] whom I knew

---

[3] Sophia Upton (L. 1223 n. 9) and her brother Arthur Percy (1777-1855), who, at the conclusion of a long career in the army (see iv. 324, 489-90), had been elected M.P. of Bury St. Edmunds (1818-26) and so had franking privileges.

[4] On 18 August (Diary).

[5] Martin Burney's unacknowledged wife Rebecca (L. 1271 n. 4), whom, according to H. Crabb Robinson, Mary Lamb had taken 'under her protection' (Manwaring, p. 299).

[6] See L. 1304 n. 20.

[7] FBA had visited Madame Campan's school in 1802 (v, L. 529). The famous educator (see *Enc. Brit.*) had died in 1822, and published in Paris in that year was

a little. No one has heard of Wm. Phillips[8] for a long time, &
no one of pretty Caroline still longer.[9] Fanny Raper was with
me last week for a few hours—always rosily handsome &
cheering.

I I entreat you, my Esther, not to think of any *instalmts.*
till you come to town—& then *remember*! the 4*th* *pt*—has
been agreed upon annually—i.e. 5 *pr* ann.—remember—
this is our bond.—unless you will do better.

I am sorry you are disappointed of Miss Reid,[10] but glad
the adoring *Miss Yeats* has some connexion with you kept
up.[11] I like Mrs. Daly mightily—& Mrs. Blagdon too.[12]

Yr. description of [*cut*] after your own courageous robbery

her *Mémoires sur la vie privée de Marie-Antoinette* ... (3 vols.), with a 'Notice sur
la vie de Madame de Campan' by J. F. Barrière. Reprinted in London (2 vols.,
1823) by Colburn, who also published a translation, the work went into numbers
of editions, one of which may have prompted EBB's queries.

[8] Son of SBP (i, p. lxx) and Molesworth Phillips of the Marines, John William
James (1791-1832) had joined the Royal Navy as a volunteer 1st class on 23 May
1805, sailed as midshipman 1805-8 on the *Jamaica* (Guernsey, Newfoundland),
1808-10 on the *Stork* (Guernsey, the West Indies, Brazil), and 1810-11 as assistant navigator on the merchantship *Minerva* (Surinam). In the years 1812-15 he
gained the ratings Master's Mate, Acting Master, Acting Lieutenant, Senior Lieutenant, sailing successively with the *Leviathan*, the *Warrior*, the *Shark*, and the
Carnation (plying between Europe and Jamaica). His active career in the Royal
Navy ended with his posting on the *Carnation*, 23 May 1818 (ADM 9/15, f. 5456),
after which he appears on the navy half-pay list until 23 November 1832 (ADM
25/ /40, f. 153).

After the Napoleonic wars, as far as can be gathered, he was a merchant sailor
on the China Seas, with a base in New South Wales, but before his death acquiring
as well possessions in Java and part-ownership of a barque, the *Elizabeth*. He was
to die in Canton in late November 1832, as may be seen from his will (PRO/
PROB/11/1834/424, pr. before the Supreme Court of New South Wales on 30
September 1833 and in London on 8 July 1834). The proceeds from the sale of
his share of the barque he left to his niece Minette Raper *later* Kingston (i, p. lxxi)
but his dogs, horses, and buggy to friends in Java.

On leaves in England he emerges from time to time in the letters of Marianne
Francis (Eg. 3704A, ff. 83-4b, 196-7b) as 'very agreeable & unaffected, relating
his adventures', chanting Portuguese airs, reading Portuguese and Spanish, and collecting books to take with him to New South Wales.

He would visit FBA on 16 August 1828 (Diary) and she would seem to have
seen him last on 28 December [?1829] when Minette 'took Uncle William to see
Aunt d'Arblay, who was extremely good natured & glad to see him & promised to
help him in a letter ... to the King as he is going to send him some very curious
Chinese chairs to put in a Chinese grotto at Windsor which the King is making'
(Eg. 3707, ff. 172-3b).

[9] Caroline Jane Burney (L. 1238 n. 20), who seems to have returned to India.
[10] Elizabeth Pickering Reid (L. 1264 n. 11). See further, L. 1373 n. 3.
[11] Charlotta Louisa Elizabeth Perrott *née* Yates (L. 1230 n. 9).
[12] See L. 1304 nn. 26, 25.

of your *all* is [*cut*] *edifying*. I hope, however, nobody *sees* the robber [*cut*] to *be* poor, & to *seem* poor, you know,— is — — &c— ¹

Adio, dearest Hettina—I only wish I could kiss you when I say Good Night, be the fashion never so old & fusty

¹3¹4   [11 Bolton Street,
25 August 1823]

To Mrs. Broome

A.L.S. (Berg), n.d.
Double sheet 4to   4 pp.   *pmk* 25 AU 1823   wafer
Addressed: Mrs. Broome, / N⁰ 9 Broad Street, / Brighton / Sussex.
Re-addressed: 47 Kings Road
Endorsed by CBFB: Sister d'arblay / ans^d aug^t 27 / 1823

Read at once the P.S.
P.S. Send to the Post Office for a Letter for Clement
Read at leisure except the P.S.

My dearest Charlotte—I may compare myself now to my poor Alex, who says he resembles the Irish Man who complained 'That he always came in time to be too late — —' —for not only Alex at 2 o'clock, but myself at about 11. arrived when the Birds were flown from Wigmore street.¹ I should have written my regret, & my desire of news, but from my knowledge of the added distress & *combustion* such a regret would cause: therefore I will wait till I can procure intelligence without fresh *turmoil* to my dearest Charlotte. Yet — — The *shortest bulletin would* be most eagerly received; & *will* be welcomed with all my heart whenever a little more *leisure* & *courage*, taking each of them a hand, make it possible you can give me Two lines. I say *two*, for though my chief anxiety is for our poor Clement, a thousand feelings urge infinite desire for *one* line relative to your dear Self.

1314. ¹ Where presumably Mrs. Broome and her son Clement Francis had taken lodgings in their visit to London (L. 1311 n. 5).

A Letter came hither 2 days ago, from Wigmore St. with a request I would forward it for Clement. As it is franked, I thought it might go safely straight forward to *Brighton Post office* in my ignorance of your individual address. Pray send for it.

I have had a short visit from Mr. Barrett & little Henry;[2] the former going to Richmond for business relative to his house[3] —the latter to Boulogne to return to his French school. Both were well, but I could gather nothing new from them of dear Clem. They were to dine & sleep at Fanny Raper's: & Mr. B[arrett] has invited the fair Hostess, her Sposo & Figlia, to spend a ᴵ Week at Ely. That place, I find, now pleases them All. Mr. Barrett speaks of his abode there with perfect sadisfaction. They have met with an old acquaintance of mine in the Wife of one of the Prebendarys, Mr. Jenyns: the latter was nephew, & I believe Heir of the famous Solmes: the former, was only Daughter of the renowned Dr. Haberden, who understood his medical art so practically well as to live to 100—within a few weeks.[4] The meeting of Mr. Barrett with *Mrs. Bruce*—civant *Mrs. Meeke,*[5] our Charlotte will probably have written to you.

[2] Henry John Richard Barrett (i, p. lxxiii), now aged 9, whom the Barretts had placed at an English school in Boulogne on their departure in October 1822. See CFBt's letter (Eg. 3706D, ff. 49b–50b): 'We have left our little Henry at Boulogne — . . . the terms were as low as those of his vulgar Richmond school & the arrangement of the house, manners of his companions &c infinitely superior.'

[3] The house at Richmond, which was to be rented or sublet during the residence of the Barretts for the year 1823-4 in prebendary Dampier's house in Ely (see L. 1304 n. 17).

[4] FBA had known in the 1780s at Streatham (see *DL* i, ii *passim*) the eminent physician William Heberden (1710–1801), the elder (*DNB*), who attended George III until his death and who in 1783 acquired a house in Windsor next door to that of Mrs. Delany. Often visiting him there and calling at least once on FB at the Queen's House (*DL* ii. 421) was his granddaughter Mary (*c.* 1763–1832), who would marry in 1788 the Revd. George Leonard Jenyns (1763–1848), vicar of Swaffham Prior, Cambs. (1787), and prebendary of Ely (1802). A third cousin of the well-known Soame Jenyns (1704-87), who died childless, the Revd. George inherited from him Bottisham Hall, near Cambridge, where in later years Julia Barrett was often to be a guest. For these matters and the character of Mrs. Jenyns, see Olwen Hedley, 'Mrs. Delany's Windsor Home', *Berkshire Archaeological Journal*, 59 (1961), 51–5; and for the farming and sporting vicar, see Leonard Jenyns, *later* Blomefield (1803–93), *Chapters in My Life* . . . (Bath, 1889).

[5] The younger daughter of CB's second wife by her first marriage, Elizabeth or 'Bessie' Allen (i, p. lxxiv) eloped at the age of 16 to Ypres with one Samuel Meeke (iii, L. 122 n. 12) and, deserting him, seems to have pursued a flagrant and unrepentant career, veiled allusions to which appear from time to time in the Burney Papers. She had married *c.* 1796 a Mr. Bruce of (?)Bristol, as yet unidentified,

Alex has had no tidings yet from the BP. of London—but the Archdeacon, kindly taking into consideration our disappointment from the sudden illness & absence of the BP. of Salisbury, has undertaken to bring forward his Name, & his sermon at St. Paul's, on the next meeting with his Lordship. The Archd^n & Mrs. Cambridge & Mrs. Baker are to come to town next Tuesday to see Mr. Angerstein's Pictures in Pall Mall,[6] & then to gratify me with a visit. I know well how much of our talk will be of dear Clem.

I have heard nothing of *Sarah-Harriet* since she so abruptly was called from her comfortable habitation in Park Street,[7] to accompany her young Pupils to Lord Crewes' in Cheshire. A sudden failure of the West India remittances forced this measure, greatly to poor Sarah's discomforture, though the disappointment was borne with commendable fortitude.

Sarah Payne & her husband are gone for about half a year to the Continent: I have seen Mrs. Admiral!!! Burney I only once since their departure, & I understand from Mr. Barrett that she is gone on a visit to Hampshire.

You have asked me about my poor faithful Ramsay:[8] a

and for a reference to her third marriage and death, see Cornelia Cambridge, A.L.S. (Eg. 3705, f. 65) to CFBt, [October 1826]: 'I heard [at King's Lynn] many painful circumstances of painful interest about Mrs Bruce's death—who is really dead after another marriage to a man who it seems married her for her money and deprived her of every comfort.—She died in I trust a happy ⟨frame⟩ of mind, writing constantly for her good Brother's [the Revd. Stephen Allen's] ministerial comfort, ⟨but⟩ indebted to him for pecuniary supplies constantly & yet under her Husband's Roof . . . She is gone to her account; and her temptations to error weighed I firmly trust.'

[6] 'I am afraid of your mouth watering', wrote Charles Lamb to Hazlitt on 15 March 1806, 'when I tell you Manning and I got into Angerstein's on Wednesday' (*Letters*, ii. 5-6):

'*Mon Dieu!* Such Claudes! Four Claudes bought for more than £10,000 . . . one of these was perfectly miraculous. What colours short of *bona fide* sunbeams it could be painted in, I am not earthly colourman enough to say; but I did not think it had been in the possibility of things. Then, a music-piece by Titian— a thousand-pound picture— . . . the colouring, like the economy of the picture, so sweet and harmonious. . . . Let me say, Angerstein sits in a room—his study . . . when he writes a common letter, as I am doing, surrounded with twenty pictures worth £50,000. What a luxury!'

In the year 1824, 'the sum of £57,000 was appropriated' by parliament 'to the purchase of Mr. Angerstein's collection of pictures for the public, as the foundation of a national gallery' (*AR* lxvi. 89).

[7] At 29 Park Street, Grosvenor Square (see L. 1291 n. 4).

[8] Elizabeth Ramsay (L. 1182 n. 3) had gone for a '6 weeks furlough' to her home in Ilfracombe in May 1822 (see L. 1288), and the maiden who supplied her

marriage off & on, because disapproved by her father, has decided my declining her return—though her Letters are most affectingly anxious to be with me again. I regret her, for her good heart & warm attachment—& perhaps may ever more!—but her insufficiencies in service would make it wrong for me to begin with her again, as she has made no attempt at attaining better experience. I still keep the young Maiden who supplied her place, but by no means intend her permanent stay, for I require a *better servant* in all ways. Should you ever meet with one, who is a good Needlewoman, & a tolerable Cook, with an *excellent* Character for principles & conduct, I should be much obliged to be *advertized* of the same.

I have had 2 or 3 Evening teas with our ingenious & valued Edward, & Fanny. Both are well. Poor Mrs. Sandford is settled, at present, with Richard & Blue, on a pick-Nick plan.[9] Fanny Raper was here yesterday, brightly blooming, & full of good humour. Lady Keith is in town, with her Daughter,[10] on their way to the continent, whither they mean travelling about for 2 years. I see the former frequently, though she sees no other person nearly, except her sisters, from the depth of her Mourning. It is a great loss I to me, & indeed to Alex also, that she leaves England for so long a time. Mrs. Waddington has been in town for a few Weeks, but is returned into Wales. She came to make preparations for the marriage of her youngest Daughter, Augusta, who is betrothed to a young man of very large fortune, son of the late Benj. Hall. M.P.[11] My NameSake is still at Rome; with 4 Children.[12]

place may have been the Hannah Langley who appears regularly in Diary (1823) for bonuses, money, tea, and cakes (L. 1329), and with FBA lately was also a 'mrs. Stains'.

[9] At the Revd. Richard Allen Burney's rectory at Brightwell (L. 1302 n. 3).

[10] Georgiana Augusta Henrietta Elphinstone (1809-92), only daughter of Hester Maria *née* Thrale (L. 1193 n. 8), who had married in 1808 Viscount Keith (1814). He had died at Kincardine on 20 March (*AR* lxv. 193).

[11] Augusta Waddington, aged 21, was to marry on 4 December 1823 Benjamin Hall (L. 1224 n. 5), son of Benjamin Hall (1778-1817) of Hensol Castle, Glamorganshire, M.P. (1806-17), F.R.S. (1812). The younger Benjamin, cr. baronet (1838) and Baron Llanover of Llanover and Abercarn (1859), represented Monmouth boroughs (1831-7) and frequently debated on the issues of the day (see

[*See p. 450 for n. 11 cont. and n. 12*].

———

I have not yet had opportunity of delivering to Mrs. Ad: Burney the Sovereign, but it is always at hand. Poor Lady Cardigan's death was very unexpected,[13] & I think will be a loss to Richmond. Her Sister is inconsolable.

———

I have very late accounts from our dear Esther, who is well, & charges me to express her true concern for you,[14] & that she does not write because she is informed Letters only harrass you while you are too much occupied to answer them. I shall promise that you will not only *understand*, but *thank* her Silence. Yet I hope—& believe you will not be sorry I have broken *mine*, as I premise I expect no Reply, & only do it to vent my own affectionate wishes & most truly say *2 literal* lines will delight me *when* you can give them, even *more* than a real Letter, because the one, *literally* done, will be as *slight* an exertion as the other would be a laborious one—& God knows how much I desire to *ease*, not further *burthen* my dearest Charlotte.—

ever & aye her's
is her faithful
F. d'A.

I *premise* I *expect no Reply.*

DNB). Lady Llanover, the favourite 'Puss' of the Bath years (ix *passim*) was to become a resentful critic of FBA's later works.

[12] Mrs. Waddington's eldest daughter Frances (1791-1876), later Baroness Bunsen (L. 1223 n. 2), had given birth to a fourth son Frederick Wilhelm on 28 April 1823 (Bunsen, *Life*, i. 201-2).

[13] Elder daughter of the 3rd Earl Waldegrave, Lady Elizabeth (i, L. 13 n. 6), Countess of Cardigan, had died on 23 June 1823. Preceding her marriage in 1791 to James Brudenell (1725-1811), 5th Earl of Cardigan, she served as Lady of the Bedchamber to the Princess Royal and, as Countess of Cardigan, Lady of the Bedchamber to Queen Charlotte (R.H.I., Windsor) until the death of the latter in 1818. Her sister Lady Caroline (1765-1831) was also at Windsor when FB arrived there as Keeper of the Robes in 1786, and kind, gentle, well bred, and amiable the newcomer thought them as they made her welcome (*DL* ii. 373, 388).

[14] EBB's letter had arrived on 15 August (Diary).

[11 Bolton Street,
post 17 September 1823]

To Mrs. Broome

A.L.S. (Berg), n.d.
Double sheet 8vo   4 pp.   *pmk* 2⟨6⟩ S⟨ ⟩ 18⟨ ⟩   wafer
Addressed: Mrs. Broome / King's Road, / 47 / Brighton.
Endorsed by CBFB: Sister d'arblay / Octr 1823 / ans^d—

A thousand thanks for this *Volunteer* Bulletin,[1] my dearest
Charlotte—I think it, *alltogether*, very comforting though in
detail very sad still. I received your dear & satisfactory long
Letter, my kind Charlotte, according to its date, & with infinite eagerness. But I write now this *little*, because its meaning
is to be *great*. I knew not how to listen to your tender entreaties, nor the really affectionate requests of our poor
Clement, as to passing a fortnight *within sound of your Call*,
when you both so urgently proposed it: but now that you
talk of a change of Coast, I feel *all-subdued* into consent. Yet
do not let that determine a removal, should the plan be
altered—as—once giving way *so far*, perhaps I may bring
my reluctant poor Nerves into complying *further*, should you
remain *wholly* where you are. But as I should exceedingly |
prefer any other part of the Coast, from my desire of only
taking You & the *sea*, without therefore *leaving* my retired
obscurity, I beg, should any alteration be fixed, to know it,
that I may accommodate my motions accordingly.

This *First*.

2dly, if our dear Clement would be better in remaining only
with you, *honestly* decide for my joining you another time.

I shall settle nothing till I hear from you.

And even then, I cannot promise to acquiesce as to your
time, though I will to your *place*: for I have engaged to be in
town to see Mrs. Angerstein when she returns from Spa, as
she is then going on to Suffolk for 3 or 4 months.[2] |

Alex, also, is not yet *gone*, though preparing to *go*.

1315. [1] Mrs. Broome's letter had arrived on 9 September (Diary).
[2] FBA had received a letter from Amelia Angerstein on the 9th, had replied on
the 12th, and had received her at Bolton Street on the 13th (Diary).

But as he will be absent 2, months, at least, during the course of that period it will be hard if we cannot *please all parties* by an arrangement for this desired Fortnight—which I shall tenderly enjoy with my ever tender Charlotte.[3]

I must have 2 rooms,—for I must Dine as well as sleep chez moi—Do not dispute this, I entreat. I shall be with you at all intervening hours as much as possible. And *You* shall always be *arbiter* of their appointment.

I tremble when I think of Cambridge!—How will he do without his unappreciable Nurse?—or shall you be able to manage to be there with him?—Defer every thing that *may* be deferred till our meeting—& do not hurry your determination with regard even to that, if inconvenient. I shall quietly wait your deliberate reply And give no *reasons*— remit that for our confabs. Merely write upon what *Place*— & *Time*, you wish the *renconter*: & I will do my best to accord to it. God bless you my Love My kind Love to dear Clement. Do not name my Scheme. I say nossing from wishing to join you quite quietly   I shall bring occupation, or my Mind would not be at ease.[4] I long to have you meet my valuable & truly constant Friend.

F. B.

P S. Mrs. Angerstein is come, & I have seen her, & [she] is gone to the Coast—I can now therefore give you *carte blanche* to fix our Time & place. See 2^d P.S.

P.S.2^d Only write *one Line* to Say *where* & *when* Answer the rest when we meet

[3] FBA was to set out for Brighton on 28 October and to return on 25 November (Diary).

[4] Presumably biographical materials for the preface to the planned edition of CB's letters.

1316 [11 Bolton Street],
29–30 September 1823

To Mrs. Locke

A.L. incomplete (rejected Diary MSS. 7342-5, Berg), 29-30 Sept. 1823
Double sheet 8vo   4 pp.
Edited by FBA, p. 1, annotated: To Keep. / for the End—
Edited by CFBt. See Textual Notes.

29. Sept[r]
Monday Night—1823

I feel very sure that not to me is left the melancholy office of writing to my dearest Friend[1]—yet to write to her is the first—the only thing I can just now do—How prepared She was—& how prepared *you* are—I dwell upon with unspeakable comfort at this mournful moment—for mournful it is —O very mournful to feel thus often the best & most precious ties of Life broken asunder. How dire must be the condition of Those who see nothing beyond the Grave![2] I always feel as if I could neither Live nor Die were I so wretched as to be persuaded this mortal machine was All that had to do either —I mean to say, that I really think so deep an horrour would pervade all my faculties that I should lose my Reason.

Tuesday. 30.—I wrote to you last Night, my sweet & dear Friend,—meaning to *causer* calmly; certain of your resignation, & wishing therefore to catch it:—but I grew disturbed, & would not write on. I wish we had been together—!

I could not have done *you* harm, feeling as I do the infinite distance of my loss from yours—yet mine is so *sensible* I to my whole frame that I know you will generously be sorry for *me* also—situated as I am, & chosen, elected as I have been by her, for a partiality that had no bounds, & that—with her

1316. [1] The dowager Lady Templetown (iii, L. 216 n. 16, and iv *passim*) had died at her home at 65 Portland Place on 29 September (Diary), aged 77.

[2] FBA is recalling the close of *Rasselas*: 'How gloomy would be these mansions of the dead to him who did not know that he should never die, that what now acts shall continue its agency, and what now thinks shall think on for ever.'

453

rare & high qualities, & delightful powers, had gained my affection to all the tenderness of Friendship—in so much as to make her kindness balsamic while her society was enlivening, was re-animating—

'Twas in *your* Name our Hearts grew to each other—in alike Loving you & adoring your revered Husband—your *matchless* — —

I was incoherent in my last, I conclude, from the incertitude it occasioned—yet I ought not now to lament it—but I was very irresolute whether or not to say I feared I had seen this exquisite Friend for the last time—I could not make up my mind as to what would be best. Yet never I ought I to be distressed with regard to *you*, my most dear & lenient Friend, for if there can be a doubt, you are sure to interpret it advantageously.—I pity my Amine my tender Amine that she cannot fly to you with her heavenly gifts of consolation— However, you are too little Self to need more consolation than the pious persuasion of Her Happiness, joined to the little prospect of her returning powers of Earthly enjoyment. There was *less* than I had supposed, for General Upton[3]— who has had the goodness at poor Miss Upton's request, to write to me himself, intimates that there were menaces of far more acute sufferings awaiting her, had she lived, than any with which she had actually been afflicted!—The *last* was perfectly serene & peaceful. I am extremely sensible of this feeling attention to me, I & the more, in looking upon it as a filial tribute of Respect to their knowledge of Her singular & most touching kindness for me.

I had not been admitted since Monday—the week before all was over—I imagine her Family were always about her —How affecting to me was that last meeting! I explained to her my long absence, & my regret—'I know it!' she kindly cried—'for I know — — your *Heart!*—' She said that with an emphasis I can never remember but with gratitude—when I was obliged to wish her good night—what blessings—what sweet blessings—mixt with fervant & re-iterated prayers to

---

[3] General Upton's letter, written on 29 September 1823, the day of his mother's death, is extant (Eg. 3698, ff. 312–13b): 'My sister Sophia has desired me to acquaint you who for such a length of time have been attached to our dear Mother, that it has at length pleased God to release her from her sufferings She expired about nine this Morng. . . .'

The Almighty—did she utter—shewing the complete self-possession with which she gave those precious benedictions, by ending them with—'You—& your dear — — son!—' She hesitated for the word, but then pronounced it quite emphatically.—Do I right—do I wrong, to enter into these details?—I hope right—for how sad am I you can ⎮

[*the next page is missing*]

1317   [11 Bolton Street,
                                          1 October 1823]

To Mrs. Broome

A.L. (Berg), n.d.
Single sheet 4to   2 pp.
Annotated in pencil, p. 1: Oct. 1 1823

I thought—I flattered myself, my dearest Charlotte, that the Spell against our living a little together was at length broken—but no!—I am almost sick in writing the *no*! When my Letter went to you, with the proposal, I was particularly well, the Weather was beautiful—& Alex just set off on his long planned Tour — — The very next Day, all was changed! Rain & Damp took possession of Sunshine & Brightness, & wholly obscured them; & a sharp pain in the Ear & beating on one side the head chaced away all my healthy acquirements, & not only stopt the *Daily* Walks that have so wonderfully hardened me from colds, but filled me with rheumatic chills & spasms that forced me to wrap up as if I had been a sheep, i.e. in woollen, & have made a '*Mobbled* Queen'[1] of me ever since, & condemned me to keep one whole side as closely roasting before the Fire as a side of Venison!

If all this should be conquered, & the Weather again be settled Fair, I will still fight hard against the spiteful Spell, & endeavour to obtain my long promised & earnestly desired fortnight with my ever dear Charlotte: but even This is not

1317. [1] *Hamlet*, II. ii.

all—another Lion stands in the way!² —Alex writes me word he is not yet decided whether to continue his Tour in the South, or to go North to Ely, to the Prebendary's House,³ or West to Bath, to a Debt-visit of 5 years owing to his Cousins & Aunt: but ˡ in either of these 2 latter cases, he builds upon finding me at Home, as he will make this his half way House for refitting. And you & I, my dear Charlotte, are two such dutiful Mothers—as Clem & Alex well know—that such a thought never occurs to us as thinking of any convenience but what belongs to a due observance of our respected little Boys. So that at all events I must wait my next Letter; which, though it may arrive to-morrow, may be put off till to-morrow week—not to say to-morrow fortnight, or three weeks, or months,—or that other to-morrow which comes in question some times in my Correspondence with my *Young Youth*, & which is vulgarly called to-morrow come never: for his part of our Epistolary intercourse finishes, sometimes, rather abruptly, with that date, i.e. without ever a word of Reply, till it can be given by Word of Mouth. The young youths of the present day, as my dear Sir Hugh observes, are pretty free & easy;⁴ however, as he further remarks, they have got to such a prodigious pitch, in the present generation, that they stand upon little ceremony in taking the liberty to hold their Parents & Relations as cheap as dirt ˡ

P S. I hope our Charlotta is well? Fanny R[a]per called the other day, & is in *hopes* to go to her with Mr. R[aper] & Minette, on the 8th S[arah] Harriet is well, & S. Payne amazingly so—she shocks the Doctors! May Clement do the same! She is best, she *shews*, in her own hands. Mrs Admiral!!! is in good health. Ed & Fanny drank Tea with me on Sunday.⁵

Poor Mrs. F. Bowdler⁶ will have a severe loss—She & Ly T[empletown] were Friends from Childhood—Should you see her, pray say I feel for her sincerely—& I shall write to

² Proverbs 26: 13.
³ To visit the Barrett family in Ely (L. 1304 n. 17).
⁴ Sir Hugh Tyrold (L. 1270 n. 8), whose remarks on the rising generation (*Camilla*, bk. 1, chap. 1) are considerably sharpened with the author's closer acquaintance with it.
⁵ On 30 September (Diary).
⁶ See i, L. 3 n. 87 and ix, x *passim*.

her as soon as I am sure where she is, at Brighton——or returned to Bath——

1318   [11 Bolton Street,
                              pre 3] October 1823

To Mrs. Locke

L., excerpt copied in the hand of CFBt (Diary MSS. viii. 7352-[3],
Berg), Oct. 1823
Single sheet 4to   2 pp.

To Mrs Lock——

                                            Octr 1823.

I have had a very kind letter from Miss Upton,[1] which like
that of her Brother[2] I receive with double satisfaction in
attributing it to a respectful tribute to the feelings of the
amiable inestimable Mother who delighted to distinguish me
by a kindness that had a charm inexpressible——a charm that
went strait to the heart & then fastened itself by clinging ties
that must adhere to its last pulsations.

My dearest Friend! have you no more Lady Templetowns

Though I have always, for so many years admired her, I
little thought 5 years ago so to be caught——& won!——I must
be grateful for what I have had. She has sweetened many an
hour of this last faded period, & her extraordinary love &
kindness have given a [|] powerful fillip to my existence. O
how she revered Mr Lock! How completely we had in unison
Two feelings!——

1318. [1] Sophia, 'bewildered', as she said, 'since the severe loss', was not able to
write at once but eventually penned the black-edged 8vo (Eg. 3698, ff. 314-15b),
asking FBA 'to Express to H.R.H. Princess Sophia our deep sense of the very kind
anxiety with which H.R.H. graciously honored us——& which alas! my poor dearest Mother was never able to hear! . . . ——to you My Dear Madam it will Ever be
a gratifying reflection that you helped to soothe many hours of suffering & made
her as she used to say 'forget *herself*'——allow me to thank you from my heart for
the very kind note My Brother had the honor of receiving from you——I know
that every word of it was *true*—— . . .'
    [2] See L. 1316 n. 3.

pre 3 October 1823

I rejoice you talk of coming to Town—the very thought of it revives me—

1319 [11 Bolton Street],
29 September–16 October 1823

To Esther (Burney) Burney

A.L. (rejected Diary MSS. 7338-[41], Berg), 29 Sept.–16 Oct. 1823
Double sheet 4to   4 pp.   *pmk* 16 OC 1823   red seal
Addressed: Mrs. Burney, / Lark Hall Place, / near Bath.
Endorsed by EBB: Oct. 17th / 1823 / answered. *Oct. 23d*
Edited by CFBt. *See* Textual Notes.

Begun. Goose Day. [Michaelmas]
Sept [29]
1823

But not a Goose Act is it to write to my dearest Esther; such writing brings Grist to my Mill such as best suits my taste. I thank you cordially for seizing every opportunity to give me double Measure. I would such offered themselves to Me more frequently.

I am now quite alone, Alex having at length begun his Excursion. He is Now somewhere on the south coast. He told me to direct my last Letter to Hastings. He has visited Dover, RamsGate, Margate, Sand Gate & *Folkstone*, whence he dates his own last, in his way to Hastings. He prefers me to give him the meeting at Brighton;[1] I have offered our poor Charlotte to join her for one Fortnight on the Coast; & I am now waiting her Answer. How you will be glad for her that Clement is amending! almost contrary to all expectation. But I am not in good courage about him, nevertheless, as his first thought is to repair to Cambridge, where his Professorship demands such hard study that I have little hope it can be followed up without a relapse.[2] His Head is utterly unfitted, by

1319. [1] FBA was to set out for Brighton on the 28th (Diary).

[2] See L. 1261 n. 3 for the offices held by Clement Robert Francis, Fellow (1820-9) of Caius College. He was to succumb to pulmonary tuberculosis, though

458

this length of enervating illness, for being exercised wholly in Science. I have frankly announced my apprehensions, & tried to warn him of his danger, which I think *more* than great, if he perseveres in this rash plan, as I think its mischief will be inevitable. Why can I not get a little of this mundane assiduity for my poor Alex, who has None! & whose health would be all the better for stated necessity of application. But he leaves every thing to arrange itself! 'tis an easy & commodious mode enough if it would succeed. But, who, except his excentric Self,—can expect that?—How different were our modes, my dear Esther, & those to whom we belonged! What of toil, anxiety & disturbance might we have been spared had such been our rule of life — — & had it prospered!—But my poor Alex has yet to learn the result. He has hitherto been so fortunate, that he is spoiled past all exhortation: I he pursues his own way, & assures me Life is not worth having on any other terms! The time will probably come when he will know & feel the contrary. He pleases so much, & with so little trouble, where he does *not* offend, that he is presently pardonned where he *does*. And this makes him deaf to remonstrance,—or, rather, *give* remonstrance in return, against the *supererogation* of my Lectures. Oh that I could make him over to an amiable, prudent, & *softly* wise, yet *deeply* wise Companion! But where may I hope to find The Paragon? She must be eminently pleasing to win his heart; she must be eminently literary to keep his society; she must be eminently œconomical to sustain his Fortune, & she must be eminently sweet-tempered to bear with his excentricities! The difficulty to discover all these eminencies is such That I am for-ever consigning him, *au lieu*, to *your* destination, for him, as next best, because Safest, of Miss Margland.[3]—Yet—if such a Paragon could be found, who would take all that toil, I do believe he would make a Partner of no usual amiability.

Oct.r 1. Edward & Fanny drank tea with me on Sunday, & were both well & chearful.—So was not I, as I fear they

suffering as well from rheumatism and other complications (see further, L. 1337 n. 4).
[3] The governess in *Camilla*.

perceived—for I have been deeply grieved by the loss of Lady Templetown, who, for the last 5 years—that is the Period of my London Residence in Bolton Street, has been to me, as far as the *recency* of our intercourse (comparative recency) would admit, another Mrs. Lock or Mrs. Delany to me—so indefatigable have been her condescending efforts to please, to sooth, & to awaken me to social life. We had been known to each other, more or less, nearly *40* years, for I early met with her at Norbury Park;[4] but though with intimacy when we met, it had I been without *suite* when we parted: till my settling here—she then sought me—O with what goodness, what patience, what persevering anxiety to bring me a little back to former times!—She never expected returns of visits—she never came in, in her calls innumerable, but after conversing in her Carriage with Ramsay, & enquiring into the state of my health & spirits — — &, finally, she devized a way to gain me, that finished in making a conquest of my heart; she proposed my accompanying her in all her visits to Eliot Vale, save [tho]se in which she remained there. This, by giving us, to & fro', 6 Hours tête à tête, joined to the sweetness of the attention, soon brought on an intercourse that heightened itself into the warmest friendship. Latterly, I went to *her* in return, whenever I pleased, by a previous Note, which brought her warm Carriage to my door. And this became a source of consolation that soon ripened into pleasure—Nay, delight; for her abilities were of the first rate order, her memory was stored with literary ornaments of the best selection, she had the highest taste for the polite arts; Music, Painting, & Poetry had her severally for a Votary; in Religion she was equally pious & liberal, resigned in her sufferings, yet open to the day-light of enjoyment whenever it was ready to break through them—& her powers of conversation, combining Wisdom with Imagination, were enchanting. She had been the earliest Friend of Mrs. Lock—even from School Girls—What a tie *that*, for each of us, when once we took to each other! Yet the great loadstone to me, & that which attracted me to her so closely, was her sense of

---

[4] FB had first visited Norbury Park in 1784 (*HFB*, p. 184), where, according to SBP's Journals (*Catalogue*), Lady Templetown and her young family were frequent visitors.

my bereavement! *he* had struck her, she said, as one of the most amiable Beings the hand of God had ever formed[5]—her pity, therefore, for me, excited all that followed,—it made her bear with my long intractable *sauvagerie* till her ¦ sympathising indulgence changed it into tender Gratitude. Her partiality to me had no bounds—& when I saw her last the benedictions she poured upon me, as she held my hands upon her breast, were so penetrating—so fervent—that they are never out of my Ears.—What a severe loss to our Mrs. Lock! —Yet no repining escapes her,—she only looks up, & looks forward to Future Junctions! Sweet Soul!—Her son William has her spare room, or I should surely offer myself to her,— & surely be accepted, as Alex leaves me a free agent. His last Letter is from Hastings, & he desires my next address may be to Brighton. I make no apology for writing all this of my dearest Lady Templetown; I know your taste, your fondness for excellence too well. I ought, however, to have reserved this swallowing subject for a Frank—but Franks occur so seldom, & This Theme is so uppermost—& I am ever so interested in all your accounts of *your* Friends, whom you make mine—⟨Adams⟩, Daly, Blagden, Hay, Beckford, *Yeats*[6] &c that I hope the feeling will be mutual.

I take great care, believe me, my kind Hetty, of my *Head*, *now*, & keep MSS. of ⟨merely⟩ a light sort for night, when alone. But I resist with all my might the proposal of the 4th of our instalment *This* October. I shall far prefer waiting till we meet. I think nothing more likely than that what passed with Ly Keith may lead to something pleasant for Fanny— Ly K. will never have it out of her mind should opportunity offer for something suitable to what I have *premised*. And nobody will be more in the way of such sort of situations, since she travels with her Daughter in her hand. I have just

[5] Lady Templetown saw something of General d'Arblay in the summer of 1798, when to be near Mrs. Locke she took a house at Leatherhead, about three miles from Norbury Park or from Camilla Cottage, the home of the d'Arblays in West Humble (iv. 182–5).

[6] The usual polite mention of EBB's friends at Bath, identified respectively in L. 1307 n. 13; L. 1304 nn. 26, 25; L. 1208 n. 4; L. 1189 n. 21; L. 1230 n. 9.

had a Letter from her from *Paris*, much delighted by her ⟨dear⟩ Girl's delight[7]——

I finish *16. Oct*ʳ Clement much *better* though ⟨not⟩ comfortably, I mean *progressively*: Charlotte sends kind Love & Thanks for your kind messages, in a hurried note just arrived by a private hand. I saw Chˢ Parr to day His Wife better.

Mrs. Admiral B[urney] returns You kind thanks & mutual regrets——but hopes next time for better luck. S[arah] P[ayne] is still abroad. S[arah] H[arriet] *ennuyed* à la morte but *mum* if she speak not *herself.* |

God bless You, my dearest Esther! Mrs. Lock leaves me this instant, & leaves her Love for this Letter. I am unfixt about Brighton from an Earache——all well

1320 [11 Bolton Street,
5 December 1823]

To Mrs. Locke

A.L.S. draft (?) (Berg), n.d.
Double sheet large 8vo with ½″ hole in the upper right corner of second leaf 4 pp.

Love & Friendship &ᶜ

I could not, my dearest Friend, execute your too kind commission with the secresy I had projected: I could get no satisfactory answer without coming to the point: & all my clandestine stratagems ended in so doing. I should otherwise, I saw, render part of your indulgent design *a little less* exquisite: & the result is that he has frankly fixed on what will

[7] See L. 1314 n. 10. Lady Keith's folio letter dated 'near Malmaison', 19 September 1823, survives (Barrett, Eg. 3699B, ff. 200-1b). 'Georgy was all Astonishment at the Splendour of the Inn [at Calais] our Room furnished with Green Satin Silk Gold Clocks & Ornaments &c wʰ one hardly sees in the best English Drawing Rooms——[In Paris] Georgina quite enchanted with all she sees ——& so struck with the Splendour of the Inns & Lodging Houses wʰ are indeed better furnished than most of our nobilitys principal Mansions. We are now again on the Wing for Geneva——taking Sᵗ Cloud the Sêve Manufactory & Versailles in our Way——'.

merit, he says, that peculiar binding as well as Mrs. Lock's peculiar kindness & goodness — — And this is
Stillingfleet's Origines Sacræ—[1]
in *Two* Volumes, alas!—but you *would* make me draw from him his real choice, & so it stands.—& *I* know you would not have thanked me ˡ to have done the thing by halves

How dear to me was your visit, my beloved Friend! *Mobbled Queen*[2] as I was, prepared for my Wilderness haunt, I could not but think, when you were gone, & I *unhuddled* myself, that what La Bruyere says of Love is equally exact of Friendship:[3]—where it is true, he says, of Love, in *awaiting* its object, nothing is good enough, elegant enough, becoming enough to display in preparation: but where the meeting is sudden, & by surprize, nothing is too ordinary, too shabby, too ill-assorted, to make us shrink from an encounter that drives the *outside* from ˡ our minds in the gratification of the *inside*.

How few give that feeling! but how genial is the predominence of such affection!

I did not hear half enough of sweetest—& I thought you had more Letters to pick out passages for me? I must hope that will be repaired soon.

The Letter is not yet come from Ely—but *next week* is fixed though not the *day*, for the excursion of Alex. He spent an Evening very pleasantly yesterday with Dʳ Ash & his family,[4] & no party whatever. For me, I have seen no one but

---

1320. [1] *Origines Sacræ; or a Rational Account of the grounds of Natural and Revealed Religion* (1662) by the 17th-century divine Edward Stillingfleet (1635-99), Mrs. Locke evidently intended as a present to Alex on his 29th birthday (18 December). The work, along with *A Letter to a Deist*, had been issued in two volumes (Oxford, 1797).

[2] *Hamlet*, II. ii.

[3] FBA is thinking of Jean de la Bruyère (1645-96), the section entitled 'Des Femmes', item 9 (iv) in *Les Caractères . . . ou les mœurs de ce siècle*, ed. Robert Garapon (1962): 'Les femmes se préparent pour leurs amants, si elles les attendent; mais si elles en sont surprises, elles oublient à leur arrivée l'état où elles se trouvent, elles ne se voient plus. Elles ont plus de loisir avec les indifférents; elles sentent le désordre où elles sont, s'ajustent en leur présence, ou disparaissent un moment, et reviennent parées.'

[4] Presumably at the home (2 Foley Place, Portland Place) of Edward Ash (*c.* 1764-1829), M.D. (1796), F.R.S. (1801), physician extraordinary to His late Majesty. His son the Revd. Edward John Ash (L. 1184 n. 6), formerly Tancred student in Divinity of Christ's and Fellow (1819), AA had known at Cambridge (see ix, L. 1064 n. 6).
'Placed in competent circumstances, and rendered independent of his profession',

my dearest Friend, & my kind Augusta, & my pretty Wilderness, & walk from the Bason in the Green Park to the top of Constitution Hill. I ¹ should like to make you see it, 'tis so much more picturesque & private & rural than there is any conceiving, unseen, that any part of a public Park can be kept. 'Tis very little frequented, but by ladies who walk for health, & children who frisk about to enjoy it.

Adieu, my dearest Friend—I trust to the young lovely Madonna for the joy of seeing you again ere long—

ever & ever yours
F. d'Ay.

1321   [11 Bolton Street,
–9 December 1823]

To Mrs. Barrett

A.L. (Berg), [*dated in error*] 9 Nov.
Double sheet 4to   4 pp.   *pmk*   9 DE 1823   red seal
Addressed: Mrs. Barrett, / at Mr. Prebendary / Dampier's, / Ely.

A model of Epistolary kindness is my dearest Charlotte,[1] kept firm to her standard of persevering Patience by a just confidence in the Affection which she knows to be invariable, though its demonstration may be a little zig Zag. *Zig Zag*, I say, for, by circuitous routes it is uniformly to be *peeped* at, though by the strait line it may not always be apparent: from Your dear Mother I have constantly News of *You*, my Charlotta, when I receive any of herself; she well knows there is no subject she can chuse that is so welcome to me, & there is certainly none on which she *dilates* so willingly—*more*

Dr. Ash was of 'retiring habits' and 'little known beyond a select circle of friends, chiefly of the literary and scientific class, by whom he was highly and universally esteemed, as well on account of his strict moral qualities as his extensive intellectual attainments' (*R.C.P.*, ii. 465). Scientific, as well as literary men, always attracted d'Arblay.

1321. ¹ Of CFBt's letters from Ely, received by her aunt on 7, 19, 27 November and 2, 16 December (Diary) only the last, dated Ely, Monday the 15th, survives (Barrett, Eg. 3702A, ff. 47–8b).

willingly, it would be correct to say; but now & then a little odd word forces its way before one is aware.

I have had the very great satisfaction of spending a month with your dearest Mother at Brighton,[2] after a separation from such intimate & comforting intercourse for, I think, more than two Years. I found her much less shaken by her long Nursery, confinement, & anxiety than I had expected. But while the Air of Brighton has braced her Nerves, perpetual occupation has saved her from the melancholy ruminations into which she is so apt to ponder — — Will You cry Look at Home, dear Aunt, look at Home?—I *do*,—& it is therefore I thus ⏐ speak. Perpetual occupation has alone kept me if not from an immediate personal farewell, at least from one far more bitter of mental alienation. And though to all my Friends—& to You amongst the kindest,—*my* occupation was one that seemed but to impress deep Affliction yet deeper, I am entirely convinced of the contrary. Where the measure of woe is so heavy as to menace overpowering either Life or Reason, believe me, my dear Girl, whatever can catch attention should be resorted to without hesitation. I will not enter into the Religious meditations which, then, led me to conceive that nothing more remained for me Here than to prepare for Hereafter; I knew not the strength of my Constitution, & concluded that my mundane Duties were over, whether for myself or for others — — But I now think there is an Organic conformation for Longevity that demands the combination of exertions for which our Earthly career seems designed. And since this has struck me, I have tried to feel & to favour, the Rights of Those I love upon my Consideration & my practice.

I delight to think of you with my dear faithful Friends the Archdeacon & his Cornelia, & to think of Them with You.— The appreciation I know is mutual. How happy Mr. Prebendary Dampier should partake of the same sympathies! My dear Brother Charles has often named to me *both* Brothers.[3]

---

[2] See further, L. 1322.

[3] The Revd. Henry Thomas Dampier (L. 1304 n. 17), prebendary of Ely, and his brother John Lucius (*c.* 1793–1853), B.A. (King's College, Cambridge, 1816), M.A. (1819), Fellow (1815), barrister-at-law (1819), Recorder of Portsmouth (1837–8).

I well remember the pretty Miss Heberden,[4] & am glad you are so pleased with her as Mrs. Jenyns. She was, *erst,* ǀ a favourite *Crony* of the, erst, beautiful Miss Port.[4]—

Poor Mrs. Waddington had left London before I received your Commission: but it shall not be lost. She is now completely occupied by preparations for her youngest Daughter's marriage, with a man, who has now 2000 p^r annum, & who is heir to *Eleven.*[5] This Daughter turns out very lovely & very clever.

⌐────┐

I have not seen our dear Fanny Raper since her return. She called while I was at Brighton, but I hope will soon redeem that mistake. I only fear we shall find no subject of Conversatio[n.] Your sweet Mother called upon me last week,[6] while transacting business in Town. She had left dear Marianne well, & was going back to her for a few days. I have now the fullest hopes of the ultimate recovery of dear Clement. All is amelioration, & so gradual as to promise permanency. My Bath Letters are cheering from my dear Sister Burney, of herself & her *progeny.* I have an Epistle rather *morne* from poor Sarah Harriet, but no hint of that unless you hear it from *1st* hand! The dullness of her life seems to require all her judgement for endurance: yet, *once begun,* it would be *ruinous* to renounce it. I was pleased with your Henry,[7] who is handsome & sprightly & pleasing: but I am constant to my dear Dick,[7] who I think will be a comfort & a Joy to you through life: though you know I never thought him the *beauty of the Family*:—but I hear so much of the *3* who bask under your immediate smiles & auspices, that ǀ I am quite satisfied with the share of

[4] In the years 1785-8 the beautiful Georgiana Mary Ann Port (GMAPW) lived with her great-aunt Delany in a house at Windsor next door to that taken in 1783 by the physician William Heberden (see Olwen Hedley, L. 1314 n. 4 and *HFB*, pp. 256-9). It was doubtless here in these years that GMAPW got to know his granddaughter 'the pretty Miss Heberden' now Mrs. Jenyns, whose visit to FB at the Queen's House is mentioned in *DL* ii. 421.

[5] See L. 1314 n. 11.   [6] On 1 December (Diary).

[7] Henry Barrett (i, p. lxxii), and his son Richard Arthur Francis (1812-81), now in the fourth form at Eton (*The Eton School Lists from 1798 to 1877* (1885), p. 119b). Dick is to emerge regularly in his great-aunt's letters as, passing through London en route to or from his parents for the vacations, he calls at her door.

that delicious but dangerous Commodity which you *& yours*
have sent forth for admiration & attraction in this mortal
World: As Alex will carry you This himself, I pass by his subject: but I shall depend upon a clandestine line or two as to
him & your Episcopal Belle.[8] You are a dear kind Love to
think so much, whether merrily or gravely, on a matter so
near my heart, nay, my peace of mind, as that of companion-
izing that dear Excentrick agreeably yet prudently. Without
the first article, he would be *uncatchable*; without the second,
he would be *undone*. Your idea seems to Unite the two requisites.

I have been shut up since my return from Brighton, with
Alex, however,—not again to seclusion!—but I shall soon
summon my ever kindly ready Sarah Payne, who is really a
charming personage. Fanny B[urney] is with her friend &
ci-*devant* pupil, Mrs. Green, in Lincolnshire.[9] Edward *sips his
Tea* with me next Sunday—when Alex will sip it with Those
who would truly flavour it to *Me*. I was sure you would feel
for my loss in my dear admirable Lady Templetown, though

[8] Elder daughter of the Very Revd. Bowyer Edward Sparke (L. 1203 n. 6),
Bishop of Ely (1812-36), by his wife Hester *née* Hobbs (d. 14 March 1836),
Hester (*c.* 1800-81) was to become the wife of Henry Pratt (1795-1860) of
Ryston Hall, Norfolk, eventually Lt. Col. of the 18th Foot or Royal Irish Regiment.
  On Thursday 11 December Alex was to set out for Ely to visit the Barretts,
and, as arranged by Archdeacon Cambridge, prebendary of Ely Cathedral, to
preach a sermon in the Cathedral pulpit. In a letter of 15 December (op. cit.)
CFBt would oblige her aunt with an account of AA's conquests in Ely Episcopal
society. On Sunday [14 December] he had 'appeared in the Cathedral Pulpit,
surrounded by the Congregations of 3 churches, who all assemble to hear the
sermon in this noble Building. the Bishop, preceded by his sword bearer, took his
Throne in state, & four Prebendaries were placed near him. Alexanders sermon
was admirably delivered, & his voice so well managed that every one c[d] hear. . . .
Mrs Sparke & all the Ladies who spoke to me were in raptures, & the AD. [Cam-
bridge] reports similar admiration from the gentlemen.' As for CFBt, she thought
the sermon 'one of the most beautiful' she had 'ever heard from him'. In the evening, on request, AA regaled the company with an earlier sermon that 'had been so
much approved by the Bishop of London' and part of another composed 'during
his late Tour'. 'The AD. admires his clear & close reasoning as much as his wonderful eloquence & power of language.' 'Miss Harwood, a friend of Mrs Rishtons, said
to me, "What a beautiful *countenance*! if I were 20 years younger, how much in
love I should be!" '
[9] Henrietta Green (L. 1293 n. 4) of Lancashire, however, not Lincolnshire.

467

you have been out of the way of knowing half its sadness: ——
—— Mrs. Baker was well,[10] & *out* the morning my sister called
here.

Adieu, my sweet Charlotta—My best comp^ts to Mr. Barrett, & Love to The Three, & kindest possible remembrances
to the Arch^n & M^rs C[ambridge]. |

Tuesday 9 Nov^r [*properly* Dec.] is the date that this de-
parts from Bolton [Street.]

This has been written for the conveyance of Alex—but he
has just requested me to save you a *mere line* from himself,
announcing that his place is taken for *Thursday* to Cambridge,
& that on Friday he builds upon paying you his Devoirs.
Thus my own projected post œconomy is rendered abortive

1322   [11 Bolton Street,
c. 16]–23 December 1823

To Esther (Burney) Burney

A.L. (rejected Diary MSS. [7354–7], p. 3 being numbered 7356,
Berg), –23 Dec. 1823
Double sheet 4to (7.3 × 9.8″)   4 pp.   *pmk* 23 DE 1823   wafer
Addressed: Mrs. Burney, / Lark Hall Place, / near BATH.
Endorsed by EBB: answered Jan—27—1824
Edited by CFBt. *See* Textual Notes.

23^d Decr 1823

How I wish, my dearest Hetty, You had half the Letters to
read that, mentally, I am perpetually writing to you!—Half?
—I had better say *half an inch* of the many *Quires* I fill to
you in that manner!—And not only in sleepless Nights, but
in heavy days, how often do I commune with you in imagin-
ing what you would say, or think, on such or such a Person
—Thing—or Feeling. But my taste helas!—for scribbling is
now all subsided into a Matter of Commerce. You would not

[10] Sarah Baker (L. 1205 n. 7), on whom Mrs. Broome must have called before
her visit of 1 December to Bolton Street.

have supposed me, perhaps, an *internal Trader*—? yet such, *Correspondentially*, I am become; for I only hold my *Pen-Epistolary*—except where some Necessity puts it into my hand, from a sense of Probity to balance accounts, or from a rapacity for Gain, to make an Exchange in my own favour. Thus, though Both your last Letters merit even double pay, I only thus slackly sit down to answer both together because I know, by all the routine of Business, in established firms, that I have no chance of receiving a *Third* Cargo till I have acknowledged the arrival of the Goods preceding. Well—this being premised, I must next tell you that I have 100 things to talk to you about, & am embarrassed by which of them to commence: whether to open with the Present Moment, according to your general taste, & so plant you by my side in Bolton Street London—(O that I could!) or whether to carry You back with me to Brighton; or whether to whisk ǀ You to & fro, with a Hop, Skip, & a Jump, by beginning at once upon my Alex?—Minor subjects rise by scores; but I feel these are the 3 you would elect; so First, where First I think will go your interest, for *Brighton*, as that includes so dear a tie to us both.

It would not be easy to tell, nor pleasant to hear—the difficulties, the repugnance I had to vanquish for this expedition. It was upwards of 4 years since I had been able to prevail with myself ever to quit This my own destined Nest, except for the short distance & urgent entreaty of Richmond & Eliot Vale—but I will not dwell on that ill-will; it was conquered by poor Charlotte's tender pleadings, aided by Alexander's vehement desires, which played the most sounding Bass to her delicate Treble: & I am now extremely glad to have been vanquished—for it could not but do me good to see the affectionate pleasure—in their different ways—with which —hardly believing their own Eyes—they received me. I spent there exactly a month,[1] & it was one of true sisterly & reciprocated consolation. She looks far better than I had dared expect, &, at times, & in certain *costumes*, really pretty still, for the sea air has restored much of her early bloom, &

1322. [1] From 28 October to 25 November (Diary).

she has recovered a degree of *embonpoint* that keeps off Wrinkles. She is weak, however, in the extreme, & incapable of walking a 1/4 of a mile, or even haft that, without being knocked up: &, her nerves & spirits are so cruelly in Unison with her poor body that the smallest ⎮ occurence unhinges her; the most ordinary circumstance seems a formidable event, & the most trivial contrariety or perplexity bewilders her into thinking that she has a weight of care upon her hands that will destroy her.——Yet no one could smile at her distresses, because she never complains; & it is only in observing, & soothing her that she can be drawn to a Vent that, then, instantly relieves & revives her:——and because, far from smiling herself at any vexations of others, there is not a moment in the day in which she is not ready wholly to set herself aside, & forget all her worries, where any opportunity presents itself for serving, at any risk, any labour, & any expence, a tormented Friend——Acquaintance or even Stranger. A kinder heart never beat in a human bosom, nor one of higher probity or sounder principle.——She procured me Chambers for myself & Alex, in a house to which she removed for that purpose; & our Drawing Room & Repasts were Pic Nic; & it was a true delight to me to pass with her those 4 Weeks, which to both flew away as 4 Days. I need not enlarge upon the comfort of my having Alex!——You will, a little, conceive that!——

Clement was the whole time at Cambridge. There is hope, now of his recovery, though not yet certainty, nor progressive Promise——poor young man! how melancholy has been his life these last 2 or 3 years! & the Malady still hovering over him——though there is an amendment that has enabled him to try change of air, scene, & *habits*——I mean, from constantly bending to inertion, to making an effort to support some employment. God spare him to his dear excellent Mother!——I believe they are now again together at Brighton ⎮ I made her fully understand all your warm interest, & all my intermediation; & she charged me with her tender Love & Thanks: but I think that things are now so ameliorated——for the present, at least——that you may give her comfort & pleasure by writing straight forward.

I saw no company——none, at Brighton. Charlotte readily

entered into my wishes; & the long illness of Clement has led
her to much shutting up herself: though not voluntarily, as
she both loves & requires society. But I was truly vexed—
nay grieved, at missing my nearly oldest Friend now in the
World, Mrs. Frances Bowdler,[2] only by a Day! Missing her
both at Brighton & here! I knew not of her motions in time
to arrange an alteration of Mine. Alex upon your representation, wrote to Mrs Maltby;[3] & Sophy, upon her's, has written
to *him*—he is Now with the Archd^n at Ely—but *purposes*
all Sophy suggests. Of Alex I have a great deal more to say,
when I write next, if he does not fulfil his real *intention* in
going to say it all for himself. So Now to *London*, as that will
be so pithy that this morsel will suffice. Know, then, I see
from time to time, Mrs. Admiral!! Burney, Sarah payne, &
Edward, & Mrs. Lock & L^y Martin, when they come occasionally to town; & 2 of the Daughters of my dear Lady
Templetown,[4] who are detained in London by affairs—and
—no! no *and* at all! This is sum total of intercourse at this
moment—except my dear faithful Diane; My MSS. I now
scrupulously arrange to be merely what is lightest & nearest
to amusem^t for the long Evenings: & all that is sacred—or
—touching—I diversify as I can in my Mornings. This is my
new history!—adieu—Be sure I Burn carefully—but the
surmize you talk of from *me*! my dearest Hetty! know I not.
Knows not *every* body that knows *You*—that your Heart is
one of the most generous in the World?—I have only room
now to add I feel quite [decided] in the reasons & their
effect *quite*—with a belief, too, [that] no blame is incurred
any where. The Thing is concluded to be *mutual*—not by
your desire, but for ⟨her⟩ convenience & affairs. Heaven bless

you my dear dear
Etty!— |

A pleasant Christmas to my Esther—& to Emily, & the
Belvederes[5]—

---

² See L. 1210 n. 23.
³ See L. 1232 n. 13.
⁴ Sophia Upton (L. 1223 n. 9) and her sister Caroline (1778–1862), who had
married on 21 August 1804 James Singleton (*c.* 1772–1855) of Mell, co. Meath.
The sisters had called on FBA on 13 December (Diary).
⁵ EBB's daughters, Amelia, Maria, and Sophia (i, p. lxix).

How much I have to answer to your interesting & dear Letters— ¹

N.B.

I only can speak of the intentions of Alex: I take no responsibility of his actions. But he says he has a Wipe to Wipe away from Sophy— ¹

I began This a week ago, at least—but put the date of the last moment.

¹323   [11 Bolton Street],
6 January 1824

To Alexander d'Arblay

A.L. (Berg), 6 Jan. 1824
Double sheet 4to   4 pp.   *pmk*   6 JA 1824   red seal
Addressed: Revd A. P. d'Arblay / Brandon Hall, / Suffolk. / If gone from Mr. / Angersteins / to be returned by post / to N⁰ 11. Bolton Street, Piccadilly

Monday—6th Jan^y—
—1824

Come to *me*, my dearest Alex! come to *me* I entreat!—

I thought not in the hurry & fullness of my distress Yesterday, that my poor Mrs. Lock had written me word—a few days ago, that *she wished to commune with me*, but was prevented by a slight cold—This cold is better — — & Day after Day I may expect her—How can I leave home without telling her not to come? — —

My dearest Alex—Come, then to me!

If you dread the *fatal* Blow alone,¹ & at an Inn, I dread it for you, too!—Come, then!—

1323. ¹ Invited by the Angersteins to Brandon Hall, d'Arblay had arrived on Tuesday 16 December, as may be seen in the letter (Berg) that Amelia Angerstein wrote to FBA on the 18th (Alex's birthday). Returning to Ely, where he spent Christmas with his cousins, he was again at Brandon Hall in January, where he encountered an alarming family crisis in the dangerous illness (an infected throat,

Last Night, late,——& I know not how, I had again a Billet from Mrs. Lock, *utterly in the dark* as to the greatness of the danger[1]——& full of gentle hope, & calm composure, & fervant friendship.——

That Angel on Earth Amelia has her own plan—should the blessed miracle you talk of be granted, & should the younger Angel be spared us, Amelia means to save her adored Mother the suffering suspence she undergoes herself: —— —— —— If *not*—she has some religious project, no doubt, of bearing the stroke *Together,* I when Each will support it for the sake of the Other.

Shall *I* thwart this heavenly plan? by an absence it would

lockjaw, etc.) suffered by the elder Angerstein daughter Caroline Amelia, now about 21 years of age, with whom, as we are soon to learn, Alex was seriously in love. The only known letter from d'Arblay himself on the subject is that dated 24 May 1824 (Barrett, Eg. 3701A, ff. 18-19), which will go far to clarify the allusions and deliberations of the next half dozen letters.

My dear Mother,

I solemnly request you to be so kind as to make known to M^{rs} A--------n the state of my feelings with respect to Miss A--------n, together with my present hopes and chances of rising in my profession—as I do not think I can ever have again so favourable an opportunity as the present, being precluded from speaking myself to Miss A--------n by the state of her health; and because any further delay w^d be ascribed to want of empressement, whereas hitherto it has only been upon principle.

Under these circumstances, I pledge myself to bear as manfully as I can any disappointment, and at all events not to make you chargeable with that which, in all human probability, is already decided, and only awaits its completion or negation in the event being made known to us. At the same time, my feelings at this moment are in a state of ungovernable anxiety, which may make me talk a great deal of nonsense backwards and forwards; but of this I beg you *to make no account*, only bearing in mind that the whole is *at my peril,* as you will only be acting *by my express desire* and earnest request.

And whether I am to succeed or fail in this most important moment that in my life has yet occurred, you alone, my dear Mother, can enable me to bear success without madness, or disappointment without despair.

Ever your affectionate son
Alex^r d'Arblay.

11 Bolton St Piccadilly
Monday morning, May 24th, 1824.

What Caroline may have felt in the matter is unknown, but six years later, CFBt, referring to the non-appearance of a second Madame d'Arblay, was to offer the opinion (Berg, 18 June [1830]): 'I think Miss Angerstein ought to have that title offered to her. Some few years ago, when we were at Ely, I am sure it would have been accepted—and why not now?' Caroline was to remain single, until, nearing 40, she would marry on 20 August 1841 the Revd. Charles Manners Richard Norman (1799–1873), Rector (1833) of Northwold, Norfolk, a relative of the 4th Duke of Rutland.

be vain to hope we could disguise, & which would prove our unbounded & uncontrolled despondency?—

Would She—the object, alive or dead, of All our Feelings, would She give her sainted approvance to any thing so decidedly as to tender & disinterested consideration of her Mother & her Grand Mother?

Those Two have always been her own First objects, with all her warm & true & zealous love for her Father, her Brothers, & her Sister; because Those Two she has always regarded as most *wanting her* tenderness, the one from fading health, the other from fading years.

Still, however, so half informed of the state of things, I write in the dark—you may have motives, as well as sensations, to set aside all obstacles.

If so, tell me, & I will still come! for I am your's, my Alex, my poor Alex, more than my own!—

But, I must have an answer again to This Letter, before I can reconcile to myself such a dangerous blow to Mrs. Lock, after Amelia's prohibition.

Do not, therefore, expect me till you have written to this present Letter. |

Unless, indeed, your Letter to-morrow should contain any unforseen reason to chace away these difficulties.

Mr. George[2] set out, after Church duty on Sunday, for his Sister. He will be a great support to All:

Pity me, my Mother, you say, my poor Alex—alas my whole soul is made up of pity for you! — — & I dare not indulge a single ray of Hope to enter my mind—at least till I hear from you again—your silence yesterday affrights all away—unless it might be owing to your conceiving I had set out—for—to the last, I shall cling, like you, to something that averts utter despair—however wide from daring to be sanguine.

NB. Should you want money, you must enquire for a country Banker, at Brandon, or at Bury, who will draw for you on Messrs Hoare.

At all events, write a line every day till we meet, or till our meeting is fixed.

But be it, if possible, Here!—

[2] The Revd. George Locke (L. 1188 n. 3).

at an Inn how tragic!— |
Finally
I supplicate you, my dearest Alexander, to take care of yourself for My poor Sake!—
see but the consequence of a neglected Cold!—And think —should you, in your misery, catch—& neglect one too!— Be Generous, my Alex, & think a little of my desolate state!
Heaven bless & preserve you — —

1324 [11 Bolton Street],
9 January 1824

To Alexander d'Arblay

A.L. (Berg), 9 Jan. 1824
Single sheet 4to   2 pp.   Page 1 has 5 lines of crosswriting   Lower left corner torn away

Friday—9th Jany 1824

In the midst of the wretchedness I unremittingly almost suffer for You & for All this most unhappy Family—except that Angel who is above all pity save for her detention!—in the midst of it all what comfort do you not give me by the sum total of your Letters & your Conduct & your feelings in this dreadful trial!—My dearest Alex!—my dear darling Alex!—more twined round my heart-strings than ever since the days of baby hood when your innocent yet fervant fondness beat with such exquisite pulsation to the bosoms of both your Parents—so dearly have you soothed even in exciting my anguish, by telling me you are *prepared for the deadly blow*, & will bear it as well as you can —, — & in assuring [m]e you will set off for me instantly — — [& n]ot stay in that scene of desolation, where you [would] then be of no use, to risk *your* senses—[&] *my* destruction.—I shall ever feel this, | ever! & with the tender solace of feeling in it your reciprocating tenderness — —

I thought—indeed, that all was over by your silence

475

yesterday—& expected your return every moment—my poor dearest Alex!

I am glad you tell me my dear—dear Mrs Lock is really *au fait*—the illusion while it can hold—is wise as well as happy! Julius¹ has it — — — yet I wish it not to *You*, as you would be so insolated for a sudden blow!—And I cannot attain it myself, as I have too acute a *double* interest to dare trust my poor frame with unprepared disappointment. I must hold up for you, my Alex, as They will, I am sure, for one another.

How sweet are all your little details of her!—You are right not to risk *asking* to see her—*your* emotion might awaken one the most dangerous. Should it be *proposed*, you must arm yourself [against] self-concentration — — I should like ⟨you should⟩ see Amine, that Mother Angel! Mother & Daug[hter] Angel, one of the three Earthly saints—but w[ ] [*tear*] ¹

You are not *Clerically* forgotten—but I know you will not move just now, so am quiet

If—as I think most likely—you were too much moved to offer any answer to these two kind messages, by the Son & by the Father—nor yet to that from the incomparable Mother by the physician² — — try to rectify the omission through the kindness of Julius—if yet not too late—

[*tear*] another Letter from me unless you desire it.

1325   [11 Bolton Street,
                                         11 January 1824]

To Alexander d'Arblay

A.L. (Berg), n.d.
Double sheet 4to   4 pp.   *pmk* 12 JA 1824   red seal

1324. ¹ John Julius William Angerstein (L. 1195 n. 14), now about 24 years of age.
² Probably Pelham Warren (1778–1835), M.D. (1805), F.R.C.P. (1806), F.R.S. (1813), 'a very sound practical physician' with an immense practice in London (*DNB*), who had been summoned to Brandon Hall at this time (see further, L. 1326).

Addressed: Revd A. P. d'Arblay. / Brandon Hall, / Suffolk. / J. Angerstein's / Esqr

You gave me great comfort, my Alex, by telling me that my Letters give some to You. God knows *yours*, are my *subsistence* at this heavy moment, although they are really heartbreaking. Yet utter suspence frightens me as much for you, as for the sweet sufferer. Alas—my loved Amelia fills me with pangs & fears that never quit me!—not for her want of Fortitude to bear the threatened catastrophe,—Religion like hers is always submissive & enduring: but from want of bodily strength to support her fatigues, joined to the view of such almost unheard of agonies. Oh sweetest Amelia! may God spare yet your precious—invaluable life—upon which the whole happiness of the whole Family hangs!—And to *me* & to *you* scarcely would her loss be less terrible! — — Dr. Warren's Letter & statement[1] would quite have revived me, had not your narrative of the *groans* & *screams* marred all its comfort:—not *All*, indeed—but O—I think but too just your fears of exhaustion! ⟨*éthesée*⟩ you say—alas, that word dies away upon my heart with sinking hopelessness! — — — Your statement of your *credence* as to a gentle preference I firmly believe: & you have relieved me from a weight of apprehension in so candidly & even sagaciously representing the probable truth of the case. I had cruelly feared you had been still under an illusion—of which you had made me completely a sharer—of a predominant attachment which, to believe just now, were almost *distracting* — — But the sum total well calculated, & pondered over in detail, breaks up that illusion, thank Heaven!—Nothing is so clear as that the First passion of the Heart is the *Filial*. Pure & sweet Angel! that to which she was born she clings to her still!— yet still I think, with you, of what might ensue on recovery —if even then health & strength should sufficiently ׀ recur to make a new tie desireable.—O my Alex! how my soul every way pities you!—accustomed *yourself* to be always watched & cherished & fostered—what would you do, when, losing that, you would only have to watch & cherish & foster another? *Ponder*, my dearest Alex, ere you commit yourself?

1325. [1] See L. 1324 n. 2.

—I mean, ere you make irrevocably plain your unhappy attachment.—The *Fortune* would be as *nothing*, to the wants, now become *necessary*, of so delicate a frame. And while her angelic *Mind* would make her bear any privation, unresisting & unrepining, *your* sense of the luxuries to which she had been brought up, & the elegancies & refinements & splendours she quitted, would make every sacrifice, where her health, or ease were concerned, mournful & depressing to you: There is no happiness with deprivations of habituated comforts where there is not Health.—Of that be certain. The one who misses, may *bear*,—but that is not Happiness!— & the one for whom the change was made may adore—& be grateful—but must lament, & be frightened—& that is not Happiness neither! — — I say all this at this critical moment, my dearest Alex, that you may put your best understanding

— — —

for you have *two* intellects,—one clear & even profound, & much spared by being seldom used.—The other—so futile, self-sufficient, & superficial, 'tis astonishing how they should come together! Yet this is the naked truth, & my opinion & prognostic place the latter, Thank God, in *decay* —the former *Now* coming out into Blossoms that are fragrant to me even here & that promise Fruits of highest flavour, & worthy preservation — — I that you may put, I say, this ᴨlatentᴨ *best* understanding into requisition at this awful moment—& suffer no ardour of immediate feeling, no emotion of immediate distress, to blind you to Futurity— While I was myself under your own illusion I had no thought but of open sympathy that should run every risk careless of consequence from depth of disappointment. But *many* things concur to assure me your statement is just—& therefore *my* Eyes open to

I write without reserve, but you must *Burn* as soon as you have answered—& tell me so, also: for I am fearful—of your leaving your papers & my Letters about, & sometimes resolve to write nothing that demands caution—yet how maintain such a resolve when the charm of your letters to me is their entire openness?—However, you are a *great deceiver* in thinking you give me 5 Letters because you give me 5 directions, for these last are *half-marginal*, so low they begin,

& so wide are the spaces between the lines. I am sure this *one*
Apparent Letter contains as much in quantity as the 5 Epistles
put together. Yet I approve not crossing—a better way,
when you write so wide, is to write again between the lines
the contrary way. But *All* ways are good, & kind, & eagerly
welcomed, that bring me your tidings, & your thoughts, &
your reflections, & your varieties at this killing period.

Indeed, my dearest Alex, I shall never forget your tender
kindness to me in writing so much when you know my whole
Heart is in *your pen*—I mean awaiting it. And for *Amelia* I
think most—though that *means* Caroline—& *both* mean
You above ˡ all. Lʸ Martin has called with a note, that her
dearest Mother will be with her to-morrow—when I shall go
to Hertford Street if she come not hither. But remember I
never shall part with a Letter of yours out of my own hand,
unless written obviously to be forwarded. So be quite unrestrained. Your writing can else do you no good to keep
pace with the good it transmits. Amine has herself told Mrs.
L[ocke] that Julius said he knows not how he should have
supported his Journey, in his terrour & grief, without your
aid! What kindness!—When it was just your own first wish!
See if I listen not to your request of writing! What a day
will be Tuesday—to-morrow—if Dr. Warren[1] goes

I love *at heart* the noble Julius—yet how wrong to *contest* with his Father—his poor wretched Father, at such a
period! to give his opinion—& *press* it, suppliantly, is all he
ought to do. Yet his affection for his sister is so beautiful in
its ardour, that I love him, I repeat, at my heart. And How
sorry I am for that truly fond Father! Mr. G[eorge] L[ocke]
is a treasure to the sick room,[2] they all so confidingly love
him. How excessively unfortunate the entrance that awoke
the sleeping angel! but the rest during the Night re-animates
a little hope!—I am amazed they do not try James's Powders[3]—can they talk of salivation, & not try them first? Is it
from *scruple? that* should be over surely. *Many* physicians
prescribe them. The late Dr. Heberden did frequently.[4] They

---

[2] As may be seen in a photograph or print in the vestry of the parish church at
Mickleham, the Revd. George Locke bore a close resemblance to his father William Locke (see iv, Plate II) in appearance and evidently also in character.
[3] For an analysis, see i, L. 7 n. 2. [4] See L. 1314 n. 4.

might search the unknown cause, & cure her!——yet alas——
they *might*——adieu——my Alex, adieu——read, answer, burn
—— ¹

For the Domestics, 1 sovereign to the chief, to deliver *for*
you; or crown pieces, or 2 1/2 crowns, given by yourself——
unless you have had Boots cleaned, &c, & then a half sovereign
to that one & nothing elsewhere

1326   [11 Bolton Street],
                                    14 January [1824]

To Alexander d'Arblay

A.L. (Berg), 14 Jan.
Double sheet large 4to   4 pp.   *pmk* 14 JA 182⟨4⟩   red seal
Addressed: Revd A. P. d'Arblay, / Brandon Hall / Suffolk. / If gone
from / J. Angerstein's / Esqr. / to be returned to / N° 11. Bolton Street
Piccadilly

                                    Wednesday——14. Jan^y

What an interesting Letter is this of Tuesday! my own dear
Alex, how you brighten upon trial!——I see you will not——
should the calamity yet arrive of a Cure *too late*,——destroy
me by your despair. You are evidently trying & preparing for
yielding to the Will of Heaven. *My* fears, like yours, are
double! first for the Cure——& next *almost* equally, for *les
suites*. What a day will This be, after a night's Watch & Judgment of Dr. Warren!¹——I shall scarcely breath to-morrow till
the post arrives.

                    ⌒

I am truly glad the James's powders were tried. Be sure she
could not send off all! some must have rested on the tongue,
& have melted to the Palate & the throat; & if the *better* has
been since, or even the *not worse*, I hope they will be insinu-
ated into use Again. Their operation, like her own malady, is

1326. ¹ See L. 1324 n. 2.

mysterious, but almost always, in desperate cases, curative.

I am in perfect unison with all your reasoning, as far as it goes.—All I demur at, is the *desireability* hence-forward!—At all events, should the blessed cure be allowed, & the Angel Amelia recover her angel Caroline, you had best be *open*, as it is *impossible* your conduct can have any other motive, or excuse, than ungovernable anxiety.

What would I not give to read the words of my matchless Amelia! *Pray* copy them, if you bring them not before you write. Without seeing *them*, or hearing something yet unheard, it appears to me you ought to come away *To-morrow* without fail. *To day* may be allowed for, as Dr. Warren's visit will be included; & to know his sentence, & its immediate effect, is a pardon-able reason. But indeed my Alex, you must make an effort to quit a spot where you are a real *intruder*, since unasked, however leniently treated, or indulgently *liked*[2]—if not *pitied*. —— for *liked* I know, thank Heaven, you are, & singularly, by all around: *pitied* is another matter! if your thoughts are devellopped, you will be quite as liable to excite *blame*, if not *sneer*, as pity, from obvious causes:—though not from the object, nor her Mother; *they* must always, internally, see that blame, if any there be, must hang on their own blindness to the manner in which you felt their favour, & had reason to think your advances were honoured with approbation. Would to God there were any way to unfathom this mystery!

Did you get my 2 last Letters[3] of the *11*th & *13*th? They

---

[2] The favour in which AA was held is reflected in Amelia Angerstein's apology (Berg) for keeping him from his mother on his birthday. She was sure, as was AA, 'that his dearest Mother would *like him to have passed his birthday here*': 'This being so settled, I have given way to the full enjoyment of the day, we have, (that is my Caroline, Julia, Alex & I) been taking a long walk together—We have had the exquisite treat of *poetry* composed in the midst of animated conversation last night, & we are to have another of molières plays, with which he so regaled us last night as I cannot tell you ... I have not, since *Westhumble childhood*, seen our Alex look bright & strong & *robust* as he does—M^r A is struck & delighted with it—& Every mental faculty & virtuous impulse seems strengthening with his strength, which may Heaven preserve—'

[3] L. 1325; that of the 13th is missing.

are so important to be read, & destroyed, or sealed up under some cover, that I write in great uneasiness from finding you have not even *read* what I said about *les Domestiques*? ¹

Pray read with attention what follows.

Whether you come away after the deepest distress be consummated, or to await here the hope of its mercifully being spared, you must alike take some leave, not rush off as you plan.

Should All fail—!—Think of Amelia & the tenderly fond Father—& judge *Their* Grief but the more deeply by your own — — & then, Write simply a few words *praying for their support*, from that Heaven which their Darling visits before them — — & let the words, on This occasion, be for Both in one—a line will do. This Give to the confidential servant, with a sovereign to distribute—or half a one to keep, if the others, this time, have done nothing for you.— And say to *him* you run away without seeing them, not daring to ask for their sight. — — — He will repeat that till it come round.

This is an exertion that Humanity, as well as the laws of Gratitude, & the feelings of sympathy, make imperious.

If, as I hope, Dr. Warren continues to sooth with distant expectation, come away *equally*, for I am *sure* your stay appears extraordinary, &, indeed, *is* so. And
in either Case,
Forbear your plan of coming Post!—

Take a Gig, or Chaise, to Burry, & come in in the first stage.

To come Post—is a thing done by no one now, who does not keep Horses, or is not sent Express for some service. Even men of quality travel in stages. They [are] as quick as Chaises; & the idea of being *Alone* is a mere phantasm—*Alone* you would be amidst thousands! You will see, hear, nobody—&, *that* way, are not likely to be seen or heard yourself. But —
— — — To come post, will seem to *publish* your intolerable Grief, as that of a declared & accepted Lover, whose despair, like that of a Husband or a Father, or a Brother, is but legitimate, though boundless affliction. ¹ Believe me, what is simple & concentrated is always most respectable, & most respected. The other way might give rise to implications that might offend, & *seem* ostentatious.

And to what should you so hurry!—alas!—an *Hour* at the most is all you would gain.—And for solitude you would be *alone* every where, till you came to the tender Mother who dissolves in grief for you while she writes these representations.

You cannot come away too soon.—Consider,—you will have as constant tidings as the *doating* Grand Mother—that pattern of pious patience with melting fondness, can herself receive. She is settled at Lady Martin's, whither I am going to her as soon as I have ensured saving the post to you. I shall leave a blank to add news of that beloved Person, & the amiable L^y Martin, before I seal.

⎯⎯⟶

All last night—having no Letter, I expected you—at least till late, when a Note from Hertford Street told me Dr. Warren was going to Brandon. I was then sure you would await him. If you do not come To-morrow, I entreat you to copy at once the words of my most dear Amelia! They will soften my terror for her. I hear nothing of the Letter to be written for her by poor Julia.[4] What did that mean?—Poor Julia I am told is heart broken, as well as that dear noble obstreperous Julius   Poor, poor Mrs. A[ngerstein]!—What anguish to have *contest* now!—how I bless the good kind Mr. G[eorge]!—

Where you say the sweet Angel *stopt*, after '*If I should recover*' I have read an account that says she added after wards 'of what avail will be my recovery to me!—' — — disentangle yourself from illusion, my dearest Alex! yet I believe in all you say, all your chances, &c—But come away—& *return* if you will.

For the World do not come away without seeing—if not Amelia, yet writing to beg *her Commands for Mrs. Lock*— & of Mr. A. to beg him to *try* to give you some commission, to the physicians, or otherwise. Do both these through Mr. Ge. L. *Nobody* else so fitting. And he will feel the *propriety* of both, after such a stay. If you cannot see them, pray Write, with a word of *apology* in your hopes ˡ *from day to day* of leaving them in less distress. But *write* & *wait an*

---

[4] Elizabeth Julia (L. 1195 n. 14), now about 18 years of age.

answer, as they may, *Both*, perhaps employ you in some commission difficult for the Post.

part 4. I am just returned from Hertford street, where I have been a little better reconciled to your long stay, by hearing you mentioned in the most affectionate manner— so take your measures *comfortably*, not *abruptly*, & by no means return without asking commissions, & hoping to be forgiven that you rested in a scene of such sorrow & affright, *wholly* domestic except your own part—but the true reason, your deep interest, & constant hope of seeing Mrs. A. will not be pleaded in vain. *No one* here has any further idea!—Mrs. Lock looks beautifully well—just so as her lovely Grand- daughter would like most to behold her before her. She keeps up *almost* unmingled *couleur de Rose*, every way. Lᵞ Martin has a fluxion, but is animated & kind as usual. All are full of Caroline.

Dr. W. is not expected till Midnight   *my* expectations are thro' you—I shall never write but in answer from expecting you by silen[ce] Heaven bless you my Alex! [Be] firm—& not ⟨elusive⟩ ⏐

P.S.

At the *Top* of my Last Letter, or last Letter but *one*, is my notion as to les—domestiques.⁵—you do not *read all* my Letters?—

¹327   [11 Bolton Street,
                          pre 19 January 1824]

To Mrs. Waddington

A.L.S. draft (Berg), n.d.
A single sheet 4to torn in half   2 pp.   8vo
Scribbling, p. 2: Cᵐ – CK / B – CZ / 6ᵐ⁻ᶜ – CK6
Edited by CFBt. *See* Textual Notes.

My dear Friend,
My warm & truly affectionate good wishes & congratula-

⁵ See L. 1325 *supra*.

tions are most sincerely Augusta's upon this happy Marriage; I beg that when next, my dear Friend, you write to the blooming Bride, you will tell her so;—& tell her, from your own long experience, that What I write or what I say, I think.

I mean, of course, where I write or speak of or from myself.

I rejoice, also, very sincerely, in your good news of your Roman Colony.[1]

The Death of Lady Templetown was indeed—at last—a happy release[2]—even to me, though I am one who linger with rivetted fondness even upon the very dregs of life in those I peculiarly love—for what, wrested from them, is existence—? &, ⟨latterly⟩ she had installed herself amongst the few who carry about with them balm for the wounded. But her sufferings had long ⟨weaned⟩ her own feelings from life; mine, therefore, must have been merely selfish still to have wished it's prolongation.

I have passed a month with my dear Sister Charlotte ⟨& hers⟩ at Brighton.[3] She is tolerably well, for Clement once more is better—though by no means as yet | radically recovered. *Our* Fanny Raper is always gay, lovely, chearful & cheering: Alex is excursioning between Cambridge with his College Friends, Ely with M⟨rs⟩ Barrett & her family, & Brandon Hall, with the Angerstein's.[4] I truly lamented missing my most valued old friend Mrs F Bowdler both at Brighton & in Bolton Street, by wayward circumstances.[5]

Mrs. Lock is well at Eliot Vale—but queer Mrs Charles— you cannot be sorry to hear is released![6]—for dreadful in all ways has been the close of her days! —— —— Adieu my Friend
F d'Ay

I say nothing of y⟨r⟩ abrupt departure except that all things previously considered it surprised me past expression.——

1327. [1] Mrs. Waddington's letter, received by FBA on 27 December 1823, had apparently given an account of the marriage on 4 December 1823 of her daughter Augusta to Benjamin Hall (L. 1314 n. 11) and news as well of her eldest daughter Frances, wife of Baron Bunsen (L. 1223 n. 2), at Rome.

[2] On 29 September 1823 (L. 1316 n. 1; L. 1318 n. 1).

[3] See L. 1322.   [4] See L. 1323 n. 1.   [5] Cf. L. 1322 and n. 2.

[6] Mrs. Charles Locke (L. 1192 n. 9), afflicted with cancer of the breast, had died in Nice (*Locks of Norbury*, pp. 310–15).

1328   11 Bolton Street,
                                    19 January 1824

To Julia Charlotte Barrett

A.L.S. (Berg), 19 Jan. 1824
Double sheet 8vo   2 pp.   *pmk* PAID/⟨   ⟩1824   wafer tear
Addressed: Miss Barrett, / at Henry Barrett's Esqr, / Ely. / at Preben-
dary / Cambridge's / or / Dampier's.

                                    19th Jany 1824.
                                    11. Bolton Street,
                                    Berkeley Square

Will my dear Julia oblige me with a few lines—though the
more the more welcome—of her very dear mama's health?[1]
My Friend Dick gave me an account every way unsatisfactory
in his little visit[2]—which I received at a terrible moment,
when I was upon the stairs, descending, to go to poor Mrs.
Lock for news of her Grand Daughter, Miss Angerstein, then
dangerously ill. She is just now pronounced out of danger by
Dr. Warren—& my Pen, as well as my heart, turns wholly to
your beloved Mama, my dear Julia. I beg you to tell me what
the illness has been, what it is called, & how it began. My
dear Dick could only say—what to say was, indeed, the only
essential thing, & the best—that she was getting well. Do not
trouble either Papa or Mama—except for their leave,—but
write all yourself, & as fully as your recollection & knowledge will permit. Give her my tender love,
                          & believe me, my dear Girl,
                              truly yours
                              F. d'A. |

Alex is but just returned from Brandon Hall, & truly grieved
by this news fr^m Ely. My best Comp^{ts} to your Papa, & love
to Hetty & Arthur.

I frank my Letter—but you must not frank Your's till
you write to your Great Niece, i.e. Hetty's, or Dick's or
Henry's. or Arthur's
                          Grand Daughter.

1328. [1] CFBt was suffering from jaundice (Ll. 1329, 1331).
        [2] Richard Barrett, aged 11, on his way from Ely to Eton (L. 1321 n. 7).

To Esther (Burney) Burney

A.L.S. (Berg), 27–29 Jan. 1824
Two double sheets 4to   8 pp.   numbered [p. 1:] II;   [p. 4:] 4;
[p. 5:] 5   [*The cover missing*]

                                        27. Jany 1824.—
                                        Bolton Street,

How sorry will be my dearest Esther to hear how I have
been prevented from preparing her a packet for this so long
projected conveyance by Alexander!—I have been—I am
still—*devoted* to our Mrs. Lock, who receives from me some
little aid,—which *she* will not call little—in supporting the
dreadful suspence between Life & Death in which Miss Angerstein has kept, unhappily, her almost adoring family during
these last 4 or 5 weeks. At this moment, all seems promising
for future recovery—but it was only *yesterday* the symptoms
of amelioration appeared. And still they are tremblingly precarious. though Dr. Warren decidedly declares the crisis of
danger to be past. The history is as follows. She went to a
dress Dinner in which she was probably too lightly arrayed—
though by no means from yielding to modish drapery, for
she is a pattern of chaste elegance without & within—but
still she caught cold; & the ensuing Sunday encreased it to
a sore throat, at Church. She neglected this at first; & soon it
became very serious—the throat swelled, the swallow was
stopt, Fever burnt in her head, & danger menaced with frightful alarm. D^r· Lynn was sent for from Bury;—Mr. Best, a
famous *medical man*, from Brandon; Mr. Dalrymple, a celebrated surgeon from Norwich:[1] but the evil continued

---

1329. [1] Called in by the Angersteins were provincial practitioners of Norfolk and
Suffolk: James Lynn (*fl.* 1823–30), physician of 76 Whiting Street, Bury St. Edmunds (*Pigot's General Directory* for 1830); Henry Best (*c.* 1774–1859) or his
son, the apothecary and surgeon Henry Waddelow Best (*c.* 1807–65) of King
Street, Thetford; and William Dalrymple (1772–1847), surgeon at the Norfolk
and Norwich Hospital.

The London physicians included, besides Pelham Warren (L. 1324 n. 2), the
fashionable Sir Henry Holland (L. 1218 n. 1) of Brook Street; Martin Tupper

encreasing, & spasms came on that caused such sufferings as to make the poor lovely young Invalid call out aloud upon Death to release her — —

Her eldest Brother, Julius, one of the finest young Men in England, both in Person & disposition & character, was sent for express from the Guards, to which he belongs, & he carried down with him Dr. Holland & Mr. Tupper, the successors to poor Mr. Chilvers,[1] who is now incapable of pursuing his prefession from some dreadful internal malady. They could do nothing—her head was on fire, & she had no ease but by a *Cap of Ice,* ǀ which was contrived for her. Her face, naturally pale, was always of the deepest rose colour. Sleep was utterly flown,—& her last hour seemed approaching, & she solicited its approach! & took leave in the most affecting manner of all her family.—Laudanum alone made existence supportable, & she took it in large dozes. The famous Charles Bell,[1] now reckoned the first anatomist, practical, of England, was now sent for. He gave some new directions, & encouraged ultimate hope of recovery. But no amendment took place. Dr. Warren was next demanded. He pronounced that there were strong motives to believe she might out-survive this dreadful malady, though at what period no man could say! The roof of her tongue was thought paralysed, as nothing could be swallowed: & the poor tongue was so parched, that at half a drop at a time, her agonised Mother incessantly moistened it with cold water. Even that became more than she could bear, & a tube was introduced—but its pain was intolerable. Then a straw

(*c.* 1779–1844), F.R.S. (1835), of New Burlington Street, who had recently succeeded to the practice of Samuel Chilver (L. 1230 n. 6), the successor of Sir Walter Farquhar (CB's physician, i, iii *passim*); and finally Sir Charles Bell (1774–1842), the 'discoverer of the distinct functions of the nerves' (see *DNB*).

'Young Dr. Somerville' was apparently James Craig Somerville (*c.* 1799–1847), M.D. (Edinburgh, 1820), who, admitted a Licentiate of the College of Physicians (1825), would be appointed in 1832 inspector of anatomy for Middlesex, Kent, Surrey, and the City of London. He seems to have been the natural son of William Somerville (1771–1860), M.D. (1800), who, entering the army as a surgeon, had accompanied General Sir James Henry Craig (1748–1812) to the Cape of Good Hope in 1795, the Mediterranean in 1805, and to Canada in 1807 (*DNB*). Returning in 1812, the elder Somerville was appointed in 1816 one of the inspectors of the army medical board and on 13 November 1819, physician to Chelsea Hospital. He had married in 1812 his cousin, later the well-known scientist Mary Somerville (*DNB*), and in his will (Somerset House, pr. 11 September 1860) suggested that she give his medical books to James Craig Somerville, apparently FBA's 'young Dr. Somerville'.

was used, to pass water upon her tongue, which was instantly sent back, as to swallow became *impossible*, & threatened choaking her by further trial! All the country Doctors pronounced the case hopeless. Her spasms caused screams & groans heart breaking, & intervals of rattling in the throat that seemed ending her sufferings with her life!—Once again Dr. Warren was summoned. He arrived at 3 o'clock in the morning, A lock jaw seemed arrived before him. Her teeth clenched, & nothing could pass between them—The Doctor determined to asartain whether this horrible stoppage were *organic*, i.e. an ossification,—or nervous,—if the former, hope was at an end,—if the latter, she was yet recoverable. He had her held by 5 persons—one at each foot & each ⌐ arm, one at the head—& then with a spoon, relentless to her cries & opposition, he made the experiment —— &, thanks to the Almighty,—he found the passage not closed irremediably!—And from that time to this, they have gone on with Hope before them, performing the painful operation of forcing asses milk, or semolina, or Beef tea, down her poor tortured throat every 4 or 6 Hours. A physician, a young Dr. Somerville,[1] lives in the house, to be the Operator. All is under the superintendence of Dr Warren.

This Day, 27th. Jany I found our beloved Mrs. Lock revived with an account that this darling sufferer had been risen from her long, long, unmade Bed, & had borne the effort beyond All expectation—They hope in about a fortnight to remove her—probably in a litter—to Woodlands, to facilitate her recovery by change of scene & air, & by being where her beloved Grandmother can help to cheer & re-animate her. I have just been with that dear person, & her two Sons, William & George, all blessing this last news, in the house of Lady Martin. The whole family have been wholly absorbed by this affliction, which has been tragical beyond description. I have in view constantly the martyrd Mother, that incomparable Mrs. Angerstein—who never quits her nursery all day, —nor at ⌐ night, but when she was so evidently on the point of being demolished, that her terrified family over-ruled her inclinations, & made her consent to leave the superintendence to her other Daughter, Julia,—who now has sat up with her sister 26 nights following!—& regularly gone into Bed for as much sleep as nature would afford her after Breakfast! what a devotion! *Night & day* thus are wholly filled up. This young lady, Caroline, is absolutely adored by all her race. Mr. J[ohn] Angerstein has renounced all the field sports, which carried him to their Estate, *Brandon Hall*, & were his sole inducement for residing there. Julius, the eldest son, has quitted his post at the Guards, & all his gay & splendid connections & amusements, & nearly *live upon the stairs*, to know the progress of Hope & Fear from minute to minute. Alexander witnessed all this in person, by happening to go to Brandon Hall, for a visit of some Days, in ignorance of the illness—Imagine his horrour to be told, at once, at the door—'Mrs. Angerstein would see *you*, sir, I am sure, if she could see any body—but —— —— Miss Angerstein is dying!' He stayed, there, nevertheless, near a fortnight, being taken in great friendship by the amiable & charming Julius—with whom, & the various medical men, he spent his time—scarcely beholding *Mr.* J Angerstein but at dinner, & *never once* my dear dear *Mrs.* A. nor Miss Julia.—I have run on with this history because it almost *absorbs* me, our dearest Mrs. Lock being here, in town, to be near to every bulletin, & to live with L^y Martin—the solitude of Eliot Vale, in such dire suspense becoming overwhelming to her spirits. I am with her all the time I have to dispose of from *indispensables*, I know how you ¹ will be interested in every word—& *wish* for particulars, as you can have them by this conveyance. *Per post* I should but have sent a paragraph—

28. Jany I have just received your long & comfortable Letter, my dearest Esther, & I am more able to write by tidings more enlivening from Brandon Hall. Miss A. has been moved, on a Sofa, to another room, where she remained while her own was aired: & she bore the exertion amazingly well. There are hopes her journey to Woodlands may be accellerated, as her strength is a little encreased, & the spasms are nearly gone: but the swallow is still the same! & *my* fear is a consumption at the end, even after a cure! for she is reduced to a shadow. —— —— ——

You say well, & most truly, let us write about what we are

thinking, & writing cannot be a task. This is a proof for I have written with real relief, knowing my dearest Hetty's deep sympathy in all that belongs to our dear Mrs. Lock— who has charged Alex with her kindest remembrances, & assurances of your interest—This is a case so strange, as well as melancholy, that of 6 physicians, one only, Dr. Warren, seemed to understand it!—Let me try to speak of something else *if possible*, if only to enable myself to write to Mrs. F B[owdler] & Mrs. Maltby,[2] *a few lines*, all for which I have leisure, by Alex.—

Alex has a Letter from Maria that has extremely pleased him—& her desire that he will go for a *period indefinite* he had anticipated; as he is in waiting for the summons of Archdeacon Cambridge, to be presented, *at last*, to the Bishop of London—& though this *may, unfortunately now*, be very soon, it may, also, be very late, as the good & truly friendly Archd[n] is kept at Twickenham by indisposition. I pressed him, Alex, however, to take this moment, with all its chances, in the *hope* that when he *does* see the Bishop, he may receive some clerical employment that may make him less Master of his Will. I

I am sure it will do him good, as well as pleasure, to go amongst you all, after this tragical visit. *En outre*, if he stayed for a more *certain period*, it would be endless in arriving, as his town engagements once begun—go on *indefinately*, one leading to another: & at present he is free, having only lived with me since his return, to recruit.—*me*, Mrs. Lock, & Lady Martin.

How I like your *Daly* society[3]—I would I could call it *Daily*—The *Name* brings to my mind to tell you that a Daughter of poor Jane Barsanti[4]—that exquisitely agreeable

---

[2] See L. 1210 n. 23; L. 1232 n. 13.   [3] See L. 1304 n. 26.

[4] Green in the memory of the Burneys still was the singer and actress 'Jenny Barsanti' (d. 1795). Daughter of the violinist and composer Francesco Barsanti (*fl.* 1690-1775), she made her début as the principal singer on 22 June 1769 in the rendition of the Anthem for which Charles Burney had been awarded the degree of Mus. Doc. (Oxford). With the impairment of her singing voice she embarked on 21 September 1772 at Covent Garden on a career as actress. So great a favourite with EBB and Maria Rishton as to be invited (along with a Burney party) to Chessington, she figures brightly in the Burney diaries of the seventies (*ED* i. 125-30, and *passim*) and in the recent account of her supplied by Highfill *et al.*, i. 359-62.

In Dublin for the winter season 1776-7, she met and later married (9 June

Girl—has lately sent to me, beseeching some pecuniary aid, from a dreadful bankruptcy, or something equivalent, that has involved her husband & 5 Children in *present* ruin, though not without hope of future restoration to prosperity. Miss Barsanti had first married Mr. Lyster, a Gentleman whose family prohibited their name from appearing in the play bills: & she had the understanding & courage equally to prohibit a *false* name from being printed: she therefore called herself, in the Play bills, *The late Miss Barsanti*; & she was respected by every body as the known *wife* of this Gentleman, who died soon after, leaving her with one Child, & no Settlement. She afterwards married *Mr. Daly*, the Manager of the Dublin Theatre—& continued to play with great applause, till she grew, like Mrs. C. Kemble,[5] so corpulent with embonpoint, that the greater quantity of her parts were forced to be relinquished—She had other business, however, for her time, in bearing 9 or 10 Children. This present daughter writes very elegantly, & in a beautiful hand. Her Husband has been with me 3 times. I have done what I could, & more than I ever did before, in remembrance of poor *Janey*: for the Daughter invoked me by her name most touchingly. I heartily hope her affairs will wear a better aspect ere long. Her husband is lively, spirited, sensible, *well bred*, & agreeable. He has been a speculatist, & unfortunate: but he is still all alive to hope.

Our dear Charlotte continues tolerably well at Brighton, with Clement: but sweet Charlotte Barrett has had the Jaundice, from which she is not yet quite recovered. Sarah Payne is reviving, from total change of system; rising to Breakfast at 8 or 9—going out in all weathers, & eating meat sparingly,

1777 in St. Martin-in-the-Fields) John Richard Kirwan Lyster, 'scion of an ancient Irish family', who, dying on 13 January 1779, left her a daughter, possibly the Mrs. Miller here in question. Mrs. Lyster married secondly *pre* 14 September 1779 Richard Daly (*c.* 1758-1813), actor and theatrical manager in Dublin (*DNB* and Highfill). The daughter, FBA's caller, may have been the wife of Robert Miller, who appears in the Docket Books of the Court of Bankruptcy (PRO, B. 4/38, Index, 61, 22 January 1824) as a Bookseller, Paternoster Row; and he appears in the Order Book (PRO B. 1 166-8) Files, R. Miller B. 3/3450 1824. London Directories (i.e. Pigot) show Robert Miller set up again in 1830 as a copperplate and lithograph printer, 14 Paternoster Row. He disappears in 1835.

[5] Marie Thérèse de Camp (1774-1838), whose career as an actress, even to the 'embonpoint' that precluded her from the comical juvenile parts in which she excelled, is given in the *DNB*; and there also, the career of the actor Charles Kemble (1775-1854), whom she married in 1806.

& indulging *in nothing*! Such a Change is astonishing—& its effect still more so, for she is youngified by it astonishingly: & she is very lively & pleasant. Mrs. Admiral—!—is pretty well. Your Fanny still in Lancaster.[6] Edward I have not been able to see this Age—which is a regret to me. Sarah Harriet is *mute*, again. Fanny Raper & Minette are flourishing.—

⌒——

With regard to your kind enquiries about my maid, I am still waiting till the Fates will give me a Ramsay for attachment—with cleanliness, *cookery*, & working accomplishments for Use. That's all! —— However, in the mean time I still keep the *interregnum* young innocent & insufficient maiden ⌐ that I have had this year & half.[7] I am sorry *your's* is so free & easy; 'tis unpleasant to *fear* being kind & *gracious*. I could count over with you the difficulties, & sometimes toil mixed with the satisfaction & pleasure of correspondent intercourse. *All* my correspondents, except yourself & Charlotte, have so much less to do than I have, or take so much more delight in Epistolary employment, that they regularly answer me by return of post—which causes me inevitably to be always in arrears, & generally over-powered with unanswered Letters—

It is very late in the night—or rather very early in the morning that I finish this, my dearest Etty—I had longed to prate longer—but these 2 sheets have been filling by bits & scraps all day —— Don't ask me to write about Miss A[ngerstein] at present, as you will hear through Alex, *if you ask him* & the cure—if performed! is expected to be as long as the illness! God spare her to her poor unhappy Mother, & angelic grandmother! she is a most exemplary Creature, highly gifted with understanding, & replete with virtues—

Make Alex remember Mrs. Maltby—M^rs F Bowdler Mrs.

---

[6] On a visit to her former pupil Henriette Greene (L. 1293 n. 4).

[7] Judging from payments (£40 per annum) shown in the ledgers of Messrs Hoare, FBA's bankers, first M⟨ary⟩ Holmes and recently Charlotte Hinton would seem to have replaced Elizabeth Ramsay (L. 1182 n. 3), who had returned to Ilfracombe in late May 1822.

H. Bowdler—Dr. Stewart[8]—Mrs. Thomas[9]—Mʳˢ Roberts *la mere*, Capt. Roberts[10]—&c—

adieu, my truly dear Etty—& God bless you!—ever ever yours—

F. d A

Your acct. of all your friends is very entertaining!

Thursday morn—29—Janʸ

1330   Lincoln's Inn *and*
                                                [11 Bolton Street],
                                  31 January–2 February [1824]

Edward Jacob
and Madame d'Arblay
To Alexander d'Arblay

A.L.S. (Berg), Saturday
Double sheet 4to   4 pp.   red seal
Addressed: Revᵈ A. D'Arblay.
This letter was opened by FBA, who on 31 Jan. and 2 Feb. wrote on the remainder of page 2 and on pages 3 and 4, and readdressed the letter: Ainslie's Belvedere / Bath. / at Mʳˢ / Bourdois   *pmk* 2 FE 1824

Lincoln Inn Saturday

My Dear D'Arblay,

After some delay Mʳ Lockhart wrote to me today.[1]—He

---

[8] Third son of John Stewart (1736–1806), 7th Earl of Galloway, the Hon. and Rt. Revd. Charles James Stewart (1775–1837), D.D. (1816), Bishop of Quebec (1826–36).

[9] See L. 1200 n. 11.

[10] Sarah Roberts *née* Gawen (*c.* 1762–1844), widow of William R. Roberts (*fl.* 1778–1802), late Captain in the 2nd (Queen's) Regt. Dragoon Guards. The Captain would have been their elder son John Charles Gawen (1787–1874), Sub-Lt. R.N., Commander (1812), Captain (1815), Vice-Admiral (4 October 1862). See also ix, L. 1011 n. 17; x, L. 1094 n. 36.

1330. [1] Brother-in-law of AA's former tutor Edward Jacob (x *passim*), the Revd. Alexander Lockhart (*c.* 1788–1831), B.A. (Oxon., 1811), M.A. (1814), rector

has I found made some alteration in his plans intending now to be absent for one month only, leaving home in the beginning of March——Perhaps under these circumstances it may not suit you to take his duty ⏐ and if so, I shall regret his fickleness I hope you may not have been inconvenienced by it.——But if you still think you should like this shorter engagement, Mr L. will be happy to consign his flock to you & wishes me to arrange with you: Therefore let me see or hear from you soon.——Pray give my respects to Mad^e D'Arblay.——

Yours truly
E. Jacob

[*By Madame d'Arblay*]

Saturday Night——31. Jan^y

This Letter, most unluckily, came while I was with Mrs. Lock, whom I did not leave till the post was gone by. Mr Jacob left it himself & they never told him you were out of town! & only said you were *out*: he desired a speedy answer.

You must weigh the Matter well, in all its bearings——The *one* month I think no obstacle, as to *time*, if it be not as to *Expence*——& as to Cold Weather for beginning visiting your flock morn^g or Even^g weigh the all with a Paper for Pro & Con. You will else never ⏐ see the *grand* preponderence, from recurring to some favourite small detail. I will give you no advice, as the event only can shew what is best: but——if *you invite me very prettily*——I will accompany you, my Alex, be the month what it may.[2]

Whatever you decide, do not write till the following morning, i.e. Thursday. A Night's rest, & fresh views, may make you repent your determination, be it what it may, if precipitated.

Let *me*, also, have a line written the same day, as my own affairs will require all the little time of February for arrangm^t

(1822) of Stone and curate of Hartwell, Bucks., planned to be away from his parishes for the month of March and was seeking a substitute. This circumstance, Jacob, now a successful barrister-at-law, with chambers in Lincoln's Inn, had evidently seized upon as an opportunity to serve his former pupil.

[2] The expense of the sojourn in Buckinghamshire is recorded in FBA's Account Book (Berg) for 1824: 'Hartwell course 14: 0. 0'.

I *will leave the rest to add Monday's News* from Suffolk.
the ⟨   ⟩

Monday 2ᵈ Febʸ I have not yet been for my bulletin but
I have just received your most comfortable & satisfactory
Letter, which carries me about with you, my dearest Alex,
from place to place: I am glad you now do justice to beautiful Bath—Brighton, with all its *agremens*, is not, as *town*, fit
to be its handmaid. Nor is any City *I* have ever visited: Brussels,[3] with all its *l'allé verte*, place Royale, Parc, &c, is completely inferiour as a whole. I rejoice my dearly loved Sister
retains all her charming qualities, & I am glad Maria has
skimmed over the 5 years so imperceptibly; but I am sorry
Sophy is still so weak ! Preach up *Bracing* to both—especially by *Example*. If you preach on Sunday, Pray do not
hurry—be grave & *dignified* but not arrogant or doctorial—
yet fear not a little phiz—animation *par ci—par là*, is *universally* successful, by keeping a Congregation awake without
snuff, or pinching the nose, or squeezing the fingers. I must
break off for my Bulletin—yet stop!—Give your address at
the post office *Ainslie's* Belvedere, with enquiry if any Letter
is arrived *without* the Ainslie, as you omitted that in yours to
Brandon Hall, & there is a *Belvedere tout simple.*

How kind is Mrs. Maltby! I hope you gave her my Billet?
& to Mʳˢ F[rances] B[owdler] & to my sister?—If not,
quick! quick! I like your Engagements, & think they will
really do you good after such tragic scenery.

The Bulletins of Thursday, Friday, & Saturday were rather
stagnant.[4] The dread Depression by no means removed, or
even lessened! but the pulse better. !

3/4 past 4. The last news is this moment come that the
dread of the removal is so imperious that the fond tender
mother is willing to relinquish it. They have therefore written
to Dr. W[arren] to tell him all the obstacles, & to demand his
positive order, from a positive conviction that she can stand
it, or his consent to its being deferred till she is better, or at

---

[3] For FBA's sojourn in Brussels in 1815, see viii *passim.*
[4] Bulletins, procured from Lady Martin or Mrs. Locke, on the recovery of
Caroline Angerstein (L. 1323 n. 1).

least better reconciled to the project. The sweet Mother writes that she is waiting with impatience unspeakable & anxiety almost intolerable the answer of Dr. W.—to which Mr. A[ngerstein] seems decided to yield. Mrs. Bouch[erett][5] & her daughter are still there. There has been a cruel return of spasm & suffering—yet the pulse continues mending. She is giving herself up entirely to noble deeds of Charity, & kind ones of generosity, & affection. She has now ordered *45 pair* of Blankets—& has no recreation but in making Lists of this sort for donation. Mrs. L[ocke] is just returned to Eliot Vale, to meet poor Cissy.[6] You stand with Mrs. L. in all y[r] first & tenderest favour: *Palpably* Be sure make your Bath Cousins go on with the lessons of your Ely ones. Julia & Hetty will take it very ill if you have induced them to throw away their precious time on an *oublieux*. Suppose you ask the opinion of Dr. Stewart as to Hertford?[7]

1331   Christ's College, Cambridge,
                        11 February 1824

John Croft[1]
and Madame d'Arblay
To Alexander d'Arblay

A.L.S. (Berg), 11 Feb. 1824
Double sheet 4to   4 pp.   *pmk* CAMBRIDGE   red seal
Addressed: The Rev. A. C. L. d'Arblay, / 11 Bolton Street / Mayfair / London /
This Letter was opened by FBA who wrote on the remainder of p. 1 and on pages 2, 3, and 4, then readdressed the letter: Ainslie's Belvedere / *Bath*. / at Mrs Bourdois. / *Bath*.   *pmk* 12 FE 1824

[5] Emilia *née* Crokatt (ii, L. 111 n. 2), stepdaughter of John Julius Angerstein (1735-1823), widow of Ayscoghe Boucherett (1755-1815) of Willingham and Market Rasen, Lincs., and one of their daughters, either Juliana (b. 27 April 1798) or Amelia Mary (b. 7 August 1790).

[6] Mrs. 'Murray' Greville (L. 1280 n. 6) *née* Georgina Cecilia Locke (L. 1192 n. 9), who presumably had returned from Nice after the death of her mother Mrs. Charles Locke (L. 1327 n. 6).

[7] See L. 1329 n. 8.

Christ College
Feb. 11. 1824

Dear d'Arblay,

The first instalment of the Diseworth fine has at length become due,[1]—I have therefore directed Mortlocks[2] to pay to your account at Messrs Hoares £27. 8. 2—being the amount of your share of the fine—

I am, dear d'Arblay,
Yours truly
John Croft.

[*By Madame d'Arblay*]

Houra! my dear Alex!—I wish you joy of this with all my heart. With a little prudence & *foresight*, you will now be able, by living with *mam*—to come forth with splendour for *April & May*, without any *tick* to lessen your disposition of your ensuing Dividend. |

The *Bulletins* have again been very bad since I wrote last! —& there has been woful disturbance—but these 2 last days there seems amelioration, & quite reviving hope. I am convinced you have *wisely* resolved, in your answer to Mr Jacob, for all sort of Reasons—but do not cast down your wisdom into fruitlessness of result by omitting to be home in time to prepare for your *Presentation*.[3] There is an outcry on that subject amongst your best Well wishers. Nothing transpires that can lead me to answer your q^y categorically enough for a Letter. My present fear is *Fanaticism*!—The Doubts ought to be removed—it is high time—meanwhile, be as gay &

1331. [1] The Revd. John Croft (L. 1232 n. 12), bursar of Christ's College, Cambridge, had sent d'Arblay the augmentation in his stipend (as Fellow of the College) accruing from the rental of the Diseworth estates in Leicestershire. These made part of the lands and revenues with which the Foundress, the Lady Margaret Beaufort, mother of Henry VII, had in 1505 endowed the College, an endowment deemed sufficient to support a Master, twelve Fellows, and forty-seven Scholars.

College estates were usually leased to a tenant for a term of 21 years, and such a transaction for the estates mentioned is recorded in the College Order Book on 23 April 1823 (Courtesy of Mr. D. R. F. Missen, M.A., College Archivist).

[2] The banking firm of John Mortlock (*c.* 1755-1816) and Co., Cambridge (ix, L. 991 n. 3). Of his four distinguished sons (see Venn), Thomas (1780-1859) succeeded his father as senior partner in the firm.

[3] To the Bishop of London (see Ll. 1329, 1331-2).

happy as you can, to bring good looks & good spirits for all your enterprizes. our dear Charlotte Barrett is still livid lipped & very weak & faint with her Jaundice, & her face is wholly colourless!—I think Ely disagrees with her, & long for her return. our dear friends in Pall Mall see only one another[4]— I have had a sweetly dear Note from Mrs. A[ngerstein]—& a very kind Message to you, of *affectionate love*, & a remembrance of your sympathy in their great sorrows.—Mrs. Lock is again at L^y Martin's—I am going to *dine* with them, *en trio*, & in a small snug room, Sr Geo[rge] being at Portsmouth. Mrs. L[ocke] is inalterable in her partial tenderness of enquiry & interest for you.—But tell me of Miss Ralles[5] —& make all the friendships you can—they sweeten Life to its end. ।

I had Yesterday a most satisfactory conference with our excellent Jacob, by appointment. He came quite *rayonant* with pleasure, from finding, by your Letter, that his good offices promised so much satisfaction; & that you accepted them with such frank alacrity.

He was very glad I should go with you, as thinking it would make your sojourn *happier*: for you know his great partiality to your Madre: but — —

Here comes the surprize,

And the quite New Compliment

(Entre Nous soit dit!)

He did not at all seem to make any point of it, or to entertain a fear of your not doing very well without her!—!—!—

His trust in the *fond* of your Character & Conduct, where you once have a *Voluntary Responsibility*, is firm as a Rock. He took the Notion early, & he adheres to it even at his own risk & peril.

He has promised me not to hurry you for Mr. Lockhart till the last moment—& to arrange all household matters with *me*.

But we completely met in idea that you should come to Town in time for seeking an introduction to the BP. of London, *coute qui coute*, before you go to Buckinghamshire. ।

---

[4] 102 Pall Mall, the dwelling of the late John Julius Angerstein (iv, L. 334 n. 4), where the family of John Angerstein seemed to be living temporarily.

[5] Possibly Ann (*c.* 1758-1842) or Lucilla Rolle (*c.* 1757-1851), who rented Camilla Cottage in 1802 (v, L. 536 n. 4).

I am so pleased with all you tell me of your good spirits & enjoyment, that I would have you stay to the *last moment*— & that, by all I can calculate, to allow of Twickenham, & perhaps *Fulham*,[6] with being presented to Mr. Lockhart, & with necessary arrangements with him & Jacob, that *last moment* may be extended to *Monday the 23ᵈ* Beyond that, you may miss what may be most essential to your future Worldly prosperity, as I happen to know that the BP. of London will be in Town from the *24ᵗʰ* to the *26ᵗʰ*—And the Archdⁿ is recovered, & *has been* in town, & will come again one of those days, on professional duty, to meet the Bishop of London.

Monday 23ᵈ is therefore the literal last moment. So you need not lose *quadrilling* it at this beautiful Fancy Ball.— Pray practice well, & exhibit fearlessly & gaily.

My best love to my dear sister—& remember me kindly to all. Don't leave my Letters about—Fire them off!—God bless you, my dearest Alex—

My sister Charlotte & Clem are both rather better—Tell it in Lark Hall place incontinently. ı

Pray Enquire whether Lady Maria Keith is at Bath[7]—& get me her La^dyship's direction. Don't forget.

1332   [11 Bolton Street,
                              post 11 February 1824]

To Julia Charlotte Barrett *and* Mrs. Barrett

A.L.S. & A.L.S. (Barrett, Eg. 3695, ff. 80–1b), n.d.
Double sheet 4to, of which part of the address panel, a segment (2.4 to 3.8 × 5.6″), is cut away   4 pp.   red seal

[6] Palace of the Bishop of London (L. 1258 n. 18).

[7] Eldest daughter of the 5th Earl of Kintore (d. 1804), Lady Maria Rembertina Keith-Falconer (1769–1851), with whom FBA made friends in Bath (ix, L. 1011 n. 31 and *passim*). Two of her letters to FBA (9 December 1818 and 25 January 1821) are extant (Berg).

Addressed: [Miss Barre]tt, / [at Henry Bar]ret's Esq / [or at the Cambr]idges / [Ely]
Docketed in pencil, p. 4: Mme D'Arblay

My dear Julia,

I thank you for your Letter, & I address this Answer to you, to shew my sense of your punctuality. Pray give my kind Regards to your Papa, & Love to dear Hetty & Arthur, & believe me, my dear Julia,

Your very affectionate Aunt,

F. d'A.

Tell Hetty, & yourself, that your scholar in Capering has so well profitted by your lessons, that he danced Quadrilles the other Night at Bath, & at a fine public Ball, from 10 O'clock till 2 in the Morning.[1] He says he is quite knocked up, & never was so tired in his life. There's gallantry to his fair Partners! I doubt not but his Cousins at Bath were obliged to buffet him well to make him practice your previous documentirings.

And Now, my dear Girl, give the following Postscript, with a gentle Kiss, to your dear Mama.

P.S. Your Letter, my sweet Charlotte, has given me so much concern, that it urges me to all that is least usual to me, Namely, a speedy Answer: for I cannot be easy without expressing my earnest wish for your hastened removal from Ely, even though fully aware of the wise & good motives which cause your hesitation. So highly I think of prudence, & so deeply of the value of œconomy, especially in the Female Chief of a young Family, that I would have every thing yield to them save Health. But What, my dear Charlotte, can come in competition with that for the Female Chief of a young Family? If said Prudence & œconomy were to save Fortunes for all the tribe, yet lose you your Health, they would be

1332. [1] Perhaps the Fancy Ball at the Assembly Rooms on 20 February, though, since d'Arblay had arrived in Bath on the 5th (*Bath Chronicle*), he could have attended the York House Subscription Ball on the 16th or the 'Batchelors Great Fancy Ball' at the York House on the 27th, attending which were a number of clerics.

poorer in their Riches than in their ǀ poverty—for they would lose what no Riches can ever purchase for them. I need not enlarge upon these words, if you will only, to save me trouble, give them their due weight by supposing me to be talking of Mrs. Angerstein: —— turn that idea in your mind, & you will then comprehend, & enforce my strong & fervant recommendation That you will not wait for *symptoms of danger*, as you hint at doing, but, since you think that Ely air disagrees with you, that you will commission Marianne to secure you an *interval House* at Richmond.

I would write this to Mr. Barrett himself, but that perhaps any sudden alarm might lead him to *hurry* you away,—& all *hurry* is inimical to delicate Nerves. Lord Chesterfield admirably distinguishes between *Hurry*, & *Haste*:[2] the latter I earnestly wish: the former I should dread.

This is the main spring of my Letter, my sweet Charlotte; & I entreat you to give it effect by the supposition I have put before you. All, then, will give way to what you will in conscience acknowledge to be the Duty of studying your own preservation.

Alas—to that dearly loved & exquisitely prized Mrs. Angerstein I have addressed nearly the same words. Her Daughter will, the physicians say, ultimately recover:—but the mother, the invaluable Mother, my trembling observations, as well as apprehensions, say will, ultimately, be the Victim! —— The Daughter, too, my dear Charlotte, is very far from making the *rapid* ǀ progress her journey to town seemed to imply. She was brought hither in a Bed constructed to go from one Corner of the Coach to the other: while the 2 other corners were occupied by her Mother & her Sister. The Physician in constant attendance, Dr. Somerville,[3] & poor Mr. Angerstein, sat on the Coach Box, to be at hand in case of sudden mischief, & Miss Angerstein's maid, & a servant of trust, went in a machine behind the Carriage, which is remarkably large &

---

[2] From her earliest years an inveterate reader of courtesy books, FB had read Chesterfield's *Letters* as early as 1774 (the year of their publication). In spite of their 'immorality', they 'contained some excellent *hints* for education', said FB (*ED* i. 314), and among the hints in deportment that she evidently approved and remembered was that in LETTER LXXVIII: 'Whoever is in a hurry, shows that the thing he is about is too big for him. Haste and hurry are very different things.'

[3] See L. 1329 n. 1.

easy. A Chaise followed close with all sort of medicines, &c. She bore the journey beyond all their hopes — — & she is essen[tially] better, since her strength & her looks seem sensibly ameliorating, but — — the swallo

[*segment of page cut away*]

Mrs. Lock is at Lady Martin's, to be near at hand to administer her angelic consolations. I see her daily. Indeed, if I were not disturbed about Ely air,—or if I loved you less, I certainly should not just now have made time to write all this.

Alex is still at Bath, but he has accepted an offer of undertaking the whole Parish duty of two Churches at Hartwell, in Buckinghamshire, for the month of March: at the opening of which I shall accompany him to the Rectory of *Mr. Lockhart*: that I may help a little, in this his first essay, as to points of Punctuality, & of schools, & the Poor, &c. &c. |

I have already spoken about the Niece of my excellent & favourite Mrs. Parker.[4] I am enquired her age & height. Is she quite grown up? Does she know useful needle word, *mending*, &c. & clear starching? & has she as little *partiality* for the soap suds as for scrubbing? Can she roast? & make a pudding & Pie?—I must state all she can—& cannot do to a lady who is much pleased with your *sbozzo* of her. How I should like her for *myself*, on account of her dear late Mistress & good aunt,[5] if I kept *two*!—But I conclude she would not *Ramsay* it.[6]

Alex is still at Bath, where all are well. Poor Fanny Burney is returned from a long visit in Lancashire,[7] after spending

[4] Mary Parker (L. 1238 n. 21), for long years housekeeper to the Cambridge family at Twickenham, and possibly her niece Mary (b. 6 August 1786), one of the six daughters of John Parker (*c.* 1750–1814) of Kew Horse Road, Richmond, and his wife Elizabeth *née* Kippen (*fl.* 1777–98).

[5] Charlotte Cambridge (L. 1305 n. 1).

[6] Elizabeth Ramsay (L. 1182 n. 3), formerly favourite maid and friend.

[7] With Henrietta Greene (L. 1293 n. 4).

half her time in nursing the *Jaundice*!—She is not yet quite *whitened*: nor one bit pinked!—the rainy season seems of a yellow Character. Sarah Payne begins to revive both in strength & spirits:[8] she is to drink tea with me to-morrow. Mrs. B. is well, but fears leaving home in the Evening. Sarah Harriet is at Crew Hall, & I hope prosperous, though not communicative.[9] Edward looked in good health last Sunday. I have seen our dear Fanny Raper only twice since she left you. Your dearest Mother, my beloved Sister, assures me that both She & poor Clement are rather gaining ground. She was wretched to think of *you* ill, & without her! My dear *God Boy*[10] came to me just as I was descending the stairs to go, by appointment, to L^y Martin—I was quite sorry to merely embrace him; but he saw a good deal of Sarah P. What a fine little fellow he is!—If Mrs Jenyns is at Ely,[11], I beg my comp^ts to her: & likewise to Miss Harwoods,[12] though I know them not, in honour of the Memory of my dear Mrs Rishton. What a history is that of Mrs. Meeke, or Bruce![13] Poor Miss Wilson has lost her Cause[14]—but with high honour & Pity public. She is very ill, poor thing! What a delectable Letter you wrote me on a certain 'well-chosen subject!'[15] No

[8] On her return from Italy (L. 1310 n. 6).

[9] A long detail of the life of a governess at Crewe Hall, Cheshire, is supplied by SHB in her letter (Berg) of 2 December 1823 to CFBt: 'Here, as I live with the girls all the morning, I put myself in mind of being at a large Hotel, where I endeavour to remain snug & detached from the other inmates till called to the Table-d'Hôte, where as in a Magic-Lanthorn, new people pass in review before one who stay for a night or two, and then are off. I begin to grow hardened to the horror of seeing so many strange faces, for, on going into the gallery before dinner, I always expect to behold three or four new phizes, which the second or third day (at furthest), give place to three or four others. . . . I just now met a house maid carrying coals upstairs, & asked how many fires there were to keep up? "Three and twenty, Ma'am."—And yet, the house is not now so full as I have known it, and the Hall stove is not included.'

[10] See L. 1328 n. 2.   [11] See L. 1314 n. 4; L. 1321 n. 4.

[12] Resident in Ely since 1818 were three Harwood sisters, originally of ?Exning, Suffolk: Maria Rishton's friend Mary (*fl.* 1789–1858), who had commented (L. 1321 n. 8) on d'Arblay's fine looks; Elizabeth (d. 11 December 1843), who would marry Captain Richard Turner Hancock (1764–1846), R.N., on 21 September 1826 at St. George's, Hanover Square; and Ann (d. 1864), mentioned in a letter (Barrett, Eg. 3705, ff. 106–7b) from her sister Mary to CFBt, dated Ely, 9 February 1826.

[13] Maria Rishton's sister 'Bessy' *née* Allen (L. 1314 n. 5).

[14] For Harriet Wilson's lawsuit, see L. 1180 n. 12.

[15] This is CFBt's letter of 15 December [1823]. See L. 1321 n. 8.

introduction has yet taken place with the BP. of London!—
I hope You will shew me your noble Ely Cathedral. —— ——
    adieu, my sweet Charlotte—ever yours with tender affec-
tion.

F. d A

1333   [11 Bolton Street,
pre 18 April 1824]

To Mrs. Barrett

A.L. (Berg), n.d.
Two double sheets 8vo (7.2 × 4.3″) the second leaf of the second
sheet cut down to 2.5″ [*perhaps before the letter was begun*]   7 pp.
Docketed in pencil, p. 1: Early in 1824

Not to write a word to my dear & generous Charlotte by
this debonnaire opportunity would be most graceless—as
when did she omit giving me another ⟨guess⟩ example?—Yet
I am hurried too much by the wish not to forsake my dear
Godboy for writing either legibly—or I fear intellectually—
But I am not able to resist this *short cut* to begging a line or
two of Bulletin, from one or other of my Charlottes[1]—as
I am very desirous to hear the Jaundice is entirely discarded.
I am sure ǀ my sweet Sister will revive & gaify with her beloved Child, & I know that no one can do so much for that
said latter person in nursing & comforting her. Our visit to
the residence & duty of Hartwell Rectory was very satisfactory to me.[2] Alex was punctuality itself in every point—he

1333. [1] Richard Barrett (L. 1321 n. 7) on his way from Eton to Ely for the
Easter vacation. As may be seen in the address of MF's letter (Berg) of 12 March
1824 to her mother, Mrs. Broome must have gone to Ely to nurse her daughter
CFBt through the attack of jaundice mentioned in L. 1329.

[2] According to plan (see L. 1331, *post* 11 February), FBA had in fact accompanied her son to Buckinghamshire, where, for the month of March, he had relieved the Revd. A. Lockhart (L. 1330 n. 1) of the parish duties of Stone and
Hartwell. The editors are grateful to the County Archivist, Mr. E. J. Davis, for his
searches of the parish registers and for other helpful materials corroborating the
accounts that FBA gave of the church at Stone and Alex's performances there.
    The infant baptized on 7 March was Charles, son of George Carter (*fl.* 1823–38),

was even *solicitously* punctual, being constantly in waiting half an Hour before hand. He went through all the duties of a Parish Priest, & for the first time, most of them, except the Matrimonial: but no one, or rather no two would be ⎮ loving enough to ask for his benediction For better for Worse. He Baptised one poor little Infant, & he performed the funeral service for another—He Churched two women, & catechised all the little Boys of Hartwell one Sunday, & all the little Girls of Stone, the neighbouring Village, on another; & He read the Prayers for the sick & dying in a poor Cottage, for a nearly expiring poor woman of the head palsey, but who retained her intellects; — — I went to the Catechising—& ⎮ to the little Funeral. You, my dear Paintress, would have made a beautiful drawing of the scene, which affected me even to tears. The Church of Stone is very Antique,[3] & stands on an eminence, with the town at its foot, & high hills, rather bleak, in every other part of the view.[4] The Infant was brought in a poor Country procession from the top of a distant Hill, slowly walking down, & then rising again to reach the Church yard. The little Coffin was held by Four young Maidens, in long red Cloaks; & the Nurse led the way, while

carpenter, who had married (by banns on 4 December 1823) Sarah Maynard of Hartwell. She was to bear in all eight children, of whom Charles was the eldest.

The infant buried on 17 March was Thomas (bapt. 24 February), son of Zacharias Thame (b. 10 December 1787) of Stone, labourer, who had married on 2 March 1818 Sarah Ashpole (*fl.* 1818–24).

[3] In 1824, before the successive restorations of 1843-5 and 1885-90, the 12th-century church at Stone was probably showing the ruinous marks of its antiquity. The church FBA saw would have boasted windows (inserted in 15th and 16th centuries), a south porch (15th century), the West Tower (14th century), South and North Transepts (13th century), and a nave and chancel, somewhat expanded and widened since earliest times, but dating back to *c.* 1170. For the 17th and 18th centuries nothing much in the way of repairs is recorded, and, as the County Archivist has noted, the church in 1824 must have been as FBA describes it, 'in a fairly decayed and ruinous state'.

[4] FBA, always extremely short sighted, rarely attempted to describe landscape, and the 'eminence' and the 'distant Hill' she mentions cannot now be descried and could not have loomed with quite the bleak prominence she suggests.

The funeral procession, however, is borne out in the records. The 'elder' child of three would have been Zacharias Thame's daughter Ann (bapt. 22 July 1821), though he had also a 5 year-old Mary (bapt. 6 June 1819). The red cloaks, seeming to suggest ceremonial robes, would have been the Sunday wear of the poor, the homespun, dyed red, the same 'Red flanes' that, worn by an oncoming group of curious women at Fishguard in 1797, the French to their terror mistook for the red coats of the regiments of the line (iii, L. 228 n. 1).

the poor Father, in tattered Garments, held an elder Child, of 3 years old, by the hand, to attend the rites. As soon as they were in sight, Alex, ˡ who had awaited them in the church porch, in his surplice, came forward, &, in measured paces, advanced to meet them at the Gate of the Church yard, which was about 100 yards: He then led the way back, reading occasionally some sentences of Scripture; & his bare head & meditative turn of features gave him a very poetical appearance, though by no means a dramatic, or irreligious one. *au Contraire*, he was deeply impressed by the Ceremony, which he performed for the first time.

Miss Angerstein is recovering, but very slowly & precariously, ˡ she is now under the command of Dr. Clarke,[5] a physician who consigns all his time, attention & study to nervous complaints in females.——

I can leave my dear Godboy no longer—& his *throat* makes him require an early departure—I shall wish to know there is no return of attack. Alex is still under the influence of a slight assault of the same. It seems epidemic, & we tremble at the very name. Pray be all carefull—adieu—adieu—if you can read this I shall be surprized—The Archdⁿ was well, & Mrs. C[ambridge] tolerably so a week ago—& Mrs. Baker & the house goes on beautifully— ˡ Fanny Raper & Minette made me a comf[ortable] visit this morning, both well—& the former very handsome.

Sarah Payne has been to Portsmouth with the Rickmans[6] —& is pretty well. Mrs. B[urney] dº Sarah Harriet wretched with bad head aches. Sends you loves through me, though I have not yet seen her — — Both well —

⁵ Charles Mansfield Clarke (1782–1857), surgeon, Lambeth M.D. (1827), F.R.S. (1825), F.R.C.P. (1836), named physician to Queen Adelaide (1830), kt. (1831). He was a brother of the eminent surgeon John Clarke (1761–1815), whose fame rests on 'the first exact description of laryngismus stridulus'. For the studies of the brothers in midwifery and women's diseases, see *DNB*.
⁶ From 1824 on the late JB's friend John Rickman (L. 1264 n. 5), the statistician, spent his holidays at Portsmouth, when 'he found it convenient to retire, even in winter, to recover from the effects of overwork'. See Orlo Williams, op. cit., pp. 226–7; and Manwaring *passim*.

To Mrs. Broome

A.L. (Berg), n.d.
Double sheet 8vo　　4 pp. [_conclusion and cover missing?_]
Docketed in pencil, p. 1: 1824

The How do do of a moment is always better than no How
do do at all to _me_, from my dearest Charlotta—& I feel as
much security of her sympathy in that feeling as in all others
that so long have bound us together. I long to know how you
are, & how the dear object that took you hence,[1] & how
poor Clement is to boot. Marianne I trust is above my solicitude—she would else share it—But I desire no augmentation of Health anxiety. Alex has had a bad & wearing cold;
caught as usual, by insufferable imprudence, since our return
from Hartwell. He dined at Greenwich, with ¦ Charles Parr, at
a great Dinner given to Burney students[2]—& the consequence
was terrible heat, &c,—&, in the fear that should not be sufficient to mischief him, he wisely left off his flannel waist-
coat that night, after a journey home on the outside the stage
at midnight—& in a season of extreme harsh weather. When
he will know the value of _not_ being ill I cannot find out,—
but the sufferings of his indiscretions make no impression for

1334. [1] To Ely (see L. 1333 n. 1) to nurse CFBt. MF was living temporarily in
Barrett's house in Richmond; and Clement Francis, rapidly succumbing to tuberculosis of the lungs and other ailments, CBFB was later to accompany to Bromley
and to Brighton.

[2] This was the annual Burney dinner (see vii, L. 652 n. 3) to which d'Arblay's
formal invitation of 1824 is extant (Berg): 'The 19th anniversary dinner of the
Noblemen and Gentlemen / Educated under the late Charles Burney and the
Revd. Charles Burney / to be held at the / Freemasons' Tavern, Great Queen
Street / Lincoln's Inn Fields / Tuesday 27 April 1824. / The Revd. Dr. Burney in
the Chair. / Dinner to take place half-past-five precisely. Ticket one Guinea each.'
　　Named were the six stewards, George Basevi (1794-1845), architect; Sir
Thomas F. Buxton (1786-1845), philanthropist, reformer; Sir George K. Rickards
(1812-89), political economist; Captain ?_later_ Admiral William Fisher (1780-
1852); and two Churchmen, the Revd. Henry North (1787-1837) and the Revd.
Edward Reginald Mantell (_c._ 1799-1884). For Warren Derry's comments on the
eminence of some of the Burney scholars, see x, L. 1150 n. 6.

amendment, severely as they try him—alas—it is fever to *me* to see his ruthless carelessness— ꞁ

Our Hartwell expedition was completely successful, in calling forth an attention of scrupulous punctuality in my poor Alex, such as he had never practiced in his life. He officiated for Mr. Lockhart, a Brother in Law of Mr. Jacob. And did every part of the Parish Priest well, save Marriage, which no cooing Turtles would call for: but I ought to except, in my plaudits, The *Banns:*[3] on the 1st Sunday he quite forgot to give them out: on the second—as they were not placed in the Prayer Book, as in town, he was going on with the service: but the Bride elect, ꞁ fearful of new delay, had planted herself close to the Clerk, & gave *him* a jog to jog the Parson! —the Clerk, looking up, pitifully whispered '*Won't* you give out the Banns, Sir?—' Alex then glided them in a little later: but when he told the Clerk, afterwards, that he was very sorry to have forgotten them the former Sunday, the Clerk grinned, & said 'I don't think the Man cared much, Sir—but Master Lockhart would be main angry, for he's very paticular.' — —

Alex is to preach next Sunday, Easter day, in Leaden-Hall Street for Mr. Knapp, a Minor Cannon of St. Paul's.[4] He preached at St. Paul's Cathedral on the C. N. Sunday in Lent:[5] his 3d Sermon there—

---

[3] According to the Banns Book (Records Office, Aylesbury), d'Arblay called banns in respect of Benjamin Monk, bachelor, and Mary Thompson, spinster, on 7, 14, and 21 March; and in respect of Richard Feasay and Elizabeth Monk, both of Hartwell, on the 14th and 21st. Banns were called for the third time for this second couple on 28 March by the Revd. Frederick Cox (*c.* 1796-1879), headmaster of Aylesbury Free Grammar School (1840), P.C., Upper Winchendon, who married them on the 30th. The first couple were married by the rector the Revd. Alexander Lockhart (L. 1330 n. 1) only on 20 May. The impatient bride-elect seems therefore to have been Elizabeth Monk.

[4] Similarly invited (see L. 1305 n. 4), AA had preached in this chapel on 11 May 1823 (Diary).

[5] Presumably *Carniprivium novum*, Quinquagesima Sunday in Lent, 4 April 1824.

1335   1 Half Moon Street,
[*c.* 15 April 1824]

To [H.R.H. Princess Sophia]

A.L.S. (Osborn), n.d.
Single sheet 8vo   1 p.

Madam,

O Yes! sweet Princess, Yes! Good Friday Evening[1] I shall feel—I dare not say more *Good*, but more *devout* I will venture to assert for spending it with so unchanged, unchangeable & kindly invariable, though so august a personage as the dear & fair Princess who, from her Childhood upwards, has so Graciously deigned to receive & to encourage the warm attachment of Her Royal Hignesses'

most obliged

most faithful, most grateful,

and most Respectfully Devoted

F. d'Arblay.

1336   11 Bolton Street,
23–25 April 1824

To Esther (Burney) Burney

A.L.S. (McGill University), 23–25 Apr. 1824
Double sheet 4to   4 pp.   *pmk* 26 AP 1824   red seal
Addressed: Mrs. Burney, / Lark Hall Place, / near / Bath.
Endorsed by EBB: Rec^d April 24th 1824 / replied to May— / favored by Maria & Sophy
Docketed in pencil, p. 1: Madame d'Arblay
                       p. 4: Letter of Madame D'Arblay / Fr Burney.

1335. [1] This reply is dated provisionally, for among the scores of notes and invitations (Berg) from the Princess, many of which are undated, no mention has yet been found of Good Friday.

Bolton St. Begun 23^d April
1824

Does my dearest Esther think me lost in the narrow, boggy, muddy, rugged, swampy, rutty Lanes—not Roads—of Hartwell Rectory?[1]—No, my dearest Etty, we have weathered these miry, shelving, slopery, slippery clay alleys, as safely, & with as much difficulty as You & I, & Co., have erst weathered those of Chesington—though not with as ample recompense![1] —*That* awaits us no more!—However, Alex, to whom all was without comparison, & quite new, & who never found out that the way was not broad, smooth, level & ordinary, was mighty content, & I, therefore, & *therein* received the best portion of Content that belongs to my present lot.

I am so much in arrears in all accounts, & I have so much to say, that my pen is disturbed where, How, & with what to begin. I have Two Letters to thank you for first; & I suppose you imagine, according to my late trading Confessions, I am waiting in the hope of 3 p^r C^t to my bargains? No, no, not quite so bad as that. I *never wait* for a *Second* — — nor *expect* it, I *assure* you, from *You*,—however spoilt on that score I may be in the habit of finding myself in general;— but you won't insist upon my saying I do not think such double & treble interest very pretty—& very generous—& very good merchandize?—no, no, cheap as you have seemed to hold all my *manoeuvres* behind the Compter, you must bear with my declining to leave off business till business leaves off me.—Pray, now, do not take advantage of this hint, & set aside your liberality, because you see you may conquer me by your *stingyness*. Besides, that is not precisely the Word that occurs to me with your idea—so do not *from mere vengeance*, compte yourself so unnaturally.

1336. [1] For FBA's sojourn for much of the month of March in the Rectory at Hartwell, Bucks., see L. 1333 n. 2; and for the lanes over Chessington Common to Chessington Hall, the resort of the Burneys in their younger days, see *HFB*, pp. 17–18, 117; and *ED* i, ii *passim*. The 'recompense' was the friend of FBA's youth, Samuel Crisp (ibid.).

How I wish you could tell me your own dear Self with what you would wish me to begin——Bath——St. Pauls——Hartwell ——Miss Angerstein——The Funds——The Charlottes——Summer plans——perspective promotion——The World at large——or our own Race in particular?——Well——as I cannot obtain an answer, I must even commence with what, at this moment, is predominant with myself, Miss Angerstein.

That long & most pitiable young sufferer recovers with a slowness & a sadness the most melancholy. Her spirits, never high, are utterly worn out by the exhaustion of her malady; & the persuasion of death has so powerfully taken possession of her mind, that nothing seems to lead ᛁ her to a belief in the possibility of her re-establishment, & she has so completely delivered herself up to religious aspirations, that the very wish of life seems absorbed in the expectation of bodily release & spiritual reward. Her lovely Mother, & still & ever lovely Grandmother are devoted to her by the most unremitting watchfulness of tenderest attentions. I tremble for them both in this prolongued & dreadful anxiety. The swallow is restored, completely, for eating as well as drinking; but not only this deep dejection of spirits pervades all her faculties, as well as dispostion; another evil, the result of all the preceding, robs her of strength for convalescence,——i.e. she has entirely lost her sleep. To this must be attributed a constant head ache, which makes it an effort to her to speak, even a monosyllable. God grant a fairer prospect ere long, or I know not how any of the three can be supported. Mrs. Angerstein seems Self-sacrificed in her attendance, & Mrs. Lock, struggling always against affliction, & chearing & comforting all around her with a determined view to happier days, is now the life of the whole house, in the midst of her own severe trials. What Angels these are! How like to that Angel we once possessed ourselves![2]——I must tear myself from this theme— or I shall give you no other——

Bath shall come next,——& the great pleasure & satisfaction you have all given to Alex during his residence there.[3] I have

---

[2] Cf. the laments for the deceased sister Susan Phillips *née* Burney, L. 1307 and n. 2.

[3] A visit of about a month to his cousins at Bath (apparently from late January to late February).

a Letter before me, written thence, by him, in which he says 'I am just going to dine with Aunt Hetty, who is looking wonderfully well, & keeping up most surprisingly her Spirit, her activity, & her pleasingness.——' Just before this, he says: 'Here I am with my amiable & agreeable cousins, who are exactly the same as I left them, only 5 years more on their shoulders, but that is not apparent in their faces—at least not in Maria's, but poor Sophy, as I expected, I have found very thin & delicate, though otherwise in pretty fair health.'— *Emily* he afterwards says, is comely, good humoured, sensible, & grown social. But before I go on with his own prate, let me come to your observations, or your friends, upon his preaching. Any resemblance to the Theatrical declamation I think undoubtedly wrong, & any to a peculiar actor, much worse. Fortunately, I have never had the distress of hearing ¦ either from him when I have been of his Congregation. 'Tis probable that being solicitous to do some Thing extraordinary, he made exertions that carried him beyond his own Mark. *Animation* I *love*, & therefore never discourage, as I think its want in a preacher is often a *doze* to the Hearer: but all *exaggeration* defeats it's own purpose by rather leading to Ridicule than to Attention. Alex is not yet the *Formed Preacher* I have hopes to see him. He is uncertain & unequal. *At times*, I own, he is all I can wish: but never so *de suite*. And this I attribute to the chasms of vague inertion which intervene from Sermon to Sermon, from his having no regular practice, & no duty that demands Responsibility: for while he only officiates occasionally, & for others, if he pleases, 'tis agreeable, but if not, 'tis *sans consequence*. However, I am so anxious he should love his profession, which alone can make him excel in it for his Congregation, or be *digne* of it for himself, that I keep all discouragement from him in his present unfixed position, lest he should return again to his Mathematics, & indulge exclusively that original propensity, which, when uppermost, swallows up every other pursuit, nay inclination. I have therefore forborne to tell him your remarks, or your friends, *for the present*; though I hoard them up for my own watchfulness, & to strengthen any similar view of such defects that may, unhappily, arise. He is much more easy to depress than to excite. This is owing to his fatal fondness of Rumination, which has consumed half his existence, already, & which, if not guarded against, will nullify all his talents.

I am most excessively gratified that you were so well pleased with his amended looks. Mrs. *M.*[4] wrote to me also, purposely to congratulate upon them. She little suspects all the *Malice* her interest inspires! Had she been younger, I really believe her danger would rather have goaded her on than restrained her. Another fair dame told me just the same thing of *herself* only yesterday—& a very dainty & fastidious judge, to boot, whom you well know, & must try to guess. ↑ How can you suppose your *Jocossities*, as you call them, can ever be ill received or ill viewed? in whatever season they arrive, they bring their own welcome by the certainty they are written in ignorance of any disaster which they may encounter, for when my dearest Hetty knows of any misfortune, who has a heart more open to its sympathy? *Pray* never rebuff them when they are so *debonnaire* as to offer themselves, for your *plaisanteries* are always to my *Goût*,—be the humour in which I receive them Grave, or Mellow.

*M*ʳˢ Miller I have *not* seen;[5] she lives at Hackney; but my help is urged by her husband, who has hopes of retrieving his affairs *ultimately*; in the mean time, he has 2ᶜᵉ again had recourse to me—& in so [ing]enuous & Gentlemanly an open & pleasing manner, that I am sincerely interested in his & her, better welfare: yet I never *meant* to apply to *You*, as they have not done it themselves: I know too well by experience the *calls immediate* to press any that are collateral. I have, at this time, involved myself in so many claims, that I have withdrawn from All that are distant to me, or I could not go on. The poor Sleepes & Mrs Sansom stand always foremost, *comme de raison.*[6] To poor good Hetty S[leepe] I have sent overplus by Mrs. Burney of Jˢ Street. & a desire she will always let me be acquainted with any illness she has, or distress.I saw her, not long since, at James St. by accident, &

---

[4] Possibly Miss Maltby (L. 1232 n. 13).

[5] The daughter of Jenny Barsanti (L. 1329 n. 4), to whom FBA had donated £2.

[6] See L. 1191 nn. 16, 17. FBA's Account Book (Berg) shows a donation of £8 in all to these indigent relatives. She seems to have denoted at least a tenth of her pension of £100 to charity.

was astonished to find how she is improved in her appearance by added years! her ordinary, house maid look, is quite passed off, to one of interesting pleasingness. Let me know, I beg, what I owe you for *Mr. Hervé,*[7] & do not jumble our accounts, by mixings & substractions, &c. Mind, now!—I have not obeyed all your injunctions, nor have I room to talk of whys & werefors, but I led Alex to read to me your Crabbes *Library,*[8] at Hartwell, & we both join in your praise. I can still enter into all authours that pass through the mouth of Alex, from my earnestness to give Zest to his own literary taste. Charlotte spent a morning with me lately, just fresh from Ely, where she has left sweet Charlotte Barrett still faint, weak, altered & unwell![9]—She writes to me chearfully of herself, but I am far from easy about her. Charlotte is gone on to Richmond. Clement is at Cambridge, rather better. Sarah Harriet drank tea with us on Thursday, pretty well, Mrs Admiral! d^o yesterday. This day, *25. April,* I expect Edward & Fanny, & will tell you how they do in some niche. Fanny Raper & Minette called last Week. What you say of correspondence & Lancashire,[10] how just! that Letter, being here answered, I have *this instant* burnt, as we agreed. Alex writes this same day to Belvedere so will speak for himself. Adieu, my ever dearest Hetty—yours most ⟨tr.⟩

affec^ly

F. d'Ay ∣

Lives still my precious Rose Tree? Ah!—the 2^d Mr. Twining is gone![11]— ∣

Edward & Fanny are both quite well. How kind & how honourable the bequest of Sr T.P.[12]

---

[7] The 'Hervé charity' (L. 1243 n. 8), later the National Benevolent Institution.

[8] *The Library* (1781).

[9] Mrs. Broome had been in Ely for the last few months (L. 1333 n. 1).

[10] A veiled allusion to Fanny Burney, the governess, and her former pupil Mrs. Greene (L. 1293 n. 4), now living in Lancaster.

[11] Richard Twining (L. 1282 n. 17) had died on 23 April.

[12] Sir Thomas Plumer (L. 1191 n. 4), eminent jurist (*DNB*), former employer of EBB's daughter Fanny, had died on 24 or 25 March. FBA had heard his defence of Warren Hastings in Westminster Hall on 24 April 1792 (i, L. 21 n. 10) and she may have learned from her niece herself of the legacy of £30 that he had left to her as a former governess to his children and of other provisions of the will (PRO/PROB/11/1684/243, pr. 27 April 1824).

11 Bolton Street,
1–5 June 1824

To Mrs. Barrett

A.L.S. (Berg), 1–5 June 1824
Double sheet 4to   4 pp.   *pmks* 7 JU 1824 7 JU 1824   red seal
Addressed: Mrs. Barrett, / Henry Barrett's Esqr / Richmond / Surry.
Scribbling in Hebrew, p. 4: Tafol Huefr / Leittrnsomd / za' morfrn

11 Bolton Street
Tuesday 1st June
1824—

My pleasure is so very great at the unexpected sight of your loved writing,[1] my sweet Charlotte, & at the perusal of so chearful a Letter, that my Pen—so tardy & sluggish in Epistolary punctuality, quite jumps into my hand to thank you.—You meet Recovery with a Grace that certainly ought to attach it to you; & doubt have I none that it visits You much quicker than your neighbours because your allurements are greater, & your welcome is more cordial. Recovery is perhaps the least spoilt Child of Prosperity, for there is, commonly, such ill Will to acknowledge any Good, such reluctance to disband our legions of Complaints, & to part from our Groans & Moans & murmurings, & all their attendant priveleges of peevishness, snapping & snarling, that I know nothing more general than to see Invalids hug their ailments as their bosom Friends.—Not so *you*, my sweet Charlotte, your desire to enliven those you love, & wish to serve, stimulates exertion in yourself, that pays its court to Recovery, & tells it that it may go far & near ere it will meet with so gracious a reception. But |

—Alack a day! I began this on the immediate impulse of pleasure from reading your welcome Letter—which was the more cheering as it arrived at the dullified moment of Alex's departure[2] — — but one interruption, which is always

---

1337. [1] CFBt had returned with her family to Richmond by 23 April (see L. 1336).
[2] Before taking up parish duties at Camden Town (see n. 7) AA had departed for a visit of a few weeks to Paris, returning on 29 June (see L. 1340).

followed by another, when not sturdily combatted, was suc-ceeded by such a possy of fellow intruders, that it is now Saturday 5th June—before I can send off my thanks, with my anxious desire that my dear Marianne will give me a fur-ther *bulletin* in a very short time.

My own *'littel Complaint'*[3] does not return—yet keeps up such a constant Bo-peep at me, that if I did not ward off surprize by the most active manœuvres of Regimen & Care, I feel sure I should soon be taken by assault. I am therefore always on the Look-out to watch & defeat my Enemy, & nearly always a Prisoner. But that is all.

I am truly grieved at the account of poor dear Clement,[4] & extremely disappointed.—& my poor dear dear Sister! 'tis cleaving her heart in twain to be separated from *You* when you are not well, though she feels, *all things* considered, Clement her first tie for a prospect of usefulness. I have this very morning heard a very high character of the abilities & wonderful successes of Mr Scott of Bromley, from the Miss Wilbrahams.[5] May this long & most I extraordinary case con-firm his fame!—

I was in hopes you were to see Dr. Walker,[6] my dearest Charlotte—but you do not mention him.—You must have very good advice indeed before you venture on a Journey, even though it be *Inland*. Mr. Barrett will, I doubt not, take all the charge of Package, Baggage, & preparation that he *Can* — — but it is always the Mistress, not the Master of the

[3] 'Cholera morbus', as FBA later diagnosed her complaint (L. 1338).

[4] Afflicted with abscessed or ulcerated legs, Clement Francis had placed him-self under the care of John Scott (1798-1846) of Bromley, Kent, R.C.S. (1820), surgeon at the Ophthalmic Hospital in Moorfields (1826) and later at the London Hospital, a specialist at this time in bandaging (*DNB*). Scott's theory was that tight bandages would prevent the infection from breaking out into running sores. H. Crabb Robinson had 'heard Coleridge explain the rationale of the treatment'. ' "By a very close pressure, Scott forces the peccant humour into the frame, where it is taken up by absorbents, and expelled by medicine" ' (Diary, ii. 295-6).

With his mother Mrs. Broome, his niece Julia Barrett, and at intervals his sister Marianne, CF was to take up residence in Bromley for the summer and autumn and to suffer the extreme pain of the treatment as described by his sister MF in her letters of this time (*Catalogue*).

[5] Daughters of SHB's former employer George Wilbraham (L. 1191 n. 7) of Delamere Lodge, Cheshire, Anna (ibid.) and her sister Emma (*c.* 1776-1855) or Elizabeth (*c.* 1784-1865).

[6] Probably Sayer Walker (1748-1826), M.D. (1791) of Norwich, whose *Obser-vations on the Constitution of Women* was published in 1803.

House, that is most in requisition for removals. Could you quickly go, with as much freedom from trouble & care & thought, as your young Guest may do, then the mere Change of Air might be serviceable: at this season, especially, when there is the least danger of damps, *unairdings*, & all the numerous host of Cold-catching articles that hover over the Journeyings of Invalids. I wish Miss Goose were a Bird of acuter qualities. She might then help on the way, & lighten it by carrolling sweet airs: but I have little hope of animals that like to herd with the Vulgar crew. If you were well, I should not despair but that you might teach her to sing in a higher sphere; & Taste that is well directed, however factitious, becomes, sometimes, habitually good. I shall be much vexed if this little Bird should be let loose from its Cage before it acquires some improvements that may mark what has been its residence.

⟶

I have not written the History of Alexander's Chapel,[7] &c, because I imagine all I could tell you would be stale, as that

[7] Working all this while in d'Arblay's favour as one who wished to find employment in London was the implementation of the Church Building Act of 1818 (58 Geo. III, c. 45), with the later Acts of 1819 (59 Geo. III, c. 134) and 1822 (3 Geo. IV, c. 72), which provided £1,000,000 for the erection of 100 parish churches at an average cost of £10,000 (but not exceeding £20,000) in populous districts within ten years. Among the thirty Ecclesiastical Commissioners appointed by Letters Patent in 1818 to carry out the programme was AA's patron, the Revd. George Owen Cambridge (L. 1190 n. 2), Archdeacon of Middlesex. For the List and for observations on the purposes and the implementation of the Acts, see Michael Harry Port, *Six Hundred New Churches. A Study of the Church Building Commission 1818–1856 and its Church-Building Activities* (1961).

Among the populous parts of London was the parish of St. Pancras, which in the census of 1831 had 103,000 inhabitants, and Camden Town, a working-class area, the Rate Books of which could almost serve as a dictionary of early nineteenth-century trades, had in 1831 nearly 10,000. Previous therefore to the Acts (*supra*) a Private Act (56 Geo. III, c. 39), passed on 31 May 1816, had provided for the building of a New parish Church (that on Euston Road) to be called *'The Parish Church of the Parish of Saint Pancras'*, the conversion of the old church of St. Pancras to a chapel to be called *'The Parish Chapel of the Parish of Saint Pancras'*, and the erection of a new chapel to be called *'Camden Chapel in the Parish of Saint Pancras'* (ss. XLII–XLV). To Camden Chapel AA would presently be presented as P.C.

The ministers of the two chapels were to be nominated by the Vicar of St. Pancras New Church, the Revd. James Moore (*c.* 1769–1846). They were to be paid 'a sum not less than One hundred and fifty Pounds, nor more than Two hundred Pounds *per Annum*' and to reside within their parishes. For AA and Camden Chapel, see further, L. 1338 n. 4; L. 1339 nn. 2, 3; and L. 1346 and notes.

sweet woman, Mrs. Cambridge,[8] I feel sure will reveal to you all my account. To the Archdeacon I am going to write as soon as I have News of Alex to give, & that intelligence, I feel equally assured, will be communicated—& therefore I avoid repetition. ⏐

Sarah Payne drank tea with me on Thursday, *pour prendre congés*: I thought she seemed well, & she was in excellent spirits with the view of Holland before her, & a perspective of Spa—Poor Sarah Harriet came also—very far indeed from well, & tame as a Dove; which made me as well as herself melancholy. She is going, with only a Maid, to Brighton, to try warm sea Baths. The Misses Crewe are to be under other care for a few Weeks at Rams Gate.[9] I earnestly hope she will return better—able to sustain her arduous enterprize. I am not easy about her—yet she does not, thank God, look *ill*, but sad, & affrighted, & reduced. She starves *too* severely. *Inanition* becomes itself an evil, & one very difficult to manage: more so than *repletion*. Poor Mrs. Piozzi literally lost her life by too acutely struggling to sustain it. She had recovered from her malady—the effects of a fall—but sunk under the weakness of too rigid a Cure.[10] Adieu, my sweet Charlotta—when I write you so long a Letter, you will not need a conclusion that talks to you of the love I bear you—

F d Ay

Is Julia still at Bromley?[11] My love to Hetty & to Arthur —but First to my dear Marianne—& my best Comp[ts] always to Mr. Barrett.

The Archd[n's] kindness & zeal for Alex would fill a whole Letter—but I hope you have heard it from M[rs] C[ambridge]. Best Love to Mrs. Baker when you are well enough to see her. ⟨Miss⟩ Angerstein is little more than *stationary*!— ⏐

Maria is looking hale, young & handsome—but poor Sophy

---

[8] Cornelia Cambridge (L. 1205 n. 6), whose letter is unfortunately missing.

[9] As may be seen in SHB's letter (Berg) of 19 June 1824 to CFBt, she was by that date at Ramsgate with 'a snug contented little party', Lord Crewe (L. 1293 n. 6), now aged 82, and the Misses Crewe (Henrietta and Annabella). Later she was to try Brighton for change of air (Ll. 1337, 1341).

[10] See Clifford, pp. 454-6; also L. 1461 n. 3.

[11] With her grandmother CBFB and her uncle CF (n. 4).

is a yellow shadow!——And poor Fanny looks ill & sallow too. Yet I hope they are both amending, tho' not amended.

P.S. You must not write again *yourself* on any account, while at Richmond——

¹338   11 Bolton Street,
                                        10–[16] June 1824

To Esther (Burney) Burney

A.L.S. (Berg), 10-June 1824
Double sheet 4to   4 pp.   *pmk* 16 JU 1824   red seal
Addressed: Mrs. Burney / Lark Hall Place, / near / Bath.
Endorsed by EBB: 1824 / answered by parcel / June 29th

(begun) 10. June, 1824
Bolton Street

Little Grace (Epistolary) as I know you allow me, with your *mechante apology* for writing to me by M[aria] & S[ophy] I do faithfully assure you, my dear Hetty, *you* were the First person to whom I meant to communicate this Good News of Alexander——[1] but before I had the time, from the general *combustion*, as Kitty Cook would say,[2] of the affair, joined to the immediate resolution of a Tour to Paris, & much remnant weakness & languor from recent illness, I was fain to grant to Sophy—what she claimed, indeed, as already done, in part, the forwarding the first intelligence. I begged her, however, to let you know I only yielded to her Letter already begun. You will probably have heard, my dearest Esther, what a severe attack I have had of the Cholora Morbus,[3] in the middle of the Night, on the 15, I think, of April. As it is now so long passed away, I shall let it go *its train* without detail, farther than to say, that though it endured but a few Hours, They were of such violent & acute suffering, that I

1338. [1] See L. 1337 n. 7.

[2] Papilian Catherine Cooke (i, L. 22 n. 4 and *HFB passim*) of Chessington Hall, whose original idiom was often adopted by the Burneys. Cf. L. 1398, par. 1.

[3] 'A disorder, attended with bilious diarrhœa, vomiting, stomach-ache, and cramps' (*OED*).

not only felt *dislocated* for Weeks after, but am even yet not quite so robust as before the assault, & forced to observe a watchful *regime*, & take libations of Gruel & of warm Toast & Water constantly! With that attention, I escape relapse.

I think Maria looks extremely well, always very handsome, & astonishingly young. Poor Sophy seemed—in her first visit, a mere sallow shadow—but, in her 2ᵈ—last Sunday, she was *whitened* amazingly, & I think & hope this tour will re-establish her.

You will but too easily—with your *connoissance de cause*, conceive the nameless sources of anxiety that accompany this opening & very arduous career of my dear Alexander:[4] he is so unused to controll, so little in habits of punctuality, so indifferent to the customs of the World, & so careless of inferences, opinions, & of consequences, that I cannot but tremble to see him advanced ᛁ at once, to the whole duty of a New Church in a New Parish, with the complete charge of the District—without some previous practice as an attendant Curate. It is not his capability that I can doubt—*that* would be affectation; but it is his *Absence* & his *carelessness* that I cannot think of without tremor. And the more, as we can no longer be wholly together—for he will not, (under a *very good living*, & a wife, to boot) give up London, it's Literature, Science, improvements, society, Libraries & public places, to live completely in a Fauxbourg, that is neither Town nor Country; for this New Chapel is between Pancrass & Hampstead.

[4] As laid down by the Private Act (56 Geo. III, c. 39) the ministers of the chapels were required, besides reading prayers, to preach or cause to be preached a sermon 'on every *Sunday* throughout the Year, and on every *Good Friday* and *Christmas Day*, and on Days . . . for public Fasts or Thanksgivings as well in the Evening as in the Morning'. 'On every *Christmas Day, Easter Day*, and *Whitsunday*, and on One *Sunday* at the least in every month [they were to] administer the Holy Sacrament of the Lord's Supper . . . and also [they] shall perform such other Duties as the Vicar . . . shall think fit to direct or appoint, except the Solemnization of Matrimony and Publication of Banns of Marriage' (s. xlviii).
As may be seen by d'Arblay's signatures in the Baptismal Registers of Camden Town (GLRO), the vicar had evidently entrusted the christenings to the curate. An extant Memorandum entitled 'Register of Baptisms / in Camden Chapel / from the Consecration of the Chapel / in July 1824. / to February 1830' gives the number as 28 for the remainder of the year 1824; 92 for 1825; and 142 for 1829. Pastoral duties, the conduct of Sunday Schools and Infant Schools, the visiting of the poor and sick are not mentioned in the Act, but with the growing social conscience in an area rapidly growing in population they must have made a heavy addition to the charge. For AA's fatigue in the duty, see L. 1401 n. 5.

His Patron, therefore, whose Church it is, Dr Moore, agrees to his only taking for himself, a study & a Bed Room, to occupy *every Saturday Night, all Sunday*, the eve of every public service day, & at *Breakfast every morning*—& then to pass the rest of his time, when secure from clerical calls, with me in Bolton Street. The Bishop of London assents to this; & the archdeacon Cambridge highly approves it. For otherwise, if he had not a real *Home* to come to in town, open to him at all hours, he would find himself forced to relinquish all Town Engagements, Instructions, pursuits, & connections. I, too, must then fall into a life of as total *seclusion* as that I have so reluctantly & so lately changed to one of only *retirement*: for Alex would, of course, adopt all the Clubs & little meetings, &c, of the neighbourhood, & I should rest alone, utterly, *every* Evening. And —— —— it would banish me wholly from my gracious & beloved Princesses—who condescend to say, they delight to have me within half an Hour's summons, & Their own Carriages.[5] Besides—I should almost wholly lose, equally, all my own dear remaining Family: our Charlotte never comes to Town, on any sort of business, that she cannot make me in her way, coming or going:—my dear Charlotte Barrett de meme:—Fanny Raper, also, cannot come, but I am in her road,—Sarah Payne & ǀ Mrs. B[urney] are within 20 minutes Very pleasant walk—(though no longer alas, pleasant to *me*!)   Charles Parr gives me a social visit 4 or 5 times in the year. Edward & Fanny spend their Sunday Evening here from time to time—& Marianne Francis, Clement, & Martin occasionally find me out —— —— But There, no one could come but *purposely*, & no such purpose could be executed but by the expence of a *Day's* leisure, coming, Going, & visit included. All this makes the plan I have mentioned the best that can be formed—& Yet —— —— 'tis fearfully I consent to my share in it. If my dear Alex had half as much consideration as he has powers of considering, how unmingled would be my satisfaction in his present prospects!—And the excessively handsome & flattering manner

[5] The visits to the princesses, submerged with the loss of FBA's Diaries for the years 1823 and 1824, had continued, as may be seen in the surviving invitations (Berg), one of the latest being of 12 April from Princess Augusta ('Will you kindly come to me tomorrow . . .').

in which the offer has been made augments its Welcome. His preaching, & his Sermon, by happy chance, happened to be of the *best* that morning he officiated in St. Pancrass Church: & great has been the sensation produced by his so immediate conquest of Dr. Moore. The Bishop of London has been much struck by it; & the Archdeacon has never done smiling his benevolent gratulations. I conclude Sophy wrote you all the particulars.

I will not talk to you of *my* sensations at seeing Maria, when thus compelled to seek Me—after the wonderful & alienating change[6] that followed my dread calamity.—Yet I thought she looked as if she wished to be well with me again, & had some inward consciousness that desired relief: she offered, however, not a word of concern, or of apology, —& I, who, the more I have been left to ruminate upon what had passed, feel the *more*, not the less offended, astonished, & wounded, could offer no cordiality—so we were both truly *biluminary* As to Sophy, she felt, or assumed to feel, as *if nothing had happened*, & was, *apparently*, quite at her ease. Maria, on the contrary, had, now & then, *stray looks*, or glances, that seemed to imply concern, & something like returning kindness. On the 2^{d} meeting there was less embarrassment. The 3^{d} was *manqué* by Rain.—I have entered inadvertently & unintentionally upon this painful & *sore* subject, which *you* & *I* had better leave alone: so turn this as a verbal confab. & think no more of it. — — |

Pray regard this Letter as *non avenu* with respect to my fears about my Alex—They must not be spread—I shall write my account free from them entirely to all but yourself. But de *tems à autre*, we both find great relief in recurring to our early habits of unfearing confidence.—Would we could do so always!—but, as you too well say, that cannot be. Embarrassed how to amuse M[aria] & S[ophy] when they purposed drinking tea with me, I looked out what yet remains of my account of Tom Thumb[7]—& I assure you I

---

[6] For an estrangement of about six years, see L. 1293.

[7] See *ED* ii. 171-9, for the production of Fielding's farce as a private theatrical at Barborne Lodge in 1777. The cast included the Worcester Burneys, their guest FB (as Huncamunca), and Mary Ann Burney, aged 7, who played the part of Tom Thumb. 'The sweet little girl looked as beautiful as an angel! She had an exceeding pretty and most becoming dress, made of pink persiam, trimmed with

could not *parcourir* it without being much moved to see how early & how fondly I had always loved Maria—who could have thought of *such* a change!

I was very much pleased with the preaching, & Doctrine, too, of Charles Ekersall,[8] last Sunday, whom I went to hear at Trinity Chapel, by desire of Alex. You have certainly —— —— What a sickly coloured season this has proved to our younger tribe, my dear Esther—I bless God you have escaped its influences—but poor sweet Charlotte Barrett rests stationary at best! She writes me a few cheering lines of herself, from time to time—but they are never confirmed by *our* sister nor by *her* sister, nor by Mrs. Cambridge, who all write me melancholy Letters about her. God preserve her!—I am writing in the dark—I will try to get you some chat ready for M. & S. of Hartwell & of BP. Salisbury, & all you mention. Miss Angerstein recovers, but so slowly as is astonishing. Something must, I fear, be wrong, & her head is always hot; & her feet always cold. Poor Thing! What a dreadful suffering illness! & Mrs. A.—sweet Mr[s] A seems sinking! in defiance of unremitting struggle to appear well!—Mrs. Lock is all well, & all admirable, & charges me constantly with her most affectionate remembrances. How you must be gratified by the Norths prodigious kindness to your Girls.[9] Adio, my dearest Hetty—Kind Love to Emily. Yours ever & aye most truly

F d A.

---

silver and spangles . . . her mantle was white; she had a small truncheon in her hand, and a *Vandyke* hat; her own sweet hair was left to itself.' A great deal of childish dialogue, FB had also lovingly recorded, though the papers she had been examining in 1824 were not published until 1889 in Annie Raine Ellis's excellent edition.

[8] The Revd. Charles (1797-1863), B.A. (Oxon. 1818), M.A. (1822), the son of John Eckersall (1747-1837) and his wife Catherine *née* Wathen (*c*. 1755-1837), the mother of eleven children who survived infancy. From 1800-17 this family lived at Claverton House, Bath, where presumably EBB had met them.

[9] After the Bishop's Palace at Chelsea was relinquished Lucy North (1775-1850), daughter of the Bishop, lived at 29 Manchester Square; and in London for the season each year were her sisters Elizabeth (1776-1845), who had married in 1802 the Revd. Thomas de Grey (1778-1839), 4th Baron Walsingham (1831), rector of Fawley, Hants (1806), prebendary of Winchester (1807), archdeacon of Surrey (1814); and Henrietta (1771-1847), wife of the Revd. William Garnier (L. 1180 n. 18), who had allowed the Revd. Richard Allen Burney the use of his rectory at Brightwell.

Wednesday. [16 June] I send this off just as M. & S. & Ed^d leave me, after a visit from Mr. & Mrs. Angerstein—all well—God bless you my Etty—

---

¹339   11 Bolton Street,
                                    17 June [1824]

To Alexander d'Arblay

A.L.S. (Berg), 17 June [1824]
Double sheet 4to   4 pp.   *pmks* PAID/18 JU 1824   F24/36
ANGLETERRE J.21 21 Juin 1824
Addressed: a Monsieur / Monsieur le Revd Alexander d'Arblay, / Hotel de Suede, / Rue de Richelieu, / A Paris. / [*on fold*]: Chez le Gouverneur des Invalides / au invalide

> 11 . Bolton Street—Berkeley Square
> *17 June.* y^r 2^d Letter just *received.*
> after anxious waiting!

My dearest Alex,

As this Letter, in all human probability, will be not only the first, but the Last, & the only one I shall write you during this separation, I must try to concentrate in it all that is most useful, or—should I find such matter—pleasing to you to hear.

1st I have had no News from or of *Dr. Moore.*[1] I conclude, therefore, that matters abide unchanged, & he has nothing either to precipitate or slacken your return. *Ergo*—I expect this will find you preparing to be on the Wing homewards.

2dly for the *Bishop of Bristol.*[2] he returned you an immediate

---

1339. [1] Vicar of St. Pancras (L. 1337 n. 7).

[2] John Kaye (ix *passim*), who, as Master of Christ's (1814-30), had consulted the statutes of the College for the clauses governing Fellows and their emoluments. A *Calendar* of 1859 for instance, mentioned fifteen Fellows, who had 'an equal claim to the College patronage, and are allowed by the statutes to hold preferment with their Fellowships, provided it does not exceed the value of ten marks, after the deductions found in *Liber Regis*' (so called after the founder of the College, King Henry VI). Fellows such as Greenall (L. 1340 n. 5) seemed to hold Perpetual Curacies along with their Fellowships, and as AA's chapel was to yield about £200 he was in the event allowed to hold his Fellowship, of *c.* £120.

answer, with an account of the *rate on the King's Bookes* by which you may, or may not, hold other employment with your fellowship. He concludes Camden Chapel to be *not* rated, & consequently secure from any doubt of eligibility: but as you were not here, I thought it best to avoid any *possible* ill consequence to enclose the Letter itself, which contained only this business, & a very civil message to your madre, straightforward to Dr. Moore, entreating a line if any difficulty occurred. No answer has come, whence I conclude all is quite right.

3ᵈ The *Archdeacon* is more & more enchanted at the *manner*, the flattering manner in which this Chapel has been obtained. He can hardly repress his surprized satisfaction that one Sermon should have sufficed, when the *intent* was only to Judge your *delivery* by that experiment; but to put your powers for making notable discourses, that might suit occasionally, his own church as well as Yours, to the test of examining sundry of your compositions: that this intent should be put by, in so handsome, so trusting a manner, upon one essay only, strikes the Archdeacon to be the greatest compliment, because the most solid one, you can receive. And he is sure it peculiarly gratifies the Bishop of London. |

But chiefly the Archdeacon has at heart suggesting to you, without loss of time, the idea of securing an *excellent* man servant.[3] One *middle-aged*,—not a raw boy, who will be always playing at marbles in your absence; nor a young second hand fop, who will wear your shirts & cravats for you, & then

[3] This was in G. O. Cambridge's letter of 12 June (Barrett, Eg. 3698, ff. 94–5b) relaying Dr. Moore's consent that AA live in Bolton Street, Mayfair, and retain in Camden town only 'a small lodging which he may use as occasion shall require'. 'But', the archdeacon went on, 'from his being thus necessarily separated . . . from you, who have hitherto been so watchful to protect him from the inconveniences that arise from those occasional aberrations of mind which belong to men of ardent imaginations, & cause them to forget the immediate object on which their attention should be fixed, I wish to suggest to you, a part of the arrangement, which as it strikes me will be essential, both to his comfort, & to the successful discharge of the Duties he is to perform. I mean his engaging a sturdy middle aged man servant, of rather methodical habits, not a fine gentleman, or a *genius*, but with a head like a wooden Dutch clock that can strike hours and quarters, and who must be allowed to sound them (respectfully) in his masters ears, & by that means, save him all the *hurry* & other inconveniences that may arise from being too late, or doing without his gown, band sermon ⟨cross⟩, or other impliments of Duty.' And the archdeacon seemed ready, if his idea was approved, to look out for such a servant.

wonder they are always in want of renewal; nor a gawky country lad, who will always be running to the ale house; but some steady man, who has known better days, but is still able as well as willing to work for something to lay by for old age; who will not be above cleaning your shoes & brushing your cloaths (which the Archd^n says will no longer be *decorous* for your *own* operation, & will look all the better for being in less learned hands!—) and yet who can write & read, to prevent mistakes in messages during your absence — — & not too weak to be competent to walk, to & fro' your two dwellings, not only for carrying backwards & forwards occasional change of apparel & of Books, but—which will be *indispensable*, to be always ready & alert to follow you to Bolton Street, in case any sudden or unexpected Clerical business should make a quicker than usual return necessary.

Without this precaution, he says, you will always be liable to some mischief from neglect or ignorance:

And *with* it, you may enjoy your *recesses* gayly & at peace.

This suggestion gives me a *repose of mind* at the opening of your new career that makes me quite bless it.

Two Rooms, & a Garret for your Man, will do; but one of the Rooms, your study, must be very pretty, for every body talks of calling upon you,—& of hearing *your organ.* |

The good *Mr. Knapp*[4] has written you a most hearty congratulation. He looks upon this, like Mr. Fortescue,[5] as a first step to high & solid Church preferment. And its being *unsolicited* strikes him as an honour that enhances nay doubles its value. He is *enchanted.*

The Hon. & Rev. *Dr. Stewart*[6] had heard of it—I know not how, & has called to congratulate you.

Sweet *Amine* calls & writes continually to obtain News of you, with a tender interest that is always touching.

---

[4] See L. 1305 n. 4.

[5] Possibly Henry Fortescue (d. 1875), who would marry on 2 November 1824 Caroline Russell (1792-1869), a sister of Henrietta Greene (L. 1293 n. 4), formerly one of Fanny Burney's pupils (see further, L. 1374 n. 11). Son of Captain Matthew Fortescue (1754-1842), he had a half-brother the Revd. William Fortescue (1788-1856), and was related to the Rt. Hon. Hugh Fortescue (1783-1861), 2nd Earl (1841), of Castle Hill, Devon, M.P. (1804-39), who had married on 4 July 1817 Lady Susan Ryder (d. 30 July 1827), whose parents CB had known (iv. 338). The Mr. Fortescue who commented on Alex's career here was probably one of these Fortescues.   [6] L. 1329 n. 8.

Dear *Mrs. Locke* came to Day, evidently embarrassed between private thoughts of drawbacks, & public delight in your honourable appointment: but ever the same in warm, animated affection.

Caroline is improving very much. She has *dined at table*, & *walked* last Sunday to Church.

Mr. Angerstein has been to see me,—& with more than usual urbanity of look & manner. He regards this as honourable & a great stimulus for the present, & promising in a high degree, if pursued so as to make friends of your flock, for the future. He spoke of you with the *greatest* kindness, but without any allusion.[7] I know not at all whether he is behind the Curtain. At all events, he is *more* than satisfied with us *both*, for he was peculiarly cordial.

Mr. Geo. L[ocke] has sent me his warmest felicitations.

All say the long walks, & healthy spot for occasional sleeping, may form your constitution so as to strengthen it for attaining *other heights* than Hampstead Hill.

Mrs. Merrik[8] quite glistened with sensibility when I recounted her the detail of the affair.

So did *Miss Upton*[9] this very morning.

Maria & Sophy are eagerly expecting you back while they are here. They drink tea with me, & Ed^d & Fanny, next Sunday. |

Imediate Business.

I am uncertain whether you will not be leaving Paris as this arrives. I am ignorant of your *furlough* from Dr. Moore: but I earnestly beg *you* to recollect it, & not to exceed it. If, however, you have only one Hour to spare, run to M. Gillet,[10] (at Mr. Laffitte's[11] you may have his direction) & present him my best Regards & Remembrances, & entreat to know whether he has the Act of Notoriety, taken by him, of the real Names of your honoured Father. Without it, we cannot *ever* make an arrangement at the Trèsor Royale; I wish you, also, to ask whether you cannot have an act drawn up to

[7] To AA's wish to propose to Caroline (see his letter of 24 May, L. 1323 n. 1).
[8] Mrs. Merrik Hoare (L. 1238 n. 22).
[9] Sophia Upton (L. 1222 n. 9).
[10] Antoine-Louis Gillet (v, L. 450 n. 7; x, *passim*), a notary, with a practice at 331, rue Saint-Honoré, Paris.
[11] Jacques Laffitte (vi, L. 590 n. 2), the banker.

constater, while you are on the spot, your being son of le feu L^t G^l comte Al. Jean Bap. Piochard d'Arblay, & of Dame Piochard d'Arblay Nee Burney, his wife? Such an act might ensure the *succession* without future difficulties. Consult with the good & friendly & kind M. de la Jaqueminiere,[12] your own *Parent*, & my constant Friend, as well as a highly loved & esteemed Relation of my revered lost husband. I wish some thing *legal* to be authenticated. *I* will repay you the expence, my dear Alex, if it be feasible: but leave *no debt* & do not forfeit your *chapel duty*, if it requires too much time. Kind M. Le Noir will advise you.[13] *If you could but write a line to Mrs. Maltby!*[14]—adieu, my dearest Alex

Yours ever ⟨from⟩
F d'A

I am delighted you have seen my beloved Friends de Maisonneuve de Maubourg & de Beauvaus—& good M^{ssrs} Le Noir & Norry,[15] & M. de la Jaqueminiere. Remember me to All. But chiefly to Mesdames de Maisonneuve & de Beauvau. I hope Maxime is in Paris.[16] I was charmed by the very Name of the Pr. Edmond.[17] May you return well—& invigorated—& fit for taking & adorning your new Post in the committee of Public Life & Reputation. Amen—!

I hope you've not forgot your plan of the consecration sermon? I shall write no more hoping this will but just catch you on the Eve of Return to Honour your appointm^t

---

[12] Louis-Charles Gillet de la Jacqueminière (v, L. 448 n. 10; x, *passim*), a cousin of the d'Arblays.

[13] L. 1189 n. 5.   [14] L. 1232 n. 13.

[15] Charles Norry (L. 1194 n. 6), the architect.

[16] 'Maxime' de Maisonneuve (L. 1195 n. 6).

[17] Edmond de Beauvau (L. 1258 n. 6).

1340   11 Bolton Street,
                                         5 July 1824

To Mrs. Broome

A.L.S. (rejected Diary MSS. 7358–[61], Berg), 5 July 1824
Originally a double sheet or possibly two double sheets 4to (7.3 plus
X 7.1″). Extant in seven cuttings, four of which were taken from a first
leaf, and three (as is shown by an address panel) from a second leaf.
Since the cuttings (supposedly conjugate) do not interlock along the
spine, it is impossible to tell whether the second group of three was
taken from the second leaf of the first double sheet with the spine cut
away, or, from the second leaf of a second double sheet, but probably
the former. The cuttings were used by CFBt for the Pasteup, described
in the Textual Notes. The discards are either missing or unidentified.
2 pp.
Edited by CFBt.

                                         5 July, 1824
                                         Bolton Street.

I was truly eager for news of you, my ever dear Charlotte,
& of Her *we* love so tenderly[1]—for surely no Aunt ever came
so *near* a Mother in her feelings as I do to our invaluable
Charlotte —— —— though I have myself been remiss of late in
writing, from the consciousness that all the interest of the
correspondence was from *your* side, as I had nothing but
repetition of repetitions to offer, of enquiry & anxious solicitude. For though I well know, and believe as my creed, my
dearest Charlotte's constant wish to have tidings of my own
health [*cut*]

[*lower part of leaf missing*] |

But, with the fore*sight* is now accompanied fore *caution*, &
I am going on too well to excite the smallest uneasiness, *believe* me.

of you your dear self, I thank God, nothing but encouraging accounts reach me. 'Tis the mercy of Heaven that gives us

1340. [1] As may be seen from the addresses of L. 1342 and from MF's letters of
this time (*Catalogue*), CFBt was by 12 July established on the Marine Parade,
Dover, and by 24 August, at Boulogne.

530

strength on these trying occasions, that we may soften off the sufferings of those we love. May it here but be extended to success as well as mitigation! — —

I think all I can gather, taken alltogether, of poor dear Clement is full of Hope, for the amelioration of his spirits, looks, & appetite, certainly prove that no under mining disease is working at any vital part.

[*lower part of leaf missing*]

Till the kind Letter of Marianne, dated 1st July, came, I had believed you set off for Brighton,[2] & waited your address in order to write to you. Tell me whether *To be left at the post office*, will suffice? Nor have I the direction of our sweet Charlotta; I beg to know it in my kind Mar[ianne's] [*cut*] bulletin which I will not solicit

[*section of leaf cut away*]

then, the Spa waters may really do her [Charlotte Barrett] the greatest good.[3] They re-instate Mrs. Angerstein when all things else fail. I am excessively glad you have contrived to send a recommendation to a clever Medical man *at* Dover. *That* may be of the highest use. I am charmed she is in a little cottage near the sea, & that she likes it. I have not answered her last very sweet Letter to me, from Richmond, because I cannot endure to add to her writing toils, & I see she cannot

[*part of line cut off at bottom of leaf*]
[*possibly another line cut off?*] |

Last—not least, you will be sure, I come to my dear Alex. He received my Letter that was to call him to a summons from the BP. of Bristol on Friday night,[4] & left Paris at 10 o'clock the next morning, & was in my room before 7 on Tuesday last: he had travelled night & day; but only passed

---

[2] Mrs. Broome was still at Bromley, where her son Clement Francis was undergoing treatment (L. 1337 n. 4). For the life at Bromley, walks, carriage rides, the air, the scenery, see MF's letter (Berg) of 29 June to CBFt ('The country is lovely & the air so pure it is quite odiferous—beautiful walks about . . .').
[3] See L. 1218 n. 1.   [4] John Kaye (L. 1339 n. 2).

through town, & I saw him hardly a moment: he looked *too* well, for he was heated into a complection by no means his own, of a bright colour. He is still at Cambridge, where is also his Patron, Dr. Moore. He will there be retained till Thursday, by an election of a new Fellow of christ's College.[5] How great will then be the bustle! the Chapel is to be consecrated the *15th* and by the Bishop of London!—& Alex is to preach the consecration sermon, which is still unthought of![6]—a style wholly new to him, & which keeps me breathless, as the Bishop of L. & Dr. Moore are Both to hear him. I must probably be in the Pew with them—but will avoid it if possible, to save my own tremors, or the force requisite to keep them in order. We have *all* to do still as to arranging his *professed residence* at Camden Town—where he must generally sleep, & always be *comeatable*, though he will Eat & Live in Bolton Street.

[*one line cut off at bottom of leaf; perhaps two lines missing.*]

I am quite *delighted* the dear & admirable Mr. Wilberforce remembers me.[7] Perhaps he will give me a Call now Parliament is asleep.

[*one line at least cut off*]

my ever dearest Charlotte—
most truly afct ever yours
Fd'Ay—

[5] Elected as Fellow of Christ's College (1824–40) was the Revd. George Shepheard Porter (*c.* 1800–67), B.A. (9th Wrangler, 1822), M.A. (1825), Fellow (1824–40), Rector of Anstey, Herts. (1839–67). He replaced the Revd. George Hutton Greenall (*c.* 1774–1845), B.A. (13th Wrangler, 1797), M.A. (1801), Fellow (1802–24), who was presented to the Rectory of Moulton, Suffolk, in 1823.

[6] See further, L. 1346.

[7] Wilberforce had first met FBA at Sandgate in 1813 (vii, L. 723), had called on her in Bath in May 1818 (L. 1227 n. 1), and again in Bolton Street (L. 1312 n. 2).

1341   11 Bolton Street,
                            2⟨1⟩ June–8 July 1824

To Esther (Burney) Burney

A.L.S. (Berg), 2⟨1⟩ June–8 July 1824
Double sheet 4to   4 pp.   *pmk* 8 JY 1824   wafer
Addressed: Mrs. Burney, / Lark Hall Place, / near / BATH,
Endorsed and docketed by EBB: answered / July 12*th* / 1824 /
reconciliation

2⟨*1*⟩ *June* 1824
Finished the
8th July

Can *I know* there is something I could communicate to my
dearest Esther that *I know* will give her pleasure, yet wait my
usual waitings?——No, my Epistolary inertness does not extend
jusqu'à là——I will hasten, therefore, to *begin*, at least, a Letter
that shall convey to her the tidings she earnestly, *I know*,
desires, that a reconciliation has taken place between Maria
& myself.[1]

You will be anxious, naturally, for some details, & I must follow the *Golden rule* in giving you some little *renseignmens*,——
though my Mind & my Time are now almost entirely occupied upon the high-impending concerns of Alex.——

I have given you already some *items* of our few,——cold——
& heartless meetings; every Sunday Evening was regularly
appropriated for a Tea party, the Sabbath being fixed by
themselves, that they might be Esquired by the ever excellent Edward. *Any* Day, I told them, would equally suit
me, if, by a line, or message, they secured my being disengaged, but I soon saw it was Ned or Nothing; nevertheless,
we made no advance, for it Rained regularly every Sunday.
When the last Sunday, the 27th June, arrived, it was fine, yet
threatened to be showery: I sent my Maiden to beg they
would not trouble themselves to call in the *morning*, as I had

1341. [1] For previous references to this alienation, see L. 1338 and n. 6.

a long visit to make after Church. And I was going, that morning, to St. Pancras New Church,[2] to hear Dr. Moore, Alex.'s new Patron.

The Mistress of the House said they were so fatigued with having ¹ gone to Bed at 1 or 2 in the morning, from some play or Opera, that she could not disturb them; but she was sure they could not drink tea with me, as she knew they were engaged out to dinner at Lady Brownlow's.[3]

————

I went to my St. Pancras, & my visits, & returned very late; & then heard that Maria had called, & seemed to be fretted at missing me; she said her Sister had been too unwell to go to the dinner party, & she, also, had excused herself; but would call again, & try to catch me, before her tea, in the afternoon, as Sophy was too much indisposed for the party *here*.—I then imagined Maria was probably engaged to James street, & would come in her way; Come she did, about 7—I received her as heretofore, but with earnest, & sincere, enquiries after Sophy. I had not yet seen Maria alone; & I thought I observed an air of trouble & agitation, yet of something indicating returning kindness. After some general talk, she said she must be gone,—but suddenly grasped my hand, & uttered, nearly with a sob, from stifled emotion 'Yet—I can't bear to leave you in this manner.—' I felt almost suffocated from surprize & rushing recollections, of all sorts—she continued to say, that she feared I was offended, but she did not know at what—I cast up my Eyes, appealing!—that she had no more intended to offend me than to offend her Mother—& had thought all was well, as I had left her, with the rest, some

[2] St. Pancras New Church, built after Greek models in the years 1817–22 by the architects William Inwood (*c.* 1771–1843) and his eldest son Henry William (1794–1843) and consecrated on 7 May 1822, was said to have cost, with fittings, organ, and all, some £70,000. For a detailed description and plan of the building, see John N. Summerson, *Georgian London* (1946), Plate LVIII and pp. 200–3; and Charles E. Lee, *St. Pancras Church and Parish* [1955].

[3] Presumably Frances (1756–1847), daughter of Sir Henry Bankes (d. 19 August 1774) of Wimbledon, and wife since 1775 of Brownlow Cust (1744–1807), cr. Baron Brownlow of Belton (1776); or possibly her daughter-in-law Caroline *née* Frudyer (1794–4 July 1824), the wife since 1818 of John Cust (1779–1853), 2nd Baron Brownlow (1807), cr. Earl Brownlow (1815).

Presents on quitting Bath — — (Those, by the way, had only been so distributed to avoid any public mark of pointed hostility, for no message whatsoever accompanied them.) Again, I cast up my Eyes, & solemnly declared I had so much horrour of incurring such another scene as ¹ I had had with her, & with Sophy, at Bath, in which I had been treated in so unjust, ungrateful, & indecorous a manner, that I would not utter one word, unless she promised to hear without contention, & only to speak & answer when I had finished. This she agreed to.—

I then recapitulated what I could *remember* of my subject of offence; telling her that the more I had thought over her conduct towards me, the more, not the less had been my displeasure at it: & that it had amounted, from her total neglect to heal it, to a real alienation—the more painful to me, yet the more profound, from the truly affectionate love I had borne her from her very birth, & had had it in my *power*, as well as *inclination*, to *prove* beyond all comparison of such power, & such proof to any other Niece, from any branch of my dear Sister & Brotherhood. — — — Looking round to her now as I spoke, I saw her so troubled, yet with looks so far from resentful of my plainness, that—suddenly moved myself by a tumultuous *turn of the tide*, I cut short my Phillipic, & offered to embrace her.—We were immediately in each other's arms—both weeping—

I offered to hear what she would wish to say—but she simply vindicated herself from the charge of *keeping away from me* 3 weeks—I accepted that justification with alacrity, —& finished by briefly running over what I had taken ill— *very* ill in Sophy, who had begun all this by being *hurt* & *angry* with *Me* for having enjoined her, in the midst of my misery, not to *bring* me Letters upon the most sacred of subjects that required *reading in* presence, & immediately.—She attempted no defence of this, nor of any thing else: I forbore, therefore, pressing upon her the strange attack they had *both* taken the liberty to make upon my removing Alex from Bath!! as well as the Letter, so nearly insulting, in which she recapitulates her *motives* for loving Alex, yet ¹ in naming his own natural claims, those due from his noble Father, & from her kind Husband, she pointedly omits mentioning his

535

Mother:——all this passed from my Mind & Memory, at sight of her changed & really touching expression of distress: her looks became to me again such as I had so long loved, & I took her once more to my heart, as the amiable, pleasing, spirited, lively & affectionate Maria I had cherished with partial love from that happy Childhood in which she had been her dear Mother's first Joy, pride, & delight. —— ——

Sophy I have not seen since; but Maria & Edward drank tea with me last Sunday, most socially & cordially. Knowing Sophy so ill, I had sent, by my maid a message to *Maria*, offering to call in S[outh] Moul[to]^n Street, if *she* could not come to me. My maid says she only saw Miss Sophy, who gave *no answer* to that proposition, except that *they had so many engagements* they could not be found after 2 o'clock, if well;—but added '*I* am *now*, indeed, always at home.'— without one word of thanks, or desire I should fulfil my proposal! And Edward came next day, to say Sophy required *utter stillness*, & had been half destroyed by a visit from *Mrs*. Gregg![4] And when Maria came, though on such perfect good terms, she took no notice whatsoever of my offer & message.

I grieve to have no good accounts to send of poor Sarah Harriet:[5] I have just received a Letter from her from Brighton, which place, alas, has rather worsted than bettered her alarming complaint. Fanny is now with her; both are expected about the end of the Week. From Sweet Charlotte Barrett I have no very recent news: the last was *rather* less bad, yet far from promising.—I expect Alex this Night from Cambridge—I *hope* it, at least—for abundant is the business to transact of all sorts, as to Camden Town. The consecration

[4] Known conjecturally to EBB and her family from summers spent in earlier years in Richmond was Maria Gosling (*c.* 1772-1847), wife of Henry Gregg (*c.* 1759-1826) of 43 Bedford Square. From 1827 until her death she appears in London Directories at the addresses 5 Park Square, Regent's Park, and Belle Vue House, near Richmond. See also *GM* xlvi (1826), 283; and n.s. xxviii (1847), 440; and wills PRO/PROB/11/1710/153, pr. 14 March 1826; and /2062/711, pr. 20 September 1847.

[5] For SHB's sojourn at Ramsgate, see L. 1337 n. 9.

will be this day week[6]—& by the Bishop of London—but Alex is to preach the Consecration Sermon. I hardly breath lest he should not be ready. He only *passed through* town from Paris. Adieu my ever dear Hetty—this is a second *feu de joie*—I am quite recovered from my late attack, though not yet un dieted nor un medicined. Miss A[ngerstein] revives. Dr Mrs. Lock, is ever yours—

God bless you—love to Emily.

affecly. yrs.

F. d'A.

1342   [11 Bolton Street],
12 July 1824

To Mrs. Barrett

A.L. (Berg), 12 July 1824
Double sheet 4to   2 pp.   *pmks* May Fair Paid 12 ⟨JY⟩ 1824
wafer
Addressed: Mrs. Barrett, Marine Parade, / Dover.

July 12—1824

My sweetly dear Charlotta must not be worried that I Frank myself—the gratification of telling her the Heart-felt comfort I have received from her Letter—which though only of a *graduating* sort gives me hope she will really find ultimate benefit by the sea air[1]—

If *Julia* could now & then send me a line it would often save me from tormenting poor Marianne, who, however, has been so amiably ready to keep me *au fait* that she has quite endeared herself to me by her Letters — — Alex is here— The new Chapel will be consecrated on Thursday by the B^p of London[2]—& Alex is now beginning his Sermon of Consecration!—I will write an account of the whole after the

---

[6] On 15 July 1824.

1342. [1] At Dover (see address), where CFBt was to remain until late August (see L. 1346 n. 2).   [2] See further, L. 1346.

following Sunday is over as soon as Julia has bribed me in her dear Mother's name with a little Dover news—God bless my sweet Girl—Best Comp^ts to Mr. B[arrett] & Love to the 3 —I am glad the Best is not quite the Worst—

adieu—

I shall hardly breathe till the ensuing *Thursday* & its following *Sunday* are over— ˡ

Edward well Poor Fanny so, so—& not braced ⟨by   ⟩

poor dear Sarah Harriet is sadly unwell indeed! — —

Maria & Sophy are gone to Brightwell

Alex—luckily—is just as Cool as poor I am *not.*—

This moment Marianne kindly calls—& gives me news. She has left Clement decidedly in fairer hopes—& my dearly loved Sister quite well—*hors* anxiety—Poor Marianne is full of Rheumatism—but looks quite well & agreeable—

I am quite recovered of all *passing* ailments—

1343   [11 Bolton Street,
                                          16 July 1824]

To Mrs. Waddington

A.L. draft (Berg), n.d.
Single sheet 8vo   2 pp.   written on a leaf of a letter that had been addressed: *To* / The Revd Alex D'Arblay / 11 Bolton Street / Piccadilly. red seal

There, still you do me justice; my still—& I believe ever dear Friend, when you confide in the inalterability of my interest for your Children. Shall I have less trust in the continuence of your good will to *my* Child? No—I desire, therefore, to be the First to acquaint you that—at length—he has got an appointment in the Church.[1] Camden Chapel has been offered to him by Dr Moore, its Patron, & vicar, with the whole of its Duty, & the care of its district, including a population of 80.000 souls. It is only 200 a year, & without house or any sort of Extras!—But though there will be no occasional emoluments, there will be neither risk nor difficulty nor *disagrèment*, for the Parliamentary Trustees (as I understand it) take all Receipts & perquisites upon themselves; The revenu, therefore, though variously worked for will be a regular, clear annuity,—which will singularly suit one so much more able to calculate Laws than to claim them. Yesterday, the 15th the Chapel was consecrated by the BP of London, before ⎮ which Alex preached the consecration Sermon: & on Sunday next, the 18, he takes possession of the pulpit &c for himself. He will have 2 Sermons to preach & the whole service to go twice through, every Sabbath.

What you tell me of the lovely & lively Bride gave me great pleasure; & not less your little account of your Roman Colony Name Sake & her family.[2]

A *Foreign* Letter tells me you have thought of visiting the latter should she go to Prussia. A fair royal writer speaks of you with animated regard.[3]

1343. [1] See L. 1337 n. 7.

[2] Augusta, wife of Benjamin Hall (L. 1314 n. 11), later, Lady Llanover; and Frances, the wife of Christian C. J. Baron von Bunsen (L. 1224 n. 2), secretary to Barthold Georg Niebuhr (1776-1831), Prussian ambassador to Rome (1816-23). On Niebuhr's resignation in 1823 there seems to have been the possibility that Bunsen would have retired with him to Bonn, instead of which he was appointed to succeed him as envoy to the papal court (Bunsen, *Memoirs*, i. 132-77).

[3] In letters (Berg) of 27 April-1 May and 24 September 1824 Princess Elizabeth, Landgravine of Hesse Hombourg, had made sympathetic mention of Mary Ann Port, whom she remembered at Windsor and whose letters she was glad to receive. 'Having loved her as a Girl, being a Girl at the same time, I could not but be interested in her . . . for you must remember that with dear Mrs Delany this girl was in the very first society ⟨coaxed⟩ up, talked up and mixed, flattered, & made such a fuss with by all those that came to the House, that it was enough to turn her brain, She loses her Aunt, has no Mother to protect, is taken in by a family who had children & felt her a burthen, & thus married to a Man who took

It is 2 years since I have had a glimpse of my valuable H & F. Bowdler—but the amiable Mrs. Hamet called upon me lately[4]—& [I] drank tea with her at my old Friend's a Cousin of Mr. Crisp, Mrs. Frodsham.[5]

Mrs. Maltby is at Tenby,[6] & will be very glad to wait on you at Llanover if you give her encouragement. She turned out a most warm & faithful friend to Alex & myself—& looks back with vivacity to the origin of our acquaintance.—.

Mrs Raper & Minette are always well, poor Clement never! & Charlotte Barret is in an alarming state! Judge the misery of my poor good sister. Adieu

1344   11 Bolton Street,
                                                 1 August 1824

To Mrs. Moore

A.L.S. 3rd person (The Hyde Collection), 1 Aug. 1824
Single sheet 4to   1 p.
Docketed, p. 1: Miss Burney—wrote / Evelina—Cecilia—Camilla. / *in 1778*— / [*in pencil*]: Ref Vo⟨   ⟩

Madame d'Arblay presents her best Compliments to Mrs Moore,[1] & is extremely sorry that a violent Cold prevents

her off to Wales, where she was in a manner buried alive from all her former friends—so that she felt *nothing* having been every thing—' 'She has had great trials in life . . . She appears quite happy with her youngest Girls marriage . . . she talks of coming over to see her Eldest Daughter should she quit Italy for Prussia which they talked of—'

[4] Emma Louisa Keith (*c.* 1786-1858), fourth daughter of Thomas Foster (b. 19 Aug. 1752) of Grove House, Chalfont St. Giles, Bucks., and wife of James Esdaile Hammet (*c.* 1781-1832), banker, of 21 Lombard Street, London. He was the son of Sir Benjamin Hammet (i. 32), a philanthropic banker of Taunton, and a grandson of the London banker Sir James Esdaile (d. 6 April 1793) of the firm styled in 1799 Sir James Esdaile, Esdaile, Hammett, Esdaile and Hammett. Presumably well-to-do, and residing for a time at Lansdown Crescent, Bath, he served for some years as Secretary to the Hervé Charity (L. 1243 n. 8), later the National Benevolent Institution, to which FBA contributed.

[5] See L. 1192 n. 2.   [6] See L. 1232 n. 13.

1344. [1] Agnes, *née* Hardy (d. 7 January 1839), 1st wife of the Revd. James Moore (L. 1337 n. 7).

her having the honour of personally expressing her sincere wishes that Health & Pleasure may attend Mrs Moore's projected excursion; & that it may allow to Dr. Moore the rest, recreation & benefit that are so highly merited & zealously earned.

11. Bolton Street,
Berkeley Square.
1st Augt 1824.

1345   49 Park Street, Camden Town,
31 August 1824

To Sarah (Payne) Burney

A.L.S. (PML, Autog. Cor. bound), 31 Aug. 1824
Double sheet 8vo   3 pp.   trimmed   *pmks* CA⟨MDEN⟩ T./1 SP 1824   1 SP 1824   red seal
Addressed: Mrs. Burney / James Street / 26 Pimlico.

31st Augst / [18]24
49 / Park Street,
Camden Town.

Will you kindly relieve me, my dear & kind Mrs. Burney, from the great uneasiness I suffer in utter ignorance how my sweet Charlotte Barrett has borne her Voyage?[1] Is your own dear Fugitive returned? whether, or no, she will have acquainted you with the state of things, & I entreat to be made a party to them. I forbear writing to my poor anxious sister,[2] whose fears are always redoubled if she believes them shared.

I was quite sorry to leave London without seeing you, but

1345. [1] The enquiry reached Mrs. Burney at a country retreat Maple Farm, where she spent a month, by which time she knew that FBA would have had news of the Barretts from their son Dick on his way back to Eton. She could only add in her reply of 28 September (Berg) that all the 'dear absentees', including presumably her daughter Sarah Payne, then travelling in Holland and Belgium (see L. 1337), were daily expected home and 'all in good health'.
[2] Mrs. Broome, CFBt's mother.

my Cold was so unmanageable, that my Minister assured me
I should never get rid of it if I came not under his District.
It is already considerably better. I almost live in the beauti-
ful environs of my pretty apartment, & I have ǀ always a
delighted Companion in Diane, though I have not always my
Minister.

I was extremely shocked & disappointed yesterday to find
that my poor sister Sarah Harriet, instead of progressively
amending, as I had left her, was again worse! She was under
her Leeches, & could not even see Me, though I had not without difficulty sought her. Dr. Paris had been before me, but
would not disturb the bleeding.[3] I did not dare, therefore,
insist. The Nurse told me *you* had seen her the day before,
tolerably well. I am impatient for to-morrow, when I shall
seek news of her. Poor—poor thing! how depressing & alarming a state is she in.

If your dear & fair fugitive be again with you, give her
my kind Love. Martin — — what shall I send to Martin?[4]
Ask him to tell me himself. ǀ My sister Burney, too, says
she has much complaint to make of him, for something, I
know not what, to be settled with Edward. Preach Reform to
him, I beg.

I wish in your Note you would name some day for coming
hither to breathe this salubrious air with me: a Chance call
has always so many chances for being unpropitious: I may be
on the route for Hygate—for Hampstead, for Kentish Town
—or lost in the various labyrinths of the Regent's park: or

[3] Sarah Harriet Burney (i, p. lxxiv), the governess, who after trying sea air and
rest at Ramsgate (L. 1337 n. 9) and Brighton (L. 1341) was now at 29 Park
Street, the house provided by Lord Crewe for his granddaughters and their governesses (L. 1291 n. 4).

The physician consulted was John Ayrton Paris (L. 1276 n. 8).

[4] 'Dear Martin has examined the agreement', Mrs. Burney replied in her affectionate letter *supra*, '& says he does not know what to think of it, but that there
is no immediate hurry. He is hard at work ⟨in town⟩ in the day, and this will continue for some weeks to come, but he will not neglect you, My dear and most
loved Sister. With regard to other business all has been settled with Mᴿ E. Burney
for some weeks back, that we can do, or know that can be done.'

She is delighted to know FBA so 'agreeably accomodated at Camden Town'
and would have been much gratified to visit her there, had her health permitted it,
but 'a severe attack of the stomach complaint I am so liable to' and the cold
weather of the last few days 'will prevent my intention of Sunday attendances at
Campden Town, which pray tell "Our dear Minister", I am vexed at'.

be off for another Park Street, to see the poor Invalid. I shall stay here some time, as—on account of my dear Minister, I shall make no other summer excursion.

Adieu, my dear *Sister & Friend*—
Believe me ever yours truly
F. d'A.

My Minister is out, or I am sure would send his Love.

I know not even whether the Spa[5]—as I hope—or Brussels, as I fear, was to finish the tour of the dear Charlotta

---

1346 11 Bolton Street *and* [49 Upper Park Street], Camden Town [*c.* 16] August–2 September 1824

To Mrs. Barrett

A.L.S. (Berg), Aug.–2 Sept. 1824
Double sheet 4to 4 pp. *pmks* OLD BOND ANGLETERRE / ⟨via⟩ CALAIS ⟨F⟩ 64 / 24 wafer
Addressed: France / à Madame / Madame Barrett / rue de La Coupe, Basse Ville / Nº 12. / Boulogne sur Mer.

Bolton Street—
Augst—182⟨4⟩

I am quite *consternated*—in the phrase of my revered Dr Johnson—at this double dealing in the small pox. In its single, original, primitive character I thought it sufficiently detestable: but to have it become wily & treacherous to boot is rather *trop fort de caffée*—Who could expect to see the small pox turn out a gay deceiver? promising so solemnly that one only visit, open, fair, nay invited, should satisfy its ardent desires, & bound its fiery love of Conquest, & then thus insidiously, thus artfully, to insinuate itself into

---

[5] See L. 1345 n. 2.

[Park Street, Camden Town][1]

Tuesday Evening.

What I was going to add, when interrupted a Week or 10 days since, I now wholly forget—for I am *consternated* in a far more serious manner—at this moment, from a visit just paid me by Mrs. *Admiral*!!! Burney, with information that my dearest Charlotte is preparing to cross the Channel.[2] And that so speedily, that there is a mere & a small chance only that a line may reach her.—Nevertheless, send I must, preferring the retort *un* courteous of receiving back my tardy Epistle to making no effort for expressing my earnest desire that my dear *Hetty*,[3] may give me a word on your arrival *across the Ditch*, (as L^y K[eith] calls it) to ¹ let me know how You have borne the passage. I cannot suffer *you*, my kind Charlotte, to take a pen for yourself—it would make me really uneasy; & I will not apply to my dear Julia, so lately an Invalid: & Mr. Barrett will be too much occupied for the impatience of my desire of promptitude. *Hetty*, therefore, must steal a moment from the Goose to give me this satisfaction.

When you *arrive* at Spa²—I have the infinite pleasure of a promise from my sweetest of sweet Friends, Mrs. Angerstein, there to seek you, & thence to send me news, through her dear Mother, of your health. If you meet—Je ne me melerai plus.

I shall be vexed to the heart if this should not reach you, first, on account of my request to dear Hetty, next from my earnestness to thank you for the truly welcome Letter which cheated me—so pleasingly—of Julia's,—& lastly, that there should be any further retard in your acquaintance with the

1346. ¹ About mid-August, as FBA is to state in L. 1348, she took lodgings at the above address in Camden Town and was to return to Bolton Street *c.* 21 October (see L. 1350).

² Following a sojourn of about a month and a half at Dover the Barretts had once more gone abroad. By 24 August letters could be addressed to them *poste restante*, Boulogne. By 4 October (see L. 1348) FBA was disappointed to learn that they had not gone to Spa, as she advised, but had visited Paris and probably, from the references to Lady Bedingfeld (L. 1350), Ghent as well. By 14 October (see L. 1350) they had returned to Richmond.

³ Henrietta Hester Barrett (i, p. lxxiii), aged about 13. Julia was about three years her senior.

consecrating dignity of Camden Chapel's Opening.[4] Alex went early, to be *dizened* in his Canonicals for the reception of the Bishop of London.[5] Mrs. Moore,[5] the lady of the Patron of the Chapel, from whom Alex had the honour of his Nomination, invited me to her pew, which of course, being that of the Vicar, is preferable to Alexander's. She is a pleasing, well bred, & still pretty Woman. The Ayles were kept entirely clear for the Ceremony, & as soon as the Mitred Carriage approached, the large folding doors were thrown open, & the Bishop was met in the Portico by Dr. Moore, at the head of a body of the Clergy,—among whom I only knew our excellent Friend the Archdeacon,[6]—by the 12 Parliamentary Trustees,[7] the Chancellor[8] (not the *Lord* Chancellor!)

[4] Camden Chapel was consecrated by the Bishop of London on Thursday 15 July.

Built after Grecian models by the Inwoods (L. 1341 n. 2), the chapel, distinguished by its solidity, neatness, and simplicity, terminates on its East and West ends semicircularly, with, on the West end, a semicircular portico supported by four Ionic pillars and roofed by a half dome. Behind the portico is a semicircular tower boasting a peristyle of six Ionic columns and topped with a short turret. For an engraving and a detailed description of the Church, its exterior, interior, and furnishings, see *GM* xciv (1824)[2], 489–90; also Summerson, op. cit., Plate LXI and pp. 200–3; and in this volume Plate I.

According to a letter of 18 November 1833 which AA sent as an adjunct to the Report he was required to make to the Ecclesiastical Revenues Commission, his chapel could 'accomodate almost 1300 persons' of which 300 could have 'free seats'. See Archives of the Church Commissioners.

In 1945 the chapel was given over to the Greek Orthodox Church (see Order of the Ecclesiastical Commissioners for England, 4 October 1945). The editor is grateful to Mr. D. A. Armstrong, Records Officer, Church Commissioners, 1 Millbank Street, for the sight of this document and other materials relating to AA's service in the parish.   [5] See L. 1258 n. 18; and L. 1344 n. 1.

[6] The Revd. G. O. Cambridge, Archdeacon of Middlesex (L. 1190 n. 2), one of the Ecclesiastical Commissioners (see L. 1337 n. 7), and signalled by Port, op. cit., p. 36, as one of the 'effective or executive members of the Commission'.

[7] Not the Commissioners (*supra*) appointed in 1818 by Letters Patent (see L. 1337 n. 7), but probably the Trustees of the Parish of St. Pancras, who by the terms of the Private Act (56 Geo. III, c. 39) were to include (s.v.) 'the Dean of the Cathedral Church of *Saint Paul*' (who was entitled to the Advowson of the Church in the Parish of St. Pancras) 'and the Vicar and Churchwardens of . . . *Saint Pancras*'. The Act set forth the manner of appointment of the others, the property qualifications necessary, and the disqualifications ('no Victualler or Person selling Spirituous Liquers . . . by retail, shall be capable of acting as a Trustee'). After that the Act delineated a length of some 50 sections the very extensive powers, duties, and responsibilities of the Trustees and set their times of meeting. Since seven is mentioned several times as constituting a quorum in the business meetings, perhaps FBA was right in the number 12.

[8] The Chancellor of the Exchequer, Nicholas Vansittart (L. 1270 n. 23), an

Camden Chapel, Camden Town, 1824

From a drawing shown in the Gentleman's Magazine of that year

the Church Wardens, Clerks, & Beadles & Vergers, & Mr Sam. Wesley,[9] the Organist.—who mounted instantly after to give his Lordship a welcome of sweet Harmony. The Bishop went into a new robing room, prepared for the purpose & his Lawn sleeves gave no small grace to the ensuing Procession, in which he read, in a sonorous & impressive, but not agreeable Voice, a portion of some of the pslams,—that were followed by responses, utterly inaudible,—owing, I imagine, to a lowly reverence i[n] the *un*mitred accompaniers: so that it seemed as if the Bishop only uttered Verses to the response of silent pauses. Alex, who began now to feel he was going to perform, for the first time, a Discourse—of which he had never heard any precedent, nor seen any example, had a look & air somewhat *drooping*, that pained me considerably as he passed by me in the suite. Imagine, therefore, whether I felt at my ease, when, after this Consecration was finished, & the Bishop had taken his seat at the Altar, & the Morning Service, which was beautifully read by Dr. Moore himself, was over, & The Two first Verses out of the 3 ordered to precede the Sermon, were sung — — when Then no Alex appeared to mount to the Pulpit. The 3^d Verse began — — & went on —& still no Alex!—the pulpit door was opened—but still no Alex! I grew so terrified that I could with difficulty forbear going forth, in the belief some accident had happened. Mrs. Moore looked at me expressively—I felt myself tremble all over—The Archdeacon, who had entered the Vicar's pew, & was seated at my other side, quite *shook*, himself, with apprehension,—he thought Alex had lost his Sermon—or had suddenly conceived a new end for it!—& Mrs. Moore believed he was siezed with affright, & could not conquer it —Finally—the last verse finished—& no Alex! Mr. Wesley ran & re-ran over the Keys, with *fugish* perseverance—& I was all *but* fainting—when, at length,—the New Camdenite appeared. I was never ǀ more relieved. The delay had been the fault of the Verger. My alarm had been so uncontrollable, that I afterwards heard it had excited a general surmize of

Ecclesiastical Commissioner, praised by Port, op. cit., p. 37, for his assiduous attendance at executive meetings.

[9] Samuel Wesley (1766–1837), 'indisputably the greatest English organist of his day' (Grove).

whom I might be—the Bishop himself whom, though distantly, I faced, enquired of the Archd^n if the lady next him was not Mme d'Arblay?—Alex delivered the prayer in a voice hardly audible, & the incomparable one of our Lord, little louder: but, whether feeling his Voice, or recovering from some tremor, I know not, all his pulmonory powers were restored as he gave out the text, which was pronounced with a fullness of tone that carried it, I should suppose, nearly to Hampstead! Imagine my delighted surprize. He sustained this sonorous quality through the whole Discourse. The instant all was over, the kind Archd^n gave me his hand, with a cordial shake, saying 'I give you Joy!—' The Committee of Trustees, &c surrounded the other side of our pew, speaking with Mrs Moore, who, when they dispersed, said 'I hope you have been gratified, Mme d'Arblay, for every body else has.—' When Alex entered the Vestry room, to make his Bow to the Bishop, his Lordship said 'I am very much obliged to you, Mr. d'Arblay; for a most excellent discourse.—' Dr Moore then came in & said, dauntlessly without waiting to be informed first of the Bishop's opinion, 'My lord, I hope you have been gratified?' 'I have been highly gratified,' he answered; & it is the Second time Mr. d'Arblay has given me gratification. I think the feeling has been general.'

I have not room—nor occasion to mention more after this. I have filled my Paper with my long promise; & few are there to whom I could with equal pleasure dilate thus minutely on such a subject. But I know my dear Charlotte's sincere & fervant interest in my Alex. I must now hold by till I gain your address.—

Camden Town. 2^d Septr The Address is just come, in exactly such a '*Stupid Letter*' as makes me long for its fellow. I send off this ms oration in[stan]tly, as it will be as new as if fresh written, for it holds the narration you have desired. I want more *detail* of your health, my sweet Charlotte, & beg it. I am quite sorry I missed my dear God-Boy[10]—I am here for some time, at the vehement desire of the *Minister* of this little Town. I think it respectable to come to such reverential

---

[10] Richard Barrett (L. 1321 n. 7).

request. If at Home, he would send you his Benediction, Be as good as you can without it till I write next. ⎸ But I grieve to know of no private conveyance—Poor—poor Lady Bedingfelt![11] how direful a change from my intimacy with her in her almost glorious happiness at Bath! Adieu, my Charlotte—Truly—Truly yrs

F d'A

I am quite provoked to have missed Dick's John Bulleries — ⎸

I am firmly of opinion Geese should not be allowed solitary walks, for fear of *Ganders*. I would oppose it solemnly, lest *consequences* should ensue that might be highly injurious —& above all I would not let innocent lovely companions still younger than the Cackler risk implications—*Therefore* I would hazard a *representation* if defied, in preference to the danger of future Reproach or Censure.

My sweet Charlotte Calls upon me—& I dislike the Cackler too much to fear her being withdrawn. But I would not have my spotless Swans confounded with any Geese, or misconstrued by any Ganders. I am shocked for my sweet Charlotte in this graceless business.

I can tell you nothing Newer than you have heard from Marian of y^r dearest Mother

N.B. After all this was written, except the *Sealing part*, came your comforting leave taking from Dover: but I have waited to this Day, 2^d Septr for your address— ⎸

My best compts to Mr. Barrett—& Love to my dear Swans —& to Arthur.

[11] Lady Bedingfeld had suffered a series of bereavements in the years 1822-3: her brother William Charles Jerningham and her eldest daughter Lady Petre (L. 1285 n. 1); a second brother Edward and his wife Emily (L. 1288 n. 3); and lost at sea on 3 November 1823, her 3rd son Edward Richard, who having entered the Royal Navy at the age of 14 as a volunteer, 1st Class (22 September 1819), sailed first on the *Phaeton*, then the *Redwing*, joining the *Spartiate* at Chatham on 13 August 1823 (PRO, ADM 11/24; 11/25). The ship was en route to Rio de Janeiro, when according to the log (PRO, ADM 53/1216), the midshipman was found missing, 'supposed to have fallen overboard during the night'. See also *Jerningham Letters*, ii. 290-1, for Lady Jerningham's comment on her grandson the 'Little Sailor Edward' and her trust in the unbounded 'Mercies of God upon youth'.

1347   49 Upper Park Street, Camden Town,
                    1–7 September 1824

To Esther (Burney) Burney

A.L. (rejected Diary MSS. 7360–[3], Berg), 1–7 Sept. 1824
Originally a double sheet 4to, from the second leaf of which five cuttings were taken as Pasteovers for the *verso* of the first leaf. A segment detached from the top of the first leaf was secured by a strip of transparent gummed paper (0.4 × 3.7″), which, lifted, has again freed the segment.   4 pp.
Edited by CFBt. *See* Textual Notes.

Park Street, Camden Town,
begun 1ˢᵗ September—1824

To begin with what is nearest & dearest to me in the last of your most welcome Letters, my dearest Etty, I must commence with giving you my hearty thanks for your assurance of meditating ere long a meeting in Bolton Street. You could not really think I could be otherwise than *delighted* by the *preparatory* measure of Ilfracomb; so I shall not open the powers of my elocution on that Theme—But Ilfracomb!— to what scenes & thoughts & circumstances did that date instantly refer in my mind![1] I am extremely glad you saw, & extremely obliged you were so kind to, my always valued, & always regretted Ramsay, whatever were her imperfections. To, & for, me she was all heart, with an attachment unbounded— but there was one cry amongst all my friends and acquaintance against her, from the unfortunate prominence of what she had of faults namely, general *negligence*—& its concomitant defects,—& therefore, as I did not send her from me, which I think I never could have done,—I deemed the event which, at her own movement, & for her own sake, took her from me to conduct her younger Brother home,[2] that which it was best to serve for our separation, unless I had had more rational hope of amending her provoking failings. However,

1347. [1] In the summer of 1817 FBA had accompanied AA and his Cambridge reading-party to Ilfracombe (x *passim*).
[2] Possibly Richard Harris Ramsay (bapt. 4 May 1800 at Ilfracombe), the son of Robert Ramsay (L. 1182 n. 3), a man of property, though a shoemaker by trade.

when she came back—unexpectedly, I might still have been unable to resist her affectionate wish of re-establishment with me, but for the engagement into which she had unreflectingly entered, & which no promises on her part could have merited dependence, after the idle & imprudent manner by which she had voluntarily been involved, unknown alike to her Parents & to myself. I shall always truly rejoice to hear of her welfare, &—poor good warm-hearted Girl, to see her, should that be possible.[3] — —

With regard to the truly extraordinary, & so nearly fatal adventure which she narrated[4]—as well as she could, having been absent at Barnstaple when it happenned—I neither wonder at your surprize I had not been my own Historian, nor at the effect upon your kind Heart of that anecdote. But thus stands the Fact:—viz— ⎮ It had chanced during my last Week at Ilfracomb, & when I had ceased sending off any Letters, save to Paris — — whither I did not dare risk its relation, well knowing I ought to tell it myself to make it heard with serenity! yet never a moment was it out of my thoughts even for Weeks;—Gratitude to Heaven for the courage & presence of mind with which I was so happily endowed during

[3] Elizabeth (ibid.) was to marry at Ilfracombe on 27 December 1827 William Pearse or Pearce (*c.* 1775–1844), of Exford, Somersetshire, evidently a very good marriage.

One evidence of her affection for the d'Arblays was in the bestowing of some of AA's names on her second son Alexander Charles d'Arblay Pearce (b. 27 October 1839), names that live in Exford still in the history of the Pearce Charity, for the interesting details of which the editors are indebted to the Revd. Henry Warren, Rector of Exford.

When Alexander Charles d'Arblay Pearce of 68 Capel Road, London, died on 25 June 1896, 'he bequeathed to the Rector and church-wardens a rent-charge on some property in Ilfracombe, N. Devon'. 'The money was to be used to pay for the upkeep of his grave in Exford churchyard and to provide charitable payments for the poor. This bequest was declared invalid in the High Court and the rent-charge was sold. After long and complicated legal proceedings, the proceeds of the sale were divided into two parts. One part was invested to produce money for the poor, and this is still known as the Pearce Charity. The other part (£75) was used to buy half an acre of land in Exford for garden allotments, the rents of which were to provide money for the upkeep of Exford churchyard and the Pearce graves in particular. The allotment went out of use several years ago and the land was eventually sold in September of [1972] for the astronomical sum of £9,400. The income from this [adds the rector] should ensure that Exford churchyard and the Pearce graves are superbly maintained in perpetuity!'

[4] See 'The Ilfracombe Journal' (x, L. 1126) for FBA's coastal adventure, when, gathering shells, she was caught by the rising tide and marooned for hours on Capstone (Plate, *DL*, vi, *facing* 330, or x, *facing* 540).

the awful *10 Hours* of Danger & Affright, & for so narrow an escape of abruptly ending my career unknown & unheard of, in becoming food to Whales or Sharks—kept alive an humble & chearful acknowledgment to the Almighty that only gave way to the all absorbing feelings that were awakened on the last return from France!—In those, every thing else was sunk —annihilated! for though, even to the latest minute—nay moment,—I never was *hopeless*, I yet saw *Danger* every Hour —every instant—But I flew from all ultimate apprehension as I would have flown from Fire & the Sword—I could suffer no one to hint a Surmize—I always said to myself *Every Recovery is possible where*—as I once energetically cried out to Messrs Tudor & Hay,[5] when they would have given me alarm,—*where the Physician who holds the reins of Life & Death is God!*—And nearly miraculous cures *have* been brought about, some of which I had witnessed. As a looker on, *I*, also, here, perhaps, might have seen That all was over! —but being such as I was, I felt a consciousness that I resisted not Preparation, but Despair — — in resisting all attempts made by others, & all inroads into my *ultimate* hopes made by my own fears, or observations.

7th Sepp^t An interruption which, happily for you! has put off my Writing till to day, has given me time to recollect your solicitations that I would forbear this afflicting—but ever ready subject — — & I will not try to finish what I meant to say. Briefly therefore to fact. I related this extraordinary adventure to mon meilleur Ami, on his return—but it so much affected him, that he could scarcely hear its detail: nevertheless, an account which I wrote of it to Her R.H. the Princess Elizabeth, he began to copy for himself—but could not finish, from indisposition! he ^l charged me, however, not to tell it to you, Maria, or any one, but in his hearing, as he wished to listen to it again when better! — — alas Alas that better never came—& my narration to you was never made! —But he enjoined me to Write it *for* his much loved Friend the Marquis Victor de La Tour Maubourg[6]—on account of his great fondness for Dogs: *for*, I can, as it was to *Mad^e de Maisonneuve*, the Sister, with whom I am in con-

[*sliced line*]   that though ^l

---

[5] See L. 1186 n. 1; L. 1180 n. 19; and ix *passim.*   [6] See L. 1192 n. 6.

[*the remainder of this page is missing*]

[*The top of the original page 4 survives*:]

I have
settled myself for some Weeks close to Alex, in Camden
Town, in apartments the smallest, but neatest & prettiest
conceivable, open on all parts to beautiful views of Hampstead, Hygate, the Regent's Park, & Primrose Hill & Kentish
Town: of which latter, the Minister & his Wife, Mr. & Mrs.
Grant,[7] found their way to drink tea with us last Week, & to
please me exceedingly. The demand for Pews, or places, in
the New Chapel, is very flattering. The best are *all* already
taken: & Alex is highly sought by the first families of the
little scattered but picturesque town. He has very little to do
as yet, except the full double service twice every Sabbath. ǀ

[*the remainder of the page is cut away*]

I have written yr. Message for Martin through his Mother,
with one of my own to exactly the same tune of compliment. ǀ

I am excessively Gratified you were so kind to my dear
feeling Ramsay—

[7] The Revd. Johnson Grant (*c.* 1774-1844), originally of Edinburgh, B.A.
(Oxon. 1799), M.A. (1805), perpetual curate of Kentish Town (1822 until his
death), and his wife Margaret (*c.* 1789-1838), whose burial is recorded in the fee
book (graveyard records) of that chapel (GLRO).

1348

49 Upper Park Street,
Camden Town,
4 October 1824

To Mrs. Broome

A.L.S. (Berg), 4 Oct. 1824
Double sheet 4to   4 pp.   *pmk* 16 OC 1824   red seal
Addressed: Mrs. Broome, / at Miss Broad's,[1] / Bromley, / Kent.

Camden Town,
49. Upper Park St.
4th Octr 1824

How long it is since I have seen the hand,—& how very
Very long it is since I have seen the dear face of my dearest
Charlotte! I am truly obliged, however, by the agency of the
kind Marianne, who has relieved me from any absolute
anxiety, by letting me know, very satisfactorily, the *state of
the case*[2]—which, — — ought I to be ashamed to say?—
I am so much more *Sisterly* than *Patriotic*, is more necessary
for my *peace* than the knowledge of the *state of the Nation*?
Nevertheless, this is by no means from supineness as to what
concerns the Good of All, & the Glory of Great Britain —
— oh no, I have them at heart most veritably—but, some
how or other, there is a certain little mean egoistical feeling
that supersedes every nobler & more enlarged view of matters
& things, just as I am going to rest, & makes my own internal
peace hang upon my last tidings or knowledge of the welfare
of my own tiny—but most dear Circle, even more than upon
that of the Great Whole.

I cannot be *surprized* that your dear Patient should be

1348. [1] Ann Broad (*fl.* 1824–45), dressmaker and milliner, Bromley, Kent.
   [2] Clement Francis (i, p. lxxiii), who had returned to Bromley to continue
treatment under the surgeon and bandager John Scott (L. 1337 n. 4). MF had
seen Scott on 29 June, 'a vulgar, good humoured man he seemed, with a cheerful
manner, brisk, brusque, & resolute' (Berg). The treatment was not in the end successful, for the abscesses continued to break out. On Sunday 16 January [1825]
CFBt was to report from Brighton (Berg) that her brother's legs were still ban-
daged, though 'not so tightly as before'. 'I think he is rather tired of Scott', and
a friend who had been 'under Scott's care for similar complaints' had advised him
to 'trust more to air & regimen & not return to Bromley'.

called back again to his Physician[2]—because to expect a regular progress of uninterrupted recovery, in a malady of so long standing, would be irrational: nevertheless, I involuntarily felt *disappointed* at the return to the direction of Bromley. Dearly, however, Mr. Scott will make me love its name when he has completed the cure, & re-animated the poor Invalid by restored health, & his beloved Nurse by I the termination of her long & painful anxiety & fatigue. The amendment that Marianne mentions in such grand & important points as Appetite, sleep, strength & looks, promises every thing *ultimately*, though, from such *in grain* causes, necessarily slowly.

How was I vexed at the excursion to *Paris,*[3] full only of temptations to imprudence & dangerous exertions, instead of a trial of the Waters of Spa, which, where they agree, have an effect like magic in the speed of their restorative qualities. Completely I agree with Marianne in her use of the words *inconsiderateness* for the syren tempt*er*, & *Cage* for the unreflecting tempt*ed*. O that our invaluable Charlotte were in wiser hands even than *her own*, where her *own* health requires Wisdom! I beg you to be so kind as to thank my dear Marianne for her open & satisfactory—as far as she had power— Letter. She gives a pretty good account of *You*, my dear love, —& I know the good your bracing Brighton always does you. I know, too, that while attending on others, where they are Favourites, we listen little to any complaints of our own: & the less we listen, the less, I believe, we suffer

Alex is well, & going on, in his discourses & their delivery & reception, as well as his partial Godmother could expect or even wish: & his absences diminish astonishingly & comfortably: but he keeps thinner than I the thinnest, by obdurately resisting all counsel for setting about his sermons early in the Week. He drives off even beginning them till Saturday,—& even then, till the Evening! This occasions him to sit up half the night, at a stretch of intellect & of toil, & a forced wakefulness, that evidently wear him to looks of consuming by 'the Midnight oil.'[4]

How perverse! In all else, he even surprizes as well as gratifies me. He has never missed one of his Religious duties,

---

[3] See L. 1345 n. 2. MF's letter to her aunt is missing.
[4] John Gay, *Fables*, Part I, 'The Shepherd and Philosopher'.

nor mistaken any professional office: & his voice is in the highest order. His Lungs, thank Heaven! are perfect: it is not, therefore, *consumption* that I fear: but a thinness from over-done exertion & intellectual fatigue that threaten *atrophy*. Heaven avert it!

He was so desirous to be settled completely in Camden Town for the beginning of his new ministry, that he might [make] *acquaintance with his Flock &* his *business,* that I have come hither myself, in the middle of August, & here mean to continue till November. I have taken a very small, but neat & beautifully situated apartment within a few yards of his own, which merits the same epithets. There is nothing in this pretty Row, upper Park Street, large enough for our being together Day & Night; but my tiny Drawing room re-ceives I him for all that is not Nocturnal, that he can spare of time, & we live together as much, nearly if not quite, as at Bolton Street, *never* separating for Meals, but when he has some Engagement amongst his Parishioners, who all seem to like him immensely. Park *Street* it is called, but is really Park *Row*, being open entirely in front to the Regent's Park, while the back has a lovely prospect of Hampstead, Hygate, Prim-rose Hill, & Kentish Town. I have received visits from the Ministers of Hampstead,[5], Kentish Town,[6] & St Martin's burying Ground,[7] & from the Wives of the two latter: as well as from the Patron Vicar & his lady,—Alex is in the utmost intimacy with them all. It is not possible to have a better beginning; both for situation, air, & neighbourhood. God ever bless my ever dearest Charlotte—& when she can write *con-veniently*—commencing as of old, & keeping a Letter on

[5] The Revd. Samuel White (1765-1841), B.A. (Oxon. 1792), M.A. (1801), B. & D.D. (1811), was perpetual curate of the parish of Hampstead from 1807 till his death. See further, L. 1431 n. 4.

[6] The Revd. Johnson Grant (L. 1347 n. 7), who according to a M.I. in the church in Kentish Town was 'Upwards of 35 years the Minister of this Chapel'. 'Powerful preacher and voluminous author', he was to die 4 December 1844, aged 71 years.

[7] The Revd. Edward Amos Chaplin (*c.* 1772-1858) of Kentish Town, B.A. (Trinity College, Cambridge, 1793), M.A. (1796), chaplain of St. Martin's-in-the-Fields Burial Ground, Camden Town (1812), Reader and chaplain at Gray's Inn (1824). He had married on 10 September 1795 Margaret Clarke (d. 1828).

The Chaplins lived in Pratt Street, Camden Town, and for some years Alex lived with them.

the stocks,—she will truly give pleasure & comfort to her most affec^te

F d'A

I beg to know whether you have any news of our good & excellent old Friend, *Mrs. Cooke*?[8] I wrote to her more than a year ago, & fear I must have given some wrong direction.

Sophy is much better—*Maria* pretty well—our dear Esther *bonnily*; but poor Sarah Harriet is Very weak & exhausted, though in good spirits,[9] & I *hope* going on *essentially* well.— My Love & kindest wishes to dear Clement. Alex joins to Him, & to kind Aunt *Gin*!—My Direction is always *Bolton Street*, whence my letters all follow when I am absent.

Sweet Charlotte has written to me. ı

I send this on to town by an opportunity—I shall return thither next Week, I believe

ı349   49 Upper Park Street,
              Camden Town, ıı October ı824

To Mrs. Locke

L., excerpt copied in the hand of CFBt (Diary MSS. viii. 7364, Berg), 11 Oct. 1824
Single sheet 4to   1 p.

To Mrs Locke

Park St Camden Town
11 Octr 1824

—— —— Yesterday brought a letter of great grief to me from

---

[8] Cassandra Cooke (L. 1182 n. 6), formerly of Great Bookham (see iii, iv *passim*), whom CBFB had met at Bath or Brighton.
[9] Sarah Harriet Burney, still apparently in Lord Crewe's house in Park Street (L. 1346 n. 3).

Madame de Maurville[1]—*our* dear—amiable Princesse d'Henin[2]
I little, indeed, ever expected to see more—here:—but still
I feel a true & faithful & very affectionate Friend lopt off by
her departure—& surely one of the most pleasing, accomplished, sensible, warm hearted, & high bred of Women,—
Innumerable are the kindnesses, the services—the good offices I owed her—She augmented all that was most cheering
to me, & helped to soften off all that was most comfortless,
during my long abode in the way of her delightful society.—
She is gone in the house of Madame de Poix,[3] while on a visit
to her!—How truly that grieves me for that excellent & most
superior woman!

1350   49 Upper Park Street,
                   Camden Town, 14 October 1824

To Mrs. Barrett

A.L.S. (Berg), 14 Oct. 1824
Double sheet 4to   4 pp.   *pmks* T.P. ⟨   ⟩ / Gt Portland St   16 OC
1824   red seal
Addressed: Mrs. Barrett, / Henry Barrett's Esq, / Richmond, / Surry.
Docketed in pencil, p. 4: death of Princesse de Henin

1349. [1] Although Mme de Maurville's letter announcing the death of the princesse d'Hénin (v–viii *passim* and vi, Plate, *facing* p. 532) is missing, surviving still
(Berg) are her letters of 9 December [1824], 26 May 1825, and others (see *Catalogue*) lamenting her loss: 'quelle perte pour moi, et tous ce qui la connaissait
mesdames de poix et de Simiane en parlent sans cesses les larmes aux yeux j y
mets les miennes et pleurons ensemble   M de lally a faite une vrai perte [elle]
etoit l'ame de sa vie . . .'.
    It was left for Mme de Maisonneuve to supply the details that on her return
from Lys she had gathered from the survivors. Feeble, thin, and in the end suffering from pleurisy, 'cette cher Princesse' had gone on a visit as planned to Mme de
Poix, and the old friends 'si en union' in gaiety and in interests, stayed up chatting
gaily till late at night. Retiring thus late, the princesse 'n'avait pas dormi une
heure qu'elle se réveilloit mourante, . . . Mad[e] de Poix et M. de Lally arrivaient
trop tard pour en être reconnue . . .'. The former, 'dans une affliction profonde',
the latter, 'dans une doleur déchirante'.
    [2] See v. 265n., vi, viii *passim*, the recollections, Ll. 1350-1, and Welvert, p. 20.
    [3] See L. 1196b n. 3.

42 Park Street
Camden Town
14 Oct[r]
1824

The circular *project*—never ending, because—from its form & nature never begun,—that has been rounding me between Camden Town and London Town ever since the dear —though not glad tidings of your return to Richmond have reached me, my dear & very dear Charlotte,[1] has impeded my writing, by impeding my power to fix any steady *strait* point for a meeting so sweetly—yet *too* kindly proposed: for I cannot bear you should come so far *merely* for my gratification. But however, finding it so difficult to get from my ever rolling & ever changing rotundity into that which Theoretically, or superficially, seems always most easy of attainment, though, practically, 'tis the most difficult & most rare, Namely The strait Path; & not yet seeing Day light to my arrival, I will no longer defer sending my blessing to my dearest Girl upon her return, & for her Letters, with my true delight that she is *stronger*; which will lead soon, I must not doubt, to her transforming her resemblance from the hue of one lilly to that of the Other. Nevertheless, warmly as I always rejoice in the prospect of seeing her, ⏐ I could not feel glad that she relinquished the bracing breezes of October by the Sea Coast of Boulogne.

I have been urged by Alex to come hither for finishing my Summer, & passing my Autumn:—But though, eventually, I have so done, intervening affairs as well as *projects*, have made my residence here always uncertain; & I cannot, at this very moment, decide whether I shall still abide here till November, or go hence next Monday.

Who, indeed, you will cry, if you are in a moralizing mood, *can?*—but that saving query should be always implied, whether detailed or not.

All, therefore, I can now suggest about a meeting which I *yearn* to have take place, is that if either business or aught gayer bring you to town, you will again become an *intrigante* in my behalf, & contrive to let me have a note the day or two

1350. [1] For CFBt's travels, see L. 1345 n. 2.

before, which shall assuredly bring me to your appointment, at Bolton Street, or, if you prefer it, in poor James Street — — for the former, I must have time to *d'avance* you, that our persons may have no chill where our minds, I feel sure, will have a glow: my apartments, at present, being shut up & Fireless. |

I have had very kind, open, & comfortable communications from dear Marianne relative to Both my dear *Lot*s & to poor Clement. I beg you to thank her most sincerely in my Name, till I can do it Myself; & very much, also, for her good intelligence of the valuable Mr. Wilberforce[2]—whom I long to again see.

I have been extremely grieved this last Week by a Letter from France, announcing my loss of a lady who honoured me with the most cordial friendship, whose Heart, open to every generous & liberal feeling that can urge leaving in the lurch all considerations—even disdainfully—of superior Rank, that might impede the freedom of mental equality, was filled with the most partial affection for me, not, indeed, like that of Madame de Maisonneuve, which makes her knowledge of my welfare, my health, & my feelings essential to her own repose; but still with a warmth as rare as it is flattering & engaging. I speak of one of whom you must have heard, though you are not likely to have seen, Madame la Princesse d'Henin.[3] She is suddenly gone—while at the house of a Friend, Madame la Princesse de Poix,[3] another woman of the most delightful & superior qualities, & who, unhappily, has lately lost her sight from a bad operation to restore it from an evil, only menaced. The particulars I do not yet know, but— little chance as there could be that we should ever have met here again, I am still sensibly grieved to lose the consciousness of the existence of such a Friend, & her lively & interesting, though not regular Correspondence. I am glad, at least, that mine, at this time, was the last written Letter— a solace I so seldom can receive. |

If you have heard any thing of poor Lady Bedingfelt,[4] when you write pray tell me. I have not been able yet to see

---

[2] MF's letter is missing, but from 1811 she spent much time at Kensington Gore as the guest of the Wilberforces.

[3] See L. 1349 nn. 1-3.   [4] See L. 1345 n. 11.

our dear Sarah P[ayne] from a hanging engagement, of the time for which I am not mistress, & which prevents my forming any for myself till it is past. Poor poor Sarah Harriet I see whenever I can, as that depends upon my own convenience in searching her for she has never been well enough to spend an hour with me here.[5] I hope she is going on *essentially* well, —but 'tis so slowly—so slowly as to demand religious patience & fortitude united. And indeed I quite honour the chearfulness of spirit with which she bears so trying a state. I have only one day known them overpowered, & then it was from a sudden impression of disappointment in cure utterly unexpected. This is only for *ourselves.*—For *Her* I feel but the truest pity, with the warmest Hope of seeing amendment. We hear no detail how Fanny supplies the Deputyship,[6] but *well*, I dare believe, from her capabilities & ambition united. I have very good accounts from Lark Hall place, & am very glad to hear that Sophy is much better. Maria *looked* as if wanting no sort of repair, when she was in town. My dear Sister has been enjoying a sail to Ilfracomb, & seen my poor good Ramsay[7]—& found her as romanticly attached as ever. I have just Written to my *other* dearest Charlotte, by Bromley,[8] therefore give you no commissions save to my excellent Friends of the New House Meadows,[9] when they return, & to my faithful Mrs. Baker. And my best Comp[ts] to Mr. Barrett & Love to my dear Julia & Hetty & Arthur. I am always sorry to have missed my dear *God Boy.*[10] I know not whether Henry be with you or not.[10] Adieu, my dear & sweet Charlotte

ever yours most truly
F d'A

I saw Fanny, very blooming, lately at poor Aunt Sarah's, & good little Minette |[11]

---

[5] Cf. L. 1346 n. 3.

[6] EBB's daughter (i, p. lxix), who, in her capacity as governess must have been substituting for SHB at Crewe Hall.

[7] For Elizabeth Ramsay (L. 1182 n. 3), the story of her marriage and of her devotion to FBA and AA, see L. 1182 n. 3 and L. 1347 n. 3.

[8] This is L. 1348.

[9] The Cambridges must have moved to their new house at Twickenham in April or May. See Cornelia Cambridge's letter to CFBt (Eg. 3705, ff. 62-3b) of 23 April *pmk* 1824.

[10] Cf. L. 1345 n. 9; and for Henry Barrett's school at Boulogne, L. 1314 n. 2.

[11] Fanny Raper (i, p. lxxi) and her daughter Minette, now aged 16.

I send this to Town by an opportunity I now *think* I shall return there Next Week

1351   11 Bolton Street,
                                              22 November 1824

To Esther (Burney) Burney

A.L.S. (rejected Diary MSS. 7370-[3], Berg), 22 Nov. 1824
Double sheet 4to   4 pp.   *pmk* 29 NO 1824   red seal
Addressed: Mrs. Burney, / Lark Hall Place, / near Bath.
Endorsed: R^d. Novr 30th 1824 / answered / Decr 2—1824
Edited by CFBt. *See* Textual Notes.

22^d Novr 1824

How very long it is since I have heard from my dearest Hetty!—I know well the retort courteous this will invite, but as that is Her affair, not mine, I cry *bis* How very long it is since I have seen her always dear hand!—If This be the only way to get at it, why then—as our dear James used to say—*here goes.*

What you tell me of your Correspondents, & your difficulty to keep pace with them, you may be very sure I can perfectly comprehend, and 'Count out line for line'—so There, we must mutually give quarter, & make allowance. But mine, of late, have been all, or almost all, swallowed up by subjects so melancholy as to incline me more than usual —*et c'est beaucoup dire*—to delay my answer to your last, till I could reply a little more in its own Colour, which was truly *de rose* to me, in bringing to life, & to kind remembrance, my long since dear, & long believed lost Mad^e de Boinville.[1] I have enquired for, & about her, ever since I *first* came to England, in 1812—when I waited upon her sister,

---

1351. [1] The widow of Jean-Baptiste Chastel de Boinville (v, L. 425 n. 8), Harriet *née* Collins (*c.* 1773–1847), self-styled '*une enfant de la revolution*' and formerly a friend of Shelley (see Cameron, iii. 275–8). She seems to have returned to England, but her letter to FBA is missing.

M. Dusseck's pupil,[2] but heard she was settled in the Country.
On my Second return, in 1815, — — you know—too well!
—how all my thoughts, as well as all my time, were absorbed:
but since my health, with apparent lengthened life, have
turned me, once again, to accept, at least, if not to seek, such
remaining ties to social chearfulness as may sweeten the
down hill passage, I have again always enquired for her of all
Berkshire people, or passengers, who came in my way,—particularly of your Richard,—but could never gather any
tidings, & concluded she was gone abroad. Your intelligence
awakened a thousand affectionate—&, alas! affecting recollections.—I had loved her as much as *any* one, I had ever
known, nearly, in the same proportion of time & intimacy—
but it was ǀ *her* misery, not *mine*, that separated us. The tale
is long, & will not bear Writing—but I have been truly glad
to receive from her, almost immediately after your last Letter, a warm & tender & very touching appeal to my former
regard, & request for its renewal. I have instantly testified my
sensibility to her returning kindness—& am rather anxious
to know whether my Letter was safely received, as it would
grieve me to the very soul that she should think me capable
to withstand a Letter such as that she has bestowed upon me:
but the address was only *Sidmouth Post office*—as she said
she was going directly to Sidmouth to pass the Winter. If you
write again, & by a more certain Direction, I entreat you to
mention this circumstance. You wish for her at Bath—How
should I be solaced to see her in London! You loved her for
reminding you of a dear—dear Sister—So did I, but not
of our Susan!—it was *you* of whom she always reminded
me: as I think I must have told you, & as I have mentioned
to her in my Letter. She was never, however, half so pretty,
as ⟨you⟩, though I believe many years younger than either of
us.—But it was a Face of the same *sort*, of the spirited &
speaking class, & much resemblance in Feature, height, &
style of dress, as well as for quickness of conception & of expression. Would to God her fates would send & fix her here!

---

[2] Harriet's sister Cornelia (d. 1814) had married John Frank Newton (1757–
1837). See Cameron, *supra*. FBA recalls that, like EBB's son the Revd. Richard
Allen Burney (i, L. 4 n. 5), she had studied under Johann Ludwig Dussek (1760–
1812), composer and pianist, who had come to England in 1789.

Now—back to my Melancholy Epistles—Almost immediately after this renovating correspondence, I had news of
the loss of two dear Friends, to whose fellow-Mourners with
myself I had scarcely finished my sorrowing marks of sympathy, ere I had a similar call for their repetition.—The first
was the Princesse d'Henin[3]—whom you have seen, when she
visited our Susan, who loved, & was loved by her with mutual
tenderness of admiration on both sides. This admirable lady,
one of the most intellectually accomplished I have ever
known, was a very principal source of all my ˡ *secondary*
comforts & pleasures during the whole of my long residence
in Paris—The Author of the *First* I need not mention!—but
for the secondary, though I was blessed & honoured & supported with *many*, Mad[e] de Maisonneuve alone stood before
Mad[e] la Princesse d'Henin. Her zeal to serve, her power to
oblige, her animation to entertain were all, & always at work
for me. She seemed to think she was paying all the obligations & favours she owed to The Lockes themselves, by
devoting to me every moment & every means she could command for use or pleasure. She presented me as her chosen
Friend to all her nearest connexions, and to all her most
splendid & all her most literary acquaintance. She procured
me tickets or places or introductions to every thing worth
seeing; she borrowed for me the Carriage of her own bosom
Friend, Mad[e] la Princesse de Poix,[3] to return visits in, or go
to dress *spectacles* in an Evening: she neither bought nor borrowed a Book that was not on my Table after her own; she
made parties to let me see the humours of French *Conversa-
tiones*, & the pleasures of French *petit soupés*,—she made
me accompany her in her country visits, that I might view at
leisure the *environs* of Paris; & she treated me with a confidence, a trust as enlivening to all my feelings, as it was flattering in its proof of her opinion.—What hours—what Days—
nay, what Weeks we have passed together,—for it was with
her I made my flight from Paris, in the 100 Days — — she
had never a party, a meeting, or any occasion of amusement
or of instruction to which I was not invited — — Can I help
being deeply affected by her loss? no,—though I had little
chance, indeed, of ever again seeing her, Here,—it was still

[3] See L. 1349 nn. 1, 2, 3.

always soothing to think of the existence, at least, of so partial & kind a Friend — — Ah! Heaven preserve my Madame de Maisonneuve! dearer yet!—dearer than all, after Mrs. Lock & Amelia; that are not of my own Kin & Kind, well as I love many still—*well*, & warmly—Letters on this event to 3 of our mutual Friends I ᴵ have painfully been writing[4]—& the task was only finished to be succeeded by another of the same mould, from the sudden death of Mrs. Merrik Hoare,[5] whom I have known, with never ceasing regard on both sides, from her 7ᵗʰ year when, as Sophy Thrale, she used to enter my chamber, after a modest tap, every morning, if at Streatham during my visits, with a Bunch of Flowers gathered in her nursery walks. She was a truly amiable creature, & her loss is very great indeed to Alex, to whom her house, society & parties were always open. To Lady Keith—to poor Miss Susan Thrale, & to Mr. Merrik Hoare I have written—persuaded my pain in the effort would at least be soothing to them, by & bye, as a tribute from one she so loved.—

The little paper that remains must come more home. Poor Sarah H[arriet] wrote me a very comfortless account of her Journey to Cheshire,—but better news is come lately & she herself believes in her recovery,—I am very happy to tell you this, for she has owned to me she was nearly desponding. Our Charlotte is still at Brighton, with her lamentable Charge, whom, however, Mr. Scott says will be well by Xmas—God grant it![6] Sweet Charlotte Barrett returned from abroad looking so revived,[7] that I felt it quite a *blessing* to see her— such had been my fears. Sarah Payne is entirely new made— she seems without complaint, & looks well with all her might,

---

[4] Letters to the princesse de Poix (see L. 1352), Mme de Maurville (L. 1349 n. 1), and to Lally-Tolendal, whose reply (Berg) of 30 November is extant (Berg): 'en vous lisant j'ai été voisin du délire. je voulais courir lui montrer cette trop admirable lettre, comme je lui montrais, comme elle me montrait toutes les Vôtres. je Voulais aller lui lire tout ce que vous me disiez sur le malheur de l'avoir perdue. Brisons, chere Madame, brisons. je sens ma tete qui se trouble. j'en suis à ne pas oser ecrire ou prononcer son nom.'

[5] Sophia Hoare *née* Thrale (1771-1824), who had died at Sandgate on 8 November. FB had first met Mrs. Thrale's daughters Susan and Sophia at their school in Kensington in August 1778 (*DL* i. 91), when Sophia would have been, as FBA remembers nearly half a century later, 7 years old. She had married Merrik Hoare (L. 1238 n. 22).

[6] But see L. 1348 n. 2.

[7] For CFBt's return from Boulogne in October, see L. 1345 n. 2.

& is in high spirits, & very agreeable. Mrs Ad^l Burney is almost always at Kingston,[8] & *There* well; but in town afresh assailed by her stomach disease, & very sufferingly. Fanny Raper & her Minette were with me on Thursday, in perfect health. Edward I have not seen for an Age, from Various impediments, & Fanny thinks ⟨of such⟩ as it suits in all respects her own convenience, without the smallest heed or enquiry, how she might suit mine. I once thought I had ⟨c⟩aught a bit of her heart—& I *tried* for it, 3 or 4 years ago—but I see, & am sorry to see, my mistake.—Mrs. Locke is in Suffolk with her —& my dear Amelia—& both well. Miss A[ngerstein] is quite recovered. Alex is well, but thin, & thinner—I am never at ease about him in my mind. But he pleases much at Camden & spends nearly half his time there. I am not happy about H.R.H. the sweet Dss of Gloucester who is very unwell —& altered![9]—

> Ever & aye yours my dearest Hetty
> F. d Ay

Your acc^t of the r⟨evived⟩ health & look[s] of your Three gives me great satisf[ac]tion. How astonishin[gl]y *young* & handsome is Maria!—Have you told her I wrote a line to her for ⟨dr.⟩ Blue,[10] who could not fetch it?—It shall go with your next Tea cady. Nothing in haste—

1352   11 Bolton Street,
                                                    [*late*] November 1824

To Mrs. Locke

L., copy in the hand of CFBt (Diary MSS. viii. 7366–9, Berg), Nov. 1824

Double sheet 4to and a single sheet 4to   6 pp.   foliated 44, 45, 46
Edited by the Press. *See* Textual Notes.

[8] See L. 1346 n. 1.

[9] Belonging perhaps to 1824 is an 8vo (Berg), written from Bagshot Park, n.d., in which the Duchess of Gloucester speaks of 'guarding against cold and damp' and of her plans for Brighton, where her 'kind Brother' (George IV) has invited her to the Pavilion for change of air and recuperation by the sea.

[10] Elizabeth Warren Burney (i, p. lxxv).

To Mrs Lock

11. Bolton St
Novr 1824

I have missed my Bulletin to my beloved Friends, & this time, I have missed it without self reproach, & that not merely through that amiable lenity which is so ready to exculpate us from all failings & defects of our own, but because I cannot in conscience send off two or 3 lines as far as Suffolk except when peculiar circumstances make them, as the last time, desired: & *more* I could not write, unless I had made them of that cast which is least congenial with that dear couleur de rose which I pray to keep unfading.——

I have been grieved at heart by the loss of my dear Sophy Hoare[1]—a loss so utterly unexpected;—I thought her built to outlive my whole remnant circle—All of letters I have written for this last fortnight have been of condolence,—long—painful, difficult.—An opportunity offering for Paris, I have addressed myself at full length to poor ┃ Madame de Maurville,[2] who is every way a dreadful sufferer by the departure of dear Madame d'Henin.[2]—Another Mr. Faunt-leroy on a smaller scale,[3] having immediately disappeared on the death of the Princesse with every *renseignement* by which her Will could be executed, & with every document for the Pension of Mad^e de Maurville, as well as with all of money she possessed, which had been placed with *le bien* of Mme d'Henin!

1352. [1] On 8 November (L. 1351 n. 5).

[2] Besides the loss of a relative and friend, Mme de Maurville suffered a pecuniary loss of some '28 mille francs' when the 'homme d'affaire' employed by the princesse d'Hénin made off with her will and all funds entrusted to him. Thus Mme de Maisonneuve in her letter (Berg) of 12–17 November: 'L'homme d'affaire de Mad^e d'hénin en qui elle avait beaucoup de confiance et qui avait presque toute sa fortune entre les mains, l'argent de M. de Lally, celui de la pauvre Mad^e de Maurville est parti [pour] L'angleterre.'

[3] The notorious banker Henry Fauntleroy (1785–1824), who, forging for large sums entrusted to the banking house of Marsh, Sibbald, & Co. of Berners Street, had invested trust funds to the amount, it was said, of a quarter of a million pounds, disposing as well of stocks, the proceeds of which he applied to his gambling debts and the support of luxurious establishments and several mistresses. He was tried, found guilty, and executed on 30 November 1824 (*DNB*). A regular reader of newspapers, FBA had apparently noted the columns at that time devoted to the trial.

This wretch was the *homme de confiance* of the Princesse & she had trusted to him every thing.——Upon her demise, Monsr de la Tour du Pin,[4] her Nephew & Executor, called upon him for delivering up his trust,——& the man suddenly decamped with his wife & Family, and, as they have since traced by Passports, I suppose, fled to England: but all was gone!——& a Will, full of [*blank*] Mad^e de M.s words are 'qu'n Testament ⎮ qui est un chef d'oeuvre de bienfaits et de bontés, où tout etoit prévû, arrangé —— —— un malheureux homme a detruit dans un instant. —— —'[5]

——How disastrous!——Mr Raper has procured & sent her, as she begged me to petition him to do, new *modeles de certificats de Vie*, by which, at least, what is to come will be secured.[6]

To poor M: de Lally I ventured to address some consolatory words,[7]——for I have long had reason to believe they were secretly married. Indeed it was the universal belief among

[4] Frédéric-Séraphin Latour de Pin (1759–1837), comte de Gouvernet (vi, L. 575 n. 2; viii *passim*).

[5] Quoted, in all probability, from the letter, now missing, that FBA had received from Mme de Maurville on 10 October (see mention of it, L. 1349).

[6] On the accession of Charles X (1824), the *émigrés* renewed their hopes of reclamations, and the request, conceivably put in the missing letter *supra*, is probably related to that of 26 May 1825 (Berg): 'Voicy, chere amie, une priore que j'aurais a vous faire et que votre cher fils coudra remplir; ce serait d avoir la bonté de faire prendre 1 extrait mortuaire de Mr de Maurville dans la paraisse de S^t pancras middlesex, mort en 1796, enterre le 2 aout, sous les noms de Jean, Louis, Bernard Bidé de Maurville . . . pour faire lever cette act absolument nécessaire pour la réclamation *de mes indemnités*. . . .'

Charles Chamier Raper (*c.* 1777–1842), now Chief Clerk in the War Office, was also called on to substantiate details of the comte de Maurville's death in England (iii, L. 237 n. 9). His wife Fanny *née* Phillips and her mother SBP, Mme de Maurville had known in England.

[7] For part of Lally's reply, see L. 1351 n. 4. Of the other letters of condolence and the replies, only that from H. Merrik Hoare (Barrett, Eg. 3698, f. 174) is known to the editors:

My Dear Madam

I was much obliged by your very Kind Note, and having now a Letter to send from Lady Keith, I take the opportunity of requesting (as one of my late Dear Sophia's earliest Friends) you will do me the Favour to accept of the accompanying small Token as a Rembrance of Her Esteem and affection—

faithfully
H. M. Hoare

York place
11 Jany 1825

The 'Token' was 'a Green mourning Ring—in memory of his sweet wife' (see FBA's annotation of the letter).

their friends; though, as the marriage took place very late, & as French Customs allowed their living under the same roof with impunity, various motives prevented its open avowal. Indirectly also, to the friend of her bosom, Mad^e la Princesse de Poix, I have written—for this fatal event took place at her house, while the poor Princesse was there, recruiting from a long illness! ¦ This packet,—which occupied my thoughts yet more than my pen, was hardly sealed—when thoughts & Pen changed their Objects, without changing their colour — — & another packet I finished & sent off only on Friday, for Lady Keith—poor Susan Thrale, & Mr Merrick Hoare—the two former drew forth very long letters as I am persuaded they will be soothing to their grief,—& the latter was not more *easy* to write, though but a few melancholy words[7]—

This detail of Facts, my dearest Friends, is not gay,—how should it be?—but 'tis less depressing than to have detailed the sentiments they caused.

Now then for a more cheerful winding-up—

I came from Camden Town very unwillingly,—but Alex was called to Cambridge to an Audit,[8] & so I took that opportunity to make a break up; for Camden Town & no Alex would be Camden Town to me no longer. But the day before I quitted it I received the highest ¦ resident honour that can be bestowed upon me—namely a Visit from one of my most dear and condescending Princesses.[9] She came by appointment,—yet her entrance was so quick that Alex had not time to save himself.—However she took the incident not only without displeasure but with apparent satisfaction, sweetly saying she was very glad to *renew her acquaintance* with him. She had not seen him since the time of his spouting, 'The spacious Firmament on high'—'Ye shepherds so cheerful & gay'—'When Princes urge us'—'Hah, Dogs! arrest my Friend before my face'—&c. all which she remembers hearing.[10] But

---

[8] By statute (L. 1185 n. 4) the audit took place within a month of Michaelmas (29 September).

[9] From the Princess Sophia, whose note of 15 October (Berg) set the hour 'Sunday after Church say 2 oClock'. 'The better day the better deed should You be able to admit / Your Grateful / Sopy' /

[10] This was on 10 April 1800, when at the invitation of the Princess Amelia, FBA brought Alex, then 6 years old, to Buckingham House (iv, L. 371 n. 2). Coached for some months, he was able to recite Addison's well-known hymn;

my dearest & kindest Friends will not be sorry to hear that, on enquiring for, & looking at the steeple of his Chapel from the Window, she said it was very pretty—but she hoped he would soon have something better.

Ah—I have never recollected till this instant that I | ought to have gone to her the next Day!—how shocking!—& now that I have the consciousness, I can do nothing, for I am lame from a little accident.—Well!—she is all goodness—& far more prone to forgive than I — — I trust!—am to offend.

— —

¹353   [11 Bolton Street,
                              late November] 1824

To ———————————¹

L., excerpt¹ in the hand of CFBt (Diary MSS. viii. 7362, Berg), 1824
Single sheet 4to   1 p.

1824.

— — I have, of late, been frequently led to see & consi-der the awfully equalizing hand of Providence in its Donations & its Privations. So contrasting are the instances that have presented themselves to my view of the *satiety* of Wealth & its Luxuries to the Wealthy who are born to their possession, with the restless *anxiety* to acquire them in those who have their own way to make for their attainment, that I am

Shenstone's 'A Pastoral Ballad'; parts of Fielding's *Tom Thumb*; and apparently Nathaniel Lee's *Theodosius*, I. i.

With his mother's memory and such early training in memorizing, Alex in later life could contribute to an evening's entertainment whole acts of Racine or other French plays, and to the gratification of Thomas Moore (20 March 1819, ii. 280) he had got 'by heart' all his long Eastern narrative *Lalla Rookh* (1817), some 5,600 lines.

1353. ¹ Possibly copied from one of the letters of condolence mentioned in Ll. 1351-2.

sometimes tempted to concur with a French Author, who brought out a Theory while I lived in Paris that I *then* disputed, of universal *Earthly* compensation respecting the Good and the Evil of *Mortal* Life.[2]—

¹354   [11 Bolton Street,
                                              late 1824]

To Mrs. Barrett

A.L. (Berg), Monday
Double sheet 8vo   2 pp.   red seal
Addressed: Mrs. Barrett, / at Henry Barrett's Esq / Richmond, / Surry.
Docketed in pencil, p. 1: Fall of 1824
Scribbled shopping list, p. 4: *Julia* / Bonnet / Jujubes / Miniatures / Silk Handfs / Hair powder / Green Sewing silk / & silk for gown

Monday.

This old Note[1] must needs go, my dearest Charlotte—but your dear lines of this morning must also have a new one.

All you say of Julia comes to my heart with approbation & pleasure. I would not *spoil* such a character, & mar such an *Education* for a thousand Worlds. Let her retain uninjured her unconscious simplicity, & beautiful innocence of moderation: yet do not think the purity I admire can lead me to withdraw my little tribute of affection: be still my Proxy both for the Presentation & the Kiss, only let them take place precisely at your own well judged time, & in your own maternal manner.

I am sure you comprehend—& will not contest me this little pleasure with the dear Girl. |

I will certainly give Hetty's mandate. Alex is at Camden Town. He drank tea with me on Saturday. He is doubly called

---

[2] Almost certainly Destutt de Tracy (v. 351), whose *Élémens d'Idéologie* (1804) FBA was reading in 1805-6 (vi. 769, 781).

1354. [1] The first note may have been written around 21 October 1824, the occasion of Julia Barrett's attaining the age of 16.

upon just now, as his friend Mr Chaplin is gone upon a Tour,[2] & has asked him to perform his *Evening* duty on Sundays, & his melancholy funereal ones on the other days.

No little Cell is yet vacated for me.

My kind Remembrances around you—& kinder still to the Core of the Circle.

I fear this wet weather will ill suit the Tourists.

I am sorry Brighton has lost its charms—it was a sort of Magnet to Health with my dear Sister.

I think my Dove *must* please Marianne, & I flatter myself they will unite permanently,[3]

---

[2] See L. 1348 n. 7.

[3] Possibly the gift of a seal, the imprint of which may be seen in detail on MF's letter (Berg) to her mother, *pmk* 6 MY 1829. Very tiny and delicate, the design is described by Linda René-Martin as 'a carrier pigeon or dove with a letter in its beak and the superscript *DEPECHE*'.

Among MF's many admirers was Frederick Doveton (*c.* 1788-1871), B.A. (Oxon. 1809), M.A. (1813), rector (1819) of South Normanton, Derbyshire, son of Frederick Doveton (d. 22 December 1815) of Blackheath and Upper Wimpole Street, whose family MF, CB, and the Barretts had known for many years.